Global

Second Edition

MARKETING

FOREIGN ENTRY, LOCAL MARKETING, & GLOBAL MANAGEMENT

JOHNY K. JOHANSSON

GEORGETOWN UNIVERSITY

Irwin
McGraw-Hill

Boston, MA   Burr Ridge, IL   Dubuque, IA   Madison, WI   New York, NY   San Francisco, CA   St. Louis, MO
Bangkok   Bogotá   Caracas   Lisbon   London   Madrid
Mexico City   Milan   New Delhi   Seoul   Singapore   Sydney   Taipei   Toronto

McGraw-Hill Higher Education

*A Division of **The McGraw-Hill** Companies*

GLOBAL MARKETING:
FOREIGN ENTRY, LOCAL MARKETING, AND GLOBAL MARKETING

This book is printed on acid-free paper.

domestic		3	4	5	6	7	8	9	0	DOC/DOC	9	0	9	8	7	6	5	4	3	2	1	0
international	2	3	4	5	6	7	8	9	0	DOC/DOC	9	0	9	8	7	6	5	4	3	2	1	0

ISBN 0-07-365863-4

Publisher: *David Kendric Brake*
Senior developmental editor: *Nancy Barbour*
Senior marketing manager: *Colleen J. Suljic*
Project manager: *Christine Parker*
Project supervisor: *Debra R. Benson*
Coordinator freelance design: *Mary L. Christianson*
Freelance cover designer: *Kaye Farmer*
Senior photo research coordinator: *Keri Johnson*
Photo research: *Michael J. Hruby & Associates*
Cover image: © *Eric Camp/Index Stock*
Supplement coordinator: *Mark Sienicki*
Compositor: *Carlisle Communications, Ltd.*
Typeface: *10/12 Janson*
Printer: *R. R. Donnelley & Sons Company*

Library of Congress Cataloging–in–Publication Data

Johansson, Johny K.
    Global marketing : foreign entry, local marketing, and global
management / Johny K. Johansson. -- 2nd ed.
      p. cm.
    Includes bibliographical references and index.
    ISBN 0–07–365863–4
    1. Export marketing. 2. Export marketing—Management. I. Title.
HF1416.J63 2000   99-33630
658.8'48--dc21

INTERNATIONAL EDITION ISBN 0-07-116961-X

http://www.mhhe.com

To my parents,
Ruth and Nils Johansson

The Irwin/McGraw-Hill Series in Marketing

ABOUT THE AUTHOR

Johny K. Johansson was named the McCrane/Shaker Chairholder in International Business and Marketing in the McDonough School of Business at Georgetown University in 1989. An expert in the areas of international marketing strategy and consumer decision making, especially as applied to Japanese and European companies and markets, Johansson has published over 70 academic articles and chapters in books. He is the author (with Ikujiro Nonaka) of *Relentless: The Japanese Way of Marketing*, HarperBusiness, 1996. He has conducted numerous executive seminars in many countries, including Japan, Germany, Sweden, Hong Kong, Thailand, and India. He has also been a consultant to companies in many countries, including Standard Oil of Indiana, General Electric, General Telephone and Electronics and Xerox in the United States, Ford Werke AG in Germany, and Honda, Mazda and Fuji Film in Japan.

Before joining Georgetown's faculty, Johansson held faculty positions at the University of Washington and the University of Illinois. He also has held many visiting appointments in several countries. He was the first Isetan Distinguished Visiting Professor at Keio Business School (Japan) and the first Ford Distinguished Visiting Professor at University of Cologne in Germany. He also has been a visiting professor at New York University, Dalhousie University, (Canada), Stockholm School of Economics, the Catholic University of Leuven (Belgium), the National Defense Academy (Japan), and the International University of Japan. In 1988 he was a Phelps scholar at the University of Michigan.

Johansson earned Ph.D. and M.B.A. degrees from the University of California, Berkeley, and his undergraduate degree (Civilekonom) from the Stockholm School of Economics. A Swedish citizen, he lives in Georgetown, Washington, D.C., with his wife Tamiko, and their two daughters, Anna and Sonja.

$\mathcal{P}$ REFACE

Global marketing is one of the most exciting fields of business today—but also one of the most challenging. This goes not only for working in it or learning about it, but also for teaching it. It requires not only a good grasp of marketing principles and an understanding of the global environment, but also how the two interact, that is, how the environment impacts the applicability of the marketing principles. Good marketing might be good marketing everywhere—but this does not mean it is necessarily the same.

The challenge when writing a text in global marketing is how to avoid being overwhelmed by all the curious and amazing differences in the marketing environment in foreign countries. These differences make things fun and enjoyable — but also frustrating, since after a while it is difficult to see if any progress has been made. It is hard to see the forest for the trees. The key is to focus on the marketing decisions that have to be made—and then deal with those environmental factors which directly impact those decisions. This is the approach taken in this text. It discusses the complexities of global marketing and clarifies the managerial roles involved, without getting bogged down by the many environmental issues which are only marginally relevant.

KEY FEATURES

When compared to other texts in global marketing, the text has three main distinguishing features:

1. There is no initial part with several chapters on "the international environment" of politics, finance, legal, and economic regions. With the exception of culture, the book covers the environmental variables on an "as needed" basis, in the various chapters.

2. As opposed to the traditional view of one "marketing manager," the typical global marketing manager's job consists of three separate tasks: Foreign entry, local marketing, and global management. Each requires different skills, as we will see. In foreign entry, in global management, and to a large extent even as a local marketer in a foreign country, the global marketer needs skills that the home market experience—or the standard marketing text—have rarely taught. The recognition of the three roles also helps dispel the notion that "there is no such thing as international or global marketing, only marketing." This sentiment has some truth to it, but mainly in the local marketing portion of the job.

3. The material is based on a theoretical foundation from the theory of the multinational firm. This is not for academic credit, but because the theory helps the marketing manager understand what drives the company expansion abroad, and helps the manager understand how and when to adapt the various marketing functions involved.

"TRIED AND TRUE" MATERIAL

At the same time as these differences may be novel, I have also incorporated much of the excellent research and teaching material that global marketers in business and academe have contributed over the years. This material is reflected not only in the chapter text, but also in the several cases which can be found at the end of each major section. My intent has been to retain and update much of the teaching and instructional material that has made global marketing such an exciting class in many business schools—and made for such an exciting managerial career—and fit the material into a structure which reflects the global marketing management tasks. I have focused on relevant material, which is timely and up-to-date, and which is not a rehash of standard marketing principles.

TARGET AUDIENCE

The text is aimed towards the executive, the MBA or senior undergraduate, neither of whom is completely new to marketing or to the global environment. I have in mind a reader who is familiar with the basic marketing principles, and who has had some exposure to the international environment and the thrust towards a global economy. I have avoided unnecessarily complicated jargon—the global marketing job is inherently complex, and any opportunity to "keep it simple" has been capitalized on.

POSSIBLE COURSES

The three-way partition of the book makes it possible to construct several alternative course outlines from the book.

- A complete course on "Global Marketing," possibly using additional cases, is the "full-course" treatment alternative.
- A shorter "Global Marketing Management" course, perhaps for executives, could go straight from the fundamentals in the first three chapters to the global management part starting in chapter 11. This is one approach I have used at Georgetown.
- An "International marketing" course could focus on the local marketing and the global management parts.
- An "Export marketing" course could select the foreign entry chapters, and then do the local marketing plus the pricing and distribution chapters in global management.
- At Georgetown I have also used the text in a second-year MBA class entitled "Foreign Market Development," for which I assign the foreign entry and local marketing parts, but only the first two chapters of the global management part.

NEW TO THE 2ND EDITION

The 2nd edition keeps the original structure (Foreign Entry, Local Marketing abroad, Global Management) which has proved successful and popular among users. But based upon user and reviewer feedback, several changes have been introduced in order to make the text more relevant, useful, and up-to-date.

There are six major changes:

1. The second chapter has been turned into a "Global Competitive Analysis" chapter.
2. An entirely new chapter (no.11) has been written on "Global Segmentation and Positioning."

3. The "Global Products and Services" chapter (no.12) now has a new and extended section on "Global Branding."
4. The last chapter on "The Future of Global Marketing" now treats the global aspects of the Internet and electronic commerce extensively.
5. The country-specific "Local Marketing Abroad" chapters have been increased from 2 to 3 based on reviews and requests from users. This part of the text has proved especially successful in project-oriented classes.
6. The cases have been updated and consolidated into longer versions. Several new cases have been added.

There are also a few minor changes:

1. The first chapter now gets into globalization of marketing right away, as many users have wanted.
2. The popular vignettes and boxed inserts have been updated, new have been added, and some deleted.
3. The marketing implications of the global financial turmoil at the end of the 1990s have been incorporated where applicable to update the text. In particular, Russia's problems have been used to caution against the blind "Global Imperative," and the potential of a more "limited global" strategic posture is discussed.
4. A number of new Power Point slides have been added to the supplements.

Even with these changes, most of what was unique about the first edition of the text has been retained, and the reader will find a similar Table of Contents and the same number of chapters (18).

SUPPLEMENTS

Teaching a global marketing course requires more supplementary material than usual because of the amount of information about foreign countries which has to be provided. No one can master it all. I am pleased to say that the editorial staff at Irwin-McGraw Hill has helped me put together what I think is a very strong resource package.

The supplements are especially designed by marketing professors, colleagues of mine, to help teachers of this course be more effective. We have taken care to offer the best supplements we could make available.

INSTRUCTOR'S MANUAL: This manual is designed to assist instructors in meeting the varied curricular and pedagogical challenges inherent in teaching an International or Global Marketing course. The manual is particularly sensitive to the needs of various kinds of global marketing classroom situations, and includes syllabus construction, pacing of topic coverage and other teaching suggestions, lecture outlines, discussion of end of chapter questions and supplemental readings based on the varying perspectives and needs of the instructor. Included in this supplement are discussions of the electronic transparencies, videos and readings.

TEST BANK: The Test Bank consists of more than 1,400 questions designed to thoroughly test the comprehension of basic terminology and concepts as well as the student's ability to apply those concepts. The material in each of the text's eighteen chapters is tested by a battery of sixty multiple-choice, ten short-answer and ten essay questions. The computerized version of the test bank, Computest 4, is available in DOS and Windows format.

ELECTRONIC TRANSPARENCIES: A large set of slides, many new to this edition including both in-text and out-of-text graphics, are available on PowerPoint software diskettes. Information about the slides is included in the Instructor's Manual.

VIDEOS: The videos are comprised of numerous segments which highlight important aspects of global marketing. The videos are intended to provide unique footage of global marketing in action.

INTERNATIONAL READINGS BOOKLET: This booklet, available in some packages, reprints current global business articles.

As in the first edition, I have tried to make the text as fun and interesting to read as possible. You will of course judge for yourself whether I have succeeded.

ACKNOWLEDGEMENTS

The first edition built upon the help and inspiration of many people. Many of these people have also been instrumental in helping me with the 2nd edition. The environment at Georgetown's School of Business is still ideal, with its emphasis on "international" as a school theme, the support of the Dean and the resources made available through the McCrane/Shaker chair, including a reduced teaching load and an outstanding assistant, Anne Walsh. Then there are colleagues like Michael Czinkota, Ilkka Ronkainen, Paul Almeida, Stan Nollen, Rob Grant, Kasra Ferdows, and Tom Brewer, friends and colleagues, and other colleagues in marketing and international business, who have provided a stimulating environment for the work. Andrea Alexander, Minako Fukagata and Hyun Jung were very able research assistants.

The 2nd edition owes much to colleagues at other academic institutions as well. In 1996/97 I spent a great sabbatical year at Stockholm School of Economics, with Lars-Gunnar Mattsson, Susanne Hertz, Ivan Snehota and their colleagues in the distribution group, and with Örjan Sölvell and his colleagues at IIB. Among international scholars, Hans Thorelli at Indiana, Tamer Cavusgil at Michigan State, Gary Knight at Florida State, David Tse at City University of Hongkong, Bruce Kogut at Wharton, and Masaaki Kotabe at Texas, now at Temple, have had a strong impact on my thinking. So have Jean-Claude Usunier at Universite Louis Pasteur in Strasbourg, Christian Homburg at Mannheim University, Masaaki Hirano at Waseda, Saeed Samie at Tulsa, Jens Laage-Hellman at Chalmers in Gothenburg, Mosad Zineldin at Vaxjo University, Israel Nebenzahl at Bar-Ilan University, Bernard Simonin, now at University of Illinois, and Carlos Garcia-Pont at IESE, Barcelona.

When it comes to global strategy, I have been greatly influenced by George Yip at Cambridge, a good friend and co-author, Warren Keegan at Pace and Nick Binedell in Johannesburg. In global branding, a new section in this edition, I have benefitted from discussions with Sandra Milberg and Ronnie Goodstein at Georgetown, Susan Douglas at New York University, Erich Joachimsthaler at Darden, Chris Macrae of the World Class Branding Network in London, Hiroshi Tanaka at Hosei University in Tokyo, Shigeo Kobayashi of Honda's Future Research group and Lia Nikopoulos of Landor Associates. On electronic commerce, another expanded section in this edition, I have learned a great deal from Bill McHenry at Georgetown, Eric Boyd of InfoCast, and Mikael Karlsson at Reson AB in Stockholm. Among marketing colleagues, I want to single out David Montgomery at Stanford, Philip Kotler at Northwestern, Dominique Hanssens at UCLA, Evert Gummesson at University of Stockholm, and John Graham at Irvine, who all have helped bridge the gap between international and non-international research in marketing.

Some of the practitioners I have had the fortune to meet and learn from should also be thanked. Flip de Jager at Volvo, Chong Lee at LG Korea, Bruce Wolff at Marriott, and John Stabb at Microlog stand out. So do Osamu Iida and Takanori Sonoda at Honda, Masumi Natsusaka at Kao-Beiersdorf in Tokyo, Masaaki Eguchi at Kao, Per Surtevall at SIFO, Stockholm, Hermawan Kartajaya of MarkPlus in Jakarta, Ulf Södergren at Electrolux, Casey Shimamoto of ExecNet, Tokyo, and Jan Segerfeldt of Segerfeldt & Partners in Stockholm. Several of my present and former students provided valuable input of one kind or another, especially Paul Lewis and Mitchell Murata at Georgetown.

I am especially grateful to the many people who have given me constructive feedback on the first edition of the book. In particular I want to thank Larry Cunningham at University of Colorado in Denver, Anthony Lowe at University of South Australia, Masoud Kavoossi at Howard, Philip Rosson at Dalhousie and Gary Bamossy at Vrije Universiteit in Amsterdam.

Special thanks are due to the case writers who graciously allowed me to use their work in the book: Tamer Cavusgil at Michigan State, Per Jenster at Copenhagen Business School, Kamran Kashani at IMD, Richard Köhler and Wolfgang Breuer at Cologne University, Tage Madsen at Odense University, Dave Montgomery at Stanford, Christian Pinson and Vikas Tibrewala at Insead, Sandra Vandermerwe at Imperial College, London, George Yip at Cambridge University, and Eddie Yu and Anthony Ko at City University of Hong Kong.

The editorial staff at Irwin-McGraw Hill deserves a great deal of credit. Nancy Barbour, Christine Parker and Karen Westover were great to work with, encouraging but also prompting me to get on with it. Harriet Stockanes in permissions, and Michael Hruby behind the photos made it clear that there is more to a book than just the writing of it. Bonnie Guy did a great job on the IM, and was fun to work with.

I also wish to express my appreciation to the following reviewers of the 2nd edition: Paul Chao at University of Northern Iowa, Dharma Desilva at Wichita State University, Jaishankar Ganesh at University of Central Florida, Kate Gillespie at University of Texas at Austin, Joby John at Bentley College, Masoud Kavoossi at Howard University, Fernando Robles at George Washington University, Sunanda Sangwan at Aston University - Netherlands, Ivan Snehota at Stockholm School of Economics, Mary Stansifer at University of Colorado - Denver, David Stewart at Memorial University of Newfoundland, and Newell Wright at James Madison University.

Finally, I want to acknowledge the debt to my family. Tamiko, my Japanese wife, and Anna and Sonja, our two daughters with U.S. passports, faced firsthand the daily challenges of living in a multicultural environment. To all these people I say thank you. I hope the effort has not been in vain.

CONTENTS

Part Two
Foreign Entry

*P*art Three
Local Marketing

P art F o u r
Global Management

Fundamentals

The globalization of today's marketplace makes many new demands on a marketer. Not only are there important decisions about which countries' markets and segments to participate in and what modes of entry to use, but a marketer must also help formulate the marketing strategies in these countries and coordinate their implementation. He or she must speak for the local markets at headquarters but also explain the need for global standardization to local representatives. It is a job in which proven marketing techniques and face-to-face contacts are invaluable and one that requires a thorough grasp of marketing fundamentals and use of global communications.

Part One of this book shows how the demands of these complex tasks force the marketing manager and his or her organization to reevaluate their marketing strategies. How would local markets abroad respond to increased standardization? How would global and local competitors respond to a globally coordinated campaign? How acceptable is a global strategy given the traditional strength of the local subsidiaries? It is not surprising that one primary concern, for both the small firm marketing abroad for the first time and the large multinational corporation trying to implement a global strategy, is the feasibility of a global marketing plan. As always, a critical issue for management is knowing not only what the company should do but what it *can* do. This is never more relevant than in global marketing with its new and unfamiliar challenges, not the least of which is communicating well and doing business in a foreign culture.

Globalizing Marketing

"Brave new world"

Your takeaways from this chapter:

1. The increase in international trade and investment, the emergence of free trade blocs, and the opening of previously closed economies have led to greater global market opportunities than ever, but also to the threat of increased competition at home.

2. Not all industries are equally fit for global strategies. Furthermore, in most cases the various marketing mix tools do not lend themselves equally to a uniform treatment. The marketer needs to analyze the globalization drivers carefully before blindly following "the global imperative."

3. In addition to seeking revenue and profit growth, the company entering a foreign market might do so to challenge a competitor, learn from lead customers, or simply diversify its demand base.

4. To compete effectively in the global marketplace requires skill building. The marketer needs to learn how to enter markets and how to manage the marketing effort in the local foreign market. To gain these skills, the global marketing manager needs to have hands-on marketing experience in one or more foreign countries.

5. The job (and career path) of the global marketing manager can be divided into three different tasks: foreign entry, local marketing abroad, and global management.

CHAPTER 1 DESCRIBES the reality facing the marketing manager in today's global firm. As trade barriers are lowered, new growth opportunities in foreign markets open up and new markets need to be entered. At the same time, foreign competitors enter local markets and previously unchallenged market positions need to be defended. The firm whose managers have a narrow view of its capabilities and its market will fall short. The purely domestic company often does not have enough managerial skill, imagination, and competence to respond to the opportunities or the threats of a global marketplace. Only by going abroad into competitive markets will a company stretch its resources and build the capability of its managers to a competitive level.

Chapter 1 illustrates how foreign markets and competitors have changed the face of marketing and how the global marketer must become more than a functional specialist. Today's marketers must develop skills that help to determine the overall strategic direction of the firm. This chapter shows how the complex new marketing can be subdivided into three main tasks—foreign entry, local marketing abroad, and global management—each task an important component of the strategic capability of the manager and the firm.

Some Books Are Really Black, White, and Read All Over

Each fall in Frankfurt, Germany, publishers gather to offer their products to the world. To do this, they sell foreign rights, that is, the right of a foreign publisher to produce and sell a book in one or more countries. Publishers at the Frankfurt Book Fair set up exhibits and spend their days negotiating with representatives from firms in other countries.

Foreign rights sales are important because many books have global appeal. Fiction, in particular, interests readers throughout the world. James Redfield's novel *The Celestine Prophecy*, published by Warner Books, was a best-seller not only in the United States but in Brazil, Denmark, Canada, and other countries. Besides fiction, business titles and New Age books interest a global readership.

Publishers do have to tailor their offerings to local needs. There's the obvious issue of language differences; when customers speak another language, the book must be translated. In addition, tastes and outlooks vary from one region to the next. Italian publishers are reluctant to buy the rights to biographies because Italians tend to read about famous personalities in magazines instead. The poison gas attacks in Tokyo's subway spurred an interest among the Japanese in books on terrorism. And at a recent book fair, a Dutch editor hesitated over Hillary Rodham Clinton's book on raising children, *It Takes a Village*. The editor remarked that she would have to see the book first because "American values are so different."

The market for many books has, of course, long been global. Writers such as Umberto Eco, Milan Kundera, Jorge Luis Borges, Kazuo Ishiguro, and Salman Rushdie are established best-selling authors even in a country such as the United States, where foreign books have found the going tough. Similarly, American books are often on foreign best-seller lists, and the number of countries involved in buying foreign rights is growing to include more developing nations. Rights to books by John Grisham have been sold to over 30 countries, including Estonia.

Driven by the globalization of the book markets, competing publishing houses are turning global too. Bertelsmann A.G. of Germany became the world's largest book publisher when it bought American Random House in 1998. The company then struck up a joint venture with book retailer Barnes & Noble, the largest chain in the United States, to build a global Internet network to sell titles in all major languages on-line. Amazon.com, the leading Internet bookseller, quickly responded to protect its turf. Later in 1998 it bought a British electronic bookstore, Bookpages, and unveiled plans for entry into Britain and Germany, striking at the heart of Bertelsmann's empire.

Sources: Mary B. W. Tabor, "Book Deals: Losing Nothing in Translation," *New York Times*, October 16, 1995, pp. D1, D8; John Tagliabue, "Nestle's Aim: New-Market Growth," *New York Times*, October 15, 1994, pp. 37, 39; Thomas A. Stewart, "Welcome to the Revolution," *Fortune*, December 13, 1993, pp. 66–68; Doreen Carvajal, "2 Book Giants in Global Deal to Sell Titles via Internet," *New York Times*, October 7, 1998, pp. C1, C9.
http://www.frankfurt-book-fair.com
http://www.warnerbooks.com
http://www.bertelsmann.de/
http://www.randomhouse.com/
http://www.amazon.com
http://www.bookpages.com

GOING GLOBAL

A lot of businesses are going global today. Ten or 15 years ago global business was mainly in the hands of a select number of multinational giants. Small and medium-sized businesses concentrated on their home markets and perhaps one or two neighboring countries. Not so any longer. Even the smallest businesses have realized that they have something to market in faraway countries, many of which have recently opened to foreign competition. Today, companies of all sizes in various industries from many countries are actively competing in the world's markets.

Behind the development toward a more global marketplace lies the revolution in global communications. Satellite television broadcasts have eliminated national borders in mass media. Fax machines and other advances in electronic telecommunications have made it possible to develop company information networks that rival government intelligence operations. Today it is possible for headquarters to participate directly in decision making in any subsidiary. Managers can direct operations any place on earth from airplanes and automobiles, and even when they're on vacation, they can be seen on the beach talking on their mobile phones.[1]

As long as world markets remain open, there is no stopping the spread of global competition. No markets are immune, as even government procurement business is opened to foreign suppliers. Deregulation and privatization confront sleepy public utilities with new and vigorous competitors, sometimes from countries in the same trading bloc.[2] Efficient foreign competitors from leading countries enter previously protected country markets and flush local companies out of comfortable market pockets. The lesson for all is that no market position is secure without attention to customer satisfaction and constant innovation.

Prominent movers in this raising of the competitive stakes have been Japanese, but companies in many other countries have risen to the challenge. European companies, aided by the European integration (EU), have consolidated and rationalized to protect themselves, and have in many cases become hunters on their own. Germany's BMW, Braun, and Beiersdorf; France's Thomson and Alcatel; Ciba-Geigy (Novartis), Nestlé, and ABB in Switzerland; Italy's Benetton; and Sweden's Ericsson are some of the success stories. Others—like Volkswagen, General Motors, Electrolux, Fiat, Olivetti, Nixdorf, and Volvo—have had their ups and downs. Operating in the new global environ-

The Nestle company's web site. Today most companies, large and small, recognize the value of creating their own homepage. The typical web site provides information about the company and its products, in different languages and with global reach. Reprinted with permission of Nestle S.A.

ment requires skills not easily mastered, especially when the traditional position was bolstered by trade barriers and government protection.[3]

North American companies have also taken up the challenge. Although many withered under the Japanese onslaught, others revived, stimulated by the new ideas learned and incorporated into their own operations. Companies such as Xerox, General Electric, and Canada's Northern Telecom have successfully reengineered their operations and raised quality, and are coming through the difficult years stronger than ever. Companies with less intense foreign competition—such as Hewlett-Packard, Microsoft, and Boeing—have kept their operations lean and their rates of innovation high, and have reinforced their global reach. Even U.S. automakers seem to be emerging from their long drought, although they have been helped considerably by the strong yen of the early 1990s. But as elsewhere, U.S. companies without international competitiveness—consumer electronics manufacturers, large steel producers, shoe makers—have had much more trouble defending their traditional market turf.

Even many Japanese companies have not fared well against international competition. Japanese markets were long protected by various tariff barriers, now removed, and also by nontariff barriers, some of which still remain. As standard economic theory suggests, such barriers often have the effect of supporting inefficient companies.[4] While Japanese automakers and electronics companies are generally very competitive worldwide, this is not the case in chemicals, pharmaceuticals, paper, medical machinery, and other industries. While rivalry among auto companies and among electronics firms is fierce, companies in less successful Japanese industries have been content with covert collusion not to compete.

The lesson is that intense competition at home and abroad forces a company to be internationally competitive. Today's global marketing manager must understand and learn from foreign competitors and from foreign customers.

This chapter will first give a historical perspective on this development, since it is important to understand where globalization "comes from." It then discusses the four main underlying forces of globalization among companies and how these forces create a need for (or constrain the potential of) global strategies. Then the discussion will shift to more pure marketing issues, starting with some needed definitions of what global marketing involves and the distinction between global products and global brands. Then the chapter describes how managers can learn a lot from doing marketing abroad, knowledge that can be put to good use in other markets as well. Finally the chapter presents the three roles that a global marketing manager plays during his or her career, and which underlie the separate parts of this book: foreign entry, local marketing abroad, and global management.

A HISTORICAL PERSPECTIVE

The global perspective in marketing has become prominent in the last 5 or 10 years. It is useful to set this development in its historical perspective.

The Multinational Phase

In the two decades after World War II, American companies emerged as dominant multinationals. While the previously warring countries were preoccupied with rebuilding their nations, American *multinational companies* (MNCs) found great opportunities in Europe, Asia, and Latin America. Maintaining control over their manufacturing and technical know-how, and overcoming tariff barriers, through wholly owned subsidiaries, the American MNCs became suppliers to the world.

In those days marketing was technically much less advanced than it is today. Because of their obvious needs, foreign markets could be penetrated easily. Since production was often localized, products could be adapted to local markets. **Multinational marketing** meant marketing to different countries with local adaptation of products and promotions. Meanwhile at home in the States, the growth ignited by the baby boom among other factors allowed companies to succeed with relative ease. Nevertheless, the size of the U.S. market, the relatively low U.S. tariff barriers, and competition between large firms stimulated development of more advanced marketing techniques.

Market segmentation, dividing a given market into more homogeneous subgroups, became a well-known conceptual tool toward the end of the 1950s, and the marketing mix with its 4Ps of marketing (product, price, promotion, and place) appeared in the early 1960s. Product positioning, the idea that a product or brand can be placed in a specific location in the consumer's perceptual map of a product category, became popular from the late 1960s onward. At the same time, marketing research techniques grew increasingly sophisticated with the impetus coming from academicians in business schools who were funded first by the Ford Foundation and later directly by companies. In the 1960s and into the 70s, the American marketers were, if not the best, at least the most technically proficient marketers in the world.

Gradually, as national markets grew and the American MNCs expanded production into new countries, these countries developed manufacturing and marketing capabilities of their own. While the American firms were still strong in new technology, they were no longer competitive in the manufacture of products embodying more standardized technology. Over time the United States became an importer of products it had originally invented, including textiles, electronics, and sports equipment. This process became known as the *international product cycle phenomenon* and retains a certain validity in today's globally integrated world.[5] It explains, for example, why a high-wage country such as Germany attempts to focus on high-technology industries. However, as increasing numbers of countries can handle high technology, companies in advanced countries may have to develop competitive advantages other than technology.

The Global Phase

The global phase, which involves much more standardization of products and integration of activities across countries than had been the case in the multinational phase, started during the 1970s but was seen as early as 1968 in a seminal article by Robert Buzzell proclaiming the advantages of standardization.[6] The phase did not get commonly recognized, however, until 1983 when Theodore Levitt published an article arguing that world markets were growing more and more homogeneous.[7]

One of the major forces behind the emergence of the global perspective was the appearance of strong foreign competitors to U.S. firms in the United States. In particular, Japanese companies had entered the U.S. market with spectacular success in markets such as autos and consumer electronics, where American firms had long held dominant positions. From the mid-1970s on, foreign firms were no longer makers of the low-technology and low-priced entries, or luxury niche marketers as some Europeans had tended to be, but competed successfully in the core of the American marketplace.

Initially, the inroads by Japanese companies were explained as a consequence of tariff and nontariff barriers in their home markets that afforded them a ready supply of cash and preferential treatment as members of industrial groupings, allowing them to pursue low-price strategies overseas. The Japanese government also prioritized certain export industries, making low-interest loans and lenient tax treatment available. This line of explanation is still maintained today and underlies the push by other countries toward further opening of the Japanese markets.[8]

Gradually, however, the explanation for the success of the foreign entrants shifted more toward business-based factors. The availability of highly educated engineers, and skilled labor, and the companies' focus on manufacturing quality became a new line of explanation. The growth of suppliers in related industries and increasingly demanding customers served to explain an increasing rate of new product innovation. The existence of rival producers and intense competition helped enhance the firms' attention to customer satisfaction.[9]

By the end of the 1980s, Porter's work on the competitive advantages of a *nation* served to codify these factors.[10] No longer was Japan a special case; successful industries and companies in other countries shared similar characteristics. Companies with well-known global brand names such as Benetton in Italy, Swatch in Switzerland, Mercedes-Benz in Germany, and Sony and Toyota in Japan were shown to owe their success to favorable productive environments in their respective home countries.

While Porter's analysis is valid, it explains only part of the global performance of these companies. The main missing part is the marketing side. How can home country factors be important in foreign markets? Levitt in 1983 argued that markets around the world were becoming more similar because of technological advances in mass communications and the increase in international travel. People everywhere now are exposed to the same products and messages, and their preferences become more *homogeneous*. Accordingly, companies that offer standardized products with low prices and high quality win out over local competitors offering adapted products at higher prices. The large-scale advantages of *standardization* mean that the global company can be profitable while selling at a lower price, and the company can amortize investments in R&D and design over many markets. Global products, although not adapted to specific local preferences, can offer a superior quality-to-price ratio. This is one reason why the Japanese succeeded against U.S. firms in the United States.

In the late 1980s and 1990s, the global phase gained increased momentum with the worldwide globalization and integration of financial markets. This development also exposed global marketers to new sources of risk (see box, "The End of the Global Imperative?").

The Success of Global Products

Although Levitt's argument was initially met by skepticism among marketing professionals, subsequent developments have tended to converge toward the global marketing view. Even if local preferences have sometimes demanded product adaptation, there have been many surprising successes for firms with standardized global products. Markets once thought to be very different across countries have been impacted by global brands. Consumer goods such as beer, food, and apparel—and service providers such as accountants, lawyers, and even retailers—are some of the categories where global firms have been successful against locals in many countries. Add to this the typically global markets in many industrial products, high-tech products, and consumer durables such as cameras, watches, and VCRs, and in some ways the markets look even more homogeneous today than when Levitt was writing. Increasing similarity of preferences has led

Picture

The End of the Global Imperative?

TOWARD THE END of the 1990s the global financial system was jolted by severe shocks. In 1997, at the threat of higher interest rates in Japan, Thai investors scurried to exchange their bahts for Japanese yen to pay for loans denominated in the Japanese currency. The baht quickly lost value and was devalued, punishing investors and Thai consumers alike. The resulting recession quickly spread to other Asian countries, then to Russia and Latin America. The close integration of the world's financial markets made it difficult to stop the spread of the turmoil.

Companies that had targeted Asian markets for expansion, such as Dell in personal computers and Coca-Cola, had to retrench and scale down their ambitions. In 1998 Malaysia virtually closed its borders to foreign capital flows, in the process making imported products prohibitively expensive for Malaysian consumers. In Russia, po-

litical uncertainties forced many companies to adopt a "wait and see" attitude toward market entry.

What does this add up to? The conclusion that many companies come to is that all-out global expansion is no longer an "imperative." Instead, companies opt for a more flexible and limited stance. In many European and American multinationals this means a focus on the markets closer to home. But once the global financial fundamentals are back in place, one can expect the push into fast-growing foreign markets to again shift into forward gear—although probably not into overdrive.

http://www.coca-cola.com/home.html
http://www.cokecce.com/
http://www/dell.com/

to the success of global products, which in turn has fostered further homogeneity of markets. Hamel and Prahalad, in a final twist, argue that in many cases new products lead and change preferences, so that the global firm should introduce many alternative new products, innovating and creating new market niches instead of trying to precisely target an existing segment.[11]

The key to success of the globally standardized products is not that they are especially cheap or that every consumer wants the same thing as everyone else. They are often the best-value products because they offer higher quality and more advanced features at better prices. They also tend to be stronger on the intangible extras such as status and brand image. But mostly they embody the best in technology with designs from leading markets and are manufactured to the highest standards. As much as they satisfy customers, they as often create new desires. In terms of the product life cycle (see Exhibit 11.10 page 359), global products will often generate new growth in mature markets, as customers return sooner for upgrades and more modern features.

SOME PRELIMINARY DISTINCTIONS

Before going further, it is useful to define some of the terms used in the book more precisely.

Global Marketing

Global marketing refers to marketing activities coordinated and integrated across multiple country markets. The integration can involve standardized products, uniform packaging, identical brand names, synchronized product introductions, similar advertising messages, or coordinated sales campaigns across markets in several countries. Despite the term *global*, it is not necessary that all or most of the countries of the world be included. Even regional marketing efforts, such as pan-European operations, can be viewed as examples of global marketing, that is, an integrated effort across several countries. The principles are roughly similar whether one talks about 10 or 50 countries.

International Marketing.

International marketing is an older term encompassing foreign trade analysis, environmental differences, and all marketing efforts in foreign countries, whether coordinated or not. There is also *foreign marketing*, meaning merely marketing in some foreign country. As described earlier in our historical perspective, *multinational marketing* meant marketing strategies that assumed all markets to be "multidomestic," or having strong local preferences, and is a predecessor term to *global marketing*, with its emphasis on standardization and integration.

In practice, these distinctions are not sharp, and the marketing activities they describe naturally progress from one to another. In order to perform the *global management* task successfully, the marketing manager needs to have some understanding of all the basics of international business and the characteristics of the market environments in foreign countries. The manager needs to have as keen a sense as possible of trade barriers, different market environments, and social and cultural biases—including, of course, his or her own. The successful global marketing manager gets intensely involved with these issues before attacking the global management job.

Multidomestic Markets

It is clear to any observer that consumers in different countries think, speak, and behave differently in many ways. The salient product beliefs, attitudes, and social norms vary considerably between markets. The extent to which quality concerns are important, the attitudes toward foreign products, and the degree to which individuals comply with social norms all affect consumers' decision making differently across countries. For example, if a Japanese shopper is often fastidious and examines a product carefully in the store, an American consumer may be more impulsive and respond to in-store promotions of new brands.

There are variations in tastes as well. If a European buyer prefers a car with a stick shift and tight cornering, a Japanese consumer likes a light touch and easy controls. If a Canadian wants a beer with a certain "body," an American may be happy with a light beer. If a Latin American woman wants strong and dark colors, a northern European may dress in lighter colors. These are preferences based on tradition, culture, or simply fashion. They are malleable within limits, but it is not at all clear whether any one firm can effect any changes alone or how long it will take. These are the differences that have made marketers say products have to be adapted.

Multidomestic markets are defined as product markets in which local consumers have preferences and functional requirements widely different from one another's and those elsewhere.[12] The typical categories include products and services such as food, drink, clothing, and entertainment, which tend to vary considerably between countries and in which many consumers prefer the local variants.

Multidomestic markets reflect underlying religious, cultural, and social factors and also climate and the availability of (or lack of) various foods and raw materials. Japanese prefer rice and dried fish for breakfast, while Europeans eat ham and cheese or coffee and croissants. Drinking beer with food is strange for the French, while tea is the standard drink at Chinese dinners. The thin-soled shoes favored by stylish Mediterranean men do not fare well in the American setting with its rugged Western traditions. And so on. These differences are based on long traditions, education, and upbringing. Western people might think that sweets are liked by young and old, but even the children in Asian countries often prefer salty snacks to sweet chocolate cake. One's taste is educated, not something one is born with.

The firm selling into multidomestic markets needs to *localize* and *adapt* its products and services to the different requirements and preferences in the markets. Levels of salt and sugar in food products might need to change, and color patterns and sizes of packaging may have to change and even be redesigned for attractiveness and taste.

Drinks need to be taste-tested and perhaps given strong communication support, educating the local consumers and trying to change their preferences, as Seven-Up has tried to do in the United States. In clothing, redesigning jeans to fit the different bodies of Asian people, widening the shoes, and shortening the sleeves are necessary steps, but the multidomestic marketer may also have to create new colors, different styles, and alternative materials. Before globalization, firms were generally multinational for a reason: The products had to be adapted to each country's preferences. Marketing could not be uniform.

Global Markets

At the same time, there are many product markets that are *not* multidomestic, such as televisions, telephones, automobiles, and personal computers. Generally speaking, these markets are not multidomestic because of the products' high-technology content. People's preferences for these kinds of products are not formed by underlying cultural or religious traditions or by climate but by differences in individual needs and wants. In multidomestic markets, segmentation by countries is natural. Not so in more technology-based products, where markets are naturally global.

Global markets are defined as those markets in which buyer preferences are similar across countries. Within each country, several segments with differing preferences may exist, but the country borders are not important segment limits. The typical characteristics of a *global market* have both customer and competitive aspects. The major *global* features to look for are the following:[13]

In customers:

Increasingly common consumer requirements and preferences as gaps in lifestyles, tastes, and behavior narrow.

Global networks with a centralized purchasing function among business customers.

Disappearing national boundaries as customers travel across borders to buy wherever the best products and/or prices are found.

Increasing agreement among customers across the globe about how to evaluate products and services and recognition of which brands are the best.

In competitors:

Competition among the same world-class players in every major national market.

Declining numbers of competitors in the core of the market as domestic companies defend their turf by specialization or merge with larger firms.

Increasing use of national markets as a strategic tool for the benefit of the firm's global network.

With global communications and spreading affluence, many previously multidomestic markets are becoming more susceptible to globalization. People all around the world now know and like ethnic foods, such as Middle Eastern hummus, Spanish paella, and Beijing duck. Stylish clothes from Armani, Levi's, and Benetton are bought in many countries. Japanese sake, German beer, and French wine compete directly as a dinner drink in many local places. Larry King broadcasts his TV talk show from Hong Kong to a worldwide audience. As multidomestic markets open up and become more global, the rest of the world is able to pick and choose among the best that the multidomestic markets offer. Increasing affluence generates a desire for variety and creates opportunities for local specialties from foreign countries.

The main differences between multidomestic and global markets are highlighted in Exhibit 1.1.[14] As can be seen, most marketing parameters in the multidomestic case

EXHIBIT 1.1 Multidomestic versus Global Markets: Key Differences

	Multidomestic markets	**Global markets**
Market boundaries	Markets are defined within country borders. Customers and competitors are of local origin.	Markets transcend country borders. Customers and/or competitors cross frontiers to buy and to sell.
Customers	Significant differences exist among customers from different countries; segments are defined locally.	Significant similarities exist among customers from different countries; segments cut across geographic frontiers.
Competition	Competition takes place among primarily local firms; even international companies compete on a country-by-country basis.	Competitors are few and present in every major market. Rivalry takes on regional or global scope.
Interdependence	Each local market operates in isolation from the rest. Competitive actions in one market have no impact elsewhere.	Local markets operate interdependently. Competitive actions in one market impact other markets.
Strategies	Strategies are locally based. Little advantage exists in coordinating activities among markets	Strategies are regional or global in scope. Great advantage exists in coordinating activities within regions or worldwide.

Source: Reproduced from *Managing Global Marketing*, by Kamran Kashani with the permission of SouthWestern College Publishing. Copyright ©1992 PWS- Kent Publishing Company. All rights reserved.

are determined by national borders, as opposed to the global case where borders matter much less.

"Foreign" Marketing

Many global companies, as disparate as CNN and Honda, have banned use of the term *foreign* in their communications. They want to avoid the sense that some countries are separate and strange. The companies want their employees to view the world as an integrated entity and not favor the home country over others. While such avoidance is useful as a device to foster a global organizational culture, this book uses the word *foreign* freely. This is because *foreign* well describes the kind of situation global marketing managers often find themselves in. For managers of a company with established presence in the world's markets, such as CNN or Honda, the various countries should be familiar enough to make use of the word unnecessary. For a textbook that teaches students how to get to that level of familiarity, however, *foreign* has just the right connotation of a slight (or severe) shock to the pre-established way of looking at the world (see box "Mercedes' Old-Fashioned Cars").

A Managerial Approach

As a final note on the managerial approach taken in this book, this text relates all important topics to the situation of the individual marketing decision maker in the firm or its subsidiary abroad. In this it differs slightly from other texts. Rather than treating the important environmental factors (political, economic, social, etc.) in separate chapters, they are brought into the decision-making setting explicitly, as additional problems or opportunities for the manager. As an example, a country's strict environmental code can be a constraint for some companies but serve to define a new market opportunity for others. Lack of commercial advertising opportunities in a country can force a company to turn to satellite TV and start developing global advertising copy.

GETTING THE *Picture*

Mercedes' Old-Fashioned Cars

ALTHOUGH MERCEDES-BENZ, the German carmaker, prides itself on the up-to-date technology it uses in its cars in the West, in other markets it is decidedly old-fashioned. Why? Because it has gone back to basics and become customer-oriented.

In Saudi Arabia, auto engines are plagued by sand entering the cylinder blocks, gradually building up deposits until the engine cracks. But not Mercedes cars. Most new cars use light aluminum alloys in their engines because their hardness increases engine performance and is fuel-efficient. By using older-style, softer steel alloys, Mercedes cars lose the efficiency race but keep running when the sand filters in. The hard silicon in the sand simply gets buried inside the softer metal of the cylinder heads.

In Poland, Mercedes' market share is on par with the Japanese cars' combined. Reason? The Poles are as rich as the oil sheiks? No. But for some models Mercedes has gone back to the old way of building cars from simple parts instead of using the integrated components and subassem-blies that have served so effectively to increase Japanese manufacturing productivity. The problem with the modern techniques is that doing your own repairs is almost impossible, and repair costs rise since, when something breaks, whole assemblies are needed to replace a broken part. This matters less in Western countries where a big part of repair costs comes from the high cost of labor, and the new subassembly can be replaced quickly. But in Poland, labor is cheap. Mercedes sells well because spare parts are simple and inexpensive, and its cars can be fixed by the owner who can take his or her time to repair the car the do-it-yourself way or have a mechanic who is affordable fix it.

Moral: "Back to basics" marketing requires imagination and an understanding of usage situations.

Sources: M. Wolongiewicz, student report, International University of Japan, June 1994.
http://www.Mercedes-Net.com/

The book does not automatically assume the global company's home market is in the United States. It covers companies headquartered in other countries and also takes a look at the United States as a foreign market. For many companies in other parts of the world, the United States is the main foreign market, and it should be of interest to Americans to recognize how they look from the outside. Incidentally, American managers who are disheartened by foreigners' in-depth knowledge of U.S. customers should keep in mind that because of the size of the U.S. market, foreign managers tend to know more about the American market than about their other foreign markets.

DRIVERS TOWARD GLOBALIZATION

Today, four classes of variables propel companies toward globalization: *Market, competition, cost,* and *government* variables are sometimes referred to as the four major **globalization drivers.**[15]

Market Drivers

Market factors are the strongest driver of global marketing. There are five major features of international markets that drive companies toward global marketing strategies. They are:

1. Common customer needs
2. Global customers
3. Global channels
4. Transferable marketing
5. Leading markets

When customers in different countries have the same needs in a product or service category, **common customer needs** become a compelling factor for companies. With

Companies serving multinational firms stress their global capability, as in this ad for DHL Worldwide Express. Courtesy DHL Worldwide Express.

technological progress and global communications, consumers in many countries are exposed to similar messages and products. For many industries, free trade and unrestricted travel have created homogeneous groups of customers around the globe. Preferences tend to become less localized or provincial and approach a *global* standard.[16] However, some markets—typically culture-bound products and services, such as foods, drinks, apparel, and entertainment—-stubbornly resist the shift toward globalization and remain multidomestic, with different customer preferences and differentiated products across countries.

Global customers are customers that need the same product or service in several countries. For example, as companies globalize, as global customers they want to buy from suppliers and vendors with global presence. This is why supplier firms in the automobile industry—such as German Bosch, Japanese Nippon Denso, and American Delco—have gone abroad. Global customers have spurred the development of global hotel chains, global ad agencies, and global communications. Hilton Hotels, McCann Erickson Worldwide, and Federal Express are prominent examples of American companies following their customers abroad, in the process putting pressure on competing local services in various countries.

Global channels, distribution and logistics firms that provide seamless transportation and storage around the world, have had a similar positive effect on the emergence of global marketing strategies. Firms can in many cases expand internationally only if the requisite developments in the channel infrastructure keep pace. Thus, the multinational integration of transportation networks, the spread of large financial institutions, the emergence of worldwide distributors of grain and other commodities, and the globalization of even seemingly localized retailers such as supermarkets (Delhaize of Belgium, for example, is now present not only throughout Europe but also in the United States) and department stores (mainly by acquiring existing stores, but also opening new stores) make it possible for marketers to sell their products through new integrated networks.

Transferable marketing involves using the same marketing ideas in different countries. This can mean the same packaging, advertising, brand names, and other marketing mix elements. As campaign ideas in one country prove successful, the global company can use the same or a slightly adapted campaign in other markets as well. This is how good ideas get leveraged. For example, Nike's successful American ad campaign featuring basketball star Michael Jordan was also used in many other countries. The multilanguage packaging of many consumer goods has made it possible to offer the same packages with the same colors and the same brand names in many countries.

Leading markets (sometimes called lead markets) are markets where products and services incorporate the latest technology, competitive rivalry is strong, and customers are sophisticated and demanding.[17] The existence of such markets and the need for the firm to be in such markets push the firm toward global strategies in order to take full advantage of the benefits gained from leading markets. Although there is no need for the marketing strategy within a leading market to be identical with the strategy in other markets, there is good reason to share market research from leading markets with markets in other countries. Thus, the firm capable of implementing a global marketing strategy can draw on lessons from competitors and customers in leading markets to design the strategy. For example, while a semiconductor firm such as Texas Instruments has trouble making money in Japan, the lessons it learns in that difficult market help it to design entry strategies and service support elsewhere in the Asian region.

Competitive Drivers

In many industries the example from competitors who go global provides a strong incentive for a firm to follow suit. Such **competitive drivers** energize an organization to match a move. It is not by coincidence that Swedish Ericsson and Finnish Nokia both attacked the American mobile phone market in the late 1990s. Also, following another company's path means that management can learn from somebody else's mistakes. Toyota's Lexus and Nissan's Infiniti luxury cars were introduced in the North American market following closely the approach used by Honda's Acura, including separate dealer networks. Also, there is legitimacy in trying to match a competitor's move, and it makes the task of convincing doubtful shareholders and reluctant subsidiary management easier. American Whirlpool's coordinated attack on the global market for home appliances (including the acquisition of Dutch Philips' appliance business) added support to the globalization efforts of Electrolux, the Swedish competitor.

On the home front, the presence of foreign competitors in a firm's domestic market increases the need for the firm to venture abroad, if for no other reason than to counterattack in foreign markets. Benetton's success in the United States has led The Gap and The Limited, two U.S. competitors, to go abroad. The emergence of strong global competitors has served to develop the necessary facilities and infrastructure for domestic companies to go global. For example, global businesses tend not only to sell their products abroad but also to transfer skills and technology across countries, making it easier for domestic companies to expand globally. The typical head of international operations at a novice entrant abroad has often been hired away from a more successful global company.

These kinds of competitive effects put pressure on companies to globalize their marketing activities. Even for the firm active in most foreign markets already, the competitive synergy achieved from synchronizing marketing across countries can be significant. Simultaneously introducing new models in several countries puts pressure on competitors, a strategy used by Microsoft when introducing new software. Monitoring competitive prices in several markets and coordinating price changes make it possible to match competitive prices in some markets and aggressively attack in others, as has been done by German automakers in the United States. Global coordination is also important when competitive signaling is to be interpreted. When Kodak was hesitant about sponsoring the 1984 Summer Olympics in Los Angeles, the news was first relayed from the London office of Fuji film to American Fuji, which immediately offered to sponsor the games at the asking price. By the time Kodak had reconsidered, the competitive coup was already a fait accompli.[18]

Cost Drivers

In industries such as automobiles that require large-scale plants to be efficient, single markets are rarely sufficient to generate **economies of scale.** Scale economies involve the unit cost reductions made possible by long series in a given plant, and to achieve this one plant often needs to supply more than one foreign market. When a new plant is established, it is often designed to assemble one model only, shipping it to neighboring countries in order to gain such scale advantages. Toyota's new Kentucky plant, for example, produces the Camry model for the NAFTA market, and the new BMW plant in South Carolina will focus on the 325 model, supplying the North American market.

Even where there are no scale economies, **economies of scope** (gains from spreading activities across multiple product lines or businesses) can push businesses to globalize. Thus, in consumer packaged goods, where the dominant global firms have small plants in many countries, they gain scope economies by marketing a wide selection of products. Unilever, Colgate-Palmolive, and Procter and Gamble have mostly uniform product lines and brand names across the EU, but have manufacturing plants in all the major European countries.

Other cost drivers include global **sourcing advantages,** which include cost savings via supply from a low-wage country, improved logistics and distribution systems, and the growth of inexpensive global telecommunications. Also, high product-development costs relative to the size of the national market and fast-developing technology serve to reinforce the need for global strategies to help recoup the investment.

These cost drivers generally induce companies to implement global strategies, and some of these strategies further encourage globalized marketing. Thus, scope economies tend to favor globally uniform brand names and communications, and improved logistics and telecommunications make it possible to manage distribution of products and services centrally. Federal Express is now well known in many places across the globe, and its computerized tracking system makes it possible to monitor the progress of shipments 24 hours a day.

The most important cost savings from global marketing are usually the gains in avoiding unnecessary **duplication** across countries. Such duplication can involve unnecessary redesign of a product for different markets, creating contradictory promotional campaigns in different markets, using localized slogans and brand names that reduce positive spillover effects, and using different packaging in different markets when all that is needed is the inclusion of more than one language on the package. These practices are all signs of potential waste that can often be eliminated without loss of goodwill. The original impetus toward global marketing is often management's desire to eliminate duplication and create better synergy across country markets.

Of course, there can also be a negative impact on global marketing from cost factors. For example, to capitalize on economies of scale in production several markets have to be supplied from a central location, creating a need for local warehousing facilities and local parts supplies. This investment may reduce some of the large-scale efficiencies. Furthermore, the large scale leads to inflexibility. For example, if a sudden change in demand creates a temporary market glut of one model and a shortage of another, a large specialized plant will be more costly to retool to satisfy the shifting demand.

Similarly, when product design is carried out in a leading market, local differences in preferences cannot always be taken into account. The same is true for prototypical advertising done in order to save money and for product-line pruning that eliminates local favorites too expensive to carry. Generally speaking, when marketing strategies are globalized to generate savings only, the local marketing effort suffers. Global marketing cannot be based on costs alone.

Government Drivers

The government globalization drivers include favorable trade policies, acceptance of foreign investment, compatible technical standards, and common marketing regulations. All of these factors have a direct and unequivocally positive effect on global marketing efforts. In the past, governmental barriers to foreign market entry kept local markets protected and made global marketing an impossibility. Despite the continued progress toward open markets and free trade, it is important to keep in mind that such barriers can be raised again and that political complications can ruin the best-laid global marketing plans.

A good example of the effect of governments on globalization is the recent introduction of **ISO 9000,** a global standard of quality certification (*ISO* stands for Industrial Standards of Operation). ISO 9000 encourages globalized marketing, since it is worldwide. Furthermore, the more countries the company does business in, the higher the return on investment in improved operations to gain certification. At the same time, the higher standards encourage uniformity of operations everywhere.

As one example, faced with myriad conflicting regulations of products and services in the different member countries, the EU Brussels Commission decided to start with a clean slate and adopt the new standards to supersede existing national standards. Of course, each product or service category (telephones, consumer electronics, autos, pharmaceuticals, etc.) has its own category-specific standards. In addition, however, the Commission developed an umbrella code in ISO 9000 that serves as a guide for all companies wanting to do business in the EU. A Board of Examiners was created to certify companies under the code, which includes requirements on the safety of facilities, treatment of raw materials, quality inspection procedures, and even customer satisfaction measures. Although approval under the code is not a legal requirement as yet, many companies, European as well as non-European, have decided to expend resources to improve their operations and gain certification. This gives them an edge over competitors not yet certified.[19]

REALISTIC GLOBAL MARKETING

Even though there might be a trend toward more global markets and toward globalized strategies, in practice it is important to keep in mind that global is not always the right answer.

The Limits to Globalized Marketing

There are four important limits to the degree a company should pursue globalized marketing.[20]

1. **Industry Factors.**   Not all industries have the right characteristics for a global strategy. That is, the four "globalization drivers" (market, competition, cost, and government) may not be conducive to a global approach.

2. **Internal Resources.** Not all companies have the required resources (managerial, financial) to implement global marketing effectively. Even if the aim is cost savings because of less duplication and larger scale in production, instituting a global marketing strategy requires some financial resources up front for the necessary investment in advertising prototypes, benchmark designs, and global communication capabilities.

3. **Different Mixes.** Not all marketing mix activities lend themselves to a global treatment. While product design can often be uniform across several countries, language and cultural barriers make it difficult to standardize salesmanship.

4. **Global Turmoil.** Close coordination of strategies across countries can make the firm more vulnerable to global financial turmoil. When financial markets tumble, as happened in the late 1990s, global integration means that no country is immune.

Differentiated Globalization

Because of these limits, a global marketing strategy that totally globalizes all marketing activities is not always achievable or desirable. A more common approach is for a company to globalize its product strategy by marketing the same product lines, product designs, and brand names everywhere but to localize distribution and marketing communications. This is the standard approach in consumer durables such as automobiles, cameras, and electronics. By contrast, consumer packaged goods companies have often gone further in their globalization effort, with worldwide ad campaigns and frequent in-store promotions in addition to a standardized product line.

Studies of the extent to which successful companies' marketing mix activities are globalized have revealed a fairly consistent pattern. A company's packaging and brand names are most likely to be globalized, followed by its media message and distribution; activities become more localized for in-store promotions, and the pattern ends with very localized personal selling and customer service functions.[21] This pattern holds for American as well as Japanese and European firms. A firm's global marketing strategy has to be flexibly implemented and take account of the different degrees to which the activities need local adaptation and personnel. Canadian and Japanese customers may prefer the same automobile, for example, but they may have different needs when it comes to after-sales support because of the different conditions of use in the two countries.

In general, the closer a marketing mix activity is to the point of purchase or after-sales service, the more need for customization. The coining of the term **global localization,** which has become a new code word in marketing strategy, is a recognition of the fact that the marketing job is not finished until products and services are used and consumed.

Stated another way, while strategy *formulation* and even *implementation* may be globalized, strategy *execution* has to be local. "What" to do and "how" to do it can follow uniform plans and guidelines, but "doing it" requires that one "speak the local language." This is why the expatriates who serve as general managers in the local foreign subsidiaries of various global companies rarely get into the action but serve more as figureheads and headquarters liaisons. For example, the management style called MBWA, management by walking around, which directly affects strategy execution, can be counterproductive when language and cultural differences prohibit effective personal communication between top managers and local employees. Even a global marketing strategy needs to keep execution local.

DEVELOPING KNOWLEDGE ASSETS

There is another aspect of globalization that influences why companies engage in global marketing. It has to do with the challenging "stretch" of individual and organizational capability involved in going abroad.

Many of today's chief executive officers consider "knowledge" to be the most basic asset of their company. **Knowledge assets** are basically intangible—brand equity, goodwill, patents, technical and managerial know-how, and so on. In today's globally competitive environment, these assets can be more powerful competitive advantages than access to land, buildings, machinery, and the like. Doing marketing in a foreign environment helps develop knowledge assets because of the exposure to new customers, new competitors, new technology, and new ways of doing things. Global companies tend to become what is sometimes called **learning organizations.**

Learning organizations are those whose competitive advantage is lodged not only in existing assets and capabilities but in the ability of the organization to innovate, to create new products, to develop new markets, to adopt new distribution channels, to find new advertising media, and to discard outdated products and tired sales routines.[22] These companies do not exist only in high-technology and high–value-added products—Microsoft, Hewlett-Packard, Mercedes, and Sony—but also in more mundane businesses such as consumer packaged goods. How does this learning come about?

To illustrate, it will be useful to relate the experiences of Procter and Gamble in Japan, and how that company had to change its ways of marketing.[23]

A well-known characteristic of the P&G marketing organization was its reliance on the **brand management** concept it helped originate. Briefly, a brand manager's task is to support the brand in the marketplace through advertising and in-store promotions, and also to coordinate shipments to warehouses and stocking on store shelves. The job also involves helping to coordinate factory production schedules with special promotional drives, to do market research, and to suggest improvements to the developmental laboratories. For P&G the system also involved direct competition with other P&G brands in the same product categories. But there was a conservative element built into the system in terms of managers' preoccupation with their existing brands.

New Products

For example, P&G evolved a system where any proposed new product needed to be thoroughly tested in laboratory clinics, by home use, and through test marketing. The tests were to be summarized in one-page memos, ideally giving three strong reasons for the advocated action (the famous "keep it simple" memos). Only if definite preferences over existing product formulations were achieved in blind tests would the company give its go-ahead. In one case, involving Pringle's potato chips, the market tests lasted well over five years. The company wanted to ensure that the product represented a discernible improvement in quality and features over existing offerings.

This system works very well in mature and relatively slow-moving markets where the premium is on incremental improvements to maintain brand loyalty, tracking competitors and customers, and rapid reaction to competitive promotions. It works less well where the competitive edge goes to the firm with the newest product innovation and where customer preferences change fast. The latter are characteristics of the Japanese marketplace, where a premium is paid for speed and flexibility, with functional quality taken for granted. Thus, in Japan P&G found it could no longer rely on a great product to be successful. It needed to be able to introduce new products more quickly.

The company tried to revamp its brand management system in Japan and placed brands under category management to avoid the individual responsibility that prohibited brand managers from taking risks. In order to speed up new-product introductions it also tried to limit "the Pringle syndrome," by making test evaluations quicker and less cumbersome. Because of the new management system, the company now is able to diffuse experiences from different countries throughout the organization faster than before. Reformulated products that succeed in one market are quickly introduced by managers elsewhere. The new compact detergents from P&G were developed in Japan and have now been introduced in most Western markets. The thinner diapers also emerged out of Japan. In both of these cases, P&G could move faster than its Japanese competitors because of its existing global network—but only after the "not invented here" syndrome typical of the narrowly focused brand management system had been eliminated.

Advertising

Long well known for TV commercials depicting P&G products as problem solvers for the harassed homemaker needing to impress her mother-in-law, the teenager looking for peer approval, or the young man who desperately needs a date, P&G went into Japan displaying Pampers diapers as a solution to a problem. Assuming that a wet baby posed a problem for the young mother, the company positioned Pampers as a new way of dealing with a hassle.

Realizing that grandmothers were important influences in Japan, the P&G commercials made sure the storyboard demonstrated approval from the mother-in-law. Understanding that the homemaker who used the convenient paper diapers could be perceived as lazy, the commercials made sure that the baby's satisfaction showed, as the baby changed from crying to smiling. The commercials also adopted a big sister–little sister format, showing how the young Pampers-using mother followed in the footsteps of the already successful mothers.

Despite such seemingly excellent fundamentals, the advertising failed. The main reason was straightforward: The young Japanese mother simply did not view the baby as a "problem." Sure, there was wetness, but this only meant that diapers had to be changed. To leave the baby unchanged after an accident was unacceptable—regardless of how "absorbent" the diaper was. Only by inventing a color-change wetness indicator could the paper diapers succeed, because then the mother could change the diapers right away after simply checking the color indicator. The indicator was convenient because it helped the mother take better care of the baby. And the Japanese mothers responded to the idea of better care, not to more convenience.

Needless to say, this benefit is contingent on the mother's not working outside of the home. But it can be transferred to Western markets by focusing separately on segments of "mother at home" households.

Distribution

Upon entering Japan, P&G learned how strongly the implementation of large-scale in-store promotions depended on sufficient channel capacity. Several distribution layers in Japan are necessary because stores have very limited space, sometimes need replenishment daily, and have little capacity to handle a rush of buyers.

The solution to the distribution problem became the invention of new-product formulations and new packaging techniques. Thus, condensed detergents now allow limited store space to be more efficiently utilized. Similarly, thin diaper designs are preferable since they lead to smaller packages. Vacuum-packing techniques are used to compact the fluffy diapers, which then pop up when the smaller packages are opened. All these innovations, born in Japan, are now used by P&G in other country markets.

Skill Benefits

Over time, P&G's Japan operation has slowly turned profitable, as trial and error has been used to hone the marketing effort. For our purposes, it is important to recognize that these experiences have helped P&G improve marketing performance in other countries. The Japan episode has built global marketing capability further in an already successful company.

It should be said that the fact that the Japanese market is different does not cast doubt on the benefits of standardization. The experience in Japan would seem to suggest that the successful company there has to customize its marketing effort. Yet the P&G Japanese innovations have been successful elsewhere, and of course Japanese companies have succeeded overseas. What does this mean?

The explanation is that Japan functions in certain product categories as a *leading market*. This means that since customers in Japan are more demanding and thus more difficult to satisfy than elsewhere, if they are satisfied, the offering has a better chance in a follower country. This is not a new notion. It is popularly expressed as "If you can succeed here, you can succeed anywhere." Cosmetics and wine in France, autos in Germany, movies and computer software in the United States, bacon in Denmark, and eel-skin in Korea, for example, all fall in this category of products that must meet demanding standards in knowledgeable leading markets. Although adjustments to product features have to be made for local conditions (such as different voltages and regulations—a process we will call "localization"), by and large preferences in leading markets are ahead of those elsewhere, and thus predictive of the future.

To summarize at this point, major benefits from global marketing include:

1. *Capitalizing on the growth potential of the foreign market and neighboring countries.* This is the most obvious benefit for a marketer.

2. *Transferring competitive information and new products from those markets to other markets*, including the home market. Management shares information across countries, and the organization has "learned."

3. *Stretching and building up the firm's marketing capability*, not only in terms of implementation and execution but also in terms of generating new ideas and concepts for strategic actions. Again, managers and the organization learn.

GLOBAL MARKETING OBJECTIVES

Given the benefits of global marketing, it is easy to see that the need to market overseas goes beyond pure marketing considerations. For example, presence in leading markets is necessary to keep track of new technological developments for tomorrow's products and services. Siemens, the German electronics giant, views its foreign market participation as one way to keep abreast of changes elsewhere and to maintain a global presence among present and prospective customers. Nissan's initial involvement in European auto markets—as well as its decision to drop the Datsun name and adopt the company name for its product line—was based partly on a desire to be better known among investors in the Eurobond market.

The main objectives the firm going abroad might pursue, often simultaneously, are as follows:

1. *Exploiting market potential and growth.* This is the typical marketing objective.
2. *Gaining scale and scope returns at home.* Longer production series and capital investment increase productivity.
3. *Learning from a leading market.* Many small market shareholders make no money in very competitive markets but learn about new technology and about competition.
4. *Pressuring competitors.* Entering a market where a firm's main competitor has a stronghold might seem doomed to failure. But increasing the competitive pressure in the stronghold market might help divert the competitor's attention from other markets.

5. *Diversifying markets.* By adding new countries and markets to the company portfolio, the firm's dependence on any one market will be lessened. Although this is often a secondary objective, many companies attempt to maintain a balance between countries ("not more than 25 percent of revenues from any one foreign market") since currency fluctuations can affect revenues severely.

6. *Learning how to do business abroad.* This is an important spillover effect from marketing in a foreign country, as we have seen. Its value should not be ignored. As a small example, entering Poland may be a first step to entering Russia, in learning how to deal with former communist countries. In the big picture, the company's knowledge assets will be enhanced by exposure to global markets and competitors.

THREE HATS

To get a better grip on the complex job faced by the global marketing manager, it is useful to distinguish between three roles he or she may assume as a company goes global and becomes more extensively involved in international markets.

The Foreign Entry Role

First there is the **export manager** in charge of international sales. In many small and medium-sized companies—but also in some larger domestically oriented companies such as department stores and beer brewers—foreign sales account for perhaps less than 10 percent of the total turnover. As orders from abroad trickle in, someone takes charge of the international sales. As the business grows, this person gradually gains status in the organization, and the foreign business needs to be managed more systematically. The marketing activities initially involve learning about how to export and how to locate reliable middlemen overseas, often carried out with little or no attention to the larger picture. But as sales grow and the potential overseas is recognized by the company, more careful screening of markets overseas becomes desirable, and the possibility of establishing more permanent representation in key markets needs to be considered.

This is the **foreign entry** phase of the marketing manager's job. The manager has to learn the intricacies of doing business overseas, of finding the right middlemen, of quantitatively and qualitatively evaluating foreign markets, negotiating for joint marketing ventures, helping to set up a sales subsidiary, and learning to understand foreign customers' product and service requirements. Internally, he or she becomes the company leader in "internationalizing" the firm. Externally, the manager becomes the company's spokesperson to the middlemen and customers in the markets entered.

These tasks verge close to a general management position, and the export manager in these companies has to shoulder more tasks than pure marketing. If the overseas entry involves manufacturing, marketing know-how is usually not crucial. But when the company enters a foreign country to gather access to markets, naturally marketers are needed. Nevertheless, many of the basic questions are organizational: setting up a logistics function and a network of middlemen, and developing reporting and control mechanisms back to headquarters. It's really basic marketing management—getting products to the customers and getting paid for them.

The Local Marketing Abroad Role

But in many countries the company can't be satisfied using independent middlemen for the marketing effort. Especially in leading markets, the company needs to be closer to the ultimate consumer. Establishing a sales subsidiary and sending some expatriates to work there is common. In this way the company can ensure that the potential of the market is exploited, that the company capabilities are properly leveraged, that customer trends are monitored, and that moves by the competition are anticipated. In addition, the expatriate marketing manager has to direct the more tactical local marketing effort.

Successful global marketers are often colorful and idiosyncratic personalities. Akio Morita, Sony's co-founder and former chairman, is famous for going against Japanese traditions, for ignoring his own staff's market research, and for an intuitive understanding of consumers in both East and West. Corbis/Bettmann-UPI

This **local marketing abroad** role involves skills largely the same as those required in the domestic setting. This is the "marketing in Germany" or "marketing in China" hat. The basic marketing skills remain those of the typical textbooks, although the environment is of course different. This is the situation that tends to teach the manager a thing or two, not only about marketing skills but also about other cultures and behaviors, and, ultimately, about himself or herself.

Because of the different environment, the local marketing effort is usually carried out with the help of several natives. In some countries, the political, economic, social, or cultural environment differs so much that the expatriate becomes ineffective and a drag on the organization. Japan is notorious in this respect, and several foreign companies have decided to rely on Japanese employees altogether. This unfortunately removes many of the learning benefits that come from operating abroad. The typical approach today is to leave day-to-day management to natives and let Western managers play a more strategic role.

In many companies, the senior managers of foreign subsidiaries are expatriates. The joint ventures and strategic alliances common today feature expatriate managers in senior positions. They have to learn that, because of the different environment, some of their marketing skills may not be applicable in the local market. Market segmentation is difficult without reliable demographic and economic data. Domestic companies may be protected by tacit agreements between government and industry. In-store promotions run up against uncooperative retailers. The local marketing abroad part of this book is intended to help the expatriate manager leverage marketing skills learned at home in this new environment.

The Global Management Role

The third hat of the global marketer, and often the next step on the career ladder, is the truly global part of the job.

Global management involves questions of global segmentation and positioning, standardization of products and services, uniform pricing around the globe, prototype advertising with a similar theme across countries, global brand names, and international logistics. The basic notion is to rationalize the global marketing operations in order to capture spillovers, scale advantages and lower costs, and to coordinate the

EXHIBIT 1.2 Global Marketing (*MATCHING SKILLS AND TASKS*)

	Marketing tasks		
Marketing skills	*Foreign entry (Part Two)*	*Local marketing (Part Three)*	*Global management (Part Four)*
Market analysis	Global market research; barriers to entry (Chaps. 4, 5)	Local buyer behavior, local marketing research (Chap. 7)	Global segmentation and positioning (Chap.11)
Formulating strategy	Mode of entry; expansion paths (Chaps. 5, 6)	Localized marketing strategy (Chaps. 8, 9, 10)	Formulating global marketing strategies (Chaps. 12–16)
Implementing and executing	Finding middlemen; negotiating with partners (Chaps. 5, 6)	Marketing in developed and developing countries (Chaps. 8, 9, 10)	Implementing global strategies; motivating locals, electronic commerce (Chaps. 17, 18)

marketing campaigns across countries for maximum effect. This is easier said than done. The main body of this book develops the promises and the potential drawbacks of global marketing in much more detail.

A GUIDE TO THE CHAPTERS

As we have just seen, the three tasks the global marketing manager may face at different levels require various marketing skills and know-how. Matching the marketing skills required against the three tasks will help you to see how the various chapters of this book fit together. In Exhibit 1.2, the major marketing skills have been divided into three parts: market analysis, formulating strategy, and implementing and executing. Market analysis typically involves marketing research to find out about customers and competitors in various markets and to forecast sales and share figures. Research skills, analytical models, and statistical techniques are important factors in this stage. Formulating strategy in terms of segmentation, positioning, and the 4Ps flows naturally from the analytical stage. Strategy formulation requires imagination and intimate understanding of customers' situations and competitors' intentions and also the firm's own capability, in order to develop viable strategies. The implementing and executing phase deals with the development of systems and operating routines that get the strategy into the field and with the control of progress and performance in the specific market. Although it is sometimes useful to distinguish between implementation ("how to do it") and execution ("doing it"), for our overview the two can be treated together here.

In Exhibit 1.2 these three main marketing skills are matched against the three tasks facing the global marketer: foreign entry, local marketing abroad, and global management. Where tasks match skills in the matrix, the main marketing problems have been identified. These are the main topics of the book's individual chapters. The book deals with foreign entry problems in Part Two, local marketing abroad questions in Part Three, and global management issues in Part Four. In Part One of the book, global marketing management skills and know-how fundamental to all global marketing tasks are introduced.

SUMMARY

This chapter has emphasized the need for marketers to develop a global mindset. As markets grow more homogeneous across countries and global competitors win out locally, there is *no avoiding globalization.* But the global marketer has to be careful in analyzing markets and competitors. If the globalization drivers are weak, with multidomestic markets and mostly local competitors, "going global" may have to be held off for the time being—although the possibility of being a pioneer should always be considered.

Firms pursue several objectives in their global expansion. Although sales and profitability are important, companies will go global in order to track, monitor, and challenge competitors; learn from lead customers and leading markets; and diversify away from reliance on a single market. Thus the marketing manager may find himself or herself in a foreign land, and the stint abroad will often seem unsettling, jarring the manager away from preconceived notions and assumed know-how. In the process, the marketing manager will gain useful experience and learn new skills, which often can be put to good use at home and in other parts of the firm's global network.

The world of the global marketer is complicated, with not only new countries but also new tasks to deal with. It is useful to simplify the situation by separating the job into three parts: foreign entry, local marketing abroad, and global management. The division is not always clear-cut, and the roles of course overlap. But the tasks involved are quite different. Furthermore, the division mirrors the career path of many present and future global marketing managers: first, helping to evaluate and enter new foreign markets; then, managing the marketing in one foreign country; and finally, coordinating the global effort back at headquarters. These three hats of the global marketer help provide the structure for this book.

KEY TERMS

brand management p. 18
common customer needs
 p. 12
competitive drivers p. 14
duplication p. 15
economies of scale p. 15
economies of scope p. 15
export manager p. 21
foreign entry role p. 21

global channels p. 13
global customers p. 13
globalization drivers p. 12
global localization p. 17
global management role p. 22
global marketing p. 8
global markets p. 10
international marketing p. 9
ISO 9000 p. 16

knowledge assets p. 18
leading markets p. 14
learning organization p. 18
local marketing abroad role
 p. 22
multidomestic markets p. 9
multinational marketing p. 6
sourcing advantages p. 15
transferable marketing p. 13

DISCUSSION QUESTIONS

1. What are the factors that seem to drive the globalization of the automobile industry? Why is the computer industry not spread more evenly around the globe?

2. Identify three product categories for which you think the markets are global. Can you find three that are multidomestic? What market data would you need to support your assertion?

3. What would a marketing manager learn in the U.S. market that could be useful in Europe?

4. After graduation, many students would like to work in a certain country, and often for a particular multinational. Using one of the Internet search machines (such as Yahoo or Infoseek), see how much information you can gather about a multinational company's organization and marketing in a country of your choice to help you decide whether it would be a good company to work for in that country.

5. Some observers argue that the coming of electronic commerce on the Internet signals the arrival of a new era of global marketing, as on-line retailers from books and music to software and outdoor gear make it possible to buy products without visiting stores. Assess how far this development has come by visiting a Web site for a retailer offering on-line shopping, and see what the limits are on which countries they can ship to.

Globalising markets

NOTES

1. Drucker, 1994, is as usual very perceptive in discussing how technology, information, and knowledge affect management.

2. Naisbitt, 1994, painstakingly documents the paradox of global economic integration coupled with political and ethnic fragmentation.

3. Lazer, 1993, spells out some of the implications of the new global order in more detail.

4. Nonaka, 1992, discusses how the creative inertia in some Japanese organizations has been overcome.

5. See Vernon, 1966. The international product cycle will be discussed in more detail in Chapter 2, which deals with foreign direct investment as a mode of entry.

6. See Buzzell, 1968.

7. See Levitt, 1983.

8. In his recent book, Chalmers Johnson reiterates this line of argument; see Johnson, 1995.

9. A prominent example of this second line of explanation is Womack et al., 1990.

10. See Porter, 1990.

11. See Hamel and Prahalad, 1991.

12. The term *multidomestic* was first proposed by Hout et al., 1982.

13. This list draws on Yip's original work, 1992.

14. Adapted from Kashani, 1992.

15. See Yip, 1992. This section draws directly on Yip's treatment of global strategy.

16. Levitt, 1983, was the first to recognize this trend.

17. More on leading markets will be presented in Chapter 4 on country attractiveness. Leading markets are often attractive despite intense competition.

18. This incident is from Johansson and Segerfeldt, 1987.

19. ISO 9000 guidelines are available directly from the EU Commission in Brussels and also from Department of Commerce offices. Consultants specializing in helping firms get ISO 9000 approval are also available in many countries. For an excellent overview of companies' response to ISO 9000 guidelines, see Prasad and Naidu, 1994.

20. This section draws on Quelch and Hoff, 1986, and Yip, 1992.

21. See Johansson and Yip, 1994.

22. The recent book by Bartlett and Ghoshal, 1992, places strong emphasis on the importance of learning in global and "transnational" organizations.

23. The references used here include Yoshino, 1990, and Natsuzaka, 1987. In addition, this section is based on interviews with Mr. Richard Laube, Advertising Manager for P&G Japan in Osaka, and with Ms. Jennifer Sakaguchi of Grey-Daiko, an advertising agency in Tokyo. A final source is a student report, "Pampers in Japan," by Mike Ando, Yasu Mori, Kazal Roy, and Masa Tanaka, International University of Japan, June 1991.

SELECTED REFERENCES

Artzt, Ed. "The Vizir Development and Introduction." Presentation at the University of Washington's School of Business, March 17, 1988.

Bartlett, Christopher A.; and Sumantra Ghoshal. *Transnational Management*. Burr Ridge, IL: Irwin, 1992.

Buzzell, Robert. "Can You Standardize Multinational Marketing?" *Harvard Business Review* 46 (November–December 1968), pp. 98–104.

Drucker, Peter. *Post-Capitalist Society*. New York: Harper & Row, 1994.

Hamel, Gary; and C. K. Prahalad. "Corporate Imagination and Expeditionary Marketing." *Harvard Business Review*, July–August 1991, pp. 81–92.

Hout, Thomas; Michael E. Porter; and Eileen Rudden. "How Global Companies Win Out." *Harvard Business Review*, September–October 1982.

Johansson, Johny K.; and Jan U. Segerfeldt. "Keeping in Touch: Information Gathering by Japanese and Swedish Subsidiaries in the U.S." Paper presented at the Academy of International Business Meeting in Chicago, October 1987.

———; and George Yip. "Exploiting Globalization Potential: U.S. and Japanese Business Strategies." *Strategic Management Journal*, Winter 1994.

Johnson, Chalmers. *Japan, Who Governs? The Rise of the Developmental State*. New York: Norton, 1995.

Kashani, Kamran. *Managing Global Marketing*. Boston: PWS-Kent, 1992.

Lazer, William. "Changing Dimensions of International Marketing Management." *Journal of International Marketing* 1, no. 3 (1993), pp. 93–103.

Levitt, Ted. "The Globalization of Markets." *Harvard Business Review*, May–June 1983, pp. 92–102.

Naisbitt, John. *Global Paradox*. New York: Morrow, 1994.

Natsuzaka, Masumi. Class report, "Kao and Procter and Gamble in Japan." University of Washington School of Business, December 1987.

Nonaka, Ikujiro. "The Knowledge-Creating Company." *Harvard Business Review*, November–December 1992.

Porter, Michael E. *The Competitive Advantage of Nations*. New York: Free Press, 1990.

Prasad, V. Kanti; and G. M. Naidu. "Perspectives and Preparedness Regarding ISO 9000 International Quality Standards." *Journal of International Marketing* 2, no. 2 (1994), pp. 81–98.

Quelch, John A.; and Edward J. Hoff. "Customizing Global Marketing." *Harvard Business Review*, May–June 1986, pp. 59–68.

Stewart, Thomas A. "Welcome to the Revolution." *Fortune*, December 13, 1993, pp. 66–77.

Urban, Glen L.; and Steven H. Star. *Advanced Marketing Strategy*. Englewood Cliffs, NJ: Prentice-Hall, 1991.

Vernon, Raymond. "International Investment and International Trade in the Product Cycle." *Quarterly Journal of Economics*, May 1966.

Womack, James P.; Daniel T. Jones; and Daniel Roos. *The Machine That Changed the World*. New York: Rawson Associates, 1990.

Yip, George. *Total Global Strategy*. Englewood Cliffs, NJ: Prentice-Hall, 1992.

Yoshino, Michael. *Procter & Gamble Japan (A)(B)(C)*. Harvard Business School case nos. 9-391-003, 004, 005, 1990.

Global Competitive Analysis

"Some like it hot"

Your takeaways from this chapter:

1. The "five forces" model of Porter is a good starting point when analyzing global competition, but it needs to be extended by considering new issues such as the split between domestic and foreign competitors and the possibility of strategic groups formed by trade barriers or regulation.

2. Because marketing strategy attempts to leverage the firm's competitive advantages, the theory of the multinational firm with its separation of country-specific and firm-specific advantages is the natural starting point for competitive strategy formulation.

3. The firm has to make sure that its competitive advantages are transferable to the new country market. This is particularly important for country-specific advantages that are not under the control of the firm.

4. Global competitors tend to have a wider repertoire and greater financial clout, which generate intense rivalry and hypercompetition.

5. A market-oriented perspective needs to be combined with a resource-based perspective when the firm is developing its global competitive strategy.

WITH COMPETITORS often the motivating force behind firms going global, the aim of Chapter 2 is to introduce some of the fundamental building blocks for analyzing global competition. The chapter first discusses the competitive environment in terms of Porter's "five forces" model. It then introduces the important concepts of *country-specific* and *firm-specific advantages* from traditional economic theory of international trade and the theory of the multinational firm. The role of marketing in leveraging these advantages is explained. The chapter applies and extends the economic principles to actual marketing examples, showing what the theories imply for global competitive strategy. The aim is to show how a few simple but powerful theoretical concepts can help guide the international marketer in developing the competitive strategy for the global marketplace.

The chapter also defines and explains the differences between a market-based and a resource-based competitive strategy, and shows how the two complement each other. The chapter ends by relating the market-based and resource-based strategies to the three functional tasks of the global marketer: foreign entry, local marketing, and global management.

Now Playing: Nike against Reebok—or against Adidas?

For the many people who obsess about sneakers—from teenage sports fans to retired executives, from elementary school girls to women lawyers—the battle has always been between Nike and Reebok. But old favorite Adidas is making a comeback.

Sneakers—or the "athletic footwear industry," to be politically correct—have never been the same since Philip Knight, the Nike founder, began peddling his waffle-soled running shoes out of his car trunk more than 30 years ago. Suddenly the fitness-minded and health-conscious new generation had a product that could take the pounding of feet against hard surfaces and protect weak ankles and tender knees. First jogging, then running, then aerobics became a craze. German Puma and Adidas, long-standing leaders of the sports shoe markets, did not respond, keeping their focus on active sportsmen and women, not wannabes, and in the process missed out on a phenomenal growth market. But British Reebok entered the fray, targeting women with an aerobics shoe that took the market and Nike by surprise. In 1987, Reebok passed Nike in annual sales.

But with global competition nothing ever stays the same. In the early 1990s Nike regrouped under Knight, placing its swoosh logo on sports superstars with massive marketing support and speeding up its R&D for new designs. Striking gold, the company came up with the airpump, a major improvement, and also signed several sports greats, including basketball star Michael Jordan. Nike's Air Jordan designs, as luck would have it created around a player who went on to become one of the most celebrated sports stars of all times, helped put Nike back into a solid lead.

Again lightning struck. By the mid-1990s, Jordan was tired of basketball and decided to get into another sport, baseball. Nike lost one of its major advantages, made worse by the fact that Jordan the baseball player bore no comparison to Jordan the basketball champion. While Michael languished in the minors, Reebok decided to launch a direct attack on Nike's hegemony in sports. Signing the new basketball star Shaquille O'Neill to a multiyear contract, and taking a page from Nike's playbook by designing a product line around him, Reebok went directly against Nike's stronghold.

This time Nike did not sit still. With Knight stepping back in to take the reins he had let go a couple of years earlier, the company launched a massive counter-campaign whose main objective was to sell Nike products for all major sports, especially soccer, and to get exposure for the swoosh logo in as many places around the globe as possible. An aggressive style pushing the swoosh and the "Just do it" slogan wherever and whenever and, especially, sponsoring the Brazilian national soccer team did make Knight unpopular among some purists, but it helped sell shoes. When Jordan returned to basketball and his Chicago Bulls won the championship again, with Shaquille O'Neill's Los Angeles Lakers out in the semifinals, Nike's victory was secure.

But even as O'Neill's contract with Reebok was not renewed, Nike's position was challenged again. In 1993 originally family-owned Adidas A.G. had put a new professional CEO in place, and a renewed sense of mission and global outlook was beginning to bear fruit. While Nike and Reebok were fighting it out for the largest shares of the global market, Adidas had begun a turnaround that by 1997 showed the company with an annual growth rate of 23 percent in sales and 27 percent in net income. At the same time Nike's marketing war had not been without costs. Nike's sales of footwear in 1997–8 showed only a slight increase, and net income was down 27 percent. Nike still dominates in terms of share and continues to control about 47 percent of U.S. sales compared with 15 percent for Reebok and 6 percent for Adidas. But Adidas is gaining even in the U.S. market where it has been relatively weak, and globally the company captures closer to 15 percent of the market compared with Nike's one-third.

Ironically, Nike's problems are compounded by what insiders call "product misplacement." When 39 members of the cult Heaven's Gate committed mass suicide in San Diego in March 1997, they all wore new black Nike shoes —so as to be able to move around Heaven easily. When a Mexico City protester burned the American flag during a May Day demonstration in 1997, he wore a Nike cap, just as O. J. Simpson did during a 1998 golf outing. And Nike's labor practices in Southeast Asia have come under close scrutiny for child exploitation, use of harmful toxins, and low wages.

The publicity resulting from its aggressive marketing campaigns and its success in the marketplace have come back to haunt Nike, the once proud antiestablishment and rebellious underdog. And in July 1998 insult was added to injury. In the World Cup final in Paris, the Adidas-sponsored French team defeated Nike's favored Brazilian team, 3–0.

Sources: Timothy Egan, "The Swoon of the Swoosh," *The New York Times Magazine*, September 13, 1998, pp. 66–70; John Tagliabue, "Once behind the Pack, Adidas Vies for the Lead," *New York Times*, March 19, 1998, pp. D1, D6; Sharon R. King, "Flying the Swoosh and Stripes," *New York Times*, March 19, 1998, pp. D1, D6; Kenneth Labaich, "Nike vs. Reebok —A Battle for Hearts, Minds and Feet," *Fortune*, September 18, 1996, pp. 58–69.
http://www.nike.com/
http://www.reebok.com/
http://www.adidas.com/
http://www.puma.com/

INTRODUCTION

The fundamental aim of business strategy is to create and sustain competitive advantage. This also holds true for the global firm. Firms will gain higher profits and superior returns on capital invested to the extent that they can build and exploit advantages over domestic and foreign competitors. Global marketers, although not the only important players, have vital roles in both the creation and the exploitation of competitive advantages. For example, marketers help create global brands, develop global advertising campaigns that communicate with target markets, and help design global channels of distribution. In doing so, they must start with an understanding of what the firm's competitive advantages are in the various markets.

A comprehensive global competitive analysis aims to determine how competitive the firm can be against domestic and foreign firms. In this chapter we separate the analysis into six components, roughly following the so-called SWOT (strengths, weaknesses, opportunities, and threats) framework:

1. An analysis of the competitive environment (opportunities and threats) in the various country markets.

2. A clear identification of the firm's country-specific competitive advantages (strengths and weaknesses).
3. A clear identification of the firm-specific advantages (more strengths and weaknesses).
4. How mobile these advantages are.
5. The best mode of leveraging the advantages in different markets to gain a competitive edge over domestic and other global firms.
6. The special case of global competitors.

The chapter also discusses the distinction between a market-based and a resource-based strategy, emphasizing the fact that firms cannot simply go for market opportunity but have to look at the resources required to compete effectively in a country market. It finishes by relating the strategic discussion to the three hats of foreign entry, local management abroad, and global management.

THE COMPETITIVE ENVIRONMENT

The analysis of the competitive environment in the various markets can be based on Porter's "five forces" model.[1] The model identifies five sources of competitive pressures on the firm in a given industry: rivalry, new entrants, substitutes, buyer power, and supplier power. The Porter analysis can be generalized to deal with global competition across several country markets.

Rivalry

The intensity of competitive rivalry between firms competing directly in a country market is the most obvious competitive force. This is the mode of competition focused on in economic theory. In global marketing it is useful to separate the competitors into domestic and foreign companies. In many industries, such as autos, this division comes close to what Porter calls *strategic groups*.

Strategic Groups

A strategic group consists of competitors with roughly similar resources and similar target markets. These two factors combine to make them follow similar strategies. In autos, the three American automakers (General Motors, Ford, and Chrysler) tend to form one group, as do the Japanese (Toyota, Nissan, Honda, and Mazda). The two German makers BMW and Mercedes also form a natural group, but Volkswagen is different, perhaps in a group with the Japanese. The groupings themselves are not necessarily important, and they change over time as mergers and acquisitions blur the borders. But strategic groups are useful for competitive analysis since they suggest the likely strategic direction the companies may take and indicate which other companies they monitor closely. When Sony introduces a new product, other Japanese electronics makers will usually follow with their own versions. In the ongoing global battle between Coca-Cola and Pepsi-Cola, when Pepsi bought Tropicana, the juice maker, Coke responded by trying to buy France's Orangina, only to be blocked by a French judge alerted by Pepsi lawyers.

Domestic Competitors

In most country markets there will be a group of domestic companies that has traditionally served the home market. In the name of national security, many nations have instituted policies aimed toward self-sufficiency in foodstuffs, transportation, industrial goods, and basic technology. For example, most governments in the past controlled telecommunications and air transportation, and subsidized farmers. With similar effects, regulations in support of small businesses and retailers, against foreign ownership, and customer sentiments in favor of local goods have in the past combined to create entry barriers for foreign firms and advantages for domestic producers.

With deregulation, privatization, and global integration through trading blocs these factors are gradually diminishing in importance. Nevertheless, these changes do not happen overnight, and the global financial turmoil at the end of the 90s has led to a backlash in some countries against free markets and economic integration. As a result, in many country markets the domestic competitors still have special advantages. The infamous "Reinheitsgebot" ("Purity decree") in Germany, an old, now amended regulation that forbade the use of artificial conservation ingredients in beer, effectively blocked foreign entry and made local production a necessity (which is why many localities in Germany still have their own local beer). And the domestic companies do not simply stand back and watch as foreign competitors enter. As late as 1998 the three large American auto companies jointly sponsored an advertising campaign encouraging car buyers to show loyalty to their fellow citizens and buy American makes.

Because entry barriers are important in determining the mode of entry into a market, barriers will be discussed in more detail in Chapter 5, "Export Expansion."

Foreign Competitors

In global markets especially, foreign entrants tend to be the most direct competitors of a globalizing firm. As was mentioned above, the foreign companies can often be analyzed as a separate strategic group, making predictions easier. This does not mean that these companies are colluding or that they imitate each other. Rather it is their strategic situation that is similar and therefore tends to suggest similar strategies. The large Korean conglomerates—such as Samsung, LG, and Daewoo—have followed the same initial OEM (original equipment manufacturing) strategy in Western consumer electronics markets to gain access without much knowledge of customer preferences.

Among foreign companies it is useful to single out global companies since their competitive resources tend to be greater than those of other firms. Because this topic is broad, the analysis of global competitors will be discussed separately in a later section. In general, to understand foreign competitors it is useful to analyze their activities in other markets. For example, to predict the likely strategy of a company such as Mars in the Chinese confectionery market it is useful to observe the company's aggressive attack on Eastern European markets.

Regional trade blocs also play a role in determining advantages and disadvantages of the foreign competitors. Foreign companies from inside a trading area have an advantage over other foreign competitors. Although the European Union is not trying to become a fortress Europe with high external tariffs (few tariffs are higher than 10 percent), the advantages of manufacturing inside Europe are such that many North American and Asian companies invest in production inside the EU. The competitiveness of the European companies is high enough that any cost disadvantage matters to non-European entrants.

Generally speaking, as will be discussed later when dealing with the analysis of company strengths and weaknesses, the nationality of the firm—and where its main production locations are—matters for country-specific advantages and disadvantages.

New Entrants

Another competitive force is the threat of new entrants into a country market. While Porter was mainly concerned with new entrants into an industry—such as Disney buying ABC television, or banks entering the securities business—the threat applies equally if not more to potential entrants into a new foreign market. In particular, it is

G E T T I N G   T H E

Picture

Citibank Looks to Emerging Markets

BANKING, both retail and commercial, has been one of the slowest areas of the economy to change in Eastern Europe. But in 1994, Citibank, the large American multinational, opened its first branch in Budapest, and its flashy decor, lavish services, and plastic cards are having an effect on traditional banking there.

Entering Hungary, Citibank decided that the best strategy was to offer upscale services not matched by any competitors. This made the bank less dependent on building volume, and the bank's research suggested that there would be enough customers for higher-margin service packages. The bank offers cash machines, still rare in Eastern Europe, but to qualify the customers need to maintain a minimum balance of $250, a little less than the average salary in the country. So far 4,000 accounts have been opened, 70% Hungarians, the rest foreign residents of Budapest.

At the high end, the bank offers special privileges to customers who maintain balances of $100,000. Beyond the rich wood veneer, peach carpet, and potted palms in the main lobby, these customers are given access to a third-floor wet bar with free drinks adjacent to the safe-deposit boxes. The bank has found 12 customers who qualify—hardly sufficient for a very profitable operation—but well suiting a prestige-raising business that generates favorable word-of-mouth advertising and intimidates potential competitors.

Sources: Bobinski, 1995; Saul Hansell, "Citicorp Announces High-Level Personnel Shifts," *New York Times*, July 1, 1995, p. D5; Jane Perlez, "Citibank in Budapest: A.T.M.'s and Potted Palms," *New York Times*, June 22, 1995, p. D7.

important that the global marketer realizes that other global companies may also enter a country market under consideration, and that the order of entry can directly affect the sales and market shares gained. This is easiest to see in emerging markets that have recently opened.

An emerging market offers the opportunity to be a "first mover" and create demand. Since domestic competition is often weak or nonexistent, the marketing task is to demonstrate how the product or service fills a need and to educate potential customers in its use. This generic marketing task can be challenging and expensive, with reluctant learners and a need for special promotional material and personal selling. But the brand has a chance to develop loyalty before competitors enter. Citibank's early entry into Eastern Europe is suggestive (see box, "Citibank Looks to Emerging Markets").

Being a first mover can create advantages but can also be hazardous. The **first-mover advantages** relative to followers include:[2]

Higher brand recognition.
More positive brand image.
More customer loyalty.
More distribution.
Longer market experience.

The drawback for a first-mover is that the market is not yet developed, which means that:

Channel members may need training.
Customers might have to be educated.
Advertising has to be more generic.
Tastes and standards are unknown and perhaps unformed.

Because of the uncertainties involved, some firms decide to become followers, waiting to see how the first entrant does before entering a new market. When they then enter, it is usually with a kind of me-too approach, trying to capture some of the first

G E T T I N G   T H E

Picture

The Global Card Game

FIRST CREDIT CARDS, then cash cards and smart cards, and now cards for the Internet—the world is turning (virtually) plastic.

The globalization of the American Express card was followed by Visa, which beat Mastercard to the global punch. Visa still has a larger global presence than Mastercard, with extensive advertising campaigns presenting Visa as a welcome alternative to the American Express card (which is not usually as attractive because of higher fees for the merchants).

Playing catch-up, Mastercard developed its own innovative strategy. Embracing the new concept of co-branded cards, Mastercard has been in the forefront of offering credit cards jointly with General Motors, AT&T, and General Electric. Purchases charged to the cards automatically add up to discounts for products from these firms, just as frequent flier miles are accumulated when flying. Coupled with another Mastercard strategic push to make people use their card for everyday shopping including supermarket purchases, Mastercard is gaining considerable business in its prime market, the United States. As the necessary infrastructure develops in other countries'

stores, the plan is to introduce similar features there as well.

Now there are also the so-called smart cards. Already available in Europe, these cards derive from the prepaid telephone cards widely used in Europe and Asia (but still not available in the fragmented American telecommunications market). The smart cards are embedded with microchips that store cash and, when used, automatically subtract from the face amount on the card. Easier to use than typical credit cards, since the balance is visible, these cards are preferred by many merchants as well as customers when paying for purchases. Several American companies, including Microsoft, the software developer, are working on developing smart cards to be used on the Internet for making payments.

Sources: Saul Hansell, "The Man Who Charged Up Mastercard," *New York Times*, March 7, 1993, sec. 3, pp. 1, 8; "Microsoft Developing Electronic Cash Card," *New York Times*, June 12, 1995, p. D4; "Revolutions: The Card That Could Rule Our Lives," *Asiaweek*, November 3, 1995, p. 52.
http://www.americanexpress.com
http://www.mastercard.com

mover's customers and also help grow the new market. When Saab entered the North American market, it positioned itself as "the other Swedish car," trading on Volvo's image. The leading French beer, Kronenbourg, attacked the U.S. market through a campaign slogan that claimed it to be "Europe's largest-selling beer," trying to capitalize on Dutch Heineken's and German Beck's rising popularity. Mastercard has been playing catch-up with some success in the global market for credit cards (see box, "The Global Card Game").

Substitutes

In new markets where conditions are very different from the home market and consumer preferences differ, the product or service can face a new series of substitutes. This is particularly true for food products and drinks. Fast food in Asia involves instant noodles, hot dogs are served as full meals with potatoes and vegetables in northern Europe, Belgians love their fritters, and so on. Milk is an unusual drink in many countries, as is coffee in others. But domestic substitutes also vary in transportation (rickshas, bicycles), clothing styles, and, of course, sports and entertainment.

In general, where markets are multidomestic, the globalized product or service need not only be adapted to local customs and preferences; it also is likely to encounter different substitutes. When McDonald's opened its first outlets in the Commonwealth of Independent States, the Russians responded with a chain of fast-food stores serving blinis and other Russian specialties. Kellogg is still trying to convince people around the world to switch from hot to cold breakfast cereals. Kentucky Fried Chicken in Japan fought successfully the habit of mothers to serve hot ramen, a noodle dish, and

A Kellogg's box of basmati flakes in India. In countries where cold cereal and milk are not immediately obvious ingredients of a breakfast, the box top needs to explain where to pour the milk and how to eat the cereal. Kellogg's® is a registered trademark of Kellogg Company. Photo used with permission.

instead convinced them to serve fried chicken, which helps build strong bodies in young children.

Buyer and Supplier Power

The last two forces identified by Porter relate to what the economist John Kenneth Galbraith has called *countervailing* power. Where the buyers are strong—either because they are few or because they have many alternatives to choose from—they have the power to counter a seller's attempts to raise prices. They simply shift their purchases or put pressure on the seller. Similar forces can be at work on the side of suppliers to the company. Where suppliers are large, or where there are few supply alternatives, the seller will be forced to pay higher prices for inputs than otherwise, squeezing profit margins.

Again, these forces carry over directly to the global case. In some countries, such as Japan where business cooperates in large networks ("keiretsus"), an entrant may find it difficult to establish the required network of distributors and other intermediaries. Domestic competitors with established networks will have a decided advantage. Similarly on the buying side, in countries with large government ownership of businesses, the only customer may be a government agency. This can be true of public utilities such as power generation and telecommunications, but other industries are also affected. For example, liquor sales and advertising are highly regulated in many countries, with public monopolies the buying agent, virtually eliminating the ability of companies to create meaningful product or service differentiation and competitive advantages.

COUNTRY-SPECIFIC ADVANTAGES (CSAs)

Turning to the analysis of competitive strengths and weaknesses, for the globalizing company it is useful to distinguish between advantages that are specific to the firm and those advantages that a firm possesses because of the country it's from or where it produces. To illustrate, producing in a low-cost European country such as Portugal—as Volkswagen does, for example—may give a cost advantage over a competitor producing in Spain—as Nissan does. But this is a country-specific advantage that can be captured by any producer in Portugal. By contrast, Volkswagen's image and brand name are assets that are unique to the company, firm-specific advantages that cannot be

G E T T I N G   T H E   *Picture*

Which Country Has What Comparative Advantage?

SINCE THE PRINCIPLE of comparative advantage applies at the country level, there have been several attempts at identifying exactly what the advantages are in different countries. A now classic example is Dunning's study in 1981, which arrived at the following conclusions: Japan—textiles, clothing, consumer electronics; United Kingdom—food and tobacco products; Sweden—mechanical and electrical engineering; United States—transportation equipment; (West) Germany—chemicals.

It should be recognized that although some CSAs persist over time (such as those based on natural resources), there will be changes as new skills among labor are developed and technological innovations force new production processes to be employed and new raw materials to become scarce.

Source: Adapted from Dunning, 1981.

duplicated by other firms. When doing competitive analysis in the global context it is important to identify whether a company's strength is firm-specific or not. If it is not, the competitive advantage is usually less sustainable since the company cannot prevent imitation.

We will first deal with **country-specific advantages (CSAs).** Since such advantages have long been analyzed in the economics of international trade, the theory of international trade is a useful starting point.

Comparative Advantage

The principle of **comparative advantage** provides the fundamental rationale for the existence of international trade. Free trade between two countries yields economic payoffs to the countries (in terms of higher welfare) provided the countries have different endowments of resources, that is, different advantages. It is not important if one country is better than another in producing all kinds of products, that is, that they have an absolute advantage. One country might have an **absolute advantage** (its resource inputs show higher productivity) for all the products involved and trade will still yield positive benefits to both countries. The requirement is simply that in one country the production involves less of a sacrifice in the output of alternative products than it does in the other country, so that there is a relative advantage in production.

The International Product Cycle (IPC)

Potentially, all of the factors that create differences in the countries' comparative advantages also create differences in absolute advantages (see boxes).

When formulating competitive strategy at the firm level, it is the absolute advantages that count. Countries as trade partners are just that, partners, and for the countries the comparative advantage principles apply—a win-win situation. But at the firm level, the company needs to have an edge on competitors, for example, through higher quality or lower cost. This is a matter of absolute advantages. And as many countries have found out, a country's absolute advantages can be erased by foreign competitors. This is the working of the **international product cycle (IPC).**

The IPC was initially proposed by Raymond Vernon in 1966, who used it to demonstrate how the manufacturing of new products in the United States shifted over time to new locations overseas and in the process affected trade patterns.[3] The process

Who Has What Absolute Advantage?

EVEN THOUGH a country has a comparative advantage in, say, labor skills, it does not follow that its labor is the most skilled. The principle of comparative advantage means only that its labor skill when compared to its other productive inputs is higher than the corresponding ratio for other countries. It is often of interest, however, to identify what countries tend to have an *absolute* advantage in the sense that its resources show high pro-

ductivity. For example: cheap labor—China, Philippines, Ghana, Indonesia, Brazil, India; skilled labor—Japan, Taiwan, South Korea, North America, and Europe; financial resources—United States, Japan; natural resources—Russia, Middle East, China; advanced technology—Japan, United States.

Source: Adapted from Dunning, 1981.

is depicted in Exhibit 2.1. In the initial stage, the innovator produces and markets the product at home to a growing home market. As production increases above the home market demands, the firm turns to exports and develops markets in other developed countries. Then, as these new markets grow and their domestic production of the product gets under way, trade shifts again to Third World markets. As the production know-how gets more widespread, however, these countries gradually develop their own manufacturing capability, helped by the processes and the technology that by now have become standardized. As low-cost production in these Third World (or newly industrialized) countries gets under way, their imports give way to exports back to the original country's market. The cycle has come full circle, and the original inventor now imports the product.

As many countries other than the United States have become adept at inventing new products and services, the international product cycle as originally developed has become outdated, and Vernon and others have amended it.[4] Today, for example, it is not uncommon to find that a country that started production of a certain innovative product continues as the foremost manufacturing site. The American supremacy in computer design is a good example. This process has been documented in detail by Porter.

National Competitive Advantages

In an important extension of the theory of competitive advantage, Porter has introduced what he calls the **diamond of national advantage.**[5] The diamond consists of four factors that make up the competitive advantage (or disadvantage) of a country:

1. *Factor conditions.* The nation's position in factors of production, such as skilled labor or infrastructure, necessary to compete in a given industry.
2. *Demand conditions.* The nature of the home demand for the industry's product or service.
3. *Related and supporting industries.* The presence or absence in the nation of supplier industries and related industries that are internationally competitive.
4. *Firm strategy, structure, and rivalry.* The conditions in the nation governing how companies are created, organized, and managed, and the nature of domestic rivalry.

Exhibit 2.2 shows how these factors interrelate. A nation's competitive advantage—and, consequently, the country-specific advantages for firms from that country—depends on the strength of each of these factors. Favorable factor conditions include the traditional endowment of natural resources that was the basis of the original theory

EXHIBIT 2.1 The International Product Cycle

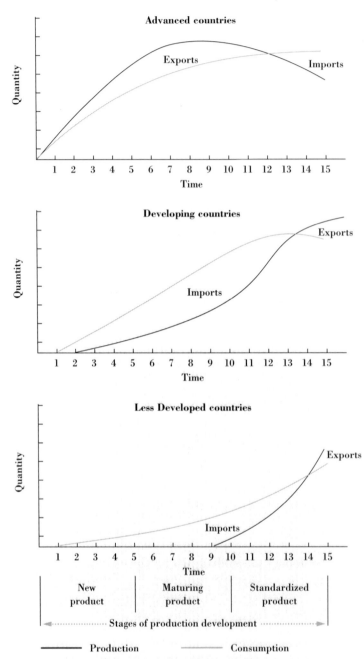

Source: Reprinted with the permission from the Journal of Marketing, "A Product Life Cycle for International Trade?" by Louis T. Wells, July 1968, pp. 1–6. © 1968 by the American Marketing Association.

of comparative advantage. Porter argues that, over time, vigorous competition in the industry will help develop stronger firms and support growth and improvement among supplier firms. Furthermore, sophisticated and demanding customers at home help hone the competitive skills of the industry further. If a country offers higher labor skills or lower wages, the multinational firm will locate production there.

Porter's is a dynamic theory, showing how over time a nation can build up and sustain its competitive advantage in an industry. While firms' reliance on factor cost ad-

EXHIBIT 2.2 Porter's Determinants of National Advantage

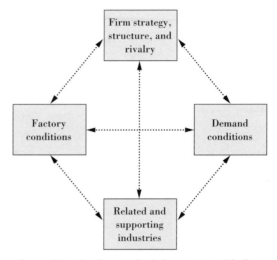

Source: Adapted and reprinted with the permission of the Free
Press, a division of Simon & Schuster, from *The Competitive
Advantage of Nations*, by Michael E. Porter, Copyright © 1990 by
Michael E. Porter.

vantages (lower cost labor, for example) can provide the initial stimulus for economic growth, other countries will appear with even lower factor costs. In order to sustain growth, the nation's competitive advantage will have to be extended by capital investments in upgraded machinery and technological development in the industry. But for a nation to sustain its advantage it is also necessary that related and supporting industries follow by upgrading their facilities and expertise (see box, "Porter's Related Industries") and that home market customers become more demanding, expecting the best.

It is important to recognize that Porter's diamond implies that a country can remain competitive in an industry even as its manufacturing costs rise. Thus, the diamond goes counter to the original IPC theory. While the IPC explains the "hollowing out" of a nation's industrial base, with manufacturing moving to low-wage countries, Porter's diamond suggests that competitive rivalry and capable business management can help nations develop new skills and renew their competitive advantages. While Vernon's IPC concludes that advanced nations will trade for standardized commodities and focus on innovation and new industries ("Get out of televisions and focus on computers"), Porter's diamond shows how the creation of favorable conditions can make a nation stay competitive in a given industry for a long time ("Automobiles is what we do best"). Actually, in most economies of the world, both tendencies are at work simultaneously.

Differentiated Competition

In a closely related theoretical development, it has been demonstrated that the trade patterns between countries depend on man-made, Porter-style, locational advantages.[6] For example, as advanced technology centers arise around strong research universities and innovative new firms, the local labor force develops skills unique to specific industries, and companies will find it increasingly attractive to locate in those areas. This **new trade theory** explains the development of high-technology areas such as "Silicon Valley" south of San Francisco, Bangalore in India, and the Stuttgart-Munich area in Germany. Similarly created CSAs include the skilled labor force in other industries, such as apparel in Italy, optical instruments in Japan, and chocolates in Belgium. These

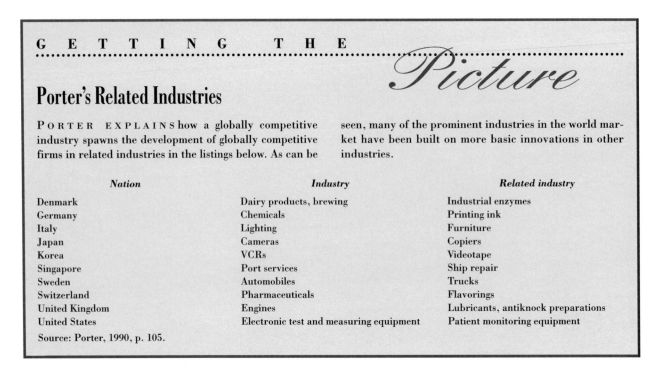

G E T T I N G   T H E

Picture

Porter's Related Industries

P O R T E R   E X P L A I N S how a globally competitive industry spawns the development of globally competitive firms in related industries in the listings below. As can be seen, many of the prominent industries in the world market have been built on more basic innovations in other industries.

Nation	*Industry*	*Related industry*
Denmark	Dairy products, brewing	Industrial enzymes
Germany	Chemicals	Printing ink
Italy	Lighting	Furniture
Japan	Cameras	Copiers
Korea	VCRs	Videotape
Singapore	Port services	Ship repair
Sweden	Automobiles	Trucks
Switzerland	Pharmaceuticals	Flavorings
United Kingdom	Engines	Lubricants, antiknock preparations
United States	Electronic test and measuring equipment	Patient monitoring equipment

Source: Porter, 1990, p. 105.

country-specific factors shift the competitive advantages away from what natural resources alone would suggest.

Of particular interest to marketers, Krugman and other "new trade" theorists point out that the products traded are generally differentiated and not homogeneous. Accordingly, international trade patterns will not necessarily follow the original theory's predictions. For example, there is a great amount of intraindustry trade between nations, with a country such as Germany both exporting and importing a large quantity of cars, for example. This still begs the question of why Germany would not produce all its desired cars and then trade for other products or services. Krugman first demonstrated how the pure theory needs to be augmented to incorporate skills developed. Differentiation leads to specialization and the creation of firm-specific advantages that come from learning by doing. German automakers become good at certain types of cars, not others. From a marketing viewpoint this is hardly surprising, since these cars tend to be differentiated and to target alternative market segments.

These ideas suggest that a country can become efficient in the production of goods in which it starts with little or no competitive advantage. As we saw in Chapter 1, at the firm level this process is variously known as organizational learning or knowledge creation.[7] It represents the process by which companies develop new resources. This learning of new skills is of course very much a theme of this text, since the global marketing manager's experiences with foreign countries serve to expand marketing know-how.

Country-of-Origin Effects

One particular country-specific advantage (that can also be a disadvantage) is the so-called country-of-origin effect. The effect refers to the impact on customers of the "made-in" label, or, more generally, the country a product or service is perceived to be from. Products or services from countries with a positive image tend to be favorably evaluated, while products from less positively perceived countries tend to be downgraded.

A number of research studies have been conducted on the impact of made-in labels.[8] In general, the studies show a pronounced effect on the quality perceptions of products, with country stereotypes coloring consumers' evaluative judgments of

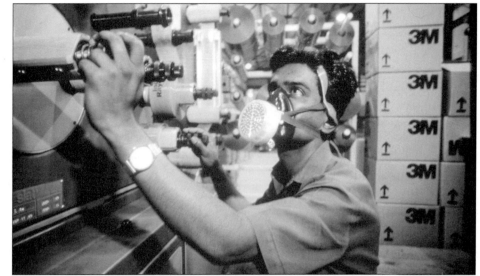

A 3M worker in Bangalore, India. A locational advantage in labor is not simply a matter of low wages. It can mean a well-educated workforce, and a concentration of firms where workers can get valuable work experience. High tech firms, such as 3M, are attracted by the quality of labor as much as by low wage rates. Dilip Mehta/ Contract.

brands. It translates into sales as well. In one study it was found that the Japanese autos' strong penetration in the U.S. market in the 1970s was based more on country advantages than on firm-specific advantages. American auto buyers bought "a Japanese car," not necessarily a Nissan or Toyota specifically.

Contrary to what one might expect, there is also evidence that these effects do *not* go away over time. Because of increased global communication consumers learn more about foreign countries, and they learn what technologies and products firms in the countries are good at. But even if country-of-origin effects do not seem to go away, country perceptions do change over time. For example, while American products enjoyed a reputation for high quality after World War II, they slipped badly in the 1970s and 1980s as superior foreign products raised customer expectations. British quality perceptions largely followed the same path only earlier and quicker, while Japanese products showed the opposite trend and the German quality image remained strong. However, given the intense global competition in many markets, there is, not surprisingly, evidence of a convergence of quality ratings in the 1990s.[9]

FIRM-SPECIFIC ADVANTAGES (FSAs)

The fundamental premise of any enterprise is that it can transform valuable inputs into even more valuable outputs. The rule for survival of a company is that it provides some desired benefit to the customer better than other enterprises do. It has a sustainable competitive advantage. Similarly, the company entering markets abroad must have advantages that outweigh the increased costs of doing business in another country in competition with domestic firms. This advantage should not be available to competitors and is, therefore, to some degree monopolistic. It is called a **firm-specific advantage (FSA)** to emphasize that it is unique to a particular enterprise. (Since different writers sometimes use different terms, Exhibit 2.3 gives some alternative synonyms for FSAs and CSAs.)

Firm-specific advantages may be of several kinds. They could consist of a patent, trademark, or brand name or be the control of raw materials required for the manufacturing of the product, access to know-how essential to the development of a service, or simply control of distribution outlets. These advantages could also include process technology, managerial capacity, or marketing skills. They might well have their source in country-specific variables, but the essential point about them is that they can be used by the company alone.

EXHIBIT 2.3 Two Sets of Synonyms for FSAs and CSAs

Level	Synonyms
Country (CSAs)	Comparative advantages: location-specific advantages
Firm (FSAs)	Differential advantages; ownership-specific advantages

From a marketing perspective it is important to recognize that the source of a firm-specific advantage can lie in specific market know-how. For example, large consumer goods manufacturers (Nestlé, Unilever, Procter and Gamble) have accumulated experience and skills in many foreign markets that give them an edge over competition. These skills include techniques for analyzing and segmenting markets, developing promotional programs and advertising campaigns, and administering massive introductory campaigns for new products and services. Similar skills in the marketing area might be said to lie behind some of Caterpillar's and IBM's successes in many markets (Caterpillar's policy that a serviceman can reach a site within 48 hours, for example) and also the close relationship with distributors nurtured by many companies in Japan.

A clear understanding of what the FSAs are is a key to the formulation of a successful marketing strategy in a country, especially for market segmentation and product or service positioning. One point to note is that the firm-specific advantage might well vary across countries. In other words, the differential advantage that products and services enjoy over competition might be different for customers in different country markets. It becomes important to identify exactly what the advantages are for the particular country. Marketing research needs to be carried out in order that customer needs and competitive offerings be properly identified and matched against the firm's product or service. Such an analysis will yield guidelines for what features need to be stressed in various countries, so as to place it in as advantageous a position vis-à-vis competitors' offerings as possible.

This logic underlies the many multinational firms' practice of providing different products or services from their complete line in different countries. In autos, few of the U.S. makes are sold abroad; they have a differential disadvantage. Many smaller European makes are not introduced in Japan where competition among small cars is intense. Black and white television sets are sold in the less developed countries (LDCs).

TRANSFERABILITY OF ADVANTAGES

A question that arises especially when marketing skills are important is the **transferability** of these skills to other countries. Not all of them can be transferred (see box, "Marketing FSAs").

Certain factors make the employment of marketing skills difficult in other countries. Where commercial television is not available, it is difficult to leverage the skills developed in the area of TV advertising. Procter and Gamble's reluctance to enter the Scandinavian markets is one illustration of this, now partly alleviated as satellite TV and new channels open up the market to TV advertising. When the FSAs are in distribution channels (as in the Electrolux case—see box, "A Marketing Skill Transferred"), going abroad might involve having to create new channels in the local market.

In some of these cases, production in the market country might make the local marketing effort easier. It could, for example, make it easier to recruit capable distributors and dealers, since host country production can be used to assure the channel members that supplies will be forthcoming.

A major difficulty in transferring marketing skills abroad is that these factors often represent intangibles, not skills "embodied" in the product itself (as technology

G E T T I N G   T H E

Marketing FSAs

Picture

MOST COMPANIES have several marketing strengths but are sometimes characterized by one or two major FSAs. Among global companies with strong marketing, the following FSAs stand out: strong brand names—Coca-Cola, Sony, Mercedes; products with state-of-the-art technology—Microsoft, BMW, Canon; advertising leverage—Gillette, Unilever, Nissan; distribution strength—Kodak, Canada Dry, Panasonic; good value for the money—Ford, Ikea, Toyota.

Other companies have marketing FSAs not easily exploited overseas: Budweiser's great brand name asset derives from an original Czech beer still brewed and sold, complicating sales in Europe. Also, its light taste relative to most countries' beers slows expansion.

German Henkel's (detergents) strong presence in the European market has been difficult to leverage elsewhere, as it depends on strong distribution and brand loyalty based on special washing traditions with respect to water hardness and temperatures used, less use of tumble dryers, and frequency of washing.

Kao's (detergents) and Shiseido's (cosmetics) strengths in distribution at home in Japan, where they have control

at both wholesale and retail levels, cannot easily be duplicated elsewhere.

http://www.coca-cola.com/home.html
http://www.cokecce.com/
http://www.sony.com
http://www.mercedes-net.com/
http://www.microsoft.com
http://www.bmw.com/
http://www.bmwusa.com/
http://www.canon.com/
http://www.gillette.com/
http://www.unilever.com/
http://www.nissanmotors.com/
http://www.kodak.com/
http://www.canadadry.com/
http://www.panasonic.com
http://www.ford.com
http://www.ikea.com/
http://www.toyota.com/crstrks@SK@M-4xgP2xMB@@.html
http://www.budweiser.com/
http://www.henkelcorp.com/searchengines/x-long.htm
http://www.kao.co.jp
http://www.shiseido.co.jp/e

typically is). The principal means of completing the transfer is by employing personnel and education of local people.[10] Because of the new environment in which expatriates have to work, and the uncertain results of the educational effort, marketing skills will often not be transferable at a reasonable cost. Conversely, where marketing skills provide the basic firm-specific advantage, the incentive to go abroad is not as strong as where the advantage rests on factors that can be embodied in the product. An exception to this rule is the growth in franchised services, in which a specific mechanism is created to transfer marketing skills. Successful service companies such as McDonald's, Kentucky Fried Chicken, and Hilton Hotels have standardized their services and relied on training local franchisees in each specific detail of the day-to-day operations, to ensure uniform quality across countries. For manufacturing companies, such an investment in technology transfer is often not necessary, since the final product embodies the advantages already.

COMPETITION AND MODE OF ENTRY

There are a number of ways in which a company can enter a given country market. They will be discussed in detail in Chapters 5 and 6 on entry strategies. In principle, three different modes can be identified: straight exporting, licensing, and direct foreign investment (in production or selling capabilities). In pure exporting the product is simply exported to a distributor appointed in the market country; licensing "transfers" some ownership advantages via a contractual agreement to an enterprise in the market country; and foreign direct investment (FDI) means the company invests money in subsidiary operations in the country.

G E T T I N G   T H E   *Picture*

A Marketing Skill Transferred: Electrolux in Japan

THE SWEDISH MANUFACTURER of vacuum cleaners, Electrolux, has long sold its product through door-to-door salesmen demonstrating the virtues of the product in the home of a prospective customer. The sales technique became one of the company's distinctive skills.

Upon entering Japan, Electrolux found negative initial reactions among the trade people toward this type of selling approach. It was said that the Japanese were not used to having unknown people enter their homes and would not allow the salesmen's entrance. Electrolux therefore decided to follow the standard Japanese approach of selling through department stores and specialty shops. For a period of several years the company attempted numerous variations on this approach, but failed to gain much market share. Domestic competitors (Toshiba, Hitachi, and others) continued to dominate the market.

Believing that with a proper demonstration of performance the price differential could be justified, management of Electrolux decided against all odds to introduce their particular selling method in Japan. After extensive training of their Japanese salesmen, the door-to-door approach was introduced. The result: an immediate success. Electrolux became a leader at the upper end of the market.

Electrolux's experience vindicates the idea that we should concentrate on doing what we do best. It also demonstrates the fact that in a new market one does not necessarily have to do things the way they have always been done, not even in a relatively isolated country like Japan.

http://www.electrolux.com/
http://www.hitachi.com/
http://www.toshiba.com/

Internalization or Externalization?

Mode of entry issues have preoccupied multinational analysts for decades. The basic question is how the company can get a reasonable payoff or return on its firm-specific advantages. Generally speaking, such a company could sell its superiority (be it in patents, brand names, or process technology) to a local buyer for use. This is the **licensing** or "externalization" option. If the market for such advantages were efficient in the sense that information was perfect, the price the firm could obtain would mirror directly the worth of the advantage in the final market. There are, in fact, a number of such contractual arrangements, some persisting over time (such as Coca-Cola's licensing of bottlers in different countries), others employed primarily in the initial stages of expansion owing to financial and other constraints (such as Mitsubishi's entry into the U.S. auto market using a tie-up with Chrysler Motor Corporation).

One problem with the licensing option is that the entering company will not have an opportunity to learn about the new market and to expand its skills repertoire. Furthermore, policing the licensee and overseeing the royalty payments (usually some percentage of sales) can be difficult. As the licensee develops the requisite skills of production and marketing, there is a risk that payments will not be made and also that the transferred know-how will be used for export production, so that over time the firm-specific advantage will gradually erode. This **dissipation** problem could be reflected in higher prices for licenses, but with less than perfect foresight it is difficult for the firm to assess the appropriate level of return. Generally, according to the theory, firms turn away from licensing because they can get higher returns on their FSAs by "internalizing" them.[11]

Where licensing is thus deemed to be too risky and learning is important, the company has a choice between exporting and foreign direct investment. Both avenues imply that the company has decided to retain control over its firm-specific advantages, by either producing at home (the export option) or investment to produce abroad (the FDI option). This is the meaning of **internalization.** In the exporting case, the firm-

Pepsi Cola's licensed bottlers target the same consumers in Moscow as elsewhere. The Pepsi entry into Russia was helped by then U.S. president Nixon, and Pepsi came to dominate the market. But the 'first mover advantages' were less than usual. After perestroika, Coca-Cola entered the market and Pepsi's image as a pre-glasnost brand allowed Coca-Cola to gain share quickly among the 'new' Russians. Sarah Leen Matrix

specific advantages are embodied in the product marketed abroad but may still need some protection against dissipation (see box, "Unique Firm-Specific Advantages: Bull Semen").

In the FDI case, the advantages are employed to generate returns in a subsidiary, and then the payoffs are repatriated by way of transfer prices or simply profit taken home.

The desire to protect FSAs has helped to give rise to the multinational corporation. The usual definition of an MNC is a firm having a number of foreign production sites and thus a number of internal markets. The pure exporting firm is usually referred to as an international company. From this perspective many of the European automobile firms are less multinational than international. For example, Mercedes and BMW build the vast majority of their cars in Germany, and the recent decision to establish assembly in the United States is a big step for both. Volvo, Renault, and Fiat have only limited manufacturing abroad—Volvo in Belgium, Fiat (previously) in Spain (Seat) and Russia. French Renault's investment in American Motors failed to resurrect the latter,

G E T T I N G   T H E   *Picture*

Unique Firm-Specific Advantages: Bull Semen

WILLARD CLARK of Worldwide Sires Inc. in California runs a very unique international business operation: He sells bull semen. Acting as a broker for nine artificial insemination cooperatives, Clark exports frozen semen of prize U.S. bulls (mostly Holsteins) to more than 40 countries, including the Commonwealth of Independent States (former Soviet Union). He is moving into China where he hopes to conquer the market for swine semen. A small business, Worldwide Sires is growing fast after grossing about $5 million in its first year.

How does Clark protect his firm-specific advantage? He does it by exclusive tie-ins with the cooperatives and by constantly keeping an eye open toward new markets (like swine semen) where his built-in advantage and company skill can be used to preempt competitive entry.

Source: Thorelli and Becker, 1980, p. 266.

Country-Specific Advantages and FDI: Rossignol

FOREIGN DIRECT INVESTMENT can be preferable to exporting even if the formal trade barriers are small. One reason is the country-specific advantage associated with manufacturing in the market country. The experience of French ski manufacturer Rossignol represents one of these cases.

As Rossignol's share of the French market reached saturation, the company sought to grow by exporting from France. But because of problems with floating exchange rates and bad experiences with dock strikes and long transportation delays, the company soon decided to turn to FDI in manufacturing. It established plants in Switzerland, Italy, Canada, Spain, and the United States, all within a span of about four years.

These sites, except Spain, were chosen because of their proximity to large ski markets (low labor costs influenced the Spain location). The company management stated: "Skiing trends change quickly, and with differences across countries. Furthermore, skiing conditions vary among countries and even (the case of Canada and the United States) between neighboring countries. With the rapid changes compounded by national and international differences, we needed to stay close to the large individual target markets in order that these trends be anticipated correctly."

Sources: Thorelli and Becker, 1980, pp. 21–23.
http://www.rossignol.com/

and Renault is now back on home ground. Contrast this with Ford and General Motors, true multinationals that have built cars in Europe for a long time, and with Volkswagen and Honda, which have a number of plants outside their home countries.

Exporting or FDI?

The choice between pure exporting and foreign direct investment (FDI) in manufacturing hinges on, among other things, the number and height of the obstacles to free trade. In the case of free trade (the situation usually associated with the original development of the theory of comparative advantage), there is no particular reason to engage in FDI just to service a market. Because of varying tariffs and nontariff barriers, however, the case for FDI is often quite strong. The investment in productive capacity induced by these types of barriers is often referred to as "import-substituting" FDI, since such barriers tend to eliminate trade. For the marketer who likes to follow the trade conflict debates between various countries, it is good to remember that FDI often replaces exports and leads to a negative trade balance.

From a company viewpoint, however, there are usually additional factors that need to be considered in choosing between exports and FDI. For example, the firm-specific endowments might not be strong enough to overcome the locational disadvantages of home production but would be if the manufacturing were done in a third country closer to the market. With the emergence of trade regions, such patterns are common; for example, EU markets are often supplied from Ireland, and the American market from Mexico.

Thus, "pure" exporting from a home base is simply a special case in which country-specific advantages at home and the firm-specific advantages are great enough to offset the locational disadvantages (including transportation costs and lack of market familiarity—see box, "Country-Specific Advantages and FDI: Rossignol").

Minimizing Transaction Cost

The emphasis on FSAs in the internalization theory can be given an equivalent theoretical interpretation in terms of Williamson's transaction cost framework. Since this framework has proved useful in determining mode of foreign entry, the theory is of relevance to the global marketer.[12]

Generally speaking, **transaction costs** are incurred when completing a transaction between a buyer and a seller. Apart from obvious costs such as transportation charges, sales taxes, and brokerage fees, there are often other costs incurred as well. Examples include costs to establish contact between buyer and seller, translations in order to communicate in different languages, the risk that the product might not follow agreed upon specifications, misunderstandings in price negotiations, and so on. These obstacles create the costs incurred by the parties in the transaction, and unless sufficient gains from the exchange are obtained, the costs may prohibit trade.

The activities that are required to overcome these barriers can be termed *market making* functions. Since specialization tends to reduce costs, a sufficient volume of transactions of a certain kind is likely to spawn different agents who specialize in these activities. The most direct examples of these kinds of institutions occur perhaps in financial markets, where banks and brokerage houses serve to link buyers and sellers across borders and rely on their global information network to spot trading opportunities in which they can fetch a profitable commission.

As an alternative to employing external agents or market makers, a firm might assume such functions itself. The seller of a product might provide the credit, storage, or insurance necessary for the completion of the transaction, while the buyer might take the responsibility for the transportation, for example. These cases of (forward or backward) vertical integration represent examples of the principle of internalization. In the framework of transaction cost theory, internalization occurs when the most efficient (least cost) means of effecting a transaction occurs within the firm itself.

As we have seen, a typical firm-specific advantage is a globally recognized brand name. From a transaction costs viewpoint, an established brand name serves to lower the cost of the exchange since the buyer can trust the quality of the product and thus "search" costs are reduced. If this trust is misplaced because company operations abroad are not properly controlled, transaction cost theory would predict that future purchases will not materialize. To ensure against such an event, the company will likely enforce rigorous quality control, possibly via FDI and 100 percent ownership. The transaction cost argument thus creates the same rationale for internalization as the FSAs do. In both cases, the aim is the protection of the benefits from the completed transaction, in one case by maintaining a sufficiently low transaction cost, in the other by protecting the FSA embodied in the brand name.

GLOBAL COMPETITORS

As we saw in Chapter 1, globalizing competitors often force a company to consider "going global." In fact, for any company contemplating a global strategy, the main rivalry will often be with other global companies. Global competitors are always a threat to enter any local market where they presently might not have a presence. In addition, the global competitor usually has greater resources available and a wider repertoire of competitive actions. These assets make for a stronger competitor and also make predictions of their actions and reactions more difficult.

Competitive Strength

Global competitors tend to possess greater financial resources than other companies, partly because it takes money to go global, but also because their presence in many countries makes it easier to raise funds in the most favorable location, usually where the company has high market share and little competition, using their brands as cash generators ("cash cows," in strategic language). Because of the challenge involved for management in a global company and the possibility of drawing on a larger pool of talent, the global competitor also tends to have access to better managerial capability. If one also remembers that the global network can be a hidden competitive asset, it is not surprising when local firms need protective legislation to be competitive.

The analysis of competitive strength should also deal with the **strategic intent** of the global competitor in any one particular local market.[13] U.S. firms that are accustomed to considering North America their primary market should remember that so do many multinational companies from other countries, such as Sony and Honda from Japan, Volvo and Saab from Sweden, and Unilever and Shell from Europe. When a global competitor enters a certain market, its intent is not necessarily profit making; as we saw in Chapter 1, the strategic objective can include a number of other goals. Since what matters to a global competitor is usually the total leveraging of the assets invested in the global network, the global firm can accept losses in one or more markets as long as the spillover to other markets is positive. And since the financial strength of the global competitor makes a long-term view feasible, such a company can wait a long time for the turnaround.

Competitive Repertoire

The broadened **competitive repertoire** of the global competitor includes first of all the capability of attacking a competitor in several markets and, in the same vein, the capability of defending a market by countering elsewhere. The global competitor can also engage in **integrated competitive moves.**[14] For example, selected price wars can be started in a few markets to occupy competitors, while new products are tested and introduced in other markets. This was the tactic of the Japanese television manufacturers as they moved into Western markets, using their home market as a testing ground for technical innovation. The global competitor can also sequence new product introductions and the roll-out of a new campaign around the globe, maximizing the effect from word-of-mouth and spillover gains from global mass communication.

It is important to recognize that the skilled global competitor does not have to yield much to domestic companies in **local presence.** The global competitor employs natives who gain considerably when the global competitor does well. Honda and Toyota dealerships have been tickets to riches for their American dealers, for example. In most countries the locals who have the territorial distribution rights for global companies such as Dunlop, Coca-Cola, and Caterpillar have done very well.

Finally, it is difficult for a domestic manufacturing company to retain the loyalty of the natives when raw materials, parts, and components are imported from foreign locations. Soon Honda is likely to employ more Americans than Chrysler, as Honda strives to become an insider in the United States and Chrysler enlarges its supplier network in Asia.

Global Rivalry

The increased strength and widened repertoire of the global competitor mean that the scope of marketing competition is enlarged. The Kodak–Fuji story is illustrative (see box, "The [Continuous] Kodak–Fuji Battle").

The Kodak–Fuji illustration shows how a global competitor can use its **global network** and its presence in many markets to make surprise competitive moves. *Global advertising* is also a competitive weapon that can pay off nicely for the global company. The Coca-Cola experience in Russia is an example. Pepsi-Cola, its arch rival, scored a coup in the 1970s when President Nixon helped Pepsi get the lone license to bottle cola in the former Soviet Union. When the Russian market opened up after the fall of the Berlin Wall, Coca-Cola had to come from far behind to catch up with ensconced Pepsi. Using globally broadcast commercials on satellite TV emphasizing "The Real Thing" and saturating advertising on CNN's global news channel, Coca-Cola established itself as the cola of the new times and relegated Pepsi to inferior status as an almost domestic Russian brand, reminiscent of the communist past. Within months, Coca-Cola had captured chunks of market share from Pepsi.[15]

G E T T I N G   T H E

Picture

The (Continuous) Kodak–Fuji Battle

BY THE EARLY 1980s Fuji film, the Japanese "poor second" competitor to American Kodak, had long tried to make a dent in Kodak's home market. Despite competitive products and successes in Europe and other foreign markets, Fuji had never been able to muster the brand awareness necessary to make it big in America. But in 1984 all that changed. As the Los Angeles Olympic Committee approached Kodak about becoming the "official" film for the 1984 Summer Olympics, Kodak managers vacillated. The potential incremental gains to Kodak awareness and goodwill hardly justified the steep $20 million price tag suggested by Peter Ueberroth, the business-oriented leader of the Olympic Committee. A small notice reporting the conflict in a British newspaper caught the attention of a Fuji manager in London, who promptly telephoned the Fuji U.S. headquarters in New Jersey. Within hours the Fuji home office in Tokyo agreed to offer Ueberroth what he asked, and Fuji became the official sponsor of the Olympics.

But the story does not stop there. The Kodak managers realized that their reluctance had inadvertently opened the door for their main global competitor. Their evaluation of the benefits and costs of the sponsorship had failed to take competitive considerations into account. A counterattack seemed necessary, partly to rejuvenate the flagging spirits within the company. Kodak management decided to launch a marketing offensive in Japan, Fuji's home market stronghold. Developing a revamped but still recognizably "Kodak yellow" package with Japanese print, and capitalizing on a superior new "200" film, Kodak saturated Tokyo with street giveaways and storefront displays. The full-court press worked. Fuji had to refocus its energies from the U.S. market and protect its home turf by matching the new film and its promotions. This was done successfully by working closely with channel members, creating entry barriers by relationship marketing. Claiming unfair discrimination, Kodak soon challenged these methods in the court of the World Trade Organization in Geneva. In 1998, however, the WTO found no unfair Fuji advantage, admonishing Kodak to simply "try harder."

Sources: Johansson and Segerfeldt, 1987; *Washington Post*, June 26, 1995, p. A12.
http://www.fujifilm.co.jp/
http://www.kodak.com/

Hypercompetition

Because of the intense rivalry between global firms in many industries, competitive advantages have become increasingly difficult to sustain. This has happened not only in high-technology industries such as computers and telecommunications where technological advances have been quickly copied and improved. It has happened as well in traditionally more slow-moving industries such as banking, retailing, and packaged consumer goods.

The cause for the erosion of advantages lies mainly in the management practices of global competitors. For example, **reverse engineering** of products, a practice initiated by the Japanese in which competitors' leading products are carefully disassembled to reveal superior engineering and design solutions, has helped equalize the performance of competing products. Nowadays the first customers for any new product or service tend to be the competitors, in athletic shoes, shampoo, or cameras.

In the same fashion, the **benchmarking** of "best practices" in services, where the operations of superior performers in terms of customer satisfaction are studied to uncover their key process steps, has meant that advantages in service quality have become more difficult to sustain. For example, McDonald's way of training its young employees has been the subject of many management seminars. When one firm **reengineers** its supply chain, by simplifying product flows and integrating electronic communication interfaces, its competitors are likely to soon follow suit. The "just in time" system pioneered by Toyota, with parts and components arriving at the assembly line just before use, has been adopted by a large number of companies outside the automobile industry, such as the Hewlett-Packard computer company.

The lack of sustainable advantages in function and quality has meant that intangible benefits have become more important. This is one reason brand image and brand equity have become so important to global companies. More will be said about global branding in Chapter 12, "Global Products and Services." It has also led at least one scholar to coin a new term: **hypercompetition**.[16]

The basic notion underlying hypercompetition is that since advantages erode, the firm has to compete by coninuously moving to new ground, in the process possibly destroying its own existing advantage (on the principle that "If we don't do it, someone else will").

RESOURCE-BASED VERSUS MARKET-BASED COMPETITIVE STRATEGY

As we have seen, when going abroad the firm usually can't be certain that the home advantages can be leveraged in foreign markets. Customers will not have the same preferences, and competitors will be different. The transfer of advantages into foreign markets is fraught with dangers: Can service be kept at the desired level? To what extent is the marketing infrastructure different? Can the product perform as well in a new environment? When is high quality no longer high quality? These are uncertainties that challenge the marketing strategic plan.

Before the recognition of the learning effects of specialization discussed by Porter and Krugman, the economic theory of international trade and the theory of the multinational firm were basically static—"equilibrium theories," in economic jargon. As we have seen, the global perspective powerfully challenges a static mindset and suggests that advantages are not a given and fixed fact. "Going global" stretches the firm's capabilities.

The dynamic benefits of foreign entry come from competing against new competitors and supplying new and demanding customers. This is what helps build new FSAs and sustain the competitive edge. Global markets are important not only for their market opportunities but also for the opportunities they offer to expand the resources of the firm. It is in the constant re-creation of the company's assets and competencies that the dynamic benefits from global marketing come. The global marketer is always learning new concepts and techniques.

Always Market Oriented?

Most students and practitioners of marketing have learned about the advantages of a **market orientation**. "Don't think of the product sold, but the customer need fulfilled." "Deliver customer satisfaction, not just what you think is a quality product." "Your dealer is also your customer." "Understand the consumer better by listening to complaints." "Don't just read research reports; go meet your customers in the store."

For the marketing manager, it is natural to think about overseas opportunities in terms of customer needs and wants. It suggests that the main issue for global marketing is whether there is a demand for the product. But this is only a start. More important, the manager has to identify what the firm has to offer abroad and whether it can deliver on the promise.

The crucial first factor for the firm is to understand the basis of its own success at home or elsewhere. The firm contemplating going abroad should identify its key strengths and whether its local success is just that, local. Only if there are good reasons to assume that some strengths are applicable in another country should the firm start examining markets abroad. It is possible to look at foreign entry in terms of learning and increasing competitiveness, but even then existing strengths and weaknesses have to be carefully assessed.

When countries are less developed as market economies, adopting a market orientation is often ineffective. The assumed infrastructure is weak or nonexistent, making "middlemen as customers" a moot idea. Customers with sophisticated needs are few and far between, making customer satisfaction a matter of providing the most basic products and services. Warranties and liberal return policies are difficult to administer and easy for customers to abuse. After-sales service can often not be offered without risky investments in new buildings and machines and additional training of dealer employees.

Knowledge-Based and Resource-Based Capability

As we saw in Chapter 1, much has been written recently on the topic of the **knowledge-based organization.**[17] Market-based explanations for sustainable competitive advantages have given way to analysis of factors internal to the firm. If competitive advantages traditionally resided in a superior offering in the marketplace, recent rapid changes in products and services have suggested to analysts that competitive sustainability lies more in a company's speed and flexibility to change products and services.[18] These knowledge capabilities are not embedded in the products themselves—their features, quality, image—but involve know-how, skills, and experiences of the company and its employees. Such know-how can be difficult to articulate and teach; it is more art than science.

Knowledge is recognized today as one of the (if not *the*) key resources of the firm. **Resource-based strategy** defines the firm not in terms of the products or services it markets, nor in terms of the needs it seeks to satisfy, but in terms of what it is capable of doing. From the resource-based perspective, the first question is what the firm can offer in terms of technology, know-how, products, and services. Only then may the issues of selecting markets and developing a competitive global strategy be successfully tackled.

An internal focus on strengths and weaknesses seems to go counter to the marketing concept, but in reality complements it. Whereas a market orientation focuses on competitive advantages in the marketplace, the resources perspective fosters a view of the company as a leveraging force for its resources. It generates an appropriate mindset of "getting a return on the assets" philosophy, in which the key management question is how the resources should be deployed to generate the best return.

A good example of how a market orientation can be wedded to a resource-based approach is the strategy adopted by Scandinavian Airlines under Jan Carlzon (see box, "SAS and Strategic Flexibility").

The Value Chain

For the global marketer, the change in perspective that comes with the resource-based view can be illustrated by the value chain concept. The **value chain** concept suggests that the firm's activities in transforming raw materials and other inputs to final goods can be viewed as a collection of complementary and sequential tasks, each adding value to the product.[19] Some tasks are in operations (purchasing, design, manufacturing, and marketing); others are support activities (finance, personnel). The concept is an elaboration of the value-added notion in economic theory, which does not specify the activities inside the firm but simply views the firm as a transforming black box between inputs and outputs.

The value chain is the "internalized" sequence of operations undertaken by the firm. The vertically integrated firm has a long value chain, while a less integrated firm focuses only on some of the operations. "Deconstructing" the value chain is equivalent to externalization. The way McDonald's, the American fast-food restaurant chain, operates in different countries is instructive. In the United States the company has externalized major activities by hiring independent firms to supply the beef, potatoes, bread, and other ingredients, and by allowing independent entrepreneurs to open franchised outlets. However, McDonald's inspects operations and keeps tight quality controls on

G E T T I N G   T H E   *Picture*

SAS and Strategic Flexibility

W H E N S A S (Scandinavian Airlines System) needed a new CEO after a dismal year in the early 1980s, it turned to Jan Carlzon, the president of the Swedish domestic airliner Linjeflyg. Savvy industry observers expected Carlzon to pursue the same strategy at SAS that he had pursued successfully at Linjeflyg: cut-rate prices and targeting the tourist class. But Carlzon surprised them.

"The international market was not the same as the domestic," Carlzon explained in his 1987 book, *Moments of Truth*. "In the international marketplace, service was a neglected but important attribute, not price." After analyzing the available airline routes and the existing collection of airplanes, he decided on a contrary strategy. SAS defined itself as the businessperson's airline, concentrated on business class excellence, and limited tourist class. This is market-based strategy.

Industry observers immediately questioned whether SAS could execute such a plan, given the airline's existing capabilities. In fact, SAS went to considerable effort to improve its service delivery resources before promoting its service. The company sent employees to customer satisfaction seminars and training sessions, gave on-the-job training, and, perhaps most important, eliminated layers of supervisors, empowering front-line people to make decisions and take initiatives. SAS was profitable within one year and was voted the world's best business airline a year later.

Alas, that was not the end. Other airlines copied the strategy, boosted their service capabilities, and soon Thai and Singapore airlines as well as British Airways and German Lufthansa could be seen advertising their preflight and in-flight service. With no airline having a distinct advantage in service anymore, competition shifted to routes and network connections, leading to a number of strategic alliances to develop global reach. SAS struck up an ill-fated deal with Continental Airlines for the U.S. market, an alliance that became a burden as Continental went into bankruptcy, and Carlzon lost his job.

Sources: Carlzon, 1987; *New York Times*, April 5, 1994, p. D2.
http://www.sas.se/
http://fly.to/linjeflyg
http://www.flycontinental.com/

all phases of business. In Europe, suppliers are also independent local producers, but some key franchised locations (including one on Paris's Champs Élysées) are owned by McDonald's itself, mainly for purposes of quality maintenance. In Moscow, McDonald's found it necessary to develop its own suppliers, since the local suppliers could not provide the necessary quality.

Exhibit 2.4 shows how two competing companies, Panasonic and Radio Shack, have configured their value chains in consumer electronics differently. While giant manufacturer Panasonic has no direct involvement at the retail level, Radio Shack, primarily a retailer, does no component manufacturing of its own. This shows how the firms' differing FSAs can be leveraged at different levels in the value chain for electronic consumer goods.

In global marketing, the stage of the value chain that can best be leveraged—and where the FSAs lodge—might not be the same as at home. For example, in markets in which the firm has limited experience or in which products are at a different stage in the life cycle, licensing a technology to a local manufacturer might be preferable to making and selling the product. Starting with a market perspective, by contrast, tends to lock management into a narrow focus on selling to foreign markets the same type of product sold at home.

This "externalization" of activities can be contrasted with the "internalization" principle discussed above that helps explain the emergence of the multinational corporation with wholly owned foreign subsidiaries. In Chapter 6, where various entry modes are discussed, strategic alliances will be seen as one example of externalization.

The value chain can change over time, as new ways of combining activities appear and entrepreneurs grasp opportunities to simplify the entire flow, from raw materials to ultimate consumer (a process called *industrial rationalization*). For example, the

Exhibit 2.4 Value-Added Analysis for Consumer Electronic Products

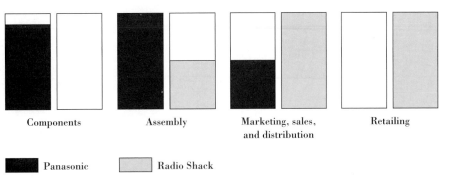

Swedish furniture retailer Ikea developed a new formula for selling home furniture. Instead of showcasing finished furniture in downtown stores and later shipping merchandise to buyers' homes as traditional furniture retailers did, Ikea created a self-service store where purchasers could bring home their furniture the same day. Designing furniture in easily assembled pieces, and locating in suburban shopping malls where customers came by car, the company has been able to offer bookcases, tables, chairs, and even beds in easily transportable cardboard boxes. The assembled showroom furniture is clearly labeled with prices, stocking numbers, and units available; and the customer can walk around and make up a buying list without assistance. Having presented the list to the cashier and made payment, while the order is relayed automatically to the stockroom, the customer drives to the back door and picks up the packaged boxes. Ikea has in fact developed a new value chain (or a new "business model"), in which the customer does more work than before. In return, the prices are much lower. Ikea soon ventured abroad and has become the first successful furniture retailer on a global scale.[20]

Role of Technology

Because of increased spending on R&D and the successful appeal of so many recent innovations, many global markets are driven by technological developments. This is true not only for high-tech computers, telecommunications, and biotechnology but for many ostensibly low-tech products such as diapers, detergents, cosmetics, drugs, and food. New and modified products are often introduced not because customers ask for them but simply because of the technological advances.

In such a market, a focus on customers will not be sufficient to sustain loyalty and sales. The firm needs to develop technological capabilities to be able to compete by introducing new products. Although such competencies ultimately have to be matched against customer needs, there is often little in the way of consumer feedback or market research suggesting potential or latent needs with any degree of reliability. Only when the product emerges on the market do needs and wants crystallize. Examples of this phenomenon are too numerous to list here (in personal computers alone, the speed of new and expanded features is astounding—and disheartening to users whose last year's unit is already obsolete).

To avoid spending resources on blind "trial and error" introductions of new products, in these cases companies often resort to close monitoring and quick imitation of new competitive offerings. As the speed of technological development has increased, intense competitive rivalries have led to a proliferation of new products in many markets, many of them "me too" variants. This reinforces rivalry, making

IKEA, the Swedish-based furniture and home furnishings specialty retailer, serves a global market. Here, a shopper visits an IKEA store in the United Arab Emirates.

strategic execution factors, such as speed and flexibility, rather than uniqueness and differentiation, which place a premium on superior segmentation and positioning strategies, the key for success. As managers often say, "If you execute well, when things don't turn out right, you know it's the strategy that is faulty. If your execution is flawed, you don't know if the strategy is right or wrong."

To repeat, the global marketing manager has to formulate the firm's competitive strategy with an eye to the firm's resources and true competencies as much as to the demand potentials in foreign markets.

COMPETITIVE STRATEGY AND THE THREE HATS

The two strategy perspectives differ in importance for the three phases of globalization.

In the *foreign entry* phase, after a preliminary assessment of the foreign market potential, the resource-based strategic perspective will dominate. The firm must decide what it has to offer, what it can do well, and how it should enter abroad. Foreign entry is frequently initiated by an order from a foreign country for a company's product. Especially in the early stages of global expansion, the assessment of the market, customer segments, and competitive offerings is often done through informal methods and by independent middlemen. The most pressing question is whether middlemen are reliable.

The *local marketing abroad* phase requires analysis of customers and competitors, the typical market-based approach to strategy. The managerial headaches usually come from unforeseen shifts in customer preferences, potential channel conflict, uncertainty about advertising effectiveness, and competitors' price cuts. The company's resources obviously make a difference when considering what kind of market strategy to implement and whether an expensive competitive battle can be sustained, but the overriding concern in local marketing is in-depth analysis of customer needs and wants, evaluation of actual and potential competitors' strengths and weaknesses, tactical decisions across the life cycle stages of the product, and issues of quality and customer satisfaction.

With *global management*, the focus shifts back to headquarters and the resource perspective. The task for the global marketing manager now is to synchronize strategic moves in various countries across the globe, standardizing products and services, coordinating activities, and timing new product entries, all in hope of synergistic efficiency. Will savings from standardization more than offset potential loss of revenues in some countries? How can subsidiary managers be soothed when a new product is rolled out in another country first? How can we get our agent in country X to report quickly any moves by competitor Y? Which are the leading markets for our product? For these kinds of questions, the firm needs to understand its strengths and weaknesses. Part Four of this book will show how the marketing manager can mold and stretch company resources into a globally effective marketing machine, using global strategies to find the optimal trade-off between local responsiveness and global scale economies.

SUMMARY

This chapter has discussed global competitive strategy. Extending Porter's five forces model, the chapter demonstrated the link between competitive strategy and the theory of the multinational with its distinction between country-specific and firm-specific advantages.

The discussion also showed how a firm's country-specific advantages related to Vernon's international product cycle (IPC), Porter's "diamond of national advantage," and Krugman's new trade theory. In the end, country-specific advantages underlie the persistence of country-of-origin effects as manifested in firms' advertising and product positioning.

Chapter 2 showed how firms translate their CSAs and FSAs into strategic advantages for the firm and how these advantages can be transferred. In particular, the chapter discussed how global competitors use these advantages to help overcome the natural disadvantage of being a foreign marketer abroad. Chapter 2 ended with a look at how resource- versus market-based strategy impacts the three global marketing tasks—the "three hats."

KEY TERMS

absolute advantage p. 34
benchmarking p. 47
comparative advantage p. 34
competitive repertoire p. 46
country-specific advantage
  (CSA) p. 34
diamond of national advantage
  p. 35
dissipation p. 42
firm-specific advantage (FSA)
  p. 39

first-mover advantage p. 31
global network p. 46
hypercompetition p. 48
integrated competitive moves
  p. 46
internalization p. 42
international product cycle
  (IPC) p. 34
knowledge-based organization
  p. 49
licensing p. 42

local presence p. 46
market orientation p. 48
new trade theory p. 37
reengineering p. 47
resource-based strategy p. 49
reverse engineering p. 47
strategic intent p. 46
transaction costs p. 45
transferability p. 40
value chain p. 49

DISCUSSION QUESTIONS

1. Identify the competitive advantages of some market leaders such as McDonald's, Nike, Swatch, and Sony. Are these country-specific or firm-specific advantages?

2. Use Porter's five forces model to analyze the competitive environment of a country of your choice (pick a product category that you are familiar with). How does a market orientation explain entry into that market? A resource-based view? Why are both perspectives useful?

3. Discuss how the transferability of competitive advantages of a service differs from that of a product.

4. Go onto an Internet interactive vehicle-buying service (such as AutoVantage), and compare the various makes offered. Discuss how the close comparisons possible on-line make competitive advantages easier to identify. What role is played by a strong brand?

5. On the vehicle Web site, keep track of your own comparisons to create a flow diagram that shows what features were accessed and at what stage (for example, price and engine power). Then compare with others in the class. What does this tell you about how potential buyers arrive at a decision on the Internet?

NOTES

1. See Porter, 1985.

2. This section draws on Lieberman and Montgomery, 1988, Kerin et al., 1992, and Schnaars, 1994.

3. See Vernon, 1966.

4. See Vernon, 1979, in particular. The later extensions involved introducing dynamic competitive conditions and firm-level rise and decline explicitly. The multinational in the early stage is an innovation-based oligopoly, turning into a mature oligopoly, and then a senescent (aging) oligopoly.

5. See Porter, 1990.

6. See Krugman, 1988.

7. See, for example, Grant, 1995, pp. 232–5.

8. A good early review is that by Bilkey and Nes, 1982. For more recent studies, see Papadopoulos and Heslop, 1993.

9. See, for example, LaBarre, 1994. In this survey covering respondents from North America, Japan, and Europe, Japan was rated highest overall in quality of manufactured products, followed by Germany and the United States. Broken down by respondents from the various regions, however, Germany scored highest among Europeans, the United States among the North Americans, and Japan among the Japanese.

10. Kogut and Zander, 1993, report on these practices.

11. The dissipation problem and the issue of getting a reasonable return on the firm's assets are headaches for managers, since licensing is a very convenient option not requiring much in terms of resources. See Rugman, 1979.

12. Williamson, 1975, is the original statement of the transaction cost framework. The application to foreign entry can be seen, for example, in Anderson and Gatignon, 1986.

13. The emphasis on strategic intent was first suggested by Hamel and Prahalad, 1989.

14. From Yip, 1992.

15. From *The New York Times*, May 11, 1995, pp. D1, D9.

16. See D'Aveni, 1994.

17. See, for example, Nelson and Winter, 1982, and Nonaka and Takeuchi, 1995.

18. See Itami and Roehl, 1987.

19. See Porter, 1985.

20. This extension of the value chain is from Norman and Ramirez, 1993.

SELECTED REFERENCES

Anderson, Erin; and Hubert Gatignon. "Modes of Foreign Entry: A Transaction Cost Analysis and Propositions." *Journal of International Business Studies*, no. 3 (1986).

Bilkey, Warren J.; and Eric Nes. "Country-of-Origin Effects on Product Evaluations." *Journal of International Business Studies* 8, no. 1 (Spring–Summer 1982), pp. 89–99.

Carlzon, Jan. *Moments of Truth*. Cambridge, MA: Ballinger, 1987.

D'Aveni, Richard A. *Hypercompetition: Managing the Dynamics of Strategic Maneuvering*. New York: Free Press, 1994.

Dunning, John H. *International Production and the Multinational Enterprise*. London: Allen-Unwin, 1981.

———. "The Eclectic Paradigm of International Production." *Journal of International Business Studies*, Spring 1988, pp. 1–31.

Grant, Robert M. *Contemporary Strategy Analysis*. 2nd ed. Oxford: Blackwell, 1995.

Hamel, Gary and C. K. Prahalad. "Strategic Intent." *Harvard Business Review*, May–June 1989, pp. 63–76.

Itami, H.; with T. W. Roehl. *Mobilizing Invisible Assets*. Cambridge, MA: Harvard University Press, 1987.

Johanson, Jan; and Jan-Erik Vahlne. "The Mechanism of Internationalization." *International Marketing Review* 7, no. 4 (1990), pp. 1–24.

Johansson, Johny K.; and Jan U. Segerfeldt. "Keeping in Touch: Information Gathering by Japanese and Swedish Subsidiaries in the U.S." Paper presented at the Academy of International Business Meeting in Chicago, October 1987.

Kerin, Roger A.; P. Rajan Varadarajan; and Robert A. Peterson. "First-Mover Advantage: A Synthesis, Conceptual Framework, and Research Propositions." *Journal of Marketing* 56, no. 4 (October 1992), pp. 33–52.

Kogut, Bruce. "Designing Global Strategies: Comparative and Competitive Value Chains." *Sloan Management Review*, Summer 1985, pp. 27–38.

———; and Udo Zander. "Knowledge of the Firm and the Evolutionary Theory of the Multinational Corporation." *Journal of International Business Studies* 24, no. 4 (1993), pp. 625–46.

Kotler, Philip; Liam Fahey; and S. Jatusripitak. *The New Competition*. Englewood Cliffs, NJ: Prentice-Hall, 1985.

Krugman, Paul R. *Geography and Trade*. Cambridge, MA: MIT Press, 1988.

LaBarre, Polly. "Quality's Silent Partner." *Industry Week* 243, no. 8 (April 18, 1994), pp. 47–48.

Lieberman, Marvin; and David Montgomery. "First-Mover Advantages." *Strategic Management Journal*, Summer 1988, pp. 41–58.

Nelson, Richard R.; and Sidney G. Winter. *An Evolutionary Theory of Economic Change*. Cambridge, MA: Belknap, 1982.

Nonaka, Ikujiro; and Hirotaka Takeuchi. *The Knowledge-Creating Company*. New York: Oxford University Press, 1995.

Normann, Richard; and Rafael Ramirez. "From Value Chain to Value Constellation: Designing Interactive Strategy." *Harvard Business Review*, July–August 1993, pp. 65–77.

Papadopoulos, Nicolas; and Louise A. Heslop, eds. *Product-Country Images: Impact and Role in International Marketing*. New York: International Business Press, 1993.

Porter, Michael E. *Competitive Advantage*. New York: Free Press, 1985.

———. *The Competitive Advantage of Nations*. New York Free Press, 1990.

Quinn, James Brian. *Strategies for Change—Logical Incrementalism*. Burr Ridge, IL: Irwin, 1980.

Rugman, Alan M. *International Diversification and the Multinational Enterprise*. Lexington, MA: D. C. Heath, 1979.

Schnaars, Steven P. *Managing Imitation Strategies*. New York: Free Press, 1994.

Thorelli, Hans B.; and Helmut Becker, eds. *International Marketing Strategy.* Revised ed. New York: Pergamon, 1980.

———; and S. Tamer Cavusgil, eds. *International Marketing Strategy,* 3d. ed. New York: Pergamon, 1990.

Vernon, Raymond. "International Investment and International Trade in the Product Cycle." *Quarterly Journal of Economics* 80 (May 1966).

———. "The Product Cycle in a New International Environment." *Oxford Bulletin of Economics and Statistics* 41 (November 1979).

Wells, Louis T. "A Product Life Cycle for International Trade?" *Journal of Marketing,* July 1968, pp. 1–6.

Williamson, O. *Markets and Hierarchies: Analysis and Antitrust Implications.* New York: Free Press, 1975.

Yip, George. *Total Global Strategy.* Englewood Cliffs, NJ: Prentice-Hall, 1992.

Three

Global Cultural Analysis

"Equal, but not the same"

Your takeaways from this chapter:

1. Culture is not only a fundamental dimension of any society but a very visible force affecting market demand as well as managerial behavior.

2. Culture is one of the major determinants of the degree to which demand varies across the globe. Where cultural differences are strong, markets tend to be multidomestic.

3. When a marketer finds it difficult to understand a customer from a very different culture, remember one universal truth: People buy what they buy for a reason.

4. Our own culture has given us certain useful behavioral skills. In new situations, those skills may be of little use and even counterproductive. This is why culture tends to affect strategy implementation and execution, "how" things are done, more than strategy formulation.

5. Cultural differences are examples of market entry barriers and can be overcome with sensitivity, hard work, and a superior product or service.

A GLOBAL MARKETER can't avoid the obvious truth that people in Hong Kong, Oslo, or Johannesburg are different, despite the growth of global travel services, global media networks, global hotel chains, and global product offerings. Since marketing is a people-oriented function, this affects the global marketer powerfully.

Culture has two main effects on the global marketer. First is the effect on demand. Differences in culture make it difficult to predict customer reactions and understand consumer behavior. Customers around the world have varying needs, face disparate economic constraints, use contrasting choice criteria, and are influenced by different social norms.

The second effect of culture is on the "soft" skills of management. National culture affects organizational culture, how managers deal with subordinates and other employees, how they negotiate contracts, how they control the independent middlemen needed to enter a foreign market, how they establish trust with joint venture partners, and how they manage distribution channels. Simply stated, culture has a direct effect on what people skills the global marketer needs in the foreign environment.

Disneyland Paris Tries to Rekindle Marketing Magic

Just a year and a half after opening its gates in 1992, the Euro Disney theme park situated outside Paris was teetering on the brink of bankruptcy. The company reported disappointing revenues and an unexpected $90 million loss for its first full year of operation. Unless it could negotiate financial help from its creditor banks and parent Walt Disney Company, Euro Disney would have to shut down. What went wrong?

At one point, Euro Disney seemed to be a promising concept: Based on Disney's success in Japan and North America, the company's theme park concept seemed to have worldwide appeal. However, park attendance at Euro Disney was less than expected, and the visitors who came did not spend much money. Perhaps most devastating to Euro Disney's bottom line was that the resort had constructed too many hotel rooms. Tourists did not book rooms for visits to the park as expected.

Disney responded by modifying its marketing approach, renegotiating the financial package, and changing the way it treated its employees. The familiar "Disney culture" was relaxed to fit the local culture and the expectations of the European managers and workers. A number of the French employees did not take lightly to the idea of being lectured about personal grooming, what makeup to use, and what clothes to wear, even coming and going to work, as they felt such demands were tantamount to invasion of privacy. And European middle managers cared more about prestige and status than the democratic ideals of American management. For these reasons, Disney eased up on its strict behavioral code.

Other changes involved adaptation of the "product." For instance, the French—over one-third of Euro Disney's visitors—expect wine with their lunch, so the park has loosened Disney's no-alcohol policy. And contrary to the eating habits of snacking Americans, the French visitors expected their lunch promptly at 1 p.m., causing long lines and some frustration. So the park opened additional restaurants to accommodate local tastes and habits. In addition, Euro Disney invested in a spectacular new ride, the Space Mountain roller coaster, reportedly the fastest Disney attraction in the world, to generate excitement and lure new visitors. Euro Disney also set more affordable prices—up to 20 percent less for tickets, food, and hotel rooms.

But the big change was a 1996 decision to disassociate the park from the "Euro" name. The Euro connotation had grown stale from overuse in various media and even turned negative with the slowing down of the pan-European economy. Instead, Disney opted for a Frenchified institution. One move was to rename the park to *Disneyland Paris*, drawing on the success with Tokyo Disneyland in Japan and doing away with all references to Euro. Another significant move was the release of a successful film adaptation of the Victor Hugo classic *The Hunchback of Notre Dame*. Produced as the typical Disney cartoon, the feature-long film became a worldwide hit, and the French theme was emphasized in cross-marketed merchandise from the film. In addition, the traditional daily parade down "Main Street" in the Disneyland Paris park was changed to feature characters, music, and songs from the movie.

Naturally, the Frenchification also included considerable upgrades in the park's restaurants and menus, and the Parisian (and Parisienne) visitor can now enjoy a truly French meal in the park, with accompanying fine wines and high prices.

The initial results of Disney's new approach have been encouraging. Judging from the nationality of the visitors, the French have adopted the American émigré as one of their own, and there seems to have been little dissipation of visitors from other European countries (who no longer need to hide their Disney memorabilia when trying to get the attention of a waiter in a Champs Élysées café). The theme park finally has begun to generate a profit. Observers are still cautious about forecasting long-term success, partly because cost pressures and the need to pay off high-interest loans have slowed down the expansion plans (including the construction of a version of a Disney-MGM studio attraction, which had been expected to draw many visitors). But with the Disney home operation in the United States doing well, such concerns will probably be temporary. Only time will tell whether the "Disney magic" has finally caught Europe in its spell, but the outlook seems better every day.

Sources: Roger Cohen, "When You Wish upon a Deficit," *New York Times*, July 18, 1993, sec. 2, pp. 1, 18–19; Roger Cohen, "Euro Disney '93: $90 Million Loss," *New York Times*, November 11, 1993, p. D4; Roger Cohen, "Euro Disney in Danger of Shutdown," *New York Times*, December 23, 1993, p. D3; "Euro Disney Rescue Approved," *Japan Times*, May 21, 1994, p. 6; Nathaniel C. Nash, "Euro Disney Reports Its First Profits," *New York Times*, July 26, 1995, p. D3; Peter Applebome, "The Medici behind Disney's High Art," *New York Times*, October 4, 1998, sec. 2, pp. 1, 38.

http://www.disneylandparis.com

INTRODUCTION

In traditional textbooks "culture" is simply seen as another environmental force that differs across countries, just like the political system, the legal and regulatory environment, the level of economic development, and so on. But for marketers culture is more than just environment; culture is a direct determinant of demand and ways to do business.

The traditional treatment depicts the environmental differences as new and unfamiliar constraints on the marketer. International marketing becomes marketing within a new set of given economic, political, legal, and cultural limits. But although this treatment might work for the other environmental factors, it does not do justice to culture. A few examples will show why. Many marketers target segments in foreign countries which belong to the same ethnic and religious (that is, "cultural") groups that are targeted at home. Export expansion often occurs into countries where a manager feels "comfortable" that is, where culture is similar. Culture affects the way to do business in a country and therefore influences who should run your subsidiary. In brief, culture does not simply set new limits on the opportunities for buyers and sellers but also helps determine their goals, preferences, and aspirations.

Chapter 3 begins by discussing the meaning of culture and how cultures differ across nations, describing the major approaches used to depict cultures. It emphasizes that culture is not simply an *underlying* driver of behavior but in fact tells us how to behave in many *concrete* ways. The chapter then explains the process by which culture affects what people do well and what they do less well, and shows how in the process managerial skills are affected.

GETTING THE *Picture*

Cultural Idiosyncrasies

AS A RULE, it is not necessary to behave as Romans do when one is in Rome (unless one is Roman). Nevertheless, for the novice manager, various kinds of cultural misunderstandings may occur.

When an Indian shakes his head, it does not mean "No" as in the West but "Yes, I understand." When a Scandinavian speaks slowly, he is serious and sure, not uncertain and deviant, as might be the case elsewhere. When an American speaks, he or she wants to make eye contact, while a listener from Japan wants to give room and avoid a direct glance.

Continental Europeans often have supper around 10 p.m. A relatively formal dinner party might not be over until 3 or 4 a.m. To leave at midnight, which is late by U.S. standards, requires a very legitimate excuse.

While Japanese consider inebriation to bring out the true person, U.S. managers tend to insist on self-control at all times. "Don't trust a man who doesn't drink" may have been coined by W. C. Fields, but it does not represent corporate America as much as some other countries.

Stylish dress sits badly in conservative American corporations. Elsewhere, the aim is often for the "bella figura," even among top managers. Of course, the Japanese blue or grey suit easily wins first prize in the race to be unnoticeable but actually serves to proclaim its wearers members of the same caste, a subconscious but prized benefit in all matters Japanese.

Sex is a tricky subject in any business circle, especially in Muslim countries but also among Americans with their Puritan roots. In European countries the topic is usually more acceptable but needs to be approached with flair ("Everyone to his taste" as Prince Orlofsky puts it in the *Fledermaus* operetta). Similarly, religion is usually a no-win topic of conversation. One reason the American insistence on human rights has encountered resistance in a country such as China is that it reflects a missionary zeal to convert others; Buddhism offers more of a "live and let live" ideology.

Sources: Durlabhji and Marks, 1993; Hall, 1976; Hall and Hall, 1990.

Then the important role of culture on consumer tastes and preferences is discussed, starting with the simple universal truth that people buy what they buy for a reason. The chapter discusses how culture is related to consumer behavior, including central behavioral concepts such as hidden motivators, emotional gratification, perceived risk, and cognitive dissonance. The aim is not to exhaust this huge and interesting topic but simply to lay the cultural groundwork for the analysis of local buyer behavior in Chapter 7 and the global segmentation discussion in Chapter 11. Chapter 3 concludes with culture's impact on the managerial tasks of foreign entry, local marketing, and global management.

At the outset it is useful to look at some examples of what culture involves (see box, "Cultural Idiosyncrasies").

As the illustrations in the box suggest, there are hundreds of potential cultural clashes every day in various parts of the world. Some of them are recognized; others are not. Every manager's behavior conveys intended or unintended meanings to his or her counterpart. **Body language**—the often unintended signals that a person projects through dress, body position, hand and eye movements, fidgeting, and so on—may provoke all sorts of culturally slanted interpretations. In countries with a homogeneous population, such as Italy, a gesture is often sufficient for information to be shared. A "Hai" in Japanese usually means "I see" rather than the more definite "Yes," which is its literal translation. A "Hai" accompanied by a slight bow is a stronger statement (unless, of course, the response is to a speaker of higher status, in which case again it simply means "I see"). And so on and so forth.

The global manager needs to learn to be a good observer of individual behavior, to become sensitized to actual and potential manifestations of cultural idioms. At the same time, the manager will begin to understand his or her own cultural heritage and biases. Just as foreign travel teaches you about a foreign country, it also teaches you about yourself. This is why the immersion in at least one foreign culture gives the manager a wider repertoire of skills and greater sensitivity to alternative behaviors. Great global marketers don't need to start from scratch in each new country, but they need to be flexible and always ready to question their own past experiences.

THE MEANING OF CULTURE

Culture is usually defined as the underlying value framework that guides an individual's behavior. It is reflected in an individual's perceptions of observed events and personal interactions, and the selection of appropriate responses in social situations. The framework encompasses *objective* reality as manifested in societal institutions and *subjective* reality as socialized predispositions and beliefs.

Culture manifests itself in **learned behavior,** as individuals grow up and gradually come to understand what their culture demands of them. "Culture" is not just an abstraction but also a physical reality. The functions of a society—the "what a society does"—are not very different across countries. Everybody has to get food, lodging, a job, money, clothes, a significant other, success, career, status, social recognition, pride, comfort, peace of mind, a center for his or her existence, power, some influence over others, and all the other things! These are the objectives of people's behavior all over the world. The relative amount of time and resources allocated to these activities may vary, but the tasks remain. The question is *how* these tasks are accomplished, and this varies a great deal across cultures.

The modern conception of culture focuses directly on observable behavior. It recognizes that culture not only predisposes the individual toward certain behavior but eliminates other behavior. Consequently, culture creates a repertoire of behavioral skills.[1] Culture directly influences what people *will* do and what people *can* do. This interpretation of culture is very useful for global marketing managers. It suggests that culture is more important for *how* managers should decide, less for *what* the decision should be. *Culture affects implementation and execution of strategies more than their formulation.*

CULTURES ACROSS COUNTRIES

What kinds of cultures are there in the world? There are several useful ways of classifying cultures across countries. First, however, one needs to recognize that cultures and countries do not necessarily go together. Countries with large populations such as India, China, Russia, and the United States are really **multicultural,** meaning that they contain a wide variety of cultures within their borders. The same goes for some smaller nations, such as the former Yugoslavia, Belgium, Canada, and South Africa. In other cases, several countries can be seen as one cultural grouping. Examples include the Scandinavian countries (Denmark, Norway, Sweden) and Latin American countries (Venezuela, Colombia, Ecuador, but not necessarily Brazil).

High versus Low Context Cultures

An important distinction between cultures suggested by Hall is that between **high and low context** cultures.[2]

In "high context" cultures the meaning of individual behavior and speech changes depending on the situation. Nonverbal messages are full of important—and intended—meanings. Even if no words are spoken, individuals communicate. And when words are spoken, "reading between the lines" is important. High context cultures require a similarity of backgrounds, a commonness of purpose, and a homogeneity in society. These result from careful enculturation and socialization starting at an early age in the family. The process continues naturally in homogeneous coun-

East meets West in Dubai. High- or low-context culture is not a matter of modern buildings or a comfortable outdoor setting, but of individual values, social norms, and subjective perceptions. Derek Berwin/The Image Bank.

tries, with one religion, one language, centralized broadcast media, coordinated educational system, and so on.

In "low context" cultures, by contrast, intentions are expressed verbally. Propositions have to be justified and opinions defended openly. In low context cultures the situation is not allowed to change the meaning of words and behavior; the context conveys little or no information. This is quite useful and effective in a country that is multicultural and where people's value systems and attitudes can be very different.

High context cultures can be found in a variety of countries, including most of the European countries, some of the Latin American countries (Chile, Mexico, perhaps Venezuela and Argentina), and many of the newly industrializing Asian countries (but not China or India). In countries with high context cultures—such as Saudi Arabia and Japan—a written contract is not always enforceable if the situation changes or if new people move into executive positions.

Americans, because of their **diversity,** have a low context culture. Low context cultures can also be found in ethnically diverse countries such as India, China, Russia, and in countries such as Australia and New Zealand with large immigrant populations that have nevertheless blended.

"Silent Languages"

In a famous article, Hall also pointed out the important role of **"silent languages"** of international business.[3] He identified the use of five different silent languages: space, material possessions, friendship patterns, agreements across cultures, and time. All of the factors have some meaning in interpersonal communication but are not necessarily spoken of. For example, one's conception of *space* relates to matters such as the distance between two people conversing. In the Middle East men will maintain an intimate distance, often too close for comfort for Westerners. *Material possessions* of course always speak volumes about one's station in life, particularly where social hierarchies are well developed so that people learn what to look for. The emphasis on well-known brands in Asian markets, for example, reflects a need to clearly identify one's position with signals other people understand.

Friendship patterns—that is, whom you treat as a friend—are not only reflective of your own cultural upbringing but also involve questions of trust and responsibility. In a business deal, it would not be strange for an American to assure a prospective partner that a third person "will agree because he is my friend." By contrast, in a country like Japan, the person might well say, "I cannot speak for him because he is my friend." *Agreements across cultures* are also interpreted differently. While Western businesspeople rely on explicit contracts and keep the letter of the law, Eastern cultures rely more on general agreement and the basic intent of the partners.

Perceptions of *time* vary considerably between even relatively close cultures, and studies have documented the varieties of problems connected with different time perceptions.[4] Latin Americans' perception of their being "on time" even when 30 minutes late for an appointment is counterbalanced by East Asians who think it safest to show up 30 minutes early, just to be on time. While northern people might not like to "waste" time on "small talk" in a business meeting, Latins tend to spend more time on nonbusiness conversation. Differing perceptions of time and its use are responsible for many problems in business negotiations, a topic to be discussed later.

It is important also to recognize that time has an additional dimension. Whether one's cultural background says so or not, in global competition "time is money," so time has a strong economic component. For example, the famous JIT or "just in time" inventory system of Toyota, the automaker, is really a "much before time" system, with supplier trucks waiting outside the plants in the early morning hours. When German supermarkets close at 6 p.m., the clerks' understanding, codified in their labor agreement, is that no checkouts will be done after that time (whereas in most other countries doors close at 6 p.m., but customers already in the store are checked out). Needless to say, in Germany store customers line up by 5:45 p.m., but in the end half-filled shopping carts are often left in the aisles or at the register. One would perhaps have expected that with increased competition through the EU integration, customer service would improve, but the outcome is still unclear.

When interpreting various cultural manifestations in different countries, the marketer needs to remember that self-referencing can be misleading. *Self-referencing* is a process by which we form judgments about others. It involves judging others' behavior against our own past experiences and our own conception of self.[5] Other information is often used when judging people—the particular setting, the other people involved, verbalized motivations, and so on. But such information, even when available, is often difficult for us to interpret when we face people from a foreign culture. Therefore, self-referencing is common when judging people from abroad; we see others through ourselves.

This can lead to misperceptions. When people dress casually while you are in a dark suit, when they avoid eye contact while you look steadily at them, when they speak slowly and you speak purposefully, when they smile while you are earnest, information comes to you, but it does not necessarily mean what you think it means. Before reaching any hasty conclusions, you must check with people familiar with the culture and perhaps bring a knowledgeable companion to any meeting. The bottom line is, learn about the culture, don't trust first impressions—and play down self-referencing in favor of more objective information. **Cultural adaptation** as a skill to be honed must be high on the manager's list of priorities, but as with all valuable acquisitions it can't be had on the cheap.

Hofstede's Cultural Dimensions

The high versus low context distinction and "silent languages" provide useful concepts by which to think about various cultures. Hofstede's questionnaire study of IBM's employees around the globe in 1980 is a much more systematic assessment of cultures across countries.[6] Although the world has changed considerably since the study was done, cultures have changed less; and judging from recent events in Eastern Europe and Russia, ethnicity and cultural roots are stronger than ever.

According to Hofstede's survey findings, countries can be classified along four basic **cultural dimensions.** The first cultural dimension is **individualism versus collectivism.** In a collective society, the identity and worth of the individual is rooted in the social system, less in individual achievement. A second dimension is high versus low **power distance.** High power distance societies tend to be less egalitarian, while democratic countries exhibit low power distance (see Exhibit 3.1).

As can be seen from the "map" in Exhibit 3.1, Australians and Venezuelans tend to be diametrically opposite each other on these two measures. While Australians are individualistic and democratic, Venezuelans are much more collectivist and believers in formal authority. It is important to recognize that the distances between countries on the map are proportional to the degree to which they differ culturally.

Hofstede's third dimension, **masculine versus feminine,** captures the degree to which a culture is dominated by assertive males rather than nurturing females. Finally,

EXHIBIT 3.1 The Position of the 40 Countries on the Power Distance and Individualism Scales

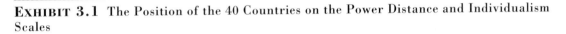
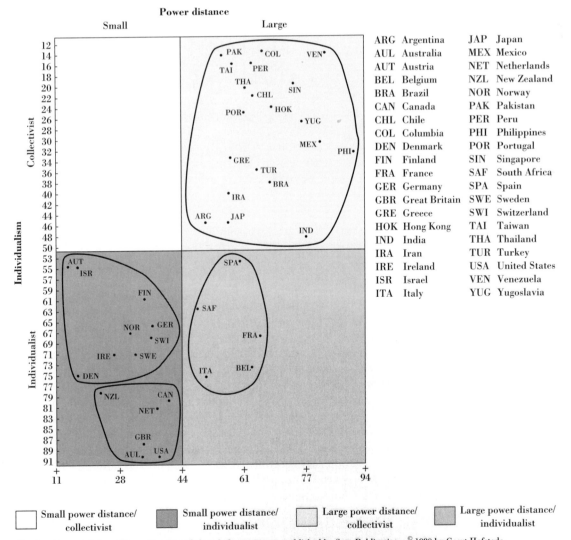

EXHIBIT 3.2 The Position of the 40 Countries on the Uncertainty Avoidance and Masculinity Scales

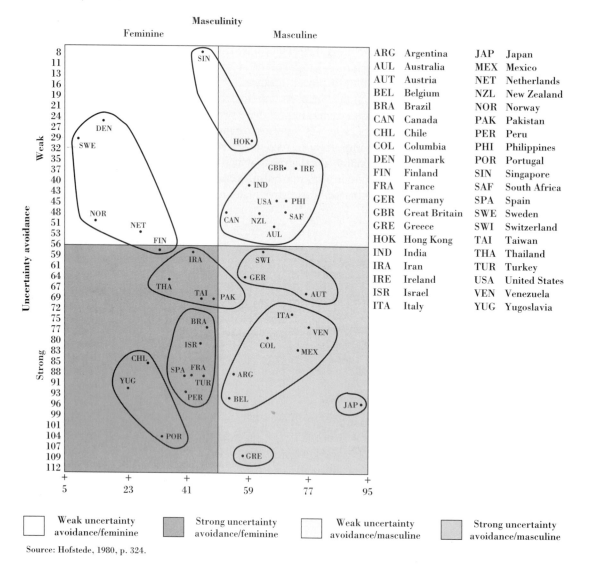

ARG	Argentina	JAP	Japan
AUL	Australia	MEX	Mexico
AUT	Austria	NET	Netherlands
BEL	Belgium	NZL	New Zealand
BRA	Brazil	NOR	Norway
CAN	Canada	PAK	Pakistan
CHL	Chile	PER	Peru
COL	Columbia	PHI	Philippines
DEN	Denmark	POR	Portugal
FIN	Finland	SIN	Singapore
FRA	France	SAF	South Africa
GER	Germany	SPA	Spain
GBR	Great Britain	SWE	Sweden
GRE	Greece	SWI	Switzerland
HOK	Hong Kong	TAI	Taiwan
IND	India	THA	Thailand
IRA	Iran	TUR	Turkey
IRE	Ireland	USA	United States
ISR	Israel	VEN	Venezuela
ITA	Italy	YUG	Yugoslavia

☐ Weak uncertainty avoidance/feminine ▨ Strong uncertainty avoidance/feminine ☐ Weak uncertainty avoidance/masculine ▨ Strong uncertainty avoidance/masculine

Source: Hofstede, 1980, p. 324.

weak versus strong **uncertainty avoidance** rates nations according to the level of risk tolerance or risk aversion among the people (see Exhibit 3.2).

As can be seen from the map in Exhibit 3.2, Australia and Venezuela are not as far away from each other this time. Both cultures tend to be dominated more by males than females, and although Venezuelans are more eager to avoid risks, the distance—and thus cultural difference—is not that great. The difficulties managers from the two countries might face in dealing with each other would likely revolve around individualism and differences in the use of power. While an Australian would act alone and treat others as equals, the Venezuelan might feel better seeking support among peers and then imposing decisions on subordinates.

In some later applications Hofstede has added a fifth dimension, **Confucianist dynamics,** to distinguish the long-term orientation among Asian people, influenced by Confucius, the Chinese philosopher, from the more short-term outlook of Western people.[7]

The Hofstede mapping of countries is useful in that it offers a snapshot of the cultural distances between countries. Marketers can anticipate the degree to which mar-

G E T T I N G   T H E

Picture

Business Here Is Business There—with a Twist

CULTURAL DIFFERENCES can be managerial headaches.

Raytheon, the U.S. chemical firm, hired Italian-Americans to manage operations in Sicily but found that this strategy did not produce the desired results. The problem related to the origins of the managers. They were from northern Italy and not very much liked or trusted among the Sicilians with their closely knit family ties.

In another case, a firm introduced a technical product into a market relatively free of competition. Anticipating few problems with the entry, the firm did not pay sufficient attention to the person chosen as its European sales manager located on the Continent. As it happened, the man chosen disliked the French and made no effort to learn either their language or culture. His treatment of the French sales force reflected this attitude, lowering morale and performance. A competing firm entering later was able to attract much of the original company's sales force and go on to become the market leader.

The standard advice in negotiations and selling is to get any agreement in writing. This advice is not so well taken in many cultures where the business decision is made at one level with a word and a handshake, and the actual closing with order specification, cost figures, and final signing taken care of later. Lack of understanding and finesse on this score lost the contract for one Western firm in Japan. Selling kitchen equipment for restaurants, the firm's sales manager pressed the president of the purchasing company for his signature on a written contract just after an oral agreement had been reached. Making two mistakes in one move, showing distrust of the oral agreement and asking for a signature at the wrong time, the manager failed to close the deal.

Sources: Hall and Hall, 1990; Salacuse, 1991.
http://www.raytheon.com

keting programs, especially communications and services, might need to be adapted to a new culture. Also, for the multinational company with different product lines in different countries, a choice can be made about which line should be introduced in a new market. For example, when Kentucky Fried Chicken expanded into Korea and Taiwan, it started with the menus already developed for Japan rather than the American selections.

Managers can also evaluate how difficult it may be to do business in a country culturally distant from their own and how much of a cultural shock they and their families are likely to get when moving to the country. As Exhibits 3.1 and 3.2 suggest, the typical American manager might find it very difficult to run a subsidiary in a country whose culture is much more oriented toward less individualism, more power distance and authority, and more avoiding uncertainties (see box, "Business Here Is Business There").

Gannon's Metaphors

In a recent book, Gannon proposed a novel way of looking at cultures.[8] He suggested the use of descriptive metaphors for different cultures, suggestive analogues that characterized cultures in such a way as to help managers anticipate what people's reactions might be in different situations. The **metaphors** offer a mental anchor for the manager who has to deal with a new culture and cannot foresee all contingencies.

In practice, it is impossible for the global marketer to learn about all cultures. According to Gannon, learning a smattering of individual "don'ts" ("Don't prop your feet on the table, don't blow your nose, don't compliment anybody's wife, don't cross your legs, don't touch your host's son's head," and so on) from the typical "how to" books is likely to create confusion when more than one culture is covered. Gannon argues that it is more effective to develop a holistic sense of a culture by creating an image (a metaphor) representing how the people think and behave. By planting the

EXHIBIT 3.3 Gannon's Metaphors

1. *American football:* Individualism and competitive specialization; huddling; ceremonial celebration of perfection.
2. *The British house:* Laying the foundations; building the brick house; living in the brick house.
3. *The German symphony:* Orchestra; conductors; performance; society, education, and politics
4. *The French wine:* Purity; classification; composition; compatibility; maturation.
5. *The Italian family opera:* Pageantry and spectacle; voice expression; chorus and soloists.
6. *The Swedish summer home:* Love of nature; individualism through self-development; equality.
7. *The Japanese garden:* Wa and shikata, harmony and form; seishin, spirit of self-discipline; combining droplets.
8. *The Chinese family altar:* Confucianism and Taoism; roundness, harmony, and fluidity.
9. *India: cyclical Hindu philosophy:* The cycle of life; the family cycle; the social cycle; the work cycle.

Source: Martin Gannon, "Cultural Metaphors," *Understanding Global Cultures*, pp. v–vii. ©1994 by Martin Gannon. Reprinted by permission of Sage Publication.

image in the back of one's mind, Gannon suggests, one can more comfortably interpret what someone in that culture is trying to say or do. If the metaphor is correct and fairly deeply understood, one's own reactions and responses can become more genuine and instinctive.

Some of Gannon's proposed metaphors are given in Exhibit 3.3. As can be seen, Gannon suggests that the metaphor of American football captures many of the features of American culture, with its emphasis on competition, specialization of individual functions, strong leaders calling the plays, and the desire for individual recognition. By contrast, Italians can be described in operatic terms, where speeches are like tenor and soprano arias, the "bella figura" of Italian dress is represented by the costumes and stage setting, and the major players are all given time to shine in the spotlight.

The German culture can be characterized by the classical symphony, with its strict discipline under a leader and skilled individuals performing together, like a well-oiled machine. And so on. However simplified such metaphors are, Gannon argues, they give the manager the right mindset with which to approach customers, distribution middlemen, potential partners—and bureaucrats!—in the foreign culture.

CULTURE AND "HOW TO DO BUSINESS"

Although the aim of business may be the same everywhere, the way to do business varies considerably across countries. The advent of global markets and global firms has to some extent reduced the disparities among countries, but it has also meant that the successful executive travels to more and more countries. Whereas in some firms a stint in the London or Paris or New York or Tokyo office serves as a step on the career ladder, in others the career stopovers are likely to include Kuala Lumpur, Mexico City, and Kiev. "Culture shock" is a potent threat to the high-flying international marketer—and his or her family.

Cultural differences affect the applicability of the experienced marketer's professional skills directly. In the new setting a great marketer is no longer necessarily a great marketer, perhaps not even a good one. The experienced marketer will often have a frustrating time getting back to the basic fundamentals of the marketing effort. When Pepsi-Cola entered Japan many years ago, it selected a young executive who had been very successful in the U.S. marketplace. His age and impetuous nature, key ingredients in his American success, set back Pepsi's introduction severely. While Coca-Cola gained market leadership with the help of Japanese leaders, Pepsi still had to recover from the initial mistake.

Situations can differ so drastically that experience is a misleading guide. Nestlé, the Swiss multinational in food products, sold its infant formula in Africa, where it was mixed with unclean water and heavily diluted, causing tragedy. Products that seem to fill needs instead create more problems.[10] Or the experienced marketer, who has learned the importance of tracking sales, may be misled in a foreign culture, resulting in disaster for the marketing effort. Reliance on store sales data might be dangerous in cultures where habitual manipulation of records has been fostered by inequitable tax regulations.

It's "back to basics" time. Some Japanese companies have a policy of sending new and untutored marketing representatives abroad, even when seasoned managers with experience of the particular country are available. The assumption is that the neophytes will perceive customers without preconceptions and be able to come up with fresh ideas. While this is an extreme approach, the point is the same: When there are great cultural differences between countries, the marketing manager often has to start from scratch again.

In short, culture influences how management skills—the way managers plan, decide, act, and control—can be applied. Not only are there obvious implications for the way managers treat subordinates and other people, but there are also definite cultural biases influencing the effectiveness of subsidiary management and the capability of marketing implementation.[11] These matters will be pursued further in the context of negotiations (in Chapter 6) and salesmanship (in Chapter 16). First, it is useful to outline briefly how culture leads to skills.

Culture and Managerial Skills

The linkage that connects national culture to managerial skills can be described as a sequence of steps.

1. Culture defines a set of acceptable behaviors and a set of unacceptable behaviors. "Don't prop your feet up on the table" and "You must wear a suit and tie" are typical examples. These form social norms for behavior. In business they form the "way of doing business."

2. Individuals learn to perform to these behavioral norms. Managers learn how to do business. These are the processes of enculturation and socialization. They determine how individuals will behave as consumers in the marketplace, how demanding they are, how they voice complaints, and so forth.

3. Over time, individuals become skilled at acceptable behaviors—and less skilled at unacceptable behaviors. They will simply not be able to engage in "learning by doing" certain behaviors. Complaining to someone making noise during a Beethoven recital is difficult for many people, since they will then be too upset to enjoy the performance anyway—a "lose-lose" situation. The savvy concertgoer will have no such qualms, because he or she has done it many times. The American marketer will be good at succinctly presenting his or her point of view, while the Japanese counterpart will be good at listening.

4. Acceptable behavior in the business firm is usually a reflection of acceptable behavior in society, especially if the company is large. In large companies employees cannot know each other personally and thus have to rely on more arm's-length relationships based on the general culture. Smaller companies can be less orthodox, with an organizational culture that is unique and unrelated to the larger society.

5. Successful managers tend to be good at acceptable behaviors—and at avoiding unacceptable behaviors. A particular organizational culture is created. Sometimes, of course, this can be dysfunctional, as when change is forced on the organization. Thus, "organizational rebels" or "change agents" often play important roles in rejuvenating companies.

6. Successes and failures in the past generate managerial "experience"—and successful behavior will be repeated elsewhere. This is because of the positive reinforcement received when behaving in a culturally acceptable way.

Managerial Styles

Because of this skill development process, culture tends to generate different **managerial styles,** that is, what is considered appropriate managerial behavior in different countries.[12] This can be illustrated with a comparison between companies from the so-called Triad: Japan, North America, and Europe. First, we need to analyze the cultures of these three regions.

As we saw in Exhibits 3.1 and 3.2, Hofstede's research produced the rough classification for the countries in the Triad seen in Exhibit 3.4. Great Britain is included among the North American countries in Exhibit 3.4 based on their respective scores in Exhibits 3.1 and 3.2. Also, because of their great differences from one another on the Hofstede maps, the European countries are divided into northern Europe (Scandinavia, Finland, and The Netherlands) and continental Europe (the rest, except Great Britain). "Context" has been added as a fifth dimension to account for differences between high and low context cultures.

According to Exhibit 3.4, the Western regions are high on individualism, as one might expect, but differ on the other three dimensions. Power distance is low in democratic North America and northern Europe, less so in continental Europe. The only region low on masculinity is northern Europe, where gender equality is more of an established fact. The tolerance for risk is higher in North America and northern Europe, while Japan and continental Europe tend to avoid uncertainty. Japan's group orientation and hierarchical society are reflected in its low score on individualism and high power distance. Japan and northern Europe are high context societies, while North America and continental Europe are less so, needing more clarification and verbalization.

How do these national cultures affect managers who are sent abroad? Some of the well-known stereotypes of various country managers can easily be derived from these dimensions.[13] One understands why Japanese travel in groups and insist on careful preparation of meeting protocols, why they listen well and slow down their decision making. Western managers can be expected to take responsibility on their own, being individually more confident and trusting their ability to solve problems and improvise. At the same time, continental Europeans tend to want clear agendas and organization of meetings, and are more likely to insist on a clear structure of agreements and solutions. The high context cultures of Japan and northern Europe make it less important to justify everything verbally and explicitly, since most managers will be able to "fill in the missing pieces" on their own. In those countries, less is more, when it comes to talking.

EXHIBIT 3.4 Hofstede's Classification of Triad Countries

	Japan	Anglo-Saxon (Canada, United States, Great Britain)	W. Europe Northern	W. Europe Continent
Individualism	Low	High	High	High
Power distance	High	Low	Low	High
Masculinity	High	High	Low	High
Risk tolerance	Low	High	High	Low
Context	High	Low	High	Low

Note: "Context" added.

Source: Adapted from Hofstede, 1980.

Managing Subordinates

These cultural differences suggest that different types of leadership skills will be needed in managing marketing overseas.

Going to a high context culture from another such culture will in general be easier than going to a high from a low context culture. Managers from a high context culture will have sensitivities to nonverbal cues that go unnoticed or are ignored by low context cultures. The person from a low context culture is easily seen as a "bull in a china shop" in a high context culture. The American managers are brought up to tolerate and respect others' convictions but are, because of their low context culture, not sensitive to nuances and not used to placing themselves in somebody else's position.

It is not surprising if people from high context cultures feel uncomfortable when managers from low context cultures arrive to run a subsidiary. People from high context cultures tend to be fine-tuned: They pay attention to nuances and omissions; they indulge the speaker and fill in the unspoken meaning on their own. In the United States, being drunk is no excuse for bad-mouthing one's boss to his face; while in a country such as Japan, that is the managers' unspoken but understood purpose of after-business drinking. The typical manager from a low context culture has no ability or will to indulge subordinates to that extent: "If words are spoken, they are meant. There is no excuse."

To help managers cope with—or, even better, avoid—such cultural clashes, most companies offer new expatriate managers (and their families) predeparture workshops and briefings about the new culture they are to encounter. As important, most companies make sure that their professional development programs are open to a multinational group of employees. In this way the managers will naturally get "cultural sensitivity training" as a side benefit from internal executive courses.

A Global Low Context Culture?

Will there be—or is there already—a **global business culture?** People in Europe and elsewhere ask why the American culture seems to be dominating other cultures in the world's marketplace. Although it is important not to confuse popular culture with culture that guides managerial behavior, it is clear that the English language and the American business schools often determine the framework. One explanation lies in the international transferability of American culture.

The American low context culture might seem heavy-handed and insensitive to non-Americans, but it travels light. Low context cultures are not as tied to the particular country of origin. A high context culture depends on common background and implicit understandings; it enables fine-tuning but also limits the repertoire. A manager from a high context culture will need time to build up business in a new country. The American businessman can move much more rapidly since the focus is on the intrinsic merits of the transaction only—good products and services, customers who need them—and less on adapting to the particular cultural environment in the new country.

In today's world markets, high context cultures are high-cost, both in terms of entry barriers and managerial inefficiency. They cherish the notion that every country is unique and no outsider can understand "us." This is possibly correct, and holding on to tradition is perhaps a desirable feature in itself. But it is counterproductive in the global economy, since it limits the inflow of new ideas into a company's managerial ranks, it reduces the pool of suppliers considered, and it keeps superior foreign goods out of markets. Globalization means that people in every country will have to decide the degree to which their own unique ways of doing business are worth preserving. These are difficult decisions. But in the global economy and the global firm, old ways don't promise success.

G E T T I N G   T H E

Picture

Shopping but Not Choosing

IN 1989 THE EAST BERLINERS were first allowed free access to West Berlin's stores. Their surprise at the variety of products was palpable. In one case a couple with two carts strolled through the aisles of a supermarket, loading up on products at every step. Queried why they bought so many units of each selection, they responded: "How can we be sure these brands will be available when we come next time?" Another couple in a shoe store was surprised to find out that sales clerks were helpful in surveying the selections, locating the right sizes, and suggesting alternatives. "The way we see it back home," they explained, "clerks are there to guard the merchandise."

Sources: *The Wall Street Journal*, February 11, 1990; "A New Brand of Warfare," *Business Central Europe*, April 1994.

CULTURE AND DEMAND

Turning to the effects of cultural forces on market demand, the first thing to note is that cultural factors are a major influence on consumer behavior. Culture is in fact a source (and a result) of significant differences in people's behavior everywhere. Understanding people from foreign cultures is often a baffling business. We see that they are born, experience childhood and adolescence, have common human needs, grow up, fall in love, establish families, work hard, and grow old. Everybody has a life. But what kind of life, and what do people choose to make of it, and why?

Of course, many groups of people are not in the position of being able to choose. A great number of people in the world live under such poor economic conditions that showing them vast choices of brands, products, or lifestyles would be pointless. They are stuck and just as likely to resent the inaccessible materialism they see advertised on the global communication highway.

But even among very poor people there are those who can and do, within limits, choose. The choices made will often astound an outsider. In a mud hut in Central Africa, where clean water is scarce, one will find a Sony TV set. In India, a paradigm of a developing country, a poor farmer is happy to show off his new Philishave electric razor. In the reopened China provinces, one can see Nissans and Toyotas navigating roads intended for oxcarts and pedicabs. And when the consumers in recently opened Eastern Europe go shopping, the result can be surprising for other reasons (see box, "Shopping but Not Choosing").

Consumption patterns are unpredictable without a feel for local culture. In affluent America, people in expensive Boss suits are happy with junk food but insist on the latest PC upgrade. In Germany, the food seems less important than unsurpassable beds; while in neighboring France, not to mention Belgium, food is a passion. The Japanese, those sticklers for quality details, seem oblivious to leaking roofs patched with plywood and corrugated sheets of plastic.

A Universal Trait in Local Form

The good news is that there is at least one simple truth about buyer behavior in all markets. *It is that most people are doing what they do for a reason.* Consumers perceive a link between behavior and desired results. Buyers do not choose products or services for no reason, even in the most fatalistic of cultures. In other words, buyers are **goal oriented.**[14]

Thus, if one can find out what people in a local market are trying to achieve, one can start to understand their behavior. The global marketer should start by attempting to find out what *motivates* buyers by asking them what and why they buy, or by ob-

Finding the Hidden Motivators

WHEN MARRIOTT, the American-based hotel chain, opened up a new luxury hotel in Jeddah, Saudi Arabia, it became an instant attraction for local luminaries and international travelers. The grandly decorated lobby with its large windows and magnificent entrance drew not only travelers and hotel guests but also local visitors. The large number of people crowded in the lobby delayed check-in and check-out operations, and long lines formed in front of the service counter. Managers of the Marriott headquarters in the United States soon determined that it was necessary to install the quick check-out system already in place in many of its hotels worldwide, which would allow the guests to leave quickly without waiting in line.

But when the system was proposed to local management, objections were immediately raised. The managers explained that the customers of the new Marriott wanted to spend time in the lobby, to see and be seen, and to enjoy the status it conveyed; the long lines supplied a simple but legitimate reason for doing this. It was decided that a more rapid check-out process would be a negative benefit, and the proposal was scuttled.

Sources: Bruce Wolff, vice president of distribution sales, Marriott Hotels.
http://www.marriott.com/

serving them buying certain products or choosing certain brands (see box, "Finding the Hidden Motivators").

Marketing research on motivation is not easily done, even in the United States, with the most straightforward customers. First, as psychoanalysis tells us, behavior has **hidden motivators,** meaning that the reason for one's behavior is not obvious. Not only are motivations willfully suppressed or denied by the buyer—choosing the rich dessert to finish the meal "just this one time"—but motivators may be unconscious—choosing colors "I like" that have been suggested by fashion.[15] The result is that direct questions often fail to uncover the true reasons behind behavior, since the buyer does not necessarily perceive these drivers consciously. He or she may very well give "sure" and "true" answers to direct questions; a fair amount of marketing research is based on the simple notion that people are willing and able to tell the truth. But psychoanalysis tells us this model can be misleading in any market.

A second consideration is that the sociocultural context within which the buyer acts influences not only behavior but also the perception of its motivators. In the West it is common to attribute choices to individual decision making. This goes well with individualism and the idea of "taking responsibility for one's own actions." In Eastern cultures it is less common to view the purchase as simply an outcome of individual deliberation. Responsibility is diffused among members of the extended family, relatives, and peers; and the decision is often justified at the group level. Individually motivated behavior is frowned on, even though it is common enough! Still, one does not want to talk openly about it or—by seeming too ego-centered—to open oneself to criticism. A similar reluctance to seem "materialistic" is of course detectable in Western countries.

A third complication is that the "means–end" relationship in buying can be more subtle than simply functional. One no longer chooses products or brands because they offer certain functions; the "demanding" customer takes those for granted. Instead the gratification is **emotional:** One likes the "look" of the new television set, the "feel" of the new car, and does not even know or understand many of the specific features. This has led marketers to say that consumers "buy the sizzle, not the steak." Thus, in some mature markets brand image and status are often assumed to be all-important. But this can be a misleading guide for a new global marketer who has to remember that quality and functionality are indeed taken for granted.[16] A global brand might be desired by local customers, but the product has to perform under local conditions, which the marketer must understand.

African villagers watching a soccer game on television. As anybody who likes sports knows, the more the merrier, and the gathering in front of a single television set is not necessarily a sign of poverty, but of a desire for a shared experience. John Chiasson/Gamma-Liaison

Perceived Risk

Most buyers make decisions under pressure. Tension comes not just from the trade-off between different features in different brands and the question of whether some extra option is worth the extra cost but from the buyer's aspirations and expectations and the expectations of relatives, peer groups, and colleagues. To an outsider, these pressures are often invisible.

The term **perceived risk** was coined by Raymond Bauer in the early 1960s to describe this tension in choosing.[17] Leon Festinger and his students at Stanford developed a related insight in their concept of **cognitive dissonance,** which describes the fearful anticipation of an emotional letdown one can feel because one might fail to make the right choice (much like the donkey in the story who starved to death unable to choose between two bales of hay).[18]

These early developments in thinking about consumers occurred in sociology. Bauer and Festinger both emphasized peer group support in the way individuals handled risk. Generally speaking, sociology is the study of the impact of social forces on individuals and how individual behavior is molded by society. As the United States developed into a premier consumer market and the individualistic tendencies of the self-centered consumer society surfaced in the 1960s, the major aim of the economic system became the gratification of the individual consumer. The preface to the 1978 edition of a prominent American consumer behavior text illustrates this:

> *One of the most remarkable developments in the last two decades is the dynamic emphasis on the consumer as the focal point of the economic system. . . . In part the awakened interest in the consumer is the result of a dramatic shift in demand-supply relationships, a change that has, in effect, placed the consumer in the fortunate position of being free to choose from many options. Thus business firms are now compelled to design and sell products that conform to the consumer's desires. "Consumer orientation" by the business firm, in turn, requires a solid basis of fact. It is not surprising, then, that analysis of the consumer has assumed a new importance.[19]*

After the 1960s, the new models of the consumer in the United States emphasized psychology and treated societal forces as constraints on the individual that could be freely adhered to or transgressed. Increasing affluence led consumers to greater economic freedom and, not surprisingly, to less reliance on family, group, or societal norms. Individuals were expected to decide what they wanted to be and then make themselves into that person. The standard American marketing textbook followed suit, with environmental forces on the consumer occupying a minor role compared to individually based perceptions, cognitions, attitudes, affect, intention, and action.[20]

But this can be misleading elsewhere in the world. Not many countries have gone through such a transformation yet. Economic affluence is still far away. Furthermore, in more socially homogeneous countries, even affluence is unlikely to engender the same tendencies toward individualism. The cultures of countries such as France, Saudi Arabia, and Japan are all based on a conception of a unique national tradition and show few signs of weakening social control even as the inhabitants grow increasingly well off. The reason is that social forces are not only negatives. They enable people to live in safety, protect individuals in need, help one get a job, alleviate the need to always justify one's actions, improve communication, generate a spirit of solidarity, and facilitate teamwork.

When a society is internally strong and orderly, social and other environmental influences on purchases are necessarily stronger. The weak social structure of the United States creates a bias in American marketing toward individual choice. Individuals are the focus, and even children are treated as decision makers. In other societies, the individual is less important. The typical man or woman dresses as he or she does because someone or something has suggested it. To understand these consumers, the global marketer has to pay attention to the sociologically important environmental influences.

Marketing and Materialism

Marketing actions are basically undertaken in the belief that more and better goods will bring an increase in consumers' standards of living, an increase in their satisfaction, and perhaps even more happiness. This assumption is often justified, but in emerging markets where capitalist dogma remains suspect, and in markets where religious and other cultural factors combine to denigrate materialism, marketers have to tread softly. For example, advertising "puffery," the use of innocuous exaggeration, may have to be avoided. What seems to be innocent play on words ("best in the West") in one context may not be seen as such in another cultural context. And many high-minded guardians of national culture will be offended by extravagant claims, regardless of merit.

When anticipating customers' reactions to new products and increased product choices, it is important to consider the very real limitations to which material affluence can generate happiness. Consumers have more products and enjoy more of the material—and also spiritual and cultural—things marketers bring. They lead "richer" lives. But richer is relative. Richer than what? As James Duesenberry, the Harvard economist, hypothesized several decades ago, the psychologically effective impact of rising incomes is that of the **relative income** (how much money one makes relative to what one's peers are making), not the absolute income level (see box, "Useful Economic Theories").

World Cup players from Europe making less than $250,000 a year are pitied in the media. In the United States, a cornerback in pro football making only $600,000 is cause for newspaper comparisons with more appreciated players.[21] Cornerbacks are by no means the highest paid players on a pro football team, and what matters is relative riches.

The fruits of progress are never distributed equally among a people, nor among nations. Even as one consumer gains, another gains more, and the first has lost, relatively speaking. This is why most of the emerging world's consumers feel under so much tension. The past had a certain order and predictability that made them feel good, and they might long for or still depend on that security, while at the same time, from the media, store windows, and their peers they know the many things available in the marketplace—things the developed world enjoys. How can they be happy without them?

Useful Economic Theories

EVEN THOUGH ECONOMISTS have been ignored by most consumer behavior analysts in recent years, traditionally, understanding consumers was the job of economists. Some of the old economic theories are useful in countries where the marketer does not have immediate access to market research data on customer attitudes and motivations.

James Duesenberry's *relative income hypothesis* states that consumers' well-being is a function of how much income they have relative to their peer groups; absolute income levels matter less. Another economist, Milton Friedman, has proposed that what determines an individual's consumption is his or her **permanent income**, defined as the regularly expected income, without "transitory" factors that lead to a temporary increase or decrease in take-home pay.

These behavioral effects are useful to keep in mind when analyzing local consumers as well as local employees. Although from a psychological perspective they are superficial, not spelling out the exact mental processes involved, they offer useful insights when more in-depth psychological data are missing. A similar case can be made for the **conspicuous consumption** concept developed by Thorstein Veblen, an economist active around the turn of the century. Conspicuous consumption refers to the notion that people make purchases of expensive brands and products in order to display their ability to afford them. Again, recent consumer behavior thinking goes further and deals with the underlying psychological processes, but the basic concept is still valid in many cultures.

Sources: Brooks, 1981; Veblen, 1899.

The bottom line is that the global entrant in a local market should recognize that the entry is not necessarily welcomed universally. Of course, some emblematic arrivals are celebrated—such as McDonald's, Coca-Cola, and Marriott. But for many potential customers, not to mention competitors, new entrants create a lot of pressure. Over time, the spread of affluence may be viewed as good, but in the short run, the potential for a backlash should always be recognized by the marketer. And it is always important that the marketer ensure that the product and service offered can solve problems as promised.

A "No-Nationality" Global Consumer?

We have already seen that high context cultures may impose a cost on consumers, while low context cultures such as in the United States tend to yield more efficient transactions. After the fall of the Berlin Wall, and the apparent "victory" of the American capitalist system, this notion was pushed further by some intellectuals who argued that we now were seeing "the end of history" in the sense that nationality and culture no longer would matter for people. All of us would be "world citizens" in the new capitalist global society.[22]

Although this (to many people) depressing vision might seem far away from marketing management, global marketers are actually likely to play a key role in stopping this development. The reason is that to marketers, nationality and culture will continue to be strong segmentation and positioning variables, even as we enter the "borderless" global era.

CULTURE'S IMPACT ON THE THREE GLOBAL MARKETING TASKS

Culture impacts the three roles of the global marketing manager in different ways. Generally speaking, when foreign entry is contemplated, the skills will involve correct interpretation of some cultural signals and a fair knowledge of local middlemen in the particular country. In the local marketing phase, the specific culture needs to be understood at a much deeper level since customer requirements and consumer prefer-

A Colgate sales rep makes a call on a store owner in Mexico City. In this kind of open-air market, where husband and wife work as a team, it is important for the salesperson to offer merchandising display tips, explain special promotions and rebates, and help unload slow-moving inventory, and also to understand who really makes the decisions. Courtesy of the Colgate-Palmolive Company.

ences have to be deciphered. When it comes to global management, the cultural issues revolve broadly around the question of the extent to which adaptation in the marketplace is always necessary, or whether cultural norms can be challenged.

Foreign Entry

Culture is intimately tied to the "way of doing business" in a country. Whether signed contracts are necessary or a simple handshake is sufficient is largely a matter of custom, or business culture. When evaluating potential importers and distributors, not only their financial standing but also their social standing often matters. Establishing trust without personal friendship is impossible in some cultures, but "friendship" may be counterproductive. There are numerous incidents of principals feeling betrayed by their friendly local middlemen in a foreign market.

Local Marketing Abroad

When we come to local marketing abroad, cultural factors relate directly to the marketplace. In addition to being an influence on managerial behavior, culture is a strong determinant of consumer demand. For the marketer it is no longer sufficient to develop cultural sensitivity and to learn to accept individuals who act in strange ways. Now culture is involved in understanding and predicting local buyer behavior (the topic of Chapter 7).

For the manager, there is now no escaping the need for firsthand personal experience of the people in the local market. Although market research reports can suggest the needs, wants, and desires of potential and actual customers, it is always necessary to interpret survey findings and related statistics in the context of the actual buying situation.

Global Management

When the task is global integration of the marketing effort across various countries, understanding cultural forces means something quite different again. *Here the marketer needs to understand the extent to which cultural forces are malleable and perhaps already changing*. The task involves less of any particular knowledge about the content of various cultures and more of an astute judgment of what the dynamics are and in which direction a country might be heading. Globalization, and any accompanying standardization, often involves going against cultural traditions.

SUMMARY

This chapter has introduced the central role of culture in global marketing management and its influence on demand and how to do business. Culture should be interpreted broadly, including not only behavioral patterns inculcated by parents and peers but practices embodied in religious institutions, ancient traditions, education, and the political process. Change in culture is slow even when people want to change because institutions aim to preserve the status quo and so cultural differences are here to stay. In organizations, the corresponding attitude is "We don't do things that way around here."

Chapter 3 discussed the frameworks for cultural analysis developed by Hall, Hofstede, and Gannon, identifying some major cultures around the world. We showed how culture helps develop certain managerial skills—and downplays others—which explains why managers from different nations tend to behave differently even though what they want to achieve is the same. This is why culture tends to affect implementation and execution more than strategy formulation, and why a degree of cultural adaptation is so urgent.

The role of culture in helping to determine consumer tastes and preferences was also discussed. The link between culture and central behavioral concepts serves to underscore the importance of recognizing cultural conditioning even where the individual buyer may state that a choice is entirely "just because I want it." Culture involves one's upbringing, education, religion, and other factors: It is good to know that those factors matter for our behavior, even without us needing to think about it every time.

And we are not all simply becoming synthesized into a globally homogeneous mass of consumers; individual differences, many deriving from our cultural heritage, matter perhaps more than ever.

The chapter also showed how the confrontation with a foreign culture is useful because it teaches managers about their own cultural biases. This self-awareness is likely to be disconcerting at first, since it challenges one's sense of identity. But if faced in a constructive spirit, it helps the individual manager to grow and to understand other people's motivations better. It teaches managers how to empathize with others and place themselves in the other's situation. This is particularly important when trying to predict how a market will react to a globally standardized product as compared with an adapted product, and managerial judgment is required to help interpret market research. It is also useful in managing marketing in countries with high context cultures where the meaning of words depends on the situation. One needs to know why and how one's foreign counterpart does what she or he does.

Culture plays a different role in each of the three marketing tasks. In foreign entry, culture has a direct impact on negotiations with potential middlemen and alliance partners. In local marketing, the question is how to treat local employees and, in particular, how consumer demand is affected. In global management, it's often "forget the cultural differences" time, and then cultural analysis is useful for assessing the amount of potential damage that can be absorbed in a strategy of standardization.

KEY TERMS

body language p. 59
cognitive dissonance p. 72
Confucianist dynamics p. 64
conspicuous consumption p. 74
cultural adaptation p. 62

culture p. 60
diversity p. 61
emotional gratification p. 71
Gannon's metaphors p. 65
global culture p. 69

goal oriented p. 70
hidden motivators p. 71
high and low context
  cultures p. 60

DISCUSSION QUESTIONS

1. An American manager can often be heard to start out saying, "Well, the way I see it . . ." while a Norwegian as often will start with, "Well, as we all know . . ." What cultural explanation can you find for this?

2. The text suggests that people buy what they buy for a reason. Why do college professors in the United States favor bag lunches while college professors elsewhere have lunch in a restaurant? Why do Americans of both sexes favor (light) trucks, while Europeans like sporty sedans with stickshifts, and Asians prefer light and smooth cars?

3. Find three examples of high context cultures and three examples of low context cultures. Justify your selections.

4. Check out the Web site of the Disney company (or some other multinational company of your choice). How many languages are available? Are the different language sites identical? What does this tell you about the company's sensitivity to cultural differences?

5. Discuss the extent to which electronic commerce (on-line purchases, Internet shopping, etc.) might be acceptable to a culture. Give examples of cultures that would be reluctant to accept electronic commerce and others that might accept it more easily?

NOTES

1. From Bellah et al., 1989. The view of culture as a determinant of behavioral skills is quite recent, complementing the more standard definition of culture as simply an underlying predisposition to behave in a certain way. The new emphasis on *skill* suggests that some people are not able to do what culture demands, even though they know what is asked. It is not easy for the new overseas manager, who is asked to eat ceremonial foods, to speak slowly, smile, and be patient, while not even understanding the language.

2. See Hall, 1976.

3. See Hall, 1960.

4. See, for example, Anderson and Venkatesan, 1994, and Levine and Wolf, 1985.

5. See Sujan et al., 1993.

6. See Hofstede, 1980.

7. See Hofstede, 1988.

8. Gannon, 1994.

9. Good examples of these cultural effects can be found in Harris and Moran, 1987, Terpstra and David, 1991, and Barsoux and Lawrence, 1991.

10. See, for example, Barsoux and Lawrence, 1991.

11. These characterizations draw on Durlabhji and Marks, 1993, Hall, 1976, and Harris and Moran, 1987.

12. Coca-Cola's success in Japan is discussed in more detail by Huddleston, 1990, pp. 177–8.

13. See "Nestlé Alimentana S.A.—Infant Formula," Harvard Business School case no. 9-580-118.

14. The idea of goal-oriented consumer behavior is by no means new; see Solomon, 1994. But it is important to keep in mind since some non-Western religions have a fatalistic bent, which tends to make human action pointless. Usunier, 1996, provides an excellent treatment of the way different cultures view human behavior and the implications for marketing.

15. Dichter, 1964, is the father of this line of reasoning.

16. See Solomon, 1994, p. 425.

17. The different sources of perceived risk are discussed further by Solomon, 1994, p. 228.

18. The original source is Festinger, Leon, *A Theory of Cognitive Dissonance* (Stanford, CA: Stanford University Press, 1957).

19. See Engel et al., 1978, p. xi.

20. This is still the typical approach; see, for example, Solomon, 1994, and the 8th edition of Engel et al., 1995.

21. From *The New York Times*, August 23, 1994.

22. See, for example, Fukuyama, 1995.

SELECTED REFERENCES

Anderson, Beverlee B.; and M. Venkatesan. "Temporal Dimensions of Consuming Behavior across Cultures." Chapter 9 in Salah S. Hassan, and Roger D. Blackwell, eds. *Global Marketing: Perspectives and Cases.* Fort Worth, TX: Dryden, 1994.

Barsoux, Jean-Louis; and Peter Lawrence. "The Making of a French Manager." *Harvard Business Review*, July–August, 1991, pp. 58–67.

Bellah, Robert, et al. *Habits of the Mind.* Berkeley: University of California Press, 1989.

Benedict, Ruth. *The Chrysanthemum and the Sword.* Tokyo: Charles E. Tuttle, 1954.

Blustein, Paul. "Giant Trading Companies Battle to Preserve Japan Inc.'s Edge." *Washington Post*, April 12, 1995, pp. A18, A19.

Brooks, John. *Showing Off in America.* Boston: Little, Brown, 1981.

Dichter, Ernest. *Handbook of Consumer Motivations.* New York: McGraw-Hill, 1964.

Durlabhji, Subhash; and Norton E. Marks, eds. *Japanese Business: Cultural Perspectives.* Albany, NY: SUNY Press, 1993.

Engel, James F., Roger D. Blackwell and Paul W. Miniard. *Consumer Behavior*, 8th ed. Chicago, IL: Dryden, 1995.

Fukuyama, Francis. *Trust: The Social Virtues and the Creation of Prosperity.* New York: Free Press, 1995.

Gannon, Martin and Associates. *Understanding Global Cultures: Metaphorical Journeys through 17 Countries.* Thousand Oaks, CA: Sage, 1994.

Hall, Edward T. *Beyond Culture.* Garden City, NY: Anchor, 1976.

———. "The Silent Language in Overseas Business." *Harvard Business Review*, May–June 1960, pp. 87–96.

———; and Mildred Reed Hall. *Understanding Cultural Differences.* Yarmouth, ME: Intercultural Press, 1990.

Harris, Philip R.; and Robert T. Moran. *Managing Cultural Differences.* Houston, TX: Gulf, 1987.

Hofstede, Geert. *Culture's Consequences.* Beverly Hills, CA: Sage, 1980.

———. "The Confucius Connection: From Cultural Roots to Economic Growth," *Organizational Dynamics* 16, no. 4 (Spring 1988), pp. 5–21.

Huddleston, Jackson N., Jr. *Gaijin Kaisha: Running a Foreign Business in Japan.* Tokyo: Charles Tuttle, 1990.

Levine, R.; and E. Wolff. "Social Time: The Heartbeat of Culture." *Psychology Today*, March 1985, p. 35.

Solomon, Michael R. *Consumer Behavior.* 2nd ed. Needham Heights, MA: Allyn & Bacon, 1994.

Sujan, Mita; James R. Bettman; and Hans Baumgartner. "Influencing Consumer Judgments Using Autobiographical Memories: A Self-Referencing Perspective." *Journal of Marketing Research XXX* (November 1993), pp. 422–36.

Terpstra, Vern; and Kenneth David. *The Cultural Environment of International Business.* 3rd ed. Cincinnati: South-Western, 1991.

Usunier, Jean-Claude. *Marketing across Cultures.* 2nd ed. London: Prentice-Hall, 1996.

Veblen, Thorstein. *The Theory of the Leisure Class.* New York: New American Library, 1899.

Cases

Case 1.1

IKEA's Global Strategy: Furnishing the World[1]

IKEA, the Swedish furniture store chain virtually unknown outside of Scandinavia 25 years ago, has drawn large opening crowds to its stores as it has pushed into Europe, Asia, and North America. Along the way it has built something of a cult following, especially among young and price-conscious consumers. But the expansion was not always smooth and easy, for example in Germany and Canada, and particularly difficult in the United States.

Company Background

IKEA was founded in 1943 by Ingvar Kamprad to serve price-conscious neighbors in the province of Smaland in southern Sweden. Early on, the young entrepreneur hit upon a winning formula, contracting with independent furniture makers and suppliers to design furniture which could be sold as a kit and assembled in the home of the consumer. In return for favorable and guaranteed orders from IKEA, the suppliers were prohibited to sell to other stores. Developing innovative modular designs whose components could be mass produced and venturing early into Eastern Europe to build a dedicated supplier network, IKEA could offer quality furniture in modern Scandinavian designs at very low prices. By investing profits in new stores, the company expanded throughout Scandinavia in the 1950s.

Throughout the following years, the IKEA store design and layout remained the same; IKEA was basically a warehouse store. Because the ready-to-assemble "knockdown" kits could be stacked conveniently on racks, inventory was always large, and instead of waiting for the store to deliver the furniture, IKEA's customers could pick it up themselves. Stores were therefore located outside of the big cities, with ample parking space for automobiles. Inside, an assembled version of the furniture was displayed in settings along with other IKEA furniture. The purchaser could decide on what to buy, obtain the inventory tag number, and then either find the kit on the rack, or, in the case of larger pieces, have the kit delivered through the back door to the waiting car.

This simple formula meant that there were relatively few sales clerks on the floor. The sales job consisted mainly of making sure that the assembled pieces were attractively displayed, that clear instructions were given as to where the kits could be found, and making sure that customers did not have to wait too long at the checkout lines. IKEA's was a classic "cash-and-carry" approach, except that credit cards were accepted.

European Expansion

In the 1960s and 70s, as modern Scandinavian design became increasingly popular, expansion into Europe became a logical next step. The company first entered the German-speaking regions of Switzerland, thereby testing itself in a small region similar to Scandinavia. Yet expansion so far away from Sweden made it necessary to

[1]Case compiled from Rita Martenson "Innovations in International Retailing," University of Gothenburg, Sweden: Liber, 1981. Richard Stevenson, "IKEA's New Realities: Recession and Aging Consumers," *New York Times*, April 25, 1993, p. F4. Kate Fitzgerald, "Ikea Dares to Reveal Gays Buy Tables Too," *Advertising Age*, March 12, 1994, pp. 3, 41.

develop new suppliers, which meant that Kamprad traveled extensively, visiting potential suppliers and convincing them to become exclusive IKEA suppliers. Once the supply chain was established, the formula of consumer-assembled furniture could be used. After some resistance from independent furniture retailers who claimed that the furniture was not really "Swedish" since much of it came from other countries, IKEA's quality/price advantage proved irresistible even to fastidious Swiss consumers.

The next logical target was Germany, much bigger than Switzerland, but also culturally close to IKEA's roots. In Germany, well established and large furniture chains were formidable foes opposed to the competitive entry and there were several regulatory obstacles. The opening birthday celebration of the first store in 1974 outside Cologne was criticized because in German culture birthdays should only be celebrated every 25 years. The use of the Swedish flag and the blue-yellow colors was challenged because the IKEA subsidiary was an incorporated German company (IKEA GmbH). The celebratory breakfast was mistitled because no eggs were served. Despite these rearguard actions from the established German retailers, IKEA GmbH became very successful, and was thus accepted, being voted German marketer of the year in 1979. The acceptance of IKEA's way of doing business was helped by the fact that IKEA had enlarged the entire market by its low prices, and some of the established retailers adopted the same formula in their own operations.

To get the stores abroad started, Kamprad usually sent a team of three or four managers who could speak the local language and had experience in an existing IKEA store. This team hired and trained the sales employees, organized the store layout, and established the sales and ordering routines. Although the tasks were relatively simple and straightforward, IKEA's lean organizational strategies meant that individual employees were assigned greater responsibilities and more freedom than usual in more traditional retail stores. Although this was not a problem in Europe and Japan (where its Japanese-sounding name also was an advantage), it was a problem in the United States.

Canadian Entry

To prepare for eventual entry into the United States, IKEA first expanded into Canada. The Canadian market was close to the U.S. market, and creating the supply network for Canada would lay the foundation for what was needed for the much larger U.S. market. Drawing upon a successful advertising campaign and positive word-of-mouth, and by combining newly recruited local suppliers with imports from existing European suppliers, the Canadian entry was soon a success. The advertising campaign was centered around the slogan, "IKEA: The impossible furniture store from Sweden," which was supported by a cartoon drawing of a moose's head, complete with antlers. The moose symbol had played very well in Germany, creating natural associations "with the north," and also creating an image of fun and games which played well in the younger segments the company targeted. The Canadians responded equally well to the slogan and the moose, as well as to IKEA's humorous cartoon-like ads poking fun at its Swedish heritage ("How many Swedes does it take to screw in a lightbulb? Two—one to screw in the lightbulb, and one to park the Volvo"), which became often-heard jokes.

The United States presented a much different challenge, as it offered a much larger market with its population dispersed, great cultural diversity, and strong domestic competition. The initial problems centered around which part of the United States to attack first. While the East Coast seemed more natural, with its closer ties to Europe, the California market on the West Coast was demographically more attractive. But trafficking supplies to California would be a headache, and competition seemed stronger there, with the presence of established retailers of Scandinavian designs.

Then, there was the issue of managing the stores. In Canada, the European management style had been severely tested. The unusually great independence and authority of each individual employee in the IKEA system had been welcomed, but the individuals often asked for more direction and specific guidance. For example, the Swedish start-up team would say to an employee, "You are in charge of the layout of the office furniture section of the store," and consider this a perfectly actionable and complete job description. This seemed to go against the training and predisposition of some employees, who came back with questions such as, "How should this piece of furniture be displayed?" IKEA's expansion team suspected that the situation would be possibly even more difficult in the United States. The team also wondered if the same slogan and the moose symbol would be as effective in the United States as it had been in Germany and Canada.

Entry Hurdles in the U.S.

The most pressing problems for IKEA entering the U.S. market was the creation of a stable supply chain. By taking an incremental approach, starting with a few stores on the East Coast of the United States with its relative proximity to European suppliers, the company ensured a successful transition from its Canadian beachhead. The company soon opened a store in southern California also, much farther away, but a large market with the kind of customer demographics—young and active—which favored IKEA's modern designs and assemble-it-yourself strategy. The California entry was precipitated by the emergence of a local imitator, "Stør," which had opened ahead of IKEA, capitalizing on the word-of-mouth generated by IKEA'S new concept.

IKEA'S early effort showed up problems because of less adaptation to the American market than customers desired. For example, IKEA decided not to reconfigure its bedroom furniture to the different dimensions used in the American market. As a result, the European-style beds sold by IKEA were slightly narrower and longer than standard American beds, and customers' existing mattresses and sheets did not fit the beds. Even though IKEA stocked European-sized sheets in the stores, bed sales remained very slow.

The American suppliers, whom IKEA gradually recruited to reduce the dependence on imports, also proved in need of upgrading and instruction in IKEA'S way of producing furniture. IKEA sent its people to the suppliers' plants, providing technical tips about more efficient methods and helping the suppliers shop around for better-quality or lower-price materials.

Promotion

While some managers helped establish the supply side of the stores, IKEA's marketing staff was busy with the promotional side of the business. Store locations had generally disadvantaged IKEA relative to competitors. Because of the huge size of the stores (typically around 200,000 square feet), the need to keep a large inventory so that customers could get the purchased furniture immediately, and the amount of land needed for parking around each store, most stores were located in out-of-the-way places—next to the airport in New Jersey in one case, and in a shopping mall 20 miles south of Washington DC in another. Thus, advertising was needed to make potential customers aware of the store location. It was thought that lower prices and selection would do the rest—positive word-of-mouth had proven the best advertising in most other markets.

But in the United States' competitive retail climate IKEA found that more focused media advertising was needed. As one manager stated: "In Europe you advertise to gain business; in the United States you advertise to stay in business." The diversity of the consumers made word-of-mouth less powerful than in ethnically more homogeneous countries. Management decided that a strong slogan and unique advertising message were going to be necessary to really bring awareness close to the levels in other countries.

The Moose symbol of IKEA, (see Exhibit 1) although successful in Germany and Canada, was considered strange and too provincial for the U.S. market, and would project the wrong image especially in California. Instead IKEA, in collaboration with its New York-based advertising agency Deutsch, developed a striking slogan that combined the down-home touch of the company philosophy with the humorous touch of the Moose: "It's a big country. Someone's got to furnish it" (see Exhibit 2).

Following the success of this advertising strategy, the company ventured further to establish itself as a pioneering store and to attract new kinds of customers. IKEA and Deutsch developed a series of eight TV advertising spots which featured people at different transitional stages in their lives, when they were most likely to be in the market for furniture. One spot featured a young family who had just bought a new house, another a couple whose children had just left home, and so on. IKEA even developed one spot that featured a homosexual couple, two men talking about furnishing their home. It was a daring step, applauded by most advertising experts and impartial observers. The campaign had a positive impact on IKEA's image—and on IKEA's sales. The company has continued the trend.

EXHIBIT 1

IKEA das unmögliche Möbelhaus aus Schweden

EXHIBIT 2

It's a big country. Someone's got to furnish it.

One 30-second TV spot showed a divorced woman buying furniture for the first time on her own.

Data on global sales and retail operations for IKEA are given in Exhibits 3 and 4. The privately held company won't reveal income figures, but it is successful in each of the market areas where it has located its U.S. stores. It is credited with being partly responsible for a shift in furniture buying behavior in the United States. Choosing furniture has become a matter of personality, lifestyle, and emotions in addition to functionality. IKEA's managers like that—they want IKEA to be associated with the "warmest, most emotional furniture in the world."

DISCUSSION QUESTIONS

1. What are IKEA's firm-specific advantages? Country-specific advantages?

2. What are the cultural factors which make expansion abroad in retailing difficult? What has made it possible in IKEA's case?

3. Describe how IKEA's expansion as reenergized mature markets around the world and changed the competitive situation.

4. What could be the cultural reasons for IKEA's problems with stores managers and employees in North America?

5. How does the TV advertising campaign initiated by IKEA overcome the entry barrier of high advertising expenditures?

EXHIBIT 3   IKEA Sales Data

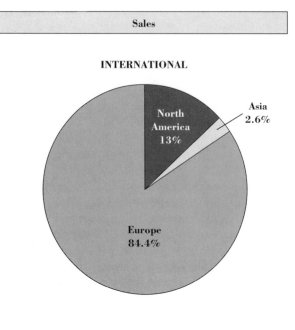

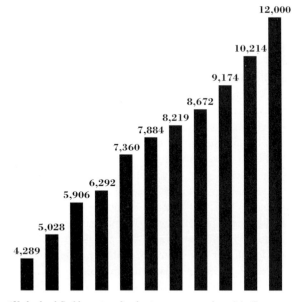

*Netherland Guilders, since Sweden is not yet a member of the Euro currency union.

EXHIBIT 4   IKEA Retail Operations

Number of Visitors (in thousands) and Surface Area

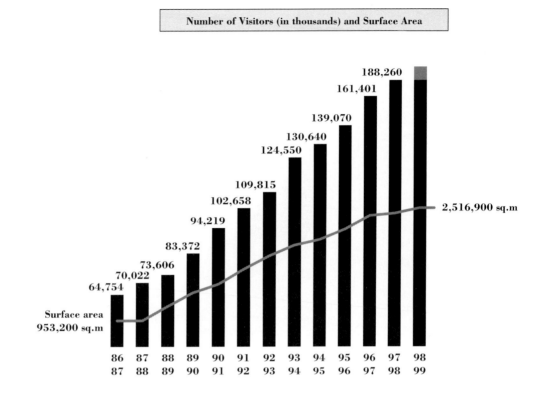

European Sales

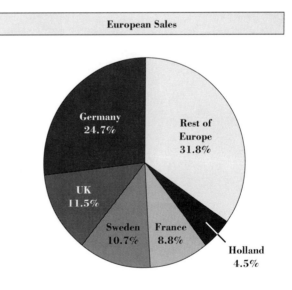

Number of active articles in an average full range store:
10,600

EXHIBIT 4 (*cont'd*) IKEA Retail Operations

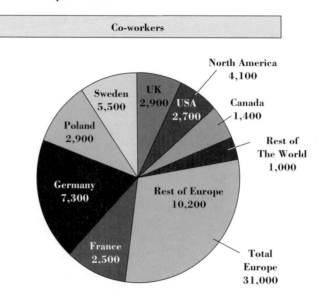

Number of co-workers world-wide: 36,400 (equivalent to 27,000 full-time)

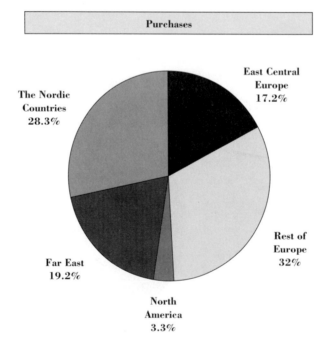

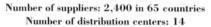

Number of suppliers: 2,400 in 65 countries
Number of distribution centers: 14

Case 1.2

Globalization Headaches at Whirlpool[1]

or Whirlpool, the Benton Harbor, Michigan, company going global "has been less than rewarding," says Russell Leavitt, an analyst with Salomon Smith Barney. Since 1994, Whirlpool, which dominates the U.S. appliance market with sales of $10.3 billion in 1998, and a 35 percent share of the U.S. market, had tried to enter the European and Asian markets. Unfortunately, this resulted in

$60 million in operating losses in Asia, in 1997, $16 million in 1998, unprofitable quarters in Europe and the redesign of half its products.

Background

Whirlpool is the leader in the U.S. appliance market ($20 billion) with brands such as Whirlpool, KitchenAid, and Roper.[2] In the U.S., General Electric (G.E.) is second, with a 32% market share, followed by Maytag, with 15%, Electrolux's Frigidaire, with 10% and Raytheon Corp.'s Amana division, with 7%. Whirlpool makes washers and dryers for Sears Roebuck and Co.'s Kenmore brand. It is also the number

[1]This case was prepared by Michèle van de Walle and Prof. S. Tamer Cavusgil, Michigan State University for class use only.

[2]Exhibit 1 provides the overall financial summary for 1996 and 1997, the development of key financial ratios over a 10 year period is shown in Exhibit 2, and regional sales and profits are given in Exhibit 3.

EXHIBIT 1 Financial Summary

(dollars in millions, except per share data)	1997	1996	% Change
Net sales	$ 8,617	$ 8,523	1.1%
Net earnings (loss) from			
continuing operations	$ (46)	$ 141	NA
Per share on a			
diluted basis	$ (0.62)	$ 1.88	
Net earnings (loss)	$ (15)	$ 156	NA
Per share on a			
diluted basis	$ (0.20)	$ 2.08	
Net earnings excluding			
non-recurring items	$ 238	$ 175	36.0%
Per share on a			
diluted basis	$ 3.15	$ 2.32	
Stockholders' equity	$ 1,771	$ 1,926	(8.0)%
Total assets	$ 8,270	$ 8,015	3.2%
Return on equity	(0.8)%	8.2%	
Return on equity excluding			
non-recurring items	12.0%	9.1%	
Return on assets	(0.7)%	1.8%	
Return on assets excluding			
non-recurring items	2.7%	2.0%	
Book value per share	$ 23.71	$ 25.93	(8.6)%
Dividends per share	$ 1.36	$ 1.36	
Average dividend yield	2.5%	2.7%	
Share price			
High	$ 69 ½	$ 61 ⅜	
Low	$ 45 ¼	$ 44 ¼	
Close	$ 55	$ 46 ⅜	18.0%
Total return to shareholders (*five-year annualized*)	6.8%	6.3%	
Shares outstanding (in 000's)	75,262	74,415	
Number of stockholders	10,171	11,033	
Number of employees	61,370	48,163	

Exhibit 2 Key Financial Ratios

(millions of dollars, except share and employee data)	1997	1996	1995	1994	1993	1992	1991	1990	1989	1988	1987
Key Ratios (4)											
Operating profit margin	0.1%	3.3%	4.5%	4.7%	6.8%	6.3%	5.4%	4.7%	6.1%	5.3%	6.9%
Pre-tax margin (5)	(2.0)%	1.2%	2.6%	3.4%	5.7%	4.7%	3.9%	2.8%	4.6%	4.9%	6.5%
Net margin (6)	(0.5)%	1.7%	2.4%	1.8%	3.5%	2.5%	2.1%	0.7%	2.8%	3.4%	4.2%
Return on average stockholders' equity (7)	(0.8)%	8.2%	11.6%	9.4%	14.2%	13.1%	11.6%	5.1%	13.7%	7.2%	13.6%
Return on average total assets (8)	(0.7)%	1.8%	3.0%	2.8%	4.0%	3.3%	2.9%	1.4%	4.9%	2.9%	6.0%
Current assets to current liabilities	1.2	0.9	0.9	1.0	1.0	0.9	1.0	1.1	1.3	1.3	1.4
Total debt-appliance business as a percent of invested capital (9)	38.5%	42.6%	43.3%	34.4%	31.6%	41.7%	46.1%	37.6%	39.2%	20.5%	19.3%
Price earnings ratio	—	22.4	19.2	23.9	21.2	15.9	16.1	22.6	12.2	18.2	9.7
Interest coverage (10)	0.7	2.4	3.1	4.0	5.0	3.4	2.9	2.0	3.6	6.2	13.6
Other Data											
Number of common shares outstanding (in thousands):											
Average—on a diluted basis	74,697	77,178	76,812	77,588	76,013	75,661	72,581	69,595	69,461	69,435	71,911
Year-end	75,262	74,415	74,081	73,845	73,068	70,027	69,640	69,465	69,382	69,289	69,232
Number of stockholders (year-end)	10,171	11,033	11,686	11,821	11,438	11,724	12,032	12,542	12,454	12,521	12,128
Number of employees (year-end)	61,370	48,163	45,435	39,016	39,590	38,520	37,886	36,157	39,411	29,110	30,301
Total return to shareholders (five year annualized) (11)	6.8%	6.3%	20.8%	12.0%	25.8%	17.0%	6.7%	2.8%	11.3%	4.4%	6.2%

(1) Restructuring and special operating charges were $405 million in 1997, $30 million in 1996 and $250 million in 1994 (Refer to Note 10).

(2) The Company's financial services business was discontinued in 1997 and the kitchen cabinet business was discontinued in 1988.

(3) Includes cumulative effect of accounting changes: 1993 — Accounting for postretirement benefits other than pensions of ($180) million or ($2.42) per diluted share and 1987 — Accounting for income taxes of $11 million or $0.15 per diluted share.

(4) Excluding non-recurring items, selected 1997 Key Ratios would be as follows: a) Operating profit margin — 4.7%, b) Pre-tax margin — 2.7%, c) Net margin — 2.6%, d) Return on average stockholders' equity — 12%, e) Return on average total assets — 2.7%, f) Interest coverage — 3.0%.

(5) Earnings from continuing operations before income taxes and other items, as a percent of sales.

(6) Earnings from continuing operations before accounting change, as a percent of sales.

(7) Net earnings before accounting change, divided by average stockholders' equity.

(8) Net earnings before accounting change, plus minority interest divided by average total assets.

(9) Debt less cash and equivalents divided by debt, stockholders' equity and minority interests less cash and equivalents.

(10) Ratio of earnings form continuing operations (before income taxes, accounting change and interest expense) to interest expense.

(11) Stock appreciation plus reinvested dividends.

EXHIBIT 3 Business Unit Sales and Operating Profit

Net Sales by Business Unit were as follows:				
Year ended December 31 (millions of dollars)	**1997**	**1996**	**Increase/(Decrease)**	
North America	$5,263	$5,310	$ (47)	(1)%
Europe	2,343	2,494	(151)	(6)
Asia	400	461	(61)	(13)
Latin America	624	268	356	133
Other	(13)	(10)	(3)	(30)
Total	$8,617	$8,523	$ 94	1%

Operating Profit by Business Unit was as follows:				
Year ended December 31 (millions of dollars)	**1997**	**1996**	**Increase/(Decrease)**	
North America	$546	$537	$ 9	2%
Europe	51	(13)	67	N/M
Asia	(62)	(70)	8	11
Latin America	28	12	16	133
Restructuring charge	(343)	(30)	(313)	N/M
Special operating charge	(53)	—	(53)	N/M
Other	(159)	(158)	(1)	(1)
Total	$ 11	$278	$(267)	(96)%

one alliance maker in Latin America in a partnership with the Brazilian manufacturer Brasmotor SA to make most of its appliances.

Global Expansion

In the 90's Whirlpool invested heavily in its overseas operations. To convince shareholders and reflect its new "cosmopolitan" face, Whirlpool's 1990 Annual Report featured postage stamps from all around the world. In 1993, the Annual Report had a tiny compass attached to the front cover and, in 1994, Chairman David R. Whitwam gave an interview to the *Harvard Business Review* entitled "The Right Way to Go Global". In 1992, Mark Gray, vice-president of technology services, was seeing the move toward globalization as a move toward standardization and product homogeneity with simplified manufacturing processes and economies of scale. Whirlpool seemed to be in a good position, it was building plants with local partners in Mexico, Brazil, and India while Whirlpool's strategy overseas was vertically integrated manufacturing.

In 1995, Whirlpool was controlling joint ventures in India and China (to make refrigerators and air conditioners) and hoping to break even in Asia in 1997. In Europe, Whirlpool had purchased Philips Electronics NV for $2 billion in 1989 as rivals such as Maytag were pulling out. Until 1989, only 10% of Whirlpool were global; after the purchase, international operations increased to 40%. To perform better in a global environment, Whirlpool tried to integrate international and domestic managers into a cohesive global team by holding worldwide leadership conferences. In 1991, 140 senior leaders participated in workshops and networked for seven days!

Whirlpool's profits hit a record $205 million in 1992 but, in April 1993, its finance company, Whirlpool Finance Corporation, took a $40 million after-tax writedown. This charge wiped out almost 50% of the unit's earnings of the past three years. 1995 was disappointing, partly due to internal issues such as manufacturing inefficiencies, start-up costs associated with production of a redesigned mid-size refrigerator and restructuring of the pan-European sales force. External pressures were also applied to the industry worldwide: unprecedented raw materials cost increases, inability to get immediate price relief, product mix erosion and intensifying competition in Europe as customers sought greater value. Additionally, Mexico's peso devaluation crisis resulted in a market decline of 40% in Mexico.

Going global is risky. In developed markets like Europe, newcomers face many entrenched players. Overcapacity is particularly endemic in Europe, where the top four appliance manufacturers have 55% of the market and new entrants face 300 local manufacturers (ready to use price wars and other tactics). Higher material costs, pinching margins, poor economic conditions as well as its own miscalculations, cut Whirlpool's profit margins. Whirlpool's name was not well known in Europe where Sweden's Electrolux dominates the market. Whirlpool did not realize the appliance business was considerably tougher in Europe than in the U.S. because of the countless variations in what consumers from different countries need and want. For example, due to very different climates, Danes need to spin-dry clothes, whereas Italians often line-dry their clothes. The British want refrigerators well constructed, the French are more concerned about the refrigerator's capacity to keep fruit and vegetables fresh, and the Spanish about its capacity to keep meats. Furthermore, Italians regard childproof safety features as vital, and Germans look for environmental features.

In Asia, Whirlpool's strategy is anchored on "five Ps": partnerships (majority-owned joint ventures, four in China, one in India), products (development of a new frost-free refrigerator platform and of a global washer), processes (all aspects of quality are included), people (foreign assignments for top members of Whirlpool's management) and a pan-Asian approach (build on commonalities between the many national markets). Whirlpool faces in China the same problem it encountered in Europe: market saturation. In developing countries like China, the risk is increased by vague laws governing taxation and commerce.

Competition

Whirlpool's rivals were also bruised by going global. Its U.S. rival, Maytag ($3 billion in sales) pulled out from Europe in 1995, giving up its six-year effort to penetrate the region. "Europe is not an attractive place to try to go in and dislodge the established players," says Leonard Hadley, Maytag's Chairman, "I am nothing but satisfied with our exit. The U.S. is still the best place in the world to make money." Hadley was instrumental in Maytag's divestment in Europe. Maytag's financial returns in Europe were only half of those they could earn in North America. Maytag is now pouring money into new products, advertising and share buybacks in its North American business. In 1993 he created a "Galaxy initiative," a lineup of nine top-secret new products, each code-named after a different planet. Most are still in the planning stage and the company won't discuss them. In 1997, Maytag launched Neptune, a front-loading washer, and the talk of the industry. In March 1998, it reached an agreement to sell its product through Sears, the outlet for a third of the appliances sold in the U.S. In September 1998, Maytag was estimating its third earnings would exceed 70 cents a share. It was expecting third quarter sales to rise as much as 20%. Despite the market downturn, its share went up from $1.81 to $46.56. Maytag is oriented to the higher end of the appliance and floorcare markets. The domestic economy's stable growth was useful because it was making consumers less price conscious. Neptune earns about $4 for every $1 Whirlpool makes on its high-end washer.

Maytag is also revising its relationship with its suppliers. During the 1998 AHAM Supplier Division Forum, Maytag's director of procurement, Mike Rosberg, described his company's 3-3-4 Initiative as a "journey" with impressive goals: 300 suppliers; 3 parts per million defect rates; and 4 years to accomplish the goals. The effort began in 1996, Maytag's supplier base was then 936. In 1998, Maytag's supplier base was approximately 870. Parts per million rates in 1996 were 10,000. In 1998, the rate was 2,800. For suppliers wanting to be among Maytag's chosen 300, Rosberg stressed the importance of partnerships. "There's been a shift away from procurement thinking and commodity sourcing in our company, to relationship sourcing." Maytag expects margins of about 135 in 1999.

General Electric (GE), with 32% of the U.S. market and 6.38 billion in sales in 1996, tried for years to dislodge Whirlpool. Its profits are bigger, with $750 million compared to Whirlpool's $300 million. GE gained two percentage points of market share in 1996. Each percentage translates into $200 million in sales. In the U.S., GE is in a nation-wide price-cutting contest with Whirlpool.

In its effort towards globalization, GE takes a different approach than Whirlpool. GE Appliances strives to be a leader in cost, speed, and international expansion, while Whirlpool decided to build a dominant consumer franchise on cost and quality, and would deal with speed later. Despite all its setbacks, Whirlpool turned out to be more successful. By 1994, GE and Whirlpool were either No. 1 or 2 in the U.S., Canada and Mexico. In 1988, both companies were leaders in the U.S. and Canada, with Whirlpool among the leaders in Brazil. In addition, GE Appliances became a leader in Colombia and Venezuela. But Whirlpool was either No. 1 or 2 in the rest of Latin America, Europe and India, as well as a leader among western firms in China. Whirlpool preempted G.E. in many of the emerging markets of the world.

Abroad, G.E. launched a strategy it called "smart bombing." G.E. executives examine each country microscopically and tailor a mix of products for marketing to each. G.E. Appliances CEO David Cote stresses that, "This industry doesn't reward investment, so we have to spend money sparingly and carefully." As refrigerators that cost $800 now sell for about $750, there is no room for pricing. G.E. bought 80% of a Chinese distribution company, Shanghai Communications & Electrical Appliances Commercial Group. Its job is to find Chinese companies capable of making GE-designed products under contract. To make sure its standards are met at each factory, G.E. flies a team of experts on "bubble assignments" from a week to 6 months to assist in quality control, technology, service, manufacturing, billing, collecting and other skills.

Total sales amounted to $20 million in 1997. With little money invested, it is a positive return on assets.

In Japan, G.E. collaborated with big discount retailer Kojima, eliminated several layers of distribution and turned American made appliances into irresistible bargains. In India and Philippines, G.E. established partnerships with Godrej, the Bombay-based top Indian manufacturer of refrigerators and laundry products, and with Philacor in Manila, the No. 2 appliance sales manufacturer in the Philippines. Both companies were healthy and sophisticated partners and surpassed G.E.'s criteria for quality and costs. In 1996, G.E. operating earnings rose to 11.8% of its $6.4 billion sales. Overseas G.E. is estimated to have made up to $320 million in profits between 1994 and 1997. G.E. also has a joint venture in Britain with Hotpoint (Britain's General Electric Company) and is trying to enter the luxury end of the European market. It buys licenses from European manufacturers to sell their products under the G.E. name. In 1996, G.E. bought a Brazilian stove maker in order to return to Latin America and compete with BoschSiemens, a joint venture between two of Germany's biggest companies, Robert A. Bosch GmbH and Siemens A.G. This German JV acquired Brazil's largest maker of cooking appliances in 1994. It has since built factories to make refrigerators and drying machines in Brazil and started construction of a refrigerator factory in Peru.

Sweden's Electrolux, with 25% market share in Europe, is part of a constellation of public companies controlled by the Wallenberg family. The global strategy Electrolux announced in 1995 was to segment geographical markets with one global Electrolux brand and three pan-European brands (Electrolux, Zanussi and AEG), as well as with local brands (Faure in France, Tricity Bendix in the UK and Zanker in Germany). Chairman Michael Treschow aimed to develop new products, such as the Euro oven (with 46 variations on a single platform) to address the fragmented European market. The company expected to double sales in its new markets (Central and Eastern Europe, China, India, Southeast Asia, Latin America and Africa) within three to five years.

In China, a $100 million investment program included a joint venture to manufacture water purifiers at a plant outside Beijing, and a joint venture to manufacture compressors and a vacuum-cleaner manufacturing plant. Only two to three percent of Chinese homes have vacuum cleaners today and it is a huge market to seize. In India, Electrolux had acquired majority shareholdings in production facilities for refrigerators and washing machines, and in Latin America, Electrolux had a minority interest in Brazil's second largest white-goods manufacturer, Refripar. But despite these successes, Electrolux recently announced a $320 million write-off to pay for shedding 12,000 workers, and will close 25 plants in several countries.

Whirlpool's global strategy

In spite of its own losses and lessons from its rivals, Whirlpool remains committed to its foreign operations. The Asian economic crisis did not threaten Whirlpool's sales since Asia accounts for only 5% of its sales. Moreover, developing countries remain a place where appliance sales are growing at double-digit percentage rates (in Brazil, the growth is 25-30% per year).

However, the financial crisis has spread in South America. Brazil doubled interest rates in October 1997 and again during the fall of 1998. As of December 1998, Whirlpool appliance sales plummeted by about 25% in Brazil, to $1 billion or about 10% of the company's 1998 revenues. Brazil is still by far the jewel of Whirlpool's global expansion strategy. Through much of the 90s it has been the company's most profitable foreign operation. Brazilian affiliates contributed 1997 earnings of $78 million compared with $11 million operating profit from the parent, but the company announced in 1998 that it would reduce its Brazilian workforce by 25 percent, resulting in the loss of 3,200 jobs. However, growth in home appliances is most likely to come in emerging markets thanks to the low penetration rate of appliances. As of December 1998, only 15% of Brazil's households owned microwave ovens. Once Brazil recovers the company projects a 5-6% growth compared to 1-2% in U.S. and Europe. The market is not following Whirlpool's optimism but recognizes that Whirlpool remains the only major white-goods maker still making money in Brazil. Paulo Periquito, Whirlpool's executive Vice-President for Latin America, is trying to cut costs and improve efficiency, flexibility and agility necessary in the unsteady Brazilian environment. He is pinning his hopes on interest rates falling gradually in 1999 and confident as to the fact Whirlpool has already survived Brazil's many debt crises, hyperinflation and military governments.

Whirlpool also intends to experiment with licensing as opposed to manufacturing. It is restructuring its international operations and spent $350 million to exit from two of its four joint ventures in China and it is reorganizing its European business. Even if it is laying off 10 percent (4,700 employees) of its corporate force hoping to save $180 million a year by the year 2000, its choice is to remain global.

Being global offers the possibility of being the first to transfer new technologies between continents and to recruit management from a more diverse pool. Whirlpool management has learned from globalization to embrace dual executive roles. The company's chief technology officer is also responsible for worldwide purchasing. Whirlpool's relationship with its suppliers has become more important as it has had to coordinate multiple product lines along geographic regions and as components makers have driven technology. Whirlpool wanted to avoid organizing the two tasks, technology and supply management, as separate functions in order to accelerate processes. People in purchasing tended to favor current suppliers but people in technical departments tend to experiment. Whirlpool concluded that an executive wearing two hats could develop and test new ideas more quickly.

Like Whirlpool, most of the appliance makers remain engaged in globalization, they are committed to dodge setbacks and try again. Despite its lack of success in Europe, Maytag decided in 1996 to reinvest abroad and put $35 million in a joint venture with China's leading washing-machine company. Another $35 million will be used to expand the joint venture operations into refrigerators.

Recent developments

Whirlpool Europe completed 1998 with a 125 percent gain in operating profit along with substantial gains in unit shipments and sales. Full-year 1998 earnings from continuing operations were up 37 percent from $226 million for the 1997 period to $310 million. Full-year 1998 net earnings were $325 million, versus a reported net loss of $15 million in 1997. Full-year 1998 sales were $10.3 billion, up 20 percent from full-year 1997 due to the consolidation of the company's Brazilian subsidiaries. In 1998 the company aggressively lowered costs and improved efficiency and productivity. Several new product introductions in clothes washing, refrigeration, air conditioning and cooking under the company's leading Brastemp and Consul brand names were made. Whirlpool Asia reported a 73 percent improvement in operating performance for 1998. The company grew its unit shipments in India as consumers continued to make Whirlpool brand refrigerators and washing machines the top choice. Exports of Whirlpool brand microwave ovens built in China rose sharply.

For 1999, the company plans further performance improvements from growing contract sales, ongoing efficiency gains and additional new product introductions including exciting new clothes washers and dishwashers. The company currently expects that U.S. appliance industry shipments in 1999 will approximate 1998 levels.

In 1999, the company expects to continue this momentum through a combination of sales growth initiatives and additional new product introductions in the clothes washing and cooking products categories. Whirlpool expects appliance industry shipments in Western Europe to grow about 2 percent in 1999. For 1999 the company believes that the Latin American economy, as well as the appliance industry, will remain under stress, as the timing of economic recovery is uncertain.

The company currently anticipates that full-year 1999 appliance industry volumes in Brazil will decline between 5 and 10 percent from 1998 levels. Whirlpool's strategy will be a combination of new product introductions, consumer focused service offerings and additional cost reductions. Whirlpool expects that its Asian business will perform soon at a breakeven level or better as unit volumes and the Whirlpool brand name continue to grow across the region.

Whirlpool's Chairman estimates that "despite continued uncertainty in Brazil, we expect operating profit to show improvement in the first quarter of 1999 and to grow between 10 and 15 percent for the full year, driven by strong performances in North America and Europe as well as a continued turnaround in Asia. In spite of difficult economic and business conditions in Brazil and elsewhere, we currently expect to deliver year-over-year net earnings growth of between 5 and 10 percent."

Challenges

It is not only abroad, but also in the U.S. market that Whirlpool and its rivals have to face new challenges due to the Department of Energy's (DOE) more stringent standards. The DOE has been prodding manufacturers to produce front-loading washing machines, which consume less water and energy than top-loaders. They are standards in Europe, and are considered to be better cleaners. However, they are also much more expensive and American consumers are not ready to pay for them. The new energy standards for refrigerators mandate a 30% reduction in energy usage for refrigerators manufactured from July 2001. The original goal was to enforce the regulation in 1998, but the Association of Home Appliance Manufacturers (AHAM) lobbied for a delay. This riled Whirlpool, which had already redesigned its line for 1998 sales, causing the company to cancel its membership in AHAM.

During the 1998 meeting of the Association of Home Appliance Manufacturers, Whirlpool's corporate vice president of global procurement Roy Armes, said the OEM has cut its supplier base worldwide by half over the past three years. Armes stressed the importance of early design efforts involving suppliers. "Today, 80 percent of the product cost occurs well before the product is produced and even before the first components are bought." Larry Spang, vice president and general manager of the laundry and specialty division at Siebe Appliance Controls opined that there is a "segment of the buying population that is paying close attention to higher end products." Emerson's Jehling challenged the appliance industry and its supply base to do "a better job of consumer analysis." And Dow's Moran said his company "is aware and sensitive to the market demand for low-noise appliances."

A summary of the Appliance Manufacturer's Major Appliance Dealers 1998 Study reveals that: 1. capacity and low noise are features for which today's consumers are willing to pay more, 2. price continues to drive the majority of appliance purchases, and 3. dealers and consumers alike are very conscious of service-oriented brands. Dealers and consumers are not yet starting to care about Design for Recyclability. The 1998 survey shows that even fewer respondents (10 percent vs. 13 percent five years ago) said that Design for Recyclability is a selling point. Even more telling is that when asked if Design for Recyclability will be a selling point five years from now, only 54 percent said yes. When that same question was asked in 1995, 74 percent answered yes.

Appliance manufacturers are also learning to probe consumers' psyches early in the cycle to design features and elements meeting the escalating needs of women (key decision-makers on appliance purchases). Consumers are more and more concerned about clean water, energy savings, softening products and water filtration in washing machines and dishwashers. Whirlpool en-

listed an anthropologist in 1995 to tap into consumer's feelings about and interactions with their appliances.

The challenges faced by Whirlpool and its rivals have not dampened Chairman Whitwam's optimism. "Everything we based our strategic plan on has happened, and we are further along than I envisioned," he said recently. "We have probably realized no more than a third of the benefits of creating an integrated global company so far. We never expected this industry to get there in the 1990's."

DISCUSSION QUESTIONS

1. To what extent is the appliance market regional rather than global?

2. What seem to be the key success factors in the appliance business?

3. Are Whirlpool's difficulties with its global strategy due to internal factors or to external factors beyond its control?

4. To what extent does Whirlpool's experience suggest that globalization is *not* a good idea in the appliance business? Explain fully.

Foreign Entry

*G*lobal marketing can be implemented only after the firm has entered foreign markets. In Part Two, we turn to the process of market entry and global expansion. Although conceptually there are many similarities between a national roll-out of a new product and international expansion to new countries, going across borders poses new difficulties.

When a business enters a foreign country, exposure to political risks needs to be managed. When products have to be shipped across borders and into another country's distribution channels, foreign middlemen have to be identified and put under contract. When transactions are across borders, exchange rate fluctuations and customs duties affect revenues. When sales have to be promoted overseas, advertising agencies with a local presence must be used. These are only some of the complications of choosing which country to enter, what mode of entry to use, and what global expansion path to follow.

Although much of the material in Part Two deals with the novice exporter, large multinationals that operate in many markets must follow the same principles. Exporting mechanics and customs barriers directly affect where a multinational will locate new facilities. An MNC will often have to change the chosen entry mode when its strategic objectives change. If political or economic conditions in a country change, an MNC will sometimes exit and then reenter as conditions improve. And for even the largest multinationals, there are usually still markets left to conquer.

Global Market Research

"But this is not Kansas!"

Your takeaways from this chapter:

1. Global market research involves not only issues of market potential and growth but also considerations of environmental factors such as political developments, trading bloc membership, competitive intensity, and entry barriers.

2. A systematic quantitative screening of candidate countries should always be undertaken when comparable data are available. This "iron law" is lessened somewhat when the entry objective is to attack a global competitor's home market or the entry is into a leading market to learn from strong competitors and demanding customers.

3. A country's attractiveness factors need to be weighed against each other systematically, and the sensitivity of the final choice to alternative scenarios of political developments and of competitive reactions should be assessed.

4. To forecast sales for a country the manager will often have to combine subjective estimates with whatever objective data are available.

5. There are many independent research agencies that provide up-to-date economic and political data on countries and regions and that will provide customized analysis on specific products and markets.

IN THEORY there are several reasons for the firm to enter a foreign market. From a pure marketing perspective, it is most natural to view expansion abroad in terms of entering new countries because of their market potential. But as we saw in Chapter 1, the firm may also enter in order to get access to a larger regional trade bloc, to learn from customers and competitors in a leading market, or to attack a competitor's major market. A country can look attractive not only because the firm can sell a lot of product but also because the firm can derive other benefits from a presence there.

Chapter 4 will outline the principles and techniques involved in systematically researching country markets for entry. Early considerations include broad political, economic, and social indicators, a matter of making sure that the "basic fundamentals" are in place. The chapter will discuss research on these environmental forces first and then proceed to the research needed to scope out the competition, domestic as well as foreign. The chapter then presents a stepwise procedure that companies use to gradually narrow down the set of candidate countries and gives a real-life running illustration of how the procedure is applied. The chapter describes various data sources, but also emphasizes the importance of firsthand experience before making a final choice. A more technical section then covers how companies forecast sales in a country.

Can KFC Be Politically Correct in India

Was it the MSG? That's what officials of Bangalore, India, said. The city government shut down India's first Kentucky Fried Chicken (KFC) restaurant, claiming that tests on chicken samples showed dangerously high levels of monosodium glutamate. Disputing the report, the Pepsico subsidiary that operates KFC in India obtained a court order to keep the restaurant open.

The problem, company managers maintain, is not the restaurant's quality. In fact, Sandeep Kohli, managing director of Pepsico Restaurants International, says, "Ours is the cleanest restaurant in the whole of India." Rather, the local government was responding to political pressure from anti-Western forces. The closing of the KFC restaurant followed weeks of protests by a local group of farmers that is associated with a broader campaign to curb foreign investments.

Ever since seventeenth-century British colonial forces acquired dominance of the country's economy, many Indians have been ambivalent about—and even hostile toward—attempts by Westerners to invest in their country. In particular, left-wing and nationalist groups have called for strict limits on foreign investment. These groups accept high-tech investments but want to exclude foreigners from operations they believe India has the capability to handle (for example, food processing, agriculture, and the production of consumer goods). Besides KFC, protesters have targeted the Coca-Cola Company, the Kellogg Company, McDonald's, and Pepsico's Pizza Hut and Frito-Lay units.

Similarly, political pressure became a great burden for the Enron Development Corporation and its $2.8 billion power plant to be built in the Indian state of Maharashtra. After five months of work and $300 million invested in the plant, which would have been India's largest power plant, the state government backed out of the contract. The cancellation of the project caused many American and other foreign investors to reevaluate the prospects of the Indian marketplace. These and other political obstacles have recently been lowered with government policies favoring economic growth and foreign direct investments (FDI amounted to US$3.2 billion in 1997–98). Nevertheless, the ruling Nationalist Party's insistence on nuclear testing and the potential of armed conflict with neighboring Pakistan keep political issues in the forefront.

In spite of any political downside, India's economic and demographic characteristics nonetheless present enormous potential. Impressed by statistics of a population of 900 million, with 200 million in the middle class, many companies remain committed to marketing in India. Hyundai Motor Company, for instance, is moving ahead with plans for a joint venture.

With up to 1,500 customers a day in its first months, KFC plans to stay in Bangalore. Comments managing director Kohli, "At the end of the day, in India as elsewhere, it is the customers who will decide."

Sources: John F. Burns, "India Effort vs. Foreign Business Upsets American Chain," *New York Times*, September 14, 1995, p. D6; John F. Burns, "India Project in the Balance," *New York Times*, September 6, 1995, pp. D1, D3; John F. Burns, "India Now Winning U.S. Investment," *New York Times*, February 6, 1995, pp. D1, D3; "Hyundai Plans Joint Auto Factory in India," *New York Times*, November 24, 1995, p. D12; Juman Dubey, "Kellogg's Invites India's Middle Class to Breakfast of Ready-to-Eat Cereal," *The Wall Street Journal*, August 29, 1994, p. 83B; "India: Progress and Plans," *Washington Post*, October 6, 1998, A13–A16.

http://www.kfc.com/
http://www.pepsico.com/
http://www.coca-cola.com/home.html
http://www.cokecce.com/
http://www.kelloggs.com
http://www.mcdonalds.com
http://www.pizzahut.com
http://www.fritolay.com

INTRODUCTION

In the global turmoil of the late 1990s, researching country markets' potential and the risks involved in entry is more critical than ever. At the same time, the possibility of relying on hard data to make serious commitment decisions to market in a country has become more difficult than ever. This is not because the data are worse than before—quite the contrary. The problem is that one can no longer be sure that past data reflect what is in store in the future. The systemic convulsions in the global financial network are threatening not only free and unfettered capital movements. They also threaten the freedom of international trade and the openness of markets, two factors much more crucial to the global marketer than free capital movement.

Even without these complications from the financial environment, it is hardly surprising to note that choosing countries to enter in a systematic way is always fraught with problems. Even though vast improvements have come with the emergence of global databases, international on-line data services, and global research agencies, market-level data quality is still usually uneven and comparable data across countries are often nonexistent. Lack of familiarity with conditions abroad means that predictions of customer preferences and long-term prospects are even more hazardous. The notion of matching the company know-how against foreign opportunities might be good in principle, but in reality it is very hard to do.

So what is a rigorous and systematic approach to country selection that is realistic? The answer comes in two parts. First, the initial screening should be based on a well-articulated vision of why the company wants to go abroad and what kinds of resources it can marshall. The nonsales objectives the company might have and any limiting constraints should be clarified and be used to screen countries out of contention as early as possible. Second, when more than one country remains in the choice set, the final choice should be made only after in-country visits have confirmed what the available published data reveal about market size, growth, entry barriers, and the competitive market shares. The iron rule is never to commit resources without firsthand information.

Chapter 4 delineates this process in more detail. It describes what market research across the world's countries involves and how to evaluate country markets in terms of *market potential* and *resource demands.* The chapter introduces systematic screening procedures and discusses how to handle various obstacles and special factors complicating the systematic process. The special cases of an entry to attack a global competitor's home market and the advantages of entering leading markets are also discussed, before the chapter describes the various data sources available. In the last part of the chapter, several different approaches to forecasting sales in a foreign country are presented.

The chapter does not deal with buyer behavior research, that is, how individual consumers and business buyers in the local markets behave. Survey research and focus groups are covered in Chapter 7, "Local Buyer Behavior."

It should be emphasized at the outset that in Chapter 4 "entering a market" means simply to make the firm's existing products or services available in a foreign country. There might be some localization requirements that force the firm to modify the offering, but basically the products or services are known. This is the typical situation a company is faced with in screening countries. The important questions of global segmentation, positioning, and standardization become issues once the company has global presence, and these issues will be dealt with later in Part Four, "Global Management."

ENVIRONMENTAL DATA

Because foreign markets present new and different marketing environments, the most valuable marketing research for the local manager is often that which deals with very simple and basic—but easily overlooked—factors.

Political Risk

For many firms the standard first question asked about a country concerns **political risks,** the danger that political upheaval will change the nation's economic rules and regulations overnight. There are many ways of analyzing the risk and of assessing the level of exposure, and the sources of information vary from very detailed statistical reports on the history of the country's political development to impressionistic tales by recent visitors to the country. The factors that need to be considered can be arranged in a descending order of importance for the investor, as in Exhibit 4.1.[1]

Political risk analysis proceeds from the first to the fourth level in the table. The data used will usually come from any one of the several firms offering political risk analysis.[2] If at any of the levels the risk is deemed unacceptable, the investment project receives a "No Go" stamp and is discontinued in favor of FDI elsewhere or simply export or licensing negotiations. Even though in several cases the economics of an FDI project are quite acceptable—in the sense that projected discounted returns well pass the hurdle ROI rate—the political risks have been great enough to stop the project. This is more likely to happen when the investment is aimed at the acquisition of raw

EXHIBIT 4.1 Political Risk Factors

Factors	Examples
Level 1: General Instability	Revolution, external aggression
Level 2: Expropriation	Nationalization, contract revocation
Level 3: Operations	Import restrictions, local content rules, taxes, export requirements
Level 4: Finance	Repatriation restrictions, exchange rates

Source: Steven J. Kobrin, "Political Risk: A Review and Reconsideration," *Journal of International Business Studies* 10, no. 1 (1979), p. 67–80. Reprinted by permission.

Political risk lowers a country's attractiveness for entry. Here Indian farmers ransacke a Kentucky Fried Chicken outlet in southern India in 1996. Nationalists opposed to multinationals in India accused the restaurant of serving food that was unhealthy and un-Indian. Wide World Photo

material or low wage costs than when the penetration of markets is at stake. But Coca-Cola's early experience in India shows that even in the latter case political risks matter (see box, "The Real Thing").

The rise of international terrorist activities is a new type of political risk. The Iran uprising, politically motivated murders in South America, and the crime wave in newly capitalist Russia have made multinational companies and their expatriate managers very uneasy and eager to purchase insurance. Although terrorism's international reach can make almost any country unsafe, as the bomb explosion at the World Trade Center in New York City showed, terrorism and escalating crime have put an especially dark shadow on certain countries' and regions' attractiveness. For example, in a December 1993 Gallup survey of British executives' evaluation of political risk in various countries, Russia was rated as "difficult" by 57 percent followed by Africa (47 percent), and South America (46 percent).[3] High-risk countries included Angola, South Africa, Zaire, Colombia, Haiti, Papua New Guinea, Turkey, and Israel's West Bank and Gaza Strip.

As governments change and new regimes come to power, political risk can be temporary, but it is important that the company make sure to follow risk indicators closely and keep them updated. Where the risk index is high, scenario planning becomes necessary, with any proposed strategy tested against alternative political developments. Predicting political change in Russia may be difficult, but alternatives can be sketched out (from "worst" to "best" scenarios) and the most robust strategy identified. Of course, "most robust" does not necessarily mean "very robust." Given the Russian tur-

G E T T I N G   T H E

Picture

The Real Thing

COCA-COLA had been marketing in India for many years when in 1977 the Indian government decreed that the secret formula for the cola and 60 percent of the equity of its Indian subsidiary must be transferred to local nationals. The equity transfer was accepted by Coca-Cola, but the company refused to divulge the formula and also insisted that it must supervise the quality control of the manufacturing process. The Indian government, set on local control, argued that this would still make the Indian company only a reseller of the American company's know-how and product. The government wanted to exercise local control over manufacturing and also stop the outflow of foreign exchange. In the end, Coca-Cola decided to withdraw from India (a small market for them in the global picture) rather than jeopardize their firm-specific advantages, leaving the market to domestic imitators.

But things change. Under the liberalization in the early 1990s following Mr. Rao's election as prime minister, foreign direct investment in India is picking up. Less restrictive investment and repatriation conditions and a booming home market have made India attractive again. In 1993 Coca-Cola decided to return, and consumers in India are now able to taste "The Real Thing" again, and not just imitations.

Sources: Dubey, 1993; *New York Times*, September 22, 1993, p. D4.
http://www.coca-cola.com/home.html
http://www.cokecce.com/

moil at the end of the 1990s it is not surprising if many firms are pulling out; even the most robust strategy is not attractive enough, given the risks involved.

Back to Basics

Once political risk has been analyzed, marketing basics can be considered. Remember that usage situations vary and they affect customer choices directly. It is not a matter of attitudes and preferences but simply "reality." Home furniture does not sell well where homes are small. Electric toothbrushes are less than useful when electricity is expensive. Small cars and thin-soled shoes make big people uncomfortable, with good reason. Placing a personal computer on the desk of an executive in many countries insults a status hard won. And so on.

It is not useful to research customer evaluation of a product if its basic functionality is not understood. One study tried to identify the demand for and desired course content of an international executive program by asking managers in Asia, Europe, and North America for rankings of various topics. The study sponsor did not realize that for many managers one major motivation to participate lay simply in the status it conferred upon the manager, independent of the content of the course, something uncovered when telephone callbacks were made.

Similarly, individual attitudes may be irrelevant when the buying determinants work at group level. In high context cultures, clothes and other personal items carry significant image connotations. Finding out through research that people are buying certain brand names because they "like the style and the quality" hides the real reason: strong social pressure. To make matters worse, this sort of cultural reason is often hidden and unconscious to the buyer and the harder for research to uncover, precisely because it's so fundamental.

Thus, in new local markets, the most valuable market research centers on very basic environmental determinants of consumption and buying behaviors. The local marketing campaign that goes wrong abroad often does so because of unexpected differences in environmental factors (different from the home market) that are missed or ignored. Especially in the early stage of local market penetration the unfamiliar environment mandates reassessment of what the firm's key success factors are. As the ex-

G E T T I N G   T H E

Picture

Market Potential in Rural Thailand

MARKET RESEARCH in some countries requires novel and imaginative methods. When the U.S. Department of Commerce wanted to evaluate the market potential for various American manufacturers in Thailand, it was faced with a dearth of data on the Thai market. "Bootstrapping" the knowledge and experience of its embassy people in Bangkok, it developed an ingenious indirect method. It linked the potential of a trade area to the presence of various social and economic institutions and created a five-level grading scale of the potential in various areas. Trade area potential was ranked according to the presence or absence of buildings—town hall, temples, train station, and schools—easily ascertained through photographs or personal visits. The more buildings, the higher the potential.

Sources: Amine and Cavusgil, 1986; U.S. Department of Commerce.

perience of the U.S. Department of Commerce in Thailand shows, research methods can be quite unconventional (see box, "Market Potential in Rural Thailand").

For market research purposes it is common to distinguish four **environmental dimensions:** (1) physical, (2) sociocultural, (3) economic, and (4) regulatory.[4]

Physical Environment

The most obvious environmental factor affecting people's behavior is the *climate*. The humidity and heat of the Eastern Seaboard of the United States in the summer (and of many other countries as well) dooms polyester fabrics, encourages air-conditioning installations, and raises property values for summer houses in cooler places like Vermont or Maine. The heat and humidity should raise air-conditioning sales also in Southeast Asia, but the soft housing construction, necessary because of the region's propensity for natural disasters, prohibits effective insulation. The cold of Russia has made furs a particularly common Russian export product, although the lack of adaptation to Western styles and to countries with less chill thus needing lighter furs has prevented further penetration of the best markets.

Sociocultural Environment

As we saw in Chapter 3, cultural influences are pervasive in most country markets and are reflected in the social class groupings and the social stratification of a society. It is not important to decide whether culture or social factors are the primary drivers. What is important is that both tend to be important when analyzing the receptiveness of a country market to a new entrant.

Social and cultural influences are of course less obvious than physical factors. The researcher needs to start by collecting quantitative data and reading newspapers, and then also making a personal visit to observe and talk to people directly. Once there, it is usually not sufficient to observe social gatherings, talk to experts and interpreters, or read treatises by natives on the behaviors of their own people. In addition, the global marketer needs to develop a tactile "feel" for the social and cultural factors by immersing himself or herself in direct contact with the locals. This is not easy without language competency, which explains why there is so much stress on learning a foreign language in the "how to do business in . . . " literature.

G E T T I N G   T H E

Picture

The Eastern European Customer

WHEN THE EAST EUROPEAN COUN-TRIES opened up after the fall of the Berlin Wall, most Western manufacturers assumed that the customers would be eager to buy their products. In many cases they were disappointed by consumers who seemed reluctant to switch to the new and better brands. Price and purchasing power were a problem, but interviews with shoppers who stayed with their old brands showed that many of them had enough money to buy the new products. According to the interviews, the problem was that the consumers could not choose between the new variants on the market, since they simply did not have enough understanding of the different features. The Western brands in shampoos, for example, offered "conditioning" and "rinse" and other features such as "two in one" and "hair repair," confusing attributes that the Eastern European customers could not translate into benefits. The solution was to change the advertising copy and to offer in-store descriptions on the shelves.

Source: M. Wolongiewicz, student report, International University of Japan, June 1994.

Economic Environment

The level of economic development is naturally a major determinant of local buyer behavior. Disposable income data are easily available from secondary sources and are, by and large, reliable. But without more information on the income distribution and the social impact of economic well-being, income-per-household data can be interpreted incorrectly. For example, in some countries there can be a dramatic difference in spending power between the rich few and the many poor. In others, there can be a seemingly strange allocation of spending among the poor away from necessities and toward relative luxury goods. One can see many television antennas among the corrugated metal and plastic sheet shacks in the barrio encircling Mexico City, for example. What research needs to uncover is the effect of income on the buyer decision-making process.

Questionnaires need to be administered in person because of low literacy levels, and questions can rarely be structured as rigorously as is standard in the West. Open-ended questions designed to elicit verbal responses and probing to generate reflective comments are common methods for exploring how purchasing decisions are made. The aim is mainly to gain information about obstacles to product purchase and effective product use, and the research is explorative (see box, "The Eastern European Customer").

Regulatory Environment

The institutional framework within which markets function is designed to enable or prohibit certain business practices, in short, to regulate the markets. It is of course very important that on-the-spot research uncovers exactly what is and is not possible under local laws and ordinances. In-store promotions, for example, are usually subject to various limitations the new local marketer needs to identify. Such research is best done through a research assistant who can contact government agencies, trade associations, and various libraries. Research also should be used to uncover the extent to which trade associations and similar networks of actual and potential competitors are present. This research usually involves the local marketer directly. For example, researching distribution in a local market is best done through lots of personal visits,

IKEA in Germany

I K E A , the Swedish furniture retailer, was able to break into Switzerland quite easily from a base in Zurich in the German language part of the country. Preliminary research—and the short cultural distance—suggested that Germany, the big neighbor to the north, would be a natural next target. But the story in Germany was decidedly different. German retailers organized a strong counterattack, with lawsuits and concerted efforts to cut off supplies. Even though the IKEA entry finally succeeded, it took the company much longer than expected after the Swiss entry. The German store regulations, although similar to the Swiss regulations, were enforced more effectively, something the research had failed to uncover. The German furniture retailers combined forces and challenged IKEA in the courts, while the fragmented Swiss retailers had acted reluctantly and independently. More research might have helped. (See also Case 1.1).

Sources: Martenson, 1981; Bartlett and Nanda, 1990. *http://www.ikea.com*

face-to-face interviews, and talking to academic experts. It is important to find out who the movers and shakers are and how their network operates. Ikea's experience in Germany is instructive (see box, "IKEA in Germany").

COMPETITOR DATA

As we saw in Chapter 2, in most markets the local marketer is faced with competition from both domestic and other foreign competitors, and research is important to identify who they are, what their strengths and weaknesses are, and how they are likely to react to a new competitor. This research is particularly useful when developing alternative scenarios of competitive reactions, for sensitivity testing of the final choice.

Strengths and Weaknesses

From company annual reports, if available, 10K or corresponding stock exchange filings, and similar sources, it is possible to get a sense of the financial capability of the competition. Recognize, however, that a company with a large consolidated financial base is not necessarily active in any one country market. It's important to judge the *strategic importance* of the market for the competition and the strategic intent of the competitors operating there.

The overall importance of the market for the competitors is usually higher for domestic companies than for foreign entrants. However, FDI in manufacturing tends to make a foreign company an "insider" in the country and thus likely to behave similarly to a domestic company. IBM Japan is in many respects a truly Japanese company, with only a handful of Western employees, and not at the top level.

Understanding the organizational structure of the competitors helps gauge their local strengths. A multinational such as Philips, the Dutch electronics company, with strongly independent country operations, is not likely to engage in massive support for a particular country's operations. By contrast, a company with a globally integrated strategy such as Caterpillar will be able to take a loss in one market and make it up elsewhere. Its country operations can draw on the global resources to a greater extent than can the Philips subsidiary.[5]

As for the local marketing efforts of competitors, research will identify whether strategies involve low prices rather than unique differentiation, will reveal the strengths and weaknesses of their distribution and after-sales service systems, and so

G E T T I N G   T H E

Picture

Microlog Goes to Europe (A)

MICROLOG INC. is a small ($12 million annual turnover) company located in Germantown, Maryland, just outside the Washington, D.C., beltway. Its business is in telecommunications. The company markets and services voice processing systems, that is, computerized electronic telephone systems that help direct incoming calls, record messages, and generally serve as an on-line mail and audio information service. Such integrated hardware–software systems saw tremendous growth in the United States in the early 1990s. Microlog is one of the many small companies that helped develop the systems. Its domestic market includes local businesses, as well as the U.S. government.

The company wants to expand overseas. Domestic markets are growing, but competition is intense. Microlog management has decided that the best strategy is to capture first-mover advantages in new and growing foreign markets such as the EU. Once a system is installed, a company will not change vendor, and the servicing brings in business. Furthermore, word of mouth from successful entry travels fast to geographically close companies.

Sources: Adams et al., 1993. Used with permission from Microlog Corporation.
http://www.mlog.com

on. This type of information is usually available from middlemen, trade magazines, and even newspaper articles. More often it's easier to "scoop out" the strengths and weaknesses of competitors than to get a handle on what motivates customers.

Competitive Signaling

The local marketer must read competitive signals to judge what competitors' future actions may be. In most markets, not only emerging ones, deregulation and the privatization of industry have led to chaotic conditions, and forecasting competitive behavior is not easy. This is especially true in high-technology areas such as telecommunications and computers where premature announcements are sometimes used to mislead competitors or foil a takeover bid.

Competitive posturing can be difficult to interpret for a new entrant, and it may be necessary to hire experienced local talent to deal with relationships with competitors, as well as with the public and with the authorities. In most countries the type of "hands off" bureaucratic stance assumed in the United States is unusual, and it becomes important for the new manager to develop a network of contacts so that communication in the trade can be facilitated. Although from one angle such networks may be seen as collusive and anticompetitive, from another viewpoint they simply represent the way business is done in the foreign industry. With the advent of strategic alliances and related cooperative alignments between companies and competitors, the local marketer needs to study and learn how the network can be used to the firm's benefit.

ENTRY EVALUATION PROCEDURE

The actual process of evaluating candidates for foreign market entry can be divided into four stages: *country identification, preliminary screening, in-depth screening,* and *final selection.*[6] The discussion of each stage will be illustrated by an actual application at a company called Microlog. See box, "Microlog Goes to Europe (A)."

Stage 1—Country Identification

In the **country identification** stage, the candidate countries are identified and listed. In principle the company can start with most of the world's more than 200 countries,

G E T T I N G   T H E

Picture

Microlog Goes to Europe (B)

TO SCREEN CANDIDATE COUNTRIES, the marketing director and his assistant first decided among three regions: Southeast Asia, Latin America, and Europe. All three regions showed promise, with increasing penetration of telephones and promising economic prospects. Southeast Asia showed the fastest growth, while Latin America was bound to get a boost from the NAFTA accord. Europe was very attractive because of the 1992 homogenization of regulations. Given their limited resources, the two managers decided to first focus on Europe, partly because of their own ease and comfort there (the manager had extensive experience in Europe, and the assistant was British). They also sensed that Europeans might be more culturally prepared for a computerized response to a telephone call than the other regions (although partially correct, later acceptance in the Southeast Asian countries proved to be even quicker).

Sources: Adams et al., 1993.
http://www.mlog.com

but most often the list includes a more limited set of alternatives. Typically the company decides to enter a particular trade area. For example, companies opt to focus on Europe or Latin America or East Asia, and then do a more in-depth analysis within each of the regions to identify where to place their sales headquarters and which countries to enter first.

The choices in this first stage are broadly based on easily available statistics on population, GNP, growth rates, and media reports on political and economic developments. It is useful for the manager to have a sense of the economic size of the countries.

Population comparisons are crucial for the global marketer to get an initial grasp of a country's potential. Indonesia has 178 million people, while Malaysia has 17 million, a big difference. The unified Germany has about 80 million people, biggest in Europe (not counting Russia), much bigger than another country with German culture, Austria, at 8 million. France and the United Kingdom have about 55 million each, while Sweden has 8 and Denmark 5 million people, much smaller markets. Hungary at 11 million is small compared to Poland's 40 million, and in Latin America, Chile at 13 million is small compared with Brazil at 150 million. Japan is 2.5 times as large as South Korea's 44 million, while another "tiger," Hong Kong, has a limited home market of 5 million people.

The country identification process at Microlog is described in the Microlog box (B).

Stage 2—Preliminary Screening

After the candidate countries have been identified, the **preliminary screening** stage begins. This involves rating the identified countries on macrolevel indicators such as political stability, geographic distance, and economic development. The idea is to weed out countries from consideration. For example, if profit repatriation or currency convertibility is questionable, the country may be eliminated. Also countries with signs of political instability may be ruled out at this stage. Generally, exchange rate volatility is an important indication of underlying economic or political problems.

At this stage, the anticipated costs of entering a market should be broadly assessed, to match financial and other resource constraints. In addition to data on transportation costs and customs duty that are comparatively easy to assemble, costs involve storage and warehousing, distribution in the country, and supporting the product in the market. These usually have to be rough estimates, drawing on industry experts and personal experience in the country.

Preliminary screening by Microlog is described in the Microlog box (C).

G E T T I N G   T H E
Picture

Microlog Goes to Europe (C)

TO COLLECT preliminary screening data on the European countries, the marketing manager asked for help from a team of MBA students at a nearby university. The five-member team collected U.N. data on the size and growth of the GNP, population size, infrastructure, and level of industrial activity from the university library. Visits to the World Bank yielded information on political risk factors, ethnic diversity, and potential language and cultural problems. Informal interviews with fellow European MBA students and faculty members with European experience were used to verify information and check indicated ratings.

The preliminary screening led to a selection of 11 countries for in-depth evaluation. The set of countries included Belgium, Denmark, France, Germany, the Netherlands, Ireland, Italy, Norway, Spain, Sweden, and Switzerland.

Sources: Adams et al.,1993.
http://www.mlog.com

Stage 3—In-Depth Screening

The **in-depth screening** stage is the core of the attractiveness evaluation. Data here are specific to the industry and product markets, if possible even down to specific market segments. This stage involves assessing market potential and actual market size, market growth rate, strengths and weaknesses of existing and potential competition, and height of entry barriers, including tariffs and quotas. Where possible, in-country segmentation should also be explored, with an eye to capturing more precise target segment forecasts. Furthermore, at this stage the company resource constraints—money, managers, supply capacity, and so on—should be revisited to make sure that contemplated entries are feasible.

Several screening criteria for the in-depth stage can be useful to the prospective entrant. Generally, studies have shown that almost all entrants use information relating to *market size and growth rate*, *level of competition*, and *trade barriers.*[7]

MARKET SIZE   A direct measure of market size can be computed from local production, minus exports, plus imports. An indirect measure can be derived from the widely available GNP measure, population size, growth in GNP, and imports of relevant goods.

MARKET GROWTH   Growth estimates can be obtained by getting the market size measures for different years and computing the growth rates. When deriving the growth rate in this manner, it is important that cyclical changes in the economy are accounted for. When the business cycles turn up, even slow-growing mature markets will show strong growth.

COMPETITIVE INTENSITY   Level of competition can be measured by the number of competitors in the market and the relative size distribution of market shares. The U.S. Department of Commerce tracks such shares for many industries in different countries in its *Market Shares Report.*[8] Competition is generally toughest where a few large domestic companies dominate the market. When existing companies all have small shares, or when foreign companies have already made successful entry, the competitors will generally be less concerned about a new entrant.

TRADE BARRIERS   Tariffs, taxes, duties, and transportation costs can be ascertained from official government publications. One problem in analyzing such data is that the level of the barriers depends on the exact specification of the goods entered. The company can often decide to do some assembly in the foreign country to avoid

G E T T I N G   T H E
Picture

Microlog Goes to Europe (D)

AFTER THE CHOICE of the 11 countries had been accepted by Microlog's manager, the team and the manager discussed the selection of in-depth screening criteria. The selected criteria involved market size, growth potential, a "loose brick" factor indicating ease of entry, competitive factors, distribution possibilities, cultural distance to the United States, technological development, likely receptivity to voice processing, and importance of the market in the EU.

Once the criteria were agreed upon, the team set about collecting data, scoring each of the 11 countries on the selected criteria. This entailed some hard legwork. For example, regulatory data of the telecommunications industry were collected from the countries' consulates in Washington, D.C., a laborious job divided among the team members. Competitive data came from Microlog's management, trade association figures, Department of Commerce publications, and computer searches across various publications. In the end, many of the ratings came from the team's (and the manager's) subjective judgments.

Sources: Adams et al., 1993.
http://www.mlog.com

high tariffs on finished products, for example, or it can decide to purchase a component from a local manufacturer in another country to get a better rate because of increased local content. Accordingly, the country rating on tariff barriers can only be assessed accurately after preliminary decisions have been made as to whether a final or some intermediate product will be shipped to that country.

The in-depth screening stage at Microlog is described in Microlog box (D).

Stage 4—Final Selection

In the **final selection** stage, company objectives are brought to bear for a match, and forecasted revenues and costs are compared to find the country market that best leverages the resources available. Typically, countries similar to those the company has already entered show lower entry costs, less risk, and quicker returns on the investments required to build up the market franchise. With a longer time horizon, less risk-averse management, and lower target rates of return, the firm can select countries that show greater long-term prospects and that promise to expand the firm's capabilities.

The firm's objectives in contemplating foreign entry can be used to assign importance weights to the various criteria, such as costs, to get a weighted sum across the criteria. There are several ways to assign scale numbers to the ratings and the importance weights. The process leads to a ranking of the countries from highest to lowest attractiveness for the firm.

The final selection stage of the team's assessments in the Microlog case is described in Microlog box (E).

Direct Experience

The final selection of the country to enter cannot and should not be made until personal visits have been made to the country and **direct experience** acquired by the managers. There is no substitute for on-the-spot information and the hands-on feeling of a new market. There are lessons to be learned from the flexibility with which the hotel staff responds to unusual requests, the language capabilities of the average person in the street, the courtesy, or lack of it, in stores, the degree to which a doctor responds to a client's questions, the ease with which a telephone connection home can be made, and the speed with which currencies may be exchanged. Countless such observations may be made on the local scene. And the visits will often have serendipi-

G E T T I N G   T H E

Picture

Microlog Goes to Europe (E)

BEFORE CALCULATING the attractiveness scores for the various countries, the team met with the manager and his assistant in order to come up with weights reflecting the importance of the various criteria for the voice processing system's market success. The cultural and linguistic similarity with the United States and the compatibility of the phone system and its regulation were judged to be particularly important. The manager had visited Europe and decided that even though the voice recordings on the system would have to be in the native tongue, for Microlog to transact business in any other language than English would be difficult. At the same time, size of the market was seen as unimportant or even slightly negative, since it was deemed that entry into a smaller market to start with might be a more manageable task for the firm. Also, in one of these meetings the ease of expansion from the entry base into other countries emerged as an important criterion.

The weights and attractiveness scores of the countries showed that the Netherlands and Ireland were rated high-est. In both cases the telecommunications market was well developed, the industry regulations were not as severe as elsewhere, and the countries seemed to be natural entry gates for the Northern European market. The Scandinavian countries, although attractive in many ways, were not sufficiently close to continental Europe to be good gateways. In addition, Sweden's Ericsson was a feared potential competitor. Germany was ruled out mainly because of its byzantine regulatory system that raised barriers and made entry costly. France's regulations were also a barrier, which was raised further by the dominance of Alcatel, the French telecommunications giant and a potential competitor. Because the team considered the Netherlands' location more favorable than Ireland's, it recommended the Netherlands for initial entry. As a second alternative for an entry into southern Europe, the team recommended Italy.

Sources: Adams et al., 1993.
http://www.mlog.com

tous effects, creating marketing opportunities not recognized before, as happens to Microlog in box (F).

SPECIAL CRITERIA

Two factors that can change the country attractiveness ratings dramatically are competitive entry and leading market status.

Competitive Attack

When the aim of the foreign entry is to attack a competitor's stronghold, the evaluation process is naturally quite different from the one presented above. The aim can be to attack a competitor's cash-generating home market or another market where a competitor is dominant. In other cases, the aim is to preempt or disrupt a competitor's entry into a new market by entering first or increasing the firm's marketing support. In either case, the choice of country is often a given. However, the firm must recognize the resource implications of fighting these kinds of battles. They may not generate much revenue and could be costly. The firm has to carefully evaluate whether the gains in other countries over time will justify these excursions. Procter and Gamble lost money for more than 10 years on its Japanese operations but was willing to do so partly to provide a competitive check on Kao, its Japanese rival.

Leading Markets

The choice of country is made differently yet again in the cases in which a company goes abroad to learn from customers and competitors in leading market countries.

Microlog Goes to Europe (F)

THE FINAL CHOICE? The Netherlands. A first trip to the European CeBIT fair in Hanover yielded several contacts, including a couple of leads to distributors in the Netherlands. Rerouting his return trip through Hilversum, the manager met with executives at Philips, the big electronics manufacturer. Philips was interesting not simply as a prospective customer but as a partner in the European market. With the kind of strong European connection provided by Philips, Microlog would be able to quickly establish credibility and create a base for future European expansion. As the manager put it: "We wanted Philips to be the long pole in our European tent." For its part, Philips' management recognized the potential value of Microlog's voice processing system and was interested in having Microlog provide an OEM system to be marketed under the Philips name in their telecommunications division. Signing a nonexclusive "best efforts" contract with Philips enabled Microlog to gain immediate credibility in Europe and obtain a strong base for further expansion via independent value-added resellers (VAR). In this way, Microlog could gain entry into several European markets by piggybacking on Philips' sales force and also selling via the VARs under its own brand name.

Sources: Adams et al., 1993.
http://www.mlog.com
http://www.philips.com

Then the company aim is primarily to gain further strengths and expand capability, and tapping market growth is only a secondary goal, at least in the short run.

Leading markets (or lead markets) are not necessarily the largest markets, but they are strong at the high end of the product line, free from government regulation and protective measures, with strong competitors and demanding customers.[9]

Leading markets are generally found in different countries for different products. Strong domestic competitors emerge because of a country's location-specific advantages, such as natural resource endowments, technological know-how, and labor skills. Over time, these advantages enable domestic firms to accumulate experience. The customers of these firms are sophisticated and demanding, making these markets bellwethers for follower markets. The U.S. personal computer market, the Japanese camera market, and the German automobile market are examples of such leading markets.

The actual location of a leading market in an industry may also change over time. This is partly a result of the workings of the international product cycle (IPC) discussed in Chapter 2. As follower markets mature and customers become more sophisticated, and as domestic producers develop new competitive skills, the follower markets may become the new leading markets. A good example is Japan in consumer electronics. Conversely, leading markets may lose their status. For as Japan rose, the United States lost its lead in consumer electronics.

An industry can have several leading markets for different segments of the total market, as in the automobile industry. In autos, Germany, Japan, Italy, and perhaps even the United States can lay claims to preeminence. However, different leading markets involve some market segmentation and product differentiation. German buyers place a premium on advanced auto technology, which is why other automakers have located engineering centers there. Italy has a well-developed luxury sports car market, and even German firms such as Porsche hire Italian designers. The Japanese provide mass manufacturing state-of-the-art knowledge, and their domestic customers get perhaps the best value for the money. The United States still provides a sophisticated market for large luxury cars, even if the domestic producers have not performed particularly well.

A British advertisement for the new SLK sportscar from Mercedes. Germany's status as a leading market for automobiles derives from its demanding customers, an efficient Autobahn system without speed limit, and the quality craft traditions of its automakers. Courtesy Leo Burnett/London

COUNTRY DATA SOURCES

Despite the important role of personal visits to the top candidate countries, most of the data used in the screening of countries come from secondary not primary sources.

A useful start when doing research is to look at the easily available *secondary data sources*, such as the U.N. publications, the OECD and GATT/WTO reports, and the Department of Commerce reports in the United States. A large number of organizations—consulates, commerce departments, newspaper and magazine affiliates, information agencies—can be helpful. The data are today often accessible through their Web sites. Some of the more prominent organizations are listed in Exhibit 4.2.

Actually, with the globalization of markets, the availability of **secondary data** (data already collected for some other purpose and readily available) on markets in different countries has grown exponentially. Internet and on-line services such as Lexis-Nexis have made it easy to access basic economic and demographic data as well as newsworthy developments. Basic data availability on-line continues to improve for companies (annual reports, for example) and for people in various regions or trade blocs (the Eurobarometer, for instance).

For more in-depth analyses, various independent firms, from advertising agencies to international research firms to electronic news media, have emerged to gather and sell information on specific industries across the globe. Leading research firms are increasingly building representation and capability to do market surveys in different countries, including the emerging economies. Some of the sources are listed in Exhibit 4.3.

In the **country identification** stage, the analysis usually has to make do with general information. A good place to start is with the United Nations annual compilation of world economic and social data, which will give a broad picture of the various countries. This can be followed by data from the U.S. Department of Commerce and other government offices, and data from international organizations such as the EU Commission, World Bank, and the International Monetary Fund (IMF).

Research on computerized data banks, CD-ROM, or on-line news services will get the most recent data and developments. The rise of the Internet, on-line services, and computerized data banks such as Lexis-Nexis has transformed the data-gathering tasks in the last few years. Magazines and newspapers can be screened in this phase as well, using key word searches to find recent articles. These data will help to narrow down *the set of countries* to consider further.

EXHIBIT 4.2 Country Data Sources

United Nations

Conference of Trade And
Development
Palais Des Nations
1211 Geneva 10
Switzerland

Publications
Room 1194
1 United Nations Plaza
New York, NY 10017

Statistical Yearbook
1 United Nations Plaza
New York, NY 10017

International business organizations

A. C. Nielsen Co.
150 N. Martingale Road
Schaumburg, IL 60173

American Demographics, Inc.
108 N. Cayuga Street
Ithaca, NY 14851

American Management Association
440 First Street, NW
Washington, DC 20001

American Marketing Association
250 S. Wacker Drive, Suite 200
Chicago, IL 60606

Burke Marketing Research
2621 Victory Parkway
Cincinnati, OH 45206

Conference Board
845 Third Avenue
New York, NY 10022

Dun & Bradstreet
World Financial Center
Building A, 31st Floor
New York, NY 10281

European Community
Information Service
200 Rue de la Loi
1049 Brussels, Belgium and
2100 M Street, NW, 7th Floor
Washington, DC 20037

Frost and Sullivan
106 Fulton Street
New York, NY 10038

Computer on-line services

America On-Line
8619 Westwood Center Drive
Vienna, VA 22182

Lexis/Nexis
Reed-Elsevier Inc.
P.O. Box 933
Dayton, OH 45401

Prodigy Services Co.
445 Hamilton Avenue
White Plains, NY 10601

Miscellaneous

Economist Intelligence Unit
111 West 57th Street
New York, NY 10019

Business Week
McGraw-Hill Publications Co.
1221 Avenue of the Americas
New York, NY 10020

Doing Business in. . . . Series
Price Waterhouse
1251 Avenue of the Americas
New York, NY 10020

Europa Year Book
Europa Publications Ltd.
18 Bedford Square
London WC1 3JN England

International Financial Statistics
International Monetary Fund
Publications Unit
700 19th Street, NW
Washington, DC 20431

Market Share Reports
U.S. Government Printing Office
Superintendent of Documents
Washington, DC 20402

Media Guide International
Business/Professional Publications
Directories International, Inc.
150 Fifth Avenue, Suite 610
New York, NY 10011

Yearbook of International Trade
Statistics
United Nations
United Nations Publishing Division
1 United Nations Plaza
Room DC2-0853
New York, NY 10017

Frost & Sullivan Inc.
90 West Street, Suite 1301
New York, NY 10006

EXHIBIT 4.3 Selected International Data Sources

The Economist Intelligence Unit (EIU): Marketing in Europe (product markets in Europe—food, clothing, furniture, household goods, appliances). EIU now also owns BI (see below).
Business International: BI database (consumption patterns in different countries).
Frost & Sullivan: Syndicated market research for various industries in different countries.
Euromonitor: European marketing data and statistics (population, standard of living index, consumption).
Bates Worldwide: Global scan (spending patterns, media habits, and attitudes in different countries).
U.S. Department of Commerce: Global market surveys (research on targeted industries); country market surveys (more detailed reports on promising countries for exports); overseas marketing report (market profiles for all countries except the United States).

In the preliminary screening phase, more in-depth data become desirable. Syndicated reports from Business International, Dun & Bradstreet, or The Conference Board should be considered. By now the data will cost money, but usually syndication keeps report costs down to reasonable levels for most firms (under $1,000). The advantage tends to be the recency of the figures: These organizations have to provide the most recent data available.

A good data source for the preliminary screening phase is the *Business International Market Report*, published annually for the last 30 years. The report gives weighted indicators of market size, growth, and market intensity for the world's markets. The *market size data* are based on a combination of measures including population size; urban percentage; private consumption expenditures (disposable GNP minus private savings); ownership figures for telephones, cars, and televisions; and electricity production. The *market growth indicator* is basically the average shift in market size over five years. The *market intensity measure* is intended to capture the dynamics of the marketplace by double-weighting the private consumption expenditures, the car ownership figures, and the proportion of urban population.

The BI indices, now published by the Economist Intelligence Unit, are particularly useful for spotting promising growth countries and thus suggest newly emerging markets where a global marketer may want to have a presence. The indices need to be buttressed by political risk indicators and some data on the degree to which the market is open and free of government interference. Such data can be obtained from the *Political Risk Yearbook*, published annually by Political Risk Services in Syracuse, New York. These data provide expert assessments of political instability in a country, including the chances of a violent change in government and the degree of social unrest. They also contain summaries of restrictions on business, such as limitations on foreign ownership and constraints on the repatriation of funds. Countries that score high on political instability and restrictions on business can usually be eliminated from consideration early.

For the most up-to-date information on the political risk situation in a country, the semiannual credit ratings published by *Institutional Investor*, a financial markets periodical, can be very useful. Published in the March and September issues, the tabulations give a quick overview of recent volatility, useful in the preliminary phase. Exhibit 4.4 shows selected volatility ratings for 1995.

In the in-depth screening stage, when data on specific markets are needed, the data availability varies by industry. Trade associations are usually the place to start, followed by government agencies. The U.S. Department of Commerce and its counterparts in other countries publish some data at the industry level, even some market share data for various countries and products. Where trade conflicts have occurred, more data tend to be available. In highly visible industries such as automobiles, computers, and consumer electronics, reasonably good data are usually available from the trade press. There are also syndicated data. Frost and Sullivan in New York, for example, provide worldwide studies of market growth and potential for specific industries. The problem in the in-depth screening stage is the lack of comparability between countries and the incompleteness of some countries' data. The dynamic potential of a country such as Italy, for example, with its large underground economy, is difficult to capture in published statistics. The lack of information serves, in fact, as a barrier to entry.

At this stage primary market research reports might be needed. Here the choice is between general agencies such as Nielsen's and Burke's and more specialized organizations. The latter can be accounting firms—Andersen Consulting, for example, does a fair amount of international market research in services—or legal professionals or industry-specific research firms (wood products, automobiles, airlines, and computer software, for example). The reason specialization occurs is simply that the research firms have to invest a great deal of time to be sufficiently well informed about the global situation for an industry, and the payoff comes when more than one client can be served on the basis of the same material. This does not mean that the firms send the same customized report to all clients, rather that the customization is done on top of a common data set for the industry.

EXHIBIT 4.4 Changes in Institutional Investor Credit Rating
for Selected Countries

Country	Six-month change in credit rating*	One-year change in credit rating†
Brazil	3.1	4.6
Canada	−1.1	−1.7
Czech Republic	3.0	6.1
Iran	−1.2	−2.3
Iraq	−0.7	0.7
Israel	1.4	4.5
Lebanon	1.7	5.1
Oman	−0.8	−0.5
Peru	2.7	6.2
Philippines	2.5	4.9
Poland	2.6	5.2
Qatar	−0.3	−0.8
Saudi Arabia	−1.6	−2.8
Slovenia	0.1	6.1
Sri Lanka	2.0	4.7
Sweden	−0.6	−0.1
Turkey	−1.2	−4.9
United States	−0.4	0.7
Venezuela	−2.9	−4.5
Vietnam	2.6	5.7

*The six-month change covers the period of September 1994–March 1995.

†The one-year change covers the period of March 1994–March 1995.

Source: *Institutional Investor*, March 1995, Vol. 29, 3, pp. 124–25. This copyrighted material is reprinted with permission from *The Journal of Portfolio Management*, a publication of Institutional Investor, Inc., 488 Madison Avenue, NY, NY 10022.

   Data on product-specific criteria can be used to cluster candidate countries into groups of high and low potential. In the Microlog case the team clustered the countries on two criteria at a time. Exhibit 4.5 shows the resulting clusters for the mapping of "Competition" against "Growth Potential." In the upper northwest corner is a cluster of countries with high growth potential and relatively weak competitive intensity, obviously presenting more opportunity than France, with so-so growth and a high degree of competition (1 strong competition). This graph alone quickly suggests why France may be a bad choice for Microlog's entry into the EU.

   The final selection stage requires no new secondary information in principle, but it is here that the subjective judgments and experiences during the visits to the prospective country play a bigger role. Now managers can substitute subjective "guesstimates" for missing data and correct other data that seem out of line. Although this may introduce bias into the final assessment, it is at least clear where it comes from. Thus, it is possible to do a sensitivity analysis and evaluate the extent to which the overall ratings vary for potential biases in either direction. This is also where the competitive research should have yielded possible scenarios for competitive reaction that can be played out against the option chosen. When door-to-door cosmetics seller Mary Kay decided to enter China, the company judged that first-mover Avon would not react defensively, since the two could grow the huge market together. The prediction proved correct, but both companies were stunned by the later political crackdown on pyramid sales that forced the firms to stop door-to-door selling in China.

EXHIBIT 4.5 Microlog's Country Clusters

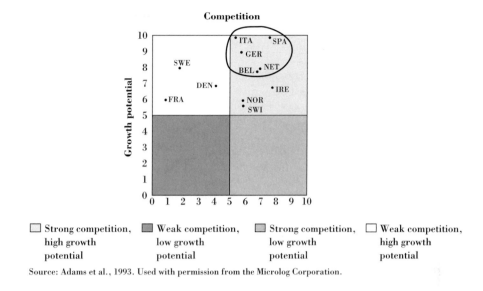

Source: Adams et al., 1993. Used with permission from the Microlog Corporation.

FORECASTING COUNTRY SALES

Up to now the chapter has dealt with research to evaluate the **market potential** in a foreign country. Such research identifies what could potentially be achieved under "ideal" conditions, while a **sales forecast** assesses what is likely to be obtained given the likely situation and contemplated strategies. Here the focus is on the derivation of sales forecasts at two levels: industry sales and market share.

The forecasting of total market sales and market share involves quite technical skills, many of which are valid in any market. But there are additional factors that need to be considered in *foreign markets*. Economic and demographic data might not be available or not be comparable because of different classifications. The marketer often has to leverage past data from other markets, including the home market, into a kind of "bootstrap" forecast of what is likely to happen in a new market. Forecasting sales in a foreign market is a matter of combining technical skills and country knowledge imaginatively.

A Basic Equation

Few companies are as fortunate as Mazda when it comes to forecasting sales in foreign markets (see box, "Mazda's Shorthand Forecast").

The Mazda approach provides the basic components that companies have to estimate in order to generate a forecast:

$$\text{Sales} = \text{industry sales} \times \text{market share}$$

The division between industry sales and market share serves to isolate what factors need to be considered. To develop an estimate of *industry sales*, the well-known determinants such as economic growth, disposable incomes, social and political developments, as well as dynamics of the product life cycle need to be incorporated. The *market share prediction*, on the other hand, relates directly to factors such as competitive situation and marketing effort. The basic idea tends to be that what affects the market size is one thing, what affects the share we get in the market is another. Although in international marketing this represents an oversimplification because of various trade obstacles (tariff and nontariff barriers), such factors can be incorporated and accounted for as we will show.

Mazda's Shorthand Forecast

E V E N   B E F O R E 1981, when their agreement to voluntarily restrict exports to the United States took effect, the Japanese auto companies had an easy time forecasting their American sales (after 1981 the Japanese simply divided their market share among themselves). Mazda, for example, was able to employ a "shorthand" type of quick forecasting method.

First, projected industry sales, in units, were polled from various sources, including economists in Washington, D.C. Second, the market share going to imports as a class was identified, also provided by these same sources. Next, the Japanese share among these imports was estimated on the evidence of past performance and projected competi-

tive developments worldwide; the Japanese Automobile Manufacturers' Association (JAMA) was instrumental here. Finally, the share falling to Mazda from the Japanese piece of the pie was estimated on the basis of in-house data and probable developments in styles and specifications, and against previous performances abroad. Computing the forecasted sales then was simple. They equaled industry sales × import share × share for the Japanese × share for Mazda among the Japanese. Time and cost to develop the forecast? Negligible. Accuracy? Almost perfect.

Sources: Personal interview with company spokesmen, Mazda North America. *http://www.mazda.co.jp/home.html*

Stage of the Product Life Cycle

An important aspect of the forecasting problem in global markets is the stage of the **product life cycle** (PLC), the S-curve that depicts how the sales of a product category (or a brand, since brands also tend to have a life cycle) progress over time (see Exhibit 11.10, page 359). The stages typically involve introduction, growth, maturity, and saturation, possibly decline.[10] These stages vary by country, even for a given product. In the early stages, relatively little data are usually available for statistically based forecasting, and more inventive methods have to be relied on. In later stages, more sophisticated methods can be employed.

In the early stage of the product life cycle, market share is usually less important: What matters is the size and growth rate of the total market. Three types of forecasting techniques can be used. One is the evaluation via a "build-up" method from industry experts and distribution channel units; another is forecasting by analogy, doing a comparison with a lead country. When all else fails, judgmental methods have to be used.

INDUSTRY SALES

The Build-Up Method

For the *introductory stage of the product life cycle* the best estimate of future sales usually comes from industry experts and knowledgeable channel members. If the company can contact some of these individuals—travel is usually necessary—an estimate of the market size can be based on their information. The **build-up** connotation comes from the fact that the market sales are estimated on the basis of separate estimates from individuals knowledgeable about certain segments of the market. These single estimates of various parts of the market are aggregated ("built up") into an evaluation of total market size.

For example, when one company attempted to forecast sales in Europe of a new consumer audio product, it divided each country market into three segments, each served by different channels. The teenage segment purchased mostly through convenience outlets. The high-performance segment purchased through specialty stores. The family user purchased through general merchandise and department stores. The company then collected estimates from each of these channels in the main European countries to build up a forecast.

Given that these estimates are subjective, it is important that the marketer gather additional information from whatever other sources are available so as to develop a sense of the reliability of the subjective estimates.

The information from the build-up method should always be compared with managerial experiences of the product in other countries—provided of course there are other countries further along the product life cycle process. In these cases forecasting by analogy has become quite popular.

Forecasting by Analogy

The basic premise underlying forecasts by **analogy** is that the sales in one "lagging" country will show similarities to sales in another "leading" country where the product is already marketed. Since the 1960s, when the theme of global interdependence and convergence first emerged strongly, such similarities have been used to forecast a similar rate of acceptance of a new product in many different countries, especially those belonging to a common regional grouping. A standard example was television: Its introduction in the United States had been shown to exhibit a growth curve replicated with minor modifications in a number of other countries (the so-called "demonstration effect"). Most examples fall within the durable category of products, where market penetration in terms of first-purchase rates is used as a standard indication of stage of market development.

According to this technique a reasonably quick and cheap way of assessing the sales potential at a given point (and for the future) in a country where a product introduction is contemplated would be to ascertain at what stage of the growth curve (the product life cycle) the product will be when entering the new market. If the product is new, the assumption is made that the growth curve will have approximately the same slope as in a "lead" country where the product is already introduced. Empirical analyses have demonstrated that the speed of adoption tends to be quite similar in new countries— but also that (because of differences in economic rates of growth) the saturation level will be lower (or higher). These differences are usually adjusted for judgmentally when the final forecast is developed.

An Illustration: TV Penetration

An example of the possible use of forecasting by analogy is provided by the introduction and market penetration of TV sets in various countries at different points in time.[11] Exhibit 4.6 shows the percent of ownership and annual increases in sales for three countries.

According to the exhibit, the penetration rate was slightly faster in the United States compared with Germany and the United Kingdom, and large annual increases occurred correspondingly earlier in the life cycle. Other countries showed different patterns. Sweden, for example, exhibited a penetration rate steeper than that of the United States, often ascribed to the "demonstration effect" of the United States and other countries in which TV stations came on the air earlier.

Exhibit 4.6 illustrates the opportunities and problems in forecasting by analogy. Yes, the patterns are the same, generally speaking. But the timing of the takeoff and rapid growth stages is different, and the lags involved are not identical. By introducing variables to explain the variations in the penetration curves it is possible to adjust the forecast by analogy to more properly reflect the likely time path.

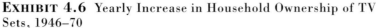

EXHIBIT 4.6 Yearly Increase in Household Ownership of TV Sets, 1946–70

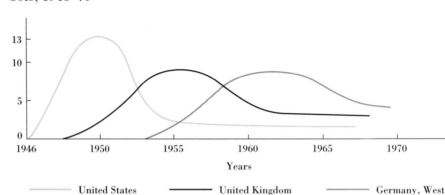

Source: Lindberg, 1982. Adapted with permission. © 1982 by the American Marketing Association.

To account for the difference in size between countries, the sales figures are usually weighted by a measure such as GNP or population size. For example, forecasted sales might be computed from an expression such as the following:

$$S_b(1995) = [S_a(1991)/GNP_a(1991)] \times GNP_b(1995)$$

where S stands for unit sales, the subscript "a" stands for the leading country, "b" for the lagging country, and there is a lag of four years (1995–1991).

In other words, the ratio of sales to GNP in the lead country in 1991 gives the unit sales per dollar GNP. By multiplying this factor into the lagging country's GNP in 1995, a sales forecast is arrived at.

It goes without saying that such a simple formula requires a careful assessment of the comparability between the two countries. What is relevant is whether there is any reason to expect the ratio between sales and GNP to differ between countries. The United States and Canada are two quite different countries in some respects, but there might be little reason to expect these differences to be very important once the discrepancy in the size of population has been taken into account. On the other hand, comparing Japan and West Germany, countries with quite comparable economic output records, might be more difficult: The TV might play a very different role in the Japanese household with the absent husband working until 11 p.m. as compared with the German household in which the larger homes and less time on the job allow the family to spend more time together. These differences might induce the suspicion that GNP will not account for differences in sales (as it turns out, the penetration ratio is lower for Germany where the typical two-income household means that no one is home during the day).

Judgmental Forecasts

If the product has no history in any comparable country (as might be the case when entering the former communist countries), analogies can be misleading. Furthermore, channel members may know too little for a build-up method to have any validity or reliability. Purely judgmental methods may have to be used.

Judgmental forecasting techniques generally attempt to introduce a certain amount of rigor and reliability in otherwise quite arbitrary guesses.[12]

THE JURY TECHNIQUE The use of executive judgment based on firsthand experience and observation in estimating foreign sales is indispensable. The **jury technique** is basically a structuring of the standard executive committee meetings, in which the members are asked to submit their separate forecasts, either before or after intensive discussion. The individual forecasts are then pooled and the results again evaluated before a final figure or range is arrived at. The concept is that a group of experienced executives would have more insights when combined than any single one. When coupled with the Delphi method (see below), the jury technique gains additional power.

It is important that whatever data exist are made available to the jury and also that staff members from overseas are included in the process. It should be emphasized that this type of managerial judgment becomes especially important in decisions involving major commitments and high risk, since then the consensus arrived at by the jury automatically assigns responsibility to the whole group, not a single individual manager. In this respect, foreign entry is more naturally the domain of several executives rather than a small number or one person with good knowledge of operations in one country but not in others.

EXPERT POOLING   There is no doubt that consultation with experts (**expert pooling**) on the country contemplated will always be a cornerstone in sales forecasting where new entry is concerned. Without a firm's having previous experience in a new country's markets, the reliance on independent experts (academicians, consulting firms, or host country nationals) is almost unavoidable. Judging from the literature on export initiation it is precisely this type of information source about market potential that best serves the process of exploring entry into a new country.

The **panel consensus,** much like the jury of executive opinion, tries to pool the available information from more than one source. The Microlog team used this type of pooling to arrive at country ratings on the selected criteria, essentially taking averages across each team member's subjective rating.

The Delphi method is a more systematic approach. It consists of a series of "rounds" of numerical forecasts from a preselected number of experts. These experts may or may not know the identity of the other members of the panel. They are asked to provide individual estimates, independently of their colleagues. The estimates are tallied, the average forecast is computed, and summary statistics (but not individual estimates) are returned to the experts. Another round of estimates is collected, tallied up, and the summary is again distributed. As these rounds continue, the feedback provided will tend to bring the estimates into line. The expert whose initial estimate is far off the average forecast will tend to converge toward the mean, unless, of course, that expert has strong prior beliefs that his or her estimate is more correct. In either case, the process gradually converges, as those with weaker opinions yield to those with strong opinions under the influence of the pressure to adjust toward the average forecast received.

The Delphi method has been discussed widely and has come in for its share of criticism. The basic problem is that "bad estimates might drive out good estimates" when the panel members show unequal degrees of stubbornness. In general, however, the type of pooling of various opinions offered by this technique has been its greatest advantage. When judgmental analysis is carried out by using several individuals with some experience or direct knowledge of a country's market, it serves to prohibit one particularly strong personality (a headquarters executive, for example, or the general manager of a subsidiary) from dominating the proceedings. The anonymity provided serves to ensure that everybody "has a voice."

Time Series Extrapolation

When the product in the market country has reached a more *mature* stage in the product life cycle, forecasting using past data becomes possible. There are essentially two approaches available for carrying out these forecasts. One is based on historical data of industry sales alone, simply extrapolating past trends into the future. The second allows for more in-depth analysis, incorporating the variables that underlie sales developments in the country. This method is based on regression analysis.

Time series data represent a form of "history in numbers." In other words, statistics are based on past performance, behavior, and developments, and the statistical analysis of the data generated by these histories will simply ferret out what happened in a more comprehensive and objective manner than subjective evaluations. Thus, the primary requirements for statistical forecasting of foreign sales are (1) that data are available, (2) that past events are relevant for the future, and (3) that statistics will be a better judge of what happened than more informal or anecdotal accounts. Although in domestic forecasting the reliance on statistical analysis often seems great (because the requisite data *are indeed* available), in international marketing all three requirements typically pose problems. For example, recent dramatic political and economic changes in Asia, Eastern Europe, and Latin America suggest that historical time series may be a poor guide for the future.

Extrapolation refers to the method by which a time series of (sales) data observed over some periods in the past is extended into the future. It represents, in a sense, the purest form of forecasting in that the concern is entirely with the future: The current level of sales provides but one data point among many. At the same time it represents a very naive form of forecasting in that the only information employed is the numbers of the sales series in past periods. The focus of the forecaster's job is on detecting patterns in these numbers to be projected into the future. There are many excellent texts on this topic, and since the international context adds little to these treatments, they will not be covered here.[13]

Regression-Based Forecasts

The first considerations in developing a **regression forecast** involve the use of some prior knowledge to develop a forecasting equation. First, the relevant dependent variable of interest needs to be determined. Is it a matter of annual industry sales, in units (the most common choice)? In dollars? The growth rate of sales per annum? The import sales alone?

Second, the forecaster must try to identify what factors will affect the dependent variable selected. For most country analyses, GNP and population figures become relevant since they tend to measure the "size" of the market. But more specific measures are often needed. How many people or firms could one consider to be potential customers, or, stated differently, what is the "in the market" proportion? If a country has a large population but few single-person households, the market for labor-saving prepared foods might be correspondingly smaller. Where a large number of small manufacturers exist, but only few large-scale corporations, the market for mainframe computers and associated software might be minimal, despite a high GNP per capita.

THE SIZE COMPONENT   It is useful at this stage to break up the independent variables into different categories. One set deals with "size": How many firms, or people, are potential customers, for example. A useful approach is sometimes to *segment* the total number into homogeneous subsets: how many heavy industry firms, how many in services, or, for consumer goods, how many households with children, how many with incomes over a certain level, how many in the big cities versus the rural areas, and so on depending on the product. This type of evaluation can usually be done using the "chain ratio rule," in which the initial figure of size is broken down by the percentages falling into the separate segments: For example, the size M of one segment may be calculated as

$$M = \text{number of households} \times \text{proportion with children} \times \text{proportion}$$
$$\text{with incomes over \$10,000 a year}$$

WILLINGNESS TO BUY   A second group of independent variables influences the willingness to buy the product. In consumer goods, need for the product among types of consumers, existing attitudes toward foreign products, and fit between product use and buyer lifestyles are all important considerations. In industrial markets, sophistication of the process technology employed in manufacturing, attitude toward foreign products, special features the product offers, and other similar considerations are relevant here. Needless to say, this portion of the analysis must be based on intimate knowledge of the country's people, be it through formal market research or personal experience.

ABILITY TO BUY   The last category relates to consumers' ability to pay for the product. Variables here are income, per capita expenditures on related products, profit performance of company customers, and other similar economic factors. It's important to identify trends in these figures so that precautions can be taken and future opportunities are not missed.

SALES PER CUSTOMER   Combining the willingness and ability to buy, one can develop an estimate of the amount of probable sales (units or money) per customer in the target segment. A typical method to use is regression, where the various factors that determine willingness and ability are regressed against sales, the data coming from other countries where the product has already been introduced.

MARKET SALES   Customers' willingness and ability to buy can now be combined into a total sales estimate. Using the market size multiplied by the average sales per customer, a simple version of the model is

$$S = M \times r$$

where r is the average sales per customer (in units or money)

FORECASTING MARKET SHARE

After forecasting industry sales it becomes necessary to predict what portion of total industry sales the particular company can obtain. This entails a forecast of market share.

Predicting Competition

Market share forecasts involve prediction of competitive moves. This requires not only knowing who actual and potential competitors might be in a given country but assessing competitors' strengths and weaknesses. Hard enough when it comes to understanding what is currently going on, when attention is directed toward the future, the forecasting problem becomes very thorny. Small wonder that subjective managerial judgment plays a relatively great role.

Market share forecasts are usually done best by breaking up the problem into its separate components. First, the likely *competitors* need to be identified, including domestic firms and multinational companies operating in the country. Second, *country-specific advantages* of the domestic companies over foreign competition should be well understood. Third, the *company's strengths* against the other firms have to be objectively assessed, particularly against other foreign firms operating in the country.

Identifying Competitors

Drawing on informal in-house knowledge and on selected contacts in the market country, a list of competitors is compiled. One difficulty is identifying what future entries may be made; here also less formal research methods will be reliable indicators. It is important that *potential entrants* be included, particularly when the product in the new country is at an early stage in the life cycle while in other countries its development has progressed further. When a competitor is already well established in other markets, entry into a new market can be undertaken quite quickly. A good example is the burgeoning auto market in Saudi Arabia that was rapidly covered by major automakers from Europe and Japan once the oil revenues had radically increased the spending power of the population.

Domestic Competitors

The fact that tariff and nontariff barriers make entry difficult by raising foreign firms' prices and giving advantages to domestic producers needs to be considered very carefully. Not-so-prohibitive existing barriers could be changed all too quickly after an entry has been successfully made, and the possibility of direct foreign investment needs to be considered at this stage. For forecasting purposes, the critical figure is the proportion of the market available to nondomestic countries ("country share"). In most countries there are (possibly unstated) limits on market capture that the entering firms can reach without inducing protectionist measures. Managerial judgment and informal inquiries might disclose what those limits are. The forecasted share might well need to be constrained a priori using this information, with the understanding that the company will have an upper limit on the share it can obtain in the market.

Apart from such political considerations, the forecaster needs to evaluate the strength of a possible "pro-domestic" attitude on the part of buyers. There is sometimes covert or overt pressure on buyers to stay loyal to their domestic companies, the "Buy American" movement being one example. In addition, there are attitude differences toward products from different countries, as well as formal requests to companies that entry into certain other countries be restricted (at the time of this writing, certain Arab states demanding that suppliers not do business with Israel, for example).

In addition to these extra-economic considerations, the forecaster needs to be aware that many domestic producers provide a product or service that is particularly well suited to the special needs and wants of the country, even though it might make little headway in the international marketplace. America's big cars, the dark beer of England, "small is beautiful" farm equipment in India may be hard to compete with in local markets. In these cases the evaluation of the competitive strengths of the domestic producers needs to be adjusted beyond a straightforward application of strengths and weaknesses of products. Needless to say, such adjustments become subjective and judgmental.

In the end, the forecaster should be able to come up with a reasonable estimate of the market share "available" to imports (import share versus domestic share). This step serves well in accounting for factors affecting market performance that are not encountered in the home market.

Foreign Competitors

How well will the company fare against other *foreign competitors* in the local market? Here more objective data are sometimes available, since these firms might have been encountered in other world markets. Motorola can assess fairly directly how well its products may perform relative to Siemens, Ericsson, or Hitachi using its experience with these companies in other parts of the globe. Market share estimates can't be assumed equal to those in other markets, but a fair evaluation can be made.

If appropriate, this last step can be broken down into evaluating foreign competitors first and then firms from the company's home country. Westinghouse might first assess a probable U.S. share and then go on to comparing itself to General Electric. We saw Mazda's approach, first identifying the probable Japanese share and then comparing its strength against Japanese competitors. This breakdown becomes particularly necessary when tariffs, quotas, and other nontariff barriers (including country-of-origin stereotyping and attitudes) differ for different home countries. A typical example would be automobiles in the EU. Semiofficial quotas help Italian and French authorities keep domestic auto firms' market shares up to protect employment. Once the "desired" domestic share has been ascertained from industry experts, the foreign automakers can focus on the remaining available market share.

SUMMARY

Chapter 4 examined how companies do global market research to evaluate countries' attractiveness for foreign market entry. The basic data on each country involves environmental data on political risk, trade barriers, economic regulation, and social and physical conditions. An assessment of domestic and foreign companies' competitive strength in each specific market being considered is also warranted.

The evaluation proceeds in stages, with an initial identification of a set of countries based on the company's strategic intentions, such as a desired presence in a particular free trade region or cluster of similar countries. A preliminary screening using broad socio-economic indicators reduces the set, after which an in-depth screening of the most promising candidates reduces it further. The chapter described the various data sources that exist for the different stages of the evaluation process. However, even though data sources have grown substantially in the last few years, the screening requires a personal visit to the top candidate countries to get a direct feel for the market and marketing infrastructure. Such "hands-on" contact by managers with the new market should never be missed, especially in situations like the one at the end of the 1990s when the financial and political turmoil is intense.

The chapter also showed how to adapt sales forecasting techniques applicable in domestic markets to foreign country markets. Despite data differences and differences in product life cycle stages, among many other factors, the standard breakdown of the forecasting problem into industry sales and market share forecasts as separate issues can be used. It needs to be modified by introducing "import share" to deal with tariff and nontariff barriers and "country share" to deal with country-of-origin attitudes.

As always, it is useful if several independent forecasts are carried out, if feasible, and the results "pooled" to arrive at the best forecast possible. This pooling effort draws on many individual judgments, based on managers' valuable direct personal experience with the country in question. The low likelihood of intimate knowledge of every country on the list makes group consensus forecasts generally superior to an individual's projections.

KEY TERMS

analogy method   p. 115
build-up method   p. 114
country identification   p. 109
Delphi method   p. 117
direct experience   p. 106
environmental dimensions   p. 100
expert pooling   p. 117

extrapolation   p. 118
final selection   p. 106
in-depth screening   p. 105
jury technique   p. 116
leading markets   p. 108
market potential   p. 113
market share forecasts   p. 119

panel consensus   p. 117
political risk   p. 97
preliminary screening   p. 104
product life cycle   p. 114
regression forecasts   p. 118
sales forecast   p. 113
secondary data   p. 109

DISCUSSION QUESTIONS

1. Company spokespeople are often heard to say, "We have to be in that market." What is a likely explanation for this statement if the market is (a) China, (b) Germany, (c) Brazil, (d) Japan, (e) the United States? Give examples of products or services.

2. What factors would you consider when helping an already global manufacturer of household vacuum cleaners choose between Mexico, India, and China as the next country to enter?

3. Access the available on-line services to create a database that would help a company decide how attractive a country market is. Product category and country is your choice.

4. Use the Web sites of companies in a given product category—such as pharmaceuticals, autos, or consumer electronics—to develop a short report on how their respective product lines overlap and compete in the global market.

5. New hi-tech products—such as the Sony Walkman was—are often said to generate their own demand. What does this imply about the possibility of forecasting sales when such a product is first introduced? How could one forecast sales for it when later entering a market such as Russia?

NOTES

1. Adapted from Kobrin, 1979, and De la Torre and Neckar, 1990.

2. These firms include, for example, Business International and Frost & Sullivan; see the discussion on country data sources and Exhibit 4.3.

3. See "War Cited as Top Risk to Business," *Chicago Tribune*, January 17, 1994, p. 1.

4. See Jeannet, 1981.

5. See Hamel and Prahalad, 1989.

6. This section draws on Douglas and Craig, 1983, and Kumar et al., 1994.

7. See, for example, Wood and Goolsby, 1987.

8. See Exhibit 4.2 for how to get these reports.

9. This section draws on Johansson and Roehl, 1994.

10. The product life cycle is discussed at length in any introductory marketing text. See, for example, Kotler, 1997, Chapter 12.

11. This example is adapted from Lindberg, 1982.

12. This section draws on Armstrong, 1985, and Makridakis, 1990.

13. Armstrong, 1985, is useful and relatively accessible for the nontechnical reader. Lindberg, 1982, and Makridakis, 1990, offer interesting applications.

SELECTED REFERENCES

Adams, Jonathan; Shubber Ali; Leila Byczkowski; Kathryn Cancro; and Susan Nolen. "Microlog Corporation: European Market Evaluation." Class project, School of Business, Georgetown University, May 12, 1993.

Amine, Lyn S.; and S. Tamer Cavusgil. "Demand Estimation in a Developing Country Environment: Difficulties, Techniques, and Examples." *Journal of the Market Research Society* 28, no. 1 (1986), pp. 43–65.

Armstrong, J. Scott. "An Application of Econometric Models to International Marketing." *Journal of Marketing Research* VII (May 1970), pp. 190–8.

—*Long-Range Forecasting.* 2d ed. New York: Wiley, 1985.

Bartlett, Christopher A.; and Ashish Nanda. "Ingvar Kamprad and IKEA." Harvard Business School case no. 9-390-132, 1990.

De la Torre, Jose; and David H. Neckar. "Forecasting Political Risks for International Operations." In H. Vernon-Wortzel and L. Wortzel, eds. *Global Strategic Management.* 2d ed. New York: Wiley, 1990.

Douglas, Susan; and Samuel C. Craig. *International Marketing Research.* Englewood Cliffs, NJ: Prentice-Hall, 1983.

Dubey, Suman. "After 16 Years Away, Coca-Cola to Return `The Real Thing' to India." *The Wall Street Journal*, October 22, 1993, sec. A, p. 9E.

Hamel, Gary; and C. K. Prahalad. "Strategic Intent." *Harvard Business Review*, May–June 1989, pp. 63–76.

Jeannet, Jean-Pierre. "International Marketing Analysis: A Comparative-Analytic Approach." Working paper, 1981.

Johansson, Johny K.; and Thomas W. Roehl. "How Companies Develop Assets and Capabilities: Japan as a Leading Market." In Schon, Beechler, and Allan Bird, eds. *Emerging Trends in Japanese Management*, vol. 6 of *Research in International Business and*

International Relations, ed. Manuel G. Serapio, Jr. Greenwich, CT: JAI Press, 1994, pp. 139–60.

Kobrin, Stephen J. "Political Risk: A Review and Reconsideration." *Journal of International Business Studies* 10, no. 1 (1979), pp. 67–80.

Kotler, Philip. *Marketing Management: Analysis, Planning, Implementation, and Control.* 9th ed. Upper Saddle River, NJ: Prentice-Hall, 1997.

Kumar, V.; Antonie Stam; and Erich A. Joachimsthaler. "An Interactive Multicriteria Approach to Identifying Potential Foreign Markets." *Journal of International Marketing* 2, no. 1 (1994), pp. 29–52.

Lindberg, Bertil. "International Comparison of Growth in Demand for a New Durable Consumer Product." *Journal of Marketing Research*, August 1982, pp. 364–71.

Makridakis, Spyros G. *Forecasting, Planning and Strategy for the 21st Century.* New York: Free Press, 1990.

Martenson, Rita. *Innovations in International Retailing.* University of Gothenburg, Sweden: Liber, 1981.

Naisbitt, John. *Global Paradox.* New York: Harper & Row, 1994.

Porter, Michael E. *Competitive Strategy.* New York: Free Press, 1980.

Smart, Tim; Pete Engardio; and Geri Smith. "GE's Brave New World." *Business Week*, November 8, 1993, pp. 64–70.

Thorelli, Hans B.; and S. Tamer Cavusgil, eds. *International Marketing Strategy.* 3d. ed. New York: Pergamon, 1990.

Wood, R. Van; and Jerry R. Goolsby. "Foreign Market Information Preferences of Established U.S. Exporters." *International Marketing Review*, Winter 1987, pp. 43–52.

Yoshino, Michael. *Procter & Gamble Japan* (A)(B)(C). Harvard Business School case nos. 9-391-003, 004, 005, 1990.

Five

Export Expansion

"Over the river and into the trees"

Your takeaways from this chapter:

1. Barriers to entry include not only tariffs, quotas, and elaborate customs procedures but also restrictive government regulations, limited access to distribution channels, and pro-domestic consumer biases.

2. Barriers to entry will sometimes force the firm to unbundle its value chain and identify intermediate products, or components of the final product, to export.

3. Export operations involve a number of activities that may be new to the global marketer. The firm can let its agent and distributor handle the local marketing, or it can control marketing by establishing a foreign sales subsidiary.

4. New export expansion usually starts with a few culturally similar countries where existing know-how can be most easily leveraged. This is often referred to as the "internationalization" of the company.

5. When rapid entry into several countries is important for competitive reasons, resource-rich exporters tend to follow a "sprinkler" strategy, entering several countries simultaneously.

AFTER IDENTIFYING various opportunities in foreign countries, the question becomes how the chosen country or countries should be entered and what strategy the global expansion should follow.

For marketing, it helps to distinguish between modes of entry that *ship the product* to the selected market and those that *transfer know-how* to the host country. *Exporting* is the standard exchange of product for money; while *licensing, franchising, strategic alliances,* and *investment in manufacturing* are entry modes that share technology and know-how with host country partners. Exporting is more straightforward and less risky, since it is expansion into new markets with an existing line of final products, while transfer of technology involves trade in markets for company know-how, an intermediate good. Selling Coke cans is simpler and safer than selling the formula. This is why many firms expanding abroad start with exporting.

Chapter 5 will concentrate on the export mode of entry and expansion. Exporting is the international equivalent of trade across geographical regions, often the preferred mode when trade barriers (including tariffs and transportation costs) are low. The local marketing effort can be directed through independent middlemen, but it is usually preferable to establish a foreign sales subsidiary.

"Made in Brazil" Becomes Badge of Pride

When it first started exporting products, the Brazilian subsidiary of Stanley Tools had to omit the "Made in Brazil" labels from at least half its products because customers had a negative impression of Brazilian quality. Five years later, only one Chilean customer wanted tools without the label.

Brazil has recently emerged as the nation with the third largest trade surplus. In other words, Brazil's exports exceed its imports to a degree unmatched by any other nation except Japan and Germany. And current available data on imports and exports do not actually show the full extent of Brazilian companies' foreign marketing because some organizations invest in foreign operations. For example, Tintas Renner S.A., Brazil's largest paint company, recently entered into joint ventures to establish paint factories in Argentina, Chile, Paraguay, and Uruguay. What happened to give Brazil this status in the world marketplace?

If "Made in Brazil" was once synonymous with shoddy work, that is no longer the case. Brazil far surpasses its Latin American neighbors in receiving certificates of quality from the International Organization of Standardization (known as ISO). Over 400 Brazilian companies have received ISO certification, which means that their products meet international standards of quality. By one forecast, 5,500 companies were expected to be certified by the end of 1997. An example of an ISO-certified company is Grupo Siemens, the Brazilian subsidiary of German-based Siemens AG. In a recent four-year period, exports from Grupo Siemens quadrupled, reaching an impressive $80 million.

Besides showing they can deliver world-class quality, Brazilian companies keep their prices competitive by improving productivity. At BASF da Amazonia S.A., productivity improvements saved the subsidiary of the German conglomerate from shutdown. The Brazilian factory now exports tapes to Europe, Latin America, and the United States. During the first half of the 1990s, Brazil's steel industry doubled its productivity to a level rivaling that of Japanese firms. During the same period, total manufacturing of Brazilian industry improved at the outstanding rate of 30 percent.

Despite being hurt by the global financial turmoil at the end of the 1990s, Brazilian companies are becoming a formidable presence in the world economy. With the encouraging reelection of President Cardozo and help from the International Monetary Fund, one can expect that foreign investors will not pull away from Brazil and that the country's exports will stay strong.

Sources: James Brooke, "A New Quality in Brazil's Exports," *New York Times*, October 21, 1994, pp. D1, D6; James Brooke, "Brazil Looks North from Trade Zone in Amazon," *New York Times*, August 9, 1995, p. D3; James Brooke, "More Open Latin Borders Mirror an Opening of Markets," *New York Times*, July 4, 1995, p. 47; Geri Smith, "Why Wait for NAFTA," *Business Week*, December 5, 1994, pp. 52–54; Diana Jean Schemo, "In a Straitened Brazil, Talk of Pay in Goods," *New York Times*, October 22, 1998, p. C4.

http://www.StanleyWorks.com

http://www.iso.ch/

http://www.siemens.de/de/

http://www.basf.com

http://www.imf.org/

INTRODUCTION

Several strategic questions arise about how to reach foreign markets and conduct an orderly global expansion. What should the mode of entry be? How fast should new country markets and new products be added to existing ones? What is the best expansion path, considering the learning and experience already accumulated? Will similar countries be preferable, or should one strike out into new ground completely? What added advantages would a product and country diversification strategy entail? How should new entries be chosen so as to maximize total benefits?

Immediate global expansion into all markets is usually not feasible. Financial, managerial, and other resource constraints often dictate a more sequential approach. Even if the company is resource-rich, prudence suggests the company take a more deliberate approach. The company needs to establish defensible market positions in each country before moving on to other countries. Foreign direct investment might be avoided at the early stages because of the risk exposure. The learning associated with exporting and doing business abroad needs to be assimilated and diffused to benefit company managers.

Chapter 5 first introduces the major modes of entry and discusses each briefly, then turns to the impact of entry barriers on mode choice, followed by the main exporting tasks involved in entering a single country. The functions of independent middlemen and the key issue of control over the local marketing effort are discussed. The effect of "cultural distance" on the internationalization path of firms' expansion and the important benefit of learning how to do business abroad are taken up. Finally, the benefits and costs of export diversification versus a focused global expansion strategy are discussed.

Modes of entry that transfer know-how are discussed in more depth in Chapter 6.

FOUR MODES OF ENTRY

It is useful to distinguish between four **modes of entry** into a foreign market: exporting, licensing, strategic alliance, and wholly owned manufacturing subsidiary. These four modes break down into several different activities. A typical breakdown is given in Exhibit 5.1.[1] These alternatives will be discussed in detail in this and the next chapter. At the outset, we take a quick look at the options available.

Exporting

Indirect exporting refers to the use of home country agencies (trading companies, export management firms) to get the product to the foreign market. "Piggybacking" is the use of already exported products' transportation and distribution facilities. Con-

EXHIBIT 5.1 Entry Modes for Foreign Markets

Exporting	*Strategic alliance*
Indirect exporting via piggybacking, consortia, export management companies, trading companies	Distribution alliance
	Manufacturing alliance
	R & D alliance
Direct exporting, using market country agent or distributor	Joint venture
Direct exporting, using own sales subsidiary	***Wholly owned manufacturing subsidiary***
Direct marketing, including mail order and telemarketing	Assembly
	Full-fledged manufacturing
Licensing	Research and development
Technical licensing	Acquistion
Contract manufacture	
Original equipment manufacturing (OEM)	
Management contracts	
Turnkey contracts	
Franchising	

Source: Adapted with permission from Root, *Entry Strategies for International Markets*, Revised and Expanded. Copyright © 1994 Jossey-Bass Inc., Publishers. First published by Lexington Books. All rights reserved.

sortia are used by some smaller exporters banding together to sell related or unrelated products abroad. **Direct exporting,** by contrast, means the firm itself contacts the buyers abroad, be they independent agents and distributors or the firm's own subsidiaries. There is also *direct marketing*, including mail order and telemarketing, a new but rapidly expanding mode of foreign entry particularly useful for small businesses and for initial entry. Since direct marketing is an outgrowth of direct mail promotion, it is discussed in Chapter 16 on global promotion.

Licensing

Licensing involves offering a foreign company the rights to use the firm's proprietary technology and other know-how, usually in return for a fee plus a royalty on revenues. Among licensing modes, **franchising** has become a well-known alternative with the expansion of global hotel and fast-food chains. In franchising, the firm provides technological expertise to the reseller abroad and also helps with the management of the franchise and often with the capital investment that is needed for start-up. The other licensing options are all similar, differing mainly in the type of know-how transmitted. **Turnkey contracts** provide for the construction of whole plants and often the training of personnel capable of running the operations; **contract manufacturing** involves hiring a firm to produce a prespecified product (jeans produced by Filipino and Chinese textile mills for overseas manufacturers).

Strategic Alliances (SAs)

Strategic alliances are collaborations between companies, sometimes competitors, to exchange or share some value activities. Examples include joint R&D, shared manufacturing, and distribution alliances. Strategic alliances in the form of **joint ventures** also involve capital investments and the creation of a new corporate unit jointly with a foreign partner. Such joint ventures have long been common especially in countries such as India, where government mandates participation by locals, and in countries such as Japan, where market access is difficult for outsiders.

Joint ventures are a type of strategic alliance in which partners create an equity-based new unit. In recent years, non-equity-based strategic alliances have become very common. An international strategic alliance is typically a *cooperative collaboration* between companies, even between potential competitors, across borders. The alliance could encompass any part of the value chain—although the focus is often limited to manufacturing, R&D, or distribution. In distribution alliances, the partners agree contractually to use an existing distribution network jointly. A typical example is the linkup between Lufthansa and United Airlines to pool route information and passengers.

Wholly Owned Manufacturing Subsidiary

When production takes place in the host country through a wholly owned manufacturing subsidiary, the company commits investment capital in plant and machinery that will be at risk in the country. This is traditional **foreign direct investment (FDI).** A wholly owned subsidiary in manufacturing can involve investment in a new manufacturing or assembly plant (such as Sony's TV plant in San Diego) or the acquisition of an existing plant (such as Matsushita's purchase of Motorola's TV plant outside Chicago). The presence of actual manufacturing operations helps support marketing activities. For example, a local plant is more likely to provide a stable flow of products, and it will be easier to adapt the products to the preferences of local customers than with a plant located outside the country's borders.

It is important to recognize that FDI usually leads to exporting. As manufacturing is established abroad through direct investment, parts and components are often shipped (exported) from the home country. About a third of U.S. international trade involves such shipments between units of the same company.[2] Although such intraorganizational transfers are quite different from market exchanges, more and more companies set transfer prices at market levels and allow subsidiaries to buy from local suppliers if quality and price are more favorable. This means the supplier plant has to engage in "internal" marketing, satisfying internal customers in the subsidiaries abroad.

A **sales subsidiary** is fundamentally different from a wholly owned *manufacturing* subsidiary. A sales subsidiary manages distribution and marketing of the product in the local market. Usually the product is exported from the home country or from another foreign plant. Volvo North America—located in Northridge, New Jersey—imports and distributes Volvos shipped from Europe.

Establishing a sales subsidiary requires relatively low levels of capital investment. Although operating costs for even a small sales office can be high in a country like Japan, with major expenditures for "general administrative and sales," the investment exposed to risk is often low. At the same time, establishing a sales subsidiary involves taking control of the marketing in the country and is thus strategically important. For marketing effectiveness, the control of the sales effort should generally be in the hands of the company itself.

THE IMPACT OF IMPORT BARRIERS

Before examining exporting and the other entry options in more detail, we look at the import barriers or entry barriers that always exist to entering a foreign market. *The height and nature of the market entry barriers directly influence the entry mode chosen by a company.* Entry barriers increase the cost of entry and constrain the options available, and where they are high, the company might have only one choice of entry mode or else have to stay out.

Entry Barriers Defined

The concept of **entry barriers** comes from the economics of industrial organization. It generally connotes any obstacle making it more difficult for a firm to enter a product market. Thus, entry barriers exist at home, as when limited shelf space prohibits a

One of Europe's traffic bottle-necks, the border crossing between France and Spain. As the EU integration continues and the customs check-points are eliminated, market entry barriers have quite literally been dismantled. Raphael Galliarde/Gamma-Liaison.

company from acquiring sufficient retail coverage to enter a market. Overseas it can mean that customs procedures are so lengthy that they prohibit an importer's fresh produce from getting to the stores before spoiling.

In global marketing it is convenient to classify the entry barriers according to their origin. Although gradually less important because of dramatic improvements in technology, *transportation costs* sometimes force new investment in manufacturing to be close to the market. Proximity of supplies and service still matters when transportation costs are high. **Tariff barriers** are obvious obstacles to entry into the country. Less visible **nontariff barriers**—for example, slow customs procedures, special product tests for imports, and bureaucratic inertia in processing import licenses—can also make entry difficult. **Government regulations** of business, domestic as well as foreign, constitute another set of market barriers, sometimes creating local monopolies. A special subset of these barriers are regulations directly intended to protect domestic business against foreign competitors.

Other barriers are more subtle. *Access* to manufacturing technology and processes, component suppliers, and distribution channels can be restricted by regulation, territorial restrictions, competitive collusion, or close ties between transacting partners. These barriers constitute artificial value chain imperfections and become important for the marketer to consider when deciding the configuration of the overseas operation. There are also "natural" entry barriers that arise because of competitive actions. Many of the typical marketing efforts—creation of brand loyalty, differentiation between products, high levels of promotional spending—are factors that, when successful, lead to barriers or defenses against competitive attack.

The Cost of Barriers

The economic costs of entry barriers are well known. The inefficiency created by barriers translates into higher prices for consumers. What this means to the marketer is that the barriers create additional costs for the foreign entrant.[3]

Regardless of the source of the barriers, their existence means that some firm or individual will have a chance to profit from a monopolistic position. This individual is sometimes referred to as a **gatekeeper,** since he or she holds the keys to the market. For example, where regulations prohibit foreign ownership of broadcast media, domestic cable companies can keep prices high and service levels low. Where a domestic company has built a viable defense for its products with a strong brand image, it can collect "rent" by charging premium prices. Where close ties in distribution channels are necessary, natives with good contacts garner considerable fees by simply arranging a meeting between two prospective partners. The cost of doing business is very high in some countries because of such barriers.

The Importer's View

This discussion suggests that an importer in a country will support the existence of barriers since barriers can give the importer a protected market position, especially when combined with exclusive distribution contracts. This has in fact happened in some countries with high trade barriers. In many Asian and European countries, for example, the possession of the exclusive rights to represent a particular global brand—such as Dunlop in golf clubs, Blaupunkt in car radios, and Canon in cameras—when coupled with restricted entry has been a virtual license to raise prices. As countries lower their tariff and non-tariff import barriers, exclusivity means less since unauthorized gray trade distributors can import the products as well. Prices come down.

But import barriers are not simply a boon for authorized importers. When trade barriers are high, the supplier company may opt to invest in production within the country, eliminating the need for an importer. Also, high barriers have to be paid for by all importers, and the importer may not always be able to pass the extra costs on to the consumer. In the end, according to their own testimony, a lot of importers would be happy to compete without the help of the government.

Tariff and Nontariff Barriers

The firm on its own or through its trade association or local chamber of commerce can attempt to lobby its own or the host government for a reduction in tariffs and nontariff barriers. Examples abound. American companies demand that the U.S. trade representative pressure Japan to open its markets. The European companies appeal to the GATT/WTO to help reduce tariffs on steel from the EU into the United States. The automobile quotas on foreign cars in Italy are under pressure from the EU Commission. These negotiations are sometimes emotional and clouded by national pride, and are always difficult.

The firm should analyze the tariff base carefully to identify how the tariff rate is calculated.[4] Most often the tariffs are higher for a complete assembly, lower for parts and components. In the early 1980s when the United States raised the tariff rate for imported trucks to 25 percent, Nissan shipped every truck in two parts, the body and the flatbed, which could be assembled in a one-step operation. In this way the trucks entered as unfinished goods, with a lower tariff rate of 2.5 percent. Such "screwdriver assembly plants" exist in various parts of the world precisely as a way of avoiding high tariffs, but governments are also learning to write more stringent classification codes for the imported parts to capture more of the rent or profit generated.

It is common to lower or even waive a tariff when the imported product or component has a certain level of "local content" or when imports involve production for reexport. The foreign entrant has an incentive, therefore, to add parts and labor from the foreign market. When such parts are not available, it is not uncommon for the entrant to help establish a supplier of the parts in the country so as to obtain the lower tariff rate. This is an example of how tariff barriers can lead to foreign investment in plants.

In general, trade barriers will lead the foreign entrant to reexamine the firm's existing integration of activities in its value chain, from supplies to final sale. It becomes important to identify if some activities in the chain need to be broken out and to internalize only those activities that cannot be done better elsewhere. For example, when

Volkswagen entered Japan, the difficulty and expense of establishing its own dealer network made the company decide to contract with a competitor, Nissan, to distribute Volkswagens in Japan. Thus, even though the barriers represent imperfections in the market, skillful management can help reduce the negative economic effects from these imperfections. As economists have shown, where trade is prohibited by tariffs, multinational production is often an efficient response, with gains for the firm and the country as well.[5]

A final tactic, increasingly employed as regional trade agreements proliferate, is to establish manufacturing in a member country in the regional trade group. Then the firm can export to the market country in the region at lower tariff rates from the transplant operation inside the region.

Government Regulations

When it comes to government regulations of business—involving questions ranging from "Who can start a business?" to "Can free product samples be sent in the mail?"—the foreign firm can do little but adapt to them. Some assistance from the home government might be available. The U.S. government's negotiation in the late 1980s of the so-called Structural Impediments Initiative (in which Japan was asked to change things like its retail store regulations) is an interesting example of intrusion into a country's domestic policies by a foreign nation.[6] The EU homogenization of a myriad of regulations is another example of how government rules are changing in the globalizing economy. In this process, a global entrant can be a catalyst.

The foreign entrant will need to study in detail the specific regulations affecting its industry and the sales of its products and services. In this process the foreign services of government offices (including the consulate abroad) and the local chambers of commerce can be of help. In other instances, the company needs to hire professional specialists who can decipher the foreign regulations. International law firms are often a good place to start.

Government regulations may be so severe and limiting that the company can do little without a native partner. As a member of a joint venture or some other collaborative alliance, the native partner can be assigned the task of carrying out negotiations with government authorities and local regulators. When Toys R Us established its operations in Japan, it selected Mr. Den Fujita, the general manager of McDonald's Japan, as its representative. The most pressing problem, getting building codes and retail regulations changed, required a strong local presence. Once in, the firm became an insider with claims on the same local protection as domestic firms.[7]

Distribution Access

In many countries it is very difficult to get members of the distribution channels to carry the firm's product. Retailers have no shelf space, they carry competing brands, and they don't trust that the new brand will sell. Wholesalers can't depend on supplies from overseas, they are not familiar with the distributor, and they need extra rebates if they are to take on a new brand. Again, tracking the new brand requires that price and packaging information be entered into the computer so that scanners will work, and so on. In many countries, including the United States, new brands need to pay a "slotting" fee—a "tip" or bribe—to get the trade interested. The difficulty of getting **access to distribution channels** means that the firm, even after successful entry, might compete with a handicap. As seen in Chapter 2, this is not an unusual situation in foreign markets (since such network ties lower transaction costs and are thus economically justified).

There is a downside to close distribution or supply ties. When the channel members or suppliers are not efficient, the ties may be more of a burden than a benefit. Thus, some smaller parts manufacturers in Japan who are suppliers for Nissan, say, lack scale economies and may not be as efficient as suppliers in South Korea, Taiwan, or even Europe and the United States, especially when the yen is very strong. In a similar vein, the vertical integration by Mercedes through its purchase of the electronic component business of AEG, one of its German suppliers, might not be very profitable if AEG quality is weak.[8] Where free market supplies are available, free competition typically ensures competitive prices and consequently lower costs.

Lack of access to distribution channels usually means that the firm has to consider a strategic alliance or even sell the product unbranded in an **OEM (original equipment manufacturing)** arrangement with a firm already established. Volkswagen distributes Toyota trucks in the EU countries. Mitsubishi cars are sold in the United States through Chrysler dealers. Taking the OEM route, Japanese Ricoh makes copiers that are then marketed in the West under the American firm Savin's brand name, although the Ricoh company has recently begun to market copiers overseas under its own name. There is also the (usually expensive) alternative of establishing a new channel. When Honda motorcycles entered the United States, the company saw fit to help train and finance new dealerships across the country.

Another access barrier is the possibility that the firm cannot hire capable local talent. Where people find working for a domestic firm preferable, either because of pay or some status-related reason, the firm may have trouble entering the market alone. This is especially striking when the market is very new to the firm, so that access to local workers is important. On the other hand, in some countries, especially developing countries, working for a foreign firm may be seen as desirable, and to that extent foreign entry is facilitated.

Natural Barriers

Competition among several differentiated brands tends to create so-called **natural barriers,** allowing strong brand names to charge a premium price over more generic or no-name competitors. This is the case in "pure domestic" markets, in which all companies compete on an equal footing (hence "natural").

Market success and customer allegiance are the factors behind natural barriers. When customer satisfaction and brand loyalty are high, or country-of-origin biases favor a domestic brand, it may be difficult to break in. Further, if advertising expenditures are large and price promotion common—typical of North American markets—the prospective entrant has to offer something special and match promotional spending. This is where firm-specific advantages are important. Natural barriers depend as much on subjective consumer perceptions as on real differences between products. Thus, it may not be sufficient to have a "superior product" in terms of objective tests. The marketing effort in the new country has to convey the superiority effectively.

Advanced versus Developing Nations

In developing countries, the important barriers are usually tariffs and other government interventions into the free market system. If the firm is able to invest in product assembly in order to get under the tariff barrier, the markets are generally less competitive and a strong position can often be gained at relatively low cost. Pepsi gained entrance to the former Soviet Union with the help of President Nixon and dominated the Russian market for colas until the fall of the Berlin Wall.

By contrast, in advanced countries it is usually natural barriers that are high. Here entry may be easier, but it is difficult to establish a strong and defensible position. This is important to remember when evaluating the firm's strategy for learning and gaining expertise in global markets. Advanced countries with open markets are a learning ground for marketing strategy and tactics. Developing countries with their tariff and nontariff barriers and myriad government regulations produce subsidiary managers with savvy about negotiations with foreign governments.

When gains have been easy because the company was one of the first foreign entrants and local protection was forthcoming, the firm may have learned less and developed less capability for more open markets. To achieve success in fiercely competitive open markets, firms have to acquire marketing skills and flexibility. In highly protected markets what matters most is skill in negotiating with government officials and powerful bureaucrats. Despite Pepsi's marketing skill elsewhere, its management in Russia seems to have been taken by surprise by Coca-Cola's entry after the Berlin Wall fell.[9]

Exit Barriers

The firm usually faces **exit barriers** after entry—nonrecoverable investments have been made, people hired, contracts signed—and if there is likelihood of a forced exit, a firm will be reluctant to commit. Another consideration for the marketer is the potential loss of goodwill accompanying withdrawal from an important and visible market. The French automaker Peugeot probably lost a great deal of brand equity (and money) in the U.S. market before finally exiting in 1992.

When future exit is a distinct possibility because of uncertainties, an otherwise attractive foreign market can be entered by choosing a less visible and less committed mode of entry, such as OEM (original equipment manufacturing) or licensing. If a global brand name might be hurt by withdrawal, the company could conceivably market the product under another name. With the advent of global markets, however, companies are less willing to forgo the advantages of leveraging a global brand name. In the era of global marketing, the company needs sufficient resources and capability to nurture and sustain its products and brands, thus surmounting exit barriers by never having to face them.

Effect on Entry Mode

In sum, barriers to entering a foreign market make entry mode decisions more complex than just the arithmetic of a simple geographical expansion.

The company can expand into some markets only by *unbundling* its know-how. That is, even though the company may want to be a player in final product markets everywhere, in country markets where government regulations or the company's lack of market knowledge would force the use of joint ventures, the company might opt only to *sell components*, so as not to give up crucial know-how. An obvious instance is China's insistence that foreign auto manufacturers entering the Chinese market team up with a Chinese joint venture partner. "Unbundling" is one of the possible outcomes of negotiations by potential foreign entrants into China's auto industry.

Where local-content requirements are high, the company may contract with a local producer to manufacture simpler versions of the products. Toshiba television sets are assembled in the Czech Republic in a plant built by Toshiba but operated by local Czechs, with Toshiba's reward being a royalty on the sales.

In other markets where distribution is complex or customer requirements idiosyncratic, the company might opt to engage in a *distribution alliance with a competitor.* Japan's Ricoh produced the equipment and let the Savin company sell the copiers in the United States in order to gain quick market penetration. The global expansion path is often more complex than simply a question of where the firm's final products will be sold.

Many companies develop managerial expertise with a particular mode of entry, and this entry mode becomes the preferred mode of expansion. Some Western multinationals have long preferred wholly owned subsidiaries, run by a home country expatriate. This mode has been sustained even when the cost of financial exposure and the growth of local management expertise weakened the rationale for it. Companies such as Union Carbide, IBM, Honeywell, Philips, and the American auto companies fall into this category. Other companies, such as small technology-based entrepreneurs, will often expand through licensing or joint ventures. The reason for one sustained company policy or another is usually that management feels more comfortable with it, having developed skills dealing with that form of overseas involvement.

Each mode of foreign entry involves quite different managerial skills. Overseeing a number of licensees in various countries is one thing, running a network of wholly owned subsidiaries quite another. Direct exporting involves learning about overseas transportation, international trade credit, tariff barriers, and so on, quite an investment for the beginner. The growth of various forms of cross-border strategic alliances in the recent past has been accompanied by the emergence of a cadre of international contract lawyers and managers skilled in international negotiations. The start-up costs of learning to manage any one of these modes of entry are considerable, and it is not surprising that companies tend to leverage their particular skills by staying with the same approach.

Consequently, even though the firm's value chain may be broken up to get under a certain country's barriers or in accordance with government regulations, its expansion path will be likely to follow the same mode of entry everywhere. Xerox and 3M are good at running international joint ventures, IBM and Ford like wholly owned subsidiaries, and Benetton and McDonald's prefer franchising. Staying with the "tried and true" leverages the company's expertise, minimizes the obstacles to entering, and maximizes the chances of success. When these companies have used another mode of entry, chances are they were forced to do so by government regulation or some other market access barrier.

THE EXPORTING OPTION

For the newcomer to the international scene, the exporting option is often the most attractive mode of foreign entry. Then, sometimes it is just through the experience of exporting that the idea of a full-fledged market entry is developed. At any rate, when unsolicited orders have started flowing in from abroad, the firm begins to pay more attention to the potential in foreign markets, and exporting becomes the natural first step.

Indirect Exporting

The simplest way to manage the firm's export business is to employ outside specialists. The firm may hire a **trading company,** which becomes the "export department" for the producer (see box, "Japan's Giant Traders").

In the United States the arrangement whereby an **export management company (EMC)** performs all the transactions relating to foreign trade for the firm has a similar character. EMCs are independent agents working for the firm in overseas markets, going to fairs, contacting distributors, organizing service, and so on. They serve basically as an external "export department" for the firm, an example of value chain deconstruction. This type of "indirect" exporting has its great advantage in the fact that the firm avoids the overhead costs and administrative burden involved in managing its own export affairs. On the other hand, there is the disadvantage that the skills and know-how developed through experiences abroad are accumulated outside the firm, not in it.

In most cases, the domestic firm wants to make only a limited commitment to its facilitating agencies, keeping open the option of taking full responsibility for its exporting at a later date. This is one reason why EMCs lead rather precarious lives. If they are too successful, the producer may decide to break the contract and internalize the exporting function.

Direct Exporting

Direct exporting has the advantage over indirect exporting in the control of operations it affords the producer. Going through an intermediary trading company, the firm may not even know in which country the product is sold. With direct exporting the firm is

GETTING THE *Picture*

Japan's Giant Traders

ALTHOUGH TOYOTA may employ more people, the biggest companies in Japan in terms of total turnover are traditionally the giant trading companies. The big traders finance salmon fishing in Alaska and sell the fish in Hong Kong, they ship iron ore from Australia to Japan and steel from Korea to Indonesia, and they ship cars to Europe and bring beer back to Japan. They are active in oil exploration, build paper mills in Peru and chemical plants in China, and organize international consortia for the exploration of minerals in New Guinea. Their take is usually a small commission or fee on the transactions created, but they also speculate in the spot market for various commodities, sometimes winning and sometimes losing. Their global information network is the envy of any spy ring, and they announced the Iranian revolution before the CIA learned about it. The largest trading companies and their sales in the Japanese heydays of 1990 are shown in the table below.

These traders are able to help many companies enter foreign markets. Thus, Marubeni was active in assisting Nissan in its initial stage in the United States, and in Algeria, Toyota trucks are still sold by a trading company.

Name	Sales (billion yen)	Employees
Itohchu	14,762	7447
Mitsui Bussan	14,179	8882
Marubeni	13,246	7418
Sumitomo Trading	13,077	6366
Mitsubishi Corp.	12,660	8552

Sources: Eli, 1991; Emmott, 1992.

http://www.itohchu.com/main/
http://www.mitsui.com/menu.htm
http://marubeni.co.jp/
http://www.sumitomocorp.co.jp/
http://www.Mitsubishi-Motors.co.jp

able to more directly influence the marketing effort in the foreign market. The firm also learns how to operate abroad. Without involvement in the day-to-day operations of overseas affairs, the firm will not generate much in-house knowledge. It is not until the firm decides to hire its own staff that a more strategic involvement in foreign markets becomes feasible.

For the direct exporter, the principal choice is between establishing a sales subsidiary or employing independent middlemen. The latter option involves an *agent* to manage sales and administration paid through fees and commissions and a *local distributor* who supplies the product to the trade and adds a markup to the cost. The choice between a sales subsidiary and independent middlemen depends on the degree to which control of the marketing effort in the country is desired and the resources the firm can muster. To strike the optimal balance, the volume of operations (current and anticipated), the firm's willingness to take risks, and the availability of suitable local distributors are critical determinants. Investing in a wholly owned sales subsidiary is a bigger commitment and requires more resources than the use of independent people. But where the market is potentially large, the firm would generally be better off with more central control of operations and, in particular, the marketing effort.

The Exporting Job

There are many separate functions to be taken care of in direct exporting. The major tasks are listed in Exhibit 5.2. The exhibit and the discussion to follow cover only the major tasks. Some of them, such as those relating to legal issues, are only marginally related to marketing, while others, such as after-sales support, directly relate to customer acceptance. Many of the functions can be handled by independent specialists who can be found through Department of Commerce contacts, at industry fairs and

EXHIBIT 5.2 Direct Exporting Functions

Product shipment	*Getting paid*
1. Transportation to the border	1. Checking creditworthiness
2. Clearing through customs	2. Getting paid in local currency
3. Warehousing	3. Hedging against currency losses
Export pricing	4. Converting funds to home currency
1. Price quotes	5. Repatriating the funds
2. Trade credit	*Legal issues*
3. Price escalation	1. Export license
4. Dumping	2. Hiring an agent
Local distribution	3. Transfer of title/ownership
1. Finding a distributor	4. Insurance
2. Screening distributors	*After-sales support*
3. Personal visit	1. Service
4. Negotiating a contract	2. Parts and supplies
Source: Adapted from Root, 1987, p. 6.	3. Training of locals
	4. Creating a sales subsidiary

conventions, through the local telephone directories, or by contacting the Consulate. Associated with these tasks are numbers of different documents needed for exporting. Exhibit 5.3 gives a list of the principal ones. They will also be discussed below.

Product Shipment

TRANSPORTATION   The shipment of the product to the border of the country is usually handled by an independent freight forwarder in combination with a shipping agency. In the typical case, freight forwarders who might specialize in certain types of products or countries pick up the product at the factory, transport it to the embarkation point, and load it onto the transnational carrier. Federal Express and DHL serve as freight forwarders in the case of express mail, and they usually own their own transportation fleets (although some shipments, such as air transport to Africa, might go by a regular airline).

CLEARING THROUGH CUSTOMS   Unloaded at the national border, the product will go from the ship or airline to a customs-free depot before being processed through customs. This depot can be a large free-trade zone, such as the one outside of Canton in China or in Gibraltar at the bottom of the European continent. From this free-trade area the product can be shipped to another country, never having crossed the border. In the typical case, the free-trade zones allow workers to further add value to the product. For example, along the U.S.–Mexican border, the so-called maquiladors are small factories located in the free-trade zones where Mexicans can be used to work on the products with no cross-border shipment. Thus, items can be shipped anywhere in the United States after the Mexican labor value is added, without having to cross customs lines.

The customs officials will process the goods for entry once a claimant appears. This is usually the buyer but can also be an independent importer or customs facilitator who specializes in getting the customs procedures done quickly. By presenting shipping documents—the **bill of lading**—the buyer or buyer's agent can get access to the goods after paying the assessed duty. The tariff rate is decided on by the local customs official on the spot. In some countries, this is where there is often a temptation for bribes, the buyer "inducing" the customs official to assign a lower tariff classification.

WAREHOUSING   After entering the country, the goods will often require storage, and there are usually facilities in the destination port to be rented. The price is often

A buyer from Super-Valu, the large U.S. food and grocery wholesaler, inspecting a sample of grapes from Chile before negotiating a price for the shipment. As Chile's reliability as a supplier of quality fruits has grown, the country's growers are able to claim higher prices for their produce. Courtesy SuperValu Stores, Inc.

EXHIBIT 5.3 Principal Documents Used in Exporting

Required by...	
Foreign customer	*U.S. government*
1. Pro forma invoice	1. Export declaration
2. Acceptance of purchase order	2. Export license (strategic goods and
3. Ocean (airway) bill of lading	shipments to designated unfriendly nations)
4. Certificate (or policy) of insurance	*Foreign governments*
5. Packing list	1. Certificate of origin
Exporting manufacturer	2. Customs invoice
1. Purchase order	3. Consular invoice
2. Letter of credit or draft (trade) acceptance	*Exporter's bank*
Freight forwarder	1. Exporter's draft
1. Shipper's letter of instructions	2. Commercial invoice
2. Domestic (inland) bill of lading	3. Consular invoice
3. Packing list	4. Insurance certificate
4. Commercial invoice	5. Ocean (airway) bill of lading
5. Letter of credit (original copy)	

Source: Adapted from Root, 1987, p. 71. Copyright © 1987 by Jossey-Bass, Inc., Publishers. First published by Lexington Books. All rights reserved.

quite high—as is the daily storage rental for goods waiting to be processed in the free-trade zone. Companies try to save money by getting the goods through customs quickly and warehoused at a less expensive location.

Export Pricing

PRICE QUOTES Export pricing quotes are considerably more complex than domestic quotes. The firm selling abroad would generally be in a stronger competitive position by quoting prices **c.i.f.** (cost, insurance, freight; that is, by accepting the responsibility for product cost, insurance, and freight, and factoring these items into the quote) rather than **f.o.b.** (free on board), which means that the buyer has to arrange shipping to his or her country. Quoting c.i.f. still leaves the buyer with the responsibility for checking and adding tariff charges and other duties; and if, in addition, the buyer has to arrange transportation from the seller's country, the transaction costs can be very high.

For products where value is high relative to weight and size, air transportation is often used. Computer software, for example, is sometimes shipped overseas by air, cash on delivery (c.o.d). In many cases the seller will force these shipments to be prepaid, however, especially after a few mishaps and, in particular, when the buyer is from a less developed country. In this way price quotes for overseas markets are very much tied into the question of trade credit.

TRADE CREDIT   The level of price quoted depends very much on what credit arrangements can be made. A high price can often be counterbalanced by advantageous **trade credit** terms, especially where the seller takes the responsibility for arranging the trade credit. For many foreign buyers, governments as well as companies, the actual price is of less concern than what the periodical payments will be. This has nothing to do with the specific countries but rather hinges on the magnitude of the money involved. Credit is of particular importance in exchanges that involve large items such as turbines, industrial plants, aircraft, and so on, in which no buyer can realistically be expected to pay the total bill in cash.

What makes the credit issue particularly interesting from a global marketing perspective is that in many cases the competitive advantages depend critically on this question. It is often a definite advantage for the seller to have strong support from a dominant international bank. The Japanese trading companies are provided such support through their affiliated keiretsu banks, which can also help organize financial support from related companies. If, in addition, the government in the home country can be persuaded to use its financial leverage to provide further credit, the competitiveness of the seller can be increased dramatically. For example, the Airbus sales are generally made at relatively high prices per plane but are accompanied by loans extended by the governments involved in the consortium (France and the United Kingdom). To compete against the Airbus it might be advantageous to offer good terms for credit payments in addition to lower prices. The Boeing aircraft company undertakes a heavy lobbying and advertising effort supporting the Export-Import Bank in Washington, D.C., partly because the bank helps the company offer competitive credit terms.[10]

PRICE ESCALATION   In general, prices abroad can be expected to be higher than prices at home for the simple reason that there are several cost items faced by the exporter not encountered in domestic sales. The factors relate to transportation costs, tariffs and other duties, special taxes, and exchange rate fluctuations. The resulting increase in price overseas is commonly called **price escalation.** An example of how this works is presented in Exhibit 5.4. As can be seen, there are several added cost items incurred when selling overseas. Shipping costs are only part of the problem: Added are applicable tariffs and customs duty, insurance, and value-added taxes. Also, the fact that several middlemen (importer to take the goods through customs, freight forwarder to handle the shipping documents, dock workers) are involved in the channel adds to the costs and cuts into the profit margin unless prices are raised.

The escalation of price means not only that prices become higher than intended but also that it is more difficult to anticipate what the final price in the market will be. The methods used to cope with the problems are several. Companies attempt to redesign the product so as to fit it into a lower tariff category, sometimes by shifting the final stages in the assembly process abroad. For example, truck tariffs for completed assemblies are usually much higher than for semifinished autos, and the industry has responded by creating a "knockdown" (KD) assembly stage consisting essentially of putting the flatbed on the chassis, "knocking it down" into place. The same formula has been applied with success to passenger autos, so that FDI (foreign direct investment) in auto production now might simply mean a "KD plant" with perhaps 20 employees.[11]

EXHIBIT 5.4 International Price Escalation Effects (in U.S. dollars)

International marketing channel elements and cost factors	Domestic wholesale-retail channel	Export market cases			
		Case 1 (same as domestic with direct wholesale import c.i.f./tarrif)	Case 2 (same as case 1 with foreign importer added to channel)	Case 3 (same as case 2 with V.A.T. added)	Case 4 (same as case 3 with local foreign jobber added to channel)
Manufacturer's net price	$6.00	$6.00	$6.00	$6.00	$6.00
+ insurance and shipping cost (c.i.f.)	*	2.50	2.50	2.50	2.50
= *Landed cost* (c.i.f. value)	*	8.50	8.50	8.50	8.50
+ tariff (20% on c.i.f. value)	*	1.70	1.70	1.70	1.70
= *Importer's cost* (c.i.f. value + tariff)	*	10.20	10.20	10.20	10.20
+ importer's margin (25% on cost)	*	*	2.55	2.55	2.55
+ V.A.T. (16% on full cost plus margin)	*	*	*	2.04	2.04
= *Wholesaler's cost* (= importer's price)	6.00	10.20	12.75	14.79	14.79
+ wholesaler's margin (33 1/3% on cost)	2.00	3.40	4.25	4.93	4.93
+ V.A.T. (16% on margin)	*	*	*	.79	.79
= *Local foreign jobber's cost* (= wholesale price)	*	*	*	*	20.51
+ jobber's margin (33 1/3 % on cost)	*	*	*	*	6.84
+ V.A.T. (16% on margin)	*	*	*	*	1.09
= *Retailer's cost* (= wholesale or jobber price)	8.00	13.60	17.00	20.51	28.44
+ retailer's margin (50% on cost)	4.00	6.80	8.50	10.26	14.22
+ V.A.T. (16% on margin)	*	*	*	1.64	2.28
= *Retail price* (= what consumer pays)	$12.00	$20.40	$25.50	$32.42	$44.94
Percent price escalation over: Domestic		70%	113%	170%	275%
Case 1			25%	59	120
Case 2				27%	76
Case 3					39%

*Indicates "not applicable."

Source: Becker, 1990. Reprinted by permission of Butterworth-Heinemann, Ltd., and the editors.

In the end, exporters learn to live with the escalated costs and avoid more outrageous customs duties by modifying the escalated products, shipping semifinished goods, and, in general, making such moves as will allow the product to fall into a relatively moderate transport and tariff classification. Having done that, they are generally on par with other importers, if not the domestic producers; and given the existence of at least some unique FSAs they are able to avoid further costly redesigns or shifting production location.

DUMPING Even though pricing on the basis of costs alone is not recommended in theory (demand must be taken into account, for example), cost-based pricing has one strong justification: It is the pricing procedure easiest to defend against dumping charges.

Dumping is commonly defined as selling goods in some markets below cost. There are sometimes good management reasons for doing that. A typical case is an entry into a large competitive market by selling at very low prices; another case is when a company has overproduced and wants to sell the product in a market where it has no brand franchise to protect. "Reverse dumping" refers to the less common practice of selling products at home at prices below cost. This would be done in extreme cases where the share at home needs to be protected while monopolistic market positions abroad can be used to generate surplus funds ("cash cows" in foreign markets). Regardless, dumping as defined is often illegal since it is destructive of trade, and competitors can take an offender to court to settle a dumping case. The usual penalty for manufacturers whose products are found to violate the antidumping laws is a **countervailing duty,** an assessement levied on the foreign producer that brings the prices back up over production costs and also imposes a fine.

The manner in which the relevant costs are used to define dumping varies between countries, reflecting the fact that economists have difficulty agreeing on a common definition. Most countries and regional groupings have established their own particular version of antidumping regulations. Under the new WTO (World Trade Organization) trade laws, the antidumping rules that are to apply to all members are more liberal than usual, making penalties more difficult to assign. The new rules, developed with the intent to support emerging countries' exports, feature: (1) stricter definitions of injury, (2) higher minimum dumping levels needed to trigger imposition of duties, (3) more rigorous petition requirements, and (4) dumping duty exemptions for new shippers.[12]

Local Distribution

FINDING A DISTRIBUTOR   The next step is to get the product into the distribution channels. The most common approach is not to try to create new channels but to use existing ones. Although there are some instances where the creation of new channels has been instrumental in a company's success (the Italian apparel maker Benetton's franchised stores in the United States, for example, and the U.S. cosmetics firm Avon's door-to-door system in Asia), in most cases existing channels will have to do. This means identifying one or more independent **distributors** who can take on storage and transportation to wholesalers and retailers. These distributors usually take ownership of the goods, paying the producing firm, and often will handle the importing and customs process, in addition to storage and distribution in the country. Generally, the firm appoints one distributor for the whole country, with an exclusive territory. However, in large nations such as the United States overseas-based companies often have two or three distributors in various parts of the country (East Coast, Midwest, and West Coast, for example).

It is crucially important for the firm to find the best distributor available. According to one report, exporters find that the range of distributor performance can vary from zero to 200 percent of what is expected.[13] There are only a few excellent distributors in any one country, and the best ones are often not interested in taking on another supplier unless offered a well-known global brand.

Identifying potential distributors can be done with the assistance of governmental agencies. Many countries maintain trade facilitation agencies to assist in the search for local distributors. The U.S. Department of Commerce, for example, will assist in identifying the names and addresses of many potential distributors in various countries and industries. But more commonly, potential distributors will be found at **trade fairs** and international conventions.

SCREENING DISTRIBUTORS   Once a few select candidates have been identified, they need to be screened on key performance criteria. In many cases a late entrant to the country market might have trouble finding a good distributor, making it particularly important that the screening process does not miss some key characteristic. The criteria include the ones given in Exhibit 5.5.

Which of these criteria are judged important and which not depends on the situation and the significance the company attaches to the criteria. For example, consumer nondurables typically require little after-sales service. The financial strength of the distributor is less important if the firm can support the company in the start-up period. Distributor strength can even be a drawback when the initial arrangements are seen as temporary, to be superseded by a more permanent FDI position if the market is as large as expected.

EXHIBIT 5.5 Criteria for Choosing Distributors

Previous experience (products handled, area covered, size)
Services offered (inventory, repairs, after-sales service)
Marketing support (advertising and promotional support)
Financial strength
Relations with government
Cooperativeness
Whether or not handling competing products

Source: Adapted from Root, 1987, pp. 63–65.

PERSONAL VISITS Once some promising leads have been developed, a personal visit to the country is necessary. On the trip managers should do three things:

> Talk to the ultimate users of the equipment to find out from which distributors they prefer to buy and why. Two or three names will be likely to keep popping up.
> Visit these two or three distributors and see which ones you would be able to sign up.
> Before making the final choice, look for the distributor who has the key person for your line. This is a person who is willing to become the champion for your new product. Experience has shown that the successful distributor is the one who has one person in the organization willing to take the new line to heart and treat it as his or her own baby.[14]

NEGOTIATING A CONTRACT The contract has to be very specific regarding the rights and obligations of the manufacturer and the distributor, the length of the contract, and conditions for its renegotiation. A checklist is given in Exhibit 5.6. The conditions under which competitive product lines might be added and the degree of exclusivity that the distributor is granted figure prominently among the rights and obligations. Although local regulations and the letter of the law naturally must be followed, the usual situation is one in which the actual formulation of these contracts hinges directly on the size and strength of the two parties.

In Western countries these negotiations tend to be rather open and confrontational so that all key points get hammered out fast, while in Eastern and other nations negotiations can be protracted, indirect, and often quite trying on Westerners' patience. Regardless, the spirit of the contract should be reflected in the subsequent actions of both the manufacturer and the distributor. Where it is not, neither of the parties will be happy. The relationship between the two should not be a zero-sum game but a win-win proposition. (See the discussion of negotiations in Chapter 6.)

Getting Paid

LOCAL CURRENCY Getting paid can be a headache, especially if the country imposes convertibility restrictions. Today in China, India, Russia, Mexico, and other countries, it is very difficult to get access to hard currencies like dollars, yen, or D-marks. The local currency is either very weak (Mexico) or not easily convertible (China, India). And despite heroic efforts to participate in global capital markets, many former communist countries (Russia, Bulgaria) still have trouble paying for their imports in hard currency.

CREDITWORTHINESS In most countries, checking on the creditworthiness of the buyer can usually be done through banking connections. Regardless, many exporters

EXHIBIT 5.6 Master Foreign Distributorship Agreement Checklist

Appointment	*Confidential information*
Appointment	*Sales literature*
Acceptance	Advertising literature
Territory-products	Quantities
Sales activities	Mailing lists
Advertising (optional)	*Trademarks and copyrights*
Initial purchases (optional)	*Subdistributors*
Minimum purchases (optional)	*No warranty against infringement*
Sales increases (optional)	*No consequential damages-indemnity*
Orders	*Product warranty*
Distributor resale prices	*Relationship between parties*
Direct shipment to customers	*Effective date and duration*
Product specialists (optional)	Effective date and term
Installation and service	Early termination
Distributor facilities (optional)	Breach
Visits to distributor premeises	Insolvency
Reports	Prospective breach
Financial condition	Change in ownership or management
Business structure	Foreign protective act
Competing products	*Rights and obligations upon termination*
List prices	No liability for principal
Prices	Return of promotional materials
Taxes	Repurchase of stock
Acceptance of orders and shipment	Accured rights and obligations
Acceptance	*Noncompetition*
Inconsistent terms in distributor's order	*No assignment*
Shipments	*Government regulation*
No violation of U.S. laws	Foreign law
Passage of title	U.S. law
Defects, claims	Foreign Corrupt Practices Act
Returns	*Force majeure*
Payments	*Separability*
Terms	*Waiver*
Letter of credit	*Notices*
Deposits	Written notice
Payments in dollars	Oral notice
No deduction by distributor	*Arbitration*
Set-off by principal	ICC rules
Security interest	Jurisdiction
	Article titles
	Entire agreement and modifications
	Entire agreement
	Modifications.

Source: Adapted from Hall, 1983, pp. 65–66. Courtesy of Unz & Co.

avoid relying on credit, not shipping goods until an intermediate bank, preferably in the seller's country, guarantees payment.

LETTER OF CREDIT   Payment in advance is traditionally done via some form of **letter of credit.** This is arranged for by the buyer. Exhibit 5.7 shows the linkages involved. As can be seen, once the buyer approaches the local bank, opening a credit line, this bank will contact its corresponding bank in the selling firm's country. This latter bank will inform the seller that a letter of credit has been issued, assuring the seller that payment will be made. Once the seller ships the goods, the bill of lading can be presented to the bank, which will contact the overseas bank in the buyer's country and pay the seller. This transaction usually takes place before the goods have reached the buyer's country. Once they arrive, the buyer can claim the goods at customs against the bill of lading sent by the bank.

EXHIBIT 5.7 Letter of Credit Model

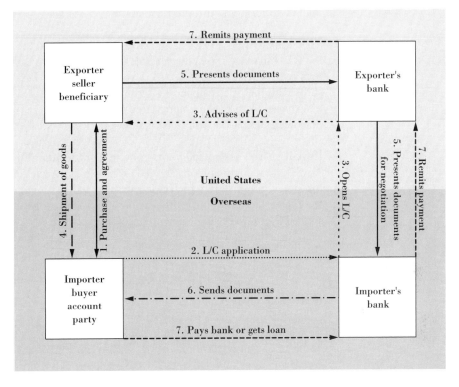

CONVERTING FUNDS   Because letters of credit involve several intermediaries and a fair amount of administrative work, the fees tend to be high. Importing companies try to reduce costs by negotiating standing letters of credit, amounting to an international credit line. In other cases, the buyer will try to induce the seller to simply accept payment within 30 or 90 days of delivery, similar to typical domestic arrangements. As international financial markets and banking institutions become further integrated, conversion to home currency and payment are likely to become less of a problem.

REPATRIATION, HEDGING   The problem of repatriating funds from a weak currency country has made financial intermediaries develop so-called swaps, through which the funds will be exchanged (at a discount) against funds elsewhere. There are also, of course, various ways of hedging against shifts in exchange rates, and many importing firms use futures options to purchase funds in a currency they know will have to be used in the future.

For the marketer, it becomes important to stay close to the financial managers in the company and make sure they are consulted before an order from a new country is accepted. Standard sales techniques—such as offering delayed payments, installment pay schedules, or no-money-down credit sales—might have to be forgone in favor of more prudent pricing schemes.

Legal Issues

EXPORT LICENSE   Many products require an **export license**—usually issued by the Department of Commerce—to be shipped out of a country. In the Cold War era, many computers and other electronics products could not be exported from the United States: Exporters could not get an export license. The issue of national security concerns was used to block many exports on the grounds that the Russians might get hold of technology with military value. Even today, when many license requirements have been voided or are approved liberally, there is often a need to get a pro forma license.

In the importing country, especially where currency restrictions are in place, import licenses are needed for many foreign products. The local Department of Commerce office will offer help on the license matter.

TRANSFERRING TITLE   The **title** or ownership to the exported goods generally follows the bill of lading. Whoever holds the bill of lading has access to the goods. The business risk—and thus exposure to normal loss, such as lack of sales in the marketplace—shifts with the title. The local distributor who borrows money to pay for the goods will be exposed to risk at the point when the bill of lading is accepted by the seller's bank—or, sometimes, as the seller's bank delivers the bill of lading to the buyer's bank.

INSURANCE   If damage to the goods occurs during transit, **insurance** questions arise. As we have seen, the recommended procedure is for the seller to quote a price c.i.f. (cost, insurance, freight), in which case the seller will arrange for insurance and shipment to the border. This simplifies the whole exporting process but also makes the seller responsible for following up with insurance claims. Alternatively, the seller can quote f.o.b. (free on board), in which case the buyer is straddled with the need to arrange for shipment and insurance. Good marketing thinking suggests that the company should quote its prices at the higher c.i.f. rate and not bother the buyer with extra work.

HIRING AN AGENT   The seller needs to pay attention to legal matters in the market country. Product liability and warranty issues can become a problem, after-sales service responsibility questions may come up, conflicts with distributors about contracted quotas and sales efforts may arise, and so on. Since most countries do not allow foreigners to work on legal questions, a company representative, an **agent,** is needed.

The agent will be the legal representative of the firm (the principal) in the local market, usually working for a retainer fee and a contract that provides hourly compensation on special cases. Exhibit 5.8 offers a checklist of things to consider when hiring an agent. Where their responsibilities involve some sales activities—such as, for example, visiting distribution outlets to monitor in-store support—agents can also be remunerated via a commission percentage of revenues. Many agents work for more than one principal, but not for competing firms. Agents can be found through the same sources as distributors.

After-Sales Support

SERVICE, PARTS SUPPLY, TRAINING   In order to support the local marketing effort, the firm needs to establish after-sales service, stock spare parts and supplies, and train local staff. These tasks are often managed by the distributor, aided by the agent. The contract specifying the responsibilities of the distributor (see Exhibit 5.6) should make clear what marketing role he or she should play, and the agent is expected to enforce the contract.

As the firm's sales in a country grow larger, control of the local marketing effort becomes a very important issue. Not only does after-sales support need to be monitored more closely, but the whole marketing program (pricing, product line offered, promotion, and channel management) might need more effective supervision. A single agent and one or two independent distributors can't usually be counted on for that kind of marketing support.

SALES SUBSIDIARY   This is when the company often decides to establish a sales subsidiary, staffed with locals and a few top managers from headquarters.

Such a sales subsidiary will run the local marketing effort, conducting market research, dealing with local advertising agencies, monitoring distributors' performance, providing information on competitors, on market demand, and on growth, and generally managing the local marketing mix—sometimes going against top management's recommendations and shared wisdom. More on this will be discussed in Part Three, "Local Marketing Abroad."

EXHIBIT 5.8 Master Foreign Agency Appointment Checklist

Appointment	*Product warranty*
Territory-products	*Effective date and duration*
Sales activities	*Effective date and term*
Promotional efforts	Breach
Introductions (optional)	Insolvency
Prices	Prospective breach
Acceptance	Change in ownership or management
Agent representations	Foreign Protective Act
Minimum orders (optional)	*Rights and obligations upon termination*
Increase in orders (optional)	No liability of principal
Agent facilities	Return of promotional materials
Competitive products	Repurchase of stock
Confidential information	Accrued rights and obligations
Reports	*Indemnity*
Operations report	*No assignment*
Credit information	*Government regulation*
Visits to agent premises by representatives	Foreign law
of principal	U.S. law
Sales literature	Foreign Corrupt Practices Act
Trademarks and copyright	*Force majeure*
Acceptances of orders and shipments	*Separability*
Acceptance	*Waiver*
No violation of U.S. laws	*Notices*
Commissions	Written notice
Commission percentage	Oral notices
Accrual	*Governing law*
Refund	*Arbitration*
Discontinuation of products	*Article titles*
Repair and rework	*Entire agreement and modifications*
Relationship between parties	Entire agreement
Subagent	Modifications
No warranty against infringement	

Source: Adapted from Hall, 1983, pp. 67–68. Courtesy of Unz & Co.

CULTURAL DISTANCE AND LEARNING

The many new tasks and foreign ways of doing business facing the beginning exporter are daunting. Understanding what has to be done is one thing: Being able to execute is another. Not surprisingly, many companies begin exporting tentatively, try to learn "on the job," and commit resources only gradually. Research has shown that "going global" for many companies simply means expanding into a few culturally similar countries. Although from a pure marketing viewpoint such a myopic focus seems counterproductive—first-mover advantages are potentially lost, for example—when the analysis is broadened to include managerial learning and organizational capabilities, the incrementalism seems more justified. Companies often can't market what they *should* market, but only what they *can* market.

The "Cultural Distance" Effect

There is a basic rule of thumb for firms when they first expand abroad. Companies find it natural to look for countries abroad where their experiences in the home market would be most useful, where the intercultural synergy would be maximized. This "reasoning by analogy" leads to selecting countries with conditions similar to those in the home market. Most of the **export expansion paths** followed by firms begin in countries "psychologically" or "culturally" similar to their own or to countries they already export to.[15] Geographical proximity plays a role but is only one part of the broader no-

Vota I "campioni d'inverno" e vinci l'estate! Courtesy Robert Bosch GMBH. "Vote for the 'Champions of Winter' and Win the Summer." Using a culturally adapted ad, the German company, Bosch, features its automobile parts product line in a contest to predict the winner of the Italian premier soccer league."

tion of "cultural distance" at the heart of expansion by gradually internationalizing (remember the Hofstede graphs in Chapter 3).

The **cultural distance** effect works so as to create very natural "biases," which are not necessarily counterproductive since they are often supported by the success of the actual entry. Factors that make for cultural proximity also make previous experience relevant, and if the company is successful in one country, it might profit nicely from doing the same thing in another similar country. In general, however, the blind acceptance of the easy cultural distance path leads to a superficial analysis of possibly very real differences among the countries and also to a predictability of company action that can be a disadvantage from a competitive standpoint.

There are numerous examples of the cultural distance effect at work. The United States and Canada are each other's most important trading partners, and many small businesses in Wisconsin, for example, trade more with Canadian businesses than with California or the East Coast. Japan's exporting companies generally started trade with the Southeast Asian countries before moving on to Latin America and Australia. Most European companies export first to their immediate neighbors, an old habit much encouraged by the establishment of EU ties.

The International Learning Curve

The cultural distance path can be justified not only on the basis that it seems to achieve a maximal capitalization on previous experience. It also allows the gradual accumulation of know-how about how to do business abroad, like following a **learning curve** that gradually increases the productivity of the managers involved. At least in the initial stages of expansion, this learning effect is a common rationale for choosing countries to enter.

Theoretically, the reason behind the pattern is mainly a desire to limit **transaction costs.** Going far away from home—in terms of geography, culture, or economic development—increases transfer costs for products and people and reduces the chances that the home market skills will be useful. However, gradually entering more countries in an expanding circle away from the home market, the company learns to do business globally, understands how to analyze foreign environments, and gains capability and a widened repertoire. In short, the firm develops new resources. Naturally, foreign market potential also matters, but in the beginning even a great potential in a psychically distant market may not be exploited because of the additional transaction costs.[16] As experience is gained, the possibilities open up, and the firm goes global.

The learning curve is also at work when the experienced international marketer eyes new and important country markets, such as the American market. For most European and other firms, entry into the U.S. market represents the capstone of success. Traditionally, the U.S. market for many products has been the biggest, most competitive, and most difficult to penetrate. Consequently, much preparation generally goes into entering it and much care is exercised in developing the appropriate strategy and tactics. As part of the preparation, companies attempt to develop skills and savoir faire by entering markets with characteristics similar to those of the U.S. market. European firms enter the U.S. market via Canada, allowing time to elapse before crossing the border. As described more fully in Case 1.1, the Swedish furniture retailer IKEA entered the European markets, established a strong position there, and waited until its Canadian operations were fully mature before entering the United States. The size and competitiveness of the U.S. market make it the "Mount Everest" of consumer markets, according to IKEA representatives.[17]

Learning periods are routinely incorporated into the expansion paths of Japanese firms (even though there are exceptions) Japanese companies tend to enter Southeast Asian markets following the minimum cultural distance path first and then, looking for diversification, enter Latin American markets (focusing on the Japanese expatriate markets). As skills and confidence grow, the companies eye the U.S. market with its great potential. Before entering it (or the European market), however, many Japanese companies will enter the Australian market to make sure they will be able to sustain penetration in a country with similar characteristics. Only with sufficient success and learning in the Australian market will they attempt to enter the U.S. market.[18]

EXPORT EXPANSION STRATEGY

After building up experience and confidence, internationalizing companies start considering a more orderly and strategic export expansion. When companies find that over 10 percent of their revenues comes from overseas markets, management starts paying more attention to overseas potential.[19] Then an export expansion strategy seems needed to manage the increasing dependence on overseas markets.

Waterfall versus Sprinkler Strategies

The export expansion path of companies typically follows one of two alternative strategies. Under the "waterfall" scenario, the firm gradually moves into overseas markets, while in the "sprinkler" mode the company tries to enter several country markets simultaneously or within a limited period of time.[20]

WATERFALL   Traditionally, the **waterfall strategy** was the preferred choice. It goes well with the cultural distance and learning patterns discussed already and also helps explain the international product cycle (IPC) process discussed in Chapter 2. After success in the home market, the company gradually moves out to culturally close country markets, then to other mature and high-growth markets, and finally to less developed country markets. This is the pattern followed by many well-known companies including Matsushita, BMW, and General Electric.

The advantage of the waterfall strategy is that the expansion can take place in an orderly manner and the same managers can be used for different countries, which helps to capitalize on skills developed. For the same reasons it is also a relatively less demanding strategy in terms of resource requirements. This is why it still is the most common approach also for newer companies such as Dell, Benetton, and the Body Shop—and as we saw in Chapter 4, also for Microlog, the fledgling voice communications company. But in fast-moving markets the waterfall strategy may be too slow.

SPRINKLER   Compared with the waterfall, the **sprinkler strategy** has the opposite strengths and disadvantages. It is a much quicker way to penetrate markets across the globe, it generates first-mover advantage, and it preempts competitive countermoves by sheer speed. The sprinkler strategy is a response to the new hypercompetition and competing on time discussed in Chapter 2. The drawback is the amount of managerial, financial, and other resources required, and the risk potential of major commitments without proper country knowledge or research.

Examples of the sprinkler approach are becoming more frequent as the competitive climate heats up and as global communications such as the Internet make access to country markets easier. The typical cases involve new-product launches by companies with established global presence such as Sony (the handheld camcorder, for example, and the Walkman), Microsoft (Windows 95 and 98), and Gillette (the Sensor, for example).

But the sprinkler strategy is also used by expanding companies to establish a global presence. For example, America Online, the Internet access provider, is launching its service simultaneously in countries in Europe, Asia, and Latin America. Catalog-based retailers such as Lands' End, Eddie Bauer, and L. L. Bean have also entered a large number of foreign countries within a limited time period. Telecommunications companies have also followed the sprinkler strategy, although partly by necessity: Not many country markets were open to foreign competitors before deregulation and privatization. The fact is that with the great advances in global communications in the last decade, the sprinkler approach has become much less resource demanding, and companies can reach almost anywhere on the globe to sell their wares.

A Comparison of Two Industries

A comparison between a mature industry such as cameras and a new industry such as personal computers will help to illustrate the trade-offs involved in choosing between a sprinkler and a waterfall strategy.

Single-lens reflex cameras constitute a product category characterized by global marketing and slow growth. A new product such as Minolta's Maxxumm needs to be introduced in most major countries almost simultaneously. Competitive lead time is short, there are considerable spillover effects across countries, and there is little need for adaptation. The major strategic task is to capture first-mover advantages in the global marketplace. A rapid sprinkler-style roll-out to the various countries is clearly called for.

By contrast, the fast-growing PC hardware market is a more difficult case. Localization of supporting software packages is time-consuming, demand fluctuates wildly in response to economic shifts, and it is important to capture increasing return by establishing local monopolies with the help of installations and service support. The global market, not surprising considering these conditions, has remained fragmented, with different companies concentrating on defending their local markets. As growth slows down and markets become more stable, one would expect a shakeout and a trend toward globalized markets with major players increasingly dominant with a waterfall strategy of expansion. The successes of American PC makers in Asia and Europe signal that this development is under way.[21]

SUMMARY

In this chapter the discussion has centered on the exporting mode of entering foreign markets and the ways companies tend to expand their global market reach. Four major entry modes were identified: exporting, licensing, strategic alliances, and wholly owned subsidiary in manufacturing. The impact of entry barriers on the choice of an entry mode was discussed. Barriers restrict the company's choices and also impact the importer's position. The chapter discussed the exporting option in some detail, showing the various functional tasks (many of them new to the typical marketing manager) that will have to be carried out if direct exporting is done.

Traditional patterns followed by exporters into foreign markets reflect the cultural distance effect and the learning curve, as the company gradually develops confidence in its ability to market abroad. Today the company needs to decide whether expansion into new countries should follow a waterfall or a sprinkler strategy. For rapidly moving markets, the firm may have to go with the quicker but also riskier sprinkler approach, entering several countries simultaneously. The firm also has to decide whether it should follow a diversification strategy or a focus strategy, selecting only those countries where potential revenues are highest. Research findings have shown that the main point is to develop a clear and coherent strategy for expansion, whether the waterfall or the sprinkler, and balance diversification against focus.

KEY TERMS

agent   p. 144
bill of lading   p. 136
c.i.f.   p. 137
contract manufacturing   p. 127
countervailing duty   p. 140
cultural distance   p. 146
direct and indirect exporting   p. 126–27
distribution access   p. 131
distributors   p. 140
dumping   p. 139
entry barriers   p. 128
exit barriers   p. 133
export expansion path   p. 146
export license   p. 143

export management company (EMC)   p. 134
f.o.b.   p. 137
foreign direct investment (FDI)   p. 128
franchising   p. 127
gatekeeper   p. 129
government regulations   p. 129
insurance   p. 144
joint ventures   p. 127
learning curve   p. 146
letter-of-credit   p. 142
licensing   p. 127
modes of entry   p. 126
natural barriers   p. 132

nontariff barriers   p. 129
original equipment manufacturing (OEM)   p. 132
price escalation   p. 138
sales subsidiary   p. 128
sprinkler strategy   p. 148
strategic alliances (SAs)   p. 127
tariff barriers   p. 129
title   p. 144
trade credit   p. 138
trade fairs   p. 140
trading companies   p. 134
transaction costs   p. 147
turnkey contracts   p. 127
waterfall strategy   p. 147

DISCUSSION QUESTIONS

1. What kind of entry barriers might be faced by Amazon.com in expanding its on-line bookselling business into European, Asian, and Latin American markets?

2. What might be the *natural* entry barriers against foreign cars, if any, in the United States? In Germany? In Japan? Any natural barriers against *foreign foods* for the same countries?

3. For an industry or product of your choice, use Internet Web sites, library sources, Department of Commerce publications, and trade publications to find out when and where the major international fairs and conventions are held. Estimate how much participation would cost for a company (registration fees, booth charges, travel, food and lodging, preparation of pamphlets, etc.).

4. How does the learning involved in internationalization add a dynamic aspect to the expansion path that exploits a firm's existing FSAs?

5. Use the Internet to locate the Web site of a global company that has recently introduced a new product, brand, or model. Then assess from the information provided whether the introduction followed a *sprinkler* or a *waterfall* strategy.

NOTES

1. Adapted from Root, 1987.

2. From U.S. Department of Commerce statistics.

3. The costs of entry barriers are not an issue of free versus managed trade. All agree that barriers cost money and that consumers have to pay more for products and services. The policy difference is rather in terms of whether the added costs are worth it for the nation, since barriers protect firms and jobs, however inefficient, at least in the short run. In the longer run, the added economic benefits from lower barriers are supposed to result in new investment and new job opportunities in competitive industries. At least that is the theory. Since the foreign marketer will be confronted with sometimes hostile reactions from workers who have lost their jobs because of trade (as has happened in Eastern Europe, Russia, and elsewhere), this theory should be kept in mind. It provides some modicum of defense for global competition.

4. The departments of commerce in different countries will have the tariff schedules for many countries and be able to give advice on how to analyze them. Also, some direct experience is, as always, useful. Watching a customs official decipher the schedules to assign the correct tariff instills some sense of humility and respect for government officials.

5. Recognizing FDI and the multinational firm as an efficient response to barriers is one of the core propositions of the modern theory of the multinational; see Buckley, 1987.

6. See Czinkota and Kotabe, 1993.

7. Personal interview with Mr. Isoda of Daiwa Securities, June 5, 1993.

8. Although the close company groupings in Japan called "keiretsus" have been acclaimed as a source of their overseas success and a barrier to foreign entry, they are now also a burden as Japan's financial crisis and recession mean that inefficient partners can no longer be supported by other members.

9. See Elliott, 1995.

10. See, for example, "U.S. Says Talks," 1987.

11. The host country governments have gradually grown in sophistication and try to stem this "loophole" in the trade barriers by requiring a certain percentage of "local content" in the value of the imported product. In autos, figures around 60 to 80 percent are typical.

12. These are only the main changes. For further information, see Horlick and Shea, 1995, and Suchman and Mathews, 1995. Effective enforcement of the new rules is still in question, especially since individual countries may not agree to the binding arbitration stipulated through the new DSM (dispute resolution mechanism). See Horlick and Shea, 1995.

13. See Beeth, 1990.

14. Ibid. offers a brief but enlightening discussion of what makes for a great distributor.

15. The cultural distance and internationalization effects were first brought out by researchers at Uppsala in Sweden; see Johanson and Vahlne, 1977, 1992.

16. Anderson and Gatignon (1986) develop the application of transaction cost theory to entry mode in depth.

17. See "Ingvar Kamprad and IKEA," Harvard Business School case no. 390–132.

18. As their annual reports show, these are the typical steps taken by Japanese firms in autos, electronics, and heavy equipment.

19. The figure of 10 percent keeps coming up in many informal conversations with executives. It is of course not a hard and fast figure—overseas potential should always be considered—but it seems that at about 10 percent of revenues, overseas markets develop enough "critical mass" to demand more attention. The actual figures for most multinationals lie closer to 50 percent even though American MNCs tend to be somewhat lower because of the large home market.

20. This terminology is suggested in Riesenbeck and Freeling, 1991. Similar strategy alternatives were suggested in Piercy, 1982, and Lee, 1987.

21. See "A Success Story," 1994.

SELECTED REFERENCES

Anderson, Erin; and Hubert Gatignon. "Modes of Foreign Entry: A Transaction Cost Analysis and Propositions." *Journal of International Business Studies*, no. 3 (1986), pp. 1–26.

"A Success Story for U.S. PC Firms." *Asahi Evening News*, July 6, 1994, p. 7.

Ayal, I.; and J. Zif. "Market Expansion Strategies in Multinational Marketing," *Journal of Marketing* 43 (Spring 1979), pp. 84–94.

Becker, H. "Price Escalation in International Marketing." Reading no. 43 in Hans B. Thorelli and S. Tamer Cavusgil, eds. *International Marketing Strategy*. 3rd ed. New York: Pergamon Press, 1990, pp. 523–26.

Beeth, Gunnar. "Distributors—Finding and Keeping the Good Ones." In Thorelli and Cavusgil, 1990, pp. 487–94.

Buckley, Peter J. *The Theory of the Multinational Enterprise.* Studia Oeconomiae Negotiorum 26. Uppsala, Sweden: Acta Universitatis Upsaliensis, 1987.

Contractor, Farouk; and Peter Lorange, eds. *Cooperative Strategies in International Business.* Lexington, MA: Lexington Books, 1988.

Czinkota, Michael R.; and Jon Woronoff. *Unlocking Japan's Markets.* Chicago: Probus, 1991.

—; and Masaaki Kotabe. *The Japanese Distribution System.* Chicago: Probus, 1993.

Eli, Max. *Japan, Inc: Global Strategies of Japanese Trading Corporations.* Chicago: Probus, 1991.

Elliott, Stuart. "At Coke, a Shift to Many Voices." *New York Times*, January 20, 1995, pp. D1, D6.

Emmott, Bill. *Japan's Global Reach.* London: Century, 1992.

Hall, R. Duane. *International Trade Operations.* Jersey City: Unz and Co., 1983.

Hanssens, D. M.; and J. K. Johansson. "Synergy or Rivalry? The Japanese Automobile Companies' Export Expansion." *Journal of International Business Studies*, Spring 1990, pp. 34–45.

Horlick, Gary N.; and Eleanor C. Shea. "The World Trade Organization Antidumping Agreement." *Journal of World Trade* 29, no. 1 (February 1995), pp. 5–31.

Johanson, J.; and J. E. Vahlne. "The Internationalization Process of the Firm—A Model of Knowledge Development and Increasing Foreign Market Commitments." *Journal of International Business Studies*, Spring—Summer 1977, pp. 23–32.

——; and ——. "The Internationalization Paradigm: A Review and Assessment." *International Marketing Review*, 1992.

Lee, Chong Suk. *Export Market Expansion Strategies and Export Performance: A Study of High Technology Manufacturing Firms.* Doctoral dissertation, University of Washington, 1987.

Piercy, Nigel. "Export Strategy: Concentration on Key Markets vs. Market Spreading." *Journal of International Marketing* 1, no.1 (1982), pp. 56–67.

Porter, Michael. *The Competitive Advantage of Nations.* New York: Free Press, 1990.

Riesenbeck, Hajo; and Anthony Freeling. "How Global Are Global Brands?" *McKinsey Quarterly*, no. 4 (1991), pp. 3–18.

Root, Franklin R. *Entry Strategies for International Markets.* Rev. ed. New York: D. C. Heath, 1987.

Suchman, Peter O.; and Susan Mathews. "Mixed News for Importers." *China Business Review* 22, no. 2 (March–April 1995), pp. 31–34.

Thorelli, H. B.; and S. Tamer Cavusgil, eds. *International Marketing Strategy.* 3d ed. New York: Pergamon, 1990.

"U.S. Says Talks with Common Market over Airbus Subsidies Are Deadlocked." *The Wall Street Journal*, December 18, 1987.

Vernon, Raymond. "International Investment and International Trade in the Product Cycle." *Quarterly Journal of Economics*, May 1966.

Six

Licensing, Strategic Alliances, FDI

"Can't we be friends?"

Your takeaways from this chapter:

1. The marketer needs to be more of a facilitator and adviser when nonexporting modes of entry are used.

2. Since licensing and strategic alliances involve transfer of know-how and therefore possible FSA dilution, the global marketer needs good interpersonal skills to deal effectively with—and control—partners in foreign countries, who may be competitors in some product markets.

3. Negotiating with potential partners to establish a relationship requires sensitivity to cultural norms, but also a secure sense of one's own culture.

4. Regardless of the product mode of entry, the firm can exercise control of the marketing effort via a wholly owned sales subsidiary.

5. The optimal mode of entry involves first finding a way over entry barriers and then making trade-offs between strategic posture and the product/market situation.

EXPORTING MIGHT BE the mode of entry into foreign markets that most closely resembles market expansion at home. But it is only one mode of entry; and because of transportation costs, tariffs, and other entry barriers, companies find it necessary to contemplate using other modes. These alternatives generally involve some amount of technology transfer and know-how sharing. The three main modes are licensing, strategic alliances, and FDI (foreign direct investment) in wholly owned manufacturing subsidiaries. The global marketer needs to understand how these modes operate and how the deconstruction of the value chain affects the marketing effort. In licensing and strategic alliances there may be no need—or no role—for local presence of marketers from the company, as the partner becomes responsible for the local effort. By contrast, FDI in a manufacturing plant might lead to a marketing effort not only in the country itself but throughout a whole trade region.

Firms Partner Up to Crack Telecommunications Market

Once upon a time, *telecommunications* meant local and long-distance phone service provided by monopolies. Today, not only are there many more ways to communicate electronically, but telephone systems are opening up to competition. Old and new firms are partnering to gain a share of foreign markets.

Despite the uncertainties surrounding the peso, an important battleground is Mexico, where existing service is notoriously bad and the long-distance market is valued at $4 billion. Mexico's telephone monopoly, Telefonos de Mexico, ended on January 1, 1997, and the Mexican government granted licenses to organizations that wanted to compete for a share of the market. To receive a license, an organization had to prepare five-year plans for investment, marketing, and finance.

The first company to receive a license was a joint venture between MCI Communications (a U.S. company) and Grupo Financiero Banamex-Accival (Mexico's biggest financial group), and this venture was the first in line to negotiate with Telefonos de Mexico and start constructing a national network. With the effort expected to cost $600 million over three years, the involvement of a financial services partner in the venture makes business sense, while MCI will contribute its technical and marketing expertise. MCI's chairman, Bert C. Roberts, Jr., is undaunted by the current difficulties plaguing the Mexican economy. He observes that organizations and individuals try to cut their expenses during a recession and that MCI's marketing strategy is generally to "[capitalize] on a situation like this."

As shown with the MCI-Banamex deal, joint ventures are the norm for entering the high-stakes telecommunications marketplace. Other joint ventures seeking to operate in Mexico include one between GTE and Grupo Financiero Bancomer (Mexico's second-largest financial group) and another between AT&T and the Mexican Grupo Alfa conglomerate.

And even bigger expansion plans are possible. Three of the largest telecommunications markets (Germany, Japan, and the United States) are now basically privatized. As more countries open up, large-scale alliances are appearing, then broken up, and then reformed, as national players from Spain, Brazil, France, and elsewhere jockey for global access and cross-country economies of scale.

In the meantime, U.S. firms are not remaining idle; they are already building partnerships. French Alcatel and Deutsche Telekom have invested in U.S.-based Sprint to create a new venture. AT&T has joined alliances with other European carriers and is also considering offering service directly to continental European customers by purchasing capacity on the lines owned by their national carriers. MCI itself was bought up by much smaller Worldcom Inc. in 1997, but the new unit continues the alliance formation strategies of the old firm with a European tie-up with British Telecom. "And the show goes on . . ."

Sources: Anthony DePalma, "MCI Wins Mexican Long-Distance License," *New York Times*, September 7, 1995, p. D5; Anthony DePalma, "Telmex Gains in Attempt to Buy Cable-System Stake," *New York Times*, June 22, 1995, p. D6; "Dutch-Swiss Team Wins Czech Phone Bid," *New York Times*, June 29, 1995, p. D7; Mark Landler, "Can U.S. Companies Even Get a Bonjour?" *New York Times*, October 21, 1995, pp. D1, D7; Elizabeth Malkin, "Mexico: He Just Might Lock You In until You Do a Deal," February 26, 1996, p. 54; Seth Schiesel, "MCI-Worldcom Match: How They'll Fit, or Won't," *New York Times*, October 3, 1997, pp. C1, C6.

http://www.telmex.com.mx/

http://www.banamex.com/banca.htm

http://www.gte.com/

http://www.bancomer.com.mx

http://www.att.com

http://www.alcatel.com

http://www.dtag.de

http://www.sprint.com

http://www.mciworldcom.com

http://www.bt.com

INTRODUCTION

Exporting no doubt introduces a new and unfamiliar set of activities for the global marketer. But complicated as exporting is to manage in a practical sense because of the number of tasks and the various middlemen involved, conceptually it is a natural extension of traditional market expansion. This is not the case for the alternative modes of entry. Licensing, alliances, and FDI all involve management skills and concepts different from the standard marketing repertoire. This chapter will cover the basic new points.

Licensing used to have a bad name as an entry mode. As we saw in Chapter 2, licensing runs the risk of dissipation; that is, a firm's know-how will easily leak to its competitors. The oft-told stories about American companies such as RCA, Honeywell, and General Electric selling technology licenses inexpensively to the Japanese after World War II only to witness the later incursions of Japanese companies into Western markets have helped put licensing in a bad light. In recent years, however, as technology sharing between competitors has become commonplace, licensing is no longer the black sheep. Also, as more countries accept the new World Trade Organization (WTO) intellectual property regime, enforcing patent protection is becoming easier. Technological leaks can be prevented more effectively now that international law is enforceable; and anyway technological change is often so fast that some licenses lose their value even before the clones and "me too" copies appear.

Still, many firms prefer to invest in wholly owned manufacturing subsidiaries abroad rather than run the risk of dissipating their firm-specific advantages and not getting sufficient upfront compensation for the use of their patented know-how. In fact, the standard definition of a multinational corporation is not simply a company that sells its products in many markets but one that also has several manufacturing and assembly plants operating abroad.

The chapter starts with a description of the typical paths of internationalization, how companies traditionally shift between different modes of entry, and the increasing role of "born global" firms. The chapter then discusses the three main nonexporting modes of entry—licensing (including franchising), strategic alliances, and manufacturing subsidiaries—in more detail. A section on establishing relationships with potential partners abroad shows how culture influences negotiation strategies. The chapter ends with a sketch of the optimal entry mode under different assumptions of company strategic objectives and market maturity.

INTERNATIONALIZATION PATHS

To get a grip on how the different modes of entry relate to one another and how companies in the real world choose between them, it is useful to go through some of the more common internationalization paths. Not to be confused with *internalization* (which says that companies exploit their FSAs internally), *internationalization* refers to the process by which a company's global expansion has taken place.

Internationalization Stages

As we saw in Chapter 5, companies historically have expanded first into countries close in terms of cultural distance. Initially, countries that are culturally similar are entered, especially ones geographically close. As more know-how and skill in international affairs are accumulated—a learning curve phenomenon—management becomes more culturally experienced and more faraway markets are explored. The firms gradually enter ever more distant countries.

As several researchers have found, this gradual internationalization sequence is reflected in the mode of entry chosen. Although companies differ, the general pattern is for gradually increased commitment to foreign markets. Several stages can be identified:[1]

Stage 1. Indirect exporting, licensing.

Stage 2. Direct exporter, via independent distributor.

Stage 3. Establishing foreign sales subsidiary.

Stage 4. Local assembly.

Stage 5. Foreign production.

Several variations of these **internationalization stages** have been proposed. For example, the early use of licensing has been questioned by proponents of the "internalization" school (Chapter 2), which places more importance on preservation of the FSAs and worries about the dissipation threat in licensing. Also, in recent years, as strategic alliances have become common, companies utilize joint ventures and alliances at almost any stage in the process. In fact, the traditional notion that firms will go global gradually and stagewise has been challenged. Following the "sprinkler" strategy discussed in Chapter 5, some firms go global from the beginning. They are "born global."

Born Global

On the basis of research among newly formed high-technology start-ups, the term **born global** was apparently first coined by a McKinsey report in 1993.[2] Born global firms are firms that from the outset view the world as one market. They are typically small technology-based businesses, and their FSAs lie in new innovations and technological breakthroughs. The entrepreneurial spirit of the founder coupled with the threat of competitive imitation and alternative technologies means that rapid internationalization is necessary to capture the first-mover advantages in world markets.

Born global firms rely on networking for most of their expansion abroad. They may start as exporters, selling to customers identified and reached through alliances and network relationships. Their FSAs involve technical eminence with substantial added value and differentiated designs. Because of limited organizational and managerial resources, the born globals tend to rely on advanced communications technologies to reach their customers in different countries—fax machines, e-mail, the Internet, and EDI (electronic data interchange). The advanced communications allow the company low-cost exchange with partners and customers. In addition, substantial market data on the Internet, previously unavailable to smaller firms, facilitate their overseas penetration. In a pioneering Swedish study of smaller firms' internationalization paths, the importance of creating a strong network of communications and logistics is similarly stressed.[3]

Born globals are typically found in business-to-business markets, where targeted sales and network relationships matter a great deal. Few of the company names are household words. Biogen, a gene splicing technology company based in Massachusetts, is a reasonably well-known born global company partly because of its controversial business. And even though companies such as Computer Network Technology, Progress Software, and Auspex Systems may not register on many marketers' radar screens, there are numerous born globals. Defining born globals as companies that went overseas within one year of their start-up, one U.S. study found that 13 percent of a national sample were born globals.[4] Because of less reliance on a large home market, some foreign companies show even more impressive figures for born global firms. An innovative Australian study found that among the sample of born global Australian firms, exports accounted for 76 percent of turnover within two years of start-up.[5]

In the end, it looks like the advances in global communication have made traditional internationalization patterns simply history. Although high-technology markets differ from those in the mainstream, there are reasons to suspect that in the future many small companies will see the world as their market from the beginning, using the Internet to research foreign countries, identify distributors and potential partners on the World Wide Web, and create alliances and relationships through e-mail and voice mail.

LICENSING

Licensing refers to the offering of a firm's know-how or other intangible asset to a foreign company for a fee, royalty, and/or other type of payment. Its advantage over exporting is its avoidance of tariffs and other levies that might be assessed against an imported product. For the new exporter, it also has the advantages that the need for market research and knowledge is reduced and that, as opposed to the use of a distributor, it is often possible to induce the licensee to support the product strongly in the market. This is because in licensing, the firm in the host country gets specific know-how from the licenser and thus is able to develop some skills on its own; it does not just resell the product as the distributor does. Licensing is therefore a form of technology transfer, but this is also its greatest weakness for the licenser. Because the licensee gets access to certain firm-specific knowledge, it will share in the competitive advantage of the licenser—and can then potentially use this knowledge in further applications other than the ones specifically stated in the licensing contract.

To avoid this **dissipation** of firm-specific advantages, the licensing firm needs to handle contract negotiations with considerable skill. Exhibit 6.1 shows some of the elements of the typical licensing contract. It is important, for example, to limit the geographical area within which the licensee might sell the product so as not to engender competition with the firm's own sales in other countries (see box, "How Not to Do It").

It is also important to make sure what the conditions for terminating the contract are, what the time limit is, and how the specific know-how is to be used. Contracts identify the level and kind of marketing support the licensee is supposed to generate and the appropriate steps to be taken should this support not be forthcoming. The licenser, for its part, pledges its supply of the requisite transfer of knowledge, including managerial and technical support, patents with or without trademark, or brand name transfer.

The royalty level and payment structure vary with different forms of licensing. **Straight licensing** of a certain technology in processing, for example, tends to bring **royalties** of 5 percent of gross revenues, sometimes more (the Disney World Corpo-

EXHIBIT 6.1 Elements of a Licensing Contract

Technology package	*Compensation*
Definition/description of the licensed industrial property (patents, trademarks, know-how)	Currency of payment
	Responsibilities for payment of local taxes
Know-how to be supplied and its methods of transfer	Disclosure fee
	Running royalties
Supply of raw materials, equipment, and intermediate goods	Minimum royalties
	Lump-sum royalties
Use conditions	Technical assistance fees
Field of use of licensed technology	Sales to and/or purchases from licensee
Territorial rights for manufacture and sale	Fees for additional new products
Sublicensing rights	Grantback of product improvements by licensee
Safeguarding trade secrets	
Responsibility for defense/infringement action on patents and trademarks	Other compensation
	Other provisions
Exclusion of competitive products	Contract law to be followed
Exclusion of competitive technology	Duration and renewal of contract
Maintenance of product standards	Cancellation/termination provisions
Performance requirements	Procedures for the settlement of disputes
Rights of licensee to new products and technology	Responsibility for government approval of the license agreement
Reporting requirements	
Auditing/inspection rights of licenser	
Reporting requirements of licensee	

Source: Hall, R. Duane *International Trade Operations*. Jersey City, NJ: Unz & Co., 1983, pp. 67–8.

ration receives 7 percent from its Japanese licensee), sometimes less. Occasionally there are also payments in the form of technical assistance fees and the possibility of lump sum royalties, paid out only intermittently. Another attractive alternative is to negotiate for an equity option in the licensee's firm, which can be exercised when further in-depth penetration into the country market is desirable.

Franchising

Special interest has arisen in recent years in **franchising,** which offers certain advantages and disadvantages over straight licensing. Franchising has become particularly popular because it allows a much greater degree of control over the marketing efforts in the foreign country.

The basic "product" sold by the franchisor is a well-recognized brand name, nurtured carefully through global advertising and promotion, including sponsorship of various events. The franchisor also provides a wide range of market support services to the franchisee, in particular local advertising to sustain the brand name, for which the franchisee usually will pay a portion of the cost. Training manuals for employees, help with product lines and production scheduling, accounting manuals, and occasional assistance with financing are some of the services provided to the franchisee. In return, the local franchisee raises the necessary capital and manages the franchise, paying an initial fee and a royalty percentage on total sales to the franchisor.

In franchising, product lines and customer service are standardized, two important features from a marketing perspective. Although cultural differences might require adaptation—in Europe, McDonald's serves beer, and in Asia, rice is added to the menu—the franchising concept works precisely because of standardization of product and service. Products should be predictably the same ("too good" can be as dangerous as "too bad" since customers rely on "what to expect"). The same for service: "Personal service" in franchising should perhaps be called "impersonal service," since even the smiles are obligatory.

Original Equipment Manufacturing (OEM)

In terms of the theory of the multinational, **OEM** usually falls in the "exporting" subcategory, involving shipments of components from home to overseas. From a marketing viewpoint, however, it fits better with licensing and strategic alliances since the company brand name is suppressed, usually not the case in exporting. OEM is like selling a generic brand, letting another firm put its name on the product.

In OEM, a company enters a foreign market by selling its unbranded product or component to another company in the market country. This company then markets the final product under its own brand name. For the supplier firm, there is little or no expense in marketing its product overseas, and the buyer gets a product ready to use and to market. The supplier has to give up its own effort to market the product overseas but often tries to change its strategy later if the overseas market for its product is strong.

Some examples will illustrate the principles. Canon provides the cartridges for Hewlett-Packard's very successful laser printers and also for Kodak's copiers, both OEM arrangements. After several years of successful market development, Canon now also markets its own copiers with success. Esco, an Oregon-based heavy machinery firm, supplies parts OEM to Mitsubishi Heavy Industries, to be distributed under Mitsubishi's name as spare parts in Komatsu and Caterpillar earthmovers.

STRATEGIC ALLIANCES

An international **strategic alliance (SA)** is typically a collaborative arrangement between firms, sometimes competitors, across borders. The joint venture is today often viewed as an equity-based SA, while new forms of alliances involve non-equity-based collaboration (partnerships, agreements to share, contractual participation in projects).[6]

SAs are a new type of entry mode increasingly prevalent in the last decade. Because they often represent collaboration between potential competitors, one effect has been to weaken the tie between ownership advantages and company control. Strategic alliances are based on the sharing of vital information, assets, and technology between the partners, even though they might in the process lose their proprietary know-how. Thus, alliances tend to be akin to licensing agreements, with the exception that the royalty and fee payments to one partner are replaced by active participation in the alliance by both partners.

The Rationale for Nonequity SAs

Since nonequity strategic alliances, especially between competitors, are a relatively new form of entry mode, it is useful to explain why they have emerged now.

The economic gains from strategic alliances are usually quite tangible. A company accesses technology it otherwise would not get. Markets are reached without a long build-up of relationships in channels. Efficient manufacturing is made possible without investment in a new plant, and so on.

However, given the risks of losing control of the firm's know-how, one wonders why alternative organizational forms—joint ventures, wholly owned subsidiaries, licensing, or mergers, for example—have proved insufficient. The reasons quoted by companies include the sheer size of the financial investments required, the speed with which market presence can be established in SAs, and the lessened risk exposure.[7]

Two other factors play a role as well. One is the crumbling of the value of control itself. As we saw above, leading know-how is being diffused faster than ever: Products and manufacturing processes embodying new technology are now readily copied through widespread reverse engineering and competitive benchmarking. Companies that have presence in most leading markets will have quick access to most new technologies. Even though patents can be policed across borders, the speed with which technology ages makes leakage less of a problem.[8]

A second factor is the new urgency about competing in several country markets at once. Having a presence in leading markets is often necessary to observe customers, monitor competitors, and disturb competitors' sources of cash. Alliances allow firms to expand the use of existing managerial resources.[9]

Hence, nonequity SAs represent more of an expansion of a company's repertoire than the replacement of existing forms of business venture. The company can now do things it could not do before. SAs allow two companies to undertake missions impossible for the individual firm to undertake. Strategic alliances constitute an efficient economic response to changed conditions.

Distribution Alliances

Since their marketing implications differ considerably, we will distinguish between three types of nonequity alliances: distribution, manufacturing, and research and development (R&D).

An early and still common form of SA is the shared **distribution** network. The tie-up between Chrysler and Mitsubishi Motors to distribute cars in the United States is one example. So are Nissan's agreement to sell Volkswagens in Japan, the licensing of Molson's of Canada to brew and sell Kirin beer in North America, and the tie-up between SAS, KLM, Austrian Air, and Swiss Air to share routes in European air corridors. More recently, the STAR alliance involving United Airlines, Lufthansa, Air Canada, SAS, and Thai Airways (and now Varig Brazilian Airlines) has been created to provide global route access and seamless booking through code-sharing agreements.

Even if the scale of these alliances is "larger than ever," these types of arrangements are not new. In the traditional textbooks they fall under "piggybacking," "consortium marketing," and licensing. Their strategic rationale usually lies in improved capacity load and wider product line for one partner and in inexpensive and quick access to a market for the other. Assets are complementary, and the partners can focus on what they do best.

One drawback of these SAs is that over time the arrangement can limit growth for the partners. The partner with the established distribution network may want to ex-

*Alliances have become
common in the
international airline
industry. They allow
different national airlines
to combine routes and
share seating codes for
seamless travel around the
world—and for valuable
frequent flier miles for the
fatigued business executive.*
Courtesy Young & Rubicam
New York.

pand its product line, competing with the other partner's products. It may want to expand into other markets, shift resources from the existing markets, and thus give less support to distribution than the other partner would find acceptable. Growth will be constrained.

As for the other partner, the arrangement hinders its learning more about the market and how to market the product in the foreign country and thus creates an obstacle for further inroads. If this partner decides to develop greater penetration in the market, adding products to the line and increasing marketing support, it might be competing with the first partner's products and also tax the capacity limitations of the existing channel network. Mitsubishi's lackluster performance in the U.S. auto market is partly due to the difficulty of working through Chrysler's dealer network and the late creation of an independent dealer network. Its growth has been stymied.

Because of such limits to growth, this type of SA does not last long when market expansion is an important goal of a partner.[10] The association can be convenient and economical, however, and when there is less pressure to grow, the alliance is justified.

Manufacturing Alliances

Another early form of strategic alliance is shared **manufacturing**. In Japan, Matsushita has agreed to manufacture IBM PCs, using up excess capacity. Volvo and Renault are sharing certain body parts and components, even though their full-fledged merger was scrapped. Saab engines are now made by GM Europe in its Opel factories (an alliance emerging from GM's purchase of 50 percent of Saab stock).

It is not always easy to distinguish these arrangements from OEM and similar agreements. The difference is that OEM arrangements are simple contracts for selling unbranded components to another manufacturer. Potentially they sell the components to many customers. By contrast, the SAs illustrated here involve the brands of both manufacturers with existing capabilities in the manufacturing of the parts; the subcontracting is a special arrangement for both partners.

R&D Alliances

SAs in R&D are different from those in distribution and manufacturing. In addition to providing favorable economics, speed of access, and managerial resources, **R&D alliances** are intended to solve critical survival questions for the firm.[11] R&D tie-ups with competitors are a means of keeping pace while making sure that competitors work toward the same technological standards. In essence, the amount of funding involved in R&D leads the company to hedge its bets and try to make sure the direction of research is the same throughout the industry. The firms have confidence in their own implementation of the new technological ideas, and marketing can be the competitive edge when technology can no longer be.

This is a striking departure from past practices, at least in the West. The R&D labs of the major companies provided the basis for their competitive edge, with supersecret research patented and policed for infringements and with full-fledged new discoveries emerging unannounced. Today, the companies are eager to announce the start of their research rather than its completion, they want competitors and customers to know what they are working on, and they listen attentively for news from competing firms. When differences in standards threaten to emerge, the firms gather eagerly under the auspices of the industry association to iron them out. As one company introduces a new product based on a new technology, customers know that competitors will announce similar products within a few months. If a competitor misses a beat, it can spell disaster.[12]

Microsoft, the PC software giant, has always made a special effort to protect the integrity of its unique software. However, recently it has decided to share some technological developments with actual and potential competitors in order to induce other software writers to use the Microsoft standard. Furthermore, it is now under pressure from several industry SAs—including one (Taligent) between Apple, IBM, and Hewlett-Packard—and Microsoft has also found it necessary to license (and "improve") the new Java network software from Sun Microsystems. However, the 1998 court case pitting Microsoft against Netscape, leader in Internet access software, and other software producers shows how fragile alliances and partnerships can be when technology evolves as rapidly as in computer software.

Joint Ventures

Even though **joint ventures (JVs)** have undeniable strengths from a marketing viewpoint, many corporations have been reluctant to enter into JV agreements unless forced to by government regulations or pressure. The JV involves the transfer of capital, workforce, and usually some technology from the foreign partner to an existing local firm, whose main contribution tends to be expertise and understanding of the local market.[13]

The transfer of technology is the main problem. Since the JV implies that equity is shared among the partners, there is a decided risk that the know-how (and thus the firm's specific advantage) will become diluted by the necessary sharing of information. The point is well illustrated by the protracted negotiations that preceded the GM–Toyota JV agreement in 1982 to produce a small car for the U.S. market. The U.S. Justice Department was reluctant to approve the agreement between two of the world's largest automakers on antitrust grounds. From Toyota's perspective there was little about car manufacturing or marketing to be gained from the venture, as compared to GM's potential gains, and the company was reluctant to share its manufacturing know-how with a competitor. However, Toyota saw the agreement as defusing the concern about Japanese imports that threatened (and still threaten) to force U.S. lawmakers into a protectionist stand. Consequently, Toyota could be indifferent to the delays caused by the U.S. government. At least for some time, the political risks could be "managed" by Toyota in this manner.[14]

MANUFACTURING SUBSIDIARIES

Foreign direct investment **(FDI) in wholly owned manufacturing** subsidiaries is undertaken by the international firm for several reasons. The aims could be to acquire raw materials, to operate at lower manufacturing costs, to avoid tariff barriers and satisfy local content requirements, and/or to penetrate local markets.[15] The last rationale is of prime interest in the marketing context.

Manufacturing FDI has several advantages in market penetration. First, local production means that price escalation caused by transport costs, customs duties fees, local turnover taxes, and so on, can be nullified or drastically reduced. Availability of goods can usually be guaranteed to resellers, minimizing potential channel conflicts over allocation decisions and eliminating delays for ultimate buyers. Location of production in the market country may lead to more uniform quality, although in some cases the basis of initial reluctance to go to manufacturing abroad may well have been the risk of lowered quality.

The most striking marketing advantage of local production is usually the ability and willingness of the company to adapt products and services to the local customer requirements. Examples include U.S. automakers' production of cars for European markets and French ski manufacturer Rossignol's location of plants in the United States and Canada. In both cases there was a desire to be closer to major markets and to be able to anticipate and quickly adapt to major changes.

There are certain distinct disadvantages to FDI in manufacturing. The major one is the risk exposure that comes with a resource commitment on the scale usually required. Even joint ventures are not free from this commitment and risk since most agreements stipulate heavy costs for one partner's withdrawal. Also, since FDI generally means the company becomes a more or less full-fledged member of the local economic and social scene, the predecision information gathering and research evaluation process is extensive. Much of this research centers on assessing the "investment climate" in the foreign country, especially the political risk (see the section on political risk in Chapter 4).

There is a potential problem in overseas manufacturing when country-of-origin effects are strong, that is, for products whose quality consumers tend to judge by the "made-in" label. In such cases, as the Toyota example shows, going abroad is not usually the preferred option (see box, "Taking the Plunge").

Research shows there can be a significant effect on product and brand evaluation from a shift in manufacturing location.[16] This can work to the disadvantage of the firm establishing production in a low-wage country where workers have lower skills. In some cases, as customers realize that what they intended to buy is actually manufactured in a developing country, they reject the product.[17]

The solution adopted by companies is to shift lower-skill operations overseas, keeping more advanced operations at home. Although companies are criticized for this strategy, it is often justified not only because it protects product quality and established brand equity but also because it is a natural step in the gradual upgrading of labor skills in the low-wage countries. Finally, companies with global brands strive very hard to ensure that quality standards are met, and research suggests that a strong brand image can override any negative country-of-origin effects.[18]

G E T T I N G   T H E

Picture

Taking the Plunge

"WITH OUR FLEET of specially built ships we would rather build the cars here in Japan and export them to the United States and Europe. There is no economic reason for us to invest in an assembly plant in those countries. Now, of course, with the European trade barriers and the U.S. protectionist voices becoming louder, we may have to make some local investment and meet the local content requirements. But how will our customers react if we cannot maintain our quality level? So, we decided to start with the joint venture with GM in Fremont to see whether we could manage the work force in the United States and satisfy our quality conscious customers. Finally, I think we have succeeded."

Sources: Toyota spokesman in 1986 before Toyota started assembly plants in Derbyshire, England, and in Kentucky.
http://www.gm.com
http://www.toyota.com

Financial Analysis

The economic analysis of the investment project usually takes the form of a discounted cash flow analysis. There is no need to go into depth here concerning this application of a well-known method. The standard approach of projecting streams of costs and revenues over the planning horizon (usually the payback period or the life span of the commitment) is directly applicable, and despite the complications involved in forecasting these series in a foreign country, the principles stay the same. The forecasting techniques discussed in Chapter 4 are directly relevant here.

On the revenue side, the possibility of using the proposed manufacturing location for exports to third (and, of course, home) countries needs to be considered. In many cases the investment calculation is complicated because the host country market is only one potential area where sales might go. Also, the forecasting of cost streams should take into account the possibility of importing subassemblies from other plant locations rather than manufacturing all components from scratch. The in-depth analysis of all these factors is beyond the scope of a marketing text.

Where political risk is low enough for the FDI project to get off the ground, it is still customary to incorporate a risk premium into the hurdle rate. Since the political risk tends to vary with regime shifts, new elections, and so forth, the risk premium needs to be adjusted over time and as new capital infusions are considered. In the discounted cash flow computations, adjustments of the discount figure should be made, generally raising the figure for each successive year.

Acquisitions

Rather than establish the wholly owned subsidiary from scratch (a **greenfield investment**), the multinational firm can consider the **acquisition** of an existing company. The advantage lies in the speed of penetration: An existing company will already have a product line to be exploited, the distribution network and dealers need not be developed from scratch, and the company can simply get on with marketing its new product(s) in conjunction with the existing line. German Siemen's purchase of compatriot Nixdorf to improve penetration in the European minicomputer market is a case in point. Another example is the purchase of American Borden by Swiss Nestlé in order to expand in the U.S. dairy food market.

The disadvantages of acquisition are many, however. In a narrow sense, the existing product line and the new products to be introduced might not be compatible, and prunings and adjustments that have to be made require reeducating the sales force and distribution channels. In general, it is not so easy to find a company to acquire that fits the purposes of entry very well. In many countries the acquisition of a domestic company by a foreign firm is not looked upon favorably by the government, employees, and other groups. From a marketing viewpoint the particular advantage of acquisition lies in the market acceptance of the company's products, gaining sales as a spillover from goodwill toward the acquired company's lines. But this benefit can be gained from a joint venture, and many of the political drawbacks of acquisitions are eliminated with a joint venture.

NEGOTIATING A RELATIONSHIP

Establishing a relationship with suppliers, with distributors and other middlemen, and with potential alliance partners involves invariably some kind of face-to-face negotiations. Foreign entry via licensing or a joint venture necessarily involves finding contract partners. Local marketing puts the marketer in direct contact with channel members who need to be convinced to carry the product. Global management involves trade-offs between local subsidiaries' autonomy and headquarters' need for standardization. **Cross-cultural negotiations** are a fact of life for the global marketer.

There are several good books on cross-cultural negotiations, and these are recommended for the prospective negotiator.[19] In general, each different culture will require its own particular approach. The Hall, Hofstede, and Gannon frameworks discussed in Chapter 3 offer some preliminary insights, but in actual negotiations more detailed advice is necessary. Following are a few basic cross-cultural generalities.

Know Whom You Are Dealing With

In most negotiations, knowing something about the cultural background of the opposite partner is considered a must. It is important to know not only the nationalities involved but also the particular ethnic background. This holds for today's obvious cases in Yugoslavia, Russia, and Belgium (Flemish versus Walloons) as well as for more subtle differences between ethnic backgrounds in the United States, Nigeria (Ibos versus Hausas), and Singapore. It is important not to treat these different subcultures as parts of the larger homogeneous unit, since differences, especially in nonverbal behavior, can be striking (see box, "Different Strokes").

But it is important never to forget that beyond cultural differences, personality can dominate cultural stereotypes. Thus, there are soft-spoken Americans, emotional Japanese, calm Brazilians, and informal Germans. But such persons may also have decided to accommodate a partner's different style, as when a Russian tries to be easygoing in a negotiation with a Brazilian. The experienced negotiator can usually diagnose the case in which the deviant behavior is genuine. And remember, without genuine behavior, **trust** is difficult to establish.[20]

Know What You Are Saying

The second caution from experts is the possibility of discrepancies between what the manager thinks he or she is communicating and what is actually received by the other party. Direct and straightforward speech still leaves many things unsaid and "plain speaking" is in many cultures a typical way to hide something (one might do well recalling Othello's "honest Iago"). If something needs to be hidden, one ploy is to stress other points strongly, deflecting attention in the same way that most magicians do their tricks. This works against the typically open and direct American negotiators who may not have anything to hide, but who are nonetheless suspect because of the haste and eagerness with which they push negotiations along.

G E T T I N G   T H E

Picture

Different Strokes for Different Folks—or a Test?

THE CONDUCT at the negotiating tables varies a great deal across cultures. Where Americans want a prompt answer, Scandinavians can take their time. By contrast, Latin Americans are likely to interrupt when they understand where a speaker is going and are prone to argue a point. Japanese often close their eyes; some even actually do sleep. Arabs may leave the table because of a telephone call and simply return later. Mexicans are notorious for arriving late. Italians pay much attention to looks and how an impressive statement can be made. The French often speak among themselves when another speaker is talking. The Germans insist on starting with background information before getting to the point. Chinese are very argumentative among themselves.

However, it is important that the negotiator recognize when cultural oddities are merely guises for delaying tactics and, in fact, represent snubs. The reason is not only the personal affront but also the question of respect for the other side. In many instances there is a subtle power gambit being played, where the foreign negotiator is being tested. By indicating that one recognizes the game, and threatening to pull out, the negotiator can often put the meeting back on track.

Sources: Graham, 1983; Hall and Hall, 1990; Salacuse, 1991.

Managers need to remember that what they may think is a harmless and friendly question may not be so elsewhere. Chatting during a coffee break and asking, "Do you have children?" can in the United States sometimes lead to a protracted explanation of a person's legal divorce and custody proceedings, whereas in a country such as Saudi Arabia it is akin to an intrusion on privacy.

All these issues teach you as much or more about your own culture's special characteristics as they do about foreign cultures.

Nonverbal communication is always a mysterious ingredient in negotiations. Research on negotiations has consistently found the other party's attractiveness to be a strong contributor to positive negotiation outcomes.[21] Although in some cases the causal direction seems to be the reverse—we like the person we have just concluded an agreement with—for the most part the effect goes the other way. If we like the appearance of someone, we are more likely to conclude an agreement. Although analysis of proposals and well-timed strategic concessions are the basic components of any successful business negotiation, most managers agree that appreciation of intangibles such as dress, looks, and nonverbal behavior can make for a much more satisfying negotiation experience and may count for more than we think. All the more so in the context of intercultural negotiations.

Know When to Say What

The typical approach by American negotiators is to take a problem-solving view of negotiations, in which the parties are oriented toward information exchange. They try to convey their own preferences and identify those of the other party by focusing on facts, asking questions, probing, and looking for specific data. Members of other cultures are more likely to assume a broader perspective and take a longer-term view of the negotiations, attempting to assess the potential of a general relationship beyond the specific contract agreement. To Americans, this is likely to be viewed as wasting time and avoiding critical issues. The difference is particularly important—American negotiators should take note of this—in foreign entry, at which time initial importing agreements may be too quickly struck and later turn out to be constraints on further penetration. Although it is difficult and time-consuming to fully evaluate the long-term consequences of a tie-up, it is important that the early negotiators not ignore the potential (or lack of it) for future and more broadly based collaboration; that is to say, spend some time and effort building relationships if necessary.

EXHIBIT 6.2 Four Stages of Business Negotiations

Stage	Japanese	Americans
1. Nontask sounding	Considerable time and expense devoted to such efforts is the practice in Japan.	Relatively shorter periods are typical.
2. Task-related exchange of information	This is the most important step—high first offers with long explanations and in-depth clarifications.	Information is given briefly and directly. "Fair" first offers are more typical.
3. Persuasion	Persuasion is accomplished primarily behind the scenes. Vertical status relations dictate bargaining outcomes.	The most important step: Minds are changed at the negotiation table and aggressive persuasive tactics are used.
4. Concessions and agreement	Concessions are made only toward the end of negotiations—holistic approach to decision making. Progress is difficult to measure for Americans.	Concessions and commitments are made throughout—a sequential approach to decision making.

Source: Adapted from John L. Graham, "A Hidden Cause of America's Trade Deficit with Japan," *Columbia Journal of World Business*, Fall 1981, p. 14.

Graham has analyzed negotiations in many cultures and identified four sequential stages that characterize information exchange in most business negotiations:[22]

1. *Nontask sounding.* This is an initial period when the conversation consists mainly of small talk, designed to get the partners to know each other better.
2. *Task-related exchange of information.* An extended period when the main issues are brought out, facts are presented, and positions clarified.
3. *Persuasion.* This is the stage when the parties attempt to make each other see the issues their way, when there is further explanation and elaboration of positions, and questioning of the other side's evidence.
4. *Concessions and agreements.* Toward the end of most negotiations is a period when mutual concessions might be made, when there is some yielding of fixed positions in order to reach an agreement.

Applying the framework to negotiations between Japanese and Americans, Graham and Sano found the significant cultural differences outlined in Exhibit 6.2.[23] As can be seen, the length and the importance of the stages differ between the two countries. The Americans use less time for nontask soundings than the Japanese, and they are brief with explanations, while the Japanese are more thorough. The Japanese are likely to wait with concessions until the very end, while the Americans move toward an agreement by gradually yielding ground. Against this background it is hardly surprising if trade negotiators from Japan and the United States sometimes seem to be in disagreement about how negotiations are progressing.

Negotiators from different cultures may be classified as proactive "A" types or reactive "B" types. Exhibit 6.3 identifies the major traits of the two types of negotiators. The **type A negotiator** starts with the easily agreed upon smaller details and works up, while the **type B negotiator** first wants to agree on the overall framework of the agreement. Most of the traits in the list are self-explanatory. The "agreement building" trait refers to the process through which the agreement is formulated. As the list suggests, the type A negotiator is a more dynamic, energetic, and risk-taking entrepreneur; while

EXHIBIT 6.3 Type A and Type B Negotiators

Trait	Type A negotiator	Type B negotiator
Goal	Contract	Relationship
Attitudes	Win/lose	Win/win
Personal styles	Informal	Formal
Communications	Direct	Indirect
Time sensitivity	High	Low
Emotionalism	High	Low
Agreement form	Specific	General
Agreement building	Bottom-up	Top-down
Team organization	One leader	Consensus
Risk taking	High	Low

Source: Chart from *Making Global Deals*. Copyright 1991 by Jeswald W. Salacuse. Reprinted by permission of Houghton Mifflin Company. All rights reserved

the B type is a slow, seasoned, mature individual who avoids risk. The A type is closer to the American managers in Exhibit 6.2; the B type closer to the Japanese managers. As Salacuse stresses, both approaches can work: Which one is best depends on the cultures involved.[24] It's when they clash that there may be trouble.

THE LIMITS TO CULTURAL SENSITIVITY

Although the advantages of understanding and adapting to a foreign culture are evident, there can sometimes be "too much of a good thing." There are limits to which the marketing manager should go to try to accommodate the foreign culture if he or she wants to be effective.

Nonadaptation

There is a case to be made for **nonadaptation.** First, it is important to recognize that when a country is ready for change, a different culture can be attractive. This is easiest to see in the former communist nations. Russians want genuine Americans, not adapted versions. They can do the adaptation on their own and expect the "real thing." The politically mandated changes in these countries have eroded the old norms and paved the way for new approaches. Here, attempting to adapt would be a mistake, since the locals want to learn from a successful foreign culture. It is important for the marketing manager to understand the historical and human context in which the firm's business dealings are taking place.

A second, more obvious caveat should be stated. There are limits to the effectiveness of cultural sensitivity as an accommodation strategy. Most transactions between buyers and sellers are based on the intrinsic costs and benefits to the parties, more than on the perceived appropriateness of the partners' dress and behavior. Once the particular needs and constraints of the prospective customer have been recognized and taken into account, even less than sensitive behavior can be overcome. Put simply, all behavioral refinements to the contrary, if the offering does not meet the needs of the buyer, there is no transaction.

There are two other reasons why attempts at adaptation to another culture can be counterproductive. First, they may be only superficial and thus lack any deeper meaning or conviction. While they are likely to engender the same kind of sympathy as flattery does, they are also clearly prone to misinterpretation and may even create distrust.[25] The businessperson who wants to establish trust needs to present himself or herself sincerely and unequivocally.

Keeping One's Center

A final reason why cultural adaptation can be counterproductive is that the manager runs the risk of losing his or her bearings. Management skills, as well as marketing skills, are learned through experience and reading. These skills are usually internalized and have become second nature to be called on at a moment's notice to evaluate a situation. When the manager is busy paying attention to his or her behavior in an unfamiliar setting, however, it is very difficult to be intuitive. It is, in fact, difficult to think. What come to mind in such situations are often only random bits and pieces of know-how, and with bad luck, the manager can come out worse in the process. It takes preparation and a certain nerve to do what one does best. To illustrate, it is useful to think of the new cultural encounter as a performance. As performing artists know well, in actual performance an individual's skills are rarely 100 percent. Rather, by practicing and preparing, the artist can make sure of success even at an 80 percent performance level. In the unfamiliar global setting, even 80 percent is a lot. As the performing artist knows, it is important not to get overly concerned with audience reaction or one loses one's center. Adaptation to the customer's culture, while a nice gesture, should not be allowed to interfere with the intrinsic merits of the proposal.

One should always try to understand one's customer or partner. But it is one thing to understand why and how the other side does things, and quite another to try to do things like that oneself. This view, finally—respect the other person's space and assume that he or she will respect yours—is the best approach. The transaction has to be based on intrinsic business merits, not on personal likes and dislikes. The notion that one should let personal likes and dislikes influence a business relationship—so popular in the early discussions of European, Japanese, and even American business—has been torpedoed as too expensive in the open competition of global markets.[26] Even in Japan, loyalties to suppliers and distributors who are not competitive have vanished into thin air as the market has opened up.[27]

ENTRY MODES AND MARKETING CONTROL

The effect of entry mode on the degree to which the firm can exercise control over its local marketing effort is not simple and direct. It is important to distinguish between the question of where and by whom the product or service is produced (which is the main concern of the preceding discussion on mode of entry) and the way the marketing is managed.

It is useful to separate three alternative ways of organizing the local marketing effort. They are, in increasing order of control, (1) independent agents and distributors, (2) alliance with a local marketing partner, and (3) a wholly owned sales subsidiary.

There is a rough correspondence between the modes of entry and the means of organizing the marketing. As we saw in Chapter 5, exporting typically involves independent agents and distributors. As we saw in the preceding discussion, the local partner in a strategic alliance is often also in charge of local marketing. FDI in manufacturing often means the creation of a wholly owned subsidiary that may also handle the local marketing.

But in practice, the picture is not so simple. For example, exporting is often undertaken from a home country plant to a wholly owned sales subsidiary abroad. This is a common organization when the local market is large and the company has had some success in the market, as in the automobile industry. European and Japanese cars are generally shipped to the U.S. sales subsidiary of the automaker. When FDI in assembly and manufacturing is undertaken, such as Nissan in Tennessee, the companies create a freestanding manufacturing subsidiary, which sells and ships its cars to the sales subsidiary.

In the case of sales subsidiaries handling the marketing, the logistics and the distribution may still be handled by independent carriers and distributors. The sales subsidiary is in charge of promotion, including advertising, pricing, market research, and the management of the channels of distribution.

It is actually quite common to find real-world cases in which the preferred marketing control mode is different from the product entry mode. Exhibit 6.4 shows some of these cases.

The example of Absolut vodka (from Sweden) sold in the United States represents an instance of pure exporting, with Seagrams functioning as the independent agent with territorial marketing control in the United States. A Toshiba-EMI joint venture in Japan markets EMI's music recordings in Japan, many localized by translations of covers into the Japanese language. Volvo cars exported to the United States are marketed by the company's U.S. subsidiary located outside of Chicago.

Licensing usually means less control over the marketing effort, as in the case of Disneyland in Chiba outside Tokyo. The Japanese marketing effort is controlled by the independent Japanese licensee. In the case of Euro Disney, in which Disney took a joint venture stake in the operation, the marketing effort is basically under the control of the local European partners. Microsoft's early entry into Japan was via ASCII, an independent licensee. However, disagreements over the local marketing strategy later forced Microsoft to establish its own Japanese subsidiary that markets the software in Japan. And Nike, the athletic shoemaker, has licensed manufacturing in Asia but controls the marketing.

To enter via a strategic alliance and then allow the marketing to be done independently is unusual, since the partner is a natural marketing agent. However, some new joint ventures in China seem to be planned according to this model. For example, in autos the marketing may have to be controlled by the Chinese government. On the other hand, for other products, with Western manufacturers establishing plants in joint ventures with Chinese government affiliated manufacturers, the marketing is managed separately by Western sales subsidiaries. An example is American Black & Decker, maker of power tools, which has its own marketing subsidiary in China.

Entering via FDI in manufacturing and then allowing independent agents to do the marketing can be illustrated through an OEM (original equipment manufacturing) agreement. Lucky-Goldstar, a Korean company, has invested in a television plant in Arkansas, which builds television sets for the Sears private label. The lack of control

EXHIBIT 6.4 Product Entry and Marketing Control Can Be Different

	Marketing control		
Mode of entry	**Independent agent**	**Joint with alliance partner**	**Own sales subsidiary**
Exporting	Absolut vodka in the U.S.	Toshiba EMI in Japan	Volvo in the U.S.
Licensing	Disney in Japan	Microsoft in Japan (initially)	Nike in Asia
Strategic alliance	Autos in China	Euro Disney	Black & Decker in China
FDI	Goldstar in the U.S.	Mitsubishi Motors in the U.S.	P&G in the E.U.

over marketing is a drawback, and in the long run most companies would like to take over the marketing and establish their own brand name as Goldstar is now doing.

Mitsubishi Motors now manufactures cars in Illinois that are marketed through its joint venture with Chrysler (although the arrangement is being gradually phased out as Mitsubishi establishes a parallel dealer network to gain more control over the marketing). The combination of wholly owned manufacturing plants and sales subsidiaries is common. Procter & Gamble operates several plants in Europe, with products marketed through its European sales subsidiaries, of which the German is the largest.

Two major lessons from these various cases should be emphasized.

1. Local marketing control often can be effectively exercised via a sales subsidiary, regardless of the entry mode of the product.

2. Even with a sales subsidiary, however, product entry mode is not irrelevant. For example, reliable and timely supplies to the local market cannot be ensured through exporting when protectionist pressures mount or when transportation is long and hazardous. Licensees may not perform as agreed, and partners in alliances may or may not prove to be good partners when conditions change.

In the end, choosing the best entry mode depends not only on marketing factors but also on the business strategy as a whole, including the strategic objectives of the involvement in the foreign market. The last section will deal with this issue directly.

OPTIMAL ENTRY STRATEGY

Which mode of entry into the foreign market should be chosen? Can an **optimal entry strategy** be found?

With all the internal and external factors taken into account, it's impossible to give a single answer to this question. A mode that offers protection from political risk (such as licensing) may offer little help with control of product quality. A mode that maximizes control over company-specific advantages (such as FDI in manufacturing) involves the maximum political risk, and so on.

The Entry Mode Matrix

One can distinguish several strategic situations and the preferred mode of entry in each. The entry strategy is affected both by company factors (the FSAs in particular) and by market factors (opportunities and threats). The company factors can be grouped into an **entry mode matrix** with three strategic postures. The market factors are different in emerging economies as compared to high-growth and mature markets. Services need to be treated separately (see Exhibit 6.5.).

STRATEGIC POSTURE   One company posture is when few resources can be dedicated to entry, the usual case when entry is the first step in the internationalization process. The major characteristic of the entry strategy then tends to be its tentativeness and the desire to keep future options open. This strategic posture will be called **"incremental."**

A second strategic posture is when the firm possesses a well-protected trade secret or patentable know-how whose potential abroad is clear, but needs to learn about the market and develop more local familiarity. This situation will be denoted **"protected".** Typical examples would include the Coca-Cola formula, the computer-on-a-chip, and electronic banking technology. In such cases there are usually real or self-imposed limits to the resources (workforce, operating capital) allocated to the entry.

In a third strategic situation the company has well-established firm-specific advantages, is large enough to encounter relatively few resource obstacles to expansion, and offers a product with definite potential abroad. This is the typical "global" situa-

EXHIBIT 6.5 An Optimal Entry Mode Matrix

Company strategic posture	Product/market situation			
	Emerging	**High-growth**	**Mature**	**Services**
Incremental	Indirect exports	Indirect exports	Direct exports	Licensing/alliance
Protected	Joint venture	Indirect exports	Alliance/licensing	Licensing
Control	Wholly owned subsidiary	Acquisition/ alliance	Wholly owned subsidiary	Franchising/alliance/ exporting

tion, with the company committed to expanding abroad without jeopardizing any of its firm-specific advantages. This will be called the **"control"** posture.

PRODUCT/MARKET SITUATION   The various product/market conditions that might prevail in the market country can be grouped into four different categories. A first distinction is between products and services. The characteristics of service markets are different from those of markets for physical products when it comes to entry mode considerations. Whereas the product embodies many of the firm-specific advantages in its physical attributes and can thus be viewed separately from the actual transaction through which ownership is exchanged, the quality and benefits of services reside in the transaction itself. This is why export of services often involves travel by professionals in various fields—doctors, engineers, consultants, and so on—to perform the service.

Among product markets it is useful to distinguish between three situations. *Emerging* markets are those recently opened up because of political changes; they show generally weak infrastructure, difficulty in accomplishing market-based exchanges, lack of distribution alternatives, and risk of default on payments. Some less developed countries also fall into the emerging category.

A second situation is *high-growth* markets, such as some high-technology markets in advanced economies and markets in many fast-growing countries, including the newly industrialized states. The main marketing issues tend to be to quickly establish presence in the country and to support the product sufficiently in the marketplace so as not to lose out against competitors. The sales growth will go to the entrant who quickly establishes leadership and captures first-mover advantages in the high-growth market.

A third situation is the market in the *mature* stage, when the name of the marketing game is market share, including dominance in at least a niche in a well-differentiated marketplace. Many markets in advanced economies are mature. The emphasis in entry of mature markets is not so much on speed of penetration as on the total amount of marketing expenditure needed to establish presence and maintain loyalty.

Optimal Modes

For preferred choices among the alternative modes, see again Exhibit 6.5.

INCREMENTAL   The resource-poor entrant that wants to stay flexible for the future will most likely be best off with exporting. For emerging markets, indirect exporting may be the only feasible option. If the market in the country is growing quickly, indirect exporting might be preferable since the start-up costs are lower and market presence can be established more rapidly. In services, the actual start-up usually requires people to be sent abroad (a form of "direct exports") but also requires some continued presence from local people, making licensing the preferred option.

PROTECTED   The firm with strong and protected know-how but without very keen interest or skills in foreign markets might also be best off with indirect exporting in high-growth markets (if speed is of the essence). An alliance with a local competitor with distribution capability might be a viable alternative. Where slower penetration is acceptable, the alliance alternative should be expanded to include the possibility of a joint venture or perhaps licensing, should a suitable partner be found. In an emerging market, against its better judgment as it were, the firm may have to accept a joint venture, keeping its partner in check to the extent possible. If the offering is a service, licensing should be the first alternative. It would run relatively low risks of dissipation because of patents or other protection and would allow the proper adaptation to local market conditions.

CONTROL   The larger firm interested in global expansion and control over production and marketing in various countries would usually do best with some type of FDI in manufacturing and local sales subsidiaries. In emerging markets, a wholly owned subsidiary may be the only viable option. If the market is growing rapidly, acquisition of (or an alliance with) a local firm may be the most advantageous alternative. Where the market is large, establishing a manufacturing subsidiary with 100 percent ownership is more easily justified. However, if there are large economies of scale in manufacturing (the case in autos but not in electronics, for example), the company would do better focusing all manufacturing in one or two plants and sourcing worldwide from there through exporting. Tariff barriers against imports might preclude such an option, of course. If the company's business is in services, the use of franchising is probably the best bet. It offers good control possibilities coupled with local adaptation (of great importance in most services) and also allows local capital to be used, an advantage from a political risk point of view.

Real-World Cases

The suggested entry modes can be illustrated with reference to some real-world examples (see Exhibit 6.6).

INCREMENTAL STRATEGY   Supervalu, a wholesaler of food products from the state of Washington, has entered the Russian food market on a small scale. An intermediary trading company located in Boston specializing in Russian trade approached the wholesaler about exporting packaged food products to Russia. The products were to be sold in a Moscow supermarket the intermediary had established. Reluctant at first, Supervalu finally agreed when the financial risk was assumed by the trading company and its Russian partner. The wholesaler is now attempting to increase its presence in the Russian market, with or without the help of the intermediary.[28]

The U.S. fishing industry, characterized by numerous small establishments, has found a large and rapidly growing market in Japan, whose supplies from northern waters have been effectively cut off by Russian ships. But, by necessity, sales to Japan are characterized by indirect exports via the large Japanese trading companies. Despite some attempts by the Americans to join together and establish some profitable processing followed by direct exports, the market knowledge and financial power of the trading companies have made the fishing industry on the American West Coast simply raw materials suppliers to Japanese processors.

A more positive experience of an incremental exporter maintaining flexibility is the case of Rossignol, the French ski maker. The initial entry into the North American market was via direct exports to American distributors. This choice was predicated on the lack of financial clout and market knowledge possessed by the company. As its experience and success in the European (primarily French) market grew, so did the recognition that the U.S. and Canadian markets were not only important but also quite different from the European in terms of skiing conditions, customer preferences, and

EXHIBIT 6.6 Entries under Different Conditions

Company strategic posture	Product/market situation			
	Emerging	**High-growth**	**Mature**	**Services**
Incremental	Supervalu to Russia	North American fish to Japan	Rossignol skis to U.S.	Dialogue to Europe
Protected	Pharmaceuticals in China	Sun Energy technology to Europe	Coca-Cola bottling; Toyota-GM tie-up	Disneyland in Japan
Control	New FDI in India	Matsushita in U.S. TV market	IBM Worldwide, autos into U.S.	Hilton, Sheraton; McDonald's

so on. The decision was then made to establish wholly owned manufacturing in both countries to enable the company to adapt its products and stay in close touch with market developments. The initial choice of direct exports allowed the company the requisite time for learning and for accumulating resources before a more committed move was undertaken.

A small consulting firm in the computer software business, Dialogue, Inc., operates out of New York City. The demand for its services abroad is growing rapidly, and the company has had problems identifying the right mode for serving this market. The strategy the company has evolved consists of service and distribution alliance tie-ups with different consulting firms in various European countries, sharing the software know-how with them through seminars and training sessions both in Europe and in New York and then using the company's established sales force and local market presence to help sell the software with the requisite quality control and backup services.

PROTECTED KNOW-HOW Western pharmaceutical companies eyeing the vast Chinese market see tremendous opportunity. There is little need for the companies to worry about leakage of formulas, since China has a very different tradition in medicine, and there are few pharmacologists educated in the West. But the unfamiliar market, the need to establish good relationships with government agencies, and, not least, the Chinese government's rules mean that joint ventures are the only entry mode for Schering-Plough, Merck, Pfizer, and the rest.[30]

The Atlas International Company of Seattle, Washington, is an export management company (EMC) specializing in sales of U.S.-developed sun energy technology. The innovating companies are too small and too unskilled at marketing abroad to be able to take advantage of the opportunities that present themselves and have turned to indirect exporting using Atlas. Many of the rapid growth markets are a consequence of government resource allocations to the sun energy field, and Atlas provides a service by keeping abreast of the rapidly developing opportunities in different countries. Nevertheless, Atlas recognizes that if any one company's exports start taking a large share of total sales, that firm will look for ways of managing "its" part of the business.

Coca-Cola's licensing of local bottlers is its standard approach in overseas markets, sometimes aided by a joint venture ownership structure. The protection of the formula is the keystone of this policy: The bottlers are given a concentrate and instructions for adding carbonated water to produce the drink but do not get access to the formula itself. Another case of a joint venture in a mature market is Toyota's tie-up with General Motors in Fremont, California, where small cars under the Chevrolet Nova name are marketed. To questions about the possible dissipation of Toyota's firm-specific know-how, the company has said little, but observers tend to agree that the effects are small. Not much of the actual know-how has been transferred, since many of the assembly tasks have been adapted for American workers. In addition, by

Delivering Coca Cola in Guangdong, China. Coca Cola's typical entry mode into foreign markets is to license independent bottlers in a franchising arrangement. But in some emerging countries Coca Cola invests directly in the bottling plants to control quality. Ron McMillan/ Gamma-Liaison.

now the technology from Japan represents quite standard process knowledge, available to most if not all carmakers in one form or other already. The basic strength of the agreement seems to be that GM gets Toyota's people to implement the new procedures and assembly technology.

In a reverse situation, Disney World agreed to license its name for use at the new entertainment park in Chiba outside Tokyo. Satisfied with a substantial 10 percent of gross sales in royalties and the provision that quality controls would be stringent, the Disney company apparently judged its expertise in the Japanese market insufficient for a wholly owned subsidiary operation. At the same time, the agreement will tend to impede the accumulation of experience abroad and thus limit the possibility of going into other Asian markets. (The company was a bit more secure in its knowledge of the European market and opted for an equity investment in a joint venture with French partners, but as we saw in the opening vignette of Chapter 3, it is encountering a fair number of problems.) Whether or not Disney World will enter any other Asian countries may be a question not only of what its top management is thinking but of what the Japanese licensee has in mind.

CONTROL POSTURE Now that India has relented on its ban on foreign ownership, many companies are coming back. Whether through greenfield investments, acquisitions, or reacquisitions of abandoned facilities, companies are establishing wholly owned subsidiaries in which they can control operations and use of their know-how. These companies include American and Japanese car firms, Korean conglomerates, and European electronics manufacturers, eager to cash in on the future growth of the Indian market.

When the American color TV market took off toward the end of the 60s, the Japanese electronics giant Matsushita (brand name Panasonic) faced the choice of establishing production in the United States or being left behind. Trade barriers were high, and Sony was already present at its San Diego plant. By acquiring the troubled Motorola TV plant outside Chicago, Matsushita at great cost managed to kill two birds with one stone. One, it acquired the desired manufacturing base in the market and could enter quickly (especially since it kept the Motorola brand name, Quasar); and two, political pressures were assuaged, especially since the Motorola plant was scheduled to close. Cost was the problem Matsushita inherited at the plant, the result of low productivity and fragmented labor–management relations. After considerable effort (including the introduction of some of the vaunted Japanese management techniques such as quality control circles), productivity was again on the rise within a spectacularly short period of time (less than one year).

The control strategy of IBM in the mature markets of Europe and Asia has been based specifically on 100 percent ownership of sales and manufacturing subsidiaries for its mainframe computers. The objectives of protecting its hard-won technical know-how and maintaining its corporate philosophy of providing outstanding service to back up its products were factors in determining the FDI strategy. In personal computers, by contrast, the company has been more willing to engage in alliances, including joint ventures. IBM's know-how in the PC field is much less on the cutting edge than in mainframes.

Scale returns in manufacturing have made automakers in Europe and Japan hesitant about setting up plants abroad. Although transportation costs to the large North American market are relatively high, all the Japanese and European automakers have followed basically the same path of direct exports marketed through wholly owned sales subsidiaries. By establishing a dedicated distribution network, an expensive and resource-consuming undertaking, the automakers can control the marketing effort without investing in manufacturing or assembly. In 1976, Volkswagen established production in Harrisburg, Pennsylvania, in order to be closer to its main overseas market, but quality problems forced the company to close the plant after five years. It was not until the voluntary quotas with Japan were enacted in 1981 that Japanese automakers started manufacturing in the United States. In 1994, both Mercedes and BMW announced plans to start manufacturing in the United States, reducing transportation costs of sports models specially designed for the North American market. When economies of scale in manufacturing are great, exporting worldwide from one or two plants is preferable, unless entry barriers to major markets are high.

The franchising of fast-food companies such as McDonald's is well known in many parts of the world. The main ingredient in this successful global expansion is the emphasis on (control of) standardized service more than the product itself (the food). This is generally true also in the companies' domestic market. The hotel chains that have sprung up in many metropolitan centers of the world, the Hiltons and the Sheratons well known to many travelers, are not wholly owned subsidiaries as one might have thought but franchise operations typically capitalized by local interests and supported by worldwide promotion and advertising.

These services aim less at a local market and more toward a global market of international businesspeople and tourists. The standardization of the service has a distinct "consumer confidence" or "trust" aspect to it: The customer using these services avoids taking chances with unknown offerings. This is why franchising, with its greater possibilities of controlling quality, is preferable to alliances or simple licensing of a trademark or brand name.

SUMMARY

This chapter first presented the internationalization stages through which a firm traditionally became a savvy global competitor. That standard pattern was shown to deviate from today's faster global expansion by the so-called born globals, smaller start-ups in high-technology fields that began exporting within a year of their founding.

The chapter then described the three main nonexporting modes of entry: licensing, strategic alliances, and FDI in wholly owned manufacturing subsidiaries. The marketer's role differs in these entry modes from that of simple exporter, since the company is marketing its FSAs directly rather than embodied in the final product. Against a historical background the characteristics of the modes were shown to depend on various trade barriers and the modes shown to provide various opportunities for the global marketer. Each mode has advantages and disadvantages for the entrant from a marketing perspective, and examples were used to demonstrate that a wholly owned sales subsidiary can be used successfully with any mode of entry.

The need to develop negotiation skills to establish partnerships was discussed and illustrated with specific examples. From a cultural viewpoint it is important to recognize how one's own words and behavior will be perceived by the potential partner. While some adaptation to the behavioral norms of a host country is necessary, too easy attempts at complete familiarity may backfire by eroding trust. Indeed, the potential mistrust generated by someone's consummate ease in a foreign culture may trigger the intuition that the fully adaptive individual's integrity is questionable, merely achieved to gain advantage. As always a high degree of judgment and sensitivity in these matters is crucial.

The question of what the optimal mode of entry should be was then discussed. The answer depends on a number of strategic and situational considerations that favor one mode over another. These considerations were summarized in a matrix of strategic market and resource situations facing the entrant into a country. Matching typical company postures (incremental, protected, or control) and typical market situations (emerging, high-growth, mature, service), the global marketer can get a feel for which mode may be preferable as a first choice. Several real-world examples were used to demonstrate the application of the choice-of-mode matrix and to show how companies have actually attempted to make entry decisions recently that are good for today and also leave room for future change and growth.

KEY TERMS

acquisition   p. 163
born global   p. 155
control posture   p. 171
cross-cultural negotiations
   p. 164
dissipation of FSAs   p. 156
distribution alliance   p. 159
entry mode matrix   p. 170
FDI in wholly owned
   manufacturing   p. 162
franchising   p. 157

greenfield investment   p. 163
incremental posture   p. 170
internationalization stages
   p. 155
joint ventures (JVs)   p. 161
licensing   p. 156
manufacturing alliance   p. 161
nonadaptation   p. 167
nonverbal communication
   p. 165
optimal entry strategy   p. 170

original equipment
   manufacturing (OEM)
   p. 158
protected posture   p. 170
R&D alliance   p. 161
royalties   p. 157
straight licensing   p. 157
strategic alliances (SAs)   p. 159
type A negotiator   p. 167
type B negotiator   p. 167

DISCUSSION QUESTIONS

1. While Disney World entered the Japanese market by licensing a Japanese company, Euro Disney (now Disneyland Paris) was established as a joint venture with European backing but with Disney holding majority control. To what would you attribute the difference in entry mode? Given the lack of early success in Europe, do you think another entry mode would have been better? Why or why not?

2. Because it is located in the Southern Hemisphere, Chile's strong fruit-growing industry has a country-specific advantage of counter-seasonal harvesting in many northern markets. What entry mode would seem most suitable for these markets? What trade barriers might Chilean fruit growers face with this entry mode?

3. How would you use networking and the Internet to help establish customer contacts abroad for a start-up high-tech company with expertise in building Web sites? What are the advantages of the Internet in distributing your final product?

4. How can control over local marketing be managed in exporting? In franchising? How can Starbuck, the specialty coffee retailer, maintain marketing control over its franchise operations in Japan?

5. In negotiations it is often said that "silence is golden." Give an example of what this might mean. What kind of culture would you expect to favor that rule, high context or low context?

NOTES

1. See, for example, Cavusgil, 1980, Czinkota, 1982, Nordstrom, 1991.

2. See McKinsey & Co., 1993. The discussion of born globals here draws on the excellent overview of the current research by Knight and Cavusgil, 1997.

3. From Hertz and Mattsson, 1998.

4. See Brush, 1992.

5. According to McKinsey & Co., 1993.

6. The terminology varies among writers. Some keep joint ventures separate from strategic alliances, arguing that the latter do not involve equity investments but are simple collaborations. From a marketing perspective, however, joint ventures and strategic alliances pose similar problems. See Contractor and Lorange, 1988, and Varadarajan and Cunningham, 1995.

7. See, for instance, Hamel, Doz, and Prahalad, 1989, and Bleeke and Ernst, 1991.

8. See Johansson, 1995.

9. See Terpstra and Simonin, 1993.

10. Bleeke and Ernst, 1991, and Parkhe, 1991, show the lack of durability of many strategic alliances.

11. Bleeke and Ernst, 1991.

12. Hamel et al., 1989, give an upbeat view of competitive collaborations.

13. See Contractor and Lorange, 1988, and Geringer and Hebert, 1991. There are many other forms of international ventures that are quite different organizationally—for example, the American Bethlehem Steel and Swedish Granges JV for the mining of iron ore in Liberia—but such alliances are of less interest here.

14. See Hamel, 1991.

15. This discussion of FDI in overseas manufacturing is necessarily brief. A lot has been written on the topic, and the interested reader can find a good comprehensive statement of the modern FDI theory in most multinational texts, including Rutenberg, 1982.

16. See Johansson and Nebenzahl, 1986.

17. See, for example, the reaction of Chrysler buyers to learning that the cars were built in Mexico (Nag, 1984).

18. See Tse and Gorn, 1993.

19. See, for example, Hall and Hall, 1990, Graham and Sano, 1984, March 1990. Schuster and Copeland, 1996, give a good overview of how effective negotiation strategies vary for different cultures and emphasize in particular the techniques for getting into the buyer's network.

20. Fukuyama, 1995, emphasizes strongly the positive role of trust in business transactions and economic success.

21. See, for example, Tung, 1988, and Graham et al., 1994. Tung's treatment illustrates many of the communication problems encountered in international negotiations.

22. See Graham, 1983, Graham and Sano, 1984, and Graham et al., 1994.

23. See Graham and Sano, 1984.

24. See Salacuse, 1991.

25. See Francis, 1991.

26. See, for example, D'Aveni, 1994.

27. See, for example, Blustein, 1995.

28. This example is from "Food Distribution in Russia: The Harris Group and the LUX Store," Harvard Business School case no. 9-594-059.

29. See Beamish, 1993.

SELECTED REFERENCES

Beamish, Paul W. "The Characteristics of Joint Ventures in the People's Republic of China." *Journal of International Marketing* 1, no. 2 (1993), pp. 29–48.

Bleeke, J.; and David Ernst. "The Way to Win in Cross-Border Alliances." *Harvard Business Review* 69, no. 6 (November–December 1991), pp. 127–35.

Blustein, Paul. "Giant Trading Companies Battle to Preserve Japan Inc.'s Edge." *Washington Post*, April 12, 1995, pp. A18, A19.

Brush, Candida. *Factors Motivating Small Firms to Internationalize: The Effect of Firm Age.* Doctoral dissertation, Boston University, 1992.

Cavusgil, S. Tamer. "On the Internationalization Process of Firms." *European Research* 8, no. 6 (1980), pp. 273–81.

Contractor, Farouk; and Peter Lorange, eds. *Cooperative Strategies in International Business.* Lexington, MA: Lexington Books, 1988.

Czinkota, Michael R. *Export Development Strategies: U.S. Promotion Policy.* New York: Praeger, 1982.

D'Aveni, Richard. *Hypercompetition.* New York: Free Press, 1994.

Francis, June N. P. "When in Rome? The Effects of Cultural Adaptation on Intercultural Business Negotiations." *Journal of International Business Studies*, Third Quarter 1991, pp. 403–28.

Fukuyama, Francis. *Trust: The Social Virtues and the Creation of Prosperity.* New York: Free Press, 1995.

Geringer, J. Michael; and L. Hebert. "Measuring Performance of International Joint Ventures." *Journal of International Business Studies* 22, no. 2 (1991), pp. 249–63.

Graham, John L. "Business Negotiations in Japan, Brazil, and the United States." *Journal of International Business Studies* 14 (Spring–Summer 1983), pp. 47–62.

—; and Yoshihiro Sano. *Smart Bargaining with the Japanese.* New York: Ballinger, 1984.

—; Alma T. Mintu; and Waymond Rodgers. "Explorations of Negotiations Behaviors in Ten Foreign Cultures Using a Model Developed in the United States." *Management Science* 40, no. 1 (January 1994), pp. 72–95.

Hall, Edward T.; and Mildred Reed Hall. *Understanding Cultural Differences.* Yarmouth, ME: Intercultural Press, 1990.

Hamel, Gary. "Competition for Competence and Inter-Partner Learning within International Strategic Alliances." *Strategic Management Journal* 12 (Summer 1991), pp. 83–103.

—; and C. K. Prahalad. "Creating Global Strategic Capability." In Hood, Neil, and Jan-Erik Vahlne, eds. *Strategies in Global Competition.* London: Croom Helm, 1988.

—; Yves Doz; and C. K. Prahalad. "Collaborate with Your Competitors—and Win." *Harvard Business Review*, January–February 1989, pp. 133–39.

Hertz, Susanne; and Lars-Gunnar Mattsson. *Mindre Foretag Blir Internationella.* ("Smaller Firms Go International"). Malmo: Liber, 1998. (In Swedish)

Johansson, Johny K. "International Alliances: Why Now?" *Journal of the Academy of Marketing Science*, Fall 1995.

—; and Izrael D. Nebenzahl. "Multinational Expansion: Effect on Brand Evaluations." *Journal of International Business Studies* 17, no. 3 (Fall 1986), pp. 101–26.

Knight, Gary A.; and S. Tamer Cavusgil. "Early Internationalization and the Born-Global Firm: An Emergent Paradigm for International Marketing." Working paper, 1997.

March, Robert M. *The Japanese Negotiator.* Tokyo: Kodansha, 1990.

McKinsey & Co. *Emerging Exporters: Australia's High Value-Added Manufacturing Exporters.* Melbourne: Australian Manufacturing Council, 1993.

Nag, Amal. "Chrysler Tests Consumer Reaction to Mexican-Made Cars Sold in the U.S." *The Wall Street Journal*, July 23, 1984, sec. 2.

Nordstrom, Kjell A. *The Internationalization Process of the Firm: Searching for New Patterns and Explanations.* Stockholm: Institute of International Business, 1991.

Otterbeck, L., ed. *The Management of Headquarters–Subsidiary Relationships in Multinational Corporations.* Aldershot, U.K.: Gower, 1981.

Parkhe, Arvind. "Interfirm Diversity, Organizational Learning, and Longevity in Strategic Alliances." *Journal of International Business Studies* 22, no. 4 (1991), pp. 579–601.

Pucik, Vladimir. "Strategic Alliances, Organizational Learning, and Competitive Advantage—the HRM Agenda." *Human Resource Management* 27, no. 1 (Spring 1988), pp. 77–83.

Root, F. R. *Foreign Market Entry Strategies*, 2d ed. New York: Amacom, 1989.

Rutenberg, David P. *Multinational Management.* Boston: Little, Brown, 1982.

Salacuse, Jeswald W. *Making Global Deals.* Boston: Houghton Mifflin, 1991.

Schuster, Camille; and Michael Copeland. *Global Business: Planning for Sales and Negotiations.* Fort Worth, TX: Dryden, 1996.

Terpstra, Vern; and Bernard L. Simonin. "Strategic Alliances in the Triad: An Exploratory Study." *Journal of International Marketing* 1, no. 1 (1993), pp. 4–25.

Thorelli, Hans B.; and S. Tamer Cavusgil, eds. *International Marketing Strategy*, 3d ed. New York: Pergamon, 1990.

Tse, David K.; and Gerald J. Gorn. "An Experiment on the Salience of Country-of-Origin in the Era of Global Brands." *Journal of International Marketing* 1, no. 1 (1993), pp. 57–76.

Tung, Rosalie. "Toward a Concept of International Business Negotiations." In *Advances in International Comparative Management*, Richard Farmer, ed. Greenwich, CT: JAI Press, 1988, pp. 203–19.

Varadarajan, P. Rajan; and Margaret H. Cunningham. "Strategic Alliances: A Synthesis of Conceptual Foundations." *Journal of the Academy of Marketing Science*, Fall 1995.

Cases

Case 2.1

Ocean Spray: Cranberries in Scandinavia?

In late 1990, the marketing department of Ripella A/S, Denmark's largest juice producer, was gathered to make a decision regarding the introduction of Ocean Spray Cranberry Drink on the Scandinavian market with Denmark on the lead market. The meeting had been called to consider an attractive proposal from Ocean Spray that Ripella become its Scandinavian agent, and to evaluate the findings from some preliminary market research in Denmark.

OCEAN SPRAY CRANBERRIES

Cranberries are small, ruby red fruits slightly bigger than peas. They have a very long ripening period of approximately 20 months from pollination to harvest. Their contents of vitamins, minerals, fiber, and organic acids are substantial, extremely wholesome, and in some cases may prevent infections. Cranberries contain very little water and sugar. The pure juice from the fruit is loved by very few people; its taste is as tart and bitter-sour as pure lemon juice. About 85 percent of the world production of cranberries is in North America owing to the optimum climatic conditions there.

The cranberry is one of the few present-day fruits that was also grown by Native Americans. The Native Americans used the fruit as food, as medicine, and as a dye. In modern times cranberries have traditionally

The Ocean Spray case was prepared by Professor Tage Koed Madsen, Department of Marketing, Odense University.

been used as a side dish, for example for Thanksgiving Day and Christmas. These holidays coincide with the fresh cranberry season from October to December. Until 1960 about 95 percent of all cranberry sales were related to these holidays. History and tradition bear great impact on the American use of cranberries.

Ocean Spray Cranberries dates back to 1912 when Marcus L. Urann, a young cranberry grower, observed that few people outside New England had ever tasted the unique little fruit. He started to sell his cranberry sauce in tins under the name of Ocean Spray Cape Cod Cranberry Sauce. At that time, the individual grower acted in his own name. Financial problems did, however, have the effect that the most important growers in Massachusetts in 1930–31 formed a cooperative under the name of Ocean Spray Cranberries, Inc. Urann was one of the promoters of this project. Today about 800 members constitute the cooperative of Ocean Spray.

Through Ocean Spray the growers invested in intensive market-oriented product development. The result showed up in the early 60s in the development of a clear, ruby, diluted juice—Cranberry Juice Cocktail—which is still Ocean Spray's core product. Many growers were skeptical about the "diluted" cranberry juice, but their skepticism was proved wrong by developments. Today, Ocean Spray is North America's leading producer of canned and bottled juices and juice drinks. Ocean Spray has been the best-selling brand name in the canned and bottled juice category since 1981, selling more than the combined total of its three biggest competitors. Annual sales reach over $1 billion. The company employs more than 2,500 people worldwide.

In 1963, Ocean Spray revolutionized the marketplace with the introduction of the juice industry's very first juice bland. CRANAPPLE® cranberry apple juice drink became such a huge success that the Cooperative continued to add to the line, including the introduction of the first low-calorie juice blends.

In 1976, Ocean Spray expanded its membership to include grapefruit growers from Florida's Indian River region. OCEAN SPRAY® grapefruit juice quickly became the number one bottled grapefruit juice. This was followed by OCEAN SPRAY® pink grapefruit juice cocktail, the very first citrus blend of its kind. To round out the grapefruit line, OCEAN SPRAY® Ruby Red grapefruit juice drink was introduced in 1991 and quickly became the most successful new product introduction in Ocean Spray history.

Ocean Spray led the way in the United States with the introduction of aseptic packaging. Now a popular mainstay of the juice section, "juice boxes" first appeared on the shelves in the U.S. in 1981 as OCEAN SPRAY® PAPER BOTTLE™ juice containers. In 1985, recognizing consumers' desire for lightweight, shatterproof containers, Ocean Spray became the first manufacturer to package juice drinks in PET plastic bottles. Since then, a new plastic gallon has been developed to fill the growing need for economical, easy-to-handle containers.

Today a number of drinks are marketed under the brand name of Ocean Spray. The most important part of the product range is based on cranberries in the form of juices, sauces, and so on. In addition, a number of blended products have been developed with cranberries blended with raspberries, apples, oranges, and grapes. Some drinks contain more sugar than others. Ocean Spray also markets pure citrus juices (starting in 1976) and apple juices (starting in 1982). The launching of the "foreign" juices was a result of the wish to better exploit the brand name of Ocean Spray. Finally, cranberries as well as citrus fruits are sold as fresh fruit. As a result of the comprehensive product development, now only about 25 percent of annual cranberry sales take place at Thanksgiving Day and Christmas.

RIPELLA A/S

Looking to expand abroad, in 1990 Ocean Spray contacted Ripella A/S and offered the company the Cranberry Drink agency for the Scandinavian market, combining Denmark's 5.2 million people with Norway's 4.2 million and Sweden's 8.2 million for a market size of 17.6 million people. The generous offer looked promising to Ripella management. Cranberry Drink had been a great success on the American market; it was a product with a high price and a good profit margin. Product development costs would be minimal if no adaptation to the Scandinavian market was necessary.

Ripella A/S was established on March 8, 1989, through a merger between Rimi (Ringe on the island of Fyn) and Apella (Odder on Jylland, Denmark's largest island), both leading juice brands in their respective local markets. Up through the 1980s both Rimi and Apella had shown strong growth. Competition was fierce, however, in the Danish market, where the consumer prices of juice were low. The idea of a merger therefore had not been unwelcome to either party. Following the merger, Rimi was applied as the premium brand name for high-quality products, and low-price products were sold under the name of Apella or as private labels. In addition, Ripella had active-sounding brand names like "Læski" for refreshing drinks to be diluted and "Pinard" for French red and white wines. Under the Rimi brand, Ripella had recently launched three new products, "Skolejuice" (School Juice), "Morgenjuice" (Morning Juice, a blended juice with oranges, apples, and pineapple), and "Dansk Æblejuice" (Danish Applejuice).

Ripella had a dominant position in the Danish juice market with a market share of about 50 percent. Exports accounted for about 20 percent of total sales of about DKK 400 million.[1] The export markets were primarily found in Scandinavia. Ripella had a staff of about 200 people, with production activities being increasingly concentrated in Ringe on the island of Fyn. Sales and marketing functions employed slightly over 20 people.

THE DANISH JUICE MARKET

In Europe, the consumption of juice had been steadily increasing up through the 80s. Germany was the dominant market with about 40 percent of overall European sales. This was partly due to the large population, partly to a per capita sale of as much as 40–50 liters annually. Only Switzerland and the Netherlands came close with per capita sales of 20–35 liters. Great Britain and the Scandinavian countries consumed about 20 liters per capita, whereas countries like France, Italy, Spain, and Portugal were as low as about 5 liters per capita.

EXHIBIT I Dnish Lifestyle Eating Habits (June 1987)

	The renewers	The unworried	The traditional	The careless	The old-fashioned	The passive	Total
Fresh fruit	*100%*	*100%*	*100%*	*100%*	*100%*	*100%*	*100%*
Daily/almost daily	78.1%	51.7%	63.0%	35.5%	51.6%	8.5%	54.6%
At least once a week	96.3	87.0	91.9	67.4	77.6	18.7	81.5
At least once a month	98.2	96.5	98.3	87.1	88.5	23.9	90.3
At least twice every half year	98.8	97.9	98.9	93.7	91.4	30.4	92.7
Never	98.9	98.3	99.0	95.4	91.8	33.7	93.3
Fruit/Orange juice							
Daily/almost daily	23.6%	20.1%	16.8%	10.5%	8.4%	1.4%	15.8%
At least once a week	52.4	48.4	42.2	24.9	18.9	4.5	37.4
At least once a month	79.7	74.3	75.1	45.1	34.4	8.2	61.0
At least twice every half year	90.1	89.0	89.1	57.4	46.3	12.4	73.2
Never	92.8	92.6	93.3	65.7	56.4	14.0	78.4

Data on Danish consumption habits as of 1987 are given in Exhibit 1 for six lifestyle segments. Danes annually drink about 3,600 million liters of liquid corresponding to about 700 liters per capita. The dominant drinks are coffee (about 33 percent), beer (about 20 percent), and milk (about 16 percent), followed by tea, lemonade/mineral water, tap water, and blended juice ("saft")/refreshing drinks ("læskedrik") in drinkable dilution (each about 6 percent); wine represents about 3 percent and juice almost 3 percent. The consumption of juice is about 50 percent orange juice, just under 40 percent apple juice, and the remaining 10 percent juice blended of various fruits and vegetables.

The latter juices are the most expensive at a consumer price of DKK 12–13 a liter, whereas orange juice usually costs DKK 7–8 and apple juice DKK 6–7. The price of apple juice is today at the same level as the price of orange juice. The cheap products (typically private labels) are generally 25–30 percent below this price level. The retail profit is 10–30 percent, depending on the brand, whereas the wholesale profit is typically 5–15 percent.

The consumption of blended "saft" and "läaeskedrik" to be diluted with water is about twice as large as the consumption of juice when you estimate the quantity in drinkable condition. The consumption is about equally distributed between blended "saft" and "læskedrik." As these products are to be diluted with about four times water, the sale of pur "saft" and "læskedrik" is somewhat lower than the sale of juice. To the consumer the prices of these products are, however, much lower. Typically one liter of blended "saft" costs DKK 8–12 in the store, depending on the qual-

ity. After dilution, the consumer price is therefore only about DKK 2 per liter of diluted drink. It is Ripella's opinion that a major part of the "saft" and "læskedrik" is consumed to quench thirst. Children often drink juice to quench their thirst. The juice consumption of adults is, however, considered the result of a desire to drink something wholesome and nourishing, particularly in the morning.

Most Danes drink juice only every once in a while. About 28 percent of all households drink juice at least once a day (heavy users); nearly 22 percent drink juice at least once a week. Quite a few (about 30 percent) drink juice about once every three months whereas about 20 percent never drink juice. As Exhibit 1 indicates, juice drinking habits vary considerably.

Generally, milk and coffee are the most common drinks, consumed daily or almost daily by about 80 percent of all households. Beer consumption is more concentrated on heavy users. Tea and lemonade are likewise consumed relatively frequently (about 30 percent of all households daily or almost daily).

POSITIONING CONCEPTS

It was natural for Ocean Spray as exporters to want the positioning of the product transferred unchanged from the American market to the new market. First, costs would be saved by not having to adapt the concept; second, Ocean Spray could use its core competence in the best possible way as the company's accumulated experience from the sale and marketing of Cranberry Drink could be fully exploited. For Ripella it seemed more natural to work with the positioning decisions from a

Danish point of view, particularly since Cranberry Drink had to fit into Ripella's existing line of products, adding an extension of strategic value.

Ocean Spray's proposal for the product positioning in Denmark was to launch Cranberry Drink as a unique, especially wholesome juice. The actual product was to be Ocean Spray's flagship, the Cranberry Juice Cocktail. The reason for picking this product was that it constituted the core of the unique "cranberry concept": the wholesome, the pure, the special taste. Based on Ocean Spray's experience in the United States, the extension of the product line with "blended products" could be effected simultaneously (few variants) or when the main product was well introduced on the market. Ocean Spray suggested the same glass packing as in the United States. In the retail outlets the product should be shelved together with other juice products. The strategy should aim for the widest possible distribution. The price level of the product should equal that of the most expensive juices, that is, a liter price of about DKK 13–20.

Ripella's product positioning concept was based on the following reasoning: The consumers were likely to perceive Cranberry Drink as a wholesome and refreshing special product of high quality. Cranberry Drink would probably be consumed in two very different situations: First, as a refreshing and wholesome product following physical exercises such as sports and gardening; second, in a cozy and relaxed environment where cranberry had the character of a nonalcoholic drink, sipped rather than gulped down. The target group of the product was envisaged by Ripella to be households/people over 18 years of age living in cities, having at least a bachelor's degree and an income above average (i.e., about 20 percent of Danish population). The company planned to market Cranberry Drink in a Pure-Pack 0.75 liter carton, priced between orange juice and special juices. An advertisement and promotion budget of just under DKK 2 million was considered necessary in the case of a product like Cranberry Drink.

At first, Ocean Spray suggested that the target group should be heavy users of juice, that is, persons drinking juice at least three times a week and preferably persons who had tasted juice based on different fruits. As their actual target group Ocean Spray wanted to focus on married women from 25 to 40 years of age, with 1 or 2 children. Furthermore, the women should have passed at least their university entrance exams and have medium-high incomes.

FOCUS GROUP INTERVIEWS

To test their alternative concepts, Ripella and Ocean Spray agreed to run six focus group interviews with a total of 48 consumers, taking about two months to complete. Ocean Spray's ad agency prepared rough sketches of advertisements showing eight alternative positioning themes and unique selling propositions.

The first focus group interviews were very general with the objective of achieving an introductory understanding of how Cranberry Drink might become part of Danish juice-drinking habits. Another objective was to illustrate the consumers' terminology related to drinks.

The subsequent focus groups were more specifically aimed at consumer reactions to Cranberry Drink and various communication concepts. The precise objective was to generate ideas about how Cranberry Drink could be fitted into the Danish market (product acceptance, target group, positioning, and so on).

LANGUAGE DIFFERENCES

The focus group interviews indicated that Danes have a different way of categorizing drinks than Americans. In the United States the concept of juice includes all drinks consisting of juice squeezed out of or extracted from fresh fruit. It is characteristic of Denmark that the consumers' terminology is more varied in this area.

The English concept of "juice" is to Danes almost exclusively attached to apples and oranges, and to Danes "juice" means 100 percent pure juice from these fruits. Actually "juice" might cover the same meaning as "saft" (syrup). However, the concept of "saft" in Denmark gives cause for some confusion. Historically, it is closely attached to home-made products and consequently the term "saftevand" has for generations been applied to drinks involving home-made "saft" diluted with water. Later "saftevand" became closely attached to industrially manufactured "blandet saft/læskedrik" (blended syrup/refreshing drink). The latter terms seem to communicate that it involves a blended product based on various fruits and containing quite a lot of sugar and possibly artificial additives. Danes attach higher quality to the concept of "blandet saft" than to the concept of "læskedrik," the latter being considered more "artificial."

Finally, the Danish vocabulary contains another concept: "most" (a sort of unfermented cider), which to Danes indicates very high-quality and pure raw materials. According to Danish law the term "most" must be applied only to cider from fruit or berries grown in Denmark. This applies for example to apples ("æble-most") and black currants ("solblærmost").

VISUAL IMPRESSIONS

The initial advertisement concepts emphasizing the unique taste, freshness, and power of the small cranberry, were quickly discarded by the first focus groups. Practically all participants were negative about their contents, calling them "too smart", "sickening," "over-American," "irrelevant," "unrealistic," and the like. One comment was, "This little berry cannot contain all that." The two concepts that were most positively received were "Goodness born of sun, sand, and ocean" and "The Cranberry country." It was considered positive to tell about the origin of the fruit. Many people were in doubt, however, as to where to find "The Cranberry country" (Canada, the United States, Japan, and northern Sweden were suggested). The small, hardy berry aroused interest. Because the text was factual, "bitter-sweet" did not seem incredible. Many got associations to a drink that was good at quenching their thirst. Illustrations of applications of the product were well accepted by all participants.

When the participants saw the actual product (in a glass bottle) and tasted it, their reactions became clearer. The look was generally judged as negative; many participants thought that the product looked thin and artificial. Some expressed the opinion that a good and wholesome juice was characterized by its content of pulp. The ruby red color seemed to signal something synthetic with lots of additives. One comment was, "It looks like a cheap summer drink." Simultaneously, to many the color red indicated something sweet and consequently not refreshing and thirst-quenching. Because of the glass bottle and the color, some people got associations to beetroots.

TASTE PERCEPTIONS

The taste was assessed by most participants as sourish and fresh (not sweet). The word "sourish" was perceived by most participants as a positive word whereas "sour" was negative. The word "bitter" was perceived very differently and might therefore be dangerous to apply. After having seen the advertisement concepts and Cranberry's strong color, quite a few of the participants were disappointed by its taste. Everybody agreed to characterize the taste as weak. Cranberry Drink was considered by practically everybody an adult drink as children would not like the peculiar taste and aftertaste that even many of the participants (adults) found unacceptable.

Cranberry Drink was perceived by most participants as a good thirst quencher that could be enjoyed alone or as a cocktail with a touch of some kind of liquor. To quench your thirst you need something cold; some mentioned ice water and others plain water. Obviously, there are two perceptions of the term "thirst." One is the thirst in which a biological need for liquid is to be satisfied, another is the lesser thirst for which you can drink something delicious. In the former case of true thirst, many thought that water was required, as otherwise it would be too expensive. There was general agreement that Cranberry Drink did not go with food with which many participants drank water. Basically, there was also agreement that Cranberry Drink was not a health drink and that is was actually not a juice, but more like a "saft." Color, taste, and consistency affected this judgment.

DISCUSSION QUESTIONS

1. What are the main differences in juice consumption between the U.S. market and the Danish market?

2. How attractive is the Danish market as a lead market for Scandinavia?

3. Judging from the focus group findings, how transferable is the U.S. positioning to the Danish market?

4. What adaptation of product and unique selling proposition, if any, would you propose for the Danish market?

5. After this research, how would you evaluate the potential for Ocean Spray Cranberry Drink in the Scandinavian market?

Case 2.2

Toys R Us Goes to Japan

Toys R Us, Inc. is a children's specialty retailer concentrating on toys and children's clothing headquartered in Paramus, New Jersey. In the early 1990s, after successful penetration of the North American market and selected European markets, company executives were formulating their expansion plans for the Japanese market.

COMPANY BACKGROUND

Toys R Us is, by all accounts, the largest toy retailer in the world, with about 20–25 percent of the U.S. market, and 2 percent of total international sales. It was founded in the late 1940s by the current chairman, Charles Lazarus, as the first "toy supermarket," and was acquired by department store chain operator Interstate Inc., in 1966. Interstate went bankrupt in 1974 after becoming overextended through buying a number of discount chains, but it continued to build more Toys R Us stores through a court-ordered reorganization. After this was finished in 1977, Interstate divested all its other assets and became Toys R Us, Inc.; Lazarus became chairman and CEO. Toys R Us grew fast through the late 1970s and 1980s by an aggressive expansion campaign which undercut existing retailers. The first Kids R Us stores were opened in 1982; and the first international stores were opened in 1984. Since going public in 1978, sales have risen every year, although earnings showed only nominal gains between 1989 and 1991.

The company operates 1,032 stores, with 581 Toys R Us stores and 217 Kids R Us stores in the United States, and with 234 Toys R Us stores operated through international subsidiaries in 18 countries. Sales in 1993 were $7.9 billion, making Toys R Us the 50th largest retailer in the world and the 22nd largest in the United States. By comparison, Japan's largest retailer, Daiei, had about $14 billion annually in sales. After-tax profits of $483 million were realized in 1993, and 18 percent of total sales and 14 percent of profits were from the international operations. Financial highlights from 1989 through 1993 are given in Exhibit 1.

COMPANY STRATEGY

Toys R Us has succeeded by using a "category killer" strategy, which combines strong advertising to promote name recognition and discounts on the most popular items (loss leaders such as diapers) to create a perception that everything is discounted, with large stores offering a wide selection of brand name merchandise. Such stores are the progenitors of the low-cost, low-service, warehouse-style discount store concept that is currently taking a large share of the U.S. market. In the United States, a computerized inventory system is used to track demand on a regional and store-by-store basis to maintain low standing inventories and capitalize quickly on trends. This system is being upgraded with even better communications technology and improved regional warehouse facilities. Toys R Us also owns and operates its own fleet of trucks, to save on shipping. Industry power from the high market share is occasionally wielded by Toys R Us to keep its producers in line. Prices on most goods are competitive with other retailers, but in general they are not deeply discounted. Over the past year, Toys R Us has used coupon promotions aggressively in the period before Christmas to increase market share over their major sales period.

TOYS R US INTERNATIONAL

The long-term strategy for Toys R Us is to expand primarily in international markets. Toys R Us International operations follow the home country strategy, but as competition from other large-volume discount-type stores is less in most of the international markets,

Case compiled from report developed by Michael Chadwick and Jeong-Soe Won, Waseda–Georgetown Graduate Business Program, Tokyo, 1994.

EXHIBIT 1 Financial Highlights *Toys "R" Us, Inc. and Subsidiaries*

(Dollars in millions except per share date)	Jan. 29, 1994	Jan. 30, 1993	Feb. 1, 1992	Feb. 2, 1991	Jan. 28, 1990	Jan. 29 1989
Operations:						
Net Sales	$7,946	$7,169	$6,124	$5,510	$4,788	$4,000
Net Earnings	483	438	340	326	321	268
Basic Earnings Per Share	1.66	1.51	1.18	1.12	1.11	0.92
Diluted Earnings Per Share	1.63	1.47	1.15	1.11	1.09	0.91
Financial Position at Year End:						
Working Capital	$633	$797	$328	$177	$238	$255
Real Estate-Net	2,036	1,877	1,751	1,433	1,142	952
Total Assets	6,150	5,323	4,583	3,582	3,075	2,555
Long-Term Debt	724	671	391	195	173	174
Stockholders' Equity	3,148	2,889	2,426	2,046	1,705	1,424
Number of Stores at Year End:						
Toys "R" Us-United States	581	540	497	451	404	358
Toys "R" Us–International	234	167	126	97	74	52
Kids "R" Us–United States	217	211	189	164	137	112
Babies "R" Us–United States	-	-	-	-	-	-
KidsWorld - United States	-	-	-	-	-	-
Total Stores	1,032	918	812	712	615	522

*After other changes as described in the *Notes to Consolidated Financial Statements.*

prices are correspondingly higher. Inventory is chosen with more than half from the Toys R Us U.S. inventory, and the rest is chosen to reflect local tastes. As of 1993, Toys R Us has started making franchising deals to enter foreign markets with local partners; deals to enter six such markets have been made, primarily in oil-rich developing countries in the Middle East. Of the 115 stores Toys R Us plans to open over this year, 70 will be in other countries.

THE JAPANESE TOY MARKET

As in many product categories, the toy retail market in Japan is dominated by small specialty stores and general retailers. Of the 29,413 stores which had toy sales as a significant percentage of overall sales in 1991, 11,628 were toy and hobby specialty retailers (including computer game shops), and 12,582 were small general retail shops; an additional 2,772 were convenience stores, and 1,227 were large toy specialty retailers; less than 500 larger general retailers made a significant portion of their income from toy sales. By comparison, in 1987 the Unites States had only 9,629 stores which fell into the specialty retailer category, and a significant percentage of total sales were made by large general retail chains such as Kmart, Sears, and Wal-Mart.

Japanese statistical reporting does not separate toys from other leisure goods, but statistics indicate that yearly sales for toys, sporting goods, and musical instruments were approximately ｜SY3.3 trillion ($25 billion at 1991 exchange rate of ｜SY130/$1) in 1991. The largest exclusive toy retailer in Japan, Kiddyland, had 1992 per store sales of ｜SY230 million ($1.8 million) from 52 stores for a total of ｜SY11.96 billion ($92 million), as compared to Toys R Us' $7.9 billion from 1,032 stores ($7.6 million per store). All in all, there are 21 toy/hobby store chains (defined as having more than one store) in Japan, with the largest, Pelican, having 71 stores.

The 29,000 toy and sporting goods retailers are serviced by a network of 5,692 wholesalers and deal almost exclusively in Japan-made products. There are upwards of 15,000 toy manufacturers in Japan, but only six of all of these (including game giants Nintendo and Koei) employ more than 50 people; the vast majority are one to two person operations. The most popular products are computer games and dolls or toys with linkages to animated television characters.

The average Japanese household spent ｜SY83,724/year in 1992 ($650) on health and leisure products (again, the two are not differentiated in statistical analyses). There are approximately 39 million households in Japan, which ranks Japan with the United States and Europe as one of the three largest and wealthiest markets in the world for leisure products. In general, they are motivated as much by quality as by price, and show a preference for established brand-name merchandise over lesser known goods.

BARRIERS TO ENTRY

Before Toys R Us entered the Japanese market, a number of issues were pointed to and voices were raised to suggest that Japan was not ready for the retailing revolution Toys R Us represented. The issues took a number of forms: suggestions that Toys R Us would not be able to get the necessary permissions and empty space it needed to open huge stores; statements that major Japanese manufacturers would not be willing to enter into direct deals with Toys R Us, instead preferring to work through middle wholesalers and preserve their traditional trade links; analyses that claimed that Toys R Us, like many other multinationals, would find that the tools which worked so well in the rest of the world would come up short when confronted with the sensitive Japanese consumer; and contentions that discount retailing was antithetical to the Japanese psyche, which linked quality with price, and so Toys R Us, by competing on price, would class themselves out of the market.

ALLIANCE WITH McDONALD'S

Toys R Us first made public its plans to enter the Japanese market in 1989, signing a high-profile alliance contract with McDonald's Japan. A new subsidiary, Toys R Us Japan, was established with Toys R Us owning 80 percent and McDonald's Japan holding the remaining 20 percent. The long-time president of McDonald's Japan, T. Fujita, came on board as vice chairman of the new joint venture, and almost the entire staff was locally hired. There are no foreign permanent employees at Toys R Us Japan's headquarters in Kawasaki City, 20 minutes outside central Tokyo. The two companies presented a formidable team to local competitors; Toys R Us, with its commanding share of the U.S. market and excellent marketing strategy, had the industry power and experience in cracking foreign markets, while McDonald's, so firmly established in Japan that it is almost considered a Japanese company by many, had the depth of market knowledge and research skills, as well as the communications lines to

the target groups of children and young families. As part of the deal, McDonald's has the right to establish a restaurant in any location Toys R Us picks for a store.

The first store was opened in Ibaraki Prefecture in December 1991, and since that time, Toys R Us has opened 15 more stores, with more expected before the end of the year. Toys R Us has relied on McDonald's market research to target suburban areas with young families as a primary growth base. City stores have so far been limited to Osaka and Nagasaki, but most stores are near enough to major cities that they can be reached within a one-hour drive. Despite the high cost of land, the stores are provided with ample parking. They are still lagging a bit behind the ambitious plan announced in 1991 to have 31 stores open by the end of the year, but are on target for 100 by the year 2000, if their luck and the lack of any serious competition holds out.

Their primary advertising media strategy is the use of colorful inserts in newspapers, rather than television or radio, which are far more expensive and scattershot, not necessarily reaching the targeted audience. Newspaper inserts for home deliveries ensure that advertising reaches the home, where mothers and children, the primary targets, are more likely to see them. It is also possible in this way to localize advertising to areas near stores; there are as yet too few stores in operation to make television a valuable alternative.

LAND AND APPROVAL

The timing of the Toys R Us market entry was fortunate. In 1989, the bubble economy was in full swing, but by December 1991, when the first store opened in Ibaraki, the economy had lapsed into recession. The slogan "Everyday Low Prices" was therefore appealing to many who were looking for value as well as quality, and the minimal level of service (no gift-wrapping) was more acceptable as fewer gifts were being given.

The entry was also well timed in coinciding with an antistructural impediments initiative by the Bush administration. The Japanese government, looking for positive PR, pushed the Ibaraki regional government to waive the "Big Store" laws under which existing retailers can veto the entry of a large retailer into the area. The first store, at 3000 square meters and offering 18,000 items in inventory, was the perfect example of what has come to be called in America a "category killer": By creating an overwhelming advantage, it is intended to stop competitors from opening opposing stores before they start.

DIRECT DEALS WITH MANUFACTURERS

As Toys R Us Japan imports more than half of its supply from the U.S., this was not the pressing issued it was first painted to be. Only one major Japanese manufacturer has signed on to ship directly to Toys R Us stores, but that one is Nintendo, which extended its American direct-shipping agreement to cover Japan as well in June 1991, before the first store in Japan was opened. On the other hand, neither is it true that, with this deal, "the Japanese toy distribution system, hit by a wave of internationalization, has taken a first step toward significant reform," as no other manufacturers have made a similar deal, and no other toy retailer has been able to crack the distribution network and deal direct. Toys R Us has adopted a flexible strategy in approaching the distribution issue, working through existing channels in Japan where necessary, but utilizing the central Kobe warehouse as a waystation so they can control their in-store inventory more precisely.

U.S. METHODS IN THE JAPANESE MARKET

Before entering the Japanese market, Toys R Us had operations in eight other countries. It drew on these experiences, especially those of its successful stores in two other Asian cultures, Hong Kong and Singapore. There was thus a willingness to be open in methods and changes; for example, although corporate policy dictates that no store should be less than 3,000 square meters, the Japan group decided that the new store in Himeji, Hyogo Prefecture, could be viable at 2,800 square meters, and succeeding stores were sometimes even smaller than that.

Just as importantly, Toys R Us was able to draw on the successful experience of McDonald's, another American firm which was able to adjust to Japanese rules while still maintaining its innovative nature (as the first Western-style fast food chain) to become a market leader. When McDonald's came to Japan, it faced and beat the same issues of establishing distribution and supply channels, and its experience was valuable for Toys R us to draw on.

LARGE-SCALE, DISCOUNT RETAIL IN A SMALL STORE MARKET

Toys R Us also copied McDonald's in another important respect: it viewed its fundamental system as a positive innovation that provided value to Japanese consumers, and marketed it as such. Toys R Us marketing, rather than focusing on "Everyday Low Prices," promised unparalleled inventory, essentially guaranteeing that even the most popular items would be in stock at all times, which small local retailers were unable to do. Rather than being forced to get up at 4 am and get in line to get the new Mortal Combat 4 the day it came out, all a consumer had to do was come to Toys R Us any time to be sure they could get the game.

The relative lack of service, while offputting to some Japanese consumers, is not unique to Toys R Us. At the same time, other discount stores such as Topos have made inroads, offering a wide selection, low prices, and economy packaging. Only Toys R Us, however, has combined the by now accepted discount store with the specialty retail niche; but given its success, it would seem likely that Home Depot, CompUSA, and other large-scale niche retailers are following the progress of Toys R Us very carefully.

COMPETITION

Interestingly, in Japan it has been two footwear dealers that have taken the lead in opening shops modeled on Toys R Us. Chiyoda's "Harrowmark" chain and Marutomi's "BanBan" are both expanding nationwide, offering low prices in line with Toys R Us, but unable to finance the same stores or inventories. The price wars that have been spawned may well cut into Toys R Us Japan's bottom line for some time. Other stores have adopted nonprice techniques to compete, such as "do-it-yourself" toy days, where children are helped to build models or stitch together dolls, or the hiring of "toy consultants" to get into kids' heads and guess the next big hit so stores can stock up.

Just as threatening is a move by smaller retailers to unite in opposition to Toys R Us. The ostensible goals of the 600 company–member Toy Shop Specialist Council (Gangu Senmontei Kai) are to research new management techniques, examine the possibility of making direct deals with producers, and cooperate to establish a new joint distribution system, all laudable goals. However, they have also taken less benign steps, approaching distributors and asking that they boycott Toys R Us for its policy of dealing direct. While they have had some successes, few distributors want to cut off hope of dealing with the toy giant, and so are taking a wait and see approach. "Distribution retribution" has not yet come to hurt Toys R Us.

COST

Toys R Us Japan, while unwilling to release operating results, has indicated that it is willing to carry a lot more debt than is the low-leverage parent firm, in line with the practices of Japanese competitors. They also leave their land on short-term leases, a concession made as part of the price of goodwill, but not a serious drawback in the current depressed land market. Despite the low rents and interest rates, in general, operating costs are three times as high as in the U.S. They also import a lot of goods, and are now profiting from the cheap dollar. However, this triple positive of cheap land, cheap money, and cheap imports will have to end sooner or later, and sharp swings upward in any or all of them will certainly have a negative effect on the bottom line.

POSITIONING

While value is important to the Japanese consumer, quality has traditionally been more of a watchword than price. Given two equivalent products, the consumer will choose the cheaper one; differentiate them and quality will win over price in most product areas in Japan. It is important for Toys R Us to steer clear of the part of the low-price zone which it veers into being equivalent to low quality. To that end, their policy of only carrying established brand name items is good, as is the marketing emphasis on inventory rather than price, but in the future, as price competitors arise, it will be important for Toys R Us to walk a fine line be-

tween becoming too expensive for the young target market it aims for and so cheap that consumers decided the store has nothing else going for it.

THE FUTURE OF TOYS R US JAPAN— LESS ROSY THAN THE PRESENT?

Discussions with Toys R Us Japan executives indicate that they feel that Japan is an almost untapped market, easily capable of supporting five times as many stores as are now in operation. At the same time, they discount the idea of competition rising to fill that niche before Toys R Us can preempt it. However, examples of other American companies that took a lead in market share, then became sanguine and saw that lead slip away, are legion. While Toys R Us to date has shown no tendency to give in to wishful thinking, it is still necessary to look at the challenges to be faced in the future. These include not only increasing competition, but also increasing costs, possible positioning problems, and the danger of a consumer and supplier backlash if the U.S.–Japan trade situation continues to deteriorate.

DISCUSSION QUESTIONS

1. What are the problems in transferring Toys R Us competitive advantages to a foreign market?

2. Why should Toys R Us internalize the firm-specific advantages rather than licensing another retailer abroad?

3. Is Japan an attractive market for Toys R Us?

4. What are the entry barriers into Japan? Any culturally based barriers, in terms of how to do business? Do you think there are any cultural obstacles to product acceptance?

5. How did Toys R Us manage to cross the entry barriers into Japan? What alternative modes of entry could have been tried?

Case 2.3

Partnering Problems: The Internationalization of the Illycaffé Company

Illycaffe was founded in Trieste, a large city in the northeast of Italy, by Francesco Illy in 1933. Frencesco Illy was a true gourmet who sought to provide his customers with the highest quality espresso coffee. By 1990 Illycaffé had a total of 150 employees and its sales had grown from 21 billion lire in 1983 to 67 billion lire in 1990.[1] It was a family-owned company whose shares were divided between Ernesto Illy (the founder's son), his wife, and their four children, all of whom occupied various management positions within the company. Riccardo Illy was marketing manager.

WHAT'S ESPRESSO?

Italy is well-known for its history, culture, art, and beauty. But Italian wine and cuisine are also part of the mystique that attracts people from around the world. Espresso coffee is an element of the cuisine and therefore of this mystique. Espresso is a symbol of the Italian culture.

What makes espresso so different from other types of coffee? There are several methods to percolate coffee: the "filter" or "napoletana" method of letting the weight of the water itself (gravity) pull it through the coffee powder; the "moka" method of creating steam pressure to push water through the coffee; the "espresso" method, which uses water at 194 degrees fahrenheit and 9–10 atmospheres of pressure. The higher the pressure, the less time it takes for the coffee to percolate; the filter method requires several minutes, while the moka method requires one minute, and the espresso method only 30 seconds. The different methods also result in different levels of caffeine in the

coffee cup; the filter method (common in North American and in Northern Europe) results in 90–125 mg. of caffeine per cup, while the espresso method produces a cup with only 60–120 mg. of caffeine.

MARKETING STRATEGY

Being a single product company, Illycaffé only differentiated its packaging of espresso coffee based on *format* (from 3kg. for professional consumption, from 125 gr. to 250 gr. for domestic consumption), on the *form* (ground coffee, beans or E.S.E. servings and on the *type* (regular or decaffeinated).

The unique preservation of the product, by the use pressurization, allowed the expansion of Illycaffé in strategic areas such as the United States, Europe, and even in Japan.

The Company's mission, which was "to delight customers around the world with an excellent cup of espresso and to do everything to improve its quality," reflected the high level of specialized experience capable of meticulously evaluating both the product level and the process level. The direction of excellence always made reference not only to the product which leaves the establishment but also to "the cup of espresso perfectly served, in every moment and in every place in the world."

Illycaffé's positioning strategy in the crowded coffee market was based on the quality concept. In order to maintain high standards, the management had patented a packaging system that was able to guarantee high levels of flavor and aroma. But the quality system was also based on the careful selection and control of the coffee beans used in production. Illycaffé used only 100 percent Arabic beans in production and had contributed to the invention of sophisticated machinery that was able to eliminate any defective beans from each batch used in

---

[1]Exchange rates fluctuated considerably during the period of the case. For analytical purposes, 1,100 Italian lire can be set equal to 1 U.S. dollar.

Source: This case was prepared by Pamela Adams, SDA Bocconi, Milano. Used with permission.

production. The company also dedicated 3 percent of annual sales to research and quality control.

The advertising and promotion policies also focused on the quality of the product, linking it to the brand name in order to increase brand loyalty. It was difficult for producers to ensure that coffee served in cafes was identified by brand. But because most consumers believed coffee made in bars and restaurants was better than that made at home, a strong presence in this segment was necessary to build the brand's image in the home segment (food retailing). Illy reinforced its brand name in cafes and restaurants by asking the owners to display Illy signs and logos both outside the premises to attract customers and inside to recall the brand name. The marketing policies and brand image established by the management helped Illy to get a premium price for its coffee, often even doubling the price of the next highest competitor in this market.

THE QUALITY PROBLEM

One of the company's major problems in maintaining its quality image was the high rate of personnel turnover in the bar and restaurant business. Many employees took on temporary positions as they were looking for other lines of work. This was true in most advanced economies, but it meant that bar operators constantly had to train new personnel in the art of producing a quality cup of espresso.

The quality depended as much on the human input and machinery as on the quality of the coffee used. According to Illy, in fact, a good cup of espresso depended on several elements including the quality of the beans, the roasting of the beans, the correct mix of roasted beans, the quantity of coffee powder used to prepare each cup of coffee, the degree to which the coffee was pressed into the filter of the espresso machine, the water temperature, the pressure at which the water was expelled during the preparation, the cleanliness of the filter, the size of the filter holes, and the quality of the water used in preparation.

The company decided that this was a strategic area for innovation and began to offer technical assistance and training/consultancy to its clients. As Riccardo Illy noted, "A good product is not enough in this market . . . You also have to teach the operators of the espresso machines how to use them in the best way if you want to guarantee an increase in sales."

THE GERMAN ENTRY

The position of Illy in Germany was somewhat different from its position in other European countries where sales were made through agents and sales subsidiaries. Originally (1974), an exclusive agreement had been signed with a German distributor. Despite the limits of this strategy, the company's sales grew from 10 tons in 1974 to 30 tons in 1978. In 1978, however, one of the major German coffee producers, Hag, approached the management of Illycaffé with a proposal to form a distribution alliance. Hag was a family-owned and family-run business with a long tradition in the coffee industry. The company produced both caffeinated and decaffeinated filter coffee, as well as a line of supplementary products such as sugar and cream. Hag had an extensive distribution network throughout Germany and had noted a growing interest in espresso coffee among its clients. The company had tried to produce its own branch of quality espresso, but had failed and was now looking for an Italian producer who would be interested in an alliance for the German market.

Ernesto Illy realized that any significant increase in sales in Germany would require much greater investments in both sales force and promotion. But 1977 had not been a profitable year in the domestic market, and the company's financial situation would not permit such investments. Nor was the existing German distributor willing to take on further commitments. Ernesto therefore decided to accept Hag's proposal. As he concluded: "This was a great offer from a significant player in the German coffee industry who believed in our product. This was all the assurance that I needed."

THE HAG-GOLDENE TASSE ERA

The contract that was signed by the two companies in 1978 gave Hag exclusive rights to the sale of Illy coffee in Germany. Illy's German distributor, in fact, was required to turn over its client lists to Hag. The job of Illy's distribution was reduced to acting as an interface between the two headquarters and to supplying smaller customers.

Illy maintained control over the brand name and the product, while Hag was given responsibility for promotion and distribution decisions in Germany. Rough sales targets were indicated in the contract (80 tons by 1980, 150 tons by 1981 and 250 tons by 1982), although Hag was under no obligation to reach these targets. No provisions were made for Illy to receive any information about the clients.

Three years later, Hag was acquired by another company in the German coffee business, Goldene Tasse. No significant changes were made in the Illy-caffé agreement as a result of this acquisition. In fact, the meetings between the two companies during these years were rare and the contract was typically renewed at the end of each period without any direct contact between the two partners.

According to the original contract, Hag had agreed to pay Illy 13.70 DM for each kilo of coffee received. The prices was broken down into two parts: one half was pegged to the price of green coffee on the international market, while the other half was pegged to Illy's production costs.

Price changes were provided for only the half related to the raw coffee: these changes could be effected only every three months according to the fluctuations in the trading price established on the international market. Requests for price increases due to rising production costs, on the other hand, could be made by Illy only once at the beginning of each contract year, and had to be supported by documentation explaining the actual cost increases.

Following the signing of this agreement in 1978, Illy witnessed a steady increase in sales. But as Riccardo complained as he looked over the records in 1990, "The sales may have been increasing, but we weren't making any money. Our selling price was too low to earn any margins and we had to absorb the high rates of inflation in Italy. Moreover, as the price of green coffee continued to fall on international markets due to the excess in supply throughout the 1980s, we had no way to raise the price of our product to Hag in any substantial way."

GLOBALIZING THE STRATEGY

As Riccardo Illy took over responsibility for the company's international activities in 1990, he quickly decided to change Illy's strategy in the European market. He was convinced that the move toward a more unified European market provided an excellent opportunity for Illy to appeal to a pan-European consumer through a standardized marketing program in line with the strategy followed in the Italian market. In order to carry out this plan, however, he understood that he needed to create a cohesive team and to bring the various subsidiaries under his direct control. The most effective way he saw to begin this process was to acquire distributors in each major market.

Once the buyout process was completed, Mr. Illy gave one of his export managers, Mr. Giacomo Biviano, responsibility for the company's activities in Europe. Mr. Biviano, a young and decisive manager with a strong background in both international marketing and administration and control, was named CEO for France and Germany, and also appointed to the supervisory board of the new company in Holland. As Biviano described it, "We needed managers who would be loyal to our ideas and would implement a standardized set of policies that were to be decided at the central level."

OWNERSHIP COMPLICATIONS

Just about this time, however, Riccardo Illy also learned that Hag-Goldene Tasse had been acquired by General Foods, a diversified multinational in the food industry, which was itself later acquired by Philip Morris International. By 1990, both Kraft, another American-based multinational in the food business, and Jacobs Suchard, a Swiss producer of coffee and chocolate with its own line of espresso, had also come under the wing of the Philip Morris group. As a result, a merger was made between Hag's coffee division, Goldene Tasse, and Jacob Suchard's coffee business in Germany. The new company, called Jacobs-Goldene Tasse, took over Hag's position as Illy's partner in the German market. Riccardo Illy immediately called for a meeting with the new partners to discuss the potential effects of the changes on the distribution agreement between the companies.

Although Hag-Goldene Tasse had its own line of espresso coffee, and Jacobs Suchard had a line of both espresso coffee and espresso pods, all of which were sold to the bar segment in Germany, Riccardo Illy underlined the fact that none of these products were of the same quality as Illy's brand of espresso coffee. At the meeting the parties agreed to continue the existing arrangement until Jacobs had time to do more research, with one significant change. To protect its quality image, Illy was allowed to have a technical assistant accompany Hag's salesmen during client visits, providing consultancy on the use and maintenance of espresso machines. Although the arrangement lasted only a few months, Illy gained some important insights from these visits. As Biviano noted, "One significant lesson we learned from these direct contacts with the clients was that it was unusual for bar and restaurant operators in Germany to demand trade credit from small suppliers. Such financing was required only from suppliers whose products represented a large share of the business, such as filter coffee and beer."

THE SECOND MEETING

Riccardo Illy and Giacomo Biviano prepared a list of changes that they wanted made in the contract for the subsequent meeting:

1. The selling price of Illy coffee to Hag-Goldene Tasse should be the same as in other European markets, and with the same payment conditions.
2. All marketing activities (especially advertising to the trade, to the consumer, and at the point-of-sales) would be managed and controlled by Illy's new German subsidiary.
3. Hag-Goldene Tasse would be granted exclusive rights to the distribution of Illy coffee in Germany, contingent on the requirement that Hag-Goldene Tasse distribute only Illy's brand of espresso coffee.
4. Clear growth objectives would be stipulated in the contract. These objectives should be in line with Illy's overall objectives for growth, and Hag should be obliged to achieve the stated objectives.
5. A unit to supervise technical consulting/quality control at the point-of-sales would be created and managed by Illy-Germany.
6. A new policy of communication at point-of-sales would be implemented through the use of Illy cups and billboards. Illy should have the authority to control the implementation of this activity through contracts and regular visits to clients.

By the end of the meeting, Jacobs Suchard and Hag-Goldene Tasse had agreed to points (1) and (4), but had refused to accept point (3). The companies did not adopt a position concerning points (2), (5), and (6). No new meeting was scheduled between the parties.

UNCERTAIN FUTURE

At the end of the current contract period in June of 1991, the manager of Illy-Germany terminated the contract between Illy and Hag-Goldene Tasse, offering an interim option to renegotiate a new contract. The option was left open until the end of August.

In the meantime, Riccardo Illy and Giacomo Biviano began to study the three major alternatives:

A. Give full responsibility for rules and distribution back to Illy-Germany and work together with the German team to establish an effective sales force.
B. Look for a new partner in Germany who could offer a solid sales network and would agree to the terms outlined in the proposal prepared for Hag-Goldene Tasse.
C. Work toward a new contract with Hag-Goldene Tasse/Jacobs Suchard.

In the latter two cases, given that it was unlikely that all of Illy's request would be accepted by any partner, it would be necessary to rank the requests in order of importance and to establish the minimum requirements for any agreement.

As the next step, therefore, the two managers had to decide whether or not to attempt to revive the piggyback agreement with Hag, to look for a new distributor, or to create their own network in accordance with their new Euro strategy.

DISCUSSION QUESTIONS

1. What created the problems with the existing distribution strategy in the German market? Was the distribution alliance with Hag ill-advised?
2. To what extent do you think the pan-European strategy shift well-founded? For example, one question is whether the espresso market is global or multi-domestic.
3. Which of the three alternatives would you recommend?
4. What negotiation strategy would you recommend for Mr. Illy when implementing the strategy?

Local Marketing

n Part Two, "Foreign Entry," we focused on how the firm establishes its presence in foreign countries. Part Three now looks at the local marketing activities in the new countries.

The marketer is no longer at headquarters but located abroad. This shift has several important consequences. First, the marketer must analyze and segment markets, manage distribution channels, introduce products and services, develop effective promotions, capture market share, and increase sales. Even though the main strategic objective of the firm's presence in the country might be to check competition, monitor leading customers, or cross-subsidize a business elsewhere, the marketing job is still to be as successful as possible within the global corporate constraints.

Second, the marketer must learn more about the environmental factors, as the political, financial, and legal restrictions on business can create unforeseen headaches. Also, the social and cultural networks among customers and competitors work in new and mysterious ways. The marketing infrastructure has developed under different conditions, so that the functions performed by wholesalers, retailers, advertising agencies, and other middlemen may deviate from

expectations. Co-workers speak a different language, pledge allegiance to their own nation, believe in a different religion, and behave in unfamiliar ways toward each other.

Third, the focus is no longer on national boundaries. The local marketer is now concerned with the *market*, and the market may or may not be the same as the nation. The market could be larger, for example, a free trade area of geographically close countries; or it could be smaller, with ethnic or urban subgroups within a country.

In our discussion of local marketing in Part Three, the manager will be seen as a marketer who is working within the special constraints created by a new and unfamiliar environment, with an arm's-length relationship to the home office. Chapter 7 presents the conceptual models underlying the marketer's understanding of customers and the marketing research necessary to analyze and understand local consumers. Chapters 8, 9, and 10 show how the different market environments in maturing, new growth, and emerging economies affect the local marketing effort. These chapters deal with strategy formulation, implementation, and execution under quite different conditions.

Seven

Local Buyer Behavior

"Buyers everywhere are the same—only different"

Your takeaways from this chapter:

1. Understanding customers abroad involves conceptual skills and imaginative rethinking more than new analytical marketing skills.

2. Existing concepts and models of consumer behavior and business-to-business buying behavior are useful tools when examining buyers in local markets abroad, but underlying assumptions need to be reconsidered.

3. Because of widely differing environmental forces surrounding product purchase and use, the core benefit of a product or service can vary considerably across countries.

4. There are numerous sources of errors in cross-cultural consumer research, including mistranslated questionnaires, strong demand effects, and poor control over the administration of surveys. However, with sensitivity and skill, marketing research techniques, including focus groups and questionnaire-based surveys, can be adapted and used in foreign cultures.

5. Regardless of the specific local motivations behind buyer behavior in different countries, delivering the promised benefits and customer satisfaction remain the goal of the marketing effort.

AS WE SAW in Chapter 3 on cultural factors, customers in different countries may want and demand the same things, but their specific product and service needs and preferences vary considerably between markets. The underlying reason is differences between cultures and socioeconomic environments, that is, the conditions under which products and services are used and consumed. These factors affect buyer behavior directly and therefore make for necessary changes in local marketing activities. A good deal of the local marketer's hard work abroad involves adjusting his or her understanding of how and why customers and competitors behave as they do.

This adjustment is not a matter of advanced marketing skills but of basic conceptual skills. To the extent they are relevant and applicable, most of the technical marketing skills required in a local market are very similar to those at home. This chapter will not deal extensively with those. On the other hand, there are *sophisticated conceptual* skills needed, especially when the local market is a leading market. To understand customers and competitors, the local marketing manager needs to develop a "theory" of what motivates the people. As a start, it is useful to get back to relatively simple models of buyer behavior—concepts about the stages of consumer decision making, how information is processed by consumers, what external influences play a role in buying decisions, and how the individual buyer handles risk taking—and reevaluate the assumptions underlying these models. Such conceptual rethinking requires a stretch of the imagination and constitutes part of the learning that goes into marketing abroad. The local marketer abroad will develop conceptual skills, fresh ways of thinking about marketing, which can in the future be usefully applied in other parts of the world. And the significant features of the buyer behavior in the home market will be understood more clearly when contrasted against buyer behavior in other countries.

A Beer Is a Beer Is a Beer?

Beer seems to be a product where consumers' subjective perceptions count for more than objective facts, and where taste preferences reveal astonishing country-of-origin effects. Two, um, cases come from Mexico and South Africa.

In 1999, at 55 million cases, Corona beer from Mexico became the most popular imported beer in the United States, handily beating perennial leader Dutch Heineken's 42 million cases. For Mexicans who regard Corona as a relatively low-class beer, the U.S. success is a mystery. But Carlos Fernandez Gonzales, Corona's new 32-year old CEO, credits marketing smarts.

Entering the U.S. market in the 1970s, Corona's sales were initially sluggish. Then the company's distributors in the U.S. hit upon the idea of focusing on two niche segments. First came the more obvious notion of targeting the millions of Mexicans living in the U.S. Then in an imaginative stroke, the company decided to target young American beer drinkers, many of whom had vacationed on Mexican beaches in Cancun, Mazatlan, and Acapulco.

Designing ads featuring attractive college-age women and men enjoying spring-break on a sun-drenched Mexican beach, and positioning Corona at a premium price between domestic and expensive import beers, the company saw sales taking off. A temporary slowdown occurred as rumors arose that Corona's light color reflected urine content (a rumor

Corona managers believe was started by competitors), but sales soon recouped, helped by the clever "hook" of suggesting that Corona be drunk directly from the bottle with a slice of lime, appealing to the irreverent "whatever" young.

Corona is going global, sales rising in several new markets, including Israel, Russia, and Japan. The company is now targeting Europe, even making inroads at the holy shrine of beer lovers, Munich's traditional Oktober Fest. Validating the globalization of markets idea, the same tropical beach ads that worked in the U.S. seem to work also in other countries.

A different kind of picture comes out of Africa. National Sorghum Breweries is a South African company that markets sorghum beer, a thick, pinkish brew with a very short shelf life. Sorghum beer is traditionally the first drink served at an African wedding or funeral. Early in the 20th century the South African government took control of brewing and sales of the traditional beer and essentially made other alcoholic beverages unavailable to black South Africans.

During the changes that transformed the country in the 1990s, the South African government decided to return the industry to black ownership. Mohale Mahanyele, who led the investor group that bought National Sorghum, saw advantages. Sorghum beer had sprung from the African culture. National Sorghum had an exclusive license to brew it. Plus, Mahanyele had fought apartheid, so consumer attitudes would be favorable.

But consumer perceptions of the product were more negative than expected. Black South Africans viewed sorghum as a drink for poor poeple. When possible, they drank other beers, preferably imports. In addition, National Sorghum had to compete with South African Breweries, the country's largest brewer. SAB was well established and courted retailers with special deals and freebies.

Following the "If you can't fight them, join them" dictum, National Sorghum developed its own lager beer, and played down the role of its flagship sorghum beer. The strategy worked. The company built its annual sales to $160 million, and in mid-1995, it sold 30 percent of the company to an Indian firm for about $1 a share—almost four times what its investors originally paid.

Apparently, when it comes to consumers and beers, it's not safe to assume anything.

Sources: Donald G. McNeil, Jr., "Not Thriving in Its Homeland," *New York Times*, October 3, 1995, pp. D1, D4; Brian Bremner, " 'Made in America' Isn't the Kiss of Death Anymore," *Business Week*, November 13, 1995; James Sterngold, "The Awakening Chinese Consumer," *New York Times*, October 11, 1992, pp. D1, D4. Wills, Rick, "The Kind of Imported Beers," *New York Times*, May 28, 1999, pp. C1, C2

INTRODUCTION

Good marketing basics are good marketing basics everywhere. Understand buyer behavior, and treat the customer right. Offer products and services appropriate to the local usage conditions, have some competitive advantage, and offer quality that justifies consumer loyalty. Empathize with the customer's situation; don't fight it. Fight the headquarters instinct that says, "What we do is what they get." Fight the kind of ethnocentric mindset that translates to "Since it's good enough at home, it's good enough here."

At the same time, it is good to remember that, as we saw in Chapter 6, it is not always true that one has to adapt to local cultural norms, do it exactly the way the locals want it, or forget about one's own heritage or pride in what one's company produces. There are times when breaking rules is good. Foreign companies successful even in idiosyncratic markets warn against overplaying the "cultural sensitivity" theme. Offering superior value to customers is as good a recipe for success in Asian, Latin American, and European markets as in the United States. *It is just that what constitutes "value" differs depending on actual usage conditions, what functions are really needed, and culturally contingent expectations about performance.*

UNDERSTANDING BUYERS

The diagram in Exhibit 7.1 demonstrates the various forces that need to be assessed when predicting buyer behavior in local markets. Apart from culture, other external

EXHIBIT 7.1 Diagram of Major Factors Influencing Local Buyer Behavior

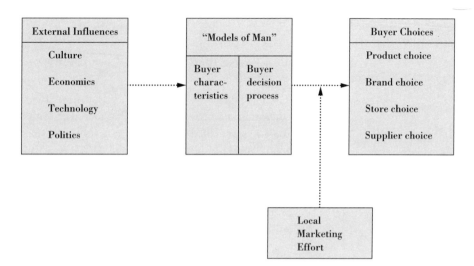

factors are important as well, including economics, technology, and politics. These and related external influences determine the overall context in which the buyer makes purchasing decisions.

The buyer box in Exhibit 7.1 involves the psychological and sociological models of man, which underlie how the marketer thinks customers should be approached. Buyer characteristics—such as personality, age, marital status, and life cycle stage—are internal determinants of behavior and will be useful when segmenting the local market. In industrial purchasing, this box also includes the characteristics of the buyer's organization. The buyer decision process relates to the way the buyer processes information and makes purchasing decisions, which is a major issue for the local marketer since processes vary across markets and cultures. Finally, as the purchasing decision is made, the firms' controllable marketing factors (including product design, price, promotion, and distribution) become important influences on the choices made.

This chapter focuses on the "models of man" that underlie local marketing decision making in consumer and industrial goods. The aim is to explain what to look for in buyer behavior in the widely different cultures the local marketer might encounter. The chapter starts by discussing how consumers in different countries are likely to go through the various steps in the buying process. A long section then deals with research into consumer behavior, how to find out what the local consumers are like, identifying what can and should be done as well as pitfalls to be avoided. The last section discusses buyers in business-to-business markets, emphasizing sensitivity to organizational culture and the pursuit of relationship marketing.

CONSUMER DECISION MAKING

An adapted version of the flowchart model of individual consumer decision making first introduced by Engel, Kollat, and Blackwell helps in the analysis of how local consumers make decisions.[1] The authors distinguish between five hierarchical stages of a consumer decision process (see Exhibit 7.2).

This flowchart can be useful to understand consumers anywhere. Buyers uncover needs or problems, look for alternative ways of satisfying their needs (where alternatives are available), evaluate the alternatives against one another, make a choice, and get satisfied or not.

EXHIBIT 7.2 Consumer Decision Process

Source: *Consumer Behavior*, Third Edition by James F. Engel, David Kollat, and Roger D. Blackwell, copyright © 1978 by The Dryden Press, reproduced by permission of the publisher.

But local market environments differ, affecting both how these steps are taken and what starts and ends the process. The flowchart can't be applied the same way everywhere. Understanding the American consumer of detergents does not mean understanding the German consumer of detergents. To paraphrase the Romanian playwright Ionesco, consumers are not consumers: In fact, detergent is not always detergent.

The Meaning of a Product

A necessary preliminary step in analyzing local consumers is to question what the product or service "means" to them. What does the product or service do for the buyer? How does it fit into the consumption and use pattern of the buyer? What are the core benefits?

This is not a question of lifestyle or preferences of the consumer but rather a question of what the product represents generically, what the **core benefit** is. And the core benefit often differs between local markets.

Some examples will clarify this. While the core benefit of an automobile may be transportation in some countries, especially large ones with a well-developed road network such as the United States, the auto is often a status symbol in less developed countries. While disposable diapers may be bought for convenience in some countries, they are used for health reasons elsewhere. A credit card may offer more security and convenience than cash in some countries, while in others it offers a chance for parents to indulge their teenage offspring.

While these benefits are intermingled in most markets, and some segments of a local market will emphasize some benefits over the others, the identification of a different core benefit is a necessary first step in analyzing local customers. Misunderstanding what the core benefits of a product are in a local market is sometimes a fatal mistake.

Because the product or service has already been marketed at home and perhaps elsewhere, most local marketers—and their headquarters counterparts—assume that the core benefits of their offerings are well known. But core benefits are not independent of the local environment. In fact, the core benefits of a product are a direct function of the environment. *The generic function of a product depends more on the local environment than on innate individual preferences.*

The core benefit of a car in the middle of Tokyo, for example, is hardly a matter of transportation. Still many families do own one to safeguard their social standing and boost their self-perceptions. Ice cream is bought for its healthy milk in India. Coca-Cola is recommended instead of local water in many countries. Disposable bottles are *not* convenient when space is limited and garbage is difficult to dispose of. Credit cards are convenient only when they are generally accepted and safe only when the charges from a stolen card can be stopped easily. Membership in a low-price food club works only when bulk storage at home is possible. Even a simple product such as apples is not the same everywhere (see box, "Fresh Fruit in Japan").

So the product often takes on a different meaning—or no meaning at all—in a local market. Thus certain products have no market, yet, in some countries. In others their core benefits have to be reformulated. In fact, the product or service itself may have to be reformulated or "localized." And, to repeat, this reformulation *is not*

G E T T I N G T H E

Picture

Fresh Fruit in Japan

O N E of the long-enduring trade conflicts between Japan and other countries has been in the fresh fruit industry. Oranges from California, apples from the state of Washington, grapes from Chile, and bananas from the Philippines are only a few of the cases where entry has been denied at the border. Japan's domestic fruit industry is small but strong politically. Gradually, however, the foreign producers have been granted entry and are doing quite well.

The typical justification for keeping products off the Japanese markets is that they do not meet the standards expected by Japanese customers. This is not because Japanese consumers want quality per se; rather it has to do with the core benefit of fruit in Japan. Until recently, fresh fruit in Japan was viewed as a specialty, even luxury product, usually bought during the gift-giving season. Thus, in the beginning, the imported fresh fruit was judged according to standards for apples at $5 apiece, cantaloupe at $40 a melon, and boxed grapes for $70, all turned out in beautifully wrapped gift sets. Not only did

the customs officials deem the imported fruit below par, but the consumer could not accept it.

It was not until fresh fruit took on the new core benefit of a daily food supplement that the imported fruit was accepted. The industry acceptance was helped by the fact that creating a new core benefit amounted to enlarging the generic market for fresh fruit, also benefiting the domestic growers.

Many of the foreign producers adopted advice by the Japanese officials about packaging, storing, and handling the fruit, as well as adhering to demands about pesticide treatments. The imported apples offered for sale in Japan today are not only less expensive than the domestic varieties but also literally the cream of the crop from the foreign producers. And in a final twist of what global markets mean, the fresh fruit offered for sale in Western supermarkets today is more healthy, better packaged, and more carefully handled than before.

Sources: Clifford, 1993; "300 Growers Protest U.S. Apple Imports," *Mainichi Daily News*, July 8, 1994, p. 5.

adaptation to consumer preferences but to the local conditions of use. The core benefits differ not because people are different but because the local infrastructure differs.

Problem Recognition

Problem recognition is what happens when an individual perceives a difference between an ideal and an actual state of affairs. The tension generates a motive for the individual to start the buying decision process in order to satisfy the need. New products often lead to tension and a recognized "problem," the way underarm deodorants suggest that "humans smell."

Because the core benefits may differ between local markets, the ability of a product or service to create a problem and satisfy the ensuing need will differ as well. The buyer may not perceive the offering as relevant or suitable, and the product will not be considered; the brand will not be included in the "evoked set." Large Western-style furniture, for example, is simply not considered in some Asian markets: It is more or less useless for the Asian consumers' needs in their smaller homes.

In other cases, the introduction of a new foreign product or service leads to an increased awareness of new possibilities. The "ideal state" is changed, the consumer is made aware of the deficiencies of what was available before, the buyer's aspiration level is raised, and the offering "educates" the consumer. The new entry has "created a need," although one can argue that at some deeper level there was a latent need for this offering.

Search

The next step in the process, a consumer's **search** for alternative ways to solve the problem, is closely related to his or her level of involvement with the product category. For products with which involvement is high—because of a large money outlay, interesting products, or high perceived risk—the search tends to be more comprehensive

Consumer behavior is a matter of learning and socialization, and in new markets companies help educate people in the proper use of their products. Here a representative of the Colgate company teaches Indian school children how to brush teeth.
Courtesy of the Colgate-Palmolive Company

and time-consuming, although previous experience and brand loyalty can reduce the effort. For convenience and habit purchases, the decision process is shorter, with little need for extensive searches or alternative evaluations.

However, the search intensity is also dependent on the perceived availability of alternatives. In markets that have been closed to trade, consumers have had less exposure to alternatives and searching for choices has not been worthwhile. The motivation to search is low, and the consumers' incentive to make an effort needs to be stimulated by the new entrant. There is often an aversion to innovations in such markets, the old product having a monopolistic advantage the consumer initially assumes is based on true superiority. No one really wants to find out that the tea they like so much is really not as good as the new varieties on the market, or that the old beloved manual SLR camera is inferior to a new automatic. The introduction of these new versions often needs to be done with a fair amount of persuasion by a credible spokesperson.

One advantage for products with high global brand awareness is that this initial distrust is easier to overcome. In fact research shows that in Internet searches, brands with large market shares and well-known names receive a majority of the hits. In many emerging markets the consumers have long waited for the arrival of these brands. There is a pent-up demand that the newly arrived global marketer can capitalize on. It is important to realize, however, that such a release will not automatically translate into future success. Once the mystique of a long-desired goal is dissolved, the consumer is likely to engage in more sober evaluation of the product's benefits.

Search and Innovations

As mentioned above, in many cases imported products represent **innovations** to the consumer. This means that the level of search activity (and acceptance of the new entrant) is influenced by the individual's psychological acceptance of new things. There are three useful categories for classifying such innovations: consumption substitution innovations, new want-creating innovations, and income-adding innovations.[2]

Consumption substitution innovations do not involve much new learning by the consumer. Already well acquainted with the product category, the consumer might turn to a new offering because of some new feature, or for the sake of variety, or because of brand image. Standard marketing know-how for mature markets—segmentation and positioning—is applicable here.

New want-creating innovations are the ones likely to create "problems" for the individual by raising levels of aspiration. Here the marketing problem is similar to a truly new product problem, with the same difficulties in educating the consumer about benefits, convincingly demonstrating how the new product satisfies the awakened wants, and then making it easily available at an acceptable price. As has been emphasized above, even if the product has been introduced elsewhere first, the local marketer can't assume that the core benefits are the same in this new market.

Income-adding innovations are the new products and services that promise to reduce the costs of solving the consumer's problem. This is a matter of not only offering lower prices but transmitting the core benefits at a lower total cost for the consumer in terms of time and money. Automated services often fall into this category. Buying an airline ticket over the phone using a credit card is generally less expensive in the total picture than for the customer to visit the travel agent personally. These kinds of innovations might have trouble being accepted in many countries not so much because the consumers "like" to talk to the agent but because the consumers can't trust the completion of the transaction, not understanding "how the system works." In addition, without proper protection from credit regulations, the credit purchase may be associated with high risk.

Thus, with new products—the typical situation for new local marketers—one can't expect that the new offering will necessarily be welcomed with open arms. For the consumer to start reconsidering loyal choices, he or she has to be given special reasons to consider a new product. This leads to the next stage of the decision process.

Evaluation of Alternatives

Once the new product or service is in the consumer's evoked set of alternatives, a *highly involved* individual will process the available information, matching the pros and cons of the alternatives against preferences.

There are several ways that consumers deal with these kinds of **multiattributed evaluations.** Consumers can, for example, use gradually less important features to successively screen out alternatives (a "hierarchical" decision rule) or consider all features simultaneously (a "compensatory" rule). The choices depend on factors such as involvement, product experience, and time pressure. For example, in Internet searches savvy consumers can spend a long time comparing different brands on a number of features as well as price. Where customers are sophisticated, as in leading markets, compensatory evaluations are likely. By contrast, in follower markets, especially in the early stages of the product life cycle, consumer evaluations tend to be more hierarchical. A desirable country of origin, or the cachet of a Levi's or Nike, can be sufficient for purchase (see box, "One People, One Mind).

Even when more attributes are evaluated, which features are important can vary considerably between markets. Part of the reason is that the core benefits can vary. While a Mercedes may be bought for its luxury status in the United States, a used Mercedes may be bought for its dependability in Eastern Europe. While Levi's are practical and functional in the United States, they may convey status in Germany.

For *low involvement* purchases, it is well known from market research that the time and effort required for a thorough evaluation of the available information are often too demanding on the average consumer,[3] who resorts to simplified rules of thumb, such as "choose the brand with the second-lowest price." Such rules are difficult to discern without consumer records, keen observation on the part of the marketer, and an understanding of the foreign culture (as well as his or her own culture).

Choice

The final choice of which alternative to select or try is influenced by social norms and by situational factors, including in-store promotions.

SOCIAL NORMS   Where group pressures to comply are strong, as in many non-Western cultures, one can expect influence of **social norms** to override any multiattributed evaluation. The social norms can be usefully analyzed by the so-called

One People, One Mind

LEVI'S JEANS seem to be in demand in every corner of the world. American tourists abroad sell their pairs to local citizens at inflated prices, and foreign tourists flock to American shopping malls to buy jeans. As trade barriers and distribution inefficiencies in different local markets disappear, the global market opens up and pricing becomes more uniform. But differences in competitive intensity and exchange rates mean that wide price differences persist, and Levi's continue to be status products in most markets except at home in the United States.

The newest development is a demand for used Levi's from the vintage years of the 1950s and 60s, when the movie star James Dean, the country-western singer Johnny Cash, and the "beat" generation's writer Jack Kerouac first established jeans as the protest wear of rebels. Roaming through flea markets around the United States, bargain hunters from Europe, Asia, and elsewhere pay cash for used jeans, repair them as needed, and resell them at home and elsewhere. A true vintage pair can fetch as much as $3,000, and many sell for as much as $100. The markets span the globe, from Finland and Poland to Australia, Japan, and Thailand.

Sources: Janofsky, 1994; Quintanilla, 1995. *http://www.levi.com/*

extended Fishbein model.[4] A flow diagram of the Fishbein model, as simplified and adapted to marketing, is given in Exhibit 7.3. Fishbein hypothesizes that a person's behavioral intention derives from the multiattributed evaluation of the alternatives but is modified by the social norms (Fishbein originally used the term *behavioral norms*) affecting the choice. The multiattribute evaluation results in an overall ranking of the alternatives in order of preference. As Exhibit 7.3 shows, the social norms involve two aspects: the social forces themselves and the individual's motivation to comply.

Social forces represent the pressures and normative suggestions that come from an individual's family, peer groups, social class, and other external forces. For example, an autoworker in Germany will face some pressure to buy a German car, regardless of individual preference. A successful pension fund manager in London is more likely to wear an expensive analog Rolex rather than a cheap digital watch however versatile and reliable.

Motivation to comply relates to the willingness of the individual to listen to what others say and think. This is very much a matter of culture. In high context and homogeneous cultures where norms are both enforceable and enforced, the motivation to comply will usually be great. Most people will know what products, features, brands, and stores are "acceptable," and adhering to the norm will have tangible benefits. Buying the right brand brings memberships, invitations, and opportunity. You "belong." Individualism, on the other hand, which represents low motivation to comply with others' demands, will be costly, since sanctions can be enforced. You are an "outsider," not unattractive in low context cultures where sanctions can't be effectively imposed. James Dean, the quintessential American outsider, is used by Levi's to advertise its jeans in Japan. Paradoxically, but not surprisingly, for the "young rebels" in Japan, wearing Levi's means that they "belong."

The high value placed by Confucian cultures on the importance of social norms suggests that, in general, Eastern cultures show much more of an impact from social norms than Western cultures. This was borne out in one study of athletic shoes comparing behavioral intentions of Koreans and Americans. As hypothesized, Koreans showed a significantly greater willingness to consider peer group influence than Americans did.[5]

SITUATIONAL FACTORS   Exhibit 7.3 also shows how the **situational factors** impact behavioral intentions. Situational factors vary from lack of shelf space and inability to get the product stocked by stores, to problems in controlling the prices faced by the ultimate buyer, to prohibitions against in-store promotions to help induce trial. There is no excuse for the local marketer not to get a firsthand look and feel for what the obsta-

EXHIBIT 7.3 The Extended Fishbein Model

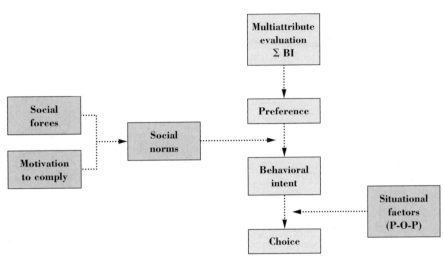

B = beliefs about product attributes; I = importance of the beliefs; P-O-P = point of purchase.

Source: Adapted from M. Fishbein and I. Azjen, *Belief, Attitude, Intention, and Behavior*, p. 334. © 1975 Addison-Wesley Publishing Company, Inc. Reprinted by permission of Addison-Wesley Publishing Company, Inc.

cles may be at this level of the decision process. This is where "the rubber meets the road," and there are numerous situational factors that could ruin the best-laid plans.

One issue needing attention is who the buyer is. Is the decision maker the father, the mother, or the children—or someone else—in the family? Who executes the decision in the store? To what extent is the choice made before the store is entered, and, accordingly, who needs to be targeted via media advertising messages?

Satisfaction with Outcomes

The degree to which consumers achieve satisfaction with their purchases also varies across cultures, as recent **customer satisfaction** surveys amply demonstrate.[6] This is not surprising, considering what factors make for high satisfaction.

The most obvious determinant of satisfaction is the actual performance of the product or service when used or consumed. But basic functionality does not necessarily mean that satisfaction is high. As we saw in the evaluation section, where product and service quality is high, basic performance is not necessarily a big factor in consumer evaluations. That the car starts in the morning is usually no cause for rejoicing—unless, of course, one's expectations are very low, as must have been the case with buyers of the notorious Trabant in former East Germany. Satisfaction is very much influenced by the **expectations** of the buyer.

Customer satisfaction tends to be high when expectations are exceeded and the consumer is pleasantly surprised. It is important to recognize that the competition existing in the local market helps set the hurdle for the new arrival's acceptance. The new entrant has to offer something new or special. This is why entries from a leading market have a better chance of success than others.

Another determinant of satisfaction is previous experience—or lack of it—with the product category. To some extent, this experience helps form the expectations about acceptable performance. In markets where products have only recently become available, expectations are based on reputation, not previous experience. This, however, does not mean that expectations are low. Unverified stories and word-of-mouth information in emerging markets have made many consumers hold unrealistic expectations about the general happiness they will experience when markets are flooded with products. Any one product's performance can generate dissatisfaction when expectations are unrealistically high.

BUYER BEHAVIOR RESEARCH

As in purely domestic marketing, to better understand the local customer requires marketing research. The typical marketing research process is shown in Exhibit 7.4. Except for the last stage, data analysis, all the stages of the research process can be affected by a foreign environment. The stages will be discussed in order.

Problem Definition

It is common to distinguish between the marketing *decision* problem and the marketing *research* problem. The decision problem in a market might revolve around the question of what to do about declining sales, and the research problem might be to assess customer attitudes and satisfaction levels. The same research might not be applicable in another market, even though the decision problem is the same.

For example, over several years the California Almond Growers Exchange was unable to penetrate the Japanese market even though there were no real trade barriers and domestic competition was weak or nonexistent. Planning to do a study of consumer attitudes toward almond nuts, the association first decided to do a marketing audit, tracing the sales through the distribution channels. The real cause of low sales was found to be the lack of distribution coverage. A deal was struck with Coca-Cola Japan, which had in place 15,000 salespeople and over 1 million sales locations throughout Japan. The association has now captured over 70 percent of a growing market.[7]

EXHIBIT 7.4 The Stages of Consumer Research

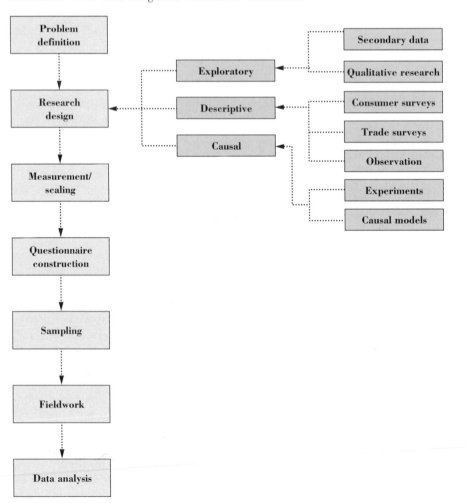

Qualitative Research

Although there are many forms of qualitative research, the well-known **focus groups** have become standard for initial exploratory research in many markets.[8] Recruiting carefully screened users and potential buyers of a product, research companies gather 8 to 10 individuals around a table to share opinions about a product or service. Guided by a moderator's questions, the participants are encouraged to voice any misgivings about a design or dislikes about a color pattern, to point to ambiguities in translated advertising copy, and so on. The responses are taped, usually on video, and the sponsoring marketer can observe the proceedings from behind a one-way mirror.

In foreign markets focus groups have the advantage of being relatively inexpensive, can be completed quickly, and can reach local pockets of the total market. Unfortunately, they can also constitute an **unrepresentative sample** because typical screening criteria are incorrect in the new environment or are not implemented correctly. For example, when the Italian maker of Campari, the aperitif, asked for a series of focus groups of "buyers" in the United States, the local research firm could not find any buyers to recruit. Agreeing to lower the screen to "users," the Campari maker was dismayed to find that the users recruited knew too little about the beverage to give any useful information. The Italian company refused to pay for the research.

These and related problems can be overcome with careful planning of the focus groups. Representativeness in terms of geographical areas is usually dealt with by selecting certain cities that are leading markets for the products. In the United States, New York and Los Angeles are often viewed as trendsetters; in Germany, it is Berlin and Munich. Few U.K. studies can avoid London, and the same is true for studies in France (Paris), Italy (Milano), Spain (Madrid), and Scandinavia (Stockholm).[9] The moderators chosen should be professionals who can identify in some way with the subjects and make them feel at ease. The amount paid should be sufficient to make a difference and thus be an incentive, but not so large as to invite praise. The screening criteria should be related to the level of market sophistication. To get consumers in emerging markets to help adapt the product is often pointless, since they usually have little experience and no confidence in their own judgment. By contrast, local users in leading markets are often ideal key informers for the adaptation of a global product.

Consumer Surveys

Surveys of relatively large ($n = 500$ and above) random samples drawn from a sampling frame of representative product users constitute the "meat and potatoes" of traditional market research. Whether administered by mail, over the phone, or in person, such surveys are used for a variety of marketing purposes, including segmentation and

"What do you like about it? How can it be improved?" A new Colgate package is tested in Brazil. As markets globalize and consumers face more choices, the importance of research increases. Courtesy of the Colgate-Palmolive Company.

Source: Doctoral researcher in anthropology at the University of California at Berkeley, at a Q&A session, June 1990.

GETTING THE *Picture*

Telling It Like It Is

THE RESEARCHER followed the family on the weekly Saturday shopping trip to the local open-air market. The goal was to document spending patterns for various household products by urban families in a large Mediterranean country. Walking by the various stalls offering all kinds of produce, clothing, and electronic products, the observer dutifully recorded the family's bargaining for a better deal and the actual prices paid. Returning home, he discussed the trip with the husband, and double-checked the figures. The husband corrected him, doubling the price for the shirt bought and lowering the price for the red wine. "But I saw how much you paid," protested the researcher. "You don't understand," responded the husband. "I can't wear such a cheap shirt, and I can't spend that much on wine." Survey responses sometimes do not match reality.

positioning, concept testing, and customer satisfaction and competitive product evaluation. But the problems with survey research methods in certain markets have been well documented.[10]

There are many cultural aspects affecting the application of the kind of direct questioning involved in the typical consumer survey. In high context cultures the idea that one can understand consumers from their responses to a formal survey is naive. Open-ended questions are often left blank by respondents in hierarchical cultures who are not used to explaining their reasoning or are afraid of being too transparent. Answering truthfully to a stranger is not necessarily proper in some nations, especially those in which an authoritarian regime has made people wary of questions. Americans have no hesitation about fabricating an opinion on the spur of the moment: Europeans will leave questions unanswered "since they have no direct experience using that product." Asked for their "perceptions" of the gas mileage of a certain car model, Japanese respondents may ask for time to check automobile specifications in a car magazine.

Face-to-face interviews are prone to bias because of **demand characteristics,** that is, respondents who try to answer in a way that satisfies the interviewer (or the respondent's own ego). Such demand pressure is handled differently in different cultures. Western people are known to either try to please ("yea-sayers") or go against ("nay-sayers") according to their attitude toward the assumed sponsor. Respondents everywhere may try to answer more or less conscientiously, often opting for the least inconvenient multiple-choice alternative. Or they may lie. For example, respondents may be eager to show off a socially desirable image (see box, "Telling It Like It Is").

One drawback of surveys can be the attitude of the respondents toward the study itself. In Western as well as Eastern societies, there will be prospective respondents who refuse to divulge any opinions simply because they "do not want to be taken advantage of," distrusting the function of market research. In more insidious cases people will consent to participate only to fake their responses so as to distort findings. To handle these problems of respondent noncooperation, the firm does well to interview the researchers carefully so as to thoroughly understand the general sentiment in the local market vis-à-vis formal questionnaires. It is also a good idea to monitor the process by observing some pilot interviews if at all possible.

Even if surveys are afflicted by a number of problems and potential distortions in many foreign markets, they can be very useful. Many examples exist of primary market research using consumers that has been successful across cultures (see box, "Axia Strikes Out").

Picture

Axia Strikes Out

IN 1988 WHEN FUJI FILM, the successful
Japanese company, attempted to diversify into blank au-
diotape and videotape, it faced a stiff challenge. It is a very
competitive global market with strong Japanese competitors such as Maxell, TDK, and Sony, plus American 3M
and Kodak, and German BASF. On the basis of the success
of its newly introduced Axia brand name in Japan, however, Fuji decided to go global. The company intended to
use the Axia brand name in the global marketplace but decided that it needed to test it against its own Fuji name.
The Fuji name had been easily beaten by Axia in Japanese
tests—Fuji was seen as "boring"—but the company suspected that other countries' consumers would feel differently about the Japanese association. Developing new
global design prototypes, the company undertook
painstaking and expensive survey research and focus
groups with consumers in the United States (New York
and Los Angeles) and in Europe (London, Paris, and Düsseldorf).

The result? Axia bombed while the Fuji name was very
attractive. In addition, the company was able to identify
differences in design requirements. For example, while
the Japanese consumers associate the color black with
high quality, American and European consumers tend to
favor silver and gold in high-quality images. Accordingly,
the "global" tapes introduced under the Fuji name are
similar between the United States and Europe, but in
Japan the name and the look are different.

Sources: Interview with an executive of the marketing research
agency hired by Fuji, November 23, 1989.
http://www.fujifilm.co.jp
http://www.maxell.com/
http://www.tdk.co.jp
http://www.sony.com
http://www.3m.com/
http://www.kodak.com/

Trade Surveys

The quickest, least expensive, and most commonly used method for learning about
customers in a market is to do a **trade survey,** interviewing people in the distribution
channels and trade associations. These people can often explain the basic segments in
the market, who the buyers are, the type of buying processes used, and the sources of
buyer information. They can answer the who, when, what, and how-much questions
but will usually not be able to more than speculate about the why. These people provide a good starting point for further data gathering and analysis.

In the United States, the use of middlemen for information about consumers is
usually limited to the sales and scanner records of retailers and wholesalers. More attention is usually given to middlemen in the business-to-business sectors, if only because there are a limited number of ways to use formal research methods on business
customers. In many other countries the middlemen are a much more important—and
perhaps the only—source of information.

In countries with less social mobility and less diversity than the United States—
and that includes a majority of the world's nations—key informants in the trade are
good sources of information about buyers. Cultural homogeneity makes it possible to
get a sense of people through a few personal interviews, since the informants usually
can speak for a large share of the population. Furthermore, social stability means that
many middlemen have been in the same position for many years, and they can speak
from experience. In the United States, by contrast, people are diverse and no one person can speak for the many subcultures. And people are likely to change jobs frequently, not building up much experience in the trade.

Interviewing middlemen is, it should be remembered, only one aspect of getting
data on the trade. Store visits to observe customers and talk to them directly, inspecting store layouts and atmospheres, and collecting sales and turnover data are other activities that yield market information.[11]

Observational Studies

Research involving **direct observation** of customers buying and using existing products can be very beneficial. Existing products give important clues to customer preferences, especially in mature markets. In markets where access is free and the customers have well-developed preferences, the sales records of the various products constitute, in fact, a shortcut to understanding customer likes and dislikes. In other words, the products themselves "reveal" consumer preferences.[12]

By analyzing best-selling products—and those that don't do so well—the local marketer can start to identify which features of a product are valued by the market and which are not. Although these points are in a sense obvious, Western marketers have been slow in exploiting this potential. The Japanese have been much faster. The Japanese successes in Western markets have not been based on thorough market research in the traditional sense.[13] Instead, they have learned about customers by analyzing the products that are successful in Western markets.

Causal Research

Causal marketing research involves more scientific methods of research design and data analysis. The aim is to establish the link between a decision variable such as price or advertising and a result measure such as brand preference or purchase. Typical research designs involve experimental methods and the estimation of links in causal models. The problems attacked tend to be the fine-tuning of price levels, the testing of alternative advertising copy and visuals, and the connection between after-sales service and customer satisfaction. The basic notion underlying the research is that the local marketer needs to understand exactly what impact the contemplated marketing activities will have on the results.

In new foreign markets this kind of research is rarely worth the costs. The decisions to be made are much too basic to need that much fine-tuning, and the action alternatives facing the local marketer are often rather crude. The exception is advertising if there is good reason to try out some alternatives because the local consumers might not be receptive to the kind of advertising coming from headquarters. *Storyboard tests* with alternative copy, for example, are not expensive and can be done quite quickly.

Measurement and Scaling

Measurement errors are likely to occur in any research, and the problems are magnified when dealing with a foreign culture. Here we can only suggest the flavor of the problems involved; expert publications in international marketing research should be consulted for further reading.[14]

In **attitude scaling,** the way of measuring an individual's intensity of feeling vis-à-vis some product or company, very basic factors can create headaches. Using numbers for scale points raises questions of cultural significance of different numbers (the number "4" carries negative connotations for some Chinese, for example, as "13" does for Westerners). It also raises questions about the validity of numbers as indicators of emotions or value ("he's a 10" may be easy to grasp for Westerners used to quantification but confusing to others). There is always the question about how many scale points should be used. Since scaling numbers are designed to reflect underlying emotions, one would like to have an approximate verbal equivalent of any number (or—complicating matters much further—does the culture have "emotions without words"?). There is also the problem of equal-appearing intervals. Even in Western applications, it is not always clear that the difference between a "1" and a "2" is equal to that between a "6" and a "7."

Picture

Getting to Know the European Consumer

DESPITE ALL THE TALK about an integrated European Union, the European consumers are hardly homogeneous. According to Tom Broeders, an independent marketing consultant in Belgium, "Europe is a collection of different cultures related to language and habits."

Marketing research in Europe must blend flexibility, intuition, and knowledge of what information resources exist in each country. Multiple sources are usually necessary. For demographic data about European consumers, researchers must rely mainly on national and regional government agencies, such as each country's national statistical institute. However, privacy concerns in some countries limit data availability. In Germany, for example, the notion of a census was rejected for many years: Germans feared government interference in their private lives.

Language differences make the creation of pan-European survey questionnaires difficult and expensive. These problems will diminish as the European nations begin providing more data for cross-national comparison and as market researchers test pan-European strategies. One example is the "Eurobarometer", a standardized questionnaire that is administered annually and collects comparable data on a number of sociodemographic, political, and economic indicators.

Sources: Blayne Cutler, "Reaching the Real Europe," *American Demographics*, October 1990, pp. 38–43; Thomas T. Semon, "Red Tape Is Chief Problem in Multinational Research," *Marketing News*, February 14, 1994, p. 7.

Questionnaire Construction

The **questionnaire** employed in the typical consumer survey needs to be carefully pretested, especially if it is simply a translation from a standardized version in another country. Translated questions are often very prone to misunderstandings, even when literally correct, because of differences in context.

The local market researcher should first translate the original questionnaire into the foreign language and then have someone else **back-translate** the questionnaire into the original language. Differences will appear, and they have to be resolved through discussions, pretests with target respondents, and repeated back translations. It is common for this process to yield a questionnaire of different length than the original, since different languages require different levels of polite indirectness. Even in the new European Union language, differences continue to create problems (see box "Getting to Know the European Consumer").

Typical screening questions such as "Do you do most of the shopping in this household?" can be ambiguous because the meanings of the words *most*, *shopping*, and *household* depend on cultural norms and the family's economic situation. These difficulties can be overcome by careful design of the questionnaire and painstaking pretesting.

Sampling

The lack of comprehensive and reliable **sampling frames** from which to sample respondents has long been holding back market research in many countries. Telephone directories are not very useful when few households have telephones. Postal addresses won't work well when people are mobile, when one address covers many individuals in extended families, and when postal service is unreliable.

However, the problems involved in getting acceptable sampling frames are being gradually solved with the emergence of service firms that specialize in developing lists for direct marketing and survey research purposes. The increasing importance of global direct marketing (discussed in Chapter 16) has encouraged American research firms to invest in the development of lists in many foreign countries, using alliances and joint ventures with local entrepreneurs. The researcher who pays for the use of such lists can ask that customized lists be developed, using standard target segmentation criteria about geographic location, income, family size, and so on. Although an emerging country such as China might still be relatively uncharted, consumers in many other countries in Asia and Latin America are becoming accessible to local market researchers.

Fieldwork

The fieldwork will typically be handled by a subcontracting market research firm, sometimes a full-service advertising agency. Here the choice is usually between a branch of a multinational firm and an independent local firm. The multinational firm has the advantage when cross-national comparability is desired. Nevertheless, the local firm will often be more cost-efficient and will sometimes have better knowledge of local situations (even if, in general, the multinational firm will be able to attract very good local talent because it can offer career opportunities abroad). Independent local firms will in many cases be part of a wider international network of local research firms, and working with local firms in many different countries can still provide cross-country comparability without too severe coordination problems.

As always, it is important that the administration of the survey be carefully monitored, since it is tempting for interviewers to cheat by returning bogus questionnaires, especially when they get paid by the number of completed interviews. But in many countries it is difficult to completely control the process. In the United States, for example, it is not always legal for a representative of the sponsor to listen in on a phone interview, or even tape it, without the respondent's explicit permission. Callbacks making sure that a respondent was interviewed can be made, provided the respondent agrees.

Finally, it is important to emphasize that as economic growth occurs, mature markets with differentiated demand requiring formal and scientific market research applications will emerge in many countries. As consumers grow more sophisticated, so necessarily must the techniques used to track their preferences.

Campbell's product research lab in Hong Kong. The Asian palate is very different from the Western and so Campbell's, trying to leverage its brand name and experience in soups, is developing new products targeting the Asian market—and will perhaps bring the successful recipes back to Western markets. Greg Girard/Contact Press Imagnes, Inc.

LOCAL INDUSTRIAL BUYERS

Marketing to local industrial buyers (business-to-business marketing) is different from marketing to local consumers. Because buyers are also people, psychology comes into play to some extent, but the organizational context makes for a different decision process.[15]

The Local Business Marketing Task

At the outset it is useful to define the local business marketer's task more precisely. Five types of business-to-business buying situations can be distinguished:

1. Buying raw materials and industrial supplies on the open market.
2. Procuring parts and components for further processing.
3. Buying finished products from an original equipment manufacturer (OEM) for resale.
4. Buying products as a distributor.
5. Buying a complete system or "turnkey" operation.

Situation 1 is important in international business but does not require much in terms of understanding buyer behavior. A typical case would be a trading company buying oil on the spot market in Rotterdam. These kinds of markets tend to involve simple exchanges, often computerized, with the buyers and sellers not in face-to-face contact.

Buying situations 2, 3, and 4 involve more in-depth contacts between buyers and sellers, and marketing becomes correspondingly more important. All three usually involve the creation of long-lasting relationships. In situation 2 the local marketer's role is that of a supplier to the buying firm, and issues of quality control and punctual delivery become important. Situation 3 is similar, but here the local marketer needs also to evaluate the performance of the buyer as a marketer of the company's finished product and to assess whether the OEM strategy is preferable to establishing its own brand. When selling to a distributor (situation 4), the local marketer needs to consider what assistance should be offered to market the product further down the distribution chain.

The purchase of a turnkey operation (situation 5) involves much wider considerations, since here the marketer usually works in tandem with other vendors. This type of situation will be dealt with further in Chapter 13, "Global Pricing," since the decisions involve negotiations about contracts and costs.

Concentrating here on situations 2, 3, and 4, which involve similar activities, the job of the local business-to-business marketer can be more clearly defined. He or she needs to establish the foreign firm as a dependable supplier to an independent business organization operating in the local market, where the buyer in the local organization is usually a native of the country. The local business uses the product for further processing or resale, in the OEM case under its own brand name. The competition consists of other suppliers, both domestic and foreign, who can also provide the parts and components, the OEM product, or the branded product to be distributed.

In this situation, a local marketer with the appropriate customer orientation has to understand the local buyer's position in the organization, the other people and factors in the organization that influence the buying decision, and the role the product (and the marketer) play in making the buyer successful in his or her organizational role. In short, the local marketer should help the buying organization succeed—and make the buyer look good. A challenging task, especially in a foreign country.

Individual Buyer Factors

Several personal factors influence how well the buyer performs the job. Typical variables to assess include age, income, and education relative to others in the organization; professional identification; personality; and, especially important in foreign markets, attitudes toward risk. In many countries, it is also important to assess the buyer's family background, and his or her past and likely future career path in the organization.

Depending on personality and underlying cultural conditioning, buyers tend to develop styles of dealing with vendors. A basic consideration is how the buyer treats the seller—as an equal or less than an equal. American marketers steeped in a democratic tradition find it hard to accept the inequality and subservience in more hierarchical societies no matter where it's exhibited, but especially when it affects them as sellers. However, it is important to recognize that despite a more advanced product or service offering, the seller is in a sense there to serve, and what is important is to serve the needs of the prospective customer. It is only when competing suppliers are nonexistent that the seller becomes the equal of the buyer. Western companies have long prided themselves on technological uniqueness, but as global competition intensifies, even aristocrats have to adopt a "customer first" attitude.

Attitude toward risk is intimately tied to an individual's willingness to change. Changing from an existing domestic supplier to a foreign supplier is usually a very risky decision. First, it is not easy to evaluate the new supplier, especially when many of the engineers and managers are foreign. Second, the reliability of supplies is questionable, since many suppliers give priority to buyers in their own country or to those with whom they have done business for many years. Third, although it is natural to start out with a small order, this is also a means by which the patience and commitment of the foreign firm are tested further. Fourth, terminating an existing domestic supplier sometimes carries with it political negatives (unemployment, plant closings), which make it more than a simple canceling of a business transaction.

Buying Process

Just as in consumer markets, the business buying process can be depicted as a sequence of steps. The flowchart in Exhibit 7.5 delineates these steps.[16]

Problem recognition can occur when quality inspections are done, when a breakdown occurs, or, in routine purchasing, when inventory controls show that supplies are low. In nonroutine cases, there follows a *need specification* phase, which determines the functions that a purchased product or service must perform. It is in this phase that reengineering often gets started. Reengineering involves questioning why the functions are necessary and whether a whole new approach might not be better. For example, rather than replace a broken water pump, why not shift to air cooling? Rather than install faster paper copiers, one company shifted the policy on internal memos to "e-mail only."

Next follows the *product specification* phase when the desired features of the product or service are specified. In this important phase existing suppliers often have an inside track, since they can ask for their particular attributes to be specified. This is a typical entry barrier, with new foreign entrants excluded because of what might seem nonessential requirements. For example, American office equipment firms selling to U.S. government offices lobby for "Buy American" rules in their business so as not to lose the government as a customer to a foreign supplier.

The next two phases are a *search for suppliers* and *proposal solicitation*. They can involve active search or passive announcements of a proposal opportunity. A major task of the local marketer is to make sure that local opportunities are effectively covered and leads followed up. Many foreign subsidiaries have local staff members in sales whose task is to scan newspaper announcements for proposal solicitations and to maintain contact, perhaps daily, with larger accounts and prospects. Since one of the drawbacks of the foreign company is the fact that it is rarely an insider getting called on by the customer, the salespeople have to be very active and often initiate contact.

The final stages involve *supplier selection*, *order specification*, and *performance review*. By this time the main preselling task has usually been completed, and the attention

EXHIBIT 7.5 Industrial Buying Process

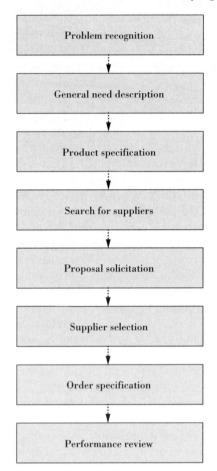

Source: Robinson et al., *Industrial Buying and Creative Marketing*. Copyright © 1967. All rights reserved. Adapted by permission of Allyn & Bacon.

shifts to closing and contracts, a domain in which the marketer often needs legal help. The performance review needs to be anticipated and designed by the time of order specification, and it is the marketer's role to see to it that after-sales service is strong enough to render a favorable review. Word of mouth spreads easily among companies in the same industry and in smaller countries, and the local marketer needs to realize that the early sales will become barometers of competitive advantage or disadvantage.

Not all the stages are passed through in each case. For example, companies often attempt to routinize many purchases after a supplier has proved its worth. So the new local marketer's sales representative often must call on a prospective buyer even though no proposal has been solicited. The fortunate marketer is present at the beginning of the stage when the product specifications are set down and can then perhaps become the sole qualifying supplier. More commonly, however, the newly arrived local marketer has to try to wrestle an account away from a favored domestic supplier.

Organizational Influences

The buyer in an organization is usually only one of the actual decision makers. Buyers are persons with formal authority for selecting the supplier and arranging the terms of purchase. The users of the product or service—engineers, designers, manufacturing managers—often have more influence on the decision of which supplier to choose. Then there are upper-level executives who have to sign off on a purchase decision. In the line-and-staff linkages between these groups there are **organizational influencers** who can wield unseen authority.

These individuals have different impact at different levels of the buying process. Users are typically more influential in the early part of the process, up through product specification. The senior executives may have real influence early when resources have to be allocated, but the signing off on the selected supplier may be more of a pro forma step, especially in decentralized and bottom-up organizations.

Although ideally a local marketer may wish to establish a strong and trusting relationship with all these parties, such a perfect world rarely exists even at home, but especially not in a foreign setting. For example, in many Asian organizations formal position descriptions tend to be vague or misleading, making it very difficult to identify key people. But it is important anywhere to try to identify the degree to which the buying decision is based on group consensus or whether there is one influential decision maker, which is quite common among Asian companies, even in Japan. In many old-style and hierarchical European companies it is common for a buyer to affect independence and entrepreneurial initiative, while in fact the decision is made by a group of senior executives. The local marketer needs to remember that it can be slightly embarrassing for a buyer to admit that others in the organization make the decision. Or, as usual, buyers may use others' alleged need for consultation as an avoidance tactic or to postpone a decision.

The group decision making involved in many industrial purchases means that cultural influences will be strong, from both the organizational culture and the culture at large. As we saw in Chapter 3, most organizations reflect the culture of the country or region where they are located, although there are instances of geocentric organizations that try to remove ethnocentric cultures from the organization (IBM, Philips, and Sony are some examples). In most instances, the local marketer, when approaching the customer, will have to be guided by both local cultural norms and the specific organizational culture involved.

Because of the complexity or unfamiliarity of organizational influences, it is not easy for the local marketer to define exactly what is needed by the buyer. Matters such as cost, quality, and dependability are usually as necessary abroad as at home but may not be sufficient to make a sale in many organizational settings. Personal rapport with a senior executive may be more useful than a demonstration of technical superiority to an impressed engineer. There are countless stories of high-tech suppliers venturing abroad only to find their welcome less than enthusiastic despite their product's obvious advantages. The stated reason is often that a foreign supplier cannot be relied on, a sort of "company security" argument. More likely, the supplier is not able to satisfy the varying needs among the several people involved in the purchase. Shifting to a new supplier, for example, often involves a loss of face for some existing procurer in the organization who has demonstrated the strength of the previous supplier (see box, "Japan's Keiretsus").

Relationship Marketing

For the local marketer contemplating the business-to-business marketing task, it is helpful to anticipate establishing a long-term relationship with the buyer and the buying organization. **Relationship marketing** is the term applied to a marketing effort involving various personalized services, the creation of new and additional services, and customizing a company's offering to the needs of a special buyer. Although the idea of relationship marketing is adaptable to consumer markets, it is obviously more applicable in business-to-business marketing.[17] The Japanese vertical keiretsus provide good examples of what relationship marketing is about. As another example, Citibank has tried to attract and build strong relationships with wealthy customers in many countries by offering extended banking hours, a separate lobby with attractive decor, comfortable seating, and sometimes free drinks.

Japan's Keiretsus: Suppliers Par Excellence

THE INFAMOUS JAPANESE "KEIRET-SUS" (industrial groups) are combinations of companies, often with interlocking shareholding, that support and aid each other. Vertical keiretsus consist of quasi-integrated value chains with suppliers, manufacturers, and distributors. The best known is probably Toyota's keiretsu, which helps implement its "just in time" supply system.

Although the high yen in the mid-1990s means that things are changing, foreign suppliers have traditionally had a hard time breaking into keiretsus. The obstacle is not simply a matter of protection and trade barriers; in fact, in order to stimulate foreign competitors, Toyota has issued guidelines in English about quality and delivery performance required of all its suppliers.

Any lingering reluctance to start using foreign suppliers in Japan has more to do with the intensive interactions between member firms and the required augmenting services routinely demanded from keiretsu members. Suppliers are expected to deliver emergency orders without extra charge, offer round-the-clock service and repairs, guarantee quality levels at "zero defect," and still price competitively. In return, manufacturers offer technical support, invest in improved supplier technology, and allow suppliers to work directly with the manufacturer's engineering groups to improve manufacturability of parts and components.

Source: *http://www.toyota.com*

ADOPT THE BUYER'S VIEWPOINT   The aim of the local marketer is to be useful to the local buying organization. As always, this means that the product or service must fill the required specifications and after-sales support must be forthcoming. Perhaps even more so than at home, the supplier must pay attention to all the influential people in the organization, not only the buyer. In some foreign countries, gift giving and so forth may come uncomfortably close to paying bribes and other unethical behavior. There is a fine line to walk as the local marketer gets acculturated. The guideline here should be the supplying firm's ethical standards and above all the individual's own standards of conduct. A good rule to adopt is whether one would do the same thing at home, considering all the possible ramifications.

ACCEPT AND DEMAND TRANSPARENCY   Since the relationship has no legally binding contract, it has to be based on mutual trust, something achievable only with openness and **transparency**—especially across cultures. Transparency means that the buyer has to be allowed to learn enough about the supplier and its operations to be able to gauge the credibility of the promises made. By the same token, the buyer needs to allow some insights into its operations and its personnel, so that communication concerning product and service modifications can flow easily. Local middlemen that can be trusted by both sides play a role here. The need for trust also excludes the use of "bribes" to middlemen, apart from the legal and ethical considerations involved in payoffs. A simply market-based relationship or arm's-length relationship is but a marriage of convenience. It does not generate customer satisfaction, provides no barrier to competitive entry, and will not help the foreign firm recoup investment made in the foreign entry.

Be proactive. Taking initiatives is particularly important when products sold involve customization. In many situations industrial products are bought as "problem solutions" in the buyer's factory or office. Slow handling of customer orders, delays in warehouse shipments, and increased customer complaints are typical of some of these problems needing solutions. In such "reengineering," the buyer is likely to need more initial help in developing a solution. Buying some PCs off the shelf, adding a truck to the fleet, or adding a telephone operator might be just stopgap solutions. In these "consultative" selling situations, the proactive marketer needs to have more expertise, invest more time studying the client's business, and provide a "system solution" (see box, "Boeing's Sales Pitch").

G E T T I N G   T H E
....

Picture

Boeing's Sales Pitch

THE BOEING COMPANY, located in Seattle, Washington, is year in and year out the United States' largest exporter. The company's planes can be found in the fleets of most airlines around the world. What kind of sales pitch sells these planes against the competition of European Airbus and some smaller competitors?

As most newspaper reports suggest, pricing (that is, financing) is perhaps the most potent marketing weapon. The Export-Import Bank of the United States is an important ally of the Boeing Company, helping to offer favorable financing terms. The product is perhaps second in importance, involving attributes such as safety record, advanced technology, fuel efficiency, and customer comfort. And the planes, although they seem to be "off the shelf" with standardized designations, same engines, and a few optional "body stretches," actually are somewhat customized in terms of seat sizes, color schemes, and cabin configurations.

In terms of service the company offers training programs for pilots and mechanics, and maintains a regular office with local staff in the cities of major customers (in London for British Airways, in Frankfurt for Lufthansa, in Tokyo for JAL and ANA, and so on). The company also helps customers in business matters only vaguely related to airplanes, such as helping sons and daughters of high officials find appropriate schooling in foreign countries. While some, if not all, of these efforts can be duplicated quite easily by accomplished competitors, Boeing relies on a trump card that in some cases is hard to match. The company gives the prospective buyer a complete system evaluation of the customer's existing fleet and route structure.

Over the years, the Boeing aerospace engineers have developed very sophisticated computer software for forecasting air traffic demand, for evaluations of various route structures, and for the identification of optimal fleet configurations. In their sales presentations, the Boeing engineers will use the software to analyze the customer's need for new aircraft, given the existing fleet and its age, and suggest additions. As a hypothetical example, if the customer intends to buy two new A320 Airbuses, Boeing might be able to show how a combination of a 747 and two 737s will be more cost-effective. The problem solution offered is validated by Boeing's years of experience and high-tech wizardry. This is proactive, relationship-building marketing.

Sources: *http://www.boeing.com/*
http://www.airbus.com
http://www.exim.gov/
http://www.british-airways.com
http://www.lufthansa.com/
http://www.jal.co.jp/
http://www.ana.co.jp/

Needless to say, such proactive relationship building requires a very strong global sales operation.[18]

It is important to keep a close watch on the costs incurred in servicing the customer. In some cases the buying firm has "turned the tables" and exploited the services of the supplier without counterbalancing through increased revenues. The Japanese subcontractors are sometimes exploited like this by their large customers, being forced to cut a greater percentage of costs than the buyer. Procter and Gamble's efforts at giving its large Wal-Mart account special attention soured when Wal-Mart unloaded costly inventory functions on P&G. When the supplier and the customer come from different cultures, such hazards are even more potentially dangerous.

As in all relationships, power becomes an issue. Bosch, the German supplier of auto components and parts to many European auto companies, strives to maintain a good relationship with its customers. But after the firm opened a modern plant in Japan for the production of ABS braking systems, customers demanded that their new ABS systems should come from the superior Japanese plant. Wanting to preserve good relations, Bosch had no choice but to consent, even though it meant curtailing production at its German plant.

Network Marketing

In industrial markets the creation of relationships between buyers and sellers has over time led to the formation of networks of independent companies. Because of the access to other members in a network, becoming a member yields additional advantages over and above those of the single relationship. On the other hand, to become a member of a network is often difficult, since it involves acceptance by several seemingly unrelated companies.

In a long series of studies, Swedish researchers have expanded the notion of networks into the international arena. Analyzing large Swedish exporters of primarily industrial products (such as Ericsson in telecommunications, Asea in power generation, Volvo and Scania in trucks, and SKF in ball bearings), the researchers have identified the critical role of **network** building in the international operations of these firms.[19]

These networks of linkages between independent firms in different countries are a source of competitive advantage in local markets. Creating a strong relationship with a foreign buyer takes on a greater strategic role than a narrow focus on the particular transaction would suggest. Over time, the seller gains further understanding of the new market, expansion into related products, and access to other potential customers. Viewing the relationship as a long-term commitment that can grow and change, the Swedish companies attempt to overcome their natural weakness of a limited home market.

In the last few years, as the increased European integration and the growth of the regional trade blocs (NAFTA, ASEAN) have encouraged consolidation of such networks, the Swedish companies have been very active in forming strategic alliances and in mergers and acquisitions. The ties between the units in the networks have become closer, and competition in the markets is often between the networks rather than individual companies. What is important to point out here is that the local marketer, when establishing a supply relationship with a local buyer, may be planting a seed for a mutually beneficial long-term relationship to help ensure survival in the new globalized economy.

IMPORTERS AS TRADE INITIATORS

Throughout the discussion of industrial buying we have looked at the exporter or market entrant as the initiator of a trading relationship. Although this is natural in a marketing text, it is important to recognize that importers can also initiate trade. The most obvious example is when a company establishes sourcing abroad. For example, when Nike locates its sneaker production in Asia, the company acts as the future importer of the planned production. When Volkswagen subcontracts with a Portugese plant for the assembly of a new van, it is the importer that creates trade, just as when H&M from Sweden sources its teenage fashion wear from Eastern Europe.

But there are less obvious cases where importers take the initiative to create exchange. Where new markets emerge and grow at a fast rate (several examples are given in the next three chapters on local marketing abroad), local businessmen are often quicker to see the potential of attracting well known foreign brand names into their countries. As we saw examples of in Chapter 5 on export expansion, global companies such as McDonald's, Levi Strauss, Toyota, Sony, Mercedes, and Dunlop owe their initial presence in many smaller countries not to a grand global strategy, but to the daring initiative shown by local entrepreneurs who convince the company to let them represent the brand in the country. The fact that one can find Heineken beer in most countries is mostly a testament to local entrepreneurs with import licenses who have approached Heineken and acquired local distribution rights. Typically, success leads to greater involvement by the parent company, sometimes leading to the contract conflicts already discussed in Chapter 5 on export expansion.

The buyers of components and supplies in large companies can of course also be the ones initiating trade from abroad. But here studies of importers' initiatives have revealed that most buyers prefer to deal with domestic suppliers. Furthermore, these studies show that a shift from domestic to foreign suppliers is often motivated by dissatisfaction with existing suppliers. In other words, industrial buyers tend to be reluctant to change to imports from a foreign supplier unless they are unhappy with their domestic sourcing.[20]

This research also shows that a major reason for the reluctance of buyers to become importers is the perceived risk associated with imports from abroad. This perception also leads importers to use different criteria when evaluating potential suppliers from abroad. While domestic suppliers are assessed in terms of quality and price of their product, foreign suppliers are also judged in terms of location and size. This underscores what has been stressed already, namely that it is very important for the supplier to demonstrate not only product quality and reliability, but also logistical capability, ensuring timely supplies.

SUMMARY

As a new local marketer, one's assumptions about reasonable buyer behavior have to be put on hold. It is important to "zero base" one's mind to the extent possible and approach buyers with an open mind. It helps to remember that most people make purchase decisions for a reason, however vague or hidden. But it is necessary to keep in mind that the core benefits of the products or services in a foreign country might be very different from what they are at home. Understanding new customers abroad often involves getting to know complete strangers.

Once the core function of the product or service has been identified, it is useful for the marketer to look at how the consumer goes through the usual steps of decision making, from problem recognition to search and evaluation to final choice and outcome. At each stage of this decision process the cultural differences between different local markets will affect how the consumer acts and what happens next. Understanding the consumer abroad involves not only relearning the role the products play in a different context but also evaluating how local peer groups and other social influences affect the consumer's decision making.

Despite the complications in doing valid buyer behavior research in many local markets, with proper adjustments the direct assessment of customer preferences in foreign markets is still a reachable goal. But the researcher has to support direct questions to customers with validations from experienced middlemen and revealed attribute preferences from observation of the products of local market-share leaders.

At the business-to-business level, buyers are constrained by the people and other factors in their company, making organizational culture an important influence on buyer decisions. Since national culture is one important source of organizational culture, but not the only one, the job of the local marketer is often to separate what he or she knows about the culture at large and what happens in the individual firm. The ultimate aim is to learn as much as possible about the main users, senior executives, and other influential people in the company, and then to use this knowledge to structure an offering that will help the buyer succeed too in a win-win relationship. Selling to industrial buyers involves creating a long-term, mutually beneficial relationship that is potentially the start of a global network.

KEY TERMS

attitude scaling p. 208
attitude toward risk p. 212
back-translation p. 209
causal marketing
   research p. 208
core benefits p. 198
customer satisfaction p. 203
demand characteristics p. 206
direct observation p. 208
expectations p. 203
focus groups p. 205

innovation p. 200
measurement error p. 208
motivation to comply p. 202
multiattributed
   evaluations p. 201
networks p. 217
organizational
   influencers p. 214
problem recognition p. 198
questionnaires p. 209

relationship marketing p. 214
sampling frame p. 209
search p. 199
situational factors p. 202
social norms p. 201
surveys p. 205
trade surveys p. 207
transparency p. 215
unrepresentative sample
   p. 205

DISCUSSION QUESTIONS

1. "Consumers everywhere are the same. Look at the way they adopt all the American products. I am sure that if the governments would only open up the markets, all consumers would in the end become just like us." Comment on this statement.

2. How would you go about doing consumer research to find if a product has different core benefits for different local markets abroad? Explain your research design.

3. To what extent do you think consumers in different countries will take to shopping on the Internet? For which part of the consumer decision process would the Internet be especially relevant?

4. What behavioral differences would you expect to find between the purchasing manager in a large German multinational and that of an American MNC in the same industry? What factors might make their behavior very similar?

5. Look for the Web sites of a few of the companies mentioned in this book. To what extent do they attempt to create a relationship with you? For example, do they offer screen savers with their logo for downloading? Do they offer more information at your request, or use the site interactively? Any differences for companies from different countries?

NOTES

1. See Engel et al., 1995.

2. See Sheth and Sethi, 1973.

3. There are many studies of "information overload," including Jacoby et al., 1974, and Keller and Staelin, 1987.

4. See Fishbein and Ajzen, 1975. An early application in marketing is presented in Ryan and Bonfield, 1975.

5. See Lee and Green, 1991.

6. Comparable satisfaction scores for various products on the market are now compiled annually for several countries, including the United States, Japan, Germany, and Sweden (see, for example, Fornell, 1992).

7. See Alden, 1987.

8. Malhotra, 1993, Chapter 6, offers a thorough discussion of qualitative research with an international flavor.

9. The actual cities chosen depend of course on the type of product involved, where the target segment is located, and what the available resources are. In general, however, foreign entrants tend to have a predilection for choosing the capital or big cities, because that is where media headquarters and opinion leaders are located.

10. See Douglas and Craig, 1982. This book and the one by Churchill, 1994, are drawn on for much of the material in this chapter.

11. Johansson and Nonaka, 1986, give examples of how the Japanese companies do this.

12. The "revealed preference" theory in microeconomics is based on the same notion.

13. The examples of the Japanese approach to marketing research here and in several other places in this chapter are mainly drawn from Johansson and Nonaka, 1986.

14. See, for example, Douglas and Craig, 1982.

15. This section draws on Robinson et al., 1967, and Rangan et al., 1995.

16. Updated from Robinson et al., 1967.

17. Some European researchers have developed the relationship marketing paradigm into a much broader approach constituting a new way to think of marketing in any market; see, in particular, Gummesson, 1995.

18. A detailed analysis of this so-called interaction approach to industrial marketing can be found in Hakanson, 1989.

19. See, for example, Hakanson, 1989, and Forsgren and Johanson, 1992.

20. See, for example, Alden, 1987, and Rangan et al., 1995.

SELECTED REFERENCES

Alden, Vernon R. "Who Says You Can't Crack the Japanese Market?" *Harvard Business Review*, January–February 1987, pp. 52–56.

Churchill, Gilbert A., Jr. *Marketing Research: Methodological Foundations.* 6th ed. Chicago, IL: Dryden, 1994.

Clifford, Bill. "Yes, Those U.S. Apple Growers Protest No Access." *The Nikkei Weekly*, April 19, 1993, p. 4.

Dichter, Ernest. *Handbook of Consumer Motivations.* New York: McGraw-Hill, 1964.

Douglas, Susan; and Samuel R. Craig. *International Marketing Research.* Englewood Cliffs, NJ: Prentice-Hall, 1982.

Engel, James F.; Roger D. Blackwell; and Paul W. Miniard. *Consumer Behavior.* 8th ed. Chicago, IL: Dryden, 1995.

Fishbein, Martin; and Icek Ajzen. *Belief, Attitude, Intention, and Behavior.* Reading, MA: Addison-Wesley, 1975.

Fornell, Claes. "A National Customer Satisfaction Barometer: The Swedish Experience." *Journal of Marketing* 56, no. 1 (January 1992), pp. 6–21.

Forsgren, Mats; and Jan Johanson, eds. *Managing Networks in International Business.* Philadelphia: Gordon and Breach, 1992.

Gummesson, Evert. *Relationsmarknadsföring: Fran 4P till 30R* ("Relationship Marketing: From the 4Ps to the 30 Rs"). Malmo: Liber, 1995. (In Swedish; English translation to appear in 1999.)

Hakanson, H. *Corporate Technological Behavior: Cooperation and Networks.* London: Routledge, 1989.

Hanssens, D. M.; and J. K. Johansson. "Rivalry as Synergy? The Japanese Automobile Companies' Export Expansion." *Journal of International Business Studies,* Third Quarter 1991, pp. 503–26.

Hochschild, Arlie Russell. *The Managed Heart: Commercialization of Human Feeling.* Berkeley, CA: University of California Press, 1983.

Hofmeister, Sallie. "Used American Jeans Power a Thriving Industry Abroad." *New York Times,* August 22, 1994, p. A1.

Jacoby, J.; D. E. Speller; and C. Kohn. "Brand Choice Behavior as a Function of Information Load." *Journal of Marketing Research* 11 (1974), pp. 63–69.

Janofsky, Michael. "Levi Strauss: American Symbol with a Cause." *New York Times,* January 3, 1994, sec. C, part 1, p. 4.

Johansson, Johny K.; and Ikujiro Nonaka. "Marketing Research: The Japanese Way." *Harvard Business Review,* March–April 1986.

—; and —. *Relentless: The Japanese Way of Marketing.* New York: HarperBusiness, 1996.

Keller, K. L.; and R. Staelin. "Effects of Quality and Quantity of Information on Decision Effectiveness." *Journal of Consumer Research* 14 (1987), pp. 200–213.

Lee, Chol; and Robert T. Green. "Cross-Cultural Examination of the Fishbein Behavioral Intentions Model." *Journal of International Business Studies* 22, no. 2 (1991), pp. 289–305.

Malhotra, Naresh K. *Marketing Research: An Applied Orientation.* Englewood Cliffs, N.J.: Prentice-Hall, 1993.

Mitchell, Arnold. *The Nine American Lifestyles.* New York: Macmillan, 1983.

Quintanilla, Carl. "Not Your Ordinary Blue Jeans: Antique Levi's May Fetch $75,000." *Denver Post,* September 7, 1995, p. C-01.

Rangan, V. Kasturi; Benson P. Shapiro; and Rowland T. Moriarty. *Business Marketing Strategy: Concepts and Applications.* Chicago: Irwin, 1995.

Robinson, Patrick J.; Charles W. Faris; and Jerry Wind. *Industrial Buying and Creative Marketing.* Boston: Allyn & Bacon, 1967.

Ryan, Michael J.; and E. H. Bonfield. "The Fishbein Extended Model and Consumer Behavior." *Journal of Consumer Research* 2, no. 2 (1975), pp. 118–36.

Sheth, Jagdish N.; and S. Prakash Sethi. "A Theory of Cross-Cultural Buyer Behavior." Working paper, Department of Business Administration, College of Commerce, University of Illinois, Urbana, 1973.

Solomon, Michael R. *Consumer Behavior.* 2d ed. Needham Heights, MA: Allyn & Bacon, 1994.

Womack, James P.; Daniel T. Jones; and Daniel Roos. *The Machine That Changed the World.* New York: Rawson Associates, 1990.

Eight

Local Marketing in Mature Markets

"The customer as King"

Your takeaways from this chapter:

1. Drawing on the product life cycle model, one can distinguish three different market environments. One is the *mature* market, where market share and customer satisfaction define the strategies. A second is *new growth* markets where the global marketer needs to participate and "all boats rise with the tide." A third is *emerging* markets where the strategic aim is market development with a long time horizon.

2. A new marketing environment usually requires some rethinking of how to apply basic principles of good marketing. The principles might be applicable, but effective execution requires adjustments.

3. Not all mature markets are the same from a marketing perspective, regardless of how similar they seem on the surface.

4. For mature markets the reader should get a better understanding of—and a more forgiving attitude toward—local marketers who claim that "our market is not the same" when *global* strategies are imposed.

5. Trading blocs become important determinants of regional market segments, encouraging the development of pan-regional products and programs.

AS WE SAW in the previous chapter, good marketing at home or in one country is not necessarily good marketing elsewhere. Since each country has its own special character, the local marketing job is never exactly the same anywhere. But in countries in some broad categories, the job is in fact more approximately the same. For local marketing purposes it is useful to divide countries into three categories: advanced economies with basically *mature* markets, newly industrialized economies (NIEs) with strong *growth* markets, and developing economies with gradually *emerging* markets. **Mature markets** include the so-called triad countries in Western Europe, North America, and Japan, and also Australia and New Zealand. The NIE **growth markets** comprise the "four Asian tigers" (Hong Kong, South Korea, Singapore, and Taiwan, the original newly industrialized countries or "NICs") and also other fast-growing markets such as Chile and other Latin American countries, several ASEAN countries, some Middle Eastern countries, Israel, and South Africa. Growth markets also include poorer Western European countries such as Greece and Portugal for which the EU membership has been very beneficial.

Emerging markets include the newly democratized postcommunist nations, including China (still communist but with a more open economy) and other developing countries (for example, India). Many emerging markets have a history of central control that still colors their approach to free markets.

This classification is not necessarily the one used by public agencies or global companies. For example, "emerging" sometimes refers to all markets outside the triad, and an emerging country such as China also shows high growth in some product markets. Furthermore, there are product markets with high growth in mature economies, especially in high-technology industries. Nevertheless, the split serves to highlight the main distinctions with marketing relevance. The correspondence to the product life cycle (PLC) is useful for marketing purposes, since the marketing problems encountered reflect the PLC stage the markets are in.

Warming Up U.S. Consumers to Unchilled Milk

Americans may think they're the world's high-tech consumers, but they've been slow to try at least one new product: ultra-heat-treated milk requiring no refrigeration. U.S. consumers generally think of milk as most nutritious and appetizing when it is cold and fresh from the dairy. The successful and long-running "Where's your mustache" advertising campaign has also helped to build the image of milk as a fresh and healthy drink.

Such ingrained attitudes are a major hurdle for Parmalat S.p.A., Italy's top milk producer, in the United States. Parmalat offers shelf-stable milk in U.S. supermarkets, but consumers are suspicious. Typically, they assume technologically sophisticated foods must be artificial. Many are afraid to drink Parmalat milk on the grounds that, to last six months without refrigeration, it must have been irradiated or laced with preservatives. (Both assumptions are false; the milk is treated only with very high heat.)

To convince consumers that its milk is safe and healthful, Parmalat relies on marketing communications. The company spends millions on television and print advertisements describing the product's convenience and health benefits. Leaflets in stores inform consumers that Parmalat preserves its milk only with heat, that little of the milk's nutrient value is lost in the process, and that modern processing techniques result in little change in taste. The milk cartons echo the message "Not Irradiated" and "No Preservatives." These efforts set Parmalat apart from U.S. dairies, which view milk as a commodity and do not advertise it.

Appealing to U.S. consumers also required Parmalat to take a fresh look at its package sizes. Whereas European consumers, with little room in their refrigerators and pantries, prefer small cartons, Americans are used to buying milk by the gallon or half-gallon. Parmalat first offered only eight-ounce and one-quart packs but has since added two-quart cartons.

Willingness to adapt and educate has helped Parmalat make inroads in the United States. Its sales rose 25 percent in a recent one-year period. It still has less than 1 percent of the American milk market, but Parmalat hopes to build its share to 10 percent—no small feat, since Americans are the world's top milk consumers.

One motive for Parmalat's expansion overseas is that sales have been stagnant in Italy, a problem that has inspired other Italian companies to try for a seat at the American table. Luigi Lavazza, Italy's largest coffee company, uses reliable follow-up service to snare American buyers for its espresso machines. Barilla S.p.A., Italy's biggest producer of pasta, and its smaller Italian competitors have enjoyed rising sales in the United States. Eager Americans are already indulging their appetites for pasta, exotic coffee, and other gourmet foods. Unlike Parmalat, these companies do not need to convince U.S. consumers to try something new: Milk on a shelf does not exactly have the glamour of steaming espresso.

Sources: John Tagliabue, "Unchilled Milk: Not Cool Yet," *The New York Times*, June 10, 1995, pp. 33–34; John Tagliabue, "Lavazza Takes a Ride on America's Coffee Bubble," *The New York Times*, July 25, 1995, p. D8; John Tagliabue, "Imported Pasta's Rising U.S. Sales Draw Complaints," *The New York Times*, September 5, 1995, p. D4; John Tagliabue, "Pasta Makers of the World, Unite," *The New York Times*, October 28, 1995, pp. 33–34; "Canada Drops Curbs on Pasta from Italy," *Journal of Commerce*, June 1, 1995, p. 3A.

INTRODUCTION

In this first of three chapters that deal with local marketing in differing environments, the focus will be on *mature* markets. Since many of the standard marketing techniques are applicable in these markets, the emphasis will be on the adaptation of this know-how to local conditions and the differences between various types of markets. *New growth* markets and *emerging* markets, especially newly democratized countries, are quite different, and Chapters 9 and 10, respectively, are devoted to them.

This chapter starts with a comparison of marketing in the three different environments. It then turns to a general discussion of local marketing in mature markets. This is followed by four special cases: pan-European marketing, marketing in Japan, in Australia and New Zealand, and in the North American market, in that order.

THREE LOCAL MARKET ENVIRONMENTS

Marketing Environment

To get a grip on the local marketing environment, it is useful for the local marketer to compare three market situations (see Exhibit 8.1). As can be seen from the exhibit, the *emerging markets* are characterized by low levels of product penetration, weakly established marketing infrastructure (especially in terms of advertising media and distribution outlets), relatively unsophisticated consumers with weak purchasing power, and weak domestic competitors. Even with high tariffs, foreign products are potentially making inroads.

New growth markets in NIEs, by contrast, show greater purchasing power and more demanding customers. Consumers can buy more than just basic products, and brand names are important. Because of a high growth rate, there are some strong domestic companies, and foreign competitors face entry barriers. These markets possess a rapidly developing marketing infrastructure.

Most *mature markets* show slow growth apart from some high-technology markets. The customers in these mature markets are pampered by strong domestic and global

EXHIBIT 8.1 Three Marketing Environments

Feature	Product/market situation		
	Emerging	New growth	Mature
Life cycle stage	Intro	Growth	Mature
Tariff barriers	High	Medium	Low
Nontariff barriers	High	High	Medium
Domestic competition	Weak	Getting stronger	Strong
Foreign competitors	Weak	Strong	Strong
Financial institutions	Weak	Protected	Strong
Consumer markets	Embryonic	Strong	Saturated
Industrial markets	Getting stronger	Strong	Strong
Political risk	High	Medium	Low
Distribution	Weak	Complex	Streamlined
Media advertising	Weak	Strong	In-store promotion

companies who compete intensely for customer satisfaction. Although some of these markets are still protected by trade barriers, customers are able to choose from among the best products in the world and tend to be confident about their ability to make informed purchase decisions, such as, for example, separating high value from high price.

Even though there are many similarities, new growth markets in the NIE countries differ from the typical growth markets in mature economies. The latter are usually driven by product innovation and high technology, while NIE growth markets result from a general economic expansion and require much less product innovation.

Marketing Tasks

Execution of the key tasks for the various marketing functions differs in these three environments. Exhibit 8.2 shows some of the main dimensions. The marketing effort by the local marketer in emerging markets tends to focus on the development of a **marketing infrastructure,** which involves enlarging market reach through improved logistics and establishing functioning distribution points. Analyzing customer needs involves primarily on-location visits to assess feasibility of entry, and a major question is whether the company should be the first to enter or wait and let others go ahead building up the infrastructure. A question mark is the degree to which disposable per capita incomes are sufficient for the market to take off, and the product offered is often a simplified and less expensive version. Often the primary aim is to make the product available in selected locations, typically urban, and then build up from there by creating awareness and positive word of mouth.

In new growth markets, the typical strategic aim of the local marketer is generic **market development** efforts involving promotional efforts to get more customers into the market and generate economies of scale for an existing product line. The aim of market research is to identify the dominant design requirements of demographic subgroups, and the local visits are meant to gain distribution in the leading channels. The product line now includes the top of the line, even though entirely new products are not yet common. Image, high price, and special service are all aspects that can be used to distinguish the offering at the high end, while the lower-end products tend to be less attractive because of the competition from domestic or other foreign brands.

In mature markets, the strategic focus for the local marketer is typically on gaining market share. This is when fine-tuning of the marketing effort is necessary; and sophisticated market research, new product introductions to develop new niches, and value-based pricing are used to appeal to a fickle and difficult-to-satisfy customer.

EXHIBIT 8.2 Dominant Marketing Dimensions

Task	Product/market situation		
	Emerging	**New growth**	**Mature**
Marketing analysis:			
Research focus	Feasibility	Economics	Segmentation
Primary data sources	Visits	Middlemen	Respondents
Customer analysis	Needs	Aspirations	Satisfaction
Segmentation base	Income	Demographics	Life style
Marketing strategy:			
Strategic focus	Market development	Participation in growth	Compete for share
Competitive focus	Lead/follow	Domestic/foreign	Strengths/weaknesses
Product line	Low end	Limited	Wide
Product design	Basic	Advanced	Adapted
New product intro	Rare	Selective	Fast
Pricing	Affordable	Status	Value
Advertising	Awareness	Image	Value-added
Distribution	Build-up	Penetrate	Convenience
Promotion	Awareness	Trial	Value
Service	Extra	Desired	Required

LOCAL MARKETING IN MATURE MARKETS

We focus first on the main issues that make a difference in the implementation and execution of traditional marketing know-how in mature foreign markets.

Market Segmentation

An important feature in mature markets is the need for *market segmentation*. In mature markets customers are increasingly particular, with well-developed preferences; they are eager to satisfy varied and idiosyncratic tastes. Small differences in products and services make a big difference to the customer. The ability of firms to target increasingly narrow niches of the market increases accordingly. New media—such as cable TV and the Internet—as well as direct marketing techniques—such as telephone shopping and catalog sales—help manufacturers target narrow consumer segments.

The fragmentation of mature markets presents an opportunity but also a headache for the foreign entrant. The opportunity lies in the fact that there will often be a part of the market that has yet to find the kind of product desired. With the large populations of Europe, North America, and Japan, even small such niches may represent a large enough market. The problem is that the foreign entrant has to spot these niches. The stereotypical descriptions of the consumers in these markets will be misleading, and conventional wisdom has to be shunned.

There are many examples of this. Baskin-Robbins has done very well in Japan, even though "Japanese do not eat ice cream standing up." Now teenagers do, even if other people don't. Armani, the Italian designer, has been very successful in the United States, even though "American men don't want to look too stylish." Businessmen wear Armani suits after hours, if not on the job. Japanese autos are a big threat in Europe, despite the notion that "Europeans drive their cars too hard for the light Japanese autos." Not all Europeans drive like Arnold Schwarzenegger. And even in a staid and mature industry such as banking, segmentation can succeed.

Product Positioning

Product positioning, the creation of a particular place in the prospect's mind for the product or service, goes hand in glove with market segmentation. In mature markets, successful products have to provide "something special."

For many foreign entrants from Third World countries, it is tempting to enter mature markets with low-end and inexpensive products. This may be unavoidable for them, but over the longer run such a strategy tends to be untenable. As industrial development progresses across the globe, other countries develop the requisite know-how and labor skill to become the new low-wage producer. In apparel, Hong Kong first gave way to the Philippines, and now China has taken over. The solution is to upgrade, positioning the products at a higher end in the marketplace. Hong Kong is now a quality manufacturer of apparel.[2]

Since product positioning is a matter of customers' perceptions, this is where image, brand name, and country of origin enter the consumers' mental picture.

A strong *brand image* conveys not only the benefits of status and recognition for the customer. It also certifies that the product will function well: Otherwise the image would have lost its luster. The global brand names that have emerged over the years represent considerable assets, or "brand equity" (much more will be said about brands in Chapter 12, which covers global branding).

The "made in" labels of foreign-made products can in the same way generate a **country-of-origin effect.** As we saw in Chapter 2, a country well known for high-quality manufacturing, such as Germany, offers an advantage to firms with products made in Germany, a country-specific advantage (CSA) in fact. When Volkswagen started the production of the Rabbit model in the United States in the late 1970s, some American customers rushed to buy the last German-made ones (for good reason, as it turned out, as the Pennsylvania plant had quality problems from the start). French fragrance products are rated highly, so in the early 1980s Shiseido, the Japanese cosmetics firm, hired Serge Lutens in Paris to do its new line of fragrances. Swatch, the very successful Swiss watchmaker, hired Italian designers for its initial line, knowing that "Swiss design" was not particularly good for styling. Companies recognize that country-of-origin effects can be useful marketing tools.[3]

As more countries develop the skills and know-how to produce quality products, one can expect such country-of-origin effects to change. The process is a matter of market success. For example, as Honda, the Japanese carmaker, successfully marketed its Ohio-assembled Accords back in Japan, the company made sure the news media knew about it. This had two results. One, it assured the American buyers that the Hondas built in Ohio were every bit as good as those built in Japan. Second, it made consumers reevaluate their perception of the ability of Americans to build reliable cars.[4]

Marketing Tactics

PRODUCT POLICIES   Many Third World countries tend toward selling a low-cost **"me too" product** in a mature market. A "me too" product is basically a copy of another product, often with simpler features and at a lower price. The key to success of a "me too" is the price sensitivity of the marketplace. A tractor from the former Soviet Union, such as the Belarus, can be sold at a discount; the main uncertainty is the necessary amount of the discount. This can usually be researched. By contrast, a completely new product offers a more high-margin opportunity but also poses a greater challenge.

The local marketer introducing a *new* kind of product to the market has the advantage of little or no competition. Being the first into a previously untapped segment generates the kind of first-mover advantage discussed in Chapter 1. Brand name recognition is often greater for the first entry. Customer loyalty and distribution networks are easier to develop. (Distribution accessibility tends to be more limited for latecomers.) Necessary product modifications can be spotted faster. Reputation as an innovator and pioneer can be capitalized on in advertising. These are firm-specific advantages (FSAs) that translate into a strong market position.[5]

Real-world examples are plentiful. The Walkman has become synonymous with Sony all over the globe, despite determined copying of the designs by other Japanese electronics firms. Swatch is still the leader in fashion watches despite attempts by Seiko, Timex, and lesser competitors to challenge Swatch's leadership. Schick is still the leader in razor blades in Japan, where it entered before the world leader Gillette.

PRICING   In mature markets it is common to think of pricing in terms of selecting a target position—high end or low end, depending on the positioning desired—and then using temporary deals and offers to attract customers—and to fight competitors—in the short term. By making the price cuts temporary, the brand can be maintained at the higher position, while still competing with lower-priced entries. Low-priced entries from the Third World countries can expect such competitive defenses from established brands.

One might think that in mature markets price would not be an important factor for consumers. However, competition in mature markets is often so fierce that pricing and discounts become very important competitive tools.

As a counterpoint, it is important to remember that positioning also plays an important role in *emerging* markets. Contrary to popular belief, high prices may not be such an impediment to market success in these countries as one would expect. By focusing their spending on a few items, even poor consumers are able to spend for luxuries. In such instances, a low price can be a drawback, since a luxury image is automatically associated with a high price. Chapter 10 deals with this question directly.

DISTRIBUTION   In mature markets the distribution system is usually well developed, and there are few or none of the infrastructure problems so common in emerging countries. But there is another problem: Getting into the appropriate channel is often very expensive and sometimes impossible.

For example, to get a supermarket chain in a mature market to add a new foreign product on the shelf takes more than dealer margins, promise of secure and timely delivery, and extensive promotional support. There are also direct payments to be made—"slotting fees"—and a very short probation period. If the brand proves itself (a matter of quick turnover) the future might be bright. But a small mistake in execution (a slipped delivery date, a faulty package, inappropriate promotional language) can easily waylay the best promise.

Entry through department stores is hardly easier. Kao, the Japanese company, spent several unsuccessful years attempting to get its cosmetics line on the floor of the large German stores. And the perfumeries that offered an alternative distribution channel proved equally resistant. In autos, where the necessity of dealer service and trained repair personnel makes entry very expensive, many companies spend years developing a network. BMW, the German carmaker, found it necessary to create its own subsidiary in Japan to help support the independent dealers that dared stock its cars. Before that, a typical dealer showroom in central Tokyo might feature one car in a small one-room window. As the Japanese began to shop for cars outside the inner city, new dealers with larger showrooms on the outskirts of Tokyo could be established.

One distribution strategy is "piggybacking." In piggybacking an existing network controlled by another company, often a potential competitor, is used to distribute the product through contracting with the competitor to move products on a fee or commission basis. Toyota trucks are sold through Volkswagen dealers in Germany. Nissan sells some Volkswagen cars in Japan. The now common international alliances between airlines often involve the sharing of reservation systems for complementary routing. The large-scale dealers selling a large number of competing auto makes, the multiple-brand electronics stores, the personal computer stores, and other similar retail innovations initiated in the United States are spreading to other

A car dealership outside of Chicago selling an American and a Japanese-made model. The Japanese penetration of the United States auto market has been helped by American dealers who recognize the scale advantages of 'dualing,' adding a second brand to attract more than one segment of a mature market. Michael J. Hruby.

mature markets. As this transformation unfolds, one can expect better access for foreign marketers.

PROMOTION   In many mature markets where market share is the criterion of success, sales promotions such as free samples, coupons, and point-of-purchase displays are used to break the habitual choice of the loyal customer. The supporting marketing communication attempts to increase the saliency of features on which the brand is superior to competitors. This leads to the kind of hard-hitting ad campaigns so often derided by foreign visitors to the United States. Because of the immense media clutter in the United States, and the proliferation of product variety, marketing communications need to have an impact during the short interval the customer is exposed.

Advertising also helps add value to the brand by creating a positive image, high recognition, strong status appeal, and so on. Advertising intended for this purpose uses more of a soft sell; such market communications tend to be favored in Europe and, perhaps especially, in Japan. When members of the distribution channels are able to furnish necessary product information (as in traditional European stores) or the consumers have time to examine products in the store (as in Japan), such softer advertising is often more effective.[5] But even in Europe the more specific and concrete benefits-oriented American style may work (see box, "American Advertising Comes to the Netherlands").

Competition

In many mature markets intense competition has produced a management focus on **customer satisfaction** (CS), a need to make sure that existing customers will stay loyal.

Typically, two things make for a satisfied customer in these markets. First there is product *quality*, in a broad sense, including functional performance factors (reliability, flexibility, and so on). Second are emotional factors, a matter of pleasing the customer. Here personal attention and after-sales service factors (delivery, warranty, and so on) become important. The idea of customer satisfaction also includes what is usually called "the surprise quotient," the degree to which the company can offer an unexpected technical feature or personal service.

While a lack of functional quality is certain to negatively affect satisfaction, managers can't assume that perfect functioning alone will produce any customer euphoria: In mature markets it may simply be taken for granted. The real satisfaction—which

GETTING THE
Picture

American Advertising Comes to the Netherlands

THE OPENING of Dutch broadcasting to commercial TV has made competition in previously staid industries more intense. An example is the insurance business. The Dutch insurance company OHRA had developed innovative services for its clients, including direct payment to pharmacies, extended evening hours, and travel assistance abroad. The company wanted to advertise these new benefits, which were offered at a 15 percent discount below competitors' prices. The problem was that the soft sell image-building advertising traditionally done in the Netherlands did not lend itself very well to explaining the new benefits. The solution was to hire a brash American agency, Direct Resources Inc. of New York. Its initial idea was to illustrate the theme "Stay ahead of the pack" by using a duck followed by ducklings—only to find that "stu-

pid duck" was a common Dutch expression. When the agency shot the commercials in New York with Dutch expatriates, the company rejected the audio portion as "obviously not real 'r's' by Dutch people."

Despite these missteps, the fundamental purpose was achieved. The commercials explained how the competitors had copied OHRA's innovations but had yet to offer the 15 percent discount. The company was able to put across its innovative image together with specific benefits—by marrying Dutch restraint to American brashness.

Sources: TeleVeronique and TV 10, 1989; *The New York Times*, August 22, 1994, p. D7
http://www.ohra.com

creates repeat business, customer loyalty, and positive word of mouth—comes from emotional factors, which are seen to yield "extra" or value-added quality. These relationships are depicted in Exhibit 8.3. A customer's typical experience with an automobile can be used to illustrate the way quality affects satisfaction in the exhibit. When the car does not start in the morning, or when the steering wheel rattles, functional quality is low. This kind of trouble leads to dissatisfaction (lower left-hand corner of the graph). Even a kind service repairer will have trouble raising satisfaction levels. On the other hand, the fact that the car starts and the wheel does not rattle does not generally lead to satisfaction: It is taken for granted.

In order to produce high levels of satisfaction, the customer needs to be given something not so obviously expected—something for which the "surprise" quotient is high. This can involve simple things such as a pickup when service is due or a cleaned-out ashtray after service is done. It can also involve semi-functional things such as more elbow room for the driver, clear instrument panels, and an easy-to-program radio. Although not necessary in a functional sense, these things often make the driver happier: They raise the emotional quality and therefore satisfaction (upper right-hand corner of the graph).[1]

In mature countries with mature markets and intense global competition, customers' expectations continue to rise, and they demand ever higher quality products and improved service—at competitive prices. This is a stiff management challenge, which must be met for the local marketer to be successful in today's mature markets.

So far we have dealt with the basic strategies for mature local markets. The local marketer has, of course, to add specifics pertinent to his or her special market environment. Four special cases follow: pan-European marketing, marketing in Japan, in Australia and New Zealand, and in North America. For ease of reading the discussion follows whenever possible the same basic outline: brief background, including foreign trade agreements; competitive situation; market segmentation; product positioning; and the 4Ps (product, pricing, distribution, and promotion).

EXHIBIT 8.3 CS and Two Kinds of Quality

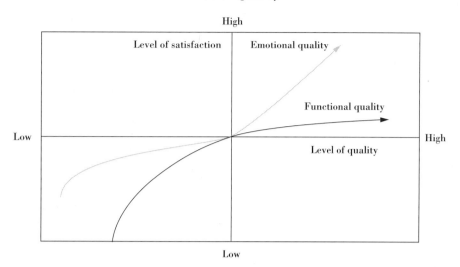

CLOSE-UP: PAN-EUROPEAN MARKETING[7]

The 1992 European integration stimulated many companies to analyze the potential of **pan-European marketing** strategies. Although pan-European marketing is not truly "local," the creation of the EU (European Union) is intended to lead to a "single market."

Background

The decision in 1986 to establish a single European market within the EU by 1992 led to a completely changed strategic environment for most businesses, European and others. Tariff barriers and customs duties were scrapped, and goods and labor were to move freely between countries. Product standards would be harmonized. Cumbersome border controls were abolished, and a common European passport was created. Commercial vehicles needed a single loading document for shipments across Europe, where before each country had its own set of documents and standards. The resulting savings were estimated at $5.8 billion. National price controls were to be eliminated, helping to create a large and unified market with competitive prices. Cars were estimated to be reduced in price by 13 percent in France, 4 percent in Germany. Prices on electric equipment were projected to come down an average of 15 percent in most countries. The increased trade and competition would foster higher productivity and an increased standard of living. A common figure quoted was that the average GDP in EU countries would be given a 5 percent boost.

Although not all the national differences in regulations were eliminated by the 1992 deadline, the EU has moved steadily closer to a fully integrated marketplace. The 1989 fall of the Berlin Wall slowed down the momentum toward EU unity as the question of Eastern European countries' membership took precedence. The EU has expanded its membership by encouraging Eastern European affiliations and accepting new members from former European Free Trade Association (EFTA) countries. Europe is steadily becoming a very large single market approaching 400 million consumers with a single currency, the "euro", in place in the beginning of 1999.

G E T T I N G   T H E   *Picture*

Bigger Is Better?

THE ARRIVAL of the euro on January 1, 1999, has set the stage for intensified pan-European tie-ups among companies. From hotel chains and automobiles to book publishers and stock markets, the name of the game is that "bigger is better." Nation-based players are now going pan-European through alliances and outright mergers with former competitors of equal size. In the first three quarters of 1998 alone, European mergers and acquisitions totaled $643 billion, about a third of that between companies of approximately equal size, an unusually high percentage.

Pharmaceutical companies were particularly active, partly in response to increasing homogeneity in national reimbursement policies for prescription drugs and also under competitive pressure from American companies. Chemical giant Hoechst of Germany merged its drug and agricultural products operation with that of French Rhone-Poulenc, and drugmaker Zeneca of Britain bought Astra of Sweden in one of the biggest mergers valued at $35

billion. But is bigger necessarily better? One problem that plagues these combinations is the difficulty of integrating different corporate cultures. Then there is always a question about who is to run the combined operations. A planned merger between two of Britain's largest pharmaceuticals, Glaxo Wellcome and Smith-Kline Beecham, fell apart when the two CEOs could not agree on who would run the merged businesses.

Sources: Anne Swardson, "Discord in Europe's Unity," *Washington Post*, October 13, 1998, p. C1; Alan Cowell, "Zeneca Buying Astra as Europe Consolidates," *The New York Times*, December 10, 1998, pp. C1, C2.
http://www.hoechst.com
http://www.rhone-poulenc.com
http://www.zeneca.com
http://www.astra.com
http://www.glaxowellcome.com
http://www.sb.com

Needless to say, for many of the large multinational companies with a long-established presence in a fragmented Europe, the changes have presented an exciting challenge. In addition to the need to coordinate marketing strategy (segmentation and positioning) and tactics (the marketing mix) across the EU, there have been questions about the appropriate organizational structure to implement the changes. Paradoxically, the challenge has been greatest for the European companies themselves.

Competition

The integration forced large European corporations to start coordinating previously independent national operations. The new rules meant that national subsidiaries had to be given stronger central direction to gain the projected savings from eliminating unnecessarily costly national differences in product designs, brand names, and promotions. It also meant that smaller plants in local countries would be closed and more efficient larger scale units created. With decades, even centuries of hostility between countries, all this was no easy task.

By contrast, many large non-European companies were unburdened by old and outdated affiliations and practices. With an existing manufacturing foothold in the EU market and global brand name recognition, many were well placed to take advantage of the integrative opportunities, be they low-cost labor in Italy, financial problems for middle-sized business as in Austria, or no-longer-protected electronics businesses in France.

For smaller European companies—and even the many large firms—the threat from these foreign entrants has been met by the creation of larger and stronger companies. The result has been a spate of mergers and acquisitions. Stella Artois and Jupiler, the two dominant Belgian beer brewers, merged. Heineken in Holland bought Amstel. German Siemens, the large maker of electronic machinery, bought Nixdorff, a computer maker. Asea, in the large-scale power transmission business, bought Brown-Boveri, a Swiss competitor. Virgin Records in London bought FNAC, a French retail firm. Where acquisitions failed or were disallowed, alliances were formed. German Lufthansa agreed with United Airlines to share routes and frequent fliers. Similarly, Swiss Air, Caledonia, and SAS agreed to cooperate.

In fact, at the corporate level, there seems to be only one strategic response possible for European firms: Get bigger and go pan-European. The response of large European retailers is one case in point. Exhibit 8.4 shows some of the retailer alliances.[8] As the exhibit illustrates, they tend to be initiated by organizations based in the larger markets, such as Germany and France. These retailers are more likely to have the financial and managerial resources required to go pan-European. The "merger mania" has been further stimulated by the 1999 introduction of the common currency, the euro (see box "Bigger is Better?").

Japanese companies have tried to decide whether a full-fledged European subsidiary is necessary and where to locate it. While Toyota made do with an enlarged presence in Brussels, Nissan established European headquarters in Amsterdam to be close to port and warehousing facilities and thus be able to better coordinate a pan-European approach. But most Japanese companies established European headquarters in the English countryside, where language and simple village customs made the transition from Japan easier.

Within Europe the Americans shifted and centralized responsibilities. Ford pulled some of the decision-making power from country heads to its European headquarters in Dagenham outside London. Product design responsibilities were centralized, and pan-European design teams were assembled in Dagenham. Financial controls and reporting back to headquarters in Dearborn, Michigan, were tightened up by a new European head, sent in from the United States. The head of Ford Werke AG in Cologne quit rather than lose power.

Rather than centralizing decision-making power within Europe, the Honeywell corporation, manufacturer of electronic measurement devices and computer controls, decided to adopt a **distributed headquarters** model with each country organization taking the European lead in certain functions. The French unit would focus on R&D, the British would handle the marketing, and the Germans would handle the existing customer support and service functions. This reorganization met with some resistance. The Xerox corporation was able to attract some of the top German development engineers from Honeywell to its German subsidiary in Düsseldorf. The Germans did not want to relocate to France and play second fiddle to the French.

Market Segmentation

As most companies developed organizational capability for a pan-European strategy, the businesses' segmentation and positioning plans followed predictably. European-wide segments were identified and targeted. Pan-European product designs and marketing communications were created to achieve the same synergistic positioning in all countries.

The experience of Volvo Trucks, one of the largest truck manufacturers in the world, is instructive.[9] Before the integration, segmentation of the European market had been localized and specific to each country. It had been up to the marketing manager of each country subsidiary to develop a segmentation scheme for the customers in that country. Because each country had special traffic regulations and transportation laws, there had been no effort to use the same segmentation scheme elsewhere. The only criterion common across countries was the carrying capacity—large trucks above 16 tons, medium-sized trucks between 10 and 16 tons, and small trucks under 10 tons. This division was dictated by Volvo's manufacturing plants but served no particular marketing purpose.

As the single market demanded greater market orientation, Volvo commissioned research that would lead to a more in-depth segmentation scheme to be used across countries. The research helped to identify different customer segments based not only

EXHIBIT 8.4 Pan-European Retailers

Retailer expansion		Cross-border alliances	
Name (origin country; turnover $billion)	Countries active in	Group (turnover $billion)	Member (countries)
Tengelmann (Germany) ($25)	Austria; France; Italy; GB; Germany; Netherlands	European Retail Alliance ($24)	Ahold (NL); Argyll (Safeway) (GB); Casino (F)
Metro (Germany/ Switzerland) ($25)	Switzerland; Germany; Netherlands; (also GB; France; Italy; Denmark; Belgium; Greece; Spain; Portugal; Turkey)	Associated Marketing Services ($52)	Ahold (NL); Argyll (GB); Casino (F); Dansk (DK); Hagen (N); ICA (S); Kesko (SF); Rina-Scente (L); Mercadona (E); Migros (Gr)
Carrefour (France) ($13)	France; Switzerland; Spain	EMD ($60)	Markant (D, NL); Selex (I, E); Uniarme (I); Socadip (F); Euromarche (F); AS-ECOL (F); Baud (F); Codec-UNA (F); Nouvelles Gal (F)
Auchan (France) ($11)	Germany; Belgium; Netherlands; Denmark; France; GB; Austria; Spain; Italy	Spar/Bigs ($26)	Spar cooperatives (D, GB, DK, A, I); Unigro (NL); Dagels (S); Tuko (SF); Unil (N)
Promodes (France) ($10)	France; Germany; Spain; Italy; Portugal	Deuro Buying ($42) Eurogroup ($48)	Metro (D, CH); Makro (NL); Asda (GB); Carrefour (F) GIB (B); Vandex (NL); Rewe (D); Coop (CH); Paridoc (F)

A = Austria	Gr = Greece
CH = Switzerland	I = Italy
D = Germany	L = Luxembourg
DK = Denmark	N = Norway
E = Spain	NL = Netherlands
F = France	S = Sweden
GB = Great Britain	SF = Finland

Source: Chris Halliburton and Reinhard Hunerberg (1993), "Executive Insights: Pan-European Marketing—Myth or Reality," *Journal of International Marketing*, Vol. 1, No. 3, p. 89. Reprinted by permission of Michigan State University Press.

on tonnage transported but also on usage situation, type of shipment, and differences in performance criteria. The usage situation distinguished between urban and long-haul transportation, allowing the company to develop special features (such as small turning radius) useful in Europe's narrow streets. Identifying common types of shipment (heavy machinery versus electronic components, for example) allowed the company to add certain loading features. Differences in performance criteria, such as speed versus fuel efficiency, helped salespeople advise the customer about which engine options to choose. These segmentation criteria were "portable" between countries, allowing the company to run a series of training and support sessions where the local

EXHIBIT 8.5 Six Basic Plus Four Potential European Segments

Cluster 1.	United Kingdom and Irish Republic (total population 60.350 million)
Cluster 2.	France, French-speaking Belgium, and Switzerland (total population 54.518 million)
Cluster 3.	Iberian Peninsula (total population 56.363 million)
Cluster 4.	Italy and Italian-speaking Switzerland (total population 71.498 million)
Cluster 5.	South Mediterranean, including Greece, southern Italy, and Island of Sardinia (total population 31.252 million)
Cluster 6.	Northern Europe and the Scandinavian Peninsula including the northern part of Germany, Flemish-speaking Belgium, the Netherlands, Denmark, Sweden, Norway, and Finland (total population 57.618 million; if former East Germany is added to this cluster, the total population will be 74.242 million)
Cluster 7.	East European countries: present Czechoslovakia, Hungary, and Poland (total population 63.771 million)
Cluster 8.	Balkan states: Turkey, Albania, Bulgaria, old Yugoslav Republics, Romania, Moldova, Cyprus, and Malta (total population 113.142 million)
Cluster 9.	Black Sea region: Russian Federation, Ukraine and Caucasian states (Armenia, Azerbaijan, Georgia) (total population 205.729 million)
Cluster 10.	Baltic region: Lithuania, Estonia, Bylerus, and Latvia (total population 17.767 million)

Source: Reprinted with permission from *International Marketing Review* 9, No. 5 (1992), "Europmarketing: Charting the Map for Globalization," by Tevfik Dalgic, p. 37.

managers and sales staff were shown how the segmentation scheme could be adapted to help their operation.

One researcher has identified six basic segments, with another four groupings added as the EU expands.[10] As can be seen from Exhibit 8.5, these clusters of countries form large markets by themselves, making it possible to gain many scale advantages without necessarily operating across the whole EU region.

Product Positioning

The shift to a pan-European market segmentation focused around the customer has taken place in many other European markets as companies find it worthwhile to analyze and target the enlarged customer base in the single market. Positioning has followed suit, partly by sheer force of the drive to a single market. There are very few products today that can maintain different images in different countries of Europe. Whereas before French wine might have been expensive, associated with a high-status image in some high-tax European countries, today most Europeans judge French wine as the French themselves do—by drinking it. Germany has had to relax its ban on artificial ingredients in beer, leaving its market open for Carlsberg, Budweiser, Molson, and other foreign beers and allowing its outstanding German beers to stand out—and the other German beers to falter.

Before integration a product such as Swatch might have had different images in different European countries; now gradually the differences are between cross-border segments, not nations. In pan-European marketing, product positioning is the same across countries, but different product lines or models target different customer segments. There are Swatches for upscale consumers and for teenagers, for business and for play. Similarly, there are different clothes, foods, and drinks for these segments. These target segments are not limited by nationality.

But a pan-European strategic response is not necessarily the correct approach for all companies in all industries. Given the right industry and company conditions, there is also opportunity in niche strategies. Research has shown three viable strategic alternatives, given in Exhibit 8.6[11]. Some companies have actually benefited by simply retreating from the market, cashing in on the existing brand and company equity and allocating funds elsewhere. More common, the alternative to a pan-European approach

EXHIBIT 8.6 Three Strategic Options

Options	Strategies	Remarks
1. Market retreat	• Sell out to pan-European player (example, Nabisco) • Seek a different, less competitive market (example, Nokia Data)	• May be preferable to a stuck-in-the-middle position
2. Pan-European competition	• Identify true pan-European market segments (example, Perrier) • Organic penetration from existing national markets (example, Pilkington) • Aggressive policy of acquisitions to complete European portfolio (example, BSN) • Cooperation with other national players to form pan-European organizations (example, Carnaud-Metal box) or alliances (example, European Retailers Association)	• May be few true segments • Excessive time required • Few winners • Complex and risky but increasingly important in "post-1992" Europe
3. Niche position	• Consolidate national position through realignment, merger, or acquisition (example, Mannesmann-VDO) • Identify new Euro-regions • Identify segments across limited number of countries (example, Campbells Biscuits) • Seek economies at component level while retaining niche brands (example, Electrolux) • Become an OEM supplier to pan-European companies	• Vulnerable to standardized Euro-products if national differences are marginal • Information access • Need to accumulate scale benefits • Organizational complexity • Vulnerable to pan-European EOM suppliers)

Source: Chris Halliburton and Reinhard Hunerberg (1993), "Executive Insights: Pan-European Marketing—Myth or Reality," *Journal of International Marketing*, Vol. 1, No. 3, p. 85. Reprinted by permission of Michigan State University Press.

is to seek out a niche or create one. Since the unification of Europe in economic terms has not been accompanied by a similar unification in terms of politics and national borders, there will undoubtedly be good opportunities for smaller firms that wish to cater to ethnic tastes and traditional preferences.

Marketing Tactics

PRODUCT POLICIES   The marketing mixes of the European marketers have moved toward uniformity as the pan-European strategies are implemented. Many companies have attempted to develop pan-European products and brands. One of the earliest examples was Procter and Gamble's "Vizir" brand name for a new liquid detergent, whose development process and success record have been used as a model for other similar efforts.[12] The lead country for Vizir was Germany, with the biggest market and

A French and German ad for Mach III, Gillette's new razor cartridge. Through standardized visual elements and use of the same selling proposition about a better shave with less skin irritation, the ad needs only language translation for pan-European use. Courtesy The Gillette Company.

the most promising test results. A global product team was organized with representatives from several European countries. Despite difficulties with cross-country coordination of introductions, delays by headquarters back in Cincinnati, and uneven support from the various country heads, the launch was a success in most countries (even though the delays allowed Henkel, the main German competitor, to catch up quickly with a "me too" product).

Today such **Euro-brands** are common and are becoming global. And even though brand names may vary because of language differences (the Snuggle fabric softener comes with at least 15 different brand names), the product itself may be identical across countries. Most packaged goods in Europe feature packaging in at least four languages: English, French, German, and Spanish. Euro-designs of durable products are also common. France's Thomson, Italy's Olivetti, and Swedish Electrolux have long designed household appliances and office products aimed primarily at the European market. But now other companies follow suit. In its Bordeaux plant Pioneer makes loudspeakers with a European design (thinner, sharper lines); Sony makes some design alterations for the European market with slimmer and elongated shapes and less flashy colors; the Mercedes product line in Europe has more models than in the United States, making finer discriminations in the intermediate range; Japanese camera companies make their European product lines unique by adding a few features demanded by customers and deleting other features (partly to enable the companies to control the gray European trade in cameras from Hong Kong and the United States).

PRICING   Other tactical marketing mix decisions are also being adapted to the new reality. Pan-European pricing is a particularly complicated issue as the single **euro currency** is introduced and companies have to set a common euro price throughout the region. Companies in some industries (such as autos) needed to price in euro by

1999 and began before that to phase in a common price level across Europe. Price differentials on the same product and brand in different countries are being minimized to avoid inducing customers to buy in a neighboring country (this so-called gray trade problem will be discussed in more detail in Chapters 13 and 14). But long-standing practices are not easily changed, especially since in many protected local markets the high prices have made some products cash cows for the distributor. Pharmaceutical companies, for example, are faced with controlled prices in many markets, with governments reimbursing patients' medical expenses. But if, because of these controls, its drugs can be bought less expensively in some countries, there is nothing to prohibit massive purchase by a foreign pharmacy for resale at higher prices. Telecommunication equipment manufacturers face similar complications, as in the case of Finnish Nokia and Swedish Eriksson. More will be said about the pricing problems in Chapter 13, "Global Pricing."

DISTRIBUTION   In addition to the rationalization of the manufacturers' sales network, retail and wholesale distribution is gradually being transformed, from locally based smaller units to large integrated organizations resembling those common in North America. The French hypermarket chain, Carrefour, has expanded throughout the EU, as have Standa's Italian-based Euromercatos. Marks & Spencer, Britain's clothing chain, is developing a pan-European presence. Belgium's Delhaize supermarket chain is attempting to expand using mergers and acquisitions in addition to new store investments. Germany's Kaufhof department store chain is also developing a pan-European strategy.

These new large units help facilitate the introduction of pan-European strategies among manufacturers. The savings created through large centralized negotiations between the manufacturer and a large distribution chain are well known in the American marketplace but are relatively new in Europe. From a marketing viewpoint, this development is likely to generate the same kind of interest in, and need for, more relationship marketing as it has in the United States.

PROMOTION   Another striking development is the increasing use of pan-European TV advertising, taking advantage of the satellites beamed across previously closed borders. As public ownership of TV broadcasting lessens and commercial air time is made available, even previously "protected" countries such as Norway and Sweden are exposed to the same mass media messages as the British, the French, and the Italians, who have long had commercial TV. Language differences are overcome by limiting copy to voiceovers, making it possible to quickly adapt a given commercial to broadcasting in a different language. This allows the local branches of the agency handling the Honda account to use the same commercial everywhere. Coca-Cola does not need many words to put across its message, and in some cases even the American English stays intact. The satellite channels feature commercials with a limited number of words, usually English. To appeal to the many different nationalities with a common theme, American Clairol uses rapid scans over pictures of women from easily recognized places in Europe, all using the same Clairol shampoo.

The Future

After the financial crisis at the end of the 1990s forced Russia to devalue, some of the pan-European marketing efforts have been slowed down while firms try to assess the opportunity in the East. Because of the slow economic growth and the subsequent political problems there, the outlook for Eastern Europe is still unclear and it is not easy to foresee what will happen. But the drive toward the single market is well under way and will only be reinforced by the arrival of the common Euro currency and the success of the companies with pan-European strategies.

CLOSE-UP: MARKETING IN JAPAN[13]

Japan's situation is sufficiently unusual that it deserves separate treatment. Despite its economic downturn in the 1990s, Japan remains one of the prime markets in the world. In addition, the competitiveness of its companies and products abroad makes an understanding of the home market situation useful. This is where the companies hone their skills.

Background

Japan is a country the size of California with 120 million people concentrated in small pockets of inhabitable land. Its economic performance in the 40 years up to the 1990s was phenomenal, per capita incomes growing from poverty level to the highest in the world. The Japanese market has still great potential for foreign firms in a wide variety of products and services: It is just very hard to succeed there.

The Japanese economy took off in the early 1950s during the Korean War as the United States pumped millions of dollars into its industry. After the war, consumers in Japan and elsewhere (from the beginning, Japan's expansion was export-led) were the beneficiaries of intense competition among Japanese domestic suppliers in many product categories. Since foreign suppliers started with the handicap of not understanding how to do business in Japan very well, especially given a difficult language, most customers in Japan, both industrial and ultimate consumers, preferred to deal with domestic suppliers. The domestic suppliers could be pitted against each other, following the old samurai tradition of feuding daimyos during medieval times.

Foreign Trade Agreements

Japan has a long history of deliberate isolation from the rest of the world, which has made it reluctant to engage in trade agreements. One reason is the country's relative isolation, geographically and culturally. Except for Australia and New Zealand, Japan is very far away from other developed countries. Its language and customs are different from others and difficult to learn or understand, even for other Asians.

This has meant that Japan is an outsider in the sense that the country is not a member of any trading bloc of significance. In addition, from the beginning the industrial policies developed by Japan's Ministry of International Trade and Industry (MITI) involved tariff protection from foreign competitors.

Today much of the tariff if not the nontariff trade protection is dismantled (although the economic problems in the 1990s have made average tariff rates rise somewhat, from 6.5 to 9.0 percent between 1993 and 1996), Japan has eased control over foreign capital investments, and consumers are more than willing to purchase foreign products. The combination of high incomes, high productivity workers, state-of-the-art technology, and success in exporting has diminished the need for protection. Pressure from American and European trading partners and the threat of protectionist countermeasures have made the Japanese eager to attract foreign products to Japan. But marketing in Japan is not all that easy. The distribution system is complex and costly, and the consumer is very demanding.

Competition

One would have thought that with the home market protected, the competition in Japan's markets would be limited. And in one sense it has been. Prices have long been "coordinated" by directives from government bureaucrats, who fear the ill effects on small- and medium-sized businesses from cut throat competition. In particular, so-called intrabrand price competition has been suppressed, meaning that a particular brand and model—Sony Walkman, say—will cost the same in all stores in Japan.

But from the beginning competition between brands from different manufacturers ("interbrand" competition) has been absolutely fierce. Inspired by the bushido or "warrior" tradition in medieval Japan and its samurais, companies from different groups have competed fiercely for customers in terms of product innovation, quality, and service. This intense competition between domestic competitors spawned the development of quality circles and "total quality management" (TQM) techniques by leading Japanese companies. Gradually, the Japanese consumers learned that functionality, reliability, and features could be taken for granted. Their choices between close competitors were based on design, brand image, and other "intangibles." Price was no object, as most stores offered the same brands at the same price.

With the economic slowdown in the 1990s, this has changed. Deregulation has allowed discount stores and "category killers" to enter in suburban locations. Tariff reductions and elimination of certain trade barriers have allowed foreign firms to enter more easily. Among consumers there is a new emphasis on price and value, more in line with the typical Western markets. With this new emphasis, the Japanese consumer markets have become more similar to other mature markets, and therefore more differentiated than previously.

Market Segmentation

The demanding Japanese customer is a hard nut to crack for the newly arrived local marketer. For example, Japanese consumers have long been accustomed to thinking that the only reason an imported product should be bought is that it provides something special. Of course, if Japanese producers were able to manufacture products that are as good or better by taking apart the foreign product ("reverse engineering") and making a similar version, Japanese consumers would often opt for the Japanese version.

Japanese consumers are, in some ways, the most spoiled buyers in the world.[14] But with the economic slowdown in the 1990s, this is changing. The Japanese are finally finding it worthwhile to get into the family car, drive to the large supermarket or out to the suburbs, and do their shopping once a week. Improved storage conditions in the home, with efficient refrigerators and freezers, make it possible to buy in larger quantities. Packaging innovations, such as condensed detergents and vacuum packs, alleviate the still severe space problems. As Jeeps and four-wheel-drive off-the-road vehicles become ever more popular, the family today has a car that can carry the purchases comfortably. The Japanese are becoming more similar to Westerners in their leisure and shopping behavior, if not in their work habits.

For each product category, there are now (1) upscale segments, (2) middle-of-the-roaders who buy the tried and true, and (3) those buying on price, looking for cheaper imports and private labels. In short, the Japanese market segments have become more similar to other mature markets. While Japanese customers were always demanding in terms of quality, service, and up-to-date technology and design, they are now also open to discounted prices. *Bargain* is no longer a dirty word.

Product Positioning

When the Japanese consumers' disposable incomes were growing, there was a considerable amount of status-oriented consumption. Well-known global brand names fetched high price premiums, especially in the luxury product categories.

Although there are still signs of this behavior, things have now changed. Less secure financially, consumers take time to evaluate products and compare prices. They have become what one informant calls "value-conscious" and don't necessarily demand the very latest (although for some product categories and for some consumers this is of course not uniformly true). Rather than focusing on brand and all the latest features, many consumers are learning to make trade-offs between what they really need to have and what the price is.

The Japanese Take To Mail-Order Buying

DESPITE CLAIMS that Japan's lack of Western imports is a consequence of Japanese consumers' reluctance to accept Western products, there are some recent successes to the contrary. Japanese have taken to ordering foreign products from mail-order catalog houses.

From its headquarters in Freeport, Maine, L. L. Bean sends thousands of catalogs to consumers throughout Japan, now Bean's largest foreign market. Sales in 1994 reached $100 million, up 66 percent from a year earlier. Clothing and camping equipment, fishing tackle and hiking boots are sold in record numbers by companies such as Lands' End, REI, and Eddie Bauer.

Still, consumer habits die hard. Japanese are afraid that sizes may be too large and hesitate when they cannot touch or feel the fabric. To overcome this resistance, L. L.

Bean, Eddie Bauer, and other companies have opened complementary store outlets in Tokyo, even though this means that customers try on the clothes and run home to order by catalog at lower prices. And quality is still a problem. "With products imported from America, sometimes the buttonholes are not sewn very well so they come apart," says Kaori Morozumi, a 33-year-old jewelry designer who spends up to $1,000 on mail orders several times a year. "These are deficiencies that Japanese products just wouldn't have."

Sources: Updike and Kuntz, 1995; WuDunn, 1995.
http://www.llbean.com/
http://www.eddiebauer.com/
http://www.landsend.com/

This does not mean lesser quality is accepted. Quality does not reside in the features of a product. For the Japanese it is not an attribute defining the product. Quality for the Japanese simply means that the product performs the promised function without fault. The many new features desired before the present slowdown were all to come with zero-defect quality, which they largely did, thanks to the vaunted Japanese manufacturing skills. When the Japanese consumer trades off features and prices today, there is no compromise with quality.

Marketing Tactics

PRODUCT POLICIES Adapting products and services to the Japanese customers' requirements has been, and continues to be, a problem. The basic demand in Japan has long been for quality products and luxury products. Western luxury brands and special cultural items with strong country-of-origin affiliation—such as Italian designs, French specialty foods, and American sports apparel—have been staple items in Japanese consumption.

This is no longer true, as incomes decline and as foreign products are entering often at lower price points. But Western quality levels are still a concern to the Japanese consumer (see box, "The Japanese Take To Mail-Order Buying").

PRICING As the distribution system opens up, imports pose a stronger competitive threat to domestic companies in Japan. Not surprisingly, price sensitivity on the part of the Japanese consumer has increased considerably in the last few years. Lower-priced imports are now more generally available in the new distribution channels, and they have put pressure on domestic retail prices. Some of these imports are private label brands of retailers. Accordingly, the consumer is faced with lower-priced alternatives not only in new discount outlets but also in established retail stores. The Japanese consumer today benefits from strong interbrand price competition and has learned from exposure to overseas markets that lower prices do not always mean lower quality.

While traditional retail outlets try to sustain premium brand prices, discount outlets have begun to sell brand name products at reduced prices, and a good deal of the brand name products are direct imports from overseas. Accordingly, while uniform prices made comparison shopping useless in the past, because of parallel imports there is now price competition within brands. Even not-so-poor consumers get price-sensitive when there are large savings to be gained.

DISTRIBUTION   The SII (Structural Impediments Initiative) and related efforts by Western powers to pry open the Japanese distribution system have won some victories, including the easing of the limiting large-store law, putting pressure on entrenched domestic marketers.[15]

The traditionally fragmented nature of the **Japanese distribution** system has frequently been noted by foreign companies. Western wholesale and retail middlemen are rationalized into large-scale units performing integrated functions; the Japanese system features several layers of small, specialized units, each handling small quantities of products. For each sale at the retail level, the product in Japan will go through many more hands, each siphoning off its fees and commissions. In 1988 the typical wholesale-to-retail ratio was 4 to 1 in Japan, while in the United States the corresponding figure was 2 to 1.[16]

For the local marketer in Japan, the cost of the system is only part of the problem. The need for frequent and close contacts between middlemen creates a preference for dealing with the same people and an aversion to change. Each middleman is treated as a customer. For a newcomer to break into an established relationship is not easy, especially if the product or service offered competes with a domestic alternative. There are still cases in Japan where a retailer is threatened with a cutoff of supplies from a domestic manufacturer or wholesaler if a competing product is added to the shelf. Although illegal and thus kept as "an understanding," the pressure can be very real. These pressures are now relenting, but they kept American cigarettes, European beer, and Western PCs off the retail shelves for a long time. The Kodak example is illuminating (see box, "Illegal Barriers").

Creating a new distribution channel is possible, but very expensive. Not only is it difficult to entice middlemen to give up their existing business, but the new people that may be attracted are often not the best. Add the cost of training and stocking and the cost of space and display locations, and the investment can be very large. It has been done successfully, as in the Toys R Us case, but one can understand why many Western firms find it too expensive a proposition.

PROMOTION   The Japanese penchant for polite indirectness has made their advertising singularly unfocused and "nonsensical." Sometimes brand names are not even mentioned, although alluded to or shown obliquely. Advertising is seen as a kind of art form, rather than a functional sales tool. Part of the reason is that the typical Japanese buyer spends more time contemplating purchases than most people in the West. Fewer housewives are working outside the home. The husband's work mates and the children's schoolmates are peer groups with which the interactions are frequent and long-standing. Add to that a distribution structure with clerks knowledgeable about their products, and there is little real need for advertising to provide information. The focus can be on entertainment and the creation of an attractive image.

But for mundane packaged goods, the advertising has shifted to more of an American style "unique selling proposition" approach. The reason is that as people encounter economic difficulties, the buyer needs specific reasons for purchasing the more expensive branded product. Image, status, and "fun" are not sufficient anymore. Thus, one can discern a clear shift toward functional advertising in Japan, also underscored by a greater willingness to speak about low prices. Economic necessity imposes itself on the advertising artistry.

The lack of store space affects promotional efforts directly. There is a need to offer smaller packages, fewer units, and faster restocking of supplies. When Procter and Gamble introduced its Cheer detergent brand into Japan using point-of-purchase promotions and dealer rebates, the consumers often found the stores sold out; there was simply not enough shelf space available to do the necessary stocking. Although the

G E T T I N G   T H E   *Picture*

Illegal Barriers—or Relationship Marketing?

ACCORDING TO the Eastman Kodak Company, makers of world-leading Kodak films, its Japanese competitor Fuji film has illegally blocked access to distribution in Japan. In a complaint lodged with the U.S. Trade Representative, Kodak charges Fuji with illegal rebates and strong-arm tactics to control the four largest film wholesalers in Japan and keep Kodak out of retail stores. Only about 15 percent of Japan's film retailers stock Kodak film, and Kodak has only 10 percent of the market compared with Fuji's 70 percent.

Fuji's view is, not surprisingly, different. It claims its rebates are legal and amount to cooperative sharing of channel members' promotional budgets. As for distribution access, Fuji film is sold everywhere, but so is Kodak film in the United States. The little green boxes are seen by Japanese everywhere from an early age. Schools receive complimentary supplies of the little green boxes for class photos, and high school students on class trips carry Fuji disposable cameras. Past tariff protection is gone, and Japanese tariffs are at zero, although American duty on imported film is at 3.7 percent. And while Fuji has 70 percent of the market in Japan, it proves nothing: Kodak has nearly 70 percent of the market in the United States. Not surprisingly, the World Trade Organization in its 1997 review of the case found no reason to intervene against Fuji.

Moral: Relationship marketing creates natural barriers.

Sources: *Washington Post*, June 26, 1995, p. A12; *The New York Times*, July 5, 1995, p. D4.
http://www.kodak.com/
http://www.fujifilm.co.jp

Japanese consumers are now able to shoulder some of the storage functions as their cars, houses, and refrigerators become larger, there is still a premium price paid for space.

CLOSE-UP: MARKETING IN AUSTRALIA AND NEW ZEALAND[17]

Australia and New Zealand are mature economies with a British heritage. Their economies have grown at a slower pace than those of the Asian countries, with growth rates at about 2 to 4 percent, typical of other developed nations. Both Australia and New Zealand have targeted Asia and in particular the ASEAN region as the future source of growth and are in the process of shifting away from their European past. In 1994 trade between Australia and ASEAN countries reached $8 billion, growing at 20 percent annually. Following in Australia's footsteps after its emergence in the 1980s from a socialist government with high tariffs and import controls, New Zealand is also targeting Asian countries. Its largest trading partner is Japan.

Australia, a vast country more than twice the size of India, has only 18 million inhabitants. Its economic base is in raw materials, in particular minerals, and in agriculture. Its ratio of exports to GDP has been relatively low because of protectionist government policies initiated after World War II; but after the election of a new Labor government in the late 1970s, Australia has gradually opened up. A free-floating exchange rate was introduced in the early 1980s as the financial sector was deregulated and foreign direct investment increased. The change has also moved Australia away from the concept of a self-sufficient economy and toward a more open marketplace, which in turn has allowed Australia's export products better access to foreign markets.

New Zealand with its 4 million people is basically agrarian. The domestic economy can be subdivided into four industries, all with substantial international involvement: forest products including paper, dairy products, meat products, and fruits. Traditionally the country has exported agricultural and forest products, and imported manufactured goods, still the dominant pattern. But economic growth and foreign direct investment by global firms have combined to make New Zealand a player in the telecommunications, information technology, and office equipment industries. Because of its small size and relative isolation from world markets, multinational companies such as IBM, Microsoft, Ericsson, Honeywell, Canon, and Philips approach New Zealand as a low-cost and low-risk test market for new products.

As a result of the growing trade exchanges, the centuries-old fear of large-scale immigration from the Asian countries seems to have waned; and in New Zealand in particular, with its Maori native culture, there is growing public acceptance of the contributions made to the economy by professionals and other immigrants from Asian cultures.

Regional Trade Agreements

Like Canada, Australia and New Zealand have traditional ties to the British Commonwealth, which gave the countries preferred trading status with the United Kingdom. When the U.K. joined the European Common Market in 1973, however, the favored trading status was lost, which led to severe economic strains and ultimately new open-market policies in both countries.

The countries are both members of the APEC (Asia-Pacific Economic Cooperation) grouping and also participate in the ARF (ASEAN Regional Forum). These are still very heterogeneous associations, far from the integrated trade area concept of ASEAN proper, but nevertheless instrumental in the trade growth with Asia (see box, "Foster's: Australian for Beer").

The two countries have close trade ties with each other, manifested in the ANZCERTA pact (Australia New Zealand Closer Economic Relations Trade Agreement). For most global marketers, the two countries can be approached as one regional market.

Competition

The relatively limited sized and the geographical distance to this region make some companies reluctant to enter the market, and thus competition is not as intense as in other mature markets. Those that do enter often produce on location to offset costs and to get under tariff and other trade barriers. But wages are high relative to many countries, not only when compared with Asia (for example, two electronics companies, Panasonic from Japan and Motorola from the United States, found manufacturing to be between 25 and 50 percent more expensive in Australia than even in Europe and the United States). These high costs suggest that in the future, as trade barriers come down, import competition will increase dramatically.

Market Segmentation

As developed and mature markets, the Australia–New Zealand region offers typical consumer markets where careful targeting and segmentation become important. Natural segmentation criteria involve cultural roots, urban versus rural, and demographics, including age. Cultural roots do not simply involve the old-world heritage from Britain, although the college sports of the British Isles (rugby, cricket) are still very much in view. It is noteworthy how soccer—a sport where England, Scotland, Wales, and Northern Ireland also excel—seems not to have caught on in Australia and New Zealand, possibly because it is less uniquely identified with the United Kingdom.

There is also a certain pioneer spirit in these countries which to some extent resembles that found in North America. For example, Australian Queenslanders are compared to Texans in the United States. This is not surprising considering the relatively late formation of these countries. Permanent European settlement of Australia began in 1788, and New Zealand's Waitangi Treaty between the Maori and the British settling their feuds dates from 1840.

The end result is that, as is typical in many mature markets, there are young people ready for the new global markets and there is an older generation nostalgic for what was. An American style might be more appealing to the younger age groups, whereas

Foster's: Australian for Beer

ONE OF THE LARGEST Australian companies is Foster's Brewing, the leading beer producer with revenues close to US$ 4 billion in 1996. Foster's operates in more than 120 countries and in 1997 was the third largest selling beer globally. It expanded vigorously into Asia in the mid-1990s and found itself with overcapacity in China as the Asian crisis hit in 1998. The company is refocusing its China strategy around its Shanghai brewery, selling off operations in Guangdong and Tianjin. It plans to use its two Vietnamese breweries as the central supply location for the ASEAN markets and its expanded facilities in India to gain first-mover advantages over other foreign brewers in that market, subsequently moving further into the Middle Eastern markets.

In its marketing communications, Foster's relies on a country-of-origin cachet, Australia being a leading market for beer consumption. In the United States its advertising focuses on the theme of "Foster's: Australian for Beer," showing stereotypical Australian characters (rugby players, hat-wearing outback men) in slightly absurd and comical vignettes, and with strongly accented Australian voiceovers. It is a strategy clearly targeting the heavy user segment among young males, of the "work hard–play hard" lifestyle that seems to come naturally to the pioneering spirit of the Australians. And so far, it seems to be working well, mate!

Sources: Russell Baker, "Foster's to Sell Two of Its Three China Breweries," *Business Times* (Singapore), August 25, 1998, p. 17; "Foster's Entry May Change Indian Beer Market's Complexion," *The Hindu*, September 14, 1998. *http://fostersbeer.com*

the older generation tends to be much more tradition-bound and in this case feel more empathy with British ways.

Product Positioning

Despite the relatively recent protectionist history in the region, global products and brands are appreciated in these markets. Part of the reason is a certain sense of deprivation because of past policies, made salient by global communications and frequent visits by people to other developed countries, in particular to Britain and the old home country.

There is still a fairly strong pro-home-country bias in several product categories, but presumably mostly because of social and cultural habits formed during the protectionist years. As always with globalizing markets, one would expect some—but not all!—of the pro-home allegiances to vanish as lower trade barriers induce competitive foreign producers to enter. The local survivors will be those who upgrade their products and stay competitive. On this count it is interesting to note that exported products from the region—kiwifruit from New Zealand and Foster's beer from Australia, for example—tend to use their country of origin in promotions abroad to create a unique positioning, drawing on the pioneering spirit of the country to position the products as fresh and irreverent newcomers.

Marketing Tactics

PRODUCT POLICIES   Most global products and services need only slight adaptation to appeal to customers in these markets. For example, the Toyota Camry, a best-seller in the U.S. market, is sold as a globally standardized vehicle, although the color preference in Australia is for dark and glossy, not necessarily the same as elsewhere. In the same way, companies in packaged goods such as P&G and Nestlé make little or no modifications of their products and may forget about those items that might need major localization changes. As for new technology, the markets are very up-to-date. A product such as mobile phones has penetrated the market particularly quickly because of difficult terrain and vast distances. Australian growth in mobile phones approached

70 percent in 1994, and by the end of the decade, the country may have the highest penetration rate in the world.

Because of its terrain, the region offers conditions for product testing that some companies take advantage of. For example, the tough road conditions in Australia's Northern Territory make it particularly useful for testing automobile suspension and new truck designs. The steep coast line on New Zealand's Southern Island spawned the bungee jumping craze.

PRICING   Because of the distance from other markets and production locations, the small market size and high labor costs that make local production inefficient, and the historically high tariff rates, prices in the Australian and New Zealand markets are relatively high. Even though tariff rates have come down from an average of about 15 percent in 1988 to 6 to 7 percent in 1996, local regulation of business is still keeping some prices up. For example, just as is traditional in many European countries, book prices are controlled to allow small stores to maintain their profit margins, a system likely to be challenged by globalizing on-line booksellers such as Amazon.com.

The upshot is that although many global products and brands are available in the region, prices tend to be higher than elsewhere.

DISTRIBUTION   Despite Australia's vast geographical expanse, its distribution is fairly efficient because its prime markets are clustered around the coastline and a few metropolitan areas, including Sydney, Melbourne, and Perth. The same holds true of New Zealand, with its mountainous interior. Where in the past the seafaring routes were key to transportation, today air travel is instrumental in connecting the local markets.

In the metropolitan areas of the two countries, the distribution system is modern and up-to-date. The shopping malls and busy streets offer the same amenities as elsewhere in developed countries. In fact, many large corporations use Australia for their regional Asian headquarters not because of its location but because of access to a well-developed infrastructure and telecommunications. For example, Dun & Bradstreet, the American financial data services company, uses its Australian location as headquarters for its Asian data distribution.

PROMOTION   When it comes to global communications media, there is very little that separates Australia and New Zealand from the rest of the developed world. In fact the relative isolation of these countries in the past because of government policies and distance from the Northern Hemisphere has made global communications particularly welcome. It's a two-way street. As global communications help open up these markets, Australia's and New Zealand's companies are fast becoming players abroad.

Global communications make it feasible to reach these markets with globally integrated promotional messages. At the same time, the countries' cultural ambivalence between the old world and the new makes for a need to segment targets. The young age segments are perhaps ready for the new media and the global program vehicles, including the Internet, CNN, American blockbuster movies, the Simpsons, and David Letterman; while older segments are likely to favor the more humorous and verbally adept British commercials and sitcoms.

In the end, it is clear that Australia and New Zealand have linked their future much closer to that of Asia. They will suffer as the Asian crisis unfolds, but also prosper as the Asian countries get back on the growth track.

CLOSE-UP: MARKETING IN NORTH AMERICA

Viewed from any perspective, the North American market (United States and Canada—Mexico is treated as part of the Latin American region in the next chapter) offers huge potential. It has a large population, with over 260 million people in the

United States and 30 million in Canada. Depending on the current exchange rate, the region has the highest or one of the highest incomes per capita in the world. It harbors a heterogeneous population with a variety of ethnic segments large enough to offer a target for many diverse products. Apart from some aberrations—steel, some agriculture, and apparel—it may be the most open market in the world. It certainly ranks as one of the most competitive markets in the world for most products. It may not be entirely correct to say so, but Frank Sinatra's words from the song "New York, New York" are perhaps applicable: "If you can make it there, you can make it anywhere."

Regional Trade Agreements

The 1994 NAFTA (North America Free Trade Area) agreement has created increased exchange between Canada, the United States, and Mexico. But the Canadian and U.S. markets were already very closely aligned through earlier free trade agreements, sometimes hotly contested. For example, the Pacific Northwest salmon fishing industry and forest industry have a long tradition of conflicts and infringement allegations between American and Canadian firms.

The ties are close also because the large Canadian multinationals, such as Seagrams in distilled liquor and Northern Telecom in telecommunications, saw the United States as their largest market. And American multinationals, such as the automobile companies, had long been locating assembly and production in the Canadian market. Honda's 1998 Odyssey minivan will be produced in Ontario, Canada, for export to the United States and Europe. European automobiles and Japanese television sets destined for the U.S. markets are often arriving across the Canadian border, drawing on preferential tariff rates. In fact, foreign firms entering the U.S. market often come across from Canada, using excellent port facilities in Halifax and on the St. Lawrence Seaway on the East Coast and in Vancouver on the West Coast. Canada is closer than the United States to both northern Europe and northern Asia.

Background

Since marketing in the North American context is what many if not most basic marketing textbooks cover, there is no need—and no room!—to discuss here all the aspects of marketing in this region. Instead, this section will focus on four aspects of the market that help make marketing there different and are not necessarily discussed in the typical marketing text. The four aspects relate to:

- Ethnic diversity.
- Religion, and the separation of state and church.
- Diffused economic activity.
- Local marketing regulations.

Although not necessarily unique to North America, these four aspects combine to create a marketing environment quite unlike that found in many other countries. They will be discussed in order.

ETHNIC DIVERSITY   A fundamental cultural factor is the region's ethnic diversity. But there is a difference between the "melting pot" of the United States and Canada's more segmented approach to diversity.

In the United States the tradition of the "cradle of freedom" symbolized by the Statue of Liberty is still strong. New immigrants from foreign countries arrive every year: In 1996 alone the number of legal immigrants was 915,900 (to which should be added an untold number of illegal immigrants). Since many of the new arrivals are poor, the cultural norm for Americans is to be helpful and to also be tolerant of seemingly strange behaviors. However, the driving concept is still the melting pot. Immigrants should be assimilated and become "real Americans." Even though this idea has come under attack in the last few years as various minorities (African Americans, Hispanics) have attempted to assert their own cultural heritage, many Americans naturally assume a "teaching" role rather than a "learning" role toward other cultures. This attitude partly explains why they sometimes appear insensitive to local cultures abroad.

Although Canadians share some of these pioneer traits, their British roots have led to a more European approach, with cultural identity, old-world customs, and different languages nursed with pride. In Canada, ethnic subgroups are still strong and supportive of their cultural traditions. The Quebecois are only the most visible example of this. Boys' soccer leagues in Vancouver can still feature matches between Italian and British teams. In the language of Chapter 3, Canada's approach to ethnic and cultural diversity is more "high context" than in the United States.

RELIGION   In North America, church and state are separated by law. The government— either federal, state, or local—can impose no restrictions on individual freedom, or freedom of enterprise, using religion as a rationale. Various religious sects have their particular customs and holidays, but it is impossible and in fact illegal to impose any constraints on commerce because it is a "religious holiday." In the United States stores can stay open 24 hours a day and 365 days of the year.

For most foreigners, such open flaunting of commerce suggests extreme materialism. Expatriates from foreign countries sometimes succumb to the "convenience" of the American markets, making it difficult for them to return home to where strict store regulations make sure that some decorum is maintained and commerce is kept in check. In many religions trade or marketing is often viewed as slightly immoral. When religion is not separated from the state, this sentiment directly affects regulations of trade. The fact is that in most countries, retail distribution is much more regulated in terms of opening hours, zoning requirements, competition, and new store locations than in the United States. In American marketing, nothing is sacred. Literally.

DECENTRALIZATION   Most countries tend to have a central government and business headquartered in close proximity. In Europe, London is the key to Britain, Paris to France, and now Berlin to a unified Germany. In Japan the headquarters of most large companies can be found in Tokyo, the capital, or Osaka. By contrast, in North America firms are spread all over the map, even into small towns. Caterpillar, a leading earthmoving machinery company, is headquartered in Peoria, a small town in Illinois. Washington, D.C., the U.S. capital, has very little big business presence (except for the lobbyists and trade associations). The 50 states in the United States and 9 provinces in Canada all claim a degree of independence from the federal center. In the United States, major economic activity and viable customer agglomerations exist in 15 to 20 large metropolitan "spot markets," including New York, Los Angeles, Chicago, and Atlanta.

While the customers in most foreign markets take their cues from the center, many American consumers are blissfully ignorant about what New Yorkers or Los Angelenos like to do or wear. One can still use these latter two areas as bellwether test markets, as foreign companies often do, but such simplifications are usually more misleading than they would be in Tokyo. Mexico City may be the key to the Mexican market, but for many packaged goods small-town Peoria is a better test market than New York or LA.

REGULATIONS   A particular headache for foreign companies entering the North American market is the prevalence of many regulatory differences between central and regional governments. As most readers will know, the French-language province of Quebec offers many challenges to standardized marketing programs in Canada, and packaging and labeling have to be dual English and French. Even brand names are affected. Procter & Gamble's Pert shampoo is Pret in Quebec. In the United States the

50 states have independent jurisdiction over several important areas affecting business, including franchising contracts, resale price maintenance, pollution control, energy, transportation, banking, and industrial safety. Thus questions of product adaptation, after-sales service, packaging, and warehousing often become quite complicated.

As in other mature markets, there are also stiff regulations protecting the consumer. Promises in advertising must be kept (unless they are "puffery," that is, extravagant and thus "obviously untrue" in legal jargon). Test data on products must be made available for objective examination. Audience figures quoted for various media need to be validated by an independent agency. Stiffer laws regarding privacy from Europe are also under consideration. And as most foreigners know, the number of lawyers in the United States is sufficient to ensure that these and other regulations are enforced.

These basic differences help explain a few of the unique features of how marketing is done in North America. Some of the differences will be highlighted.

Competition

The United States is by most measures one of the most competitive markets in the world. Its huge potential has attracted many of the strongest multinationals, helped by relatively low trade barriers in many industries. But because of competition, success does not come easily. For the many successful foreign entrants, there are many that have found success elusive. Mercedes and BMW have succeeded where Peugeot and Rover have not. Adidas and Puma have found the going tough, while Reebok's early success has been difficult to sustain. The Body Shop and Benetton have had trouble keeping their U.S. operations in the black. While Sony, Honda, and Toyota have been consistently strong in North America, the same cannot be said for Mitsubishi, Nissan, and Mazda. And so on.

Although there are many reasons for such failures, one underlying factor is often the marketing complexity fostered by the cultural diversity in North America. The diversity in both the United States and Canada is not simply reflected in varying customer preferences but also makes for complexity in marketing communications. Simple messages can be misinterpreted and misunderstood, and there is less agreement on fundamental values than elsewhere. Add the fact that so many competitors vie for attention, and the end result is that marketing budgets need to be much larger than elsewhere. Novice foreign marketers are often baffled and have a hard time understanding the huge amount of advertising required for successful entry into the North American market.

Market Segmentation

Because of the maturity of the North American market and the large geographical area covered, *market segmentation* is a "natural." For segmentation purposes cultural identity can serve as a useful criterion even in the United States. Marketers target the Hispanics in larger cities with advertising on Spanish-language cable TV stations such as Univision, and African American audiences are targeted through advertising on prime-time shows featuring African American actors.

Product Positioning

Diversity has helped keep the American culture "low context" and "young." In positioning, premium is placed on direct and straightforward explanations. If nothing is said, nothing is meant. If you can't hear or understand what was stated, you had better ask for a repeat. For products with a mass audience it also makes it reasonable to communicate the positioning in concrete terms so as to be sure that "they get the message," since shared cultural norms may not exist. Subtle sales pitches get nowhere fast; hard sell becomes the norm. By contrast, the Canadian approach treats differences in cultural norms with much more sensitivity—and more soft sell. Still, individual consumers are

4

assumed to make rational purchase decisions based on the trade-offs between various attributes or benefits, just as they or their forefathers might have done when they weighed the pros and cons of moving to these countries.

Marketing Tactics

PRODUCT POLICIES Market size, affluence, and diversity have meant that the North American market offers a dizzying array of choices of products and services. Affluence and diversity not only help explain the wide assortments of products offered in stores or the ethnic variety of restaurants. They also help explain the emergence of the United States as a champion of fast foods. Pioneers, as contrasted to more established citizens, have many things to do and cannot spend too much time on unproductive activity. Also important is the fact that fast food represents a "least common denominator" offering for a diverse society, the kind of energy replenishment that everybody can partake in. McDonald's is the United States answer to the communal sharing of food in more traditional societies.

PRICING The attractiveness of the North American market has made it a very competitive arena for many domestic and foreign producers, with consumers reaping the benefits in terms of favorable price-to-quality ratios. For example, many foreign tourists, including Canadians, find prices in the United States cheaper than at home, even for their own countries' products. Free trade works.

The freedom from restraints on trade affects prices in many ways. Resale price maintenance ("fair trade") is usually illegal under the Robinson-Patman Act. To deny off-price outlets product shipments because they undercut prices is an offense. Competition is encouraged between brands but also intrabrand, between retail outlets. In the United States the same pair of Ralph Lauren eyeglass frames can be sold in two different stores with a 50 percent difference in price (see box, "Why Americans Are Price-Sensitive").

In most other countries such discrepancies would perhaps suggest to the buyer that the cheaper version is counterfeit. It might be in the United States as well—but so, alas, may be the more expensive version in the other store (the problems of counterfeits will be dealt with in Chapter 12, "Global Products and Services").

DISTRIBUTION The great size of the North American continent and the wide spread of its people would seem to be the main cause for the large-scale stores and the nationwide chains that have made distribution in the United States very efficient. The creation of efficient transportation highways, the ownership of automobiles, national broadcast networks, and the technological developments in packaging and storage techniques, including plastic wrapping and the refrigerator, made the large-scale supermarkets and nationwide distribution possible.

But this has also meant that distribution channels carry more clout in the United States than in many other markets. For a foreign entrant used to a more fragmented system, it is surprisingly easy to gain coverage of the North American market quickly, provided an agreement can be reached with one of the large nationwide distributors or chain stores. The problem is that such an agreement can be very expensive to reach. Conversely, in many other markets national distribution may be difficult to attain without negotiations with many local small and independent channel members. For the North American marketer used to the simpler system at home there is little preparation for such distribution headaches.

PROMOTION North American communications *media* are in principle not that much different from media elsewhere, but the use of advertising and commercials is greater. The United States shows larger advertising expenditures per capita than any other nation, including Canada (Japan is a distant second). Clutter is a real problem for advertisers since it is hard for one ad to get noticed. Nevertheless, advertising is absolutely necessary for consumer goods to reach any penetration in American markets; TV advertising, in particular, serves as the "great equalizer" carrying the mes-

Why Americans Are Price-Sensitive

WHEN JOHN KENNETH GALBRAITH published *The Affluent Society* in the 1960s, his assertion was that prices do not matter much in a society where people are affluent. This led many foreign observers to assume that in America, the land of milk and honey, prices do not matter. Many of them were surprised to find that, in fact, the United States may have the world's most price-conscious consumers. The Japanese, for example, have long been wondering why Americans are so focused on price.

The explanation is simple. It has to do with something called *intrabrand competition*. Intrabrand competition means competition between two offerings of the same brand.

In the U.S. marketplace, suggested retail prices can usually not be enforced. Attempting to not ship to stores that undercut suggested prices is illegal, and this is enforced through the justice system with its many lawyers. The principle is that any store legitimately selling coffeemakers should be able to feature Braun models. The price they charge is theirs to decide, not Braun's. Nor can Braun charge the store a higher price than it charges other similar stores—again, a law that is actively enforced. When a big cost-cutting retailer begins to offer Braun's products, the company can try to avoid shipping, claiming lack of supplies or some other problem, but such defenses have been challenged successfully in courts and do not usually hold up.

The result is that a Braun automatic coffeemaker that in a department store retails for, say, $95 can be had at a cost-cutting suburban warehouse for $49.95. A Ralph Lauren eyeglass frame at $250 in the city can be had for $129 across a state line. London Fog coats are sold at a 40 percent discount in off-price outlets. And these are not copies but the real thing (although knockoffs are also a big market). American consumers are price-sensitive for good reason, and American stores have also wised up, many promising to pay the difference if the customer can find the same product at a lower price elsewhere.

Source: *http://www.braun.com/*

sage to the many different segments in the market. Foreign brands frequently have to spend 5 to 10 times more advertising per dollar sales in the United States than at home. The big market is there for the taking—but at a steep price.

The wide media choices available to North Americans are partly another result of the diversity. Cable TV offers 50 or more channels in many areas. TV programming is accordingly varied, and many programs cater to special subgroups in the population. In contrast to most other countries, there are no government-owned noncommercial broadcasting stations, an expression of the desire to keep the government out of unduly influencing the population. This also means, of course, that there is no commonly accepted view of events or issues but that each citizen is forced to take responsibility for whatever opinions he or she may have. In the United States, it is rare to hear someone refer to the kind of "As we all know" evidence that forms such an important part of arguments in high context cultures.

SUMMARY

In the mature markets of the advanced countries local marketing should become "just marketing." It can, but with a twist. Even among the triad nations of Western Europe, North America, Japan, Australia, and New Zealand, there are plenty of differences the marketer must take into account. This chapter has spelled out some of the more obvious differences but has really only scratched the surface. The local marketer has to develop a more in-depth sense of the local marketing scene in order to be effective.

Market segmentation is usually a "must" in mature markets, and in these open markets competition is intense. New entrants will often have to use niche strategies, positioning their products not in the core of the market but in a specialty area. Even when the entrant is a strong core brand in a leading market, the differences between mature markets can be great enough that the niche approach is preferable. On the other hand, when the product is new, the entrant has a chance to develop a new market and gain favorable first-mover advantages, something which takes resources, focus, and continuous monitoring of penetration.

KEY TERMS

country-of-origin effects
  p. 227
customer satisfaction   p. 226
distributed headquarters   p. 233

Euro-brands   p. 237
Euro currency   p. 237
Japanese distribution   p. 242
market development   p. 225

marketing infrastructure   p. 225
"me too" products   p. 227
pan-European marketing
  p. 231

DISCUSSION QUESTIONS

1. From library research (including the Internet), identify how a product and brand of your choice is advertised differently—or similarly—in a European country and North America. Are the differences (similarities) related to differences (similarities) in positioning?

2. Use the Internet and company Web sites to find out the competitors in the Australian/New Zealand market for beer. Which global brands are present, and which are not?

3. Other than offering low prices, what can a Third World country do to get its products accepted by consumers in a mature economy? Can you find an example of a successful entry from such a country?

4. What are the reasons why entry into the Japanese market is so expensive?

5. Use news media and on-line access to track the impact of the single European currency introduction in January 1999. What seem to be the main marketing implications from the euro's arrival? How has the forced pricing in both national currency and the euro been handled by the various companies?

NOTES

1. See Albrecht, 1992, and Fornell, 1992, for a fuller presentation of what customer satisfaction involves in different markets.

2. The diffusion of manufacturing technology that drives this development exemplifies the Vernon international product cycle (IPC; see Chapter 2).

3. Country-of-origin effects have been the focus for a number of research studies for three decades or so. The sustained findings are that made-in labels matter for customers' quality perceptions. While consumers often protest that where a product is from does not matter, they still use country of origin as a clue to quality. It is less common, apparently, that consumers buy things because of some patriotic feeling. See Papadopoulos and Heslop, 1993.

4. As the multinational companies expand their manufacturing operations across the globe, the same process can be expected to make customers reevaluate their stereotypes of the countries. So, Indonesian-made calculators won't raise any eyebrows. What seems to be happening, according to research by David Tse and others at the University of British Columbia, is that a strong brand name serves to reassure the buyer. A Hewlett-Packard printer made in Malaysia is still an H-P product. A BMW Z3 roadster built in South Carolina is still of German quality. A Sony TV made in San Diego is still a Sony, and to many consumers, its positioning is still that of a "Japanese product." See Tse and Lee, 1989.

5. See Kerin et al., 1992.

6. See Johansson, 1994.

7. This section is based on Cecchini, 1988, on Quelch et al., 1991, on Johansson, 1989, and on updated material from various newspaper sources.

8. From Halliburton and Huenerberg, 1993.

9. From "Volvo Trucks Europe," case no. 17 in Kashani, 1992.

10. See Dalgic, 1992.

11. From Halliburton and Huenerberg, 1993.

12. See Bartlett, 1983.

13. This section draws on Johansson and Nonaka, 1996. Thanks are due to Kennedy Gitchel for reviewing and updating the material.

14. Fields, 1989, paints a vivid picture of Japanese consumers.

15. This section draws on Johansson and Hirano, 1995. The structural impediments initiative (SII) was an agreement in the early 1990s between the United States and Japan to dismantle distribution and other barriers that prohibited entry into each other's markets.

16. See Czinkota and Woronoff, 1991, p. 91.

17. This section draws on FitzRoy, Freeman, and Yip, 1998, and on Cartwright and Yip, 1998.

SELECTED REFERENCES

Albrecht, Karl. *The Only Thing That Matters.* New York: Harper Business, 1992.

Bartlett, Christopher A. "Procter & Gamble Europe: Vizir Launch." Harvard Business School, case no. 384–139, 1983.

Cecchini, Paolo. *The European Challenge 1992.* Aldershot, UK: Woldwood House, 1988.

Cartwright, Wayne; and George S. Yip. "New Zealand—Resource Play." Chapter 15 in Yip, 1998.

Chadwick, Michael; and Sue Won. "Toys-R-Us in Japan." Project report, Waseda-Georgetown program, Summer 1994.

Czinkota, Michael R.; and Jon Woronoff. *Unlocking Japan's Markets.* Chicago: Probus, 1991.

Dalgic, Tevfik. "Euromarketing: Charting the Map for Globalization." *International Marketing Review* 9, no. 5 (1992), pp. 31–42.

Dreifus, Shirley B., ed. *Business International's Global Management Desk Reference.* New York: McGraw-Hill, 1992.

Fields, George. *The Japanese Market Culture.* Tokyo: The Japan Times, 1989.

FitzRoy, Peter; Susan Freeman; and George S. Yip. "Australia— Asian Future." Chapter 14 in Yip, 1998.

Fornell, Claes. "A National Customer Satisfaction Barometer: The Swedish Experience." *Journal of Marketing* 56, no. 1 (January 1992), pp. 6–21.

Halliburton, Chris; and Reinhard Huenerberg. "Pan-European Marketing—Myth or Reality?" *Journal of International Marketing* 1, no. 3 (1993), pp. 77–92.

Halliburton, Chris; and Ian Jones. "Global Individualism— Reconciling Global Marketing and Global Manufacturing." *Journal of International Marketing* 2, no. 4 (1994), pp. 79–88.

Johansson, Johny K. "Japanese Marketing Strategies for Europe 1992." Paper presented at the Conference on "The New Japan— U.S. Relationship," New York University, New York, April 4–5, 1989.

_____ ."The Sense of 'Nonsense': Japanese TV Advertising." *Journal of Advertising* 23, no. 1 (March 1994), pp. 17–26.

_____ . and Ikujiro Nonaka. *Relentless: The Japanese Way of Marketing.* New York: HarperBusiness, 1996.

_____ . and Masaaki Hirano. "Japanese Marketing in the Post-Bubble Era." *International Executive* 38, no.1 (January–February 1995), pp. 33–51.

Kashani, Kamran. *Managing Global Marketing.* Boston: PWS-Kent, 1992.

Kerin, Roger A.; P. Rajan Varadarajan; and Robert A. Peterson. "First-Mover Advantage: A Synthesis, Conceptual Framework, and Research Propositions." *Journal of Marketing* 56, no. 4 (October 1992), pp. 33–52.

Kotler, P.; L. Fahey; and S. Jatusripitak. *The New Competition.* Englewood Cliffs, NJ: Prentice-Hall, 1985.

Papadopoulos, Nicolas; and Louise A. Heslop, eds. *Product-Country Images: Impact and Role in International Marketing.* New York: International Business Press, 1993.

Quelch, John A.; Robert D. Buzzell; and Eric R. Salama. *The Marketing Challenge of Europe 1992.* Reading, MA: Addison-Wesley, 1991.

TeleVeronique and TV 10. "Launch of Dutch Commercial TV Good News for U.S. Distributors." *Television/Radio Age* 36 (July 24, 1989), p. 19.

Tse, David; and W. Lee. "Evaluating Products of Multiple Countries-of-Origin Effect: Effects of Component Origin, Assembly Origin, and Brand." Working paper, Faculty of Commerce, University of British Columbia, Vancouver, Canada, 1989.

Updike, Edith Hill; and Mary Kuntz. "Japan Is Dialing 1 800 BuyAmerica." *Business Week,* June 12, 1995, pp. 61, 64.

Womack, James P.; Daniel T. Jones; and Daniel Roos. *The Machine That Changed the World.* New York: Rawson Associates, 1990.

WuDunn, Sheryl. "Japanese Do Buy American: By Mail and a Lot Cheaper." *The New York Times,* July 3, 1995, pp. 1, 43.

Yip, George S. *Asian Advantage: Key Strategies for Winning in the Asia-Pacific Region.* Reading, MA: Addison-Wesley, 1998.

Nine

Local Marketing in New Growth Markets

"The future is now"

Your takeaways from this chapter:

1. As Western markets have matured, new growth markets in Asia, Latin America, and elsewhere have become the new sources of growth for global companies—and for their own domestic firms as well.

2. Despite the recent global turmoil, many of these countries still have strengths as markets and producers and sustained potential for the longer run.

3. Trading blocs play a great role for these economies because as stand-alone markets they tend to be too small for targeting—and because the blocs provide advantages for their own exports.

4. Marketing in a high-growth market in a newly industrialized economy is not the same as marketing in a high-growth market in a mature economy. There is less stress on new-product development and more on generic market development for existing products.

5. Because of pent-up demand in many of these markets, standardized global products and brands can be successful. But as markets evolve and affluence grows, customers very quickly become more similar to the fickle consumers in mature markets, demanding adaptation and customization.

CHAPTER 9 DEALS with local marketing in the context of fast-growing markets in countries that are recently appearing (or, in the case of Latin America, reappearing) as players in the global marketplace. The chapter discusses these new markets in terms of opportunities for global marketers, but it is useful to remember that they also serve as sourcing locations for multinational firms (as we saw in Chapter 5's opening vignette about Brazil's exports, for example). This means that many companies are relatively familiar with the cultures involved and how to do business in the countries. It also means that manufacturing technology has been transferred, and many of these countries have viable domestic firms that can be strong competitors in their home markets as well as export markets.

The chapter stays close to the traditional marketing model involving market segmentation, product positioning, and the 4Ps. It first deals with these markets at a general level and then goes into more detail for two special cases: Latin America and the new Asian growth countries.

Cartoons Capture Kids' Hearts from Guadalajara to Guangdong

Betty Cohen, president of the Cartoon Network and TNT International, has a friend who grew up in Mexico, and like many children, she enjoyed watching cartoons. When Cohen's Mexican friend moved to the United States, she was astonished to discover that Fred Flintstone could speak English as well as Spanish.

People around the world have sought out popular entertainment born in the United States for years. Although the United States has lost its dominance in marketing the "hardware" of entertainment—televisions, VCRs, CD players, and so on—consumers are still eager to snap up the "software," from audio recordings to movies.

Marketers are therefore crafting strategies to expose U.S. popular entertainment and culture to new audiences, and they target children's programming as a market ripe for global expansion. Fox and Nickelodeon are creating new shows with partners abroad, while other companies are tailoring existing products to foreign markets. Fred Flintstone and his animated colleagues of Hanna Barbera are owned by the Cartoon Network, which has teamed up with Ted Turner's TNT cable network as Cartoon-TNT to provide global television programming. Cartoon-TNT has 28 million subscribers in Europe, 2 million in Asia, and 4.5 million in Latin America. The Cartoon Network offers up its huge cartoon library as a global product, adapting cartoons by dubbing them in several foreign languages. It also uses ratings data to select offerings for particular regions.

Hollywood also has been targeting its movies to eager audiences in developing countries. Movie studios have been experiencing flat profits domestically but have enjoyed rapid growth in Latin America and Southeast Asia, and China's huge population offers tantalizing opportunities for expansion. When Walt Disney Company originally released *The Lion King* there, it expected to gross $3 million. The movie surpassed all expectations, grossing that much in just 10 days, and subsequently the company doubled its forecast.

Unfortunately for U.S. popular entertainment and culture marketers, consumer demand is only one facet of the global marketing environment. Selling popular entertainment and culture in developing nations also poses some challenges.

China, for example, heavily taxed the revenues generated by *The Lion King*, cutting deeply into the movie's profits. In addition, studios must contend with a slow-moving government bureaucracy wary of exposing the country to foreign entertainment. Furthermore, piracy is rampant in many places, including Hong Kong and Thailand. Consumers there can buy unauthorized videos, CDs, and other products without generating any royalties for the artists or studios. The Motion Picture Association of America has pegged losses to piracy of movies alone at well over a billion dollars annually.

Still, enormous potential remains. Already, MTV has become the world's top brand of music videos, CNN is number one in television news, and ESPN sports has become a global leader. It's just a matter of time before Fred Flintstone is speaking "Taglish" (a mix of English and the local Filipino language Tagalog).

Sources: Lawrie Mifflin, "Can the Flintstones Fly in Fiji?" *The New York Times*, November 27, 1995, pp. D1, D4; Seth Faison, "A Chinese Wall Shows Cracks," *The New York Times*, November 21, 1995, pp. D1, D4; John Huey, "America's Hottest Export: Pop Culture," *Fortune*, December 31, 1990, pp. 50–53ff.

http://tnt.turner.com/
http://www.fox.com
http://www.nickelodeon.com/
http://www.disney.com/
http://www.mpaa.org
http://www.mtv.com
http://www.cnn.com
http://www.espn.com

INTRODUCTION

The local marketer in a **newly industrialized economy (NIE)** with fast economic growth faces a situation not unlike that of early marketers in mature markets. Although some of the markets are small in terms of population—Hong Kong and Israel at about 5 million, Singapore at almost 3 million—others are in the range of the European mix of populations, or between Chile's 14 million and Korea's 44 million.

The new growth markets comprise a varied set of countries. In addition to Southeast Asian and Latin American countries, one can also include several Mediterranean countries, South Africa, and now also several of the Eastern European countries. The main focus here will be on the Asian countries (except China and India, which will be dealt with in Chapter 10) and Latin America.

Two Kinds of Markets

For global marketing purposes, it is useful to distinguish two kinds of new growth countries. There are those that are relatively rich in natural **raw materials,** but where the majority of the people have suffered pain inflicted to equal degrees by **authoritarian political regimes** and **colonial domination.** Broadly speaking, this is the history of many Latin American countries and also South Africa. The growth of consumer demand in these countries is fueled by a more even distribution of the wealth created by their natural resources. Many of these peoples have witnessed at close range the affluence made possible by capitalism, but have not been able to share in it before. Their outlook as consumers is cautiously optimistic, with the fear of renewed autocratic rule still very real.

Another kind of new growth market involves countries that have turned toward Western-style capitalism more recently, with the help of foreign direct investment. Not so well endowed with natural resources, their wealth creation has been spurred by multinationals locating export-oriented plants to take advantage of low **labor costs.** Included are several of the Asian countries and to a lesser extent Israel. These countries are newcomers to economic affluence and tend to be basically optimistic about the future.

Although the global financial turmoil at the end of the 1990s has shifted these general sentiments downward, the basic distinction remains. The Latin American growth markets tend to be strong for consumer durables and related products as households

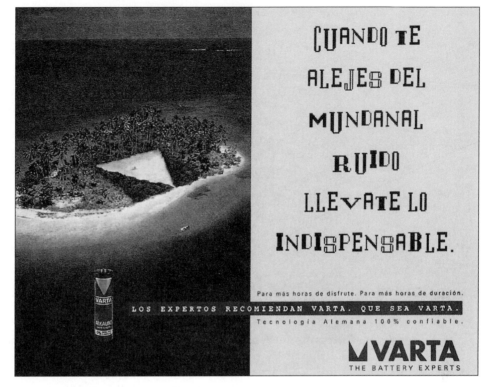

Creating brand name recognition is important in new growth economies. This Venezuelan ad for Varta batteries reinforces the distinguishing triangle, which symbolizes Varta's focused power and alludes to the tranquility that comes with long life. Molina Silva Publicidad.

improve their living conditions and attempt to create a better quality of life for children and extended families. Meanwhile Southeast Asia has been the source of phenomenal growth for Western luxury products and global brands, as the newly acquired wealth is channeled into hedonic consumption and individual gratification.

The difference in economic and political history between these countries is generally related to differences in religion and culture. While the Catholicism of Latin America has emphasized submission to authority and acceptance of the essential pain of ordinary life, the Buddhism of Asia offers fatalism and an emphasis on the basic insignificance of individual life. While Christianity preaches original sin and guilt, Buddhism offers meditation and transcendence of worldly constraints. Although these distinctions are oversimplified, they suggest clues as to why consumer demand in some new growth markets seems more frivolous than in others.

The Role of Trade Blocs

For many new growth markets, membership in **trade blocs** plays a very important role. There are two basic reasons for this. One, it makes the country more attractive to foreign investors, since manufacturing plants can be located there and receive preferential treatment for exports to other member countries. This is a key factor behind Malaysia's and Thailand's economic growth, fueled by membership in the ASEAN grouping. It helps in particular where components and parts need to be shipped between different assembly plants of a multinational. The large Toyota automobile plant in Indonesia exports to other ASEAN markets but also receives parts and supplies from its subsidiary operations in other ASEAN countries. Separating its manufacturing of engines, transmissions, and components between the different ASEAN countries to gain scale advantages, Toyota manages to obtain a preferential treatment for cross-shipments at half the regular tariff rates.

A second factor increasing the importance of trade blocs for the new growth countries is the enlarged market potential. Mercosur membership allows Argentina, a country with a population of less than 30 million, to boost its market size to close to 150 million, adding Brazil, Paraguay, and Uruguay. Market entries and foreign investment that could not be justified with a smaller population can be attracted much more easily. Conversely, the lack of a trade bloc among geographically close neighbors will be a drawback for a region. In the Middle East, for example, the Arab request that entering multinationals not deal with Israel has made it difficult to realize the full growth potential for the small Israeli economy.

The relationship between trade bloc membership and growth is of course reciprocal. New growth usually occurs when the trading blocs are created. At the same time, growth is necessary for the country to show sufficient promise—passing the critical takeoff point for sustained growth—in order for other countries to see the benefits of a trade bloc. If the country's economy is weak, its domestic businesses will fear and fight new entrants, and prospective bloc members will hesitate to partner with an inferior candidate. Africa is a good example of this vicious circle. Apart from their seemingly intractable tribal conflicts, the weakness of their domestic economies and market demand has prohibited many African countries from pursuing effective trade coordination and forced potential leaders such as South Africa to look elsewhere for markets and investments.

Market Segmentation

Despite these fundamental differences, there are several marketing similarities among these new growth markets. As we saw in Exhibit 8.1 of the previous chapter, new growth markets are in the growth phase of the product life cycle, which makes them attractive for entry. Certain markets might seem mature—food, basic household products, apparel—but there is generally potential for new variants and more international offerings. Other markets might be embryonic and in the introductory stage, including leisure products and services, Western furniture, and frozen food. But as incomes are rising, people in these countries are demanding the variety and experiences offered by the markets in more mature economies.

Product Positioning

Market segmentation in these countries differs from that in the developing countries primarily in the degree to which a **core middle class** is developed. The emergence of such a core group of consumers with some spending power in the NIEs means that segmentation techniques are directly applicable. In some cases, the requisite basic information—demographics, incomes, location—is unreliable because of large but hidden extended families, a desire to avoid taxes, and increased mobility of the populace. But as economic growth continues, consumer segments can be defined based on spending according to preferences and not only in terms of necessity, that is, not just according to "needs" but to "wants." It becomes important to recognize this and augment the official data available with primary data collection and personal observation and interviews.

In new growth markets it is easy to observe the attention given to well-known **brand names.** Many people from these countries are aware of foreign products, either through travel or through the global communication network. Global brands carry a cachet, and companies capitalize on this by high-profile promotions, including very visible outdoor and transit advertising. However, this does not mean that these customers are necessarily gullible; rather they are open to indulging themselves occasionally. For more basic and essential products and services—foods, household appliances, autos—the demand for quality and performance can be as high as in an advanced market.

These countries often use **foreign technology** and capital to fuel their growth, which tends to create a certain advantage for foreign entrants since they represent the "real thing." Unlike more mature markets, domestic products tend to be seen as less desirable, even though their functional performance may be superior. This **"neocolonial"** attitude on the part of the customers does not mean that one particular foreign country is necessarily favored, although one is struck by the apparent preference for

European styles in Argentina, Japanese products in Korea, and for anything British in Hong Kong and Singapore. The country-of-origin effect generally reflects how the economic development of these countries has depended on these supplier countries to a great extent; and, consequently, the products on the market tend to come from these countries.[1]

Marketing Tactics

The 4Ps in new growth markets can often be handled with a minimum of adaptation from more mature markets.

PRODUCT Basic localization to make sure the product functions well (adapted electric currency, smaller package sizes, translation of directions, etc.) is necessary in these markets, and customers can be as demanding as elsewhere. But since there is often a cachet to being "foreign" for certain segments and occasions, the "no adaptation" option should be given serious consideration. It is important that the brand name be strongly supported; generic products in these markets rarely stand a chance against the domestic variants.

PRICING Pricing is important but can largely reflect the same considerations as in the advanced markets—demand, costs, competitive conditions. If the unique selling proposition involves status positioning, a high price is warranted. These markets are growing, and people are ready to spend money. At the same time, it is important that price not be too limiting: Building a brand franchise with a large and loyal following is very much the name of the game.

DISTRIBUTION Distribution and service activities should also be viewed for the potential long-range benefits. Distribution is very important and warrants larger margins and more support services than elsewhere. Participating in a growth market usually involves spending money to increase the number of outlets, the coverage of segments, and the response to competitive threats. These markets are not cash cows yet. Except for the upper niche of luxury consumption, they will not really produce a large net cash flow until later.

PROMOTION Products and services should be supported for the future potential benefits they offer. Creating a strong image for a brand is important. Sharing information and building trust among customers for industrial products is similarly important. The sales personnel need to be careful not to divulge trade secrets that can be used by domestic producers against the innovating firm. The NIEs have often shown themselves impervious to international copyright laws and patent enforcement. Microsoft, the large U.S. software producer for personal computers, has had a policy of avoiding entry into Korea, Hong Kong, and Singapore because of these countries' copyright infringement practices (pirated Microsoft software still finds its way into these markets).

Nevertheless, with free trade issues still politically salient in attractive markets such as the United States and Canada, the NIEs will find it necessary to curb such activities in order to be part of the global trade system. Thus, promotional support, tie-ins with local representatives, and an open mind in regard to sharing with and trusting locals will be more justified in the future than in the past.

CLOSE-UP: **MARKETING IN LATIN AMERICA**[2]

These general considerations provide a starting point for the local marketer in an NIE. But more details on local conditions are needed to formulate, implement, and execute marketing strategy. Two major growth regions will be discussed in more detail. First, the Latin American market, and then, the new Asian growth markets.

G E T T I N G   T H E

Picture

Latin American Surge

LATIN AMERICA'S drive toward free trade is surging. In customs lanes at the international airports of Rio de Janeiro and Sao Paulo, the police simply wave through thousands of passport bearers from Argentina, Paraguay, and Uruguay, Brazil's common market partners in Mercosur. Jets that shuttle hourly between Sao Paulo and Buenos Aires carried 1.3 million passengers in 1994, twice as many as four years earlier. Four times as many business executives from Mercosur countries visited Brazil than executives from the United States.

Further north, the United States, Canada, and Mexico have agreed with Chile to start negotiating that country's entrance into an expanded NAFTA. In a mid-1995 meeting of 33 trade ministers from the Americas in Denver, the delegates agreed to start working on the creation, by 2005, of a hemisphere-wide customs union, the Free Trade Area of the Americas.

Since free trade talks are expected to take years, a complementary building block that crosses trade barriers more easily is taking shape: Latin American multinational corporations. Telecommunicaciones de Chile has invested in telephone companies in Argentina, Colombia, Peru, and Venezuela. Tintas Renner S.A., Brazil's largest paint company, has joint venture partners in Argentina, Chile, Paraguay, and Uruguay. In recent financial ventures an Ecuadorean bank bought a Colombian bank, a Colombian bank bought a Venezuelan bank, and a Chilean bank bought a Bolivian bank. In 1995 there were 300 Brazilian and 170 Chilean companies operating in Argentina.

Sources: Brooke, 1995; Smith, 1994.

Latin America is coming back as one of the growth markets of the world (see box, "Latin American Surge").

The economic growth is fueled by regional trading blocs, a political shift toward increased democracy, and a gradual emergence from a large debt burden in several of the countries. For the local marketer, of special importance is the culture (religious and ethnic heritage), which affects communication strategy in particular, an uneven income distribution, which strongly affects segmentation, and a drive toward pan-regional marketing. More on this below; first, some background information.

Market Environment

Latin America is a geographical area that stretches from Mexico down through Central and South America to Cape Horn. It is tied together by a common cultural heritage of native Indians, colonial dominance by Spain and Portugal, and the Roman Catholic Church. The language is Spanish except in the largest country, Brazil, whose 160 million inhabitants speak Portuguese. The total population is 460 million, of which Mexico accounts for 86 million.

Latin America exhibits a varied ethnic mix of descendants of the ancient, highly developed civilizations of Incas and Aztecs and the conquering Europeans—largely Spanish and Portuguese, but also German, Italian, and British. There are also African, Asian, and Polynesian influences and a significant Japanese presence in Peru and Brazil. These varied influences combine uneasily, with ethnic heritage strongly linked to social class. There is great disparity between the political, social, economic elite and the often illiterate, poor peasants of Indian heritage. Society is stratified with two classes: very rich and very poor. This has given rise to political/military instability, a history of revolutions and coups, and terrorism as a means of changing the status quo. Economic progress should serve to lower this propensity for violence, and there is some indication of a growing middle class.

The Roman Catholic Church is still the most important **religious influence;** it has been shifting from its traditional role of supporting the oligarchy to supporting movements for social justice. There has been some growth in Protestantism and an evangelical movement (principally Pentecostal), heavily influenced by TV evangelism from the United States. The shift toward Protestantism goes hand in hand with the industrialization and urbanization of Latin America and the cultural shift toward democratization and self-reform.

Overall the region is poor, with at least 50 percent of wealth controlled by 20 percent of the people in almost all the countries in Latin America. Affluent consumers with buying power equivalent to that in developed countries are only about 10 to 20 percent of the population in most countries. Broadly speaking, these are countries in the process of moving from an agricultural to an industrial society.

Regional Trade Agreements

Several regional trade agreements affect marketing in Latin America directly by enhancing the opportunities for regionwide marketing strategies. The major agreements are as follows:

LAIA—LATIN AMERICAN INTEGRATION ASSOCIATION This agreement between all South American countries and Mexico expands a previous free trade agreement (LAFTA) into a customs union with free flow of goods and a common tariff rate toward nonmembers.

ANCOM—ANDEAN COMMON MARKET In February 1993, Bolivia, Colombia, Ecuador, and Venezuela began operating a common market. ANCOM means reduced tariffs, increased intraregional trade, free factor mobility, and a political climate more favorable to foreigners. Peru has now also been added to the group.

MERCOSUR—SOUTHERN CONE COMMON MARKET A common market consisting of Argentina, Brazil, Paraguay, and Uruguay. With the economies of Brazil and Argentina performing well, this has become perhaps the strongest grouping in Latin America. The member countries have agreed to establish a common external tariff (in 1998 still at a relatively high average level of about 20 percent) and lower tariffs for intraregional trade. There have been problems in adjusting internal tariffs on a smooth schedule (in 1995, for example, Uruguay had 950 products listed as "exceptions" to the common agreement), but the sheer growth of the countries has generated a strong momentum in internal trade. For example, the Brazilian shoe industry benefits from supply of less expensive Argentine leather, while competition from Argentine wheat has reduced Brazilian wheat production by a third compared with levels before the agreement.

NAFTA—NORTH AMERICAN FREE TRADE AREA The 1994 ratification of NAFTA has meant that Mexico has moved closer to its northern neighbors. But rather than seeing this as a step away from the Latin American region, from a marketing viewpoint Mexico has become a natural entry gate to the larger Latin American market for North American businesses. This would be reinforced with the proposed admission of Chile to the trade agreement.

Market Segmentation

Market segmentation in Latin America is often based on the simple distinction between **urban versus rural** population, combined with age and income level. A typical rule of thumb says that 80 percent of the purchasing power is in urban areas, with 20 percent in rural areas.

Urban Latin America also has a young, style-conscious segment. Approximately 56 percent of Latin America's population is under the age of 24. Many young adults live with their parents and spend disposable income on luxury and semiluxury items. The youth market can have a large influence on the buying patterns of their parents and other consumer groups. Trying to capture the future potential of this market, MTV (Music TV) Latino is targeting the still small but rapidly growing Latin American pay-TV market and cable TV is growing rapidly.[3]

In rural Latin American markets the cultural heritage of poverty and sometimes fatalistic religion creates a large tradition-bound family-oriented core customer segment. Authority is centered in the father, with a culture of "machismo" and the strong male figure. There is still a willingness to leave things to destiny and chance, to view the future as inevitable, and to put off till tomorrow (the well-known "mañana") anything that can wait and hope that it will take care of itself. But change is under way, and the global marketer should not assume that this tendency makes it unnecessary to answer requests and fill orders on time.

Product Positioning

Companies targeting affluent urban buyers can generally apply the strategies used in more mature markets. The urban segment is a status-conscious and aspiring market with working- and middle-class households spending a large portion of their income to upgrade the quality of life for their families through appliances, TVs, VCRs, and so forth. Global brands and products carry the usual cachet—and sticker prices. One company, Prosdocimo in Brazil, was a leading competitor in the home appliance business for many years. Now bought up by European Electrolux, its products have been upgraded in line with the rising affluence of the Brazilian market, and the brand name has been changed to the higher status name of Electrolux.

Marketers targeting the huge pool of low-income consumers have a tough challenge. Successful mass marketing can possibly be achieved through creative packaging (small-volume, low-price units), taking new product rollouts one step at a time, establishing one product firmly before launching another, and spending heavily on advertising.

Companies also have to rethink their strategies for reaching outlying markets/ rural populations in Latin America. Face-to-face interviewing and observation are generally necessary to gauge reaction to promotions and products. It is very important to be sensitive to religious, political, ethnic, and cultural issues. Cultural idiosyncrasies—such as symbolism of certain colors, flowers, and animals—have to be reckoned with in advertising and promotions. In some rural areas consumers have not had extensive contact with the developed world.

Marketing Tactics

PRODUCT POLICIES During the growth of the 1990s the Latin American marketers, whether domestic or foreign, have continually upgraded their products and services. The process has been driven by two factors. One is the increased competition from foreign producers as domestic markets have been opened. A second driver is the implementation of trade agreements between Latin American countries, opening neighboring countries to within-region exports.

A typical example is the beer industry. Major international beer companies, including Anheuser-Busch and Miller from the United States and Labatt's from Canada, have focused on Latin America as a new growth region. Investing in brewing capacity in these countries not only increased supply but also introduced modern brewing techniques and global brands, putting pressure on the local brewers. As a result, the locals consolidated and upgraded their brewing facilities, and many started exporting to other countries. Not surprisingly, and typical of this type of new growth markets, generic demand increased sharply as beer consumption soared. While in 1990 annual beer consumption in South America was 37 liters per capita, the 1998 figure was over

50 liters, leaving room for both global and local brands, such as Brazil's favorite, Brahma, with almost 50 percent of the Mercosur beer market.[4]

Apart from obvious localization changes such as using Spanish (and Portuguese for Brazil) on packages and instruction booklets, these markets so far require fairly limited product adaptations. But it is important that the right choices among a company's assortment be chosen. Latin American people can be much more serious and formal than Western managers might expect. For example, when J. C. Penney, the American lower-end department store, entered Chile in 1996, it offered expensive lines in the flashy colors popular in more tropical markets such as Miami and Mexico. After a disappointing performance, the store replaced American managers with local talent, put greater emphasis on less expensive and more functional items, and went after Chile's growing maternity market. Sales picked up, and soon Penney opened a second store.[5]

Overall, however, the pent-up demand is for global brands and products that have been seen on television broadcasts of sports and entertainment events. In time, as the markets move closer to maturity and pan-regionalism, one can expect to see a need for more specific targeting of Latin American consumers and their specific tastes. That demand will to some extent be satisfied by advanced local companies, but one would also assume that global marketers will find the market sufficiently attractive to want to develop pan-regional products for Latin America as well.

PRICING   As long as the historical inequality in incomes holds in Latin America, global entrants will have to focus on the urban markets, leaving the lower price end of the range to local companies. This means that the standard advice for foreign companies is to price products slightly higher to create a semi-upper-middle-class image attractive to upwardly mobile families. As the middle class is developing rapidly, however, the foreign companies have found it useful to avoid too high a skimming price, instead extending the price range from the high end (for the top-of-the-line products) to include also the mid-range prices.

The real potential in Latin America being the huge middle market, it is not surprising to see that many mid-range producers are doing increasingly well. Wal-Mart discount drugstores and Home Depot's hardware "category killer," both American retail chains with middle-of-the-road products at affordable prices, have done well in targeting the new middle class. But here the local producers and retailers are also active, and the competition can be fierce. Sears, Roebuck, with long-standing presence throughout Latin America, was forced to withdraw from Chile in the early 1980s. Local chains such as Sodimac Homecenter offer comparable products and matching prices—and are more attuned to the local market.[6]

There are also plans for a common Mercosur currency. If implemented, this will directly affect prices because of the need to have transparent uniformity in different country markets.[7] If the brief experience in Europe is any guide, the effect will be to force companies to price at relatively lower levels than previously in most countries, a sort of "lowest common price" level based on prices in the most competitive market.

DISTRIBUTION   Distribution in Latin America is moving toward the larger integrated units and the chain concept common in Western markets. For example, large supermarkets with expanded assortments of leisure products and home appliances—so-called hypermarkets—are growing in importance. Carrefour, the French chain of hypermarkets, has a large presence there.

In terms of establishing distribution at the time of initial entry, barriers exist. Some find that a weak infrastructure creates problems (see box, "Getting Started in Mexico").

Foreign companies have found that it is a mistake to rely on selling products through large and established Latin American distributors, who may only take on

G E T T I N G   T H E

Picture

Getting Started in Mexico: Amway Finds Localization Leads to Rapid Growth

WHEN ENTERING MEXICO, Amway, the American direct home sales company, had to modify its system to conform to local laws and adjust for the lack of service infrastructure.

First was a change in the organizational system to avoid responsibility for social security payments and income tax withholdings for its individual distributors. Each Amway distributor must therefore register as an individual business so that there is absolutely no labor connection with the company.

Instead of the home delivery from a central warehouse used in the United States and Europe, the lack of adequate service by shippers in Mexico forced Amway to use eight distribution centers in six cities. It also works with a Mexican express delivery company for service to areas not covered by its own depots.

One challenge was the inadequate telecommunications system. The Mexican telephone company's (Telmex) rapidly expanding toll-free 800 service couldn't keep up with Amway's needs for quick order taking from its distributors. Service is still relatively inefficient and expensive. Also, Amway has had trouble securing a dedicated line for computer communication between HQ in Monterrey and outlying distribution centers.

Trademark registration and health authorization processes for imported products cause significant delays: Average wait is up to three months versus one month in Europe.

Sources: Dreifus, 1992; American Chamber of Commerce in Mexico, 1992.

products that are easy to sell and who do not have a commitment to specializing in their products. For North American firms, joint ventures with strong local partners are advisable at entry to help open up the doors to Latin America's clubby business world. Some companies, such as the Philadelphia hospital company AMSCO, avoid allowing middlemen to define their markets and concentrate on learning the market and getting to know the end customers firsthand.[8]

Tropicana Dole Beverages International, now a unit of Pepsico, entered the South American market by launching its Pure Premium Orange and Grapefruit juices and Pure Tropics line of fruit juice blends in Argentina. Tropicana has a joint venture with La Serenisima, Argentina's largest dairy and a partner with similar high-quality products and brand loyal customers. Tropicana entered into Argentina because of its strong economy, concentration of affluent consumers, and lack of premium chilled juice competitors. Argentina is also to be used as a springboard for entry into other Mercosur markets.[9]

PROMOTION   In general, Latin America is no longer in its infancy in terms of knowledge and awareness of world-class brands and products. Globally established brands have invested considerably in raising brand awareness and creating a market presence, and smaller local brands have had to fight for their existence.

Among urban consumers, research has shown that adult Latin Americans want detailed product information in advertising and tend to reject image-oriented ads. They want to understand immediately what the commercial is for and what it claims to deliver. Product demonstrations and testimonials are effective.[10]

Television commercials often revolve around family life, as households frequently have three generations under one roof. Women have been shown to respond well to commercials that convey a sense of pleasing the family through traditional roles of caring for the home and making meals. The Hispanic culture is upbeat and happy, and Hispanics react most favorably to ads that portray them as colorful and lively.

An Argentine advertisement for Tropicana orange juice, emphasizing its purity. The Spanish language ad is a logical pan-regional advertisement as Tropicana expands from its Argentine entry point to the rest of Latin America. Courtesy Tropicana.

Sponsoring the popular daytime soap operas on television allows the advertiser to reach a huge audience of women of all ages. For the male audience, sponsorship of movies or sporting events is also fruitful. Endorsements by well-known entertainers or athletes can be powerful. Cafe Pele, named after the soccer star, has been very successful for Brazilian coffeemaker Cacique de Alimentos. When Gatorade featured soccer star Pele in a TV commercial in which he was seen drinking Gatorade after a game, no words were necessary. Sales took off, and success was ensured throughout the region.

In rural areas marketing communications are dominated by the need to overcome illiteracy. High illiteracy rates mean that there is a need for product identification through nonverbal/pictorial means. The accompanying music becomes very important: Brazilian commercials typically rely heavily on the popular dance music of the region. Package shape and design become very important. Repetition of identical posters and reinforcing the product and its name are useful, accompanied by easily memorized music.

As for sales promotion, because many retailers do not accept cents-off coupons, inducing new product trial is a challenge. Companies have used inventive promotional tools such as vans and sound trucks stationed at markets to play music and offer free samples to passersby.

Major Country Markets

Latin America has four major markets. Argentina, Brazil, and Mexico have large populations, while Chile has the highest per capita GDP. Some marketing highlights are discussed below.

ARGENTINA   In the early years after World War II Argentina was one of the 10 richest countries in the world, on a per capita income basis. Politics changed that, but in the 1990s the country is coming back as inflation has been reined in, markets have been opened, and foreign direct investments have significantly increased. The country has a highly sophisticated industrial and agricultural sector, making it able to withstand the

Tango at Harrod's

IN 1913, AS EUROPE lurched toward the Great War and faraway Argentina with its agricultural resources and prime beef was one of the high-potential countries in the world, Harrod's, the great London-based department store, built a branch in downtown Buenos Aires. Its glory faded after the Peronistas had reduced the potential for luxury consumption in Argentina, and in 1960 the owners sold the store to an Argentine company. But the Londoners apparently forgot to check the fine print carefully. The 1913 holding company contract gave the store the right to "carry on in the Argentine Republic and elsewhere in South America." By selling the store, Harrod's had also sold the South American rights to its name.

Throughout the 1990s, as economic growth made the Latin American market increasingly attractive, Harrod's made furious attempts in court to get its name back. But the courts held fast, and in 1998 Harrod's name in South America was the confirmed property of the Argentine company Harrod's BA, Ltd. Now only seen on the old store in Buenos Aires, Harrod's name and stores will soon appear elsewhere in Latin America's major capitals—under Argentine ownership and with a special department for tango outfits.

Sources: Faiola, 1998; Schemo, 1998.

Latin American repercussions of the Mexican currency crisis of 1995 and maintain free markets. Its membership in Mercosur has served to attract foreign companies such as IBM and General Motors looking for entries into the larger region.

Increased purchasing power has contributed to record sales in consumer markets. With their European heritage and past affluence, the Argentine consumers are highly sophisticated and oriented toward Western products and global brands (see box, "Tango at Harrod's").

The 11 million people in the larger Buenos Aires metropolitan area serve as a lead market not only for the rest of the country but also for the larger Mercosur region. It can be very competitive. One example is the soft drink market (seventh in the world in per capita consumption and growing at 8 percent per year for the past 10 years). Fierce competition exists between Pepsi and Coke for brand penetration and customer loyalty. Both companies are targeting young consumers and installing large numbers of vending machines as well as sponsoring rock concerts and special promotions. After nearly reaching bankruptcy during the years of hyperinflation and price controls, Pepsi has recently been relaunched in Argentina, achieving a 39 percent market share. Coke has responded by restructuring its distribution channels to work more closely with supermarket chains, bars, restaurants, and other retailers.

BRAZIL   Brazil is the largest of the Latin American countries with about 160 million people. Under President Cardoso's regime, past restrictions on inward investment and capital movements have been lifted, runaway inflation has been stopped, and the country has become a Latin American engine of growth again. Brazil generates a third of South America's economic output and is a major consumer of its exports. For example, in 1996 Brazil absorbed almost 90 percent of Argentina's exports.

The currency devaluations in Asia and Russia at the end of the 1990s have also threatened Brazil's real and the country's attraction for foreign investors, but the longer term future looks bright.[11] In 1998 there were over 300 joint business projects under way with Argentine companies alone, and more than 70 percent of Brazilian exports were of manufactured goods, including automobiles from Brazilian plants of Volkswagen, Fiat, General Motors, Honda, and Toyota.

CHILE   Chile with its 14 million people is perhaps the most vigorous example of recent Latin American growth, and its consumer markets are booming. Over $200 million was invested in new shopping malls in 1994. One-fifth of the Chilean population currently frequents shopping malls (versus three-fifths in the United States). The new shopping malls range from a $59 million luxury mall to Chile's very first outlet mall, where one-third of the new stores will be foreign chains.[12]

As elsewhere in Latin America, credit card issuers are helping to fuel growth in spending by lowering the minimum household income required to obtain a card (for instance, Banco Santander requires only $500 to $600 monthly income, versus $1,000 previously).

MEXICO The 90 million people of Mexico make the country the second largest market (after Brazil) in Latin America. Its membership in NAFTA and its resilient comeback after a severe slump and peso devaluation in 1995 have reinforced foreign investors' confidence in the country despite various political problems and ethnic disturbances. In the past many foreign companies (Japanese and European in addition to American) located plants in Mexico to serve the Latin American market. With the advent of NAFTA, capacity at these plants is now increased to serve the North American market as well. The economy is also given a boost from Mexican workers in the United States who send money back home to their families and relatives.

The Mexico City metropolitan area, home to almost 15 million people, provides a major market for global brands and upscale consumer goods. As in so many other countries where business and government are concentrated in the capital city, Ciudad de Mexico is a trendsetter for the rest of the country but also atypical in its cosmopolitanism. For example, a 24-hour home shopping network was introduced in Mexico City in 1993, and many of the world's major retailers can be found there (although Home Depot, the American hardware superstore, scrapped plans for Mexico in the 1995 crisis and instead went into Chile in 1998).[13] Some marketers are successful with the integrated marketing approaches common in mature markets to reach consumers. For example, the Kellogg's cereal company sponsored a conference on nutrition and fiber that generated a large amount of publicity. This was followed by an equally successful introduction of recipes and nutrition messages on cereal boxes.

Pan-Regional Marketing

Some observers argue that the Latin American market is **pan-regional** and that a marketing strategy aimed at the Latin American region overall will be effective.[14]

Advertising agencies such as McCann-Erickson and DDB Needham believe that there is a strong trend toward increased regionalization and integration in Latin America.[15] They anticipate that this will lead to more pan-regional advertising and media buying. However, cross-border advertising is currently hampered by the media infrastructure, which is still very localized and not very extensive in some countries.

Two American companies' Latin American strategies can be used to demonstrate how global marketers are approaching the region (see also the globalization of Goodyear's Latin American advertising discussed at the end of Chapter 15).

BURGER KING IN LATIN AMERICA Burger King, the fast-food restaurant chain, has expanded into Mexico, Brazil, Chile, Peru, Argentina, Colombia, and Puerto Rico during the last few years. This expansion has taken the form of joint ventures, franchise agreements, and alliances with U.S. consumer products companies such as Coca-Cola. Burger King spent about $5 million in advertising annually to introduce its name into the region.

The company's objective in expanding in Latin America is to "think globally and act locally." It has established headquarters for the Latin American division in Miami but is also setting up corporate offices in the local markets including Rio de Janeiro, Mexico City, and São Paulo.[16]

IBM IN LATIN AMERICA IBM's long-term strategy for Latin America includes spending millions of dollars to bring computer technology to local schools in 11 countries. In five years, IBM has provided 800,000 children with access to computers and has trained more than 10,000 teachers. This program is intended to enhance the company's image and also create a market with loyal future customers for its products and services.

The computers are purchased by institutions and private firms and then donated to the schools. IBM contributes in the form of teacher training and technical support and has invested millions of dollars in its Latin American Research Center, which advises countries on designing and implementing educational programs.

In Venezuela, IBM and Procter and Gamble have designed a donation scheme called Future Mission, where students, parents, and teachers collect proof of purchase seals from P&G products and redeem them for computer equipment for their schools. An extensive advertising campaign including press, radio, direct mail, TV, and in-store computer demonstrations has publicized the program.

In the end, however, it is misleading to believe that Latin America is a single, borderless market like what the European Union aspires to be. Manuel Mencia of the Beacon Council, a Florida economic development group, says that non-Latin Americans tend to ignore that "what divides Latin Americans is much more important than what binds them."[17] Marketers may do better understanding one country's culture at a time and, for the time being at least, emphasizing localization.

CLOSE-UP: MARKETING IN THE NEW ASIAN GROWTH MARKETS[18]

Up until July 1997 when the Thailand currency (the baht) was devalued, setting off a worldwide financial crisis, the Southeast Asian countries had been the fastest growing economies in the world through the 1990s. Annual growth rates for the region typically ranged between 5 and 10 percent, significantly above the 2 to 4 percent growth rates of the mature economies (see Exhibit 9.1). With the precipitous fall in the exchange rates as investment capital fled the countries, growth rates were sharply down and even negative in 1998. With Japan's reawakening, however, one can expect the region to bounce back and resume its economic progress.

The countries of primary interest here are South Korea, Taiwan, Hong Kong, and the original ASEAN members (Indonesia, Malaysia, the Philippines, Singapore, and Thailand). As emerging markets, China and India will be discussed in Chapter 10. Even though all of these countries suffered significant economic damage at the end of the 1990s, caught in the grip of financial crises and currency devaluations, in the longer run they are likely to return as high growth-markets.

Market Environment

As can be seen in Exhibit 9.1, these countries vary in size from Indonesia's almost 200 million people to Singapore's 3 million. Several are ethnically homogeneous (Taiwan, Korea), while others (Malaysia, Singapore) are populated by several racial groups (Chinese, Indian, Malay). They also vary in geographic scope, from the city-states Hong Kong and Singapore to Indonesia's and the Philippines' archipelagoes with a vast number of islands. Indonesia alone possesses an estimated number of 13,700 islands, it has the world's largest Muslim population (over 170 million), and its people speak some 250 regional dialects. Their economic performance also differs, the longer established "four dragons" (Korea, Taiwan, Hong Kong, and Singapore) clearly outperforming relative newcomers such as Thailand, Indonesia, and the Philippines. In 1995 Hong Kong and Singapore had per capita incomes (adjusted for purchase power parity) higher than that of Japan and just behind those of the United States and Germany, a remarkable feat.

One common characteristic of these countries is a sort of love-hate relationship with Japan. Most were occupied by Japanese forces in World War II, and some, such

EXHIBIT 9.1 Key Statistics of Asia-Pacific and Other Economies

	Population 1995 (millions)	GNP 1995 (U.S.$ billions)	GNP (PPP*) 1995 (U.S.$ billions)	Per capita GNP 1995 (U.S.$)	Average GDP growth 1995–1997 (%)†
Asia-Pacific					
Japan	125.5	4,975	2,775	39,640	2.8
South Korea	44.9	436	514	9,700	7.7
China	1,200.2	744	3,505	620	10.5
Taiwan	22.0	246	279	12,265	6.0
Hong Kong	6.2	144	142	23,200	4.9
Singapore	3.0	80	68	26,730	7.2
Malaysia	20.1	78	181	3,890	8.3
Thailand	58.2	159	439	2,740	7.2
Indonesia	193.3	189	735	980	7.5
Philippines	66.6	72	196	1,050	5.5
India	929.4	316	1,301	340	5.9
Vietnam	73.5	18	96‡	240	9.0
Australia	16.1	339	343	18,720	3.3
New Zealand	3.6	52	59	14,340	3.5
Other					
United States	263.1	7,098	7,098	26,980	3.2
Germany	81.9	2,253	1,644	27,510	2.9
Mexico	91.8	305	588	3,320	2.0
Poland	61.1	170	330	2,790	6.4

*Purchasing power parity.
†Includes estimates for 1997.
‡Gross domestic product.

Source: Adapted from Yip, 1998, p. 2

as Korea, had been under Japanese domination before. At the same time, the recent economic resurgence of these countries has been modeled on the Japanese pattern, basically an export-led expansion. In addition, the Japanese multinationals have invested heavily in the Asian countries, with operations ranging from sourcing of raw materials (Indonesian lumber, oil) to technology products such as automobile components and computer chips (Malaysia, Thailand). Despite the occasional animosity against Japan because of atrocities committed during the war, the Japanese businesses are basically well positioned and welcomed in these countries.

Regional Trade Agreements

There are several regional trade agreements among these countries that offer good starting points for pan-regional strategies.

The Association of South East Asian Nations, or ASEAN, was created in 1967. It includes Indonesia, Malaysia, the Philippines, Singapore, and Thailand, with Brunei added in 1967, Vietnam in 1995, and Myanmar and Laos in 1997. Originally a political union, it has evolved into a free trade area, although Malaysia's 1998 decision to close its border to foreign capital threatens to change this.

There are looser groupings as well. APEC (Asia-Pacific Economic Cooperation) is a large association that spans both sides of the Pacific from Canada and Chile to Australia. ARF, or ASEAN Regional Forum, is an extension of the ASEAN bloc to include Russia and Cambodia. These groupings represent tentative efforts to extend the region politically and economically, and have been slowed by the turmoil at the end of the 1990s.

In 1992 ASEAN countries met to formalize a far-reaching trade agreement, forming the ASEAN Free Trade Area (AFTA). Created to match the emergence of the European Union, the principal result was a preferential tariff rate no higher than 5 percent between member nations (with the ultimate aim of reducing tariffs to 0 percent), reduction of nontariff barriers, and a common external tariff rate. The AFTA development is a significant step toward creating the kind of common market one finds in Europe's EU and Latin America's Mercosur, and it is likely that "Pan-AFTA" products and marketing campaigns will gradually emerge.

Market Segmentation

The economic upswing in the Asian high-growth markets has led to the emergence of a significant middle class, in Thailand known as the "have somes." Its size varies with the population and the level of growth. In Korea, with a 1995 GDP ranked eleventh in the world, the majority of the 45 million inhabitants can be classified as middle class, while less than 15 percent of Indonesia's 200 million people are middle class. Most of these people live in the urban areas. In fact, the core of the market for global companies is in the large metropolitan areas, from Bangkok and Jakarta to Manila and Seoul.

However justified from an economic perspective, avoiding the rural areas where people tend to be less well off can create some political problems. Multinational entrants cannot always count on a welcome with open arms, especially from governments with socialist leanings. So far the Asian growth markets have been led by pro-Western capitalist governments, but the financial crises at the end of the 1990s threaten to change this. In 1998, for example, Malaysia closed its door to free capital flows, essentially cutting itself off from the foreign money that had so far fueled much of its growth. One would expect that once the capital flows are again freed up, the multinational entrants would have to pay attention not only to economic fundamentals but also to the social problems in these countries, just as the World Bank has urged them to do.[19]

Segmentation in most of these markets does in fact have to start with the underlying cultural, ethnic, and religious roots. The cultures in these countries vary a great deal. People in Hong Kong and Singapore are basically Chinese but also cosmopoli-

Shopping in warehouse stores at discounted prices is becoming a global phenomenon as chains go into new growth markets. Here shoppers in Malaysia push the limits of their carrying capacity at Makro, a Dutch-owned retail chain. Munshi Ahmed.

tan. Taiwan and Korea each have quite unified national cultures, while the Philippines' long relationship with Western Catholicism and more recent American ties have made for a very special culture. South Asia generally exhibits a mix of Chinese, Indian, and native cultures.

Product Positioning

The most visible products for these markets are perhaps the global luxury brands (Gucci, Chanel, Dunhill, and others) positioned at the upper end of the market, skimming the demand from the very affluent and the occasional buyers who want to indulge themselves. Before the financial turmoil, there was no doubt about the continuing fascination with status and premium prices. These countries are relative newcomers to economic prosperity, and with little stigma attached to hedonic pleasures in their Buddhist credos, it was natural to follow the "If you've got it, flaunt it" maxim. It is not surprising to learn that in 1996–97 as much as 40 percent of the sales of European luxury goods makers came from Asia (although this changed during the financial crises in 1997–98).[20]

The Asian markets' desire for **global identification** has made many multinationals with more mundane products use global standardization in their positioning strategies as well. In addition to Lux soap, Unilever has introduced well-known brands such as Lipton tea, Persil detergent, and Pepsodent toothpaste using essentially global campaigns. Procter & Gamble's Pampers diapers, Pantene shampoo, and Whisper sanitary napkins are also positioned with limited adaptation.

But as in the case of Toyota, Unilever, and P&G, to appeal to the less affluent core segments, multinational companies are forced to offer less advanced, localized products. The companies also use acquired local brand names to help establish local identity and supply the lower end of the market. Then there is the need for more specific adaptations because of country-specific factors. For example, American Motorola used a global campaign in Korea to position its cellular phone as leading in technology. But the appeal of "a world everybody dreamed of" made little sense in mountainous Korea where Motorola's older technology was inferior to that of Samsung's newer technology. In 1995 Samsung's domestic Anycall brand took over market leadership from Motorola's global Microtech series.[21]

Marketing Tactics

PRODUCT POLICIES The emphasis on these markets as followers of global mature markets makes standardized product policies natural. Nevertheless, there are some idiosyncratic factors that product policies need to pay attention to.

Product Design Because of limited storage space in the homes, many of the products for these markets need to be localized by offering smaller package sizes. Furthermore, as in Japan, buyers prefer slimmer designs, and robustness is not as important an attribute as elsewhere. Basically Asian people tend to be less dominating toward their possessions, taking a caring approach as opposed to the cruder "use and discard" attitude common in the West. This also means that style and finish are more important than elsewhere. Again the Japanese market and its products provide good illustrations. One reason the Japanese companies have a country-specific advantage in the Asian markets is simply that their home market is similar to that of their neighbors.

Product Line The Asian consumer is generally more eager to achieve **"a harmonious whole"** than Western individuals. In clothing, for example, Asian customers aim for "the complete look," wanting all parts of their outfit coordinated. While this desire has some vague cultural background in collectivist "groupthink" and traditional aesthetic norms from the Orient's imperial past, it also reflects an underlying uncertainty among consumers about Western-style dress codes, as in "Exactly what goes with what?" Retail stores and apparel makers have turned this problem into an opportunity by providing head-to-toe outfits, from hats and scarves to dresses, skirts, stockings, and shoes, creating within a single store and brand environment a complete line of inter-related products. A New York designer like Anna Sui develops whole ensembles specif-ically tailored to the Asian woman.[22]

The same desire for **full-line policies** has long inspired the Japanese manufac-turers in consumer electronics, cameras, and autos. In Western markets such a pol-icy goes well with brand loyalty and the notion that once you have bought a brand, you should be able to stay with it as your needs change or your income goes up. In Asia, the notion is broadened to the idea that the brand defines who you are. This is not so far-fetched even in the West, especially for some market segments such as teenagers. But in Asia, where individualism and egos are not so highly developed, one's material possessions clearly signify one's worth. Firms that make sure that their product line offers complementary products and upgrades will do better and can price accordingly. In Korea, the Philips company from Holland offers a product line from small electronic tools to home appliances and advanced state-of-the-art TVs and VCRs, to more sophisticated microchip products, all with distinctive European designs and well-recognized brand name. Despite the presence of domestic giants Samsung and LG, Philips can charge premium prices about 10 to 15 percent higher than the competition.[23]

New Products   At first glance, there are few compelling reasons for the introduction of new products specially designed for the Asian markets. The buyers are basically ea-ger to get access to the products they see available in mature foreign markets. These are not lead markets but followers. Their insistence on the "whole harmonious pic-ture" also makes an attempt to introduce a single new product less likely to succeed. Furthermore, because of the newness of the market, there is a lack of independent judgment on the part of buyers, and without the endorsement of success elsewhere, a new product will not be easily accepted.

But the Asian countries can serve as **leading markets** for the emerging markets dealt with in the next chapter. That is, the global marketer can use the lower-end prod-uct line extensions carried out for the Asian market to get a foothold in China, Russia, and other emerging markets. In addition, the experience with the upper end and the middle classes in the new growth Asian markets may well be transferable to emerging markets, especially China and India, where underlying cultural and ethnic segmenta-tion criteria suggest similarities. And, to be sure, in some products such as watches and cameras, Hong Kong, Singapore, and Seoul are joining Japan as lead markets for the West.

PRICING   In Asia as elsewhere, the global marketer faces a choice between a high **"skimming price"** strategy and a lower **"penetration price"** strategy. As we have seen, the natural positioning of a global brand entering the market is at the upper end of the price range, a skimming strategy. To penetrate the core of the market a lower price is necessary. To justify this price without losing the strength of the high-end brand name, companies develop the lower-end product alternatives discussed above. In addition, some companies acquire a local manufacturer with a local brand.

These are not particularly unique pricing policies for Asia, but changing price po-sition there without losing loyalty is not easy. The entry price will lock in the brand's positioning. In the West one can shift the price level for the brand downward, as in P&G's 1996 decision to set an "everyday low price" for several of its brands, or the Marlboro "Friday night massacre" in 1994 when Philip Morris lowered prices on its world-leading cigarette. But in Asia the repercussions would likely be more severe, be-cause it would ruin the brand loyals' sense of what the brand stands for and would hurt the "whole harmonious picture."

Pricing in the Asian region also needs to take into account the risks of gray trade. Many of these markets have a long-standing inclination to engage in pirating and cross-shipment of products, especially top global brands. Although this danger is lessened as the countries achieve economic growth, the lack of effective copyright protection and the Japan-induced predilection for technology diffusion rather than technology protection have made it difficult to erase these practices completely. The upshot is that multinationals need to make sure that prices in the Asian region are not entirely out of line with those in other parts of the world, especially if the brands and products sold are pretty much the globally standardized versions.

DISTRIBUTION Many observers agree that the most visible sign of economic growth in the Asian markets is the dynamism of the urban retail sector. Modern department stores dominate the vibrant shopping areas not only of Hong Kong and Singapore but also of Bangkok and Kuala Lumpur. Hypermarkets attract large crowds in Taipei, and just as in the "Mall of America" in Minnesota, shopping malls in Manila have become entertainment centers with ice rinks, cinemas, and children's playgrounds. Personal computers can now be bought through superstores as shopping has become a social activity and old mom-and-pop small stores rapidly disappear.

Outside of the big cities, however, several of these countries still suffer from a weakly developed infrastructure, including underdeveloped transportation networks and weak retail structures. Transportation gets especially difficult in countries like Malaysia, the Philippines, and Indonesia where large and disconnected archipelagoes make distribution costly, time-consuming, and risky, what with the uncertainties of a tropical climate and accompanying weather patterns. Even in the immediate surroundings of the big cities, crowding and overstretched city budgets make for less than optimal distribution conditions, especially in the south, where one can still see very picturesque and quaint rickshas in the street. But as in Hong Kong and Singapore, the capitals of the Asian countries are modernizing rapidly with high-rise buildings downtown, broad avenues, clean streets, and global symbols of achievement, as in Kuala Lumpur's aspiration to erect the highest building in the world.

PROMOTION By and large the promotional strategies employed by multinationals in Asian markets have been only minimally adapted from elsewhere. As with their product policies, the rationale is the pent-up demand for Western products. But even though positioning messages, unique selling points, brand names, and slogans may stay the same, companies have had to adapt to the local language, and in many cases used native endorsers, including local sports heroes and television stars.

In the Philippines where many natives speak English, global campaigns often use "Taglish," a mix of English and the local Filipino language (Tagalog). Global advertising campaigns by Unilever and Procter & Gamble use Tagalog and local movie and native personalities to reach housewives and their maids, many of whom may be illiterate.

Not all promotional tools can be directly extended. For example, sales calls to the home, a standard approach employed by Japanese auto companies in Japan, cannot be used in Taiwan where the intrusion is considered too great. At the same time the family is the decision-making unit for cars, creating a dilemma. The solution has been to attract the whole family to the showroom, with the help of inducements such as toys for the children as well as flowers for the wife, a generally pleasant atmosphere with soft music, clean windows and carpets, and a seating area for relaxed contemplation of the new cars.

Major Country Markets

SOUTH KOREA One of the original Asian NIEs or "four dragons" (together with Taiwan, Hong Kong, and Singpore), Korea has 45 million people and in 1995 a per capita income on par with many European countries. This makes Korea a worthwhile stand-alone market for many products (although market entry barriers can be high— see box, "Marketing in Korea").

G E T T I N G   T H E   *Picture*

Marketing in Korea

NOT ALL NIES are the same when it comes to marketing. While a country such as Taiwan has high trade tariffs and little regulation of how to do business, South Korea has lower tariffs; but when it comes to marketing regulations, it is considered by some observers to be one of the most restrictive countries in Asia. For example, most aspects of promotion are heavily regulated: how, what, when, and where. Price cuts should not exceed 60 days per year, any one individual period being limited to 15 days for a manufacturer, 7 days for a retailer. Any one business can have only four promotions per year. The price cuts have to be related to the product value according to a complicated formula. Commercial TV is available, but until 1995 the advertising industry was strictly local. Liberalization of TV time buying and the advent of cable and satellite TV promise to increase competition for local agencies, which lag behind their foreign counterparts.

Distribution, a key element of the marketing mix since promotional tools are limited, has its own share of regulations. For example, store limits have been at 300 square feet for foreigners, roughly the size of an average 7-Eleven store. A liberalization package, passed on July 1, 1993, as a first step in a campaign to gain World Trade Organization membership for Korea, has led to increased store construction in the big cities by Korean entrepreneurs eager to position themselves ahead of an expected foreign influx. Most foreign firms enter via joint ventures, needing a local partner to handle the regulatory obstacles if not the business itself. Price Club/Cosco, the American warehouse retailer, established links with Shinsegae, and its low prices are revolutionizing the market—30 percent below Korean competitors.

With liberalization and deregulation, one can expect the Korean consumer to follow the Japanese example, just as its manufacturers have, once the financial crisis is over.

Sources: Boddy, 1994; Taylor, 1994.

An additional argument in favor of Korean entry is a pent-up demand for Western goods as preferred over Korean products. For example, foreign fast-food restaurants, including KFC and Pizza Hut, increased sales by 63 percent in 1996 compared with the previous year. An astounding 80 percent of small home appliance sales in the same year went to foreign makers like Philips and French Moulinex in competition with Korean giants Daewoo, Samsung, and LG.

Western companies such as France's Carrefour in retailing, German Siemens in white goods, American Tower Records, and a number of Japanese companies are getting increasingly active in Korea as distribution regulations are gradually eased. Despite the economic difficulties in 1998, Korea seems to be on a strong growth path in the long run.

TAIWAN   The overriding question at the end of the 1990s for Taiwan's 18 million people is the relationship with mainland China, which wants to incorporate Taiwan under a "one China" rule. Depending on the outcome of that political struggle, the Taiwanese market may or may not be viable for foreign entry, especially with a relatively small population.

In the recent past Taiwan had relatively high tariff barriers behind which its small- and medium-sized companies have used a low-cost and highly efficient workforce to create a vigorous export industry. As affluence has increased, the low-wage emphasis has given way to a stress on skilled labor and high-technology products—personal computer maker Acer is a prominent success story in Taiwan—again supported by government. This development has allowed entry barriers for many consumer products and services to come down. Many of the large MNCs are active in Taiwan (P&G, Unilever, the Japanese automakers, etc.). Just as in Korea, loosening regulations in distribution have allowed foreign retailers to enter, and in Taipei one can now see Japanese-owned 7-Eleven convenience stores, volume discount stores such as Makro from the Netherlands, the Wellcome supermarket chain from Hong Kong, and other foreign chains.

Taiwan is considered to have particularly exacting customers, which makes the country useful as a test market for new products targeting Asia. For example, in 1990 P&G designated Taiwan the lead country for the introduction of its new Pantene Pro-V shampoo-and-conditioner product. After success in Taiwan, the product was successfully rolled out in other Asia-Pacific countries.

HONG KONG   The 6 million inhabitants of Hong Kong have long been the most affluent of the East Asian people, except for the Japanese, and its central hub location has made it a natural entry point for many companies venturing into Asia, especially mainland China. Because of its international flavor it is not a typical Asian market, but like New York in the United States, Hong Kong still serves as a lead market and trendsetter for the rest of Asia.

The 1997 changeover of Hong Kong from a British Crown Colony to a Special Administrative Region of China has so far not forced any changes in this role. Even though there has been a shift of some company headquarters from Hong Kong to Singapore, and some people left Hong Kong or shifted resources to other locations before 1997, the city is still strong and vibrant. The relatively small population makes it a less attractive stand-alone market, but high-end luxury goods makers such as Vuitton, Hermes, Armani, and Cartier still do good business in Hong Kong, especially since the financial turmoil at the end of the 1990s seems to be contained quite successfully by the city's financial rulers.

Pan-Regional Marketing

The Asian markets naturally lend themselves to **pan-regional** strategies because of their cultural similarity and parallel development paths, with Japan as the lodestar. However, the differences in economic development are still large enough to make implementation of standardized products and communications strategies often premature. What sells well in Seoul and Hong Kong might still be out of reach for people in Malaysia and Thailand. In addition, as we have seen, the religious factor plays a role, limiting the applicability of uniform advertising and other communications.

The trading blocs, however, offer a good starting point for pan-regional strategies. Although the APEC grouping is too loose and heterogeneous to be an effective market area, ASEAN, in particular after the expanded 1992 AFTA Trade Agreement, constitutes a natural regional market, with low internal tariffs and acceptance of foreign capital and goods. One would expect pan-AFTA strategies to be very viable in the future.

Because of the large distances in Asia (Tokyo is as far from Singapore as London is from New York), industrial activities—and thus markets—tend to concentrate around regional transportation hubs, where raw materials, plants, and skilled labor come together. These "growth triangles" (or "growth polygons," to be more correct) can be found around Hong Kong and southern China; around Singapore (called SIJORI for Singapore, Johore in Malaysia, and Riau in Indonesia); between Korea, Japan's Kyushu island, and China's North East coast (the "Yellow Sea" triangle); and in several other places. Actively supported by local and national government planners, these growth polygons have become the preferred development path of Asia and naturally serve as leading markets within the larger trading areas.

SUMMARY

New growth markets in the NIE countries differ from the typical growth markets in mature economies. What is important is further market development, helping to increase the total market size. As the markets evolve, the global marketer needs to shift from infrastructure and distribution issues to developing product lines and communication strategies that are sensitive to local culture, language, and religion. It is also important to continue adaptation of packaging and pricing to accommodate smaller budgets. To take advantage of opportunities in the new growth markets of the NIEs, the local marketer needs to gradually shift from a basic localization strategy to a more mature market strategy involving product development and targeted communica-

tions. This effort will benefit from working closely with local partners.

In terms of economics there are many basic similarities among these new growth markets, but their cultural, ethnic, and political heritages differ considerably. Most of them share a basic pent-up demand for products and brands from mature markets, which global communications have revealed to them. At the same time the distinctions in terms of religion and culture make for important differences in means of communication. The disparity between the Buddhist Asian and the Catholic Latin American countries dealt with here reflects the Kipling words that "East is East, and West is West—and never shall the twain meet." The global marketer tries to prove Kipling wrong.

KEY TERMS

authoritarian political regimes
   p. 256
brand names p. 258
colonial domination p. 256
core middle class p. 258
foreign technology p. 258
full-line policies p. 272
global identification p. 271
harmonious whole p. 271

labor costs p. 256
leading markets p. 272
neocolonial p. 259
newly industrialized economies
   (NIEs) p. 256
pan-regional Asian marketing
   p. 275
pan-regional Latin American
   marketing p. 267

penetration price p. 272
raw materials p. 256
religious influence p. 260
skimming price p. 272
trade blocs p. 257
urban versus rural population
   p. 261

DISCUSSION QUESTIONS

1. For a product category of your choice (select one with which you might want to work, for example), search in news media and on-line data sources to generate a market evaluation for an Asian or Latin American country (your choice again!), in the new global financial situation.

2. Discuss the major factors that affect market acceptance of a new consumer product in a Latin American country. In an Asian country. Any similarities?

3. Use the Web sites of PC manufacturers to do an analysis of the competitive situation facing Acer, the

Taiwanese PC maker, when expanding into other Asian countries. Is Acer's Taiwanese origin an advantage or disadvantage?

4. What are the reasons why entry into the Korean market is so expensive?

5. Why might a successful North American marketer not be the best one to head the company's marketing effort in Latin America? What about in Asia? What kind of person is needed, and how would he or she be trained?

NOTES

1. Papadopoulos and Heslop, 1993, discuss many of these remnants of the past in Chapter 2 of their book.

2. This section draws on Garten, 1997, and on research assistance by Kerri Olson, Ernesto Priego, and Huyn Jung.

3. These data come from the *Crossborder Monitor*, February 16, 1994.

4. See Kotabe and Arruda, 1998.

5. See Krauss, 1998.

6. From Krauss, 1998.

7. See Capell, 1998.

8. From Barks, 1994.

9. From "Tropicana Enters South American Juice Market," PR Newswire (PRN) on ProQuest Business Dataline, February 21, 1994.

10. See Sanchez, 1992.

11. See Schemo, 1998.

12. From *Crossborder Monitor*, November 24, 1993, p. 2.

13. From Krauss, 1998.

14. See, for example, *Crossborder Monitor*, April 21, 1993.

15. See Turner and Karle, 1992.

16. See Rosenberg, 1993.

17. From Barks, 1994.

18. This section draws on Yip, 1998, on Garten, 1997, and on Lasserre and Schuette, 1995. Thanks are extended due to Chong Lee and Stephen Gaull from whose research part of this section is also drawn.

19. See Landler, 1998.

20. From Steinhauer, 1997.

21. From Jun and Yip, 1998, p. 73.

22. From Steinhauer, 1997.

23. See Jun and Yip, 1998, p. 76.

SELECTED REFERENCES

American Chamber of Commerce in Mexico. "Setting Up a Distribution Operation: How Amway Adapted Its Direct Sales System to Mexico." *Business Mexico 2* (January–February 1992), pp. 22–23.

Barks, Joseph V. "Penetrating Latin America." *International Business*, February 1994, pp. 78–80.

Boddy, Clive. "The Challenge of Understanding the Dynamics of Consumers in Korea." In *Meeting the Challenges of Korea: The 1994 AMCHAM Marketing Seminar*. Seoul: American Chamber of Commerce in Korea, 1994, pp. 7–12.

Brooke, James. "More Open Latin Borders Mirror an Opening of Markets." *The New York Times*, July 4, 1995, p. 47.

Capell, Kerry. "What a 'Euro' Could Do for the Latins." *Business Week*, April 13, 1998, p. 46.

Dreifus, Shirley B., ed. *Business International's Global Management Desk Reference*. New York: McGraw-Hill, 1992.

Faiola, Anthony. "Harrods By the Si." *Washington Post*, June 8, 1998, pp. D1, D7.

Garten, Jeffrey E. *The Big Ten: The Big Emerging Markets and How They Will Change Our Lives*. New York: Basic Books, 1997.

Jun, Yongwook; and George S. Yip. "South Korea—New Prosperity and Agony." Chapter 3 in Yip, 1998.

Kotabe, Masaaki; and Maria Cecilia Coutinho de Arruda. "South America's Free Trade Gambit." *Marketing Management*, 7, no. 1 (1998), p. 39.

Krauss, Clifford. "Despite Uncertain World Markets, a Big U.S. Retailer Bulls into Latin America." *The New York Times*, September 6, 1998, sec. 3, pp. 1, 11.

Landler, Mark. "2 Asian Economies Seek to Keep Global Markets at Bay." *The New York Times*, September 12, 1998, pp. C1, C2.

Lasserre, Philippe; and Hellmut Schuette. *Strategies for Asia Pacific*. London: Macmillan, 1995.

Papadopoulos, Nicolas; and Louise A. Heslop, eds. *Product-Country Images: Impact and Role in International Marketing*. New York: International Business Press, 1993.

Rosenberg, Sharon Harvey. "Burger King Maps Move into Latin America." *Miami Daily Business Review*, December 13, 1993, p. A1.

Sanchez, Jacqueline. "Some Approaches Better Than Others When Targeting Hispanics." *Marketing News*, May 25, 1992, pp. 8, 11.

Schemo, Diana Jean. "In a Straitened Brazil, Talk of Pay in Goods." *The New York Times*, October 22, 1998, p. C4.

Smith, Geri. "Why Wait For NAFTA?" *Business Week*, December 5, 1994, pp. 52–54.

Steinhauer, Jennifer. "Design Houses Lament Asia's Faltering Economies." *The New York Times*, December 23, 1997, p. A22.

Taylor, John. "The Critical Elements of Sales and Distribution." In *Meeting the Challenges of Korea: The 1994 AMCHAM Marketing Seminar*. Seoul: American Chamber of Commerce in Korea, 1994, pp. 23–28.

Turner, Rik; and Delinda Karle. "Shops See Unity of Latin America." *Advertising Age*, April 27, 1992, pp. I-4, I-38.

Yip, George S. *Asian Advantage: Key Strategies for Winning in the Asia-Pacific Region*. Reading, MA: Addison-Wesley, 1998.

Ten

Local Marketing in Emerging Markets

"Sleeping giants wake up"

Your takeaways from this chapter:

1. To take advantage of the opportunities in emerging markets, the marketer needs to get back to the basics of what marketing is supposed to bring to people.

2. In emerging markets there are a variety of marketing environments that a local marketer might encounter, and every national market is different. However, emerging countries are usually characterized by political uncertainty, and direct foreign investment can be very risky.

3. A functioning marketing infrastructure, especially an effective distribution system, is crucial. When one is lacking, the local marketing effort has to help build it.

4. The political heritage of the newly democratized countries means that middlemen and consumers often have a very ambivalent feeling about free markets, simultaneously both expecting too much and not wanting to accept the uncertainties they bring. The local marketer from abroad becomes an educator about free markets.

5. The emerging markets are not all the same and do not even necessarily move in tandem. For example, in the late 1990s as Russia faltered, China and India still held their own.

IN THIS, the third of three chapters on different marketing environments, the challenges posed by emerging markets are discussed. *Emerging markets* include the newly democratized postcommunist nations, including Russia and Eastern Europe, China (still communist but with a more open economy), India, and other developing countries. Although some of the discussion will cover developing countries in general, the focus will be on "newly democratized countries" (NDCs). In these markets the heritage of a centralized planning economy means that marketing activities are suspect, marketers need to be legitimized, and there is a traditional supremacy of producers over consumers. Marketing becomes an act of rebellion against the old order and places people's mindsets under stress. The standard injunction of good marketing practice—satisfy the customers with good products and services—still applies. However, there is a lot of basic education about the workings of the free market system needed (among competing producers, middlemen, and customers) before marketing action can be effectively implemented. Marketing is a tool of the capitalist system, and the marketing manager becomes its foot soldier and standard-bearer.

Partners and Persistence Are Leaven for Chinese Bakery

For Ray Tsaih, an American businessman born in Taiwan, operating a $2.2 million baker on the outskirts of Shanghai, China, is full of surprises. In fact, *surprise* (his own word) is a positive way to think of the challenges Tsaih has faced since he first began negotiating arrangements for the business.

Knowing that personal relationships are the key to marketing success in China, Tsaih started by signing on a joint venture partner, a company owned by the city government. For its share of equity in the enterprise, the partner contributed a plot of land and no cash. However, not even a local partner could guarantee good service from the electric company. A month before the factory was scheduled to open, the utility said it was still building the power grid and would be late plugging in the factory. Once the plant was operating, a freezer and some electric dough mixers were destroyed in two power surges.

With new parts from Japan, the bakery got running again, but the Shanghai government informed Tsaih that his business, Shanghai Cheerful Food Company, needed a permit before it could use its delivery trucks. Unfortunately, the number of permits is limited. Tsaih had to pay another company to "borrow" its unneeded permits.

By then, seven months had passed, and many small bakeries had sprung up in Shanghai. Tsaih had to scrap his initial small-scale marketing plan to sell frozen dough to local retailers. He needed a less crowded niche and that meant operating on a larger scale. He negotiated an arrangement to sell buns to Kentucky Fried Chicken outlets in Shanghai. To win the contract, Tsaih had to agree to several changes, including replacement of his (new) ovens and quadrupling his delivery fleet.

Finally, Shanghai Cheerful Food Company was in business, selling 80,000 hamburger buns, cakes, and other products a day. Still, the "surprises" continue. Turnover is high, and government officials are apt to look for special favors.

Tsaih's challenges are hardly unique or limited to small businesses. General Motors, too, depended on local partners to establish a foothold in China, and GM had to give the Chinese extensive access to its advanced technology. With challenges like these, why are businesspeople flocking to China? The economy's growth and its sheer size offer a potential that is just too mouthwatering.

Sources: "In Shanghai, Executive Finds, Success Requires a Thick Crust," *Journal of Commerce*, May 17, 1995, p. 6A; Edwin Mc-Dowell, "Business Travel," *New York Times*, September 20, 1995, p. D6; Edward A. Gargan, "Asia Guide Calls Local Partners Key to Success," *New York Times*, November 14, 1995, p. D4; Keith Naughton and Pete Engardio, "How GM Got the Inside Track in China," *Business Week*, November 6, 1995, pp. 56–57.
http://www.kfc.com
http://www.gm.com

INTRODUCTION

Emerging markets as defined here comprise Russia and the newly democratized post-communist nations, China (whose communist government has eased central control over the economy), India, and other developing countries. Among typical **developing** countries are many of the poor nations in Africa (Nigeria, Zambia, Tanzania), Asia (Pakistan, India, the Philippines), and Central America (Nicaragua, Guatemala). They are defined primarily by *low per capita income levels* and are discussed here together with the newly democratized countries (NDCs) mainly because they share a severe *lack of marketing infrastructure.*

This chapter will first deal briefly with some general problems of marketing in developing countries and then concentrate on marketing in the newly democratized countries (NDCs), especially Russia and Eastern Europe. We then discuss the special cases of marketing in China and India.

LOCAL MARKETING IN DEVELOPING COUNTRIES

Marketing in the typical developing country faces a number of special problems engendered by the poor economic conditions, the low educational levels and high illiteracy rate, and the general apathy of the populace. Western marketing activities tend to assume a substantial and economically strong middle class, something usually lacking in developing countries. Local marketing in such countries becomes a special challenge.

The macroenvironment in the typical developing market is characterized by *uncertainty*, and thus "environmental scanning" becomes part of the job for the local marketer. Radical political change can develop quickly, and financial risk tends to be great. Convertibility problems, black markets, and exchange rate fluctuations tend to lessen the value of revenues. The possibility of abrupt changes in tariff rates and other trade-impeding measures creates a need for constant vigilance. It becomes necessary for the local marketer to work with international lending agencies such as the World Bank and the International Monetary Fund (IMF) and to use insurance agencies such as the Overseas Private Investment Corporation (OPIC).[1]

Because developing markets have typically not had access to many consumer products in the past, consumer needs tend to be basic and easy to identify. However, the same lack of products has also made for a poorly advanced **marketing infrastructure.** Distribution channels are few and show low productivity, and communication media are limited in reach and coverage. Marketing research, therefore, rather than focusing on the buyer, is more usefully focused on the feasibility of various marketing activities. The well-known problems Nestlé faced with its baby formula products in African countries underscore this point. Although mothers were pleased with the product, the lack of clean water with which to mix the formula made it dangerous for the infants.[2]

Market Segmentation

In these markets *income level* represents the basic segmentation criterion, and the market for upper-end status products from the West is often potentially lucrative because of an uneven income distribution. But the effective income measure is not necessarily defined in terms of salary or wages per household but rather in terms of *access to foreign or convertible currency.* For example, government bureaucrats may not be paid much in Uganda, but they may have better access to convertible currency than a local small entrepreneur. On the other hand, the secondary (or black) market for foreign currency may offer the small entrepreneur access to hard currencies but at a price premium.

Once income level has been identified, the standard demographics may be used to segment the market. But the relatively low level of customer sophistication makes segmentation unnecessary on any other basis than geography. "Where" the customers are is the second question after income has been taken care of. And usually the most promising market is the urban population of big cities.

It is important not to be too casual about the emergence of more sophisticated tastes and preferences on the part of the customers. In most markets even relatively poor buyers have some aspirations concerning emotional satisfaction, a desire to get more than just functional performance from a product. In relatively low-priced items, for example, it pays to adapt to local tastes (see box, "African Romance").

Furthermore, contrary to popular belief, high prices may not be such an impediment to market success in these countries as one would expect. For example, by focusing their spending on a few items, consumers are able to afford some luxuries. In such instances, a low price can be a drawback, since high prices are automatically associated with a luxury image.

It is useful to recognize that upscale positioning—targeting an upper, more status-oriented niche of the market—can play an important role in newly democratized countries. But in *developing* markets such luxury desires tend to be exactly that, only developing. Gradually, as the markets shift into growth, the consumers will develop their individual preferences.

Product Positioning

The developing market environment makes product policy a key issue. At the core of the market customer needs tend to be basic and domestic alternatives weak, the initial offering usually consists of standardized simpler selections from the existing product lines. Limited features also make it possible to sell through low-service outlets; the reliability that comes with standardization alleviates the need for extensive after-sales service. General Motors uses this strategy. The company has developed a special automobile for use in rural areas in Southeast Asian countries such as the Philippines, where dirt roads are common. The chassis can be constructed from steel bars that come in a kit and require only simple tools for assembly. The engine and transmission are then mounted on the frame together with two seats and a canopy. The vehicle is cheap, runs high off the ground, and is easy to repair. It's perfect for the market (although with rising incomes and better roads, countries such as Malaysia have increasingly turned to more sophisticated Japanese cars assembled in neighboring Indonesia or Thailand).[3]

Pricing

Price policies in developing markets are dominated by the balance between affordability and upper-end positioning. Thus, pricing often fluctuates between maintaining a *skimming price,* which will yield a high-end positioning and possibly quick payback, and a lower *penetration price,* which ensures affordability but also lowers margins and endangers

G E T T I N G   T H E
Picture

African Romance

"THE SUN WAS SETTING far, far away, casting a mysterious glow on Ebrie Lagoon. From her villa, Vanessa Toulay, a former hostess for Afrique Air, watched the sunset with sad, downcast eyes. . . . A gin and tonic in his hand, Christian Magou stood in front of a bay window in his bachelor pad in Deux-Plateaux. He gazed longingly at the stars twinkling in the sky, unable to get Vanessa's bewitching smile out of his mind. . . ."

Another Harlequin romance set in a far off and mysterious land? Well, almost. It is a scene from "Un Bonheur Inattendu," or "Unexpected Happiness," one of six titles in *Adoras*, a new series of African romance novels published in the Ivory Coast and marketed in several of the countries of formerly French West Africa. The difference with Harlequin is small, but telling: The writers of the novels are African, as are the characters and the settings of the stories.

To be sure, the arrival of the typical Harlequin novels into stores and kiosks in Abidjan, the capital of Ivory Coast, jump-started the romance market. The Canadian publisher of romance novels sold 193 million books in 1991 on six continents and in 20 languages. But the enterprising director of *Adoras*, Meliane Boguifo, spotted a weakness in the typical Harlequin offering: The Prince Charming was always blond and blue-eyed, and the

Beauty Queen would blush. Neither description rings any bells for West African readers.

The writers for *Adoras* make sure that the love triangles depicted fit what its readers can identify with. For example, Vanessa and Christian exchange glances not over candlelit French dinners but over plenty of couscous and tchepdiene, a Senegalese dish. The backdrop is Abidjan, West Africa's most modern city with skyscrapers and highways built around Ebrie Lagoon.

But even with the drive to be truly African, the *Adoras* series makes one exception: The writers' pseudonyms are exotic and akin to the Harlequin style. As Ms. Boguifo explains: "Marketing research showed that names like Christopher Hill and Carmen P. Lopez had more credibility than purely African names." It seems that some country-specific advantages still accrue to the more established purveyors of romance.

Sources: Norimitsu Onishi, "The Africans Fall Heavily for Amour and All That," *The New York Times*, December 11, 1998, p. A4; John A. Quelch, and Nathalie Ladler, *Harlequin Romances—Poland*, Harvard Business School, case no. 9-594-017, 1993.
http://www.harlequinromance.com/

the most desirable position. Striking a middle ground, many companies opt for a relatively high price that eliminates some buyers but offers the firm first-mover advantages in terms of image and brand loyalty.

The lack of purchasing power means that the marketer often must find ways of offering a simpler product paid for through innovative financing. A washing machine can be sold to a communal village, for example, with several families helping to foot the bill. Smaller and less expensive packages of shampoos sold by Unilever are popular in many of these markets. Soft drinks and packaged foods often come in smaller sizes as well, as do cigarettes (it is not unusual for someone to buy or sell one cigarette, for example) and beer cans. Store credit to customers is common, forcing manufacturers and distributors to offer liberal credit terms in turn.[4]

Distribution

Distribution is usually the most critical area facing the local marketer in the developing country. In fact, unless effective ways of distributing the product can be found or created, market entries might be thwarted and the economic growth of the developing countries will not take off. On the other hand, cheap labor and personal service are usually readily available in developing markets. Where established logistical systems are weak, one can often pursue alternative routes using cheap domestic labor.

For example, where telephone systems are unreliable, messengers on bicycle or Vespas are often able to carry on. Lack of fast road systems can be compensated for by slower river traffic and hand-carry services. Overcrowded mass transportation systems

With capitalism, outdoor advertising has come to Russia. A central Moscow subway entrance creates the kind of heavy pedestrian traffic pattern that entices outdoor advertisers to go all out. Wide World Photo.

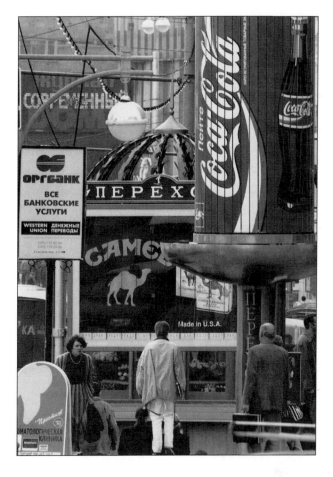

are avoided by taking taxis to faraway destinations. In developing markets personal service is a "convenience good" for many people and a necessity for the upper crust of society, including the expatriate manager in a multinational firm.[5]

Marketing organization and control is a difficult management problem in overseas business, regardless of the environment. In developing markets things get particularly difficult, since the local professional skills tend to be lower than elsewhere.

Promotion

Promotion in developing markets is initially limited because of the lack of broadcast media. However, as such media become available, the effectiveness of promotional messages can be considerable because of the lack of other advertising: There is less clutter. Of course, this is not true for outdoor advertising, which is an often effective means of establishing brand awareness and image. It is important to keep in mind the level of literacy; in developing countries the notion that "a picture is worth a thousand words" should be taken literally.

CLOSE-UP: MARKETING IN RUSSIA AND EASTERN EUROPE

The strong economic growth in Russia during the 1990s was fueled by huge investments of foreign capital. But the persistently low prices on world markets for its oil, a failure on the part of the government to collect taxes to pay workers, and apparent corruption were factors that left the country without sufficient reserves of hard currency when the Asian crisis spread and risk-averse investors began to pull back their capital. The resulting 1998 devaluation of the Russian ruble by 34 percent and the country's defaulting of its external debt sent shock waves through the world's financial markets. Nevertheless, Russia remains in the long term a potentially strong market. Its prospects are also supported in no small measure by the strength of the other Eastern European nations, which have weathered the storm well so far.

The defining characteristic of Russia and the Eastern European countries is their emergence from a communist-dominated political system, with state control of production and planned markets. From a marketing perspective, there are three major features that set these **newly democratized countries' (NDC)** markets apart from those of the typical developing country.

1. *Basic needs satisfied.* Although these countries may be poor in per capita income by Western standards, the most basic needs of the population have in the past been satisfied through the government planning system. The consumers in these countries have not been starving (except during some drought years), and they have been able to buy clothing, shoes, housing, soap and detergent, and sometimes even televisions and automobiles. Since most of these products have been produced domestically, they may not be up to world standards, but the people had their needs met. This is especially important considering that some of the NDCs have very large populations (Russia and China, for example).

2. *Education and social control.* These countries have usually offered their citizens a solid basic education, strong social control, and a secure life. At the same time, they have inculcated, intentionally or not, an aversion to the capitalist system and free markets. The people in these countries are not illiterate, they understand logic and numbers, and they have considerable pride in past accomplishments by their country. They have some hope for a better future and can be energized by the new prospects for individual growth.

3. *No free market.* What these people don't have, on the other hand, is a clear understanding of what a free market system entails, and they have trouble appreciating the magnitude of the changes of mindset required. Placing the consumer ahead of the producer is inconceivable to someone reared on the Marxist theory of labor value. Teaching Russian retail clerks that customers are important takes a lot of patience. For consumers, making a choice between three alternative coffee brands is a new and sometimes disconcerting experience.

These factors make the marketing manager's task different in NDC economies. But these markets also share characteristics with other developing markets, adding further complexity. The marketing infrastructure is typically weak. Channels of distribution are few and provide few service functions. Communications media are often still controlled by the state, and advertising is frowned upon. Customers do not have much purchasing power, and foreign currency is difficult to come by except for a few privileged groups.

International Support

NDC economies share many of the typical problems of developing countries: underdeveloped legal and financial institutions, uncertain political leadership, generally low purchasing power for foreign products, and so on. As in the case of developing countries generally, assistance from **international agencies** plays an important role in economic progress.

International institutions such as the United Nations, the World Bank, and the IMF play important roles in many NDC markets. The functions of these international agencies—lending capital, technical assistance, and economic planning help—have been mobilized to support the transformation of many of the Eastern European countries into free market economies. The European Bank for Reconstruction and Development (EBRD), created by the European Union, was developed expressly to support the Eastern European countries. These international agencies are important facilitators and guarantors of foreign investments for improving the basic infrastructure (road construction, electric power, and telephone service) and factories. From a marketing perspective they can be seen to help create a more favorable demand situation. The markets for products and services in the construction and telecommunications industries, for example, depend directly on loans from international agencies such as the World Bank.[6]

Political and Legal Factors

In NDC markets it is necessary to treat political and legal factors as part of the economic landscape. Since communism banned private property, a complete legal system required to create and sustain orderly free markets is often not in existence. The result is that some fundamental marketing activities have a loose legal basis.

For example, marketing usually involves the exchange of products and services for money (or other goods and services). When the transaction is completed, the ownership of a product passes from the seller to the buyer. Each has important rights— based on explicit and implicit contracts—concerning product use, fulfillment of payment obligations, delivery times, return rights, and so on. This legal machinery is often not yet in place in NDC economies, making binding transactions difficult to enforce.

Export controls are another political-legal problem area for the marketer. During the Cold War it was important to control trade with adversarial nations, especially in technology-intensive products. In the West, export controls became common for goods traded to any communist country, and even some nonaligned nations such as India.

The administration of the control regime was the task of COCOM, the multilateral coordinating committee for export controls. After the fall of the Berlin Wall, the importance of export controls diminished, and in the spring of 1994 COCOM was dissolved. This did not mean the end of export controls, however, since there continues to be a need to control the proliferation of various weapon systems to belligerent countries. A new international control regime is being developed by the United States and other countries, and the marketer of technology-intensive products should not expect an export license to be automatically granted for NDC markets.[7]

The **political risk** in these countries primarily involves the chance that the regime will revert to communist rule or some similar centralized economic system. Although most commentators seem to agree that such a reversal is unlikely, the local marketer needs to keep close watch on these developments.[8] It is important that contacts with knowledgeable insiders be established so that developments can be monitored. This is not only the job of the general manager of a local subsidiary or branch. Since marketing is the function in the firm that consistently relates to the external world, it is incumbent on the marketer to demand that salespeople and distribution channel members track and report new developments.

Politics also influences the **attitudes toward the free market system.** The situation in NDC markets varies to some extent between countries. Central Europe has a different political heritage than the former Soviet republics in Asia. Some of these differences have marketing implications. For example, in China communism came into power only in 1947, while the Russian October Revolution was in 1917. As a consequence, in China the precommunist days of more free market entrepreneurship, including the Kuomintang of Chiang Kai-shek, can be remembered by a part of the population. In addition, there are many Chinese living and working abroad, with sustained ties to relatives in the homeland. The overseas Chinese are successful in many free market economies, and they can help the transformation to a free market system in China. This is less true for the countries of the former Soviet republics, including Belarus and the Ukraine.[9]

Because of the length of the period of communism in Eastern Europe, there are fewer remnants of the capitalist past in these countries. Education in economics by its reliance on Marx has been effective in discrediting the free market system. In addition, the obvious successes of Soviet Russia—Sputnik, military weaponry, the achievements in high culture, the strong sports teams—have inspired justified pride in the communist system. The dismantling of the Berlin Wall was a result of economic failure; but for many of the people in these countries, economics is not everything. Marketing is not well understood by these people, and when they see it in action, they don't always like it. "Hard sell" promotions, for example, are likely to backfire, not only among older consumers.[10]

Market Segmentation

The local marketer in NDC economies may find it useful to define the market served in terms of **ethnic market segmentation** of subgroups among the population in each of the countries. For example, the ethnic Hungarian minority in Slovakia may have preferences similar to those in Hungary and Moravia. Despite the breakaway of many countries from the former Soviet Union, Russia is still home to many ethnic minorities who are represented also in other Eastern European countries.[11] In China, the province of Szechwan with its 350 million inhabitants and different food and cultural traditions from the rest of China may provide a sufficient market by itself.

As the transition toward a market economy progresses, the NDC consumers will undoubtedly move closer to their Western counterparts. A 1998 study showed that they already have—among the teenage segment. Another market segmentation study of Russian consumers found that more than half of all men and women could be categorized as independent, ambitious, or self-reliant, all traits uncommon in communist days (see Exhibit 10.1).[12] As the exhibit shows, the 150 million consumers in the Russian market can be grouped into five different segments. Apparently Western products are often preferred in some groups. A economic progress proceeds, one would expect actual sales to follow in the not too distant future.

Product Positioning

One question for the new local marketer in an NDC is whether to lead with the upper or lower end of the product line. Most indicators—income, usage conditions, needs—would suggest that these markets would be best served with a more basic product at the

EXHIBIT 10.1   A Psychographic Segmentation of the Russian Market

	Kuptsi (merchants)	Cossacks	Students	Business executives	"Russian souls"
Percent of all men	30%	10%	10%	25%	25%
Percent of all women	45%	10%	5%	10%	30%
Dominant traits	Reliant, nationalistic, practical, seeks value	Ambitious, independent, nationalistic, seeks status	Passive, scraping by, idealistic, practical	Ambitious, Western-oriented, busy, concerned with status	Passive, follows others, fears choices, hopeful
Likely preferences	*Car:* Volkswagen	BMW	2CV	Mercedes	Lada
	Cigarettes: Chesterfield	Dunhill	Marlboro	Winston	Marlboro
	Liquor: Stolichnaya	Rémy Martin	Local vodka in Smirnoff bottles	Johnnie Walker	Smirnoff

Sources: *The Russian Consumer*, 1992; Elliot, 1982.

Picture

American Standard in Russia

AMERICAN STANDARD, the New Jersey–based multinational, is the world's largest manufacturer of bathroom furniture, with strong market presence in many countries. Its early entry into Russia was not so successful, however.

An initial market survey of demand in Russia in early 1991 suggested that the main market, new construction, would be slow and closed to outside vendors for the time being. The company decided to target reconstruction, the renovation and upgrading of old apartments in Moscow and St. Petersburg for office use by Western firms.

American Standard decided that the Russian private entrepreneurs who took on the renovations would mainly be interested in the low-end equipment, which would lower building costs. Accordingly, the company brought in its low-end product line, priced competitively. The products did not move. The entrepreneurs wanted the top of the line. They went to European competitors for their upscale products. Price was no object. The reason? The builders figured that the Western companies would be willing to pay top dollar for their offices. And they were right. In 1994 central Moscow was perhaps the world's most expensive business district, where prices of $15,000 to $20,000 per month for a small office were not unheard of.

Sources: Lloyd, 1994; Personal interview with Eric Crabtree, vice president and director, CMT Moscow, Construction Marketing and Trading, Inc., Washington, D.C., October 20, 1994. *http://www.americanstandard.com*

low end of the price scale. However, being the first company to offer a more advanced product can yield first-mover advantages. Furthermore, the lower end typically pits the entrant squarely against existing domestic brands, regardless of how uncompetitive they may be. In addition, the few upscale customers may prefer the most advanced high-end product (see box, "American Standard in Russia").

Marketing Tactics

PRODUCT POLICIES   In NDC markets customers tend to feel ambivalent about their domestic products. On the one hand, they know that new offerings from outside are often superior. Still, they do not necessarily want to give up the old brands. The reasons are not only sentimental remembrances of things past or country-of-origin affections. They also realize that if the products are not bought, the domestic factories can't stay open and they will lose their jobs. And it is not easy to evaluate the many competing brands when previously only one or two choices have been available.[13]

PRICING   Entering global brands will typically be able to command a price premium over existing local brands. But for the typical Western firm the primary task is not to skim a small existing market but to develop the market generically with new and superior products from leading markets. This means that a better strategy will be to price at a lower penetration level, keeping it sufficiently affordable to induce trial and continued usage.

For most firms the long-term prospects of these markets matter much more than short-term payoffs, leading firms to establish a penetration price level. With the ruble's devaluation in 1998, however, many firms have found it necessary to take a short-term view, raising prices on their exports to Russia to offset the fact that ruble earnings have lost more than half of their value in U.S. dollars. Fortunately, many of the Eastern European countries seem to weather the storm better, leading firms to stay in for the longer run rather than withdraw from these markets completely.

DISTRIBUTION   A big problem that the new local marketer faces in typical NDCs is a wasteful and dysfunctional distribution system. Because the economies were closed off to outside competition, ineffective systems for delivery of products and services

G   E   T   T   I   N   G   T   H   E

Picture

P&G Goes to Russia

WHEN RUSSIA OPENED up its borders to Western products, the giant multinationals in consumer packaged goods quickly started to reconnoiter the potentially huge market. But the initial delegations of top marketing executives soon came to realize the difficulty of selling through the existing distribution channels. Weak transportation systems, inferior storage facilities, and out-of-date warehousing operations created costly inefficiencies in the delivery of the products to the stores. And in the stores the limited shelf space, the dull gray atmospheres, and the sullen clerks made for a dreary shopping experience, even though the stores had been recently privatized.

Accordingly, the first tasks for a company such as P&G in Russia involved creating a much more efficient and modern distribution network. Investing in existing facilities and new warehouses, helping to improve transportation fleets and parking space, and training store employees were some of the measures taken. P&G even invested in improving port facilities in St Petersburg and sent its products by ship rather than trucking through country border stops.

Sources: *New York Times*, July 23, 1994, pp. 1, 43; Lloyd, 1994. *http://www.pg.com*

have been left in operation. Marxist ideals hold that only production has value, and unfortunately distribution was seen as unworthy of serious attention. Furthermore, the priority was on industrial products over consumer goods, which means that the entire marketing infrastructure (the logistics of distribution, the media of communications, and the means of transferring payments) in consumer products is particularly weak.

Weak Infrastructure   It is mostly the deficiencies of the marketing infrastructure that make it difficult for the local marketer to penetrate NDC markets. The functions provided by middlemen are weak or nonexistent, and the local marketer can't expect to rely very much on independent middlemen. This creates a need for localization by augmenting the product sold. For example, since electricity is often in short supply and rationed with frequent blackouts, electric appliances might need to be redesigned with a buffer battery that kicks in when cutoffs occur. Similarly, digital alarm clocks, radios with push-button station memory, coffeemakers with preset timers, and rice cookers with warming features are all products that might need to be redesigned. In some cases complete battery function is preferable; battery radios without a recharger are still best-sellers in many NDC markets.[14]

It is important to find out what functions the existing channel members can and can't perform, and to what degree it is necessary to create entirely new channels for products, services, and communications. Procter and Gamble's experience in Russia is instructive (see box, "P&G Goes to Russia").

To accomplish the job, the local marketer sometimes has to think about reconfiguring the firm's *value chain*. For example, in addition to localizing the product, services that at home are provided by independent operators may need to be added to the value chain. To service vacuum cleaners and other household appliances, Western firms at home often depend on small entrepreneurs who run their own independent operations and service several makes. In NDC markets, the required know-how may not yet be diffused enough to rely on independents. Instead, the Western entrant has to help create such a service network and train the staff.[15]

Marketing Education   In NDCs the marketing manager must be prepared to do a lot of on-the-job training and **educating of middlemen** and others in basic marketing principles and practices, and in how to distribute, sell, and service the product effectively. There is also a secondary audience consisting of actual and potential customers, as well as domestic competitors. Finally, many government bureaucrats need to be informed about free markets, although this part of the educational process is usually handled during the initial negotiations before starting to do business in the country.

Broadly speaking, the aim of the education is to demonstrate the role of marketing in the free market system. It is necessary to elaborate on principles taken for granted and self-evident to the Westerner. Thus, before the marketer can serve as a teacher, he or she may have to study some of the basics of the system at home.

The marketer first of all has to explain the basic functioning of a product or service to the middlemen involved in the distribution chain. Many products have no counterpart in the NDC markets, or their advanced character requires explanation and instruction in use and service. Furthermore, how to listen to customer questions, how to offer product information, and how to give after-sales support are all "naturals" for the Western marketer that he or she must now give some thought to. The Japanese incursion into American and Western markets has served to educate even Western middlemen about these basic prerequisites of effective marketing.

The marketer in NDC economies needs to be able to explain how the roles in the distribution chain have changed with the emergence of free markets. Now the idea is to perform efficiently—to help move the products through the chain with speed, respond quickly to demand shifts, and be alert to competitors' moves. Gone are the days when the suppliers and the customers were captive: Now only the best can survive. The marketer needs to explain—"teach"—that in the free market system costs need to be controlled and revenues have to cover expenses. It is "Welcome, brave new world" for the middlemen.

Service Training   The new teaching will be heresy to many and will seem to go against many things in their past experience. The middlemen will have ingrained ideas about what is appropriate and may find it difficult to accept the new ways. It becomes important that the "teacher" explain why these changes are necessary. Of course, the market and competitors are the new "teachers," but the manager can't wait for mistakes to show up before taking action. Luckily, people are generally willing to try the changes, having seen how badly the previous system performed. For example, the successful Western cosmetics firms' marketers in Eastern Europe train the in-store sales personnel, teaching them how to care for a customer and, in the process, teaching them how to take care of themselves.[16]

Practically speaking, the local marketer needs to:

1. Develop training programs for store personnel, focusing on how to treat customers.

2. Prepare manuals and pamphlets describing products and services and helping middlemen devise appropriate facilities and procedures for the transportation, storage, and shelving of the product.

3. Help the middlemen develop a tracking and cost accounting system to make it possible to trace shipments and locate where in the chain there may be a problem such as overstocking.

4. Make sure that product localization in terms of design and packaging also takes into account the needs of the middlemen. This often involves educating the home office about special requirements, such as different sizes and packaging of existing products.

5. Distribute instructional videotapes and other educational material to various members of the distribution channel, explaining why customers are so important in the free market system and why marketing is as important as manufacturing.

PROMOTION   Marketing communications often have to be revised in NDC markets. The common advertising media—television, magazines, newspapers—may not be available or may have only limited reach. Because of the immaturity of the market, many products are new and any communication needs to stress simple functional explanations. People who have not seen a 10-speed bike need some instructions and explanation of its advantages over the domestic clunker that has served so well for 30 years—and justification for the high price. The solid education of the people, however, will make the requisite advertising copy quite easy to develop. The average Russian is quite capable of processing information.

Lack of **credibility of advertising** claims is a problem. In previously totalitarian countries people maintain a healthy disrespect for public announcements and mass communication. This naturally reduces the power of advertising, at least in the short run until its benefits in terms of new products and services materialize. By contrast, word of mouth is often considered more reliable and effective than mass media. This can have its own negative consequences. In Poland, for example, a rumor that P&G's Head and Shoulders shampoo made your hair fall out turned out to be particularly difficult to put down. In some of these markets, domestic companies sometimes resort to such "dirty" campaign tricks as they see their protected advantage dissipate.[17]

When the political, economic, and social fabric is undergoing the kind of revolution seen in newly democratized countries, old values are crumbling along with the political system. There is a need for the country and its people to learn what a free market system is about. To change the old order, communications have to be open and the old implicit understandings reexamined. The American insistence on transparency of transactions helps tear down the labyrinthine networks and closed systems that in many NDCs have made corruption and exploitation of the common man and woman prevalent. The American way with marketing is an agent for democracy.

Still, the hard-hitting approaches used in some American advertising could lead to a backlash when applied in an NDC market. On the one hand, cynicism and suspicion can be a problem. On the other hand, people are not used to the "puffery" associated with much of American promotion and may take assertions of "best" and "most" at face value. This potential downside risk of the free market experience will taper off in intensity as the people gradually become more insensitive to preposterous assertions and reap the benefits of new ideas and new products. In the meantime, the local marketer will do well to temper some of the more obvious excesses of American advertising.[18]

Russia at the Crossroads

The situation in Russia at the end of the 1990s deserves special attention.

Although hit by the Russian problems at the end of the 1990s, several of the Eastern European countries withstood the global financial crisis quite well. While Russian economic growth was negative in 1998 at about −4 percent, Poland's continued upward with a robust 5 percent, Hungary at 4 percent, and the Czech Republic down but still at 1 percent. The reason? Since the fall of the Berlin Wall, the Eastern European countries have been diversifying their economies away from their giant Russian neighbor (Russia has approximately 150 million people) to the east. And with the help of Western capital, the move is succeeding.

A case in point is Poland. In 1988 the former Soviet Union took a good 25 percent of Poland's trade, or $6.3 billion. By 1996 the amount was down to $4.2 billion, or a 6.8 percent share, while Poland's total foreign trade had increased almost 2.5 times. About 70 percent of the production was intended for export to Western Europe. Polish consumer markets were also picking up, with wages rising at an annual rate of about 5 percent, keeping pace with growth in GDP.[19]

Meanwhile Russia is mired in an economic downturn that is threatening to turn the political sentiments of the people against open and free markets. Ironically enough, Russia's natural resources in gold, oil, and gas, which placed the country in an advantageous position compared with Poland, have become its undoing. The resources attracted foreign capital investment, but without the legal and economic infrastructure in place, control over the use of capital became difficult. Although the details are unclear, it seems the capital had to be channeled via old political networks, and some of it ended up in unproductive corruption and mafioso hands. With President Boris Yeltsin in weak health, Russian political leadership was not very strong, and local governments exercised considerable freedom. When the Asian financial markets tumbled, and foreign investors became more risk-averse and short-term oriented, Russia simply did not have enough reserves to counter the run on its ruble. The 1998 devaluation of 34 percent and the ensuing default on foreign debt hurt large investors all over the world.

That, briefly, seems to be the bad news. The good news is that although many businesses are reconsidering their commitment to the Russian market, for most the overriding consensus seems to be that this is a temporary crisis and the long-term potential of the Russian market is still strong. However, their exports to Russia have come with sharply increased ruble prices to counter the devaluation. Not suprisingly, many Western companies—from American Nabisco with its supermarket snack foods like Ritz crackers and Oreo cookies to Italy's Fiat with cars assembled in Russia—are recording sharp downturns in sales as Russian consumers can no longer afford the prices with their devalued rubles.

The Russian markets have in fact turned back to a barter-style economy, with products exchanged to avoid taxes and, more importantly, to make up for lack of hard cash and counter the sharp loss in the ruble's value. For a global marketer, this shift is understandable: People act to preserve what little they have, and when their money is no good, global marketers are also forced into countertrade options—but it is nevertheless a very threatening problem. In particular, the global marketing approach offered in this book suggests that the global marketer allocate resources carefully and enter those markets where opportunity for rewards (either immediate in terms of revenues or long term as a first mover in a takeoff market) outweighs the costs and the risks involved. This economic logic also suggests that "exit" is always an option. One would hope that instead the Western firms find it possible to see Russia through these bad times, staying in the market even if the rewards in rubles have lost most of their value.

In Russia the political risks are high as Yeltsin's health falters. One hopes that the Russian crisis is temporary and that the authoritarian regimes of the past will not make a comeback. But one also has to acknowledge that with the misery visited upon the Russian consumers, it is understandable if the political sentiment is shifting back to the "good" old days of communism and closed markets.[20]

CLOSE-UP: MARKETING IN CHINA[21]

China and India are two large and important emerging markets deserving further treatment. Both countries can be viewed as "developing," and both have features similar to NDCs. But China is not (yet) a democracy, and India is not a *new* democracy. They present some very special problems for the local marketer. These problems have mostly to do with the political legacy of the countries, and much of the discussion about the NDCs above is relevant for China and India. In what follows, only the additional peculiarities of the marketing environment in the two countries will be highlighted. Let's start with China.

China's Market Potential

China has a population of 1.2 billion, the largest in the world. The number of people and the growing economy make China a large importer of machinery, production equipment, technology, telecommunication equipment, aircraft, and raw materials for industrial production. The Chinese government has expanded its importation of agriculture-applied technology, fertilizers, industrial raw materials, and technologies and

G E T T I N G   T H E   *Picture*

"Guess Who Is Knocking?"

IN APRIL 1998, door-to-door selling was banned in China, putting an end to the successful market penetration of Amway, direct marketer of a wide variety of inexpensive household products, and cosmetics sellers Avon and Mary Kay. The Chinese government claimed that direct sales techniques worked like a religion, making people passionate about new ideas—something the government abhors.

For the American companies, one of their largest international markets was suddenly "off limits." Amway alone had 80,000 distributors in China who sold $178 million worth of products in 1997, accounting for 21 percent of the company's total sales. All three companies stopped their door-to-door selling activities—including recruiting new salespeople—by end of April. Throughout the summer, the companies negotiated with the Chinese government to work out new deals that would allow them to stay in China. Their basic argument was that the law was aimed against fly-by-night direct selling companies, which had a shady past in China, and not against well-established companies selling reliable products. By early June, Avon had negotiated a deal with the government in which the company would operate as a wholesaler to Chinese retail stores, with plans to convert its 75 supply branches into actual retail outlets.

If you can't fight them, join them.

Sources: Ligos, 1998; "Penetrating the Great Wall," 1998.
http://www.amway.com
http://avon.avon.com
http://www.marykay.com

---

equipment for energy, transportation, telecommunication, and industrial renovation programs. Importation of consumer products is expected to grow because of recent tariff reductions, from 40 percent in 1988 to about 20 percent in 1998, still high by international standards. China is not a member of the World Trade Organization, but the 1998 granting of continued "Most Favored Nations" (MFN) status with the United States promises to help the Chinese economy to achieve further export-driven growth. In 1998 the annual bilateral trade deficit with the United States alone stood close to $60 billion.[22]

With its underlying strength in natural resources and able and disciplined workers, the Chinese economy has so far been relatively untouched by the Asian crisis. Strong central leadership by its communist rulers combined with a "hands-off" policy toward Hong Kong, its new Special Administrative Region, has made devaluation of the won unnecessary. But the country's rulers can be unpredictable (see box "Guess Who Is Knocking?").

Despite the size and potential of the Chinese market, its fast-growing purchasing power is still low. The per capita income in 1992 was equivalent to US$224; in 1993, $380; and in 1995, $620, steadily growing at a speed of 10 percent annually. As economic progress continues, the huge market potential for Western products will presumably come closer to realization. One sign of this is the fact that the (interminable) Kodak–Fuji battle for supremacy of the world's photographic film market continues apace in China. In 1998 Kodak unveiled plans for the investment of US$ 1 billion in two existing Chinese plants for film production, in order "to slow the advance of Fuji" in the world's largest market.[23]

Entry Barriers

The Chinese government is by most measures the greatest entry barrier into China. It controls importation through various measures: import license controls, protective tariffs, foreign exchange control, and government-controlled foreign trading companies.

IMPORT LICENSE CONTROLS   The Ministry of Foreign Trade and Economic Cooperation (MOFTEC) is the main regulatory organization governing the current import-licensing system. China uses a centralized system to restrict imports of consumer and luxury goods in order to conserve foreign exchange for other items. Among the 10,000 import product categories, 53 are on the import license control list, covering various consumer products, raw materials, and production equipment. In 1992, 16 categories were removed from the list in an effort to meet World Trade Organization (WTO) requirements, and the Chinese government promised to eliminate two-thirds of the listed categories in the next two years.[24]

PROTECTIVE TARIFFS   From 1986 to 1998, China adjusted tariff rates several times and continues to do so. However, its 1998 rate of 20 percent is still much higher than both the average 5 percent for the developed countries and the average 13 percent for the developing countries. The government has promised to continue tariff reduction until it meets the average level of the developing countries. At the Asia-Pacific Economic Cooperation Forum in November 1995, Chinese President Jiang Zemin pledged to cut import tariffs by 30 percent.[25]

FOREIGN EXCHANGE CONTROL   In January 1994, China implemented a new exchange rate system. Its official exchange rate was brought into line with the more market-driven rate that applied on the foreign exchange swap market. After the unification the rate stayed stable at around 8.4 to 8.5 yuan to the U.S. dollar, compared with a trading rate at 8.7 to the dollar just before the change.[26]

Foreign exchange is controlled by the State Administration of Foreign Exchange Control, which supervises the allocation of the foreign exchange quota and the operation of the Foreign Exchange Swap Center. The swap center makes it possible for enterprises to have access to foreign exchange. With a foreign exchange quota, one can obtain foreign exchange at the official exchange rate. The quota is allocated based on criteria such as the importance of the project and the enterprise's record of foreign exchange generation.

The Foreign Exchange Swap Center is an institution through which entities with excess quota can trade off their foreign exchange with those who need it. Contrary to the stable official exchange rate, the swap rate varies from day to day.

FOREIGN TRADING COMPANIES   With the ongoing reform of China's foreign trade system, the government-controlled trading companies have lost their monopoly to the mushrooming local trading companies and the industrial firms. The foreign-invested companies are automatically granted foreign trade rights.

In general, China's foreign trade system is undergoing a big reform, and most of the effort is geared toward the goal of gaining WTO status. To become a member of the WTO, China needs to:

Unify its foreign trade policies, laws, and regulations.

Clarify its foreign trade policies, laws, and regulations.

Reduce tariff and nontariff barriers.

Promise a price reform timetable.

Accept selective protection provisions prior to price system reforms.

All the reforms or readjustments have to be made in order for China to become a WTO member.

Special Economic Zones

Five limited areas called **Special Economic Zones** (SEZs) have been established by the Chinese government to attract foreign investment in production for export. They are Shenzhen, Zhuhai, Shantou (all in the Guangdong province in the South), Xiamen (in Fujian province), and Hainan (in Hainan province). Besides these five, the Pudong New Area in Shanghai is entitled to similar preferential policies as an SEZ. To attract investment, the corporate tax rate within SEZs is only 15 percent compared with a

G E T T I N G   T H E   *Picture*

Pirated Rock Music

WALKING AROUND the streets of Beijing or Shanghai—as well as New York and Paris—it is easy to spot the vendors who sell cheap copies of many branded products from watches to compact disks. Most of these pirated copies come from Southeast Asia, where small entrepreneurs have long found it lucrative and relatively risk free to produce knockoffs of well-known products. Compact disk copies of famous rock stars are a common target since the artists are very popular in China. Western record producers have started to engage private investigators to track down factories and vendors guilty of these copyright violations. In one case, Walt Disney Company won a victory in Beijing Intermediate Court with a $77,000 judgment against Chinese companies that were producing children's books based on Disney's animated films.

Even so, Chinese government officials have been reluctant to engage in active prosecution. The reason? The legal system is not yet ready to handle these cases, and going to court is complicated. Furthermore, many of these entrepreneurs have good contacts with the ruling party; and even though the China market is opening up, the communists are still in power.

Sources: Ecenbarger, 1994; *New York Times*, August 18, 1994, and May 17, 1995.
http://www.disney.com

national rate of 33 percent. Also, enterprises within the zones enjoy some tariff exemptions.[27]

The SEZs serve to bring in foreign manufacturing jobs, with Chinese workers staffing the assembly lines. The products are intended for reexport, helping the government to generate hard foreign currency. But it has also meant increased penetration by foreign products in China. Although the products imported into those areas are not allowed outside the zones' borders, many are smuggled into China, copied, and sold. The difficulty of controlling this black or gray trade and widespread **copyright infringement** practices mean that the authorized distributors find themselves competing with local **counterfeits and pirated copies.** Pirated compact disks are a case in point (see box, "Pirated Rock Music").

Hong Kong's Role

The 1997 Hong Kong handover from British to Chinese rule has had surprisingly little impact on economic policy so far, since China has exercised restraint in dealing with the former British colony. Many European and American companies enter China from Hong Kong, where many sophisticated **Hong Kong trading companies** are familiar with both Western business practices and Chinese language and culture. Trade fairs, exhibitions, and technical seminars are commonly used to promote awareness among trading middlemen and mainland customers.

To identify potential customers, the in-charge industrial ministries in China need to be approached, which is difficult to arrange without a strong and well-connected Hong Kong intermediary. Although the ministries can no longer decide which products to buy, they are still influential over the factories and purchasing decisions. In addition, much information—such as plant size and capacity, purchasing potential, and financial records—can be found in the ministries.

Most foreign companies find themselves in a difficult position. They have to deal not only with their Hong Kong agent and the foreign trading companies in China but also with their Chinese end users' requests for service. In general, the end users select the foreign supplier, and the foreign trading companies sign the contract as agents for the factories.[28]

Even with the use of the Hong Kong traders, the local marketer from abroad needs to consider employing a Chinese national to balance the decision-making power. With

Matsushita's man in Beijing, Yoshiya Kuse (center), runs a joint venture TV-tube plant—including a kindergarten for the children of the workers. Alan Levenson.

a Chinese employee, it is possible to communicate directly with the end users and get feedback from the market without relying entirely on the intermediate traders. The Hong Kong trading company can then concentrate on handling the administrative and organizational arrangements with the Chinese trading company, while the marketing manager gathers market information and stays close to the customer.

A typical mode of entry for foreign companies is a direct **joint venture with Chinese partners,** also possibly established with help from Hong Kong. The Chinese partner usually does some assembly to reduce the effect of tariffs and other barriers. In autos, for example, an import tariff of 180 to 200 percent for vehicles coupled with restrictive government policies forces the joint venture route and shared assembly.[29]

Market Segmentation

A natural first segmentation criterion in China is geographic region. Philips, for example, the Dutch electronics maker, subdivides the country into four regions: eastern China (with Shanghai as the center), northern China (with Beijing at the center), southern China (with Guangzhou as the center), and western China (with Chengdu as the center). These are also natural market groupings in that languages and dialects, food and drink preferences, and even ethnic roots vary across the regions.[30]

A second segmentation is the urban/rural split in the typical emerging market pattern. Mainly because of the weak infrastructure in these emerging countries, the urban population offers a much more accessible marketplace than the rural areas. Along the same lines is the income differential. If there is an emerging middle class, it will come in the cities first. The rise in per capita income is most rapid in Shanghai, Beijing, and

Guangzhou: Here there are segments with enough funds to provide a market for some of the Western luxury products.

The young people segment, the teenagers and the college-age students of both sexes, represents the Chinese version of the global youth segment. Less affluent than many of their counterparts elsewhere, they do aspire to many of the same world-class branded products—and might resort to counterfeiting to satisfy their needs.

Product Positioning

With indirect exposure to Western communications and media via Hong Kong and from overseas Chinese, the China market is open for global brands and standardized campaigns. But for effective penetration, some localization is usually necessary. In particular, there is a need to revisit the company brand names and how they will translate into the Chinese kanji characters. Coca-Cola had to change its original transliteration from one meaning "dry mouth full of wax" to one signifying "happiness in the mouth" when read and spoken. Sprite beat 7-Up because its Chinese name came out as "Snow Jade," while 7-Up had to fight against a transliteration that in Shanghai suggested "death from drinking." It is small wonder if a foreigner hears some familiar brand names with slightly out-of-the-ordinary sounds added to get the right touch for the Chinese consumer.31

Marketing Tactics

PRODUCT POLICIES   The quality gap between foreign and local products is still large, although the technology transfer in the joint ventures is helping to reduce the difference. As is typical in NDCs and other developing markets, Chinese customers cite two reasons for buying a foreign product: (1) no availability of similar products on the domestic market and (2) the superior quality of the foreign product. Because of high tariffs, a foreign product can seldom compete with a Chinese product on a price basis.

For most Chinese acquiring foreign-made products is a novel experience. With very few choices for four decades, the Chinese are eager to see what is in the stores. Their limited experience leads them, predictably, to rely on famous brand names. In a wide range of goods surveyed, well-known brands accounted for as much as one-half of intentions to choose.[32] Like the Japanese, the Chinese consumers tend also to be brand loyal, making for a definite first-mover advantage among competing foreign firms.

Reflecting the rise of a more affluent consumer, a new consensus has developed about the "four big things" (*shi da zen*), the four products everyone aspires to. In the 1970s, they were a bicycle, a black-and-white television set, a refrigerator, and a washing machine. In the 1990s they have become a video camera, a CD hi-fi system, a personal computer, and an air conditioner.[33]

PRICING   The relatively low per capita income makes China and the Chinese price-sensitive customers.[34] But low income is only half the story.

Although things are gradually changing, most Chinese customers are price-oriented out of habit. They are not willing to pay more for alleged superior quality because from experiences in the past they assume a uniformly low quality level for all products. This is not an entirely mistaken assumption either today. Many products are still in short supply, and some domestic companies are still in the "quantity, not quality" frame of mind nurtured during the central planning era.

Because of the high tariff rates, prices are still high for products with imported content. For example, a Chinese-assembled Volkswagen Santana car costing around US$14,000 on world markets sold in China for 180,000 yuan ($20,000).[35] For pure imports, the difference is even greater. Strikingly, still one of every two cars running on China's tough roads is imported.

Rude Service in China

PERSONAL SERVICE in China is still below par. The past top-down, in-your-face attitude of service providers toward customers is still alive and well. It has gone far enough that the Chinese government, true to its style, recently banned 50 common phrases that the rude clerks are not to use when dealing with customers. The list is instructive as a reminder of the changes a market orientation imposes on a noncapitalist society. Selected items are:

1. If you don't like it, go somewhere else.
2. Ask someone else.
3. Take a taxi if you don't like the bus.
4. I don't care whom you complain to.
5. If you're not buying, what are you looking at?
6. Buy it if you can afford it; otherwise, get out of here.
7. Are you buying or not? Have you made up your mind?
8. Don't you see I'm busy? What's the hurry?
9. I just told you. Why are you asking again?
10. Why didn't you choose well when you bought it?
11. Go ask the person who sold it to you.
12. If you don't like it, talk to the manager.
13. The price is posted. Can't you see it yourself?
14. No exchanges; that's the rule.
15. If you're not buying, don't ask.
16. It's not my fault.
17. I'm not in charge. Don't ask so many questions.
18. Didn't I tell you? How come you don't get it?
19. If you want it, speak up; if you don't, get out of the way. Next!
20. Why don't you have the money ready?
21. What can I do? I didn't break it.

Past habits die slowly.

Sources: Faison, 1995, Engardio, 1996.
http://www.microsoft.com

DISTRIBUTION   The weak infrastructure in the huge China country makes "national rollouts" a logistical impossibility. Even the regional segments will constitute too large an area for effective penetration. Roads are unpaved, flooding is common, and railroads reliable but slow. Air transportation is a necessary option for many firms. And with the growth of mobile telephone communications, the lack of communication lines is partly overcome. It is small wonder that Motorola, Ericsson, and Nokia all consider China an immense future market.

Many of the distribution channels are controlled by the government, again creating some obstacles to a focused distribution effort and affecting service levels negatively (see box "Rude Service in China"). For example, department stores are typically state-owned, leaving little possibility for firms to offer individual achievement incentives. Multinationals therefore hire promotional staff to assist in store stocking, selling, and service, an expense that a company such as Philips finds worthwhile and necessary to generate acceptable sales levels of its electronics goods.

As in the past, personal contacts play an important role in sealing a transaction. The Chinese customers value the **guanxi**, or "mutual good feeling and trust" between old friends.[36] Personal selling is a necessary tool to establish good channel relationships. And this sentiment has been successfully exploited by new foreign entrants into China's insurance market (see box, "Selling Life Insurance in China").

PROMOTION   Advertising is strictly controlled by the Chinese government, and censorship is severe. For instance, an advertisement that showed the Statue of Liberty was deemed unacceptable, and so was one that featured the word *Hollywood*, apparently viewed as a subversive influence. Advertising is constrained also because the penetration of media, especially television, is still limited. Nevertheless, entering multinationals such as Coca-Cola rely heavily on television advertising to create awareness and

Selling Life Insurance in China

IT MAY COME as a surprise in a country where communists are in power and food and housing are in principle guaranteed, but China has long had a viable life insurance industry. A traditional family focus has encouraged savings and risk sharing, and when the one-child-per-family policy was enacted by Chairman Mao, the demand for life insurance to protect the one offspring rose further.

Naturally, in the past, the industry has been a government monopoly. Not surprisingly, service was deficient. Each month, a person would have to stand in line to pay the premium, and if late, a penalty would be charged. Only a straight insurance policy was available, with no interest and no options to borrow against the policy.

Enter the American International Group, whose chairman had wooed the Chinese government officials since his first visit to China in 1975. American International, or "Friendly Nation" in its Chinese incarnation, is the only foreign insurance company allowed to market its product in China. In Shanghai it sells life insurance policies that pay interest after 5 years. The policies can be borrowed against after 3 years and are fully refundable after 20 years. The sales agents are young Chinese ladies who have adapted the now outlawed door-to-door sales techniques to the Chinese situation.

The "Friendly Nation" ladies visit offices, where underemployed workers do not mind being interrupted. They sell to the boss first, so the authority-conscious employees know it is acceptable to buy. They appeal to parents to buy insurance for their children. And they sell to women.

"I go for the women," says Lily Hua, an agent, flashing a mischievous smile. "You sell a policy to a man and the next day he may come back and ask for a refund because his wife objected. That never happens when I sell to a woman."

Sources: *New York Times*, April 4, 1995, pp. D1, D5; Yuen, 1995; Ligos, 1998.

good will among consumers and the trade. And, not the least, the advertising serves to signal to the prospective buyers that the new product comes in fact from the advertised firm and is not a counterfeit![37]

Print and outdoor advertising does play a larger role, as do in-store factors. The consumers have time to browse and search for brands in the stores. Their lack of experience with variety leads them to trust a brand they know, have tried, and found satisfactory, generating a strong first-mover advantage for foreign entrants. They will also look for a brand they have only heard of—especially if the information came through advertising on the commercial TV stations.

Continuous Change

As news media report, China continues to change. This change is reflected not only in a two-digit economic growth rate but also in the frequent revisions of government policies, the privatization of state-owned monopolies, and reform in the foreign trade system.

Change brings fresh opportunities. The economic growth in China has opened up a vast potential market. Change also brings problems, as the Tiananmen Square events of 1989 demonstrated. Most foreign marketers find it challenging to operate on such a moving stage, but the stakes may well be worth it.

CLOSE-UP: MARKETING IN INDIA[38]

Market Potential

India has close to 900 million citizens. Since 1947, when British colonial rule ended, it has been the world's largest democracy. Despite religious and ethnic violence in India, the country's leaders have continued to be elected through a democratic process, without the military coups that have plagued less fortunate Third World countries.

India's educational system is a heritage from British colonial rule, with advanced English-language instruction that is the envy of many other countries. Unfortunately for the country, a large portion of its elite can't find an outlet for their productive capability in the developing home country and have found it necessary to emigrate to Western countries, where their education is put to good use. In these Western countries the Indian immigrants constitute a large ethnic minority at the upper end of the income scale. For example, in 1990 Indians were the ethnic segment of the U.S. population with the highest median income. As socialist policies and government controls give way to privatization and free markets, domestic opportunities for India's citizens will multiply, and one can expect the country to show much stronger economic growth than in the past.

The Socialist Era

Indian industry did not develop much under British colonialism, which exploited the country's raw materials, precious gems, textiles, tea, and exotic foodstuffs. When the British granted independence to India in 1947, the country split into predominantly Muslim Pakistan (East and West) and India. The two main industries, cotton and jute, suffered tremendously as the manufacturing and raw material supplies were split between the two countries.

After 1950, when Nehru became prime minister, India developed a socialist leaning attempting to develop industry on three fronts: a massive public sector based on the Soviet experiments with state-run industry, a small joint sector with private participation, and a private sector consisting of business houses that had made it rich during British rule. Because of their traditional regional monopolies, the private sector companies were the only successful part of the economy. Lack of competition led to little development.

During the next three decades, India had very high tariff and nontariff barriers against foreign imports. Both the public and private sectors developed considerable corruption and bureaucratic inefficiencies, remnants of which still plague the political and economic functioning of the country.[39]

Domestic products were of poor quality with marketing activities aimed mainly to inform the customer of the products' existence. The Indian consumer had very little choice: What mattered mostly was that the products were durable. There was some foreign participation, and several multinationals—including Coca-Cola, Colgate, Ciba-Geigy (now Novartis), and General Electric—had limited presence through equity collaborations with Indian firms. However, during those three decades most information coming to India about foreign goods was via the Indian emigrants abroad, who sent back gifts of higher-quality foreign goods. Consequently, in popular imagination, anything having a foreign-made label was seen as having high quality.

During this period there were restrictions not only on the flow of products but, more importantly, also on inbound **technology transfer into India.** The private companies advertised the fact that they had been in business for 30 years, and they often had regional monopolies. The advertising media were limited to radio and print. There were little or no market segmentation efforts except along geographic lines. There was almost no research and development into new technology with the exception of government-sponsored R&D into weaponry and nuclear power. *Products on the Indian market hardly changed from 1950 to 1980.*[40]

Free Markets

In 1977 the left-wing party led by Morarji Desai came to power and soon implemented even more extreme socialist policies. Foreign equity shares had to be decreased and multinationals' technology shared. These policies caused a mass exodus of foreign companies from the Indian market, led by Coca-Cola. Desai's party was defeated in the next election.

From 1980 onward, in an effort to modernize the economy, then Prime Minister Indira Gandhi started to allow foreign investment, alliances, and technology transfers. Foreign firms were allowed to have a stake of up to—but no more than—26 percent in the equity of a joint venture. Among the first collaborators to enter India were Japanese motorcycle companies Yamaha, Kawasaki, and Honda, creating competition with domestic automakers. Later, Japanese electronic firms began to enter. To maintain market share, almost all domestic companies started collaborating with multinationals. Market success during this period depended directly on which company had the best international collaboration. Goods were expensive, since the foreign firms wanted to make sure that their returns were sufficient, given the uncertain prospects in the Indian market. The technology offered, although advanced according to Indian standards, was internationally substandard.

The further **liberalization in India** in the early 1990s led by Prime Minister Rao and continued by Prime Minister Vajpayee has eliminated the ceiling on the share of foreign ownership. The return of Coca-Cola, General Electric, and other Western companies has been a tremendous boost to the Indian economy. Although the **political risk in India** remains high because of ethnic and religious violence, the country is showing strong economic progress and revitalized domestic firms. The U.S. Department of Commerce has proclaimed India one of the new export priorities and has led trips of businesspeople to the country. As of 1998, the annual growth rate stood at 6.5 percent, well above the average of mature economies.[41]

With increased competition from entering multinationals, local companies are finally starting to deliver products to suit consumers' needs rather than expecting the consumer to adapt to their products. As competition has increased, domestic companies have become more aggressive in their marketing policies as well. Competition is now on the basis of product features, quality, image, price, and so on.

Market Segmentation

During the 1980s the Indian market started to divide into two large segments: a still impoverished rural population and an increasingly well-off urban middle class. As the new opportunities pulled people away from the countryside, cities became huge metropolitan markets, and towns grew into cities. This trend was strengthened after the further market-opening measures of the early 1990s. The disposable income of the Indian middle class has increased considerably. Not only has there been strong economic growth but trends in family planning have changed, with households having fewer children. This has also meant that in many families the wives, often well-educated, have started contributing to the family income. Traditional habits are changing, and the Indians are even starting to have cold cereal for breakfast (see box, "Basmati Flakes in the Morning").

Product Positioning

Exposure to new products and services has increased the appetite for further purchases. The Indian consumer who was earlier focusing on the durability of products has now started buying products as symbols of status and success. Consumers are becoming more demanding. Products that were earlier a luxury now have become necessities. Cable TV has entered Indian homes, and households have more than one car. Foreign automakers compete for the privilege of tying up with domestic automakers.

As the liberalization of the economy continues, Indian companies are being forced to become more efficient. Drawing on the large pool of talented and well-educated people, the domestic industry is now surging ahead. Foreign companies are also eager to utilize the local expertise. Motorola, the American cellular phone company, has been awarded a "plum" contract to provide cellular phone service to the Indian public and can easily find local engineers and MBAs who are familiar with both the technology and the market.

G E T T I N G   T H E   *Picture*

Basmati Flakes in the Morning

K E L L O G G, the American cereal company that made cornflakes a staple of many Western children's breakfasts, is scoring again. This time it is having success in India with corn, wheat, and basmati rice flakes, which are selling faster than hotcakes in Bombay. The key is an intensive advertising and promotional campaign designed to make Indian consumers change their breakfast eating habits.

A $450,000 multimedia campaign included three 30-second TV spots featuring a family around the breakfast table addressing the problem of overeating as well as the effects of a bread-and-butter diet and skipping breakfast. The campaign "does leave behind a suggestion that current fried breakfasts are not the best you could provide for your family to begin the day," says Anil Bhatia, senior vice president-general manager at Hindustan-Thompson Associates.

Kellogg also plans to sponsor a TV special featuring a panel of nutritionists, dieticians, and physicians on the government-run Doordarshan Network. The company is already sponsoring "Kellogg's Breakfast Show," a morning talk show that runs daily on radio. The first guest celebrity was Sushmita Sen, Miss Universe 1994.

Kellogg is also sponsoring two message boards on the main Bombay commuter thoroughfare featuring healthful advice from medical experts. Informative and copy-heavy ads are being placed in English and local-language newspapers as well as women's magazines and health periodicals.

"The Indian market is similar to the Mexican market because the Mexicans also used to consume a hot, savory breakfast," says Damindra Dias, Kellogg India's managing director. "We are saying, 'Take the right food. Don't fill yourself with fat the first thing in the morning.'"

Sources: Dubey, 1994; *Advertising Age*, November 14, 1994, p. 60.
http://www.kelloggs.com

Marketing Tactics

PRODUCT POLICIES   Multinational firms entering India have gradually come to learn two things: One, the market demands a full line of products. Two, there is a significant first-mover effect at work. The full-line policy requirement derives from the increasing competitiveness of the local firms and from the long-time involvement in India by some large multinationals, including Matsushita, ABB, and Unilever. These companies have acquired first-mover advantages in the Indian market, and as new multinationals enter after liberalization, the newcomers face an uphill battle against the "old India hands." Procter & Gamble, which by default entered India with its 1986 purchase of Richardson-Vicks, has decided to gradually introduce all its brands into the market. Philips, the European electronics company, introduced a product each month for 18 months from 1994 to 1995, and the company has now captured 13 percent of the Indian television market, in competition with strong Japanese and domestic joint ventures.[42]

PRICING   Even though global brands are very attractive to the emerging Indian middle class, they can no longer count on an automatic price premium when competing against strong local products. As in so many other markets, the majority of the consumers in the middle-income group are generally price-sensitive. Several multinational companies entering India, including Reebok, incurred losses before realizing this fact. Unilever, the large packaged goods company with a long and successful record in India, keeps overhead costs under strict control to allow prices to be lowered and still capture positive margins.

Price level is especially important when brand name is less known. This also affects global companies whose brands might not be well known yet in India. For example, Procter & Gamble, a relative newcomer in India, struck up a short-lived but useful entry alliance with Godrej Soaps, a local company with a better known name. P&G gained quick access to distribution and recognition through Godrej and could gradually introduce its global brands into the market at acceptable prices.[43]

DISTRIBUTION   Distribution channels and stores are developing more efficient networks, and capacity is expanded. But a weak infrastructure in a vast country is still one of the drawbacks to doing business in India, and companies are having to assist with structural improvements.

[handwritten margin note: companies invest in India to makes it's own infrastructure to do a good business.]

Matsushita, the Japanese electronics giant, has invested heavily in building a viable distribution network for its products. Dividing the large country into geographical sales territories, Matsushita built large warehousing facilities at strategic points in the network to ensure adequate supply and inventory of finished products and parts for its Panasonic brand. Matsushita has also invested in training its Indian dealers in retail service, inventory management, and customer service programs. Borrowing a page from its strategy at home in Japan, the company expects all its dealers to become exclusive Panasonic dealers by the year 2000.[44]

PROMOTION   Advertising and marketing agencies are now booming. Advertising in India does not include direct attacks on the competition (it is prohibited by law), though it is often implied. Many multinationals have to modify their global advertising campaigns to meet local Indian tastes and the various local dialects. For example, Motorola, the American mobile phone company, advertised its pagers with traditionally dressed commodity traders. The increased penetration of television has made TV advertising very popular, but in terms of cost-effectiveness other media such as print and outdoor ads will often be superior.

Corporate advertising also is on the upswing. Showing how marketing can help reposition previously protected companies, giant industrial conglomerates like Tatas and Birles—companies that make and sell everything from candy to industrial machinery—advertise defensively what they do for local communities.

A leading industrialist, Rahul Bajaj of Bajaj Autos, proclaimed in the preliberalization period: "We are a Third World country; our consumers do not expect very high quality."[45] Unless political forces intervene, such sentiments are a thing of the past in India's marketplace. The Indian consumers have developed expectations similar to those in more advanced economies.

SUMMARY

Developing countries are characterized by low disposable incomes, low educational levels, and a general apathy among the people. Market potential in these countries is often low, and trading with these countries often involves intermediaries such as specialized trading companies and international financial institutions like the World Bank and the IMF. Also, the local marketer has to be prepared to evaluate and accept countertrade offers.

Internally, these countries have an overriding need to develop a more effective marketing infrastructure, in particular a functioning distribution network. But to accomplish this more is needed than a mere infusion of capital and know-how. The local marketer has to become a teacher of sorts, educating middlemen as well as consumers about how to do effective marketing.

The NDC markets differ from those in other developing countries in that the political systems have long attempted to provide the basic conditions of a decent life and good elementary education but have also emphasized production instead of consumption and have pursued a consistent strategy of hostility to capitalism. These background factors make these markets different and in some ways more difficult to penetrate. The idea of consumer sovereignty, so basic to the Western market systems, is foreign to people who have been taught that labor is the supreme value. The notion that consumers must be satisfied by producers is hard to accept, and a service orientation is difficult to inculcate in retail clerks. The local marketer in these nations becomes a foot soldier and a teacher in the struggle to bring the marketing concept to these budding free markets.

But consumer psychology in NDC economies is changing rapidly as economic progress continues. As new products appear, people change their attitudes and preferences, and traditional habits give way to new lifestyles. Over time, unless the political situation reverses itself, customers in the NDC markets can be expected to become more similar to their compatriots in more mature markets.

KEY TERMS

attitudes toward free markets in NDCs   p. 285
copyright infringement   p. 294
counterfeits and pirated products in China   p. 294
credibility of advertising   p. 290
developing markets   p. 280
educating middlemen   p. 288
ethnic market segmentation   p. 286

export controls   p. 285
guanxi   p. 297
Hong Kong traders in China   p. 294
international agencies in NDCs   p. 284
joint ventures with Chinese partners   p. 295
liberalization in India   p. 300
marketing infrastructure   p. 280

newly democratized countries (NDCs)   p. 284
political risk in India   p. 300
political risk in Russia   p. 285
Special Economic Zones in China   p. 293
technology transfer to India   p. 299

DISCUSSION QUESTIONS

1. How strong would you say the evidence is that the emerging markets will sooner or later have the same kind of consumers as mature markets? What will the role of national differences and culture become? How do entry barriers stall the process toward similarity?

2. What are the basic functions of an effective distribution system in mature markets? As on-line shopping across country borders becomes feasible and accepted, what are the demands on the countries' distribution systems (including customs duties) that need to be handled? How well and by whom are these functions likely to be performed in an NDC market such as Russia?

3. Access one of the Web sites for Amway, Avon, or Mary Kay. What do they say about their operations in China

and other emerging markets? Check out other direct marketers with pyramid-type sales organizations, such as Nuskin, and see what they do in these markets. What are the pros and cons of being a distributor for such a company in an emerging country?

4. What factors would you think are particularly important for a marketer of cosmetics to teach retailers in the stores of NDC markets? If you are a marketer of automobiles?

5. What factors in your own country's typical consumer advertising do you think will not be the same in an NDC economy? How do consumers in your country and the NDC learn about new product features?

NOTES

1. This is of course much too brief a discussion to do justice to the range of agencies and services available and what the firm can do to mobilize support for its overseas endeavor. The extent of support differs by region, country, and industry. More will be said below in the context of the newly democratized countries (NDCs), but this chapter can only scratch the surface. There are specialized books and directories available, and the interested reader can start by consulting, for example, the sources listed in Chapter 4.

2. See "Nestlé Alimentana S. A.—Infant Formula," Harvard Business School, case no. 9-580-118.

3. This example is from "General Motors' Asian Alliances," Harvard Business School, case no. 9-388-094.

4. See *The Russian Consumer*, 1992, and "A New Brand of Warfare," 1994.

5. For more on this perspective, see "Gillette Keys Sales," 1987.

6. These brief paragraphs on international support for NDCs can be pursued further by the interested reader; see note 1 above.

7. See Czinkota, 1994.

8. Events in Russia have created some anxiety, but as of mid-1998 progress was still being recorded. See, for example, Tagliabue, 1998.

9. See "GE's Next Century," 1993, and Tagliabue, 1998.

10. See *The Russian Consumer*, 1992.

11. See, for example, "Cosmetics Companies," 1994.

12. From Elliott, 1992, *The Russian Consumer*, 1992, and Jagger, 1998.

13. See "A New Brand of Warfare," 1994.

14. See Yan, 1994, and also "What Clinton Won't Find," 1994.

15. See "A New Brand of Warfare," 1994.

16. See ibid. and "Cosmetics Companies," 1994.

17. From "A New Brand of Warfare," 1994.

18. For an informative view on advertising strategy in the new Russia, see *The Russian Consumer*, 1992, and Jagger, 1998.

19. From Tagliabue, 1998.

20. For a pessimistic outlook, see Kvint, 1998. LaFraniere, 1998, details the severity of the crisis for the average Russian consumer.

21. This section draws on Lee and Yip, 1998(1). Thanks are offered to May Guo for drafting the section and to Mingxia Li for reviewing and updating it.

22. See "China: Special Report," 1995, and Lee and Yip, 1998(1).

23. See "China's Low-Cost Loans in Doubt," 1995, and Lee and Yip, 1998(1).

24. See "China: Trade Regulation," 1995.

25. See "China Tariff Cut Seen," 1995, and "Peugeot Chief," 1995.

26. See "China Pledges," 1995.

27. See "No Holiday," 1995.

28. See "Actel Signs Unique. . . .," 1998.

29. From Lee and Yip, 1998(2).

30. See Lee and Yip, 1998(1).

31. See note 30.

32. From Yan, 1994.

33. See note 30.

34. See note 21 above. Also "Chinese Bikes," 1995.

35. See "China Expert," 1994.

36. About the role of "guanxi" in marketing relationships, Davies et al., 1995, are very informative.

37. See note 30.

38. This section draws on Ramachandran and Yip, 1998. Thanks are offered to Ashwani Gujral for drafting the section and to Sachin Anand for reviewing and updating it. Unless otherwise noted, the country statistics are from United Nations and the U.S. Department of Commerce publications.

39. The 1995 problem with the massive power project in the state of Maharashtra is a reminder of the political risks involved.

American company Enron was awarded the contract by the Indian government, but a new state government challenged the agreement and forced a renegotiation. See "Enron, India to Begin Talks," 1995.

40. This is the popular imagination in India. There were changes: For example, already by 1980, India did have electronic word processors and some personal computers, brought in by expatriates from abroad. But the relative stagnation in, for example, automobiles, where the models remained unchanged over a 30-year period, is a striking testament to the power of trade barriers to retard economic growth.

41. See Ramachandran and Yip, 1998, and "India: Progress and Plans," 1998.

42. See Ramachandran and Yip, 1998.

43. See note 42.

44. See note 42.

45. From "Foreign Car Makers," 1994.

SELECTED REFERENCES

"Actel Signs Unique as New Distribution Partner for Hong Kong/China." *Business Wire*, September 3, 1998.

"A New Brand of Warfare." *Business Central Europe*, April 1994.

Babakian, Genine. "Smirnoff Pop Chart Causes Russian Flap." *Adweek* 36 (August 7, 1995), p. 14.

Beck, Simon. "Trade Go-Ahead to Boost Ties, Says Clinton." *South China Morning Post*, July 24, 1998, p. 7.

"China Expert Sees 'A Car in Every Garage' by 2010." *Reuter European Business Report*, April 6, 1994.

"China Pledges Three-Stage Currency Convertibility." *Reuter Asia-Pacific Business Report*, February 11, 1995.

"China's Low-Cost Loans in Doubt." *The Age (Melbourne)*, March 30, 1995.

"China: Special Report—The Long March to Market Economy Continues Unabated." *Lloyds List*, November 24, 1995.

"China Summit Opportunity." *Washington Times*, October 22, 1995.

"China Tariff Cut Seen to Slash Surplus by $10 Billion." *Reuters, Limited*, December 10, 1995.

"China: Trade Regulation." *EIU ViewsWire*, October 30, 1995.

"Chinese Accused of Pirating Disks." *The New York Times*, August 18, 1994.

"Chinese Bikes Being Dumped in U.S." *Los Angeles Times*, May 20, 1995.

"Cosmetics Companies Stake Out Eastern Europe." *The New York Times*, October 11, 1994.

Czinkota, Michael R. "Export Controls: Providing Security in a Volatile Environment." Working paper, MKTG-1777-13-994, School of Business Administration, Georgetown University, 1994.

Davies, Howard; Thomas K. P. Leung; Sheriff T. K. Luk; and Yiu-hung Wong. "The Benefits of 'Guanxi': The Value of Relationships in Developing the Chinese Market." *Industrial Marketing Management* 24 (1995), pp. 207–214.

Dubey, Suman. "Kellogg Invites India's Middle Class to Breakfast of Ready-to-Eat Cereal." *The Wall Street Journal*, August 29, 1994, p. 83B.

Ecenbarger, William. "There's No Escaping Us: The Sun Never Sets on America's Pop-Culture Empire." *Chicago Tribune Sunday Magazine*, February 13, 1994, p. 16.

Elliott, Stuart. "Sampling Tastes of a Changing Russia." *The New York Times*, April 1, 1992, p. D1.

Engardio, Pete. "Rethinking China," *Business Week*, March 4, 1996, pp. 57–65.

"Enron, India to Begin Talks." *The Oil Daily*, November 3, 1995, p. 5.

Faison, Seth. "Service with Some Bile." *New York Times*, October 22, 1995, sec. 4, p. 4.

"Foreign Car Makers Make Drive for India's Middle Class." *Washington Post*, September 17, 1994.

"Gauging the Consequences of Spurning China." *The New York Times*, March 21, 1994.

"GE's Next Century: China, India, and Latin America." *Business Week*, April 12, 1993.

"Gillette Keys Sales to Third World Tastes." *The Wall Street Journal*, April 2, 1987.

Hays, Constance L. "RJR Nabisco Braces for Drop in Russian Sales." *The New York Times*, September 30, 1998, pp. C1, C19.

"In Polish Shipyard Signals of Eastern Europe's Revival." *The New York Times*, July 4, 1995, pp. 1, 46.

"India: Progress and Plans." *Washington Post*, October 6, 1998, p. A13.

Jagger, Steven, "Smells Like Teen Spirit." *Brand Strategy*, June 19, 1998, pp. 8–9.

Kvint, Vladimir. "The Last Days of Boris Yeltsin." *Forbes*, September 7, 1998, p. 145.

LaFraniere, Sharon. "'Every Day We Are Angry': Russian City Discovers the High Price of Free Market." *Washington Post*, September 13, 1998, pp. A1, A40.

Landler, Mark. "2 Asian Economies Seek to Keep Global Markets at Bay." *The New York Times*, September 12, 1998, pp. C1, C2.

Layne, Rachel. "Kodak to Invest $1 Billion in China in Attempt to Slow Fuji's Advance." *The San Diego Union-Tribune*, March 24, 1998, p. C–6.

Lee, Kam Hon; and George S. Yip. "China—Enter the Giant." Chapter 4 in Yip, 1998(1).

———— and ————."Hong Kong—A New Role." Chapter 6 in Yip, 1998(2).

Ligos, Melinda. "Direct Sales Dies in China: Door-to-Door Sales Banned." *Sales & Marketing Management*, August 1998, p. 14.

Lloyd, John. "Survey of Russia." *Financial Times*, June 27, 1994, p. VIII.

Michaels, James W. "The Elephant Stirs." *Forbes*, April 24, 1995, pp. 158–59.

"Missing Out on a Glittering Market." *The New York Times*, September 12, 1993.

"No Holiday for HK Pro-Labor Group." *United Press International*, December 16, 1995.

"Penetrating the Great Wall: Entry of Direct Marketers into the Chinese Market." *Target Marketing*, June 1998, p. 26.

"Peugeot Chief Urges China to Protect Car Market." *Reuters, Limited*, December 8, 1995.

"Radio Advertisers Tune In to Russia's Middle Class." *The New York Times*, August 12, 1994.

Ramachandran, K.; and George S. Yip. "India—Giving Multinationals a Chance." Chapter 12 in Yip, 1998.

Siegle, Candace. "Crap Shoot." *World Trade* 6, no. 10 (November 1993), pp. 64–66.

Tagliabue, John, "Tilting but Standing as a Big Domino Falls." *The New York Times*, October 6, 1998, pp. C1, C4.

The Russian Consumer: A New Perspective and a Marketing Approach. New York: D'Arcy Masius Benton and Bowles, 1992.

"What Clinton Won't Find in Russia." *The New York Times*, January 10, 1994.

Yan, Rick. "To Reach China's Consumers, Adapt to *Guo Qing*." *Harvard Business Review*, September–October 1994.

Yip, George S. *Asian Advantage: Key Strategies for Winning in the Asia-Pacific Region.* Reading, MA: Addison-Wesley, 1998.

Yuen, Darrel K. S. "China: The Next Life Insurance Frontier?" *National Underwriter* 99 (May 22, 1995), pp. 2, 17.

Cases

Case 3.1

Daloon A/S[1]
The Catering Market in Germany

At the end of 1992 managing director Hemming Van was able to look at a year that had brought new and great challenges to Daloon A/S. After a couple of years with large expansions and rapid growth he was proud to ascertain that 1992 was the year when the flagship within the fast food sector, McDonalds, the American burger chain became a Daloon customer.

Daloon differs from most of the Danish food industry in that the company's business concept is not based on the processing of specific raw materials, it is based on a product concept, i.e. Chinese pancake rolls. Hemming Van's father, Sai-Chiu Van, came to Denmark in 1935, and at the beginning of 1960, in basement premises, he made 240 rolls for a stall in Tivoli Gardens in Copenhagen. That year Sai-Chiu Van sold about 50,000 rolls to various small restaurants and wine bars, and the foundation was prepared for the firm now employing almost 250 persons, producing almost 150 million rolls and selling a total of about 300 million DKK in 25 countries.

The German market has seen a virtual explosion in sales in recent years. Sales have almost quintupled since 1988 and today the German market is as important to Daloon as the Danish and British markets, each representing about 30 percent of Daloon's total sales. Two major customers carry much weight in Germany, i.e. Aldi (that became a customer in 1989/90) and McDonalds that in September/October 1992 implemented a very successful campaign selling China rolls produced by Daloon.

The recent years' rapid growth means that the firm is about to live up to the name of Daloon, the Chinese word for "The Great Dragon." Compared with McDonalds the 'dragon' is, however, still small. Daloon's remaining customers likewise keep getting larger owing to the concentration taking place in the retail trade as well as among catering wholesalers. The future perspectives outlined are both interesting and frightening. Interesting, because the growth possibilities are great; frightening, because Daloon becomes more and more dependent on fewer and larger customers. Life may become very risky in the future. Will the present shareholders run the risk involved in growth? How much is Daloon to grow? Is the German McDonalds campaign to be copied in other countries? Is the success to be exploited vis-à-vis other catering customers?

DALOON A/S

Daloon is the world's largest producer of spring rolls. Its product portfolio comprises a wide range of rolls with different fillings—making up the largest share of the product list. In addition to spring rolls, the company produces samosas, savoury souffles, cabbage and meat rolls, ice cream pancakes, and Danish doughnuts. On-going product development has been adapted to consumer demands and is one of the reasons why Daloon is able to export so extensively—to more than 25 countries at present.

Daloon has a strict policy for all its products. This is reflected in:

- a high, uniform level of quality
- use of first-class ingredients

[1] Prepared by Professor Tage Koed Madsen, Department of Marketing, Odense University, as a basis for discussion rather than to illustrate either effective or ineffective management. It is based on information made available by Daloon A/S. The case is not to be used or reproduced without prior permission. The exchange rate is approximately DKK5/U.S. $1.

- quick and easy preparation of products sold
- easy portioning
- no colourings, flavourings or preservatives added.

Daloon's strict product policy is highlighted on the packaging, where the quality and many uses of the product are illustrated in words and pictures.

Exhibit 1 shows the key financial data for Daloon from 1986 through 1992. Exhibit 2 is an excerpt from its 1992 annual report, performance results, threats and opportunities.

Daloon's internationalization process began in 1970, i.e. at a time when the individual markets to a much smaller extent than now were characterized by

EXHIBIT 1 Daloon koneernens hovedtal (*MAIN FIGURES OF THE DALOON GROUP HAUPTZAHLEN DES DALOON KONZERNES) DALOON A/S, DALOON FOODS (UK) Ltd, DALOON LEGENSMITTEL GmbH, DALOON FOODS (USA) Inc.*

	1986	1987	1988	1989	1990	1991	1992
Afsætning, 1.000 tons Sales, 1,000 metric tons/Absatz, 1.000 Tonnen	8,8	9,0	9,5	10,0	13,0	13,9	15,4
	Mill. DKK	*Mill.DKK*	*Mill.DKK*	*Mill.DKK*	*Mill.DKK*	*Mill.DKK*	*Mill.DKK*
Nettoomsætning Net turnover/Nettoumsatz	155,6	162,5	185,4	190,7	260,9	286,6	308,3
Eksportandel Export share/Exportanteil	61%	59%	65%	63%	69%	69%	69%
Investering i materielle anlægsaktiver Fixed assets investment/Investition in mat. Anlageaktiven	16,6	12,2	8,7	34,9	15,0	83,2	10,5
Afskrivning på materielle anlægsaktiver Fixed assets depreciation/Abschreibung mat. Anlageaktiven	7,7	8,7	8,7	7,3	11,2	13,1	15,5
Resultat af ordinær drift Operating profit/Resultat des ordentlichen Betriebes	18,6	14,8	19,8	24,5	41,5	45,9	45,5
Årets overskud før skat Pre tax profit/Jahresüberschuß vor Steuern	15,9	14,0	20,0	20,4	42,1	43,7	39,2
Selskabsskat Corporation tax/Köperschaftsstenern	6,3	3,8	8,3	6,6	16,1	16,1	12,9
Årets resultat Result of the year/Jahresresultat	9,6	10,2	11,7	13,8	26,0	27,6	26,3
Samlede aktiver Total assets/Gesamte Aktiven	122,6	133,5	147,7	180,9	220,4	282,9	310,7
Egenkapital* Capital and reserves/Eigenkapital	48,2	58,3	68,5	83,0	108,8	134,1	104,9
Nøgletal Key Figures/Schlüsselzahlen	%	%	%	%	%	%	%
Overskudsgrad Profit ratio / Überschußgrad	$\frac{\text{rets ordin re overskud}}{\text{Oms tning}}$ $\frac{\text{Operating profit before interest and tax}}{\text{Turnover}}$ $\frac{\text{Ordentl, Jahresresultat vor Z insen und Steuern}}{\text{Umsatz}}$	12,0	9,1	10,7	12,8	15,9	16,0	14,7
Soliditet Solidity / Kreditwürdigkeit	$\frac{\text{Egenkapital}}{\text{Sam lede aktiver}}$. $\frac{\text{Netcapital}}{\text{Total assets}}$. $\frac{\text{Eigenkapital}}{\text{Gesam te Aktiven}}$	39,3	43,7	46,4	45,9	49,4	47.4	33,7
Antal beskæftigede Number of employees/Anzahl Beschäftigte	156	164	178	176	224	235	256
***Aktiekapital** Share capital/Aktienkapital	Mill DKK 3	Mill DKK 3	Mill DKK 3	Mill DKK 3	Mill DKK 3	Mill DKK 2	Mill DKK 2

Exhibit 2 Annual Report 1992

ANNUAL REPORT 1992

The Daloon Group can in retrospect look upon 1992, noting that the general expectations for the development of the Company have at large been fulfilled. It was expected that the year would be one of consolidation following the major capacity expansion in Nyborg in 1991, and that the earnings would not compare with the two previous years, due to increased depreciations and interest costs. This has been the case, but the earnings are still satisfactory.

SALES DEVELOPMENT

The German market has now taken the position of Daloon's largest, this especially due to one of the leading international fast food chains placing a large single order with Daloon. The prospects are still positive despite the difficult economic situation in Germany.

Sales on the Danish and English markets, however, have not really developed throughout the year despite launches of new products. The reason for this is to be found in the uncertainty surrounding the two countries' association with the European community and the general economic climate.

Special efforts have been made with regard to the South European markets towards the end of the year with a range of new pancake roll variations, and we expect a positive reaction during 1993. The Scandinavian markets are still not very accessible due to import duty, and competitiveness has been weakened by the devaluation of the Norwegian and Swedish currencies.

In conclusion, the Company has every reason to be satisfied with the achieved results, but notes with concern the continuously weakened situation on the European markets. Daloon must monitor its production costs very closely, and at the same time carry out the necessary product development and adaption. This is the only way in which the Company can meet the demand for increased earnings from the trade.

GENERATION CHANGEOVER

The founder of Daloon, Mr. Sai-Chiu Van, decided in 1992 to complete the generation changeover in the Company in order to eliminate all uncertainty regarding the future ownership situation. Daloon will forthwith be run as a family owned business in order to maintain the independence, flexibility and short decision process, which the shareholders consider necessary for future expansion and earnings.

international competition and co-operation across national borders. Up through the 1970s Daloon did not have the required capital resources to head directly for the consumer market. That was the major reason why the catering market was always the first target at the entry of a new national market. The retail market was considered too unstable, unreliable and expensive to enter. An exception was, however, made in Switzerland where Migros became a co-operation partner as early as the beginning of 1974.

Today Daloon has more substantial capital resources and much better development resources internally. This means that the firm is now better capable of entering the retail market directly. This was made in Spain in 1990 when Daloon concluded a private label agreement with one of the most important retail chains.

It is characteristic of Daloon that a brand name strategy as well as a private label strategy is pursued. Fundamentally, it is the opinion of the Daloon management that the earning opportunities are just as good as a specialized private label supplier as they are as brand name supplier. This goes for the consumer market as well as the catering market. Frequently, life is easier in the catering market as most catering wholesalers are not very particular about the products carrying producer names or the name of the individual wholesaler. Brand identification is not the decisive factor in obtaining customer loyalty; many other qualities in the wholesaler's market offer are of a more decisive nature and the brand name is therefore not a dominating competitive parameter for them.

PRODUCTS

The basis for practically all activity at Daloon is the fundamental product concept that comprises many different aspects of "rolls." It is a standardized product in the sense that the outside of all rolls is made practically of the same sort of pancake. There is, however, some variations to the effect that some rolls are to be prepared in a deep-fat-frier (declining sales) whereas others can be prepared on a frying pan or in the oven. At present efforts are being made to develop a roll that is micro-wavable. The problem related to micro-waving is that the rolls do not get crisp when micro-waved. The development so far indicates that the rise in the number of microwave ovens does not represent a threat to Daloon's sales of the existing products.

The filling of the individual types of rolls varies (savoury rolls, China rolls, pizza rolls, gourmet rolls, etc.). In some cases the filling contains different meat products whereas other rolls contain only vegetable filling. Low-calorie rolls are marketed under the name of 'Daloon-Light.' The continued product development at Daloon has the effect that the rolls are today considered wholesome fast food providing the consumer with great flexibility when preparing the food. Rice, salad, vegetables, etc. can be chosen by the individual consumer to go with the rolls.

Daloon puts great emphasis on supplying a wholesome and uniform high quality product. This means that Daloon is very meticulous in the selection of proper raw materials and takes great care that they can be seen as well as tested in the finished product. Furthermore, efforts are made to use as few additives as possible (colourings, flavourings, preservatives, etc.). It is considered an advantage that the firm has no ties to raw material producers as the composition of the raw materials in the filling may be changed without any problems. This results in great flexibility and negotiation strength vis-à-vis the raw material suppliers. The raw materials cost about 20 percent of the amount (excluding VAT) the customer is to pay for a Daloon product.

The production machinery is tuned in such a way that the optimum balance is being sought between achieving advantages of scale and maintaining product change flexibility. In practice, this means that the individual process lines are arranged so that the outside (the pancake) of the rolls are practically the same for all rolls whereas the filling can be changed very quickly. In that way it is possible to produce relatively small series of specialized rolls without losing the low-cost advantages of large-scale operations. Daloon has developed a substantial part of its machinery—and has taken out the corresponding patents.

The top-selling roll weighs about 100 gram. However, in the catering market a number of 150-200 gram rolls are sold, particularly to industrial canteens in Germany. For the McDonalds campaign in Germany, Daloon furthermore developed a special roll of about 20 gram (thumb-size). The sale of rolls constitutes about 85 percent of total Daloon sales. In addition to this the product programme includes soufflés, cabbage meat rolls, Danish doughnuts and pancakes with ice. A growth in soufflé sales is expected, particularly on the catering market. It is frequently easier to introduce a new product to this market as the menu is composed by the chef. This has the effect that the product is presented 'live' on the counter to the individual consumer, thus increasing his motivation to buy.

At Daloon the product development department recently merged with the quality control department as it was frequently hard to distinguish between fundamental product development and minor adaptations (belonging to quality control). In the day-to-day activities it was considered much more appropriate to deal with such questions generally. This means that all product related decisions are dealt with by Daloon's product development group consisting of the R&D manager, the technical manager, the sales manager, the financial manager and the managing director. The group convenes regularly. The individual salesmen have direct access to the members of the group. This has the effect that feedback from the market can be incorporated very quickly in the internal product development and product adaptation work.

COMPETITION

It is difficult to define Daloon's market because the rolls and also the other Daloon products are considered highly varied substitutes by the consumers, on the consumer market as well as the catering market. In principle, all fast food products compete with Daloon's products. This applies of course to other rolls and soufflés, etc. but also sausages, pizzas, breaded fish and all possible ready-made dishes or dishes that are easily and quickly prepared and that can be bought in flexible portions. It offers advantages and disadvantages. The advantage is that the sales opportunities are practically unlimited seen from a company of the size of Daloon's.

The disadvantage is that it is often difficult to point out direct causes of possible declining sales as it is impossible to point to a direct cause in the market. For Daloon it means that no special importance is attached to the traditional analyses of market shares, consumer familiarity with Daloon's products and repurchase percentages, they rely much more on the personal contact to the actors of the market when Daloon assesses its own position in the market.

In the European market only four producers supply rolls that are directly comparable with Daloon's rolls. The firms in question are four Dutch companies that individually are smaller than Daloon, but combined they are bigger. Compared with them Daloon has a production technical lead and is capable of producing at lower costs. In addition Daloon has established much stronger sales organizations in Scandinavia, Britain and Germany than these competitors. The Dutch companies were started in the same way as Daloon, namely by a person immigrating from the Far East and starting a production of rolls. The Dutch firms, however, have their roots in Indonesia where the rolls are somewhat drier than in China. The Dutch firms have stuck to this tradition. Additionally their fillings contain more chicken and more bean sprouts as these raw materials are relatively low-priced in the Netherlands.

Furthermore, a line can be drawn from Paris over Southern Germany marking the north-south border line in Europe as to the perception of what a roll is or should be like. France, for instance, is characterized by the Vietnamese cuisine with its tradition for rolls with much thinner pancakes and a more minced meat type filling including prawns and crabs. Such rolls are not part of the Daloon programme at present, but Daloon is now in the process of developing this type of roll. The French agent has for several years urged Daloon to produce such rolls. At Daloon they have, however, had their hands full product developing on the basis of the requests made by their own salesmen. This is one of the reasons why Daloon has been reluctant to start development activities aimed especially at the French market.

THE GERMAN SITUATION

It was very difficult for Daloon to make sales and marketing work on the German market up through the 1970s and the 80s. As a matter of fact the retail market was about to drop out early 1989 and the catering market was stagnating. On the retail market an important reason for the imminent collapse was that the oven rolls introduced were inferior. The finished ready-made roll had neither a structure nor a presentation that came up to the consumers' expectations. This was due to the fact that rolls were not adequately pre-treated by Daloon. The consequences were failing sales and delisting by the chains.

Following intensive product development activities Daloon could in 1989 offer the market new and improved rolls that were pre-fried by Daloon in Nyborg and which could easily be prepared in an oven. The new assortment was introduced to Aldi and Aldi took in the products as a mixture of brand name and private label; the package was specially developed for Aldi, but carries Daloon's name and logo. From the outset the products sold well in the Aldi stores and this meant that other chains were included among the customers (with genuine private labels). Aldi's great success had the effect that the consumer market now suddenly accounted for the majority of Daloon's sales in Germany, which is still the case. In Nyborg the consequences were very tangible as the German progress was the major motive behind the decision to invest 80 million DKK in new manufacturing equipment which was ready for production at the end of 1991.

THE CATERING MARKET

In the German catering market Daloon pursues a brand name strategy as well as a private label strategy, dependent on the requests of the individual customer and the opportunities available. Most distinct is, however, the brand name strategy. Daloon has been active in this market since 1970 and sales have developed quietly and steadily over the years, however by a giant leap in recent years. Even before the reunion Daloon had extended its activities to include also former East Germany by the employment of a junior salesman. The German catering market is more accessible to Daloon than the Danish market in that Germans traditionally have a hot meal at noon.

Daloon's target groups are as follows:

- industrial and staff canteens (i.e. within industry, insurance, banking, etc.)
- university canteens, etc.
- institutional canteens (hospitals, nursing homes, etc.)
- military canteens

This segmentation of the market is the result of various circumstances. The fundamental target group is industrial and staff canteens representing the most important market potential. Very often the canteen customers work hard physically and this must be reflected in the choice of the canteen. University canteens are special in that the customers are almost exclusively young people who often have attitudes and eating habits deviating from the average German. Within institutional canteens it is often so that the food is prepared in a centrally located kitchen and then delivered to the different wards of the institution. The composition of the menu must reflect the special demands made by such wards. Military canteens are a relatively new target group. The reason for this is that the former practise of letting the soldiers be in charge of the preliminary preparation of the food has been abandoned. Now the kitchen staff must be paid and this results in demands for more pretreated products in these canteens. A corresponding development has been ascertained by Daloon in other target groups where reductions have taken place in the kitchen staff. In that way "time has been on Daloon's side"; this also goes for the more general acceptance of convenience food.

DISTRIBUTION CHANNELS

The target groups mentioned are served by a total of about 300 catering wholesalers of whom about half carry Daloon's products. As Daloon products are carried by the major wholesalers, this corresponds to somewhat more than half the sales in this part of the German catering market. An ever increasing concentration is taking place among wholesalers. During the latest ten years the number of independent wholesalers has been halved and Daloon expects a corresponding reduction within the next ten years. Part of the concentration is caused by mergers, part by some wholesalers growing big enough to oust others that simply have to close down. City Grossmarkt is an example of a wholesale firm that has grown rapidly in recent years. Furthermore, more and more wholesalers enter into some sort of purchase co-operation.

Generally, the wholesaler is in charge of the entire distribution of Daloon's products just like invoicing is always effected via the wholesaler. In a few cases where quantities are extraordinarily large, Daloon delivers directly to a canteen. Daloon has its own warehouse in Paderborn. From this warehouse deliveries are effected twice a week to wholesale warehouses all over Germany. These warehouses carry stocks and deliver to the individual canteens. The wholesalers have their own agents influencing the individual canteens. Dependent on sales each wholesaler has between 1 and 80 salesmen in the field. The small and medium-sized wholesalers are regional whereas the major ones are national, covering the entire German market. The trend is that more and more become national as the small wholesalers are the ones ousted. The small canteens are increasingly being served by Cash & Carry stores like Metro.

Daloon is only a small unit in the assortments of the wholesalers. A large wholesaler may carry 5-6 Daloon articles out of a total number of 4,000 articles in the wholesaler catalogue. This means that Daloon cannot expect the individual wholesaler to make a special effort for Daloon's products. Daloon must work in the field on its own and influence the decision-makers of the individual canteens. Traditionally, Daloon has done so by participating in the great gastronomy fairs in Germany as well as in the so-called Hausmessen (house fairs), fairs held locally by the wholesaler for chefs and the like. Annually Daloon participates in about 50 so-called house fairs. The chefs used to place orders during these house fairs, but this is not very much so any more. This likewise makes it necessary for Daloon to get into closer contact with the canteens in other ways.

INDUSTRY TRENDS

Simultaneously, competition has grown keener within convenience products. The four Dutch competitors are strong in the Ruhr district where eating habits better match the Indonesian rolls. The Dutch firms of course try to oust Daloon in other parts of Germany. Simultaneously, recent years have offered a number of new launchings. National German producers like Pfanni, Packfisch and Hanna have launched potato dough with filling, puff paste with meat and vegetable filling, cordon bleu with chicken, etc. Danish Prime is active with meat balls, lasagna, etc. The Unilever firm VandenBerg has developed a fish roll with vegetable filling. These are all examples of products competing more or less directly with Daloon's rolls. The large actors in the market like VandenBerg, Iglo and Oetkers are furthermore independent of wholesalers as they distribute directly to medium-sized and large canteens.

In addition to the ordinary catering wholesalers Daloon co-operates with more specialized actors on the catering market. A substantial customer is ARA which is a system gastronomic firm. Daloon's brand name products are included in the ARA menu sold by the ARA's sales organization especially to small canteens and the like. A minor customer is Lickart specializing in vegetable products. Daloon's vegetable products (rolls and soufflés) are included in Luckart's assortment as private labels. For Daloon this represents new opportunities in the consumer market as the firm is free to exploit the product concepts developed for Luckart over the years.

STRENGTHENING THE LOCAL ORGANIZATION

Daloon's response to the development has been to increase the direct contact to customers. Since 1988 the staff of the German sales subsidiary has been increased substantially. This increase has been made possible by the increased earnings on the German market being the result of the acquisition of Aldi as a customer in 1989/90. At that time it was decided to invest earnings in an intensification of the sales and marketing activities in the German market, particularly the catering market. The sales subsidiary is in charge of all sales in Germany, i.e. to both the consumer and the catering markets. In 1988 the subsidiary had a Danish manager and three regional salesmen (Germans). Today there is a Danish manager, three sales managers, four junior salesmen (customer advisers) as well as two secretaries (the latter nine are German). The new employments in the sales subsidiary have resulted in a much more intensive Daloon customer contact.

The three sales managers supervise direct sales to the catering market and are responsible for negotiations with catering wholesalers as well as retail chains. In addition to this, they participate in general sales drives, including the preparation of the magazine "DALOON Report—Informationen, Ideen und Tips" posted to all customers in Germany. The three junior salesmen are all fully trained cooks and are in direct contact with Daloon's most important target groups in the German catering market. It is their job to visit chefs and other decision-makers at the individual end-customers to demonstrate new products, advise the customers in the applications of the Daloon products, put up advertising signs and the like in canteens, cafeteria, etc. and furthermore to be in constant touch with minor catering wholesalers.

INCREASED SALES EFFORT

Daloon influences the canteen decision-makers more and more actively. The firm has started to visit the wholesalers to get the names and addresses of the wholesaler's most important customers. Daloon then offers to join the wholesaler's salesmen when calling on customers or is allowed to visit the chefs to influence them with information on the application of the products (recipes, etc.). This initiative has been welcomed by the wholesalers. The four junior salesmen may each typically visit about 200 canteens every month. In addition to their advisory activities they also take orders during these visits. The orders are then forwarded to the wholesaler. It is Daloon's experience that this direct customer influence has been definitely advantageous. The direct influence is supported by advertisements in professional papers and by direct mail campaigns forwarding new recipes to selected target groups among the customers. Finally, the DALOON Report magazine also supports the influence on the canteen decision-makers.

The junior salesmen also participate in the so-called house fairs and together with the sales managers they influence the wholesale salesmen at meetings where Daloon tries to familiarize these salesmen with Daloon products and their applications by means of video shows and tastes. The same things take place at meetings in various chef clubs. All things considered Daloon's German sales and marketing department is much more well-organized today than it was in 1988 when it was not nearly so effective. At that time the sales managers had to be in charge of everything which made their activities very diffuse.

CUSTOMER FEEDBACK

Being cooks the junior salesmen are able to look at the matter from the customer's point of view and thus contribute greatly to promote the customers' understanding of opportunities offered by the Daloon products as well as to feed important information from the market back to the Daloon organization.

The model for this form of organization was transferred from the Danish market. In Daloon's opinion it offers a number of advantages. Firstly, it secures a much more effective influence on customers just as it is very easy to get out into the field and test new ideas and support the Daloon programme. Secondly, the close contact to catering customer secures that the feed-back from the market is exploited very quickly and much more efficiently in Daloon's internal organization. One of the reasons for this is that the market information goes directly back to Daloon and does not 'disappear' in a report from one of the wholesaler's salesmen. Furthermore, the information obtained from Daloon's own salesmen is considered more reliable and thus carries greater weight internally than information received from an external agent. Market information from the firm's own salesmen has the effect that Daloon feels more obliged, and thus also to a much higher degree willing, to act on the feed-back received. It is not that Daloon does not trust its representatives in other markets, but somehow the weight of what is said is much more felt when the information from the market comes from somebody "in the fold."

CLOSE TO THE CUSTOMER

The close contact to the catering market customers has been of great importance. The personal contact to chefs at university canteens has for example resulted in a material change of the soufflé products. Previously, the soufflés were sold in aluminium bowls and were to be baked on location in the canteen kitchen. This meant that the canteens had the problem of discarding several thousand aluminium bowls. The students found this great waste of aluminium bowls environmentally wrong. Daloon changed the product that is now prebaked in Nyborg. This means that the aluminium bowls are no longer required. It is Daloon's opinion that the personal contact to the market is an important advantage for development. If such feed-back on product drawbacks is canalized to Daloon through independent wholesalers' salesmen reports they do not have the same effect in Daloon's internal product development group.

It is typical for Daloon that feed-back from the market is by and large received through the personal contacts of the sales force in the market. Actual formal market analyses are very rare.

THE MCDONALDS OPPORTUNITY

For a number of years Daloon has nourished the idea that McDonalds might represent a potential customer. Within the company most considered this idea purely Utopian, however, they were intrigued by the wish to become a supplier to this fast food market flagship. Some years ago Daloon's German sales department had a meeting with McDonalds' purchase department and presented Daloon's product programme. It was to no avail at the beginning, but the sales manager in Southern Germany was persistent in his efforts to 'persuade' McDonalds German purchase department located in Munich.

In February 1991 a request was received from McDonalds to develop a 20 gram pancake roll. Daloon's development department dispatched samples, but no reply was received. In November 1991 a renewed request was received specifying the filling of the roll.

Daloon replied that the firm was unable to produce so small rolls with the existing process lines; Daloon's enthusiasm had cooled slightly off following the total lack of reaction to the samples forwarded in February. In Nyborg the general attitude was: Forget it.

The sales manager in Southern Germany pushed hard, however, because he was of the opinion that McDonalds was serious this time. After some internal discussions and turmoil Daloon decided in February 1992 to give it a chance and the development department was given ten days to test the possibilities. The reply from this department was: It is possible with some investments being made in the machinery. McDonalds wanted to run the campaign in September/October 1992 and would be needing 15 million rolls in August with an option for an additional 3 million rolls if the campaign became a success. To live up to such requirements Daloon had to start production in April. Late February, Daloon hardly knew what product was to emerge from the efforts. Various products were suggested by Daloon and McDonalds purchase department came to a decision: a purely vegetarian China roll.

THE CAMPAIGN CONCEPT

McDonalds Germany wanted to profile the chain through a China week with a special menu consisting of six small Daloon rolls, fresh Peking salad and Chicken McNuggets "Shanghai." The customers were furthermore offered the opportunity of picking special sauces, namely a China sauce, a soya sauce or a Kung Fu sauce (a sharp fruit sauce). In addition to this the usual assortment was of course available in the McDonalds burger bars. Daloon was to deliver the rolls in transparent plastic bags each containing 48 rolls, packed in cartons with six plastic bags in each. Delivery was to be effected to McDonalds two central warehouses in Germany that were in charge of the redistribution to the individual burger bars.

During the final negotiations McDonalds made the offer that Daloon could have its name and logo on all the material printed for the campaign (advertising signs outside the burger bars, light boxes inside, on tray mats, etc.). After a negotiation 'time-out' of ten minutes Daloon presented an offer which was later accepted by McDonalds. Daloon has been very happy with this solution that has created an image effect in the German market. At a catering exhibition in Munich during the campaign Daloon had many comments regarding the co-operation with McDonalds and Daloon is convinced that this will make it easier to sell the concept of 20 gram rolls to other catering customers in Germany. The only thing annoying Daloon is that the offer made by Daloon was in the form of a price reduction and not as a fixed 'contribution to advertising' as the campaign became such a success that the latter contribution would have been less expensive for Daloon.

Mid-April the final order arrived from McDonalds, a Dutch and Far East competitor to Daloon were eliminated as they could not guarantee the delivery of the quantities requested by McDonalds. The summer was extremely busy at Daloon. Until mid-August, when delivery was to be effected, the production of rolls took place in regular shifts, permanent over-time and permanent weekend shifts. Production and packaging problems were solved as they arose by changes in the machinery. When the campaign had lasted only three days, it was registered as a success by McDonalds: the option of the 3 million rolls was ordered together with an extra order for an additional 8 million rolls. Production plans at Daloon again had to be rearranged drastically, and the good intentions of the staff were tried as they had to go back on overtime. Working to the utmost of its capacity, Daloon succeeded in delivering the order to the entire satisfaction of McDonalds.

CAMPAIGN EXECUTION

The campaign co-operation presented a very intensive and exciting period for Daloon. McDonalds German purchase department pursued a very systematic and consistent line when the agreement was concluded. The fundamental attitude of McDonalds was all along that Daloon had to be prepared to meet all the requirements made. No excuses for delays and the like would be accepted. The attitude was: 'We pay a good price so we want the product as agreed.' It was a feather in Daloon's cap that no problems arose. Several times during that period the great flexibility in the purchase of raw materials and production turned out to be of great importance; the flexibility and loyalty of the staff likewise. Daloon does not consider it unlikely that McDonalds would like to rerun the campaign in Germany. Considering the good results of the first campaign, Daloon feels confident that its possibilities of becoming the supplier again are good.

At the end of the campaign McDonalds German purchase department participated in a strategy meeting in Chicago together with colleagues from divisions all over the world. The very progressive German department presented its great success with the China

week and Daloon's rolls. This has had the effect that Daloon is to supply rolls for a corresponding campaign in Britain in February/March 1993. The concept (product, prices, printed campaign material, etc.) will be identical with the German concept. Furthermore, McDonalds in the Netherlands and Sweden are very interested in copying the success. For Daloon this means that the investments made in the form of special machinery constructions for the small rolls and the general product development can be exploited in full.

Daloon is free to offer the concept of the small rolls to other catering customers, apart from direct customers to McDonalds, such as Burger King. Furthermore, Daloon has on its own refrained from selling the small rolls with the 'McDonalds' filling to other customers.

FUTURE MARKETING STRATEGY

The catering market has a smaller potential than the consumer market, it is likewise less risky as there are no high listing fees or similar initial costs related to supplying to a customer. The risk in the catering market is, however, increasing owing to the continued reduction of the number of wholesalers. By way of example the development in Britain has during the latest 3-4 years been as follows: from comprising one large, quite a few medium-sized and a network of small regional wholesalers, the wholesalers now comprise one enormous, a couple of large ones and much fewer small regional wholesalers. Among the latter three to four disappear every year, either because they close down or are acquired by the large wholesalers. Additionally, internationalization is beginning to appear, the largest British catering wholesaler has for example acquired firms in France. Germany also sees a concentration among catering wholesalers.

In spite of its rapid growth Daloon has maintained a very flat organization with short and direct communication lines. The result is great flexibility and quick reaction to market changes. Productionwise Daloon is also very flexible as demonstrated by the McDonalds campaign. Hemming Van is convinced that it is a good idea to maintain the great flexibility within production; it turned out to be of vital importance during the co-operation with McDonalds. But what about sales and marketing? The development Daloon has been through in Germany has definitely been positive, however, the overheads of running the sales subsidiary have doubled. If one of the major customers drops out, the cost level within sales and marketing are not immediately adjustable. Reducing the activities of the sales subsidiary will probably also mean a substantial reduction in sales to catering wholesalers because it will no longer be possible to influence the decision-makers of the medium-sized and large canteens in the way practised today.

The experience from Germany indicates that it has been right to invest in the direct contact to customers. Sales have increased, Daloon's market knowledge has increased, and the product programme has been adapted much more to the German market. According to Hemming Van these are important elements in the strong competitive position Daloon has obtained in the German market. Simultaneously, he feels that the close customer contact will become even more important in future when the individual wholesalers grow larger. Will the close contact to the canteens not help balance the increased power of a large wholesaler? Will it be one of the ways in which Daloon can protect itself from the negotiation power of large customers? Is the proper way perhaps to invest in an additional expansion of the sales and mar-

keting departments at Daloon? If so: What new activities should Daloon concentrate on solving? What can help increase and stabilize sales through the catering wholesalers?

DISCUSSION QUESTIONS

1. What are the firm-specific advantages of Daloon over its competitors? The country-specific advantages? Any disadvantages?

2. Why was the German market so difficult for Daloon to enter? What was required to make entry successful?

3. How well did Daloon adapt its marketing organization to the requirements in the German market? How did Daloon try to create a strong relationship with and loyalty among its customers?

4. How did Daloon gain McDonald's Germany as a customer? How would Daloon leverage this foothold into other European countries?

Case 3.2

Levi Strauss Japan K.K.: Selling Jeans in Japan

In May 1993, Mr. A. John Chappell, President and Representative Director, Levi Strauss Japan K.K. (LSJ), was contemplating a conversation he just had with the National Sales Manager and Managing Director, Mr. Masafumi Ohki. They had been discussing the most recent information regarding the size of the jeans market in Japan. It appeared that after two years of market shrinkage in 1990 and 1991, the market contracted further in 1992. Al-

though LSJ was still increasing its share of the market, Mr. Chappell was disturbed by this trend and wondered what new strategies, if any, LSJ should pursue.

LEVI STRAUSS ASSOCIATES

General

Levi Strauss invented jeans in San Francisco in the middle of the nineteenth century gold rush. At that time Levi Strauss made pants for the gold miners that would not rip apart when miners filled their pockets with gold. Since then, the company bearing the founder's name had been faithful to the guiding principle—"Quality Never Goes Out of Style"—and had built a strong reputation and broad customer base.

Levi Strauss Associates (Levi Strauss) designed, manufactured, and marketed apparel for men, women,

This case was prepared by Elizabeth Carducci and Akiko Horikawa, second year MBA students, and Professor David B. Montgomery, Stanford University Graduate School of Business, as the basis for class discussion rather than to illustrate either effective or ineffective handing of an administrative situation. The authors gratefully acknowledge the cooperation and assistance of Mr. A. John Chappell and Mr. Masafumi Ohki of Levi Strauss Japan, and Mr. David Schmidt and Mr. S. Lindsay Webbe of Levi Strauss International.

© The Leland Stanford Junior University, 1994.

and children, including jeans, slacks, jackets, and skirts. Most of its products were marketed under the LEVI'S® and DOCKERS® trademarks and are sold in the United States and throughout North and South America, Europe, Asia, and Australia. In 1992, Levi Strauss was the world's largest brand name apparel manufacturer. Sales of jeans-related products accounted for 73% of its revenues in 1991.

Levi Strauss International

Levi Strauss International (LSI), which markets jeans and related apparel outside the United States, was organized along geographic lines consisting of the Europe, Asia Pacific, Canada, and Latin America divisions. In terms of sales and profits, Europe was the largest international division. Asia Pacific was the second largest, particularly due to the strong performance of its Japanese and Australian operations. Sales growth in LSI was faster than in the domestic division. The following table gives the breakdown of domestic and international sales for the recent years.

Levi Strauss—Domestic and International Sales (in millions of Dollars)

	1989		1990		1991	
Domestic	$2,395	66.0%	$2,560	60.3%	$2,997	61.1%
LSI	$1,233	34.0%	$1,686	39.7%	$1,906	38.9%
Total	$3,628		$4,247		$4,903	

In 1991, LSI was more profitable than the domestic operations on a per unit basis. LSI was generally organized by country. Each country's operations within the European division was generally responsible for sales, distribution, finance, and marketing activities. With few exceptions, Canada, Latin America, and the Asia Pacific divisions were staffed with their own merchandising, production, sales and finance personnel.

The nature and strength of the jeans market varied from region to region and from country to country. Demand for jeans outside of the US was affected by a variety of factors, each of varying importance in different countries, including general economic conditions such as unemployment, recession, inflation and consumer spending rates. The non-US jeans markets were more sensitive to fashion trends, as well as being more volatile than the US market. In many countries, jeans were generally perceived as a fashion item rather than a basic functional product and were higher priced relative to the US. Internationally, LSI maintained advertising programs similar to the domestic programs,

modified as required by market conditions and applicable laws. Advertising expenditures for LSI were $108.4 million (5.7% of total sales) in 1991, a 21% increase from 1990.

JAPANESE JEANS INDUSTRY ENVIRONMENT AND TRENDS

Jeans Market

Jeans were introduced into the Japanese market before World War II. Yet, the first market boom occurred right after the war, when U.S. forces brought a large supply of jeans into the country. The second growth spurt in the market for jeans was in the mid-1970s concurrent with the United States bicentennial. During this time, being American was in vogue, greatly enhancing the demand for American culture and products. The third boom, in 1986, was fueled by the increasing popularity of the casual fashion look among Japanese youth. This fashion trend, along with more leisure time, greatly increased the market for jeans, resulting in a doubling of output from 26 million pairs in 1985, to more than 50 million pairs in 1990[1] (compound annual growth rate of 14%). However, the trend was towards slower growth, and the market actually shrunk in 1991. The growth in total production of jeans from 1987 to 1991 is given in Exhibit 1.

The financial results of major jeans manufacturers in 1992 indicates that the market continued to shrink following 1991. Yet, towards the end of 1992, some companies started to see the market revive. After the last couple years of market contraction, the jeans industry seemed to be revitalized due to the development of new dying techniques (such as antique look jeans), as well as the development of jeans made of new fabrics such as light ounce denim and rayon. In addition, some of the smaller jeans manufacturers which targeted the women's market were experiencing double digit growth in sales.

Competitive Environment

During this period of rapid expansion, LSJ grew 35% annually, more than twice as fast as the market.[2] As a result, LSJ currently enjoyed the highest share of any single brand at 16% of total market sales. Still, there

---

[1]"Fashions Come and Go, But Blue Jeans Never Fade", *The Nikkei Weekly*, August 17, 1991.

[2]"Fundamentals Lend More-Than-Casual Look", *The Nikkei Weekly*, September 14, 1991.

World Maps

ALASKA
(United States)

GREENLAND
(Denmark)

Reykjavik
ICELAND

CANADA

Montreal
Toronto
Detroit
Boston
Chicago
Philadelphia
New York
Washington
San Francisco

UNITED STATES

Los Angeles

Dallas

ATLANTIC
OCEAN

Houston

MEXICO

Miami

BAHAMAS

Monterrey

CUBA

DOMINICAN
REPUBLIC

Mexico City

BELIZE
HONDURAS

HAITI

JAMAICA

PUERTO
RICO
(U.S.)

GUADELOUPE
DOMINICA
ST. LUCIA

HAWAII
(United States)

GUATEMALA
EL SALVADOR

NICARAGUA

COSTA
RICA

PANAMA

Caracas

VENEZUELA

TRINIDAD &
TOBAGO

GUYANA
SURINAME

Bogota

COLOMBIA

FRENCH GUIANA
(France)

ECUADOR

PACIFIC
OCEAN

PERU

BRAZIL

Lima

BOLIVIA

Belo Horizonte

PARAGUAY

Sao Paulo

Rio de Janeiro

C H I L E

Porto Alegre

Buenos Aires

URUGUAY

ARGENTINA

FALKLAND
ISLANDS
(U.K.)

1 The Americas

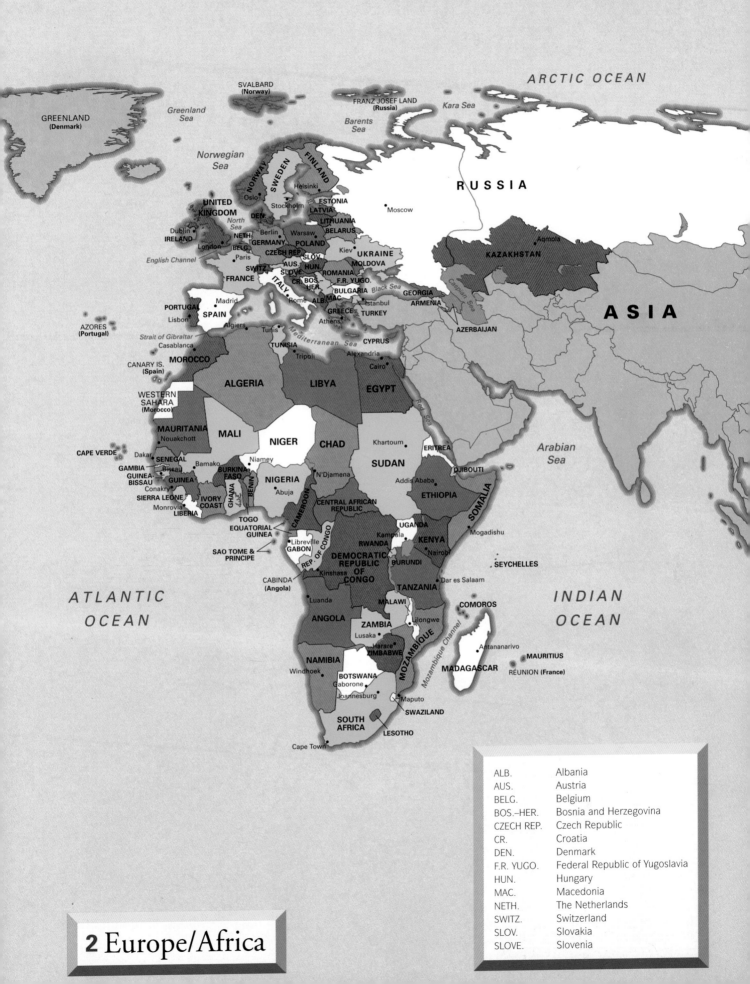

ARCTIC OCEAN

GREENLAND
(Denmark)

*Greenland
Sea*

SVALBARD
(Norway)

FRANZ JOSEF LAND
(Russia)

Kara Sea

*Barents
Sea*

*Norwegian
Sea*

NORWAY

SWEDEN

FINLAND

Helsinki

Oslo
•Stockholm

RUSSIA

Moscow

AQmola

KAZAKHSTAN

UNITED
KINGDOM

DEN.

ESTONIA

LATVIA

LITHUANIA

BELARUS

*North
Sea*

Dublin
IRELAND

NETH.

BELG.

London

GERMANY

Berlin

Warsaw

POLAND

Kiev

UKRAINE

English Channel

FRANCE

Paris

SWITZ.

CZECH REP.

AUS.

SLOV.

SLOVE.

HUN.

MOLDOVA

ROMANIA

CR. BOS.–
HER.

F.R. YUGO.

ASIA

PORTUGAL

ITALY

Rome

ALB.

MAC.

BULGARIA

Black Sea

GEORGIA

ARMENIA

Caspian Sea

Lisbon

Madrid

SPAIN

GREECE

TURKEY

Istanbul

Athens

AZERBAIJAN

AZORES
(Portugal)

Algiers

Strait of Gibraltar

Casablanca

TUNIS

TUNISIA

CYPRUS

Mediterranean Sea

CANARY IS.
(Spain)

MOROCCO

Tripoli

Alexandria

Cairo

Red Sea

WESTERN
SAHARA
(Morocco)

ALGERIA

LIBYA

EGYPT

*Arabian
Sea*

MAURITANIA

Nouakchott

MALI

NIGER

CHAD

Khartoum

ERITREA

CAPE VERDE

Dakar•

SENEGAL

Bamako•

Niamey

SUDAN

DJIBOUTI

GAMBIA

Bissau

GUINEA-
BISSAU

BURKINA
FASO

N'Djamena•

Addis Ababa•

ETHIOPIA

GUINEA

Conakry•

NIGERIA

Abuja•

SIERRA LEONE

IVORY
COAST

GHANA

BENIN

TOGO

CAMEROON

CENTRAL AFRICAN
REPUBLIC

SOMALIA

Monrovia•

LIBERIA

EQUATORIAL
GUINEA

UGANDA

Kampala•

KENYA

Mogadishu•

SAO TOME &
PRINCIPE

Libreville•

GABON

RWANDA

•Nairobi

REP. OF CONGO

DEMOCRATIC
REPUBLIC
OF
CONGO

BURUNDI

SEYCHELLES

CABINDA
(Angola)

Kinshasa•

Dar es Salaam•

TANZANIA

ATLANTIC
OCEAN

Luanda•

MALAWI

COMOROS

INDIAN
OCEAN

ANGOLA

ZAMBIA

Lilongwe•

Lusaka•

Antananarivo•

MAURITIUS

Harare•

ZIMBABWE

MOZAMBIQUE

Mozambique Channel

MADAGASCAR

RÉUNION (France)

NAMIBIA

Windhoek•

BOTSWANA

Gaborone•

SWAZILAND

Joannesburg•

Maputo•

SOUTH
AFRICA

LESOTHO

Cape Town•

ALB.	Albania
AUS.	Austria
BELG.	Belgium
BOS.–HER.	Bosnia and Herzegovina
CZECH REP.	Czech Republic
CR.	Croatia
DEN.	Denmark
F.R. YUGO.	Federal Republic of Yugoslavia
HUN.	Hungary
MAC.	Macedonia
NETH.	The Netherlands
SWITZ.	Switzerland
SLOV.	Slovakia
SLOVE.	Slovenia

2 Europe/Africa

ARCTIC OCEAN

Kara Sea

Laptev Sea

East Siberian Sea

RUSSIA

EUROPE

KAZAKHSTAN

MONGOLIA

Lake Baykal

Sea Of Okhotsk

Bering Sea

Shenyang

Sea of Japan

Black Sea

Caspian Sea

UZBEKISTAN Tashkent KYRGYZSTAN

Beijing

NORTH KOREA

JAPAN

Ankara

TURKMENISTAN TAJIKISTAN

Tianjin

Seoul

Tokyo

TURKEY

Tehran

CHINA

SOUTH KOREA

Osaka

SYRIA

IRAN

PACIFIC OCEAN

LEBANON

Baghdad

AFGHANISTAN

Lahore

Shanghai

ISRAEL

IRAQ

KUWAIT

PAKISTAN

Delhi

Chongqing

East China Sea

JORDAN

Persian Gulf

OMAN

NEPAL

BHUTAN

Taipei

BAHRAIN

Karachi

Calcutta

Dhaka

Guangzhou

TAIWAN

QATAR

SAUDI ARABIA

UNITED ARAB EMIRATES

OMAN

INDIA

BANGLADESH

MYANMAR

Hanoi

Hong Kong

MACAO (PORTUGAL)

Red Sea

Bombay

Yangon

LAOS

VIETNAM

Philippine Sea

YEMEN

Arabian Sea

Hyderabad

THAILAND

South China Sea

Manila

AFRICA

Madras

Bay of Bengal

Bangkok

CAMBODIA

PHILIPPINES

Bangalore

Ho Chi Minh City

PALAU

SRI LANKA

Colombo

FEDERATED STATES OF MICRONESIA

BRUNEI

Kuala Lumpur

MALAYSIA

INDONESIA

PAPUA NEW GUINEA

SOLOMON IS.

SINGAPORE

INDIAN OCEAN

Jakarta

Surabaya

Port Moresby

Coral Sea

VANUATU

AUSTRALIA

Sydney

NEW ZEALAND

Melbourne

Wellington

Tasman Sea

3 Asia/Australia

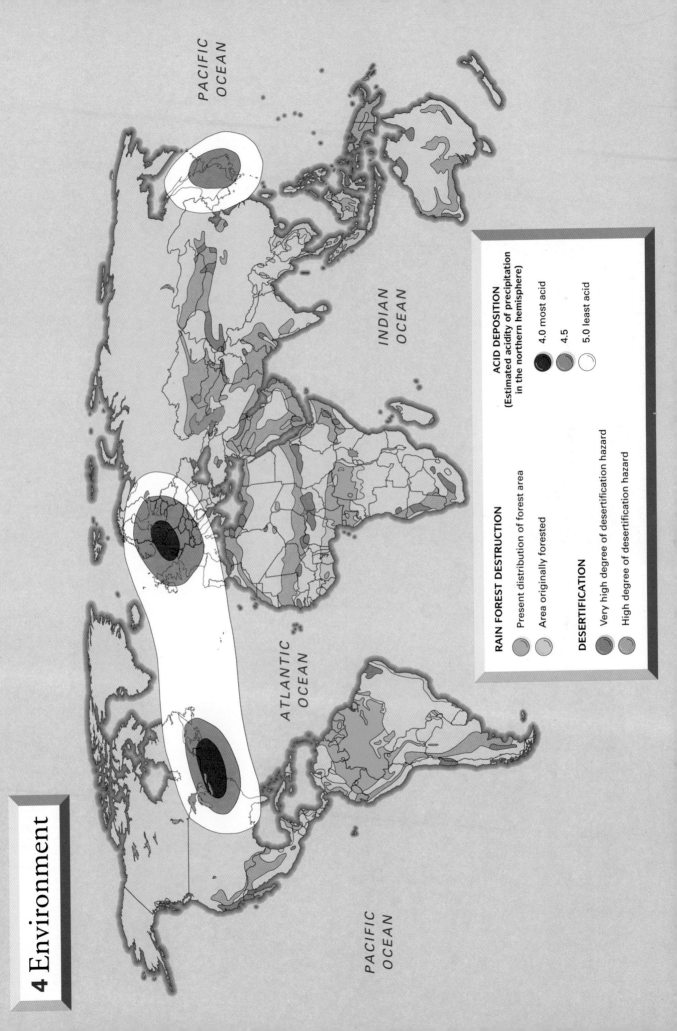

4 Environment

PACIFIC OCEAN

PACIFIC OCEAN

ATLANTIC OCEAN

INDIAN OCEAN

RAIN FOREST DESTRUCTION

Present distribution of forest area

Area originally forested

DESERTIFICATION

Very high degree of desertification hazard

High degree of desertification hazard

ACID DEPOSITION
(Estimated acidity of precipitation in the northern hemisphere)

4.0 most acid

4.5

5.0 least acid

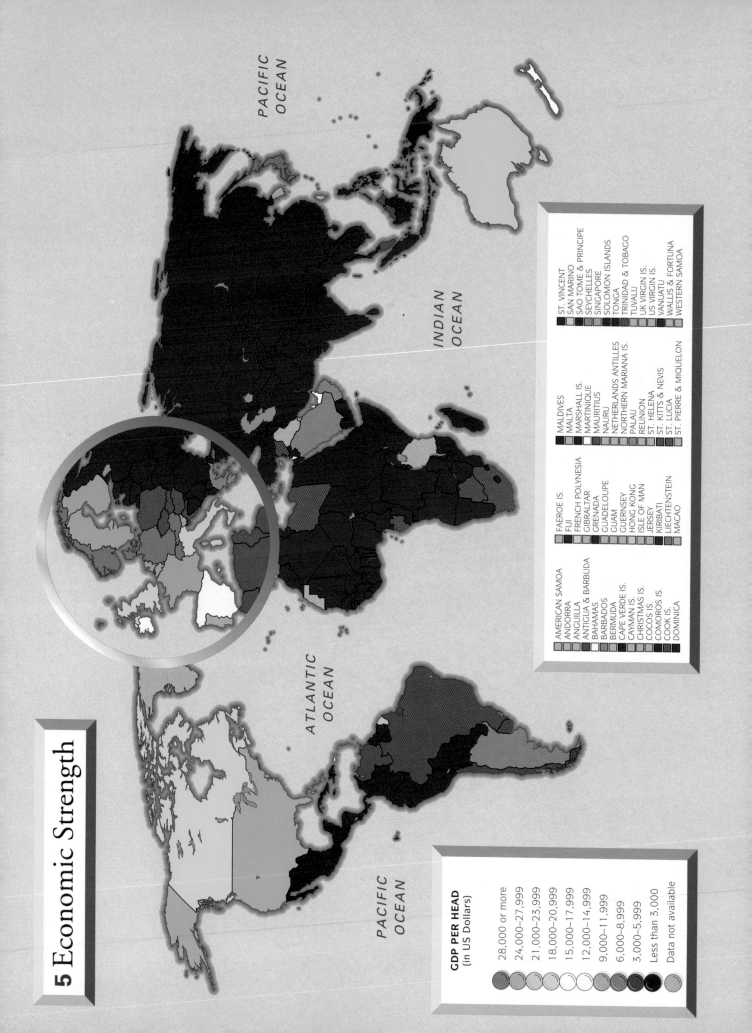

5 Economic Strength

GDP PER HEAD
(in US Dollars)

- 28,000 or more
- 24,000–27,999
- 21,000–23,999
- 18,000–20,999
- 15,000–17,999
- 12,000–14,999
- 9,000–11,999
- 6,000–8,999
- 3,000–5,999
- Less than 3,000
- Data not available

PACIFIC OCEAN

ATLANTIC OCEAN

PACIFIC OCEAN

INDIAN OCEAN

AMERICAN SAMOA
ANDORRA
ANGUILLA
ANTIGUA & BARBUDA
BAHAMAS
BARBADOS
BERMUDA
CAPE VERDE IS.
CAYMAN IS.
CHRISTMAS IS.
COCOS IS.
COMOROS IS.
COOK IS.
DOMINICA

FAEROE IS.
FIJI
FRENCH POLYNESIA
GIBRALTAR
GRENADA
GUADELOUPE
GUAM
GUERNSEY
HONG KONG
ISLE OF MAN
JERSEY
KIRIBATI
LIECHTENSTEIN
MACAO

MALDIVES
MALTA
MARSHALL IS.
MARTINIQUE
MAURITIUS
NAURU
NETHERLANDS ANTILLES
NORTHERN MARIANA IS.
PALAU
REUNION
ST. HELENA
ST. KITTS & NEVIS
ST. LUCIA
ST. PIERRE & MIQUELON

ST. VINCENT
SAN MARINO
SAO TOME & PRINCIPE
SEYCHELLES
SINGAPORE
SOLOMON ISLANDS
TONGA
TRINIDAD & TOBAGO
TUVALU
UK VIRGIN IS.
US VIRGIN IS.
VANUATU
WALLIS & FORTUNA
WESTERN SAMOA

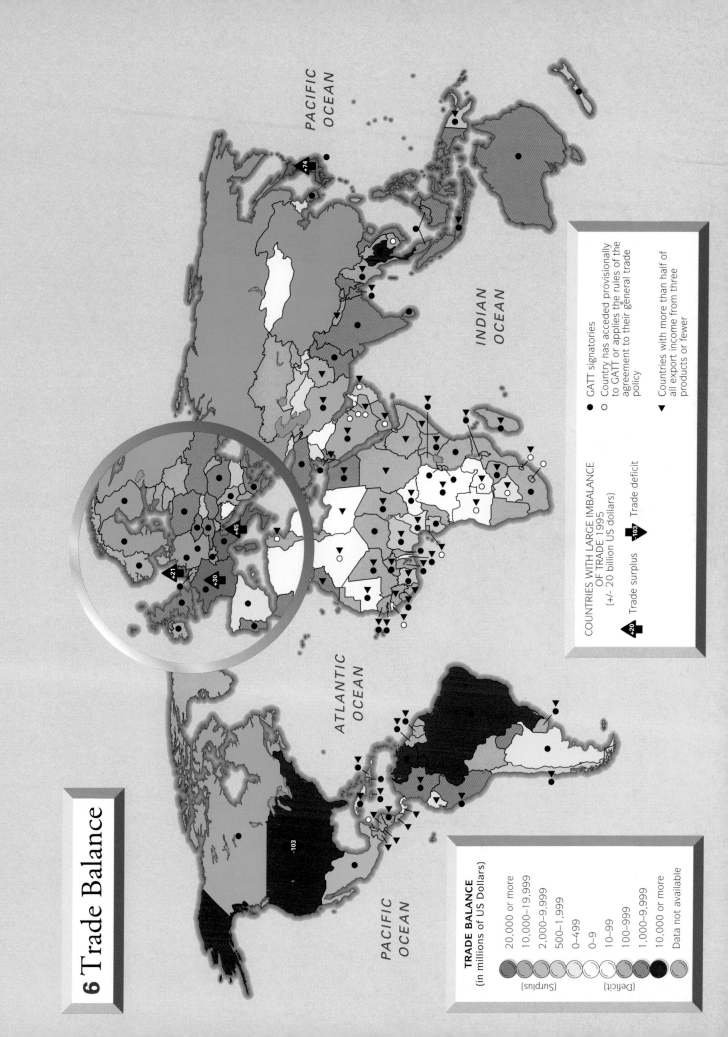

6 Trade Balance

PACIFIC OCEAN

ATLANTIC OCEAN

PACIFIC OCEAN

INDIAN OCEAN

TRADE BALANCE
(in millions of US Dollars)

(Surplus)
- 20,000 or more
- 10,000–19,999
- 2,000–9,999
- 500–1,999
- 0–499

(Deficit)
- 0–9
- 10–99
- 100–999
- 1,000–9,999
- 10,000 or more

- Data not available

COUNTRIES WITH LARGE IMBALANCE OF TRADE 1995
(+/- 20 billion US dollars)

+20 Trade surplus

-103 Trade deficit

- ● GATT signatories
- ○ Country has acceded provisionally to GATT or applies the rules of the agreement to their general trade policy
- ▼ Countries with more than half of all export income from three products or fewer

-103

+74

+45

+21

+30

-103

7 Energy Consumption

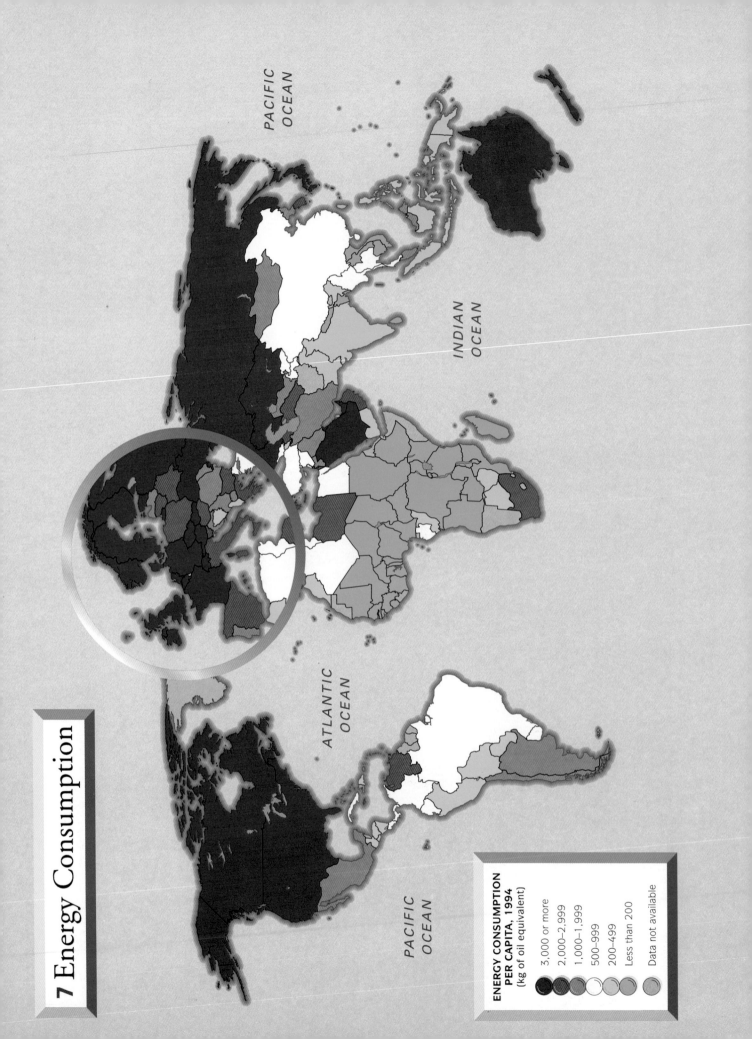

PACIFIC
OCEAN

INDIAN
OCEAN

ATLANTIC
OCEAN

PACIFIC
OCEAN

**ENERGY CONSUMPTION
PER CAPITA, 1994**
(kg of oil equivalent)

3,000 or more

2,000–2,999

1,000–1,999

500–999

200–499

Less than 200

Data not available

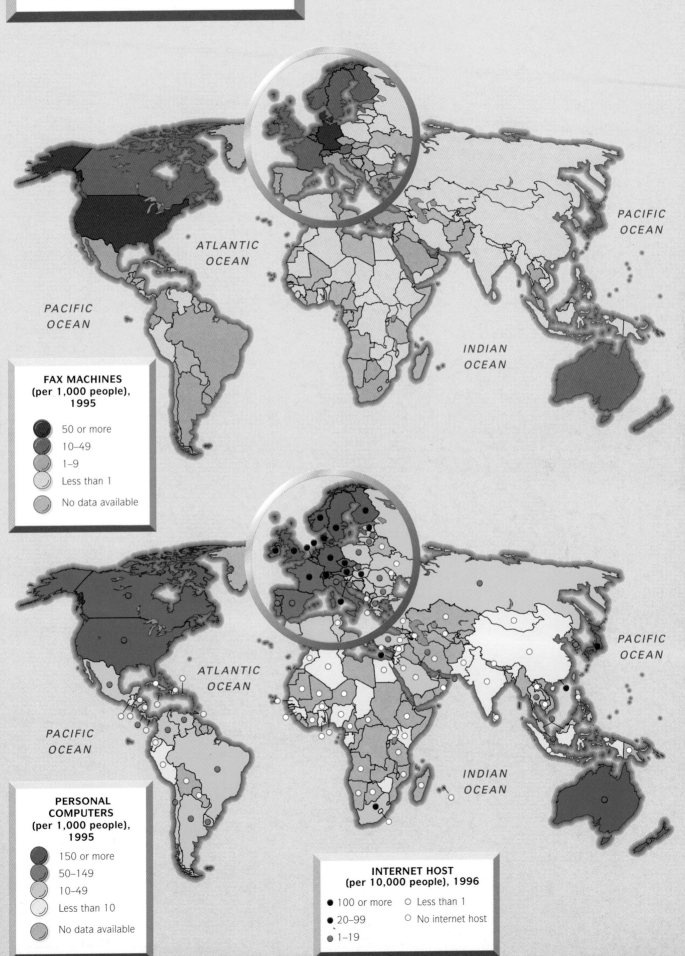

8 Telecommunications

PACIFIC OCEAN

ATLANTIC OCEAN

PACIFIC OCEAN

INDIAN OCEAN

PACIFIC OCEAN

**FAX MACHINES
(per 1,000 people),
1995**

- 50 or more
- 10–49
- 1–9
- Less than 1
- No data available

PACIFIC OCEAN

ATLANTIC OCEAN

PACIFIC OCEAN

INDIAN OCEAN

PACIFIC OCEAN

**PERSONAL
COMPUTERS
(per 1,000 people),
1995**

- 150 or more
- 50–149
- 10–49
- Less than 10
- No data available

**INTERNET HOST
(per 10,000 people), 1996**

- 100 or more
- 20–99
- 1–19
- Less than 1
- No internet host

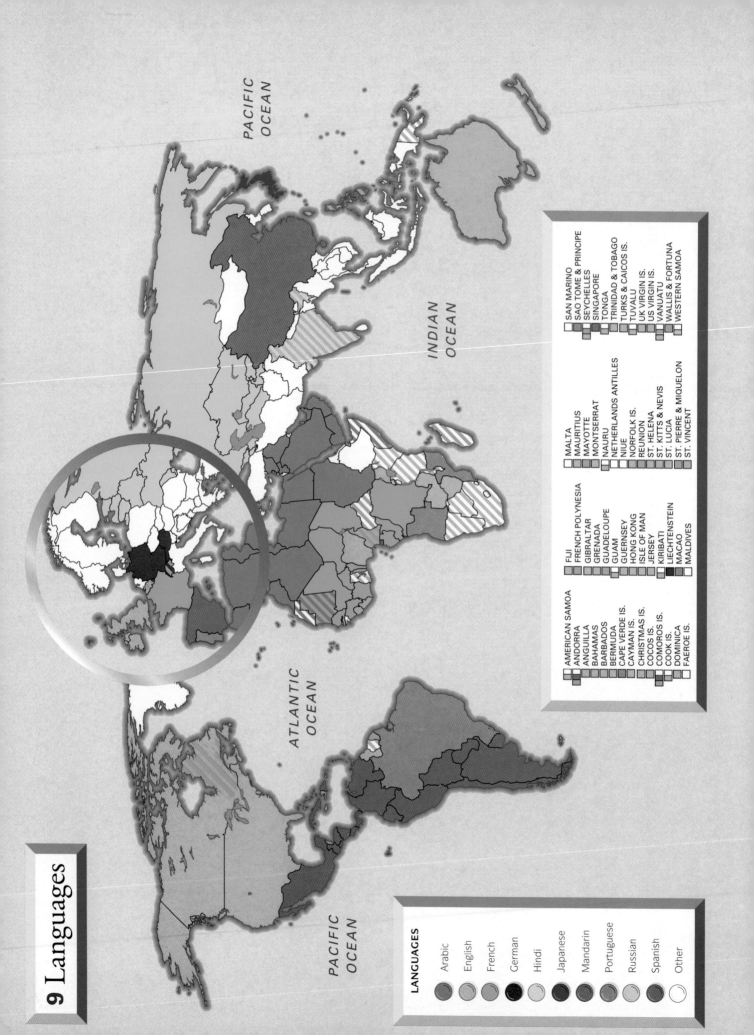

9 Languages

PACIFIC OCEAN

PACIFIC OCEAN

ATLANTIC OCEAN

INDIAN OCEAN

LANGUAGES

Arabic
English
French
German
Hindi
Japanese
Mandarin
Portuguese
Russian
Spanish
Other

AMERICAN SAMOA
ANDORRA
ANGUILLA
BAHAMAS
BARBADOS
BERMUDA
CAPE VERDE IS.
CAYMAN IS.
CHRISTMAS IS.
COCOS IS.
COMOROS IS.
COOK IS.
DOMINICA
FAEROE IS.

FIJI
FRENCH POLYNESIA
GIBRALTAR
GRENADA
GUADELOUPE
GUAM
GUERNSEY
HONG KONG
ISLE OF MAN
JERSEY
KIRIBATI
LIECHTENSTEIN
MACAO
MALDIVES

MALTA
MAURITIUS
MAYOTTE
MONTSERRAT
NAURU
NETHERLANDS ANTILLES
NIUE
NORFOLK IS.
REUNION
ST. HELENA
ST. KITTS & NEVIS
ST. LUCIA
ST. PIERRE & MIQUELON
ST. VINCENT

SAN MARINO
SAO TOME & PRINCIPE
SEYCHELLES
SINGAPORE
TONGA
TRINIDAD & TOBAGO
TURKS & CAICOS IS.
TUVALU
UK VIRGIN IS.
US VIRGIN IS.
VANUATU
WALLIS & FORTUNA
WESTERN SAMOA

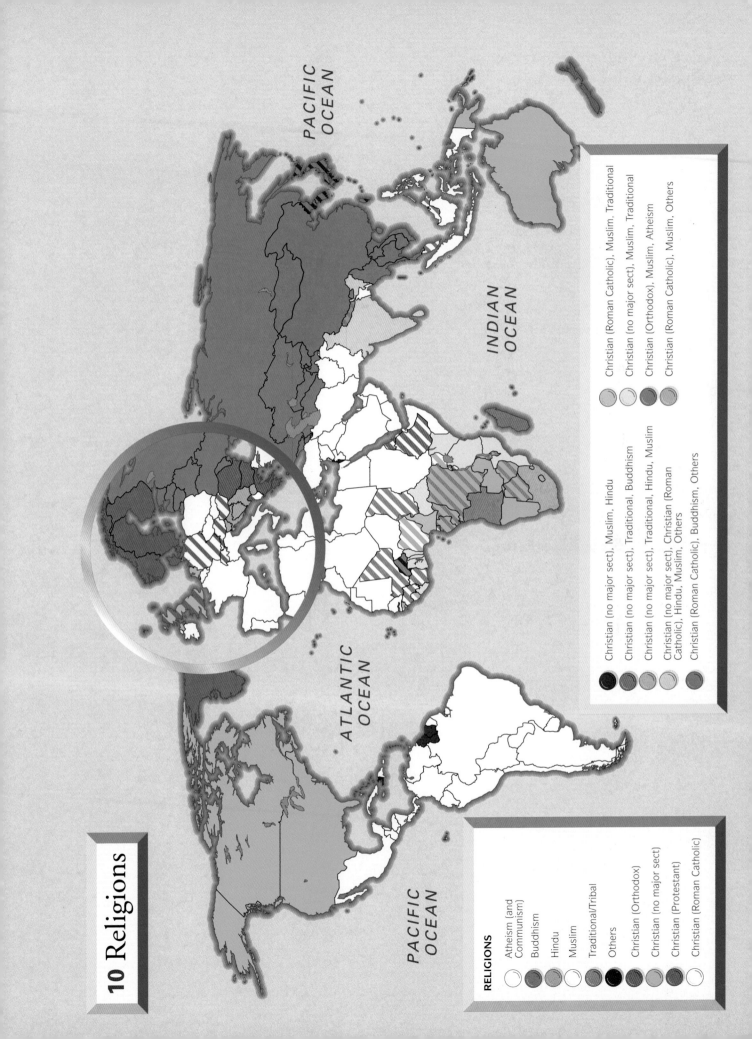

10 Religions

RELIGIONS

- Atheism (and Communism)
- Buddhism
- Hindu
- Muslim
- Traditional/Tribal
- Others
- Christian (Orthodox)
- Christian (no major sect)
- Christian (Protestant)
- Christian (Roman Catholic)

Christian (no major sect), Muslim, Hindu
Christian (no major sect), Traditional, Buddhism
Christian (no major sect), Traditional, Hindu, Muslim
Christian (no major sect), Christian (Roman Catholic), Hindu, Muslim, Others
Christian (Roman Catholic), Buddhism, Others

Christian (Roman Catholic), Muslim, Traditional
Christian (no major sect), Muslim, Traditional
Christian (Orthodox), Muslim, Atheism
Christian (Roman Catholic), Muslim, Others

PACIFIC OCEAN

ATLANTIC OCEAN

INDIAN OCEAN

PACIFIC OCEAN

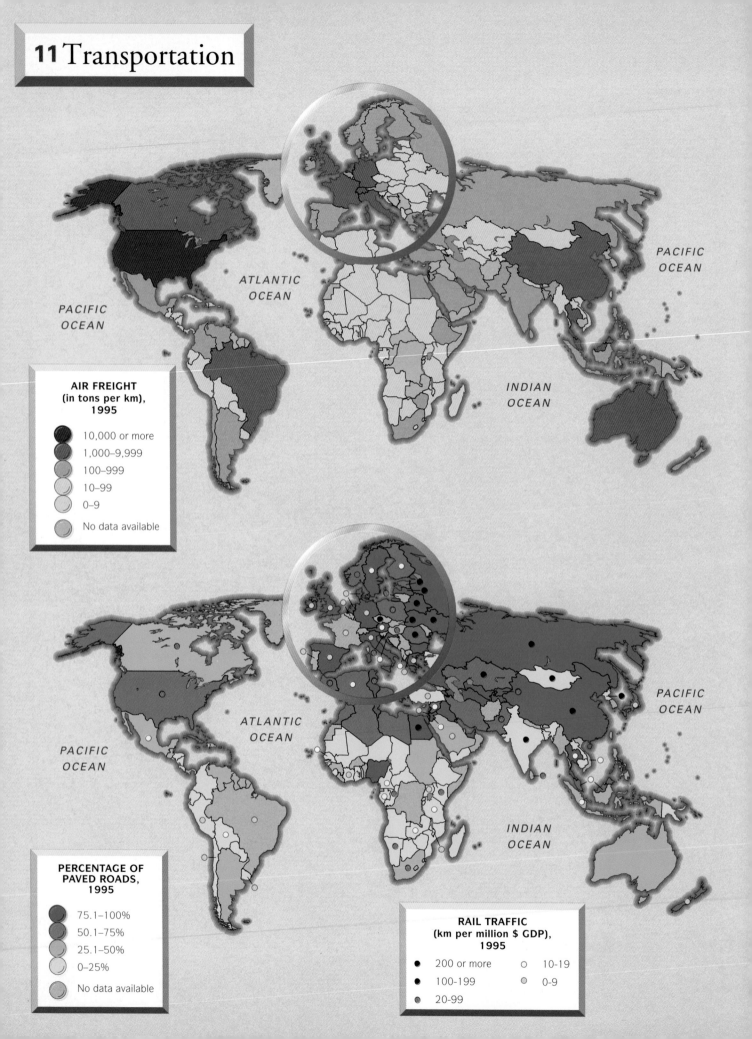

11 Transportation

AIR FREIGHT
(in tons per km),
1995

- 10,000 or more
- 1,000–9,999
- 100–999
- 10–99
- 0–9
- No data available

PACIFIC
OCEAN

ATLANTIC
OCEAN

PACIFIC
OCEAN

INDIAN
OCEAN

PACIFIC
OCEAN

ATLANTIC
OCEAN

PACIFIC
OCEAN

INDIAN
OCEAN

PERCENTAGE OF
PAVED ROADS,
1995

- 75.1–100%
- 50.1–75%
- 25.1–50%
- 0–25%
- No data available

RAIL TRAFFIC
(km per million $ GDP),
1995

- 200 or more
- 100-199
- 20-99
- 10-19
- 0-9

EXHIBIT 1: Size of the Japanese Jeans Market

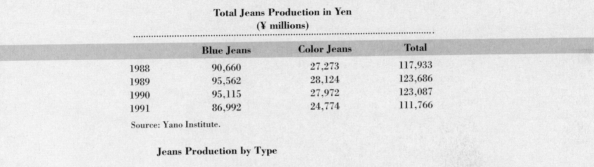

	Units of Total Jeans Production					
	Blue Jeans		Color Jeans		Total Jeans	
	Units	Growth	Units	Growth	Units	Growth
1987	36,924		15,186		52,110	
1988	43,274	17.2	12,904	(15.0)	56.178	7.8
1989	45,614	5.4	13,310	3.2	58,924	4.9
1990	45,401	(0.4)	13,238	(0.5)	58,639	(0.5)
1991	43,864	(3.4)	12,946	(2.2)	56,810	(3.1)

Source: Japanese Jeans Manufacturing Association (JJMA)

Notes: These numbers include imports, but not exports, thus are an appropriate proxy for market size. Also, these production quantities are more than LSJ estimates based on annual consumer surveys. For example, in 1991, LSJ estimates the total market size to be 45 million pairs, while the JJSM indicates 25% more. As JJMA's figure is based on self reporting by each of the jeans manufacturers, it is likely to be inflated over the actual sales quantity.

Total Jeans Production in Yen
(¥ millions)

	Blue Jeans	Color Jeans	Total
1988	90,660	27,273	117,933
1989	95,562	28,124	123,686
1990	95,115	27,972	123,087
1991	86,992	24,774	111,766

Source: Yano Institute.

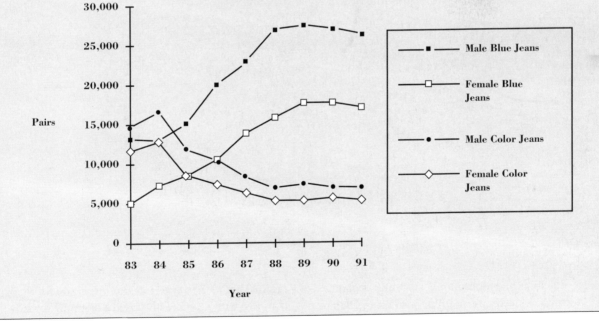

Jeans Production by Type

was fierce competition for market share with the five other large brands in the jeans market: Lee, Wrangler, Edwin, Big John and Bobson, due to the fact that all of the brands marketed similar product lines (emphasizing basic blue denim jeans, followed by other basic jeans, fashion jeans and chino pants) targeted at essentially the same customer segment. Also, all the American brands marketed their products by emphasizing the image of Americana.

Sales figures for the six largest jeans manufacturers are given in Exhibit 2. These figures show that the market share of the three large domestic Japanese brands,

EXHIBIT 2: Sales and Income Data for Jeans Manufacturers

Sales of Top Six Jeans Brands (¥ million)						
	1988	1989	1990	1991	1992	1993E
LEVI'S	15,425	21,508	28,855	35,056	37,626	38,600
Edwin (incl Lee)	30,342	33,579	38,250	38,534	37,099	
Lee			5,000(e)	6,300(e)	6,500(e)	10,000
Wrangler	11,715	13,550	15,367	16,972	17,847	
Big John	13,939	16,472	18,163	17,674	17,421	18,400
Bobson*	13,190	15,578	18,187	18,277	16,403	
Other	90,439	98,674	103,689	108,363	111,327	
Total	175,050	199,361	222,511	234,886	237,723	

Net Income of Top Five Jeans Manufacturers (¥ million)						
	1988	1989	1990	1991	1992	1993E
LEVI'S	3,585	4,421	6,124	7,058	6,532	6,280
Edwin (incl. Lee)	2,592	3,445	3,365	3,045	3,039	
Wrangler	596	631	1,118	1,127	802	
Big John	881	1,358	827	781	346	
Bobson	531	812	1,413	883	346	1,250
Other	1,814	3,023	2,380	2,416	925	
Total	9,999	13,690	15,227	15,310	3,141	
					14,785	

Return on Sales of Top Five Jeans Manufacturers (%)						
	1988	1989	1990	1991	1992	1993E
LEVI'S	23.2	20.6	21.2	20.1	17.4	16.3
Edwin (incl. Lee)	8.5	10.3	8.8	7.9	8.2	
Wrangler	5.1	4.7	7.3	6.6	4.5	
Big John	6.3	8.2	4.6	4.4	2.0	6.8
Bobson	4.0	5.2	7.8	4.8	5.6	
Other	2.0	3.1	2.3	2.2	2.8	
Total	5.7	6.9	6.8	6.5	6.2	

Notes: (1) Includes sales of jeans and tops.
(2) Bobson merged its sales affiliates in 1990, therefore, the financial statement has not been published since then. The figures since 1990 are taken from a report by the Yano Institute.
(3) Since Edwin does not break out sales of Lee brand, Lee sales numbers are estimates provided by LSJ.
(4) 1993 estimates for LEVI'S and Lee provided by LSJ. 1993 Big John figures estimated by Big John.

Source: Company Financial Statements. Yano Institute.

Edwin, Big John and Bobson was currently declining. LSJ, however, moved up from fifth position in 1986 to second position following Edwin in 1990 with a market share of almost 13%, and in 1991 LSJ became the top selling brand with approximately 15% of total jeans sales.

Following is a brief description of each of LSJ's major competitors.

EDWIN In addition to marketing its own brand of jeans, Edwin, the largest domestic manufacturer, also marketed Lee jeans under a license agreement with VF Corporation, the U.S. company which owns the Lee brand. Edwin wanted to increase market share of its original brand, however, Lee was important for them to compete with Levi's. This posed a dilemma for Edwin, since the Lee brand was cannibalizing the Edwin brand. In 1992, for the first time, LSJ exceeded Edwin in the total sales amount as shown in Exhibit 2. The figures for Edwin include revenues from Lee and Liberto brands. Edwin was also planning to sell a new Italian brand called Fiorucci beginning in the autumn of 1992.

BIG JOHN Sales and net income were expected to increase after two consecutive years of decrease. This was due to the success of their new product line, the "antique collection." The company expected the blue jeans market to grow again in 1993. Since blue jeans was Big John's major product line, the company believed it was well positioned for growth in 1993. In May 1993, the company was to begin construction of a new headquarters which would enable it to effectively concentrate the cutting, distribution, trading, and kids clothes sections into one location.

WRANGLER JAPAN Wrangler, also a jeans brand of VF Corp., was produced and sold through a license agreement with Wrangler Japan, a joint venture between Mitsubishi and Toyo Boseki. Sales began to pick up in September 1992, especially in the women's jeans market which was growing at double digit rates.

BOBSON Bobson's sales target for 1993 was ¥20,000 million. The company had been incredibly successful in the women's jeans market. As a result, from October 1992 to January 1993, sales in that segment increased 40% over the same period of the previous year. The company expected 1993 to be a growth year.

Up to this point, Levi Strauss' U.S. competitor, VF Corporation, had chosen to operate in Japan solely under licensing arrangements. However, there was speculation that the VF Corporation was planning to shift its marketing strategy from licensing to direct sales. This could drastically change the competitive market in the near future. Market experts predicted that the Japanese jeans market would eventually be dominated by the three major American brands: Levi's, Lee, and Wrangler.

New Emerging Segments

In 1990, Wrangler Japan Inc. tried to reinforce its traditional image by marketing "revival jeans," which featured natural dye extracted from the indigo plant. These indigo blue jeans, named Vintage Wrangler, were made of 100% denim and hand dyed. They were priced at ¥30,000 (approx. $242.00), but were selling well.[3] LSJ also introduced reproductions of its 5033BSXX and 701SXX styles, popular in the 1950s and 1960s, which were priced at ¥48,000 ($384.00) in September 1991. Yet, it was reported that LSJ cannot make these jeans fast enough to satisfy the demand.[4]

On the other hand, well-preserved second-hand jeans were in high demand, some selling for more than ¥500,000 ($4,000.00). About 30 to 40 stores had

opened specializing in used jeans from the United States made in the 1940s, 1950s, and 1960s. One store owner indicated that the most popular items were priced slightly below ¥100,000 ($800.00).[5] However, the slowing growth in demand seemed to indicate that oversupply was becoming a problem and that the market was close to saturation. According to the National Sales Manager of LSJ, the second-hand trend was supported primarily by jeans enthusiasts and may not last long.

Sales of women's blue jeans registered a phenomenal 109% growth between 1985 and 1989, increasing from 8.5 million to 17.8 million pairs a year. With the forecast that the young men's market was stabilizing, all the companies were looking at the potential in the market for women's jeans, creating fierce competition in that category.[6]

Changing Distribution Channel

Unlike the U.S., Europe, and other countries in Southeast Asia, jeans sales in Japan were still predominantly through jeans specialty stores. In other countries, jeans specialty stores had already lost market share to large national chains (such as Sears and J.C. Penney's) and to discounters (such as Walmart and Kmart). The successful speciality stores in the US were those who had been able to develop their own brands, such as The Gap and The Limited.

Although there had not been a similar shift in the Japanese market (from specialty stores to national chains), the shift was occurring within the jeans speciality shop channel. The structure of this channel seemed to be changing with the emergence of a new type of jeans shop. Traditionally, jeans shops were located in urban areas and sold only jeans (both factors placing a constraint on store size). Recently, new chain stores had been built in the suburbs which were usually five to seven times larger and might carry other products besides jeans. These jeans stores had proliferated at the expense of the smaller jeans stores. Their success was partly a result of their emphasis on sales promotions, ability to stock a full line of products and the unique store designs. Two such chains, Marutomi and Chiyoda (the two largest shoe store chains), entered the jeans retail market four to five years ago and now boasted retail stores in excess of 200 each. This emer-

[3]"Fashions Come and Go, But Blue Jeans Never Fade," *The Nikkei Weekly*, August 17, 1991.

[4]"Vintage American Products Attract Japanese Rebels," *The Nikkei Weekly*, December 7, 1991.

[5]Ibid.

[6]"Fashions Come and Go . . .," op.cit.

gence of jeans specialty store chains had saved this category from losing market share following those in other countries.

In 1992, approximately 250 new stores were opened, most of which were large-scale suburban stores of the type described above. Even though the peak was over, an additional 230 stores were likely to open in 1993. This consists mainly of Chiyoda's 75 to 85 "Mac House" stores and Marutomi's 100 "From USA" stores. In some suburban areas, the increasing number of stores had started to stimulate competition for local market share. For example, as the city of Tsukuba, a growing suburban area outside of Tokyo, 10 jeans stores (including those under construction) ranging in size up to 4,500 square feet were clustered in 3.1 square miles. Many retailers, therefore, were attempting to differentiate themselves by increasing customer service and being more selective in what product lines they would carry. Yet, with the slowing down in the jeans market, compounded by the recession, the excessive increase in jeans retail space was worsening the inventory turnover leading to inventory surpluses.

Potential Impact on Pricing

Thus far, most of the distribution channels, including jeans specialty stores, department stores and even national chain stores, had maintained the suggested retail price. National chain stores such as Daiei and Itoh Yokado had discount stores as their affiliates, yet, these discount stores had different supply routes and sold different products. This enabled Daiei and Itoh Yokado to maintain the retail price suggested by jeans manufacturers.

A similar change in channel structure had occurred in the distribution of business suits, where sales of department stores and specialty stores in the cities had suffered due to the emergence of larger men's shops in the suburbs. In this case, price competition was increasing between the discount stores (the "category killer"), but not between the national chain stores as had occurred in past. National chain stores had not entered the price war but were stuck in the middle between the discount stores (at the low end) and the specialty and department stores (at the high end).

If this held true in the jeans industry, national chain stores would not likely begin competing on price. Also, department stores and traditional jeans specialty stores (with few stores) were unlikely to discount. However, the new jeans specialty stores with many outlets, giving them strong purchasing power against manufacturers, might begin competing on price. These stores, which have expanded rapidly, were experiencing increasing competition and inventory surpluses, creating a ripe environment for price competition. The eventual outcome depended somewhat on how jeans manufacturers would react to discounting, should it occur, and on the sales policies of traditional jeans specialty stores.

LEVI STRAUSS JAPAN K.K.

Overview

Levi Strauss entered Japan with the opening of a branch office of Levi Strauss (Far East) Limited (Hong Kong) in April of 1971. Prior to this, its presence was limited to a minimal level of sales generated by importers. The Hiratsuka Distribution Center was opened in November of 1973, and in June 1974, Levi Strauss began domestic production of jeans products.

In December of 1975, Levi Strauss began selling through wholesale agencies, in addition to its direct sales to retailers. Levi Strauss also began importing products from the U.S. in 1978. In the same year, the reporting line of the Japanese office was changed from Hong Kong to LSI headquarters in San Francisco.

In 1982, Levi Strauss Japan K.K. (LSJ) was established as an independent operating company. Another important milestone occurred in June of 1989, when 4.1 million shares of LSJ were listed on the Tokyo OTC market in an initial public offering. This sale brought in $80 million, while still leaving Levi Strauss with an 85% share of the Japanese company's equity.

LSJ's strategy has been to maintain consistency and a long-term view. With a strong emphasis on advertising, constant new product introduction in addition to traditional styles, systems development, good relationships with suppliers, contractors, wholesalers, and retailers, and personnel training, LSJ has successfully built its position in Japan.

This position is largely due to LSJ's marketing strategy described below.

1. Target young male customers and advertise extensively through TV commercials and men's magazines, creating the image that LEVI'S jeans is cool American casual wear.

2. In order to have extensive accessibility, contract with various kinds of sales outlets from small specialty jeans shops, mainly located in urban areas, to national chain stores which have larger sales space, mainly located in suburbs.

3. Provide not only the traditional jeans imported from the United States, but also new jeans which are in line with current fashion and sewn to fit Japanese physical features. See also Appendix 2 "The Jeaning of Japan" *Business Tokyo* (February 1991).

PERFORMANCE

LSJ experienced sluggish sales until around 1984. Since then year-on-year sales has been increasing by approximately 35% every year until it slowed down to 20% in 1991. The company expects this slower level of growth to continue in the short term. In 1991, LSJ sales were ¥35.056 billion with profits of ¥7.058 billion. LSJ is planning to raise its market share to cover 20% by fiscal 1995.

LSJ experienced a decrease in profit in 1992, due to an increase in indirect marketing costs, including depreciation from investment on the distribution center and system development. Yet, LSJ still posts an impressive 17.4% return on sales, far higher than its competitors, and nearly three times the industry average. In 1993, the company expects sales growth to be moderate, therefore it expects a further decrease in net income.

Employing the strategy described above, LSJ successfully increased sales volume through stimulating the jeans market, It enjoys constant demand not subject to the whims of fashion or the changing season. LSJ has been successful in establishing the reputation of high quality products and brand image, allowing them to sell higher end products than their competitors. This high quality, premium product strategy was successful since it capitalizes on the Japanese economy (with one of the highest GNP per capita and significant growth).

On the cost side, LSJ is very efficient in the sense that it does not have a factory requiring huge capital expenditure, but instead, contracts out all its production in Japan. As a result, it does not have to worry about potential costs associated with downtime, equipment improvement, and workers compensation both in monetary and non-monetary terms. Moreover, LSJ has a very small sales force to cover all of Japan. As a result, LSJ's sales-to-employee ratio is ¥180 million ($1.4 million), which is roughly three times the average of its rivals.[7] Another strength of LSJ is its no debt strategy to alleviate risk due to interest rate fluctuations. Since its IPO on the Tokyo Stock Exchange, the stock price has been constantly increasing to the current P/E ratio of 50.[8]

Products

Product lines sold by LSJ consist of tops (shirts, jackets and sweatshirts), men's and women's basic jeans, other basic jeans and fashion jeans. There are approximately 18 kinds of men's basic jeans (excluding multiple colors), 10 kinds of women's basic jeans, 20 kinds of other basic jeans (including 5 for women), and several fashion jeans. Other jeans consist of trendy jeans products and fashion jeans consist of cotton (non-denim) pants. The sales breakdown is as follows: 20% from tops, 20% from women's jeans, 40% from basic men's jeans and 20% from the remainder.

Belts, accessories, shoes, socks, bags and kid's jeans are sold by another company under a license agreement. In addition, apart from traditional styles, product managers in LSJ design new styles which are in line with the fashion at the time. New products are introduced twice a year in spring and in autumn. Occasionally, product innovations developed for the Japanese market are later introduced into other markets. This was the case for "stone-washed" denim jeans and the Dockers line, which were successfully introduced in the U.S. after being developed and introduced in Japan.[9]

While LSJ does not own its own production facilities in Japan, all its domestically produced clothing is made by contracted factories which produce only Levi Strauss products. These contractors sew jeans products from denim purchased by LSJ from various domestic textile manufacturers and from trading companies. Currently, the domestic production accounts for 50% of the total products sold in Japan, while 30% is imported from the United States and 20% from Southeast Asia, mainly from factories in the Philippines.

It is interesting that until 1978 the company sold only domestic- and Asian-made jeans products in

---

[7]"Fundamentals Lend More-Than Casual Look," *The Nikkei Weekly*, September 14, 1991.

[8]Ibid.

[9]Geoffrey Duin, "Levi's Won't Fade in the Japanese Market," *Tokyo Business Today*, April 1990, p. 46.

Japan. Then realizing the importance of having the original U.S.-made jeans, the company started to sell some U.S.-made products (specifically the 501 product line) in Japan. According to Mr. Ohki it was crucial to send customers a message that LSJ is selling "real" American products. Yet, the domestically made jeans products actually fit Japanese bodies better, which partially contributed to the company's success in the early years.

Distribution

The company first established its distribution center in Hiratsuka, Kanagawa in November 1973, two years after establishing operations in Japan. However, LSJ recently reconstructed its distribution center in order to enhance customer service by improving the quality and quantity of warehouse and shipping facilities. In October 1990, it completed the first stage of reconstruction, including installation of the computer controlled warehouse system named AS/RS (Automated Storage and Retrieval System). Automation of picking and shipping areas, which are controlled along with the automated warehouse, was completed in May 1991. These renovations greatly improved the storage capacity and more than doubled the daily shipping capability. They also enabled the company to handle small quantity, frequent, short-term delivery orders. In addition, LSJ has installed automated ordering systems at some of the national chain stores, allowing for better inventory control and quicker response.

The company has two distribution channels, one is direct sales by sales personnel, and the other is wholesale by sales agencies. Currently, 53% of total sales comes from direct sales made by 40 LSJ sales personnel located in the four sales offices. Using 1991 sales data to calculate the revenue generated by the direct sales force, the average salesperson generated ¥464.5 million (approximately $3.7 million) of revenue in that year. This demonstrates the extraordinary productivity of LSJ's sales force. The remaining 43% comes from 13 domestic sales agencies.

Sales of LSJ products occur through four kinds of sales outlets. LSJ's sales personnel and sales agencies both have contact with these key outlets consisting of: (1) major nation-wide jeans shops such as Big American and Eiko; (2) major nation-wide department stores, from the prestigious Mitsukoshi Department Store to Marui, a department store specifically targeted to the younger generation; (3) national chain stores such as Daiei, Itoh Yokado, and Seiyu; and (4) nation-wide men's shops such as Iseya. Most of LSJ's sales occur in jeans shops (70%), with the remaining sales fairly evenly split among department stores (12%), national chain stores (10%) and other stores (8%).

Currently, LEVI'S were sold at fewer sales outlets than some of their domestic competitors. For example, 5,000 stores carry the LEVI'S brand, while more than 10,000 stores sell the Edwin brand. Although LSJ receives a higher percentage of its sales through traditional jeans shops (70%) than the market overall (60%), there is very little difference between LSJ distribution patterns and that of the other top brands.

LSJ's effort to be a Japanese company can be observed from its strategy of building good relationships with its sales outlets. LSJ provides various services to each outlet store, from giving advice on product displays and in-store arrangements to organizing seminars and handing out sales manuals. Japanese department stores rely heavily on the manufacturers to provide sales staff, forcing LSJ to place 160 employees in department stores as sales clerks. However, this necessity allows LSJ, and other Japanese manufacturing companies, to gather information regarding customer preferences.

Pricing

Historically, LSJ was positioned as a price leader, charging 15 to 20% higher than competitors for similar jeans products. However, about 10 years ago, competitors raised their prices to match LEVI'S (pricing of LEVI'S remained flat), allowing LSJ to greatly increase their market share. Today, compared to competitive brands such as Edwin, Lee and Wrangler, LSJ has a similar price range for its jeans products. Even so, the average product price which LSJ's customers pay (¥7,900 = approximately $63.20) is about 5 to 10% higher than the average price received by competitors. This is due to the fact that LSJ customers are willing to buy more expensive types of jeans.

Wholesale price varies by distributor due to the rebate scheme. However, the average price charged to sales outlets is 55% of retail, while sales agents pay about 50% of retail on average. LSJ charges a higher wholesale price to the department stores in order to offset the cost of LSJ employees who work as sales personnel in those stores. However, there is no significant difference in retail price across the various distribution channels, since retail outlets so far have maintained the suggested retail price.

EXHIBIT 3: LSJ Magazine Advertising 1991 and 1992

1991 LSJ Magazine Advertisements			
Magazine	Type	Readership Profile	Number of LSJ Ads. 1/91-12/91
Popeye	Fashion	Young males, 18–23	22
H D Press	Fashion	Young males, 18–23	24
Men's Non No	Fashion	Young males, 18–23	20
Fineboys	Fashion	Young males, 18–23	15
1992 LSJ Magazine Advertisements			
Magazine	Type	Readership Profile	Number of LSJ Ads. 1/92-10/92
Popeye	Fashion	Young males, 18–23	18
H D Press	Fashion	Young males, 18–23	17
Men's Non No	Fashion	Young males, 18–23	17
Fineboys	Fashion	Young males, 18–23	11
Asahi Weekly	News	White collar males, all ages	1
Shincho Weekly	News	White collar males, all ages	1
Bunshun Weekly	News	White collar males, all ages	1
Bart	News	Young, white collar males	1
Non No	Fashion	Young single females	1
Pia	Entertainment	Young males/females, <35	1
Dime	New Product Intro	Affluent males, 30-40	1
Sarai	Housekeeping	Married females, 25-35	1
Number	Sports	Males, all ages	1

Advertising and Promotion

Similar to the strategy employed by Levi Strauss in the U.S., LSJ emphasizes a pull strategy spending heavily on advertising to increase demand. Since 1976, LSJ has been spending approximately 6% of total sales on advertising (TV and print) compared to an industry average of 4%.[10] It uses James Dean as an advertising character in order to establish the image of the young, active American. Its target customer has traditionally been young men, aged 16 to 29, who have grown up with, and maintain a good image towards, American products.

When LSJ first launched its campaign in 1984 with the slogan "*Heroes Wear LEVI'S*," its main purpose was to increase the awareness of the LEVI'S brand. The ads showed movie scenes in which James Dean, John Wayne, Steve McQueen and Marilyn Monroe wore jeans, while a famous movie announcer Mr. Haruo Mizuno, read the slogan. In 1985, the slogan was changed to "*My Mind, LEVI'S*" and, in 1987, the "*The Original LEVI'S*," both of which were intended to project traditional American values and a pioneering spirit with a more familiar nuance. The current slogan, "*Re-Origin*" was launched in 1989 to emphasize the revival of traditional jeans. Since the very beginning, the company has recognized the Japanese purchase mentality towards imported goods—Japanese are willing to choose imports and even pay more for these goods—and has been maximizing its marketing by appealing to this psychology.

LSJ focused on TV commercials and magazine advertisements which accounts for 65% of the total promotional budget. Of this advertising expense, approximately 70% was used for TV commercials, and 30% for magazine advertisements. The company used mass media effectively based on differences in features. For TV commercials, LSJ used an advertising agency in order to maximize reach and communicate the company's image to a larger audience. In contrast, the company created its magazine advertisements mostly in house, since the goal of the magazine ads was to increase consumers' understanding of its products and to appeal strongly to certain target customer segments (see Exhibit 3 for the audiences targeted). In terms of cooperative advertising with sales outlets, LSJ was consistent with other Japanese manufacturing companies which tended not to use this method as much as U.S. companies.

LSJ also published seasonal product catalogs named "LEVI'S BOOK" and placed them in outlet stores in order to introduce new products. Two million

[10]"Fundamentals Lend More-Than Casual Look," *The Nikkei Weekly*, September 14, 1991.

LSJ Promotional Expenditures

Point-of-
Purchase
25%

LEVI'S Book
10%

Television
50%

Magazines
15%

copies of this catalog were produced twice a year accounting for 10% of LSJ's promotional expenditures. The remaining 25% of promotional expense was used for direct communication with customers at the point of purchase. By these consistent advertising and promotional activities, the company was trying to increase (1) awareness of the LEVI'S brand, (2) understanding of its products, and (3) the willingness to buy.

FUTURE CHALLENGES

LSJ's major challenges, resulting from the changing market and retail environment were:

- how to continue to grow faced with a contracting market;

- how to respond to the changing structure of the distribution channel; and

- how to develop and implement a pricing strategy given the current retail environment.

First, the traditional market for jeans in Japan had peaked and was likely to continue to shrink or remain flat. The number of young people was decreasing due to the lower birth rate, shifting the demographics to an older population. For the last twelve years, the birth rate each year, had been the lowest ever recorded, a trend which was expected to continue.[11] Also, the average frequency of jeans purchased per person per year in Japan was a meager 0.5 compared to the 1.5 in the US.[12] This was due to the fact that high schools in Japan require students to wear uniforms, so there was significantly less time and chance to wear jeans. These

[11]1992 Statistics Handbook. Statistics Bureau, Management and Coordination Agency; Ministry of Health and Welfare.

[12]"Fundamentals Lend More-Than Casual Look," *The Nikkei Weekly*, September 14, 1991.

trends would further impact the market size of the young male segment, the traditional market which jeans manufacturers (including LSJ) have targeted.

In addition, Mr. Ohki brought up the issue of selection criteria for retailers and sales agents. The distribution channel was undergoing structural changes, and Mr. Ohki believed that LSJ needed to evaluate and possibly revise their distribution strategy. LSJ was very selective in choosing its retailers and had historically focused their distribution on traditional urban jeans specialty shops. However, there were many new, large stores opening in the suburbs which were carrying jeans, amongst other items. Although LSJ did sell their jeans in some of these new stores, they had not pursued this new channel as aggressively as some of their competitors.

Mr. Chappell realized that increasing the number of stores would improve LSJ's reach and possibly help to stimulate the overall market. However, this could have a serious impact on LSJ's image. LSJ had spent years developing a premium product image which had catapulted them to market leader. Besides their product and advertising strategies, this image had also been cultivated by their selectivity in choosing retail outlets and sales agents. Not only did this ensure that LEVI'S would have a good image with the consumer, but it also was the only way LSJ could influence the retail price. Mr. Chappell feared that a decision to expand the number of retail outlets would have a negative impact on LEVI'S prices and might even result in discounting. This could seriously affect the premium product image LSJ had worked hard to foster over the years.

DISCUSSION QUESTIONS

1. What are the key success factors (KSFs) in the Japanese marketplace?

2. To what extent do the Levi Strauss' FSAs and CSAs match the KSF's? How has Levi's been able to leverage its country-of-origin to become a leading brand? Can other American jeans do the same?

3. How would you explain the apparent success of LSJ's advertising campaign stressing American values in Japan?

4. List the pros and cons of the different distribution alternatives facing LSJ. Which one do you think has the best chance of succeeding?

5. Would you retain the premium positioning of Levi's in Japan? Why/Why not?

Case 3.3

Colgate-Palmolive: Cleopatra in Quebec?

The Canadian launch extravaganza in February 1986 began with cocktails served by hostesses dressed like Cleopatra, the queen of ancient Egypt. Then followed a gala dinner with a dramatic, multimedia presentation of the new brand, ending with the award-winning commercial and these words:

> Today the memory comes alive,
> a new shape rises up, a new texture,
> a new standard of beauty care
> worthy of the name it bears,
> Today the memory frozen in ancient stones comes alive . . .
> Cleopatra.

Each of the retailer guests had received an exclusive, golden, three-dimensional pyramid invitation to the launch, and expectations were high. The retailers were sick of discounted brands, all basically the same, and were looking for something different and exciting. Finally, the new soap Cleopatra was revealed to the audience of nearly 1,000—a huge turnout by Canadian standards—and the response was overwhelmingly positive.

So enthusiastic was the audience, that by the end of the evening the Colgate-Palmolive salespeople had received orders for 2,000 cases. Bill Graham, the divisional vice president of marketing for Canada, and Steve Boyd, group product manager, agreed that the night had been a grand success and that Cleopatra's future looked very rosy.

THE FRENCH EXPERIENCE WITH CLEOPATRA

Cleopatra soap was first introduced in France in November 1984. By May of the following year, the brand had reached an amazing market share of 10%, despite its 23% price premium compared with other brands. In fact, Colgate-Palmolive's biggest problem was keeping up with demand. By the end of 1985, market share shot up to 15%. Cleopatra had actually become the number one brand in France.

Cleopatra's success in France received a great deal of publicity within the organization. Encouraged by the experience, the Global Marketing Group, situated in New York, set out to find other markets for the product. They reasoned that if Cleopatra had worked well in France, it should do likewise elsewhere in the world.

Canada, especially French-speaking Quebec, seemed like an obvious choice to the Global Marketing Group. At the annual update meeting in New York, the group strongly recommended to the Canadian management that a test be done in Canada to see if Cleopatra was a proposition for them.

THE REACTION OF THE CANADIAN SUBSIDIARIES TO CLEOPATRA

The idea of a market test for Cleopatra was greeted with mixed feelings by the Canadians. Some managers, such as Stan House, assistant product manager, were enthusiastic, especially because they knew that Steve Boyd, group product manager for Canada, was convinced it would work. In Boyd's opinion, Canada could show the people in New York that the same formula would do as well or even better than in France.

Other managers, like Ken Johnson, were more skeptical. They resented having a brand thrust on them. Johnson believed that what Canada really needed was a strong "national" brand, and he doubted that Cleopatra could ever be that.

Nonetheless, a decision was made to proceed and test the Canadian market. One fundamental question had to be answered: Was there reasonable certainty that Cleopatra would be accepted by consumers in Quebec? Two types of research, both conducted in Toronto, tried to answer that question. The first study was among a "super group" of articulate professional women, specially chosen and brought together for the event. They were introduced to the product, its price,

This case was prepared by Professor Sandra Vandermerwe, with the assistance of J. Carter Powis (MBA, IMI 1988–89). Copyright © 1990 by the International Institute for Management Development (IMD), Lausanne, Switzerland. Not to be used or reproduced without permission.

and the advertising; then they were asked to discuss their likes and dislikes openly. On balance, the results were positive; the women seemed to like the soap and the concept.

The second research study used more typical consumers; these people were exposed to the proposed advertising for Cleopatra and then were asked whether they would buy it. Fifty percent said they would. They were also given a bar of soap to try at home and were phoned a week later for their reactions. Sixty-four percent of the group who used the soap said they would buy Cleopatra as soon as it was available on the shelves.

The research confirmed the feelings of Boyd, and most of the marketing team in Toronto that Cleopatra could indeed be a winner. Immediately, plans were made for an early launch the following year.

The Canadian marketing team was determined not to allow Cleopatra to go to war with all the other brands. They felt something had to be done to reverse the negative profit trends that had been brewing in the industry for some time. This was the ideal opportunity. They would position Cleopatra as the premium-quality, premium-priced soap and differentiate it from all the others. They wanted to avoid having a price war at all costs.

SOME BACKGROUND ON COLGATE-PALMOLIVE CANADA

Colgate-Palmolive, a multinational consumer packaged goods corporation operating in 58 countries, marketed a variety of personal care and household products worldwide. With annual sales of $5.7 billion, many of its brands were global leaders. For example, Colgate toothpaste was number one and Palmolive soap was number two in the world in their respective markets.

The Canadian subsidiary opened its doors in 1912, and since then had grown into a $250-million-a-year corporation. Together with two competitors, Procter & Gamble and Lever (both $1-billion subsidiaries of their parent companies), they dominated the aggressive and innovative personal care and household market sectors in Canada.

Colgate-Palmolive Canada manufactured and marketed a wide range of personal care and household products inside Canada and also supplied brands to the United States and Puerto Rico. The major products marketed in Canada were as follows:

Personal care products	Household products
Colgate toothpaste	Palmolive liquid soap
Colgate toothbrushes	Palmolive automatic dishwasher
Colgate mouth rinse	soap
Halo shampoo	ABC detergent
Irish Spring soap	Arctic Power detergent
Palmolive soap	Fab detergent
Cashmere Bouquet soap	Baggies food wrap
Cleopatra soap	Ajax cleanser
	Ajax all-purpose liquid cleanser

The Colgate-Palmolive head office and manufacturing facility were both located in a building in Toronto. Sales offices were in each of the six major regions across Canada, namely the Maritimes, Quebec, Ontario, the Prairies, Alberta, and British Columbia.

Marketing was organized at the head office under a product management system, whereby each person was responsible for a brand or group of brands and reported to a group product manager who, in turn, was responsible to the vice president of marketing. The brand managers made decisions on all aspects of marketing planning and execution, from market research to consumer and trade promotion. The product managers made sure that their brands received the needed resources from the head office.

THE STATE OF THE CANADIAN SOAP MARKET

In 1986, the soap market in Canada was worth $105 million to manufacturers. This revenue figure was projected to grow by 4 to 5% in the years ahead. The Canadian soap market was probably one of the most competitive in which Colgate-Palmolive competed—a fact that even the average consumer could see each time he or she turned on a television set or opened a magazine.

The competition would continue at the store level, where limited shelf space was at a premium. Because of the intense competition, retailers were all-powerful. They literally could pick and choose with whom to do business. Inside the store, a brand's fate was in their hands; they decided what to promote, which prices to cut, and how to allocate shelf space.

Competition was extremely fierce for some of the following reasons:

1. Volume growth in the market had slowed and coincided with the growth of the Canadian population (1.0–1.5% annually). No further rapid expansion was expected.

2. The only method of survival for the many new brands and new variants of existing brands was to steal share from other products in the market.

3. Competition from no-name and private label products had increased.

4. Technological advances were slowing, and relaunches were increasingly "cosmetic" in nature (new color, new fragrance, etc.).

5. Consumers had a group of "acceptable" brands that they were willing to purchase (usually 3 or 4 in number). Buying decisions within this group were based on price. There were 15 mainstream brands, along with 20 to 25 minor ones, fighting to become one of these "acceptable" choices.

6. Trends toward larger bundle packs had developed (more than one bar of soap packaged and sold as a unit), reducing the number of purchases each consumer made during the year. For example, in the skin care segment, twinpacks (two bars sold together) were becoming the norm, whereas the refreshment segment was dominated by three- and four-packs, and the utility segment by four-, five-, and six-packs.

7. Competition was based on price, as there were no real competitive advantages or meaningful differences among most brands, and because of increased pressure from the retail trade to meet competitive deals and prices.

8. Liquid soaps had entered the market and held an 8% share. Based on current consumer reaction, the maximum share was not expected to grow beyond 10% in the future.

For most consumers, "a soap is a soap is a soap," with few perceivable differences among brands. Bombarded by advertising in every conceivable type of media, consumers mainly bought the "acceptable brands" on price. Therefore, becoming and staying an "acceptable brand" was where the ongoing competitive battle among the various brands took place.

The soap market was divided into three distinct groups: the skin care segment, the refreshment segment, and the utility segment (see Exhibit 1). The skin care market was the largest of the three segments, which were split as follows:

	1985 (%)	1986 (%)	1987 (%)
Skin care	37.3	38.4	38.8
Refreshment	34.9	33.4	32.3
Utility (price)	27.8	28.2	28.9

EXHIBIT 1 Market Segments and Brand Advertising Claims, 1986

Segment	Brand	Advertising copy claim
Skin care	Dove	For softer, smoother skin, try Dove for 7 days
	Camay	Skin care as individual as you are
	Caress	The body bar with bath oil
	Cleopatra	New soap: rich as a cream, sensual as a perfume
	Aloe & Lanolin	Good for skin because it has natural ingredients
	Palmolive	Not advertised
Refreshment	Zest	Zest leaves you feeling cleaner than soap
	Coast	Coast picks you up and pulls you through the day
	Irish Spring	Fresh fragrance, double deodorancy
	Dial	You will feel clean and refreshed all day long
Utility (price)	Jergens	Not advertised
	Woodbury	Not advertised
	Cashmere Bouquet	Not advertised
	Lux	Not advertised
	Ivory*	Ivory is 99 44/100 pure soap

*Ivory competes with different creative executions in each of the three segments.

Source: Colgate-Palmolive Canada.

Exhibit 3 contains details of market share for each of the three large companies and their competitors. Although there were at least 15 mainstream brands (Exhibit 2), only 4 had managed to create a really distinctive niche.

In the skin care segment, Dove had been advertised for years as the facial soap. It had a loyal customer base, mainly because of its unique formulation and moisturizing capabilities. Low on additives and scent, it was seen as the "Cadillac" of this segment and was priced accordingly.

Ivory was an "institution" in the Canadian soap market, with its 100-year heritage and ever-powerful "I use it because my mother used it" pure soap positioning. The market leader, it successfully competed with all three markets.

Irish Spring, made especially for men, did well in the male market as a refreshment soap, although females used it as well. Consumers associated its strong scent and high lathering capability with cleaning strength.

Zest was also positioned in the refreshment segment. Seen as the "family brand that gets you cleaner than soap," it was low in additives and perfume. It

EXHIBIT 2 Category Market Shares
(Quebec)

	1985	1986	1987 YTD*
Colgate-Palmolive			
Irish Spring	6.2	6.0	6.5
Palmolive	3.7	3.6	6.4
Cashmere Bouquet	3.3	3.4	2.8
Cleopatra	0.0	0.9	1.1
Total:	13.2	13.9	16.8
Lever			
Lux	4.3	6.0	8.3
Dove	7.1	9.6	10.8
Caress	1.5	1.7	2.9
Other	3.9	2.7	1.2
Total:	16.8	20.0	23.2
Procter & Gamble			
Ivory	28.2	24.9	22.9
Zest	4.9	6.1	4.7
Coast	5.6	5.5	6.4
Camay	6.4	5.3	2.6
Other	0.1	0.1	0.1
Total:	45.2	41.9	36.7
Jergens			
Aloe & Lanolin	2.4	3.2	2.6
Woodbury	0.3	0.8	1.4
Jergens	5.4	5.4	5.4
Total:	8.1	9.4	9.4
Canada Packers			
Dial	2.4	2.4	3.2
Other	0.1	0.0	0.0
Total:	2.5	2.4	3.2
Other	14.2	12.4	10.7

Note: Market share is calculated on an equivalent case basis.
*Year end is the October/November share period. Therefore, 1987 YTD
(year-to-date) is made up of two bimonthly share periods: December/
January and February/March.

Source: Colgate-Palmolive Canada.

especially appealed to people in "hard water" areas of the country. Its detergent formulation allowed it to make special claims against other brands, such as "it rinses clean and doesn't leave a soapy film."

THE QUEBEC MARKET

Quebec is Canada's second largest province in population and the largest in geographical size. The 6.7 million people (or 26% of Canada's total population) are clustered throughout the southern portion of this immense region, which is 2.5 times the size of France.

Unlike the other nine provinces whose populations are of British ancestry, Quebec has a population that came originally from France. In fact, over 80% of the 2.3 million households in Quebec list French as their mother tongue. Needless to say, with this unique culture, marketing strategies sometimes differ from those used in the rest of the country.

Quebec accounts for 28% of the Canadian soap market volume and is, therefore, slightly overdeveloped in proportion to the country's total population. The major brands and their positions in the Quebec market are similar to those throughout the rest of Canada. The exceptions are Zest, which does poorly because Quebec is mainly the soft-water market, and Lux, which has done extremely well due to its strong European image.

THE CANADIAN CLEOPATRA MARKETING STRATEGY

Cleopatra looked like an excellent prospect for Canada. Not only was it a premium quality product in all respects, but it complemented Colgate-Palmolive's Canadian product line and had a past history of success. If launched, the product line would include Irish Spring, well positioned and strongly niched in the refreshment segment; Cashmere Bouquet, performing well in the utility segment; Palmolive soap, positioned as the all-family skin care bar; and Cleopatra, the premium quality skin care brand worthy of competing with the segment leader, Dove.

After considering these facts as well as the positive research results from the two analyses, Colgate-Palmolive decided to launch Cleopatra as the "premium quality, premium priced beauty soap." The marketing team, however, decided that it would not be financially feasible to launch Cleopatra like any other soap, where ultimately its success would be determined by its ability to compete on price. Although the marketing team knew the risks, they wanted to avoid having to rely on retailers and being forced to offer large trade allowances and discounts. They wanted the demand to come directly from the consumers, by generating their interest in Cleopatra through strong media and consumer promotions.

This approach was very different from the industry norm, where manufacturers traditionally paid large sums of money to retailers just to get the product listed in their "accounts order books." Then, manufacturers would have to pay even more in discounts and allowances to have a showing in the retailers' weekly advertising fliers. Once management decided to forgo these payments, it was critical for the company to make the best possible media and consumer promotion schedule for the launch.

The company set an ambitious objective: a 4.5% market share for 1986; 100% distribution of the product with retail accounts; maximum shelf presence, defined as the same number of facings as the current segment leader Dove; proper shelf positioning, which meant being next to Dove; and, finally, maintaining Cleopatra's premium pricing strategy.

To make the strategy work, especially since targets were based on an 11-month first year, the company knew it had to get both consumers and salespeople enthusiastic about the brand. Therefore, it was essential to generate excitement from day one. The promotion had to be very powerful. In fact, it had to be so good that consumers would demand the brand and force retailers to stock it. That meant the emphasis would be on advertising. Television was chosen as the most obvious way to focus resources and create an impact and instant awareness among the target group—women between the ages of 18 and 49. The campaign, which the marketing team wanted to be "an event," began the first week in May.

The budget was set to make Cleopatra the number one spender in the entire soap market. The objective was clear to all: ensure that Cleopatra gets the most "share of voice" in its category in Quebec, which amounted to 15%. In other words, for every 100 minutes of advertising for soaps, 15 minutes would go to Cleopatra.

The Quebec TV commercial was the same one used in France, with one or two minor and hardly noticeable modifications. This commercial, shot in Rome on a very elaborate set, had been one of the most memorable aspects of the French marketing strategy. It showed the Egyptian Queen taking a perfumed bath. The feedback from consumer research in France had been particularly positive, and the commercial had received a number of awards for excellence.

Equally important in the marketing strategy was sales promotion, always popular with the average Canadian consumer. Since the team's research had established that 64% of the market would buy Cleopatra after trying it at home, the first and foremost aim was to be sure that people tried it. Thus the promotion campaign, scheduled to run from May to October, centered on the product being tried. Approximately 250,000 households in Quebec received free bar coupons that could be exchanged for a free bar of soap at the nearest store. All stores were fully informed.

There was also the "Cleopatra Gold Collection and Sweepstakes Promotion," which offered consumers a wide range of popular and fashionable costume jewelry at very reasonable prices. For example, one could send for a necklace and earrings that cost only $12.99. Consumers who bought the jewelry received forms and were automatically entered into the grand prize draw, a chance to win a Cleopatra-style, 14-karat gold necklace worth $3,500. Research among current brands on the market showed that mail-in offers and sweepstakes were very successful with consumers, and management had high hopes that this promotion would stimulate interest in the brand. The promotion began in August and ended with the draw in early January 1987.

Since Cleopatra had been positioned as the premium quality brand in soap, no discounts were offered. Single cartons were packed 48 to a case, at a price of $41.71. Cleopatra's pricing strategy was to be higher than Dove, historically the most expensive brand. (Comparative prices are shown in Exhibit 3.)

The product itself had been developed in France, with no changes made for the Canadian market. As it turned out, Cleopatra was the finest quality soap made by the company in Canada. Its unique formulation contained the best ingredients, including the equivalent of 15% beauty cream, which delivered a rich, creamy lather and was noticeably soft on the skin.

The perfume, blended in France, was said "to produce an unforgettable fragrance." The soap was also carved into a special shape to make it easy to hold and use. The Cleopatra logo was stamped on the ivory-colored bar—another differentiating feature intended to convey quality, luxury, and prestige. The bar was slightly larger than the French product, to conform with the other Canadian brands.

Each bar of soap came in its own gold-colored laminated carton, a difference from being wrapped in paper as in France. The laminated material was unique in that it not only reflected light, which made it stand

EXHIBIT 3 Price and Trade Discount Structure

	Cleopatra	Dove
Case size*	48 × 140g	48 × 140g
Case price	$41.71	$39.72
Unit cost	0.87	0.83
Regular selling price	1.29	1.19
Off-invoice allowance	—	3.00
Deal unit cost	—	0.77
Feature price	—	0.99

Note: The average manufacturer's price for Cleopatra was 87 cents per single bar, compared with an average manufacturer's price of 31 cents per single bar for all toilet soaps.

*Dove is also available in a twinpack (24 × 2 × 140g case size)

EXHIBIT 4 Performance to Date (Quebec)

	1986											1987		
	Feb.	Mar.	Apr.	May	June	July	Aug.	Sep.	Oct.	Nov.	Dec.	Jan.	Feb.	Mar.
Shipments (cases):														
Forecast (000s)	3.0	5.0	5.0	15.0	15.0	6.0	5.0	10.0	7.0	9.0	10.5	8.0	7.5	7.5
Actual (000s)	3.6	3.0	0.4	2.5	2.1	1.3	0.6	0.9	1.3	0.7	1.7	1.9	0.9	1.2
% Achieved	120	60	8	17	14	22	12	9	19	8	16	24	12	16
Market share[a]	0.1		0.7		1.1		1.7		1.8		1.1		1.1	
Distribution[b]	44		51		65		68		69		69		72	
Out-of-Stocks[c]	4		3		5		2		3		1		4	

[a]Bimonthly market share is calculated on an equivalent case basis (i.e., all brands' case packs are made equivalent based on weight, and market share is then calculated as a percentage of this base).
[b]Bimonthly percentage of accounts in Quebec where the brand is listed.
[c]Bimonthly percentage of accounts in Quebec where, at the time of audit, the brand was sold out.

Source: Colgate-Palmolive Canada.

out against the other brands on the shelves, but it also prevented the perfume from escaping.

THE RESULTS OF THE CANADIAN LAUNCH

Due to the launch, sales had started off with a bang. On the first evening along, 67% of the first month's objectives had been achieved. But from then on, the brand started missing its targets.

Steve Boyd had warned his team not to expect an instant miracle. After all, the Quebec soap market was one of the most competitive, and it took time to establish a brand. As the retail trade had been so positive at the launch, he felt sure that things would eventually pick up. The results, however, continued to be discouraging well into the first year. Cleopatra simply was not selling and could not seem to reach the explosive growth everyone was anticipating and expecting to be "just around the corner."

After 13 weeks, the advertising commercial had created an awareness of 63%, the highest in the skin care segment. At that time Camay was at 49%; Dove, 24%; and Aloe and Lanolin, 13%. By the end of 1986, Cleopatra had achieved its "share of voice target"— that is, the number one position in advertising intensity in Quebec. By the end of the promotion period, the free bar coupon had been distributed to households throughout Quebec, and 21% of the coupons had been redeemed. The sweepstakes, however, had been disappointing: only 1,500 people had entered by the December deadline.

Market share reached only 0.9%, peaking in October/November at 1.8%, compared to the 4.5% goal. Sales, which were expected to reach $3,775,000, were only $755,000. Instead of a $389,000 positive contribution to sales, contribution was negative $442,000. (The performance figures for 1986 and for the first

EXHIBIT 5 Profit and Loss Statement (000)

		Actual 1986	1st Quarter 1987
Sales	$	755	167
Margin[a]	$	477	108
	%	63.2	64.8
Trade[b]	$	53	12
	%	7.0	7.2
Consumer[c]	$	401	34
	%	53.1	20.3
Media[d]	$	465	94
	%	61.6	56.3
Total expenditures	$	919	140
	%	121.7	83.8
Contribution[e]	$	(442)	(32)
	%	(58.5)	(19.2)

[a]Includes direct product costs, freight/warehousing, etc.
[b]Includes all expenditures directed to the retail trade.
[c]Includes all consumer promotion expenditures.
[d]Includes cost of developing a commercial, plus air-time.
[e]Contribution toward allocated overheads and operating profit.

Source: Colgate-Palmolive Canada.

EXHIBIT 6 Consumer Research on Brands (Quebec)

	Brands (total random sample)[a]				
	Aloe & Lanolin	Camay	Cleopatra	Dove	Palmolive
Brand awareness (%)[b]	54.4	98.5	73.5	99.5	96.1
Brand in-home (%)[c]	3.5	15.2	6.9	23.9	7.4
Ever tried (%)[d]	12.3	86.3	14.2	83.5	65.2
Brand used[e]					
All of the time (%)	1.5	8.3	2.9	12.3	3.9
Most of the time (%)	0.5	3.9	1.5	5.4	3.9
Occasionally (%)	7.4	47.6	8.8	46.6	36.3
Stopped using (%)	2.9	26.5	1.0	19.2	21.1

[a]Total random sample—204 respondents.
[b]Question: Have you ever heard of _____ ?
[c]Question: What brands do you have in your home now?
[d]Question: Have you ever tried _____?
[e]Question: Do you use _____ ? If yes, would you say you use it all of the time, most of the time, or occasionally? If no, did you use _____ at some time in the past?

Source: Tracking study, Colgate-Palmolive Canada.

EXHIBIT 7 Consumer Research on Best Brands (Quebec)

Brands best for . . .[a] Brand	Being good value for money Total sample[b]	Cleo triers[c]	Being mild and gentle Total sample	Cleo triers	Having a rich, creamy lather Total sample	Cleo triers	Having a pleasant fragrance Total sample	Cleo triers	Moisturizing your skin Total sample	Cleo triers	Suitable for the whole family Total sample	Cleo triers	Leaving skin soft and smooth Total sample	Cleo triers
Aloe & Lanolin	11	2	31	9	8	0	13	0	27	2	13	1	19	1
Camay	40	11	31	7	50	9	53	13	28	7	32	10	41	10
Cleopatra	10	30	8	33	27	51	21	53	15	31	6	23	20	49
Dove	26	13	53	29	63	31	51	16	39	20	49	21	68	24
Palmolive	36	18	20	5	12	5	19	9	9	3	43	19	19	4
All	26	10	5	5	19	2	29	5	2	4	6	5	5	8
None	22	7	28	8	8	0	6	2	38	19	25	12	15	2
Don't know	33	8	28	3	17	1	12	1	46	13	30	8	17	1

Note: The two sets of data are from separate panels (i.e., the 99 Cleopatra triers are not included in the total random sample of 204 respondents).

[a]Question: Which of these five brands—_____, _____, _____, or _____—is best for "Being good value for the money" (for example).

[b]Total random sample = 204 respondents.

[c]Cleopatra trier sample (people who have tried Cleopatra in the last 6 months) = 99 respondents.

Source: Tracking study, Colgate-Palmolive Canada.

332

EXHIBIT 8 Consumer Research on Attitudes Toward Cleopatra

	% of triers[a]
Likes Cleopatra[b]	
The smell/good/nice/pleasant/perfume	29
Makes a lot of suds/foam/suds well	26
Mild perfume/light	22
Miscellaneous	21
Softens skin/soft for skin/leaves skin smooth	20
It's mild/good for skin/the mildness	19
The smell/perfume lasts/leaves nice smell on skin	12
It's creamy/creamier	11
The fresh smell/refreshing	10
It's soft/as silk/like satin/like milk	7
Dislikes Cleopatra[c]	
Price too high	20
Too strong a smell/contains too much perfume/harsh	17
Too harsh a soap/not mild enough	12
It melts too fast	10
The smell/the smell left on skin	7
Irritates the skin/burns skin/too much perfume	6
Dries the skin	5
Miscellaneous	5
Doesn't suds enough/not enough foam	3
Doesn't moisturize skin	3

Note: Only the 10 most frequent responses are shown here

Note: For many French Canadians, the level of perfume is perceived to vary directly with the cleaning strength and harshness of the product.

[a]Cleopatra trier sample (people who have tried Cleopatra in the last 6 months) = 99 respondents.
[b]Question: Given that you have tried Cleopatra, what are your likes and/or dislikes of the brand?
[c]42 respondents had no dislikes.

Source: Tracking study, Colgate-Palmolive Canada.

EXHIBIT 9 Consumer Research, Usage

Questions asked of users[a]	% of respondents
Do you plan on buying Cleopatra again?	
Regularly	27
Occasionally	66
No intention to buy again	7
Do you use Cleopatra every day?[b]	
Yes	41
No	59
What part of the body do you use Cleopatra on?	
Face only	3
Body only	76
Face and body	21
Who uses Cleopatra in your household?	
Yourself only	65
Others	35
How often do you use Cleopatra?	
Regularly	33
Occasionally	67

[a]Questions asked of those who have tried Cleopatra in the last 6 months (Cleopatra trier sample = 99 respondents).
[b]Showers outnumber baths 4 to 1 in the province of Quebec.

Source: Tracking study, Colgate-Palmolive Canada.

EXHIBIT 10 Consumer Research, Advertising

	% of respondents[b]
Main pont recall[a]	
It's a beauty soap/soap for women	22
It's perfumed/contained perfume	18
It's mild/a mild soap/mild as milk	16
Contains cream/milk/oils	15
Cleopatra/beauty linked together	14
Cleopatra/Egyptians linked together	14
It suds well/lots of lather	10
Fresh smell/it's refreshing	8
Smells good/nice	5
Makes skin soft/smoother skin	5
Note: Only the top 10 responses are shown here.	
Reaction to Cleopatra after seeing advertising[c]	
Positive	41
Negative	13
No reaction	46
Intention to try Cleopatra after seeing advertising[d]	
Yes	37
No	63

Note: Questions c and d were asked of those in the total random sample who had seen the advertising but who had not tried Cleopatra at the time of the study.

[a]Question: Do you recall Cleopatra advertising? If yes, what were the main points of the ad?
[b]Number of respondents out of the total random sample who recalled Cleopatra advertising = 128.
[c]Question: What is your reaction to Cleopatra?
[d]Question: Do you intend to try Cleopatra?

Source: Tracking study, Cleopatra-Palmolive Canada.

EXHIBIT 11 Consumer Research, Trial

Reaons for not trying Cleopatra?*	% of respondents
Not available where I shop	29
Haven't needed any soap	21
Too expensive	19
Happy with my present brand	19
Has too much perfume in it	16
I don't think about it	10
Miscellaneous	9
Waiting to get a coupon	6
It's new	4
Don't know	4

Note: Only the top 10 responses are shown here.

*Question: Why haven't you tried Cleopatra soap? (Asked of those who have seen the advertising and had originally intended to try the brand.)

Source: Tracking study, Colgate-Palmolive.

three months in 1987 are shown in Exhibit 4. The financial losses of 1986 and the first part of 1987 are presented in Exhibit 5.) Distribution also fell short of expectations, and presence and shelf positioning gradually deteriorated to the point where Cleopatra was placed on the bottom shelf next to generic soap. The sales force, however, did manage to restrict any discounting of the brand.

Over the first year, some small-scale research had been done in stores to determine consumer reaction, but nothing else had taken place. By January 1987, it was clear that some serious market research was needed, and a full-blown tracking study was commissioned.

Two panels from Quebec were chosen: a random sample of 204 consumers and an oversample of 99 Cleopatra "triers." Over 90 questions were asked to obtain key information on brand awareness, usage, brand ratings, likes and dislikes, advertising recall, and trial information (see Exhibits 6-11 for the results).

THE DILEMMA OVER CLEOPATRA'S FUTURE

Steve Boyd fumbled with his papers as he listened to Bill Graham, divisional vice president for marketing Canada, say, "I can't understand it. It was a star performer in France. The French loved it, and Quebec is, after all, part of the French culture. Why has the brand flopped so badly?" Boyd knew that for Cleopatra to succeed as a major brand in Quebec and perhaps in all of Canada, as the Global Marketing Group had first suggested, he had to react quickly to rectify the situation. But how?

The research results on Cleopatra lay on the table. Product Manager Ken Johnson and Assistant Product Manager Stan House had been over the research with Boyd to try and solve the Cleopatra riddle. But they could not agree about what should be done. Johnson wanted to scrap the brand. He said that Cleopatra was just plain wrong for Canada and should never have been launched there in the first place. He believed there was no point in letting more good money chase a loser. House was adamant that what the brand needed was time. He accused Johnson of being shortsighted and impatient. It was, he believed, totally unrealistic to expect a new brand to succeed overnight, and Cleopatra had only been on the market a little over a year. With a sizable investment and some patience, House believed they could recreate momentum and achieve a target of 4.5% market share.

The Global Marketing Group in New York was convinced that there was nothing wrong with the brand but that implementation had been poor. They proposed rethinking the basic strategy and suggested that perhaps Cleopatra should not be positioned as a skin care product at all, competing head on with Dove. A smaller niche might be more sensible.

Boyd knew that he had three options:

- Admit defeat and discontinue the brand.
- Continue the strategy with minor modifications if necessary, and try to get a 4.5% market share by giving it more time and support.
- Alter the strategy or even the product itself.

Boyd could not help feeling that he should try to find a way to make Cleopatra work. Giving up would be such a shame. Yet, with retailers literally pulling the brand off the shelves, did he really have a choice?

DISCUSSION QUESTIONS

1. What are the similarities between the French and the Quebec markets which suggests acceptance for the Cleopatra after the French success? Any significant differences which would alert you to potential problems ahead of the launch?

2. How would you evaluate the positioning of Cleopatra in Canada? Any alternative options?

3. Evaluate the promotional launch and the advertising campaign. Were mistakes made that could have been anticipated?

4. On the basis of the consumer research data collected, what is your diagnosis of what went wrong?

5. If you were Steve Boyd, which of the three options would you pursue? Justify your choice.

Global Management

After the company has expanded into foreign markets and become confident in several local markets, there is usually a need to integrate the global network and develop a global strategy. There are many reasons for this. On the cost side, unnecessary duplication (meaningless differences in product designs, separate advertising campaigns, different brand names) is wasteful. On the demand side, global communications make for homogeneous preferences and positive spillovers from global brand names. Global competitors often force other firms to go global as well.

Part Four deals with the globalization of marketing management, that is, how a firm coordinates and integrates its local marketing efforts globally. Chapter 11 focuses on global segmentation and positioning questions and explains how a globalized marketing mix can satisfy customers and be effective against local competitors. Chapter 12 discusses the management of global products and services, including how firms standardize products and services and how global brands are managed. Chapter 13, which covers global pricing, shows how companies have tried to come to grips with price coordination across borders, including the problem of arbitrage opportunities because of fluctuating exchange rates. Global distribution is covered in Chapter 14, with a discussion of the massive changes in global logistics technology.

The next two chapters deal with global advertising and promotion. Chapter 15 on advertising gives the pros and cons of globally uniform ads and shows how the emergence of global agencies has facilitated global advertising. Chapter 16 covers other promotional tools, including public relations, publicity, and trade fairs, and also discusses personal selling and the increased importance of direct marketing for global commerce. Chapter 17 treats the organizational problems that arise when global marketing is undertaken and the question of how to motivate local subsidiary managers. Chapter 18 concludes coverage of global management and ends the book by discussing the future potential of global marketing, including the threat from protectionist forces and the potential of the Internet as a global marketplace.

Eleven

Global Segmentation and Positioning

"Pick and choose"

Your takeaways from this chapter:

1. Segmentation and positioning have strong benefits and should be seriously considered at all levels (for groups of similar countries, trade regions, continents, the globe).

2. Even if analysis reveals that markets are essentially multidomestic, the marketer has to assess the probability of future convergence of preferences, especially in response to the introduction of global products or services.

3. Microsegmentation within a country does not necessarily have to limit itself to finding similar segments in all markets. Even if the segments differ in terms of demographics or some other criteria, a global product or global positioning message might work.

4. The advantages of global products and brands in terms of features, image, and quality often outweigh the fact that they are not always perfectly tailored to local tastes.

5. Local-only products and services still have opportunities in the marketplace, above all in specialty niches and as alternatives for variety-seeking consumers.

FORMULATING AND IMPLEMENTING a global marketing strategy is a complicated task. Even an accomplished marketing manager with experience in local markets abroad can have trouble sorting out the many complex issues involved. The best global companies use a systematic and structured approach that begins with market segmentation, both at the macro (across-country) level and at the micro (within-country) level. The marketing program is then coordinated across the selected target markets so as to generate a unique and consistent positioning in the various markets. Good market data on customers and competitors across the globe make the task easier. But insightful analysis of such data requires some imaginative rethinking about customers and competitors.

When the Whole World Is Just Too Big

In May 1997 Pepsi-Cola, the chief global competitor to Coca-Cola, announced a cutback in its international expansion. The company issued a statement saying that "in [international] markets where the business proposition is not sustainable, we have to make the difficult decision to move on." The announcement specifically concerned the company's departure from South Africa, where its headline-grabbing reentry from a couple of years earlier had gone astray. Awarding the new South African franchise to a group of well-known African Americans, including pop stars Whitney Houston and Michael Jackson, Pepsi-Cola targeted the mainly nonwhite markets outside of the major cities. But problems with distribution coverage, crucial in soft drink marketing, soon arose as rival Coca-Cola's marketing muscle was flexed. For example, at a Pepsi-sponsored tour of South Africa by Whitney Houston, Pepsi-Cola was barred from the concert arenas since Coca-Cola already had the concessions. In the end, the investing group's relative inexperience in business coupled with weak infrastructure and lack of management expertise in South Africa led to the decision to exit.

Pepsi-Cola has developed a kind of "limited global" approach that involves focusing on some key markets while forgoing others. The company is building a new soft drink plant in Russia, its fifth in the territory, and has entered an alliance with Brahma, Brazil's largest brewer, giving Pepsi tremendous distribution in a huge market. It also signed an extensive franchise bottling agreement with Norway's Pripps Ringnes, for distribution and sales in nearly all of Norway. But the company has ceded some markets, not only South Africa. For example, in Argentina Pepsi's largest international bottler ran into financial difficulties, and in Venezuela its bottler of more than 40 years switched to the Coca-Cola company. The limited global approach is based on the motto that "we focus on markets where we can prosper alongside Coca-Cola rather than trying to defeat it."

Other companies follow similar limited global strategies. As detailed in Case 1.2, Whirlpool, the American manufacturer of "white goods" (kitchen home appliances), acquired Philips white goods division as a means of quickly creating a strong presence in the pan-European market. But Whirlpool ran into the same problem with divergent preferences and high coordination costs that had already afflicted Philips' performance. After absorbing losses, the company has started cost-cutting efforts in Europe and in 1998 turned its aim toward expansion in India and China. In Ranjangaon near Pune, India, a new R&D facility has been built at a cost of $5 million to support its increasing manufacturing capacity. The company already produces refrigerators in Faridabad near Delhi and washing machines at a plant in Pondicherry in the south of India. It is investing in a new plant in Ranjangaon that will build 400,000 non-CFC (chlorofluorocarbons) frost-free refrigerators annually.

In contrast to Whirlpool's global orientation, in the mid-1990s the Maytag company, a home appliance maker from Newton, Iowa, decided to pull back from its losing foreign entries to focus on the American home market with new products and innovation. Raising operating margins from 9.1 to 14.6 percent, with profits at $280 million in 1998, up 324% from 1992, the company is likely to get back into global markets by the turn of the century, under a new CEO from Procter and Gamble.

Especially with the global financial turmoil at the end of the 1990s, "going global" is no longer (if it ever were) a simple "imperative" that all businesses should follow. It is now a matter of picking and choosing where to focus the firm's marketing efforts.

Sources: Adite Chatterjee, "Whirlpool's Asian Interests," *Appliance*, May 1998, p. 26; Pablo Galarza, "The Man Who Fixed Maytag," *Money*, November 1998, p. 57; "Pepsi-Cola's International Focus Looks Sharp," *Beverage Industry*, May 1998, p. 8.
http://www.coca-cola.com
http://www.cokecce.com
http://www.pepsiworld.com
http://www.whirlpoolcorp.com
http://www.maytagcorp.com
http://www.pg.com

INTRODUCTION

The globalization of marketing usually takes place after the company has international experience in multiple markets. At the corporate level, globalization typically involves three separate activities:[1]

1. Integrate sourcing, production, and marketing.
2. Allocate resources to achieve a balanced portfolio and growth.
3. Coordinate marketing activities across countries and regions.

At the business level, this coordination is usually accompanied by a certain degree of standardization of the marketing mix. In fact, as we will see in Chapter 12, large numbers of globalization decisions facing managers center on the issue of standardization versus locally adapted products and services.

This chapter covers how marketers analyze markets to identify segmentation and positioning opportunities for globalization. To get a firm handle on the managerial questions faced in the chapter, it first introduces Keegan's and Levitt's alternative approaches to global marketing strategies and shows how they are related to different market characteristics. The chapter then describes how macrosegments of countries can be useful as a preliminary step in market segmentation. Next, the potential of microsegmentation—that is, identifying and targeting homogeneous customer segments across countries—is evaluated against the kind of market data that might be available.

The chapter then deals with the product positioning questions, focusing on the issue of how a global entrant to a new country market might impact local customers. A discussion of **embryonic markets** where positioning maps are in flux and targeting therefore is difficult follows. In the final section Keegan's strategy alternatives are extended and used to analyze the various targeting strategies implemented by global companies.

GLOBAL STRATEGY DECISIONS

The segmentation and positioning decisions facing the global marketers are different from those faced in local markets. The basic question is the extent to which segmentation and positioning strategies can be extended from one country to the next.

Keegan's Global Strategies

In an early seminal article, Keegan suggested that there are typically four marketing alternatives to be considered when global strategies are contemplated.[2]

The most common strategy is **product–communications extension,** simply extending the existing product line, pricing policies, advertising appeals, and promotional themes to the new countries entered. This approach naturally involves lower expenditures and is convenient but does not always work. It fits a company such as Coca-Cola, since consumer preferences and competitive conditions for colas tend to be similar across countries. On the whole, though, it works best where cultural distances are small and is a natural for a company adopting a focus strategy to expansion.

A second marketing alternative is **product extension–communications adaptation.** When product usage is the same or similar to that in the domestic market but the need to be fulfilled is different, the product line can be extended but the communications must adapt. This involves repositioning a global product. The Minolta Maxxumm, a leading automatic single lens reflex (SLR) camera, is a good example. The global product is identical in terms of technology and design, but the positioning varies across countries. In Japan and Europe it is a camera for serious amateurs, young adults who are interested in the technology. In the United States, on the other hand, the camera's appeal is to a broader group of people, including families and older adults.

A third strategy, **product localization–communications extension,** can work well when product usage changes but positioning is the same. The well-known Exxon slogan "Put a Tiger in Your Tank" has worked well across the globe for many years. The gasoline itself, however, has been adapted by the use of additives to account for differences in climate, season, and performance requirements in various countries.[3]

The fourth strategy alternative is **dual adaptation,** involving both product localization and communications adaptation. This case is most likely to be necessary when a diversification strategy is attempted, entering countries where usage conditions and positioning requirements differ. This alternative involves higher costs and often more uncertainty as well, since cultural distance is likely to be larger and market know-how less. Benetton, the Italian apparel maker, has faced this problem in Southeast Asian markets. Because people's body proportions are not the same the world over, and because the preferred range and intensity of colors also differ, the designs have to be altered. Also, attempts to extend Benetton's politically charged European advertising have met with resistance from local retailers whose customers are willing to buy the Italian design image but not the societal concern.

Keegan suggests a fifth strategy alternative, **product invention,** which he recommends for global companies. It involves developing entirely new products for the market abroad and is less common as an entry strategy since it presupposes thorough knowledge of market conditions. Global companies with presence in many countries often do this. The Nissan Primera was developed for the European market, the Volkswagen Rabbit was developed for the American market (on the European Golf platform), and Procter and Gamble's Vizir detergent was developed for Europe.

Lipton, the quintessentially British company now owned by Unilever, has long been a global player. Here it is sold in the Ivory Coast. Lipton's tea bags, packages and labels might be the same everywhere, but its distribution is adapted to local conditions. Peter Hince.

Levitt's Homogeneous Markets

In 1983, over 10 years after Keegan's article, a strong argument for companies to globalize marketing without much adaptation was made by Ted Levitt.[4] Levitt argued that markets were becoming more homogeneous because of two factors: **global communications** and rapid **technology diffusion.** With satellite TV broadcasts beaming the same programs all over the world and with instantaneous global telecommunications, the world will supposedly move inexorably toward greater homogeneity of markets. At the same time, the increasing speed of technological innovation and diffusion makes today's products soon outdated by the onslaught from global competitors able to incorporate the latest product inventions. The joint effect of these two forces makes a global product or brand not only a potent competitor but the preferred alternative.

This point of view generated controversy and induced rebuttals from a few marketing academicians as well as practitioners. The basic counterargument was that although these forces are at work, the world's markets are as yet far from homogeneous.[5] Many domestic producers are still marketing competitive products that could be dislodged only by even more attractive offerings tailored to local conditions and tastes. Furthermore, the advantages of scale have become diminished with the emergence of computerized flexible manufacturing systems that can produce many different product models and versions without incurring extra costs. The experience in the European appliance industry suggests that globalization has some limits (see box, "Globalization Frustrated").

Three Homogenizing Forces

Today, despite the global financial turmoil at the end of the 1990s, most academicians and practitioners agree that in many markets the globalization forces are winning the battle. In addition to Levitt's two globalization forces (global communications and technology diffusion), there are three other drivers of the global convergence of preferences:

1. *Dynamic preferences.* Customer preferences are not fixed once and for all but are dynamic and open to change, especially in open and free markets.
2. *New products.* A major determinant of the direction of the preference change is the new products on the market.
3. *Leading markets.* As we saw in Chapter 4, there are markets that lead and markets that follow, depending on the product category, the competition, and the customers. New standard-setting products are usually first introduced and tested in leading markets, then diffused to follower markets.

These three forces need to be discussed in more depth.

G E T T I N G   T H E

Picture

Globalization Frustrated

GLOBALIZATION FAILED in a case presented by Baden-Fuller and Stopford in 1991, who analyzed the performance of regional and national competitors in the domestic appliance market in Europe. Here was an industry seeming to offer great promise for globalization as the EU integration proceeded with removal of tariff barriers and tedious customs procedures and the creation of common technical standards. Analysts predicted a convergence in consumer tastes, and large companies (such as Swedish Electrolux and Italian Zanussi) joined forces to gain scale advantages and rationalize production, marketing, and distribution.

The researchers found that during the 1980s the firms focused on one national market (such as Hotpoint in Britain and Thomson in France), outperformed the large global players (Electrolux and Philips) in terms of return on sales and on capital employed. The reasons were sev-

eral. First, the predicted convergence of tastes failed to materialize. Tastes did change in the various countries but not toward the same standard.

Second, the local companies maintained high standards in distribution and after-sales service, making it costly and time-consuming for the global firms to enter the national markets. Third, the retail sector in Europe was not regionally integrated, which limited the possibility of transferring systems and know-how to support retail sales. The scale returns and cost savings to standardization could therefore not be realized.

Sources: Reprinted with permission from *Strategic Management Journal* 12, Spring 1979, "Globalization Frustrated: The Case of White Goods," by Charles W. F. Baden-Fuller and John M. Stopford, pp. 493–507. Copyright 1979 by John Wiley and Sons, Ltd. *http://www.electrolux-usa.com*

DYNAMIC PREFERENCES   Much of standard marketing thought is based on the assumption that customer preferences are stable or at least predictable. Most market research is designed to find out what consumers want, not what they might want. However, consumers themselves find it hard to articulate what they want. Few people could have conceived of a handheld calculator before Hewlett-Packard introduced it. New Zealand's kiwifruit was not desired until it appeared. On the other side, negative surprises such as lack of acceptance of a new product are often ascribed to faulty market research when the real problem is that preferences have changed by the time the product is introduced.

This means there is little point arguing whether customers in a particular local market have different preferences from those elsewhere. They do, probably. The appropriate question is, "In what way and how fast will these preferences change?" To think that the Japanese will never drink wine is the same as assuming Americans will always drive big cars. Sure, there are differences between countries today, but what about tomorrow? When and how did the Americans become the largest market for opera and Brie cheese?[6]

NEW PRODUCTS   There are many drivers of changing preferences. Word of mouth, mass communication, usage experiences, and store visits are some of the typical sources of information that change preferences. And they have something in common: They all involve exposure to new products. Customer preferences are changed as new products are introduced.

New products make preferences change, especially innovative new products. Where they are based on assessed customer preferences, they tend to represent only incremental modifications, such as the New Coke or this year's new Buick. Only rarely can customer desires be more than a general guide to new-product development. The incrementally modified product can be dominated by a new innovative product that changes customer preferences in unexpected ways. When the sporty new Buick Reatta was introduced in 1988 after painstaking and sophisticated consumer research on desired features, it was quickly derailed by the introduction of the Mazda Miata, a much

Gillette's World View: One Blade Fits All

GILLETTE, the American razor blade manufacturer, is one company that believes in global standardization. As Mr. Alfred M. Zeien, the chairman and CEO, states: "The most important decision that I made was to globalize. We decided not to tailor products to any marketplace, but to treat all marketplaces the same. And it worked in most countries."

Mr. Zeien's globalization principles were honed when he ran Gillette's German subsidiary Braun, maker of electric razors and appliances such as coffeemakers and hi-fi equipment. When he arrived in Frankfurt in 1968, the German home market accounted for 90 percent of Braun's revenues. When he left for Gillette's headquarters in Boston in 1978, Braun revenues had more than tripled, with 65 percent coming from non-German sales. Mr. Zeien discovered that he could sell Braun merchandise outside Germany on the strength of the brand name without redesigning the product (except for localization aspects such as electrical rewiring). Traveling out of Frankfurt and exploring markets on every continent, Mr. Zeien learned about different kinds of people. "But," he says, "I did not find foreign countries foreign. They have distinctive characteristics, but they are not foreign. When people shop they do not think very differently from each other."

This simple insight is perhaps not equally apt for all products, but Mr. Zeien gambles that shoppers in Malaysia and Singapore, the site of Gillette's regional headquarters for Asia, will buy the same upscale Parker fountain pens (a Gillette product) as French shoppers at Printemps—and for the same price or more. "We are not going to come out with a special product for Malaysia," he says.

Sources: Uchitelle, 1994; Lim, 1993
http://www.gillette.com
http://www.braun.com

---

smaller and less expensive sports coupe that changed the nature of the market. The Miata was designed "on a hunch" by a British racing fan who convinced Mazda's management to take a chance on a new concept.[7]

LEADING MARKETS   The new products and marketing programs underlying global marketing do not have to be "shots in the dark," however. When it comes to product specifications, companies use leading markets to identify what features to include—and which to exclude—for their globally uniform product lines. Leading markets can be found in the countries with the most demanding customers and the most advanced technology. For most companies, identifying the leading markets in the industry is easy: It is usually one or two of the largest markets, with the most maturity and the most intense competition. In autos, Germany is one leading market; in consumer electronics, Japan; and in computers, the United States.[8]

Leading markets are important in determining which new products will be successful and which company's design will set the next standard. These markets help the global marketer, who can suggest the new designs to the local follower markets. Even though global marketing often involves some standardization of a product or service, this does not mean that the company compromises on features. Rather, the best designs from a leading market, the ones with outstanding ratings on the major salient attributes, are the successful global products. This goes for cars, ice cream, movies, computers, hotels, consumer electronics, and many other categories. Scale and scope economies make it possible to offer state-of-the-art features at affordable prices (see box, "Gillette's World View").

Business Markets

The globalization drivers affect not only consumer goods. Many industrial products have long been sold in global markets. This is especially true of raw materials such as petroleum, rubber, and minerals, but also true of fabricated products such as steel, semiconductors, and plastics. Of course, tariff barriers protecting domestic producers have tended to create artificial local markets with high prices, but these business markets tend to be inherently global.

Since most industrial products are bought as intermediate goods and used to produce final goods, the degree of globalization of their markets depends intimately on the degree to which manufacturing technology is widespread. Purchasers of automobile or electronic components have similar requirements in most parts of the world, and the sellers of these components are forced to shift from a multidomestic to a global perspective. High-quality suppliers to Japanese automakers have now begun selling components to American and European carmakers. Volvo buys transmissions from an Isuzu supplier, and Ford's small engines come from a Mazda subsidiary. Strong European and American suppliers counter by marketing their products to Japanese companies. Air-conditioning units in Hondas are manufactured by Americans, and German Bosch sells its ABS braking system to Japanese auto manufacturers. The Bosch systems come from its manufacturing subsidiary in Japan, whose quality control is up to Japanese standards. This has created a problem for Bosch at home, since its German customers (Mercedes and BMW) have requested braking systems to be supplied from the Japanese subsidiary, not from the local plant, which initially had lower quality standards.[9] Customers in global markets are likely to look for the best deal anywhere.

MACROSEGMENTATION

The Keegan and Levitt contributions provide a good basis for a discussion of global segmentation and positioning. While markets grow ever more globalized, and customer homogeneity increases, within each country individual choices and preferences also become more varied. This means that segmentation and positioning strategies have to become more sophisticated.

With more than 200 independent country markets to consider, many exporters find it difficult to develop a comprehensive global attack. Therefore companies tend to break down the field into trade blocs such as the EU, NAFTA, or ASEAN—or simply geographical regions such as Southeast Asia, Oceania, the Middle East, and Western Europe—and treat these markets as relatively autonomous organizational units. Alternatively, the country data discussed in Chapter 4 are revisited to discern possible synergies and untapped opportunities. The typical question is which countries seem to go together from a market opportunity standpoint. This is a form of macrosegmentation.[10]

Macrosegmentation consists of grouping countries on the basis of common characteristics deemed to be important for marketing purposes. These variables typically include sociodemographic data on population size and character, disposable income levels, educational background, and primary language(s), as well as indicators of level of development, infrastructure, rate of growth in GNP, and political affiliation. The choice of variables must take into account the possible lack of data comparability across many countries and will generally vary across products (for industrial products, a manufacturing intensity index is often used as an indicator of general level of economic activity, for example).

Clustering Countries

To identify regional groupings (macrosegments) of countries, it is possible to use computerized techniques such as **cluster analysis.** Clustering maps show a picture of which countries are similar and which are far apart (recall Hofstede's similar approach to culture discussed in Chapter 3). To incorporate more than two criteria at a time, it is common to do an initial factor analysis before clustering the countries. The factor analysis helps combine all the criteria into a manageable few dimensions, although at the price of making interpretation of the dimensions less clear. The interested reader is referred to the many available statistical texts.[11]

EXHIBIT 11.1 A Two-Dimensional Country Clustering Map

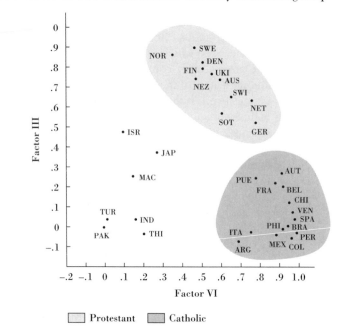

Factor number	Name and number of descriptors	Selected descriptors
I.	Aggregate economic, of level of development (47)	Gross national product, radios in use, passenger kilometers flown
II.	Population size (31)	Total midyear population
III.	Personal economic, or standard of living (32)	Income per capita, newsprint consumption per capita, birth rate (negatively related)
IV.	Canada—conditions on which Canada ranks highest (12)	Newsprint production, visitor arrivals in the U.S., geographic area
V.	Linguistic affinity (10)	Adults who read English or speak it
VI.	YC—Code for private descriptors (11)	Brand and industry sales of a consumer product, number of Roman Catholics
VII.	International participation (22)	Membership in international organizations, foreign tourist arrivals, airfare to Tokyo
VIII.	Trade capacity (12)	Exports, number of Protestants
IX.	Climate or price stability (10)	Sunny days per year, temperature of key city, price index (negative)
X.	Mortality (5)	Infant death rate, number of Moslems

Source: Charles Ramond. *The Art of Using Science in Marketing.* New York: Harper & Row, 1974. Copyright © 1974 by Charles Ramond. Reprinted by permission of HarperCollins Publishers, Inc.

An example of a country clustering map is provided in Exhibit 11.1. As can be seen, at this level the groupings usually turn out to be similar to the East–West and North–South categories typically employed in U.N. policy analyses. Although such groupings should not be mistaken for final market segments, these very broad indicators serve to illustrate strength of markets and socioeconomic distance to the home market.

In one application, Cavusgil used six variables (population growth, median age, number of children per household, infant mortality, life expectancy, and GNP per capita—all available in published U.N. data) to come up with market-based clusters of countries.[12] He then proceeded to name the clusters and to describe their distinguishing features. Fi-

Exhibit 11.2 A Market-Oriented Clustering of World Markets

Cluster	Demographic make-up	Marketing implications
Dependent societies Most countries in Africa, Asia, and a few in South America	Population growth: 3% Median age: 16 Children: 5+ Infant mortality: 100 per 1,000 births Life expectancy: 40 years GNP per capita: less than $300	Demand goods and services related to food, clothing, housing, education, and medical care. Investments related to extractive activities (agriculture and mining) are undertaken. Government/state economic enterprises are the major buying groups. Poor infrastructure and access to rural markets are major impediments.
Seekers Most Latin America; some in Asia (Indonesia, Thailand, Philippines), and some in Africa (Morocco, Tunisia, Egypt)	Population growth: 1.5 to 2.5% Median age: 20 Children: 4+ Infant mortality: 50 to 100 per 1,000 births Life expectancy: 60 years GNP per capita: less than $900	Infrastructure-related projects are high priority (construction equipment, machinery, chemicals, etc.). Good opportunities for technology sales and turnkey projects. Independent trading groups and a few large holding companies have much influence. Increased urbanization but a "mass market" does not yet exist.
Climbers Brazil, Venezuela, Portugal, Mexico, Taiwan, Malaysia, Turkey, South Korea	Population growth: under 1.5% Median age: slightly higher than 20 Children: 2 to 3 GNP per capita: Less than $2,000	Industrialization and service sector expenditures assume greater importance. Private enterprises have become more dominant than the state agencies. Good opportunities for joint ventures and technology agreements. Growing mass market.
Luxury and leisure societies United States, Canada, Japan, United Kingdom, Australia	Zero or very little population growth Median age: 30+ Children: 2 Reaching maximum longevity GNP per capita: greater than $8,000	Substantial discretionary income and availability of credit. Restructuring of economy. Maturing markets. Intense competition. Relocation away from large population centers.
The rocking chairs West Germany, Switzerland, Luxembourg, The Netherlands	Fertility rates below replacement level Median age: 37 Children: less than 2 Peak life expectancy GNP per capita: greater than $10,000	Dominance of service economy and high-technology sectors. Highly segmented markets. Ideal distribution and communications channels.

Source: Cavusgil, 1990, pp. 206–7. Reprinted by permission of Butterworth-Heinemann, Ltd., and the author.

nally, he outlined the marketing implications. The results are presented in Exhibit 11.2. As can be seen, even these relatively crude measures are useful to judge country attractiveness, uncover market opportunities, and suggest interesting marketing implications.

The use of broad economic indicators in macrosegmentation has been challenged by marketers who argue that these indicators are too general to be really predictive of buyer behavior and market response. In an effort to test the predictive ability of the country groupings based on broad economic, social, and political criteria, one study examined the new product diffusion pattern for three products (color TV, VCR, and CD players) in different country clusters.[13] If the clusters are useful, one would expect the new product rate of penetration to be similar for the countries in a cluster and different across clusters. The study found little evidence of this. The new product diffusion patterns varied within clusters, and some countries from different clusters showed similar patterns. The study concluded with a caution, however. The clusters can still be useful in other ways. In particular, echoing other studies, the authors suggest that clusters of countries can be useful to gain scale economies in the execution of marketing research, in uniformity of packaging, in simplifying logistics, and in similar promotions. Overall, managerial judgment is necessary to fully evaluate the benefits of these broadly defined clusters.

Less general variables have been used for macrosegmentation, depending on the purpose of the segmentation. In an imaginative study for the purpose of developing reactions to a global advertising campaign, two researchers clustered countries on the basis of "think" and "feel" variables.[14] The "think" variables included cultural and regulatory variables that suggested the population's inclination to approach communications on a "left brain" critical reasoning basis. For example, countries with low tolerance for risk and with strong regulation of advertising content score high on the "think" dimension. The "feel" dimension captured the degree to which a country's population tends to be impulsive, wants excitement, and becomes emotionally involved with products and people. On the basis of the resulting mapping of countries (see Exhibit 11.3), the authors were able to define clusters where the advertising appeals should use rational arguments and a lecture format, and other clusters where the appeal should be primarily emotional and dramatic. Again, however, these techniques need to be matched against managerial judgment; for example, Italy is shown to prefer "high think" and "low feel" advertising, contrary to what most cultural analysts would suggest (see Gannon's metaphors in Chapter 3, for example).

EXHIBIT 11.3 "Think" and "Feel" Country Clusters

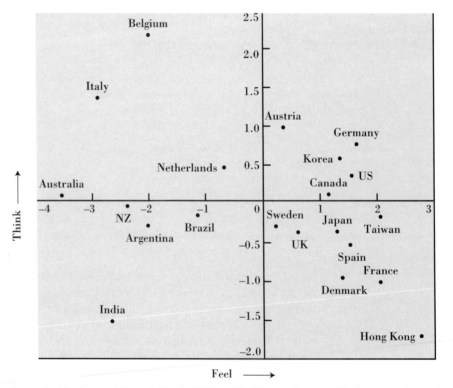

Source: Fred Zandpour and Katrin R. Harich, "Think and Feel Country Clusters: A New Approach to International Advertising Standardization," *International Journal of Advertising* 15 (1996) p. 341. Copyright Advertising Association.

Diversification versus Focus Strategy

The clustering approach to macrosegmentation leads generally to the identification of *similar* markets. However, in developing a global strategy, some companies make a conscious effort to be a player in *different* markets. This is done in order to balance market countries so that the international "portfolio" of countries provides **diversification** protection against the risk of large losses. This has become increasingly important with the global financial turmoil spreading quickly through tightly integrated markets.

Examples of diversification strategies are common. Volvo, the Swedish carmaker, limited its U.S. market involvement to 25 percent of total output for many years. In personal interviews with top management, Toyota executives reported feeling uneasy when their exports take more than 50 percent of their home market demand.[15] The recent tendency is for Japanese exporters to limit their unit shares going to the U.S. market, not only in autos but in electronics. The fear of too great a reliance on the U.S. market is palpable, especially at times when the United States seems to be vacillating in its adherence to free trade.

However, even though there may be strong diversification benefits from entering several markets or regions, a case can be made for **focusing** on a few similar markets in the same cluster. These markets can be given more attention and market positions fortified. Since the countries are relatively similar, spillover effects can be shared more easily. Product lines can be the same. Good advertising copy is more likely to play well in a similar country. How should a company strike a balance between diversifying and possibly overextending itself versus being too dependent on a few single markets? Exhibit 11.4 shows some of the market factors that need to be considered.[16]

As can be seen in the exhibit, high-growth markets require more marketing support for a brand, and a focused strategy tends to be desirable. On the other hand, instability and competitive rivalry in the market increase the benefits of diversification. When decisions have to be custom-tailored to the local market, there is greater need for focus. The "marginal sales" condition refers to the shape of the sales response curve as marketing expenditures are increased. If the markets respond strongly to an increase in expenditures (the sales response curve shows a region of increasing returns), it will pay to focus and spend more, since every dollar spent brings in more sales.

Empirical research has shown that generally diversified strategies tend to lead to greater *sales* abroad, while concentrated or focused strategies tend to result in somewhat higher *profitability*.[17] One prime determinant of profitability is whether the firm can identify and track cost effectiveness, something that is easier in focused strategies. In firms aiming for diversification, sales objectives and market orientation tend to be

EXHIBIT 11.4 **Market Factors Affecting Choice of Market Portfolio**

Factors	Diversify if:	Focus if:
Growth rate	Low	High
Demand stability	Low	High
Competitive lag	Short	Long
Spillover	High	Low
Need to adapt product	Low	High
Need to adapt promo	Low	High
Marginal sales	Diminishing	Increasing
Need for control	Low	High
Entry barriers	Low	High

Source: Adapted with permission from Ayal and Zif, 1979, p. 88. © 1979 by the American Marketing Association.

more important than costs, leading to greater sales. In either case, global strategies proved more successful for companies whose objectives were clearly articulated than for companies with more diffuse objectives.

MICROSEGMENTATION

In microsegmentation the global marketer is faced with the task of selecting similar target segments within the set of countries selected in the macrosegmentation stage. Again the basic question is to find target segments with high demand potential for the firm's products or services and then to assess whether global coordination and uniformity may be feasible.

Differing segments exist, of course, in all markets. People's lifestyles, usage levels, demographics, and attitudes vary among any population. But to be useful for marketing purposes, targeted segments have to possess certain characteristics. They have to be:

1. Identifiable (what distinguishes them?).
2. Measurable (how many belong to each segment?).
3. Reachable (how to distribute to and communicate with each segment?).
4. Able to buy (can they afford it?).
5. Willing to buy (do they want it?).

It goes without saying that each of these requirements, except possibly the last one, can be difficult to satisfy in emerging and less developed markets. If, in addition, the potential customers in these markets have only weakly developed preferences—because of a lack of exposure to products and services—research to identify market segments will be akin to searching for Atlantis, the mythical sunken city.

Segmentation Criteria

The formation of microsegments can be based on many different criteria. The most useful **segmentation criteria** are those that accomplish three things:

1. The criteria help give a clue to what *influences* the segment's buying behavior, both consumption level and choice between competing brands. "Political party affiliation" may be a less useful criterion than "Number of children" from this perspective.
2. The criteria should be reflected in published data so that the *size* of the segment can be calculated. "Lifestyle" may be less useful than "Level of education" in this regard.
3. The criteria should help identify the *media* through which marketers can communicate with the segment. This requirement suggests that "Teenagers" is a more useful criterion than "Social class."

In reality, firms tend to use several criteria in combination. The most common bases for global microsegmentation are the following (in order from the most basic country factor to more specific market factors):

ECONOMIC   The most basic global segmentation criterion is still economic development. Even for low-priced consumer necessities such as detergents, soap, and toothpaste, level of GDP per capita matters. The reason is that it is difficult to globalize marketing mixes where package sizes have to be downsized, distribution channels are different, and some communications media are unavailable.

DEMOGRAPHIC   The age and family structure in different countries also play an important role in determining global segments, especially in terms of size. The fact is that

The Bodyshop, Anita Roddick's small cosmetics store that grew to a global empire, targets the same consumers everywhere. However, the segment of women who also care about environmental and social issues varies in size across countries and affects the level of success achieved. Courtesy The Body Shop.

for many consumer products, age and family size are strong determinants of consumption levels. As in the case of economics, published data are usually available and quite reliable. But they rarely determine the choice between competing brands. Demographics, like economics, help determine consumption levels, but they do not always satisfy the first requirement of a good segmentation criterion, that is, influence choice between competing brands.

CULTURE Even though a lot has been said in the media about the emergence of global segments of people with no regard for nationality and culture, the reality is that people care about their identity. Famous companies such as Benetton, Nike, Levi's, and British Airways have promoted their universality only to find that customers still want to be recognized for what they are, and they want their brands to reflect that. Thus, global segments are still often defined in terms of culture: Benetton's target is generation X, Nike's runners are "rebels," Levi's targets are the American "wanna-bes" in foreign countries, and British Airways targets Anglo-Saxon businesspeople around the world. These segments are no longer bound by country borders, but they have a strong cultural identity nevertheless. Furthermore, culture influences choice between competing substitutes more than actual consumption levels.

BENEFITS The most clear-cut segmentation criteria are those that focus on the benefits sought. In general, different people may look for different benefits, but global segments can be identified that are looking for roughly the same benefits. Anita Roddick's Body Shop seems to have identified a global segment that looks for "green" products in personal care, with benefits in terms of both functional quality and environmental care. The problem in using benefits sought for segmentation is that it requires good understanding of the local markets, solid marketing research, and a product that scores high on the specific benefits sought. It also works less well in technology products, where consumers do not have enough product understanding to give useful information about benefits. Often—as in the Body Shop case and in other cases such as Swatch watches, PC software, and mobile phones—consumers do not comprehend the benefits until the products have been introduced on the market.

LIFESTYLE As economic development takes place, and buying behavior involves more than simple necessities, consumers start developing their own lifestyle. They choose products and brands on the basis of what they want, not simply on what they need. Customers become more sophisticated and fickle, and markets move toward the maturity stage. Their AIOs (attitudes, interests, and opinions), not economics or demographics, determine what they choose.

EXHIBIT 11.5 Selected International Data Sources

> *The Economist Intelligence Unit (EIU):* Marketing in Europe (product markets in Europe—food, clothing, furniture, household goods, appliances). EIU now also owns BI (see below).
>
> *Business International:* BI database (consumption patterns in different countries).
>
> *Frost & Sullivan:* Syndicated market research for various industries in different countries.
>
> *Euromonitor:* European marketing data and statistics (population, standard of living index, consumption).
>
> *Bates Worldwide:* Global scan (spending patterns, media habits, and attitudes in different countries).
>
> *U.S. Department of Commerce:* Global market surveys (research on targeted industries); country market surveys (more detailed reports on promising countries for exports); overseas marketing report (market profiles for all countries except the United States).

In the European market, the research agency RISC has developed the following six pan-European lifestyle segments (the relative size of the segments in percent):[18]

Traditionalists	18 percent
Homebodies	14 percent
Rationalists	23 percent
Pleasurists	17 percent
Strivers	15 percent
Trendsetters	13 percent

Because it is not tied to a specific product category, this type of general lifestyle segmentation, although suggestive for creative advertisers and copywriters, does not always link directly to particular consumption choices. It is typically employed in combination with other segmentation criteria.

SEGMENTATION RESEARCH

The kind of large-scale market segmentation studies common in the United States, Japan, and Western Europe are relatively rare in other places around the globe. This is not only because they are expensive and require advanced analytical techniques. They also suffer from the problems of collecting data from individual respondents, as discussed in Chapter 7. And in many markets they are not necessary, because the markets are not mature and the buyers' preferences are not yet differentiated.

But in mature markets in developed countries there is always a payoff to researching market segments. And such research does not always have to be so large-scale or expensive. With the advent of global markets and global communications, there are sources for secondary data that can serve as very reasonable indicators of potential segments (see Exhibit 11.5). Bates Worldwide, for example, the global ad agency headquartered in New York, publishes its "Global Scan" database every other year. The database covers 20 countries and offers demographics and socioeconomic data for subgroups of the population of the various countries. The Euromonitor is another source that offers data on attitudes and opinions in addition to socioeconomic data on the European countries. The so-called VALS (Values and Lifestyles) program initiated by Stanford Research Institute has been expanded internationally, identifying lifestyle segments of many developed markets.[19]

Although such data will necessarily be only a crude start, they can give the marketer a good sense of the market segments, especially when compared with the market at home. Since in many cases the introduction of a new global product will create its own segment, there is perhaps less need for in-depth research than is common in the

EXHIBIT 11.6 International Market Researchers (1997)

	Non-U.S. revenue (million US$)
A. C. Nielsen	$1082
IMS Health	602
Research International	241
Milward Brown	124
Information Resources	90
NPD Group	88
VNU Marketing Info. Services	65
NFO Worldwide	49
MRB Group	48
PMSI (Pharmaceutical Marketing Services)	40

Source: Reprinted with permission from the May 25, 1998, issue of *Advertising Age*. Copyright, Crain Communications, Inc. 1998.

pluralistic and diverse markets of the United States. But in most developed countries, many of the large research firms have branches that can carry out local research as advanced as that at home. The largest firms are given in Exhibit 11.6.

GLOBAL PRODUCT POSITIONING

In some ways, global positioning is no different from positioning in any market. For a given target market, the firm has to identify what attributes and benefits the customers look for and how the product or service measures up on these features against competition. But there is one principal difference with globalization. The global marketer is looking for cost savings and demand spillovers from coordination and global products and brands. This means there are limits to how much features and communications can be customized to consumer preferences. What the global marketer needs to find out is how far he or she can stray away from buyer preferences before sales and market shares get punished. For this assessment it is useful to understand something about the psychological processes that underlie product positioning.[20]

Product Space

The **product space** map that helps define a product's or brand's position is constructed from four sets of data.

- **Salient attributes.** First are the data on what attributes are "salient," that is, what a customer looks for in a product. For example, in considering automobiles, individuals may look for handling, gas economy, comfort, reliability, and so forth.
- **Evoked set.** A second set of data involves identifying what brands are considered by the buyer, in other words, what is the "evoked" set. These are the brands (car makes, say) that compete for this buyer's purchase.
- **Attribute ratings.** The third set of data shows how the individual rates the brands in the evoked set on the salient attributes.
- **Preferences.** Finally, the fourth set of data involves how the brands rank in terms of overall preference.

Statistical techniques such as factor analysis can be used to summarize the data and to plot the competing brands in a diagram. In psychology, these diagrams are usually called *perceptual maps*, while marketers tend to use the term *product space*.

An example of a product space for automobiles is given in Exhibit 11.7. The axes of the diagram are described in terms of the various attributes that people consider important. The location of the various automobiles on the axes—their "position" in product space—is derived from people's ratings of the cars on the various attributes. For example, a Lincoln scores high on "Has a touch of class" and is also high on "Appeals to older people." The map also shows the preferences of different market segments through "ideal points" circles. The size of the circles reflects the size of the market segment. The location of the circles—which is derived from people's expressed preferences—shows what kind of attributes would appeal to the segments. For example, the relatively small segment 5 would like a "Sporty looking" car that still "Has a touch of class."

The distances in the diagram between makes reflect the degree to which they compete. For example, the Lincoln seems to compete more with Cadillac than with Mercedes, but not at all with VW. Similarly, the cars that are located closer to a segment are better positioned to capture that segment. Lincoln most likely would sell better in the relatively small segment 4, really a niche segment, than in the largest segment, number 1.

These implications need to have some credibility or "face validity," helping managers to trust the results. As always with market research, managers need to exercise judgment in relying on the kind of advanced data analysis represented by the product positioning technique. Some portion of the results should match what managers already know.

Positioning a New Brand

So far we have dealt with the basic application of positioning methods. In global positioning, managers typically introduce a product or brand into one or more new markets. Before dealing with the full global case, it is useful to analyze first how customers tend to receive *any* new brand entering into an existing market.

Four psychologically different effects on buyers' perceptions can be distinguished when a new product or service is introduced on a local market:

- *Perceptions stay intact.* Perceptual maps and preferences remain unchanged, with the new entry simply added.

EXHIBIT 11.7 Market Positioning Map of Selected Automobile Brands (1984)

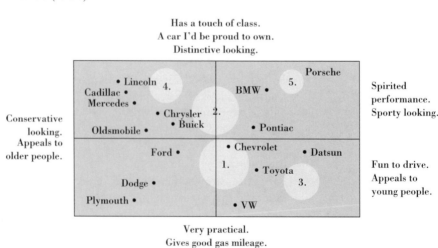

Source: John Koten, "Car Makers Use 'Image' Map as Tools to Position Products," *The Wall Street Journal*, March 22, 1984, p. 31. Reprinted by permission of *The Wall Street Journal*, © Dow Jones & Company, Inc. All rights reserved worldwide.

- *Extended product space.* Perceptual scales are extended.
- *Additional features.* New perceptual dimensions are added.
- *Changing preferences.* Buyer preferences are changed.

In practice all four processes can be at work simultaneously, often at counterpurposes and therefore creating tension. Most people tend to resist changes, but are also curious about new things.

PERCEPTIONS STAY INTACT   The traditional idea of product positioning was that new entries simply were added somewhere in the consumer's existing perceptual maps. This is still the basic rationale behind the use of these maps. Identify the existing competitive positions and consumers' ideal points and then target a "hole" in the market where no competitor is positioned.

Exhibit 11.7 shows a product space map of the American automobile market in the beginning of the 1980s.[21] The Japanese Toyota and Datsun (now Nissan) are positioned inside the third largest segment in the market. This segment desires good gas mileage and a car that is both sporty and fun to drive—preferences that the Japanese-made cars had already targeted in their home market. But even though these two makes were well positioned relative to American models, there is also a "gap" open (segment 3)—a gap that Honda was to fill.

EXTENDED PRODUCT SPACE   In practice it is unlikely that customers' perceptual maps stay unchanged when a new product or brand enters the market. More often than not the introduction of new "stimuli" (again using the standard consumer psychology terms) will change the perceived product space. The space gets elongated or compressed, and new dimensions might be added.

The elongation of the dimensions defining the product space occurs when the new entrant offers more of the salient features. This happens frequently, since the global products often incorporate the *newest technology*.

The introduction of the Honda Accord in the U.S. auto market illustrates the extension of product space. Exhibit 11.8 shows a positioning map from 1982 with the Accord and several competing models included.[22] As can be seen, the Accord offered a

EXHIBIT 11.8 How the Honda Accord Extended the Product Space

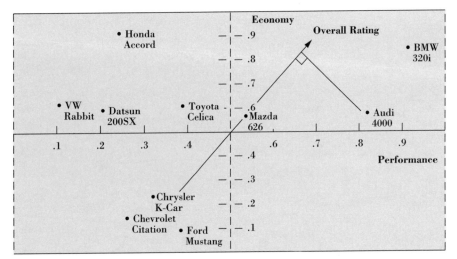

Source: Johny K. Johansson and Hans B. Thorelli, "International Product Positioning," *Journal of International Business Studies*, vol. 16, no. 3 (Fall 1985), pp. 57–75. Reprinted by permission of the *Journal of International Business Studies*.

unique mix of characteristics, being much more economical than even the Japanese competitors. As the overall rating vector shows, the BMW was the preferred choice, but the price was much higher for that car. The American makes were not competitive in this market segment without large rebates.

With extended spaces the benefits desired by consumers are available in greater amounts than before. The convenience, functioning, storage, shopping, and other aspects of the purchase and use of the product have improved because of advances in technology incorporated in the new products.

ADDITIONAL FEATURES   Because of the advances in technology, there is also a strong possibility that the new entrant offers novel features as well. This means that the product space is changing, with new salient dimensions added. Products that do not offer the new features (digital audio, antilock brakes, low cholesterol) will be left out of the consumers' evoked sets. Older brands, often local-only, are now mispositioned. They might not even register in the appropriate evoked set any longer. The main players are global.

The advances in technology restructure the space in another way. Features that in the past could be had only by giving up other features can now be accommodated without sacrifice. In the product space, previously mutually exclusive features have become independent dimensions, enlarging the benefit space. In automobiles, comfort can now be had without compromising fuel economy. Safety does not require heavy car bodies. Noiseless air-conditioning is available. These innovations are not necessarily limited to global products—but the advantage of the global product is that it can incorporate these advanced features at a reasonable cost to the consumer, because of *scale economies*.

Again the American automobile market offers an instructive illustration. Exhibit 11.9 shows the market in 1968, before the two oil crises in the 1970s. As can be seen, there is little evidence of miles-per-gallon or economy as a buying criterion. This can be contrasted with the earlier map in Exhibit 11.7. In Exhibit 11.7 "economy" was emerging strongly, opening up a window for the Japanese entrants. At the same time, there was no need to give up on sporty performance, as would have been the case in 1968.

CHANGING PREFERENCES   Finally, a new product or brand can also induce changes in customer *preferences*. Actually, as we mentioned earlier, a shift in preferences

EXHIBIT 11.9 Illustration of Joint Space of Ideal Points and Stimuli (1968)

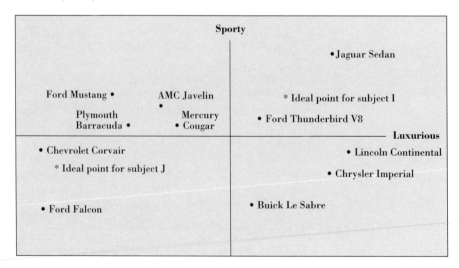

Source: Paul E. Green and Donald S. Tull, *Research for Marketing Decisions*, 3d ed. (Englewood Cliffs, NJ: Prentice-Hall, 1975), p. 611. © 1975. Adapted by permission of Prentice-Hall, Inc., Upper Saddle River, NJ.

can be brought about by various factors, including global communications, changing fashions, and social and national movements, such as the emergence of a "Green" political platform. Japanese carmakers received a "windfall gain" when the oil crises of 1974 and 1978 made consumers look for more fuel-efficient cars. L. L. Bean, the U.S.-based catalog retailer of outdoor gear, has been boosted internationally by the increased emphasis on healthy living and extended amounts of leisure time.

Of equal interest for positioning analysis, the driving factor behind the changes in preferences can be the introduction of products offering new benefits. The change might not be immediate, and in fact, the first reading may be negative. Early market reactions to the Swatch watch were negative, before the notion of a *fashion* watch became accepted. Honda's Acura Legend was considered a "failure" one year after its U.S. introduction, and the idea of a Japanese luxury car did not catch on until Acura's excellent service shifted competition to dealer service and customer satisfaction. Toshiba's laptop computers were rated low at first because of weak picture resolution, but their portability and ease of use soon converted users. These products set *new standards* and became the preferred choices for some segments, often creating new markets in the process.

Positioning a Global Brand

How are global brands of products and services received in local markets abroad according to the positioning framework? The simplest answer is that because they often embody the latest technology, they will naturally have the kind of effects on the perceptual space already discussed. They might tap into an existing "hole" in the market, they may extend the space, and/or add new dimensions. But they can also change preferences directly, even though they may seem mispositioned in the existing product space.

MISPOSITIONING   A drawback of a global product or brand is typically that it is not adapted to the actual preferences in a particular foreign market. In marketing language this means that it is **mispositioned** relative to the preferences or ideal points of the consumers in their perceptual space.[23] This is why local managers often claim that adaptation is necessary because "in our market customers are different."

Why would customers buy a mispositioned offering if they have alternatives closer to their ideal? The usual answer is a *lower price*. This is one reason why one can see so many "special discounts" in various markets around the world, as firms try to sell products that customers don't really want. But as many marketers have learned, inducing the customer to purchase a less desirable product by offering a discounted price often leads to customer dissatisfaction, as the favorable discount is soon forgotten but the less desirable product remains.[24]

BRAND IMAGE   Another and more common reason why mispositioned global products are attractive to potential consumers is *brand image* and status. While local products and services may be better adapted to the market, the global competitor with a strong brand name offers "value added," which the locals can't easily match. For conspicuous consumption, to impress someone special, or simply to lower perceived risk and cognitive dissonance, a well-known global brand name will often do much better than a local brand (see box, "Bunge & Born").

Traditionally, consumers' tastes and preferences were formed by brands and products they could see, touch, and buy. With *global communications*, things have changed. Global media and sponsorship of events ensure that many people will be exposed to a brand name even before they have seen the real product. For example, advertising on the Superbowl in 1998 reached an estimated 150 million people. Although some countries blacked out the commercials, there were considerable spillovers from satellites and direct TV. The 1998 World Cup drew an audience of over 250 million viewers for a month; although not all of the audience resided in the target market for Mars' Snickers candybar, many more people are now aware of the Snickers name. The fact is that a brand name can cross trade barriers much more easily than a product or service. This

---

Bunge & Born: Creating Brand Awareness

BUNGE & BORN S.A. is South America's largest consumer goods company, a multinational especially strong in food products. As the Latin American market improves, the company is facing increased competition from domestic producers and imports in the various country markets. Says Ricardo Esteves, a director of the company: "During high inflation the fear was simply to be able to get the products, and you did not worry about quality or price. Now the shopper is comparing local goods with imported goods and other brands. So we have to produce better products at more competitive prices."

The solution? Uniform standards of products from the various country subsidiaries. And establishing strong regional brand awareness. "Before people would buy whatever pasta was on the shelves, even though they did not know what little company made it," says Mr. Esteves. "But people want to feed themselves better; they are looking for better taste, more purity, as well as a company that will stand behind the product. We want them to look for our brand."

Sources: Nash, 1994; Robinson, 1989.

---

means that a pent-up demand for a branded product in a protected market can easily be created by global communication of the brand name.

Global brands are brands that are well known throughout the world's markets. Examples include Swatch, Mercedes, Nestlé, Coca-Cola, Nike, McDonald's, Sony, and Honda. *Local brands*, by contrast, are well known and strong in some particular market but unknown in others. Examples include retailers such as Delhaize in Belgium and Giant foods in the United States; Luxor electronics in Scandinavia; Morinaga, a food processor, in Japan; the Tsing Tao beer from China; Prosdocimo appliances in Brazil; and so on.

For younger people, global brands such as Coca-Cola and McDonald's have become as familiar as the local brands. The advantage of a local-only brand—in the immediate recognition and subliminal identification that come with familiarity and tradition—is then achieved also by the global brand. As one little boy from Hong Kong happily exclaimed upon arriving in Los Angeles: "They've got McDonald's here too!" It is not surprising that many of the global segments in consumer goods refer to markets for children and teenagers—toys, dresses, shoes, music. For them, "tradition" means last year's styles.

In consumer psychology terms, the global brand effect on positioning usually involves social norms that change preferences in favor of the global brand. If the buyer's motivation to comply with social norms is high—a matter of cultural factors, as we saw in Chapter 3—the global brand will be preferred. In Exhibit 11.7, Mercedes, whose positioning relative to segment 4 is weaker than Lincoln's, is a good example. The mispositioning is not compensated for by price—the Mercedes being more expensive than the Lincoln—but by brand image and the status conferred upon the owner.[25]

COUNTRY OF ORIGIN   Similar to a brand effect, the country-of-origin effect discussed in Chapter 2 can also influence perceptions and affect the position of a product or service. On the basis of the "made-in" label or the home country of the brand, the country-of-origin effect tends to be either a strength or a drawback, depending on how the consumer views the country.

Research shows that the country-of-origin effects on positioning perceptions are generally justified on the basis of objective data. In autos, for example, performance tests and expert ratings confirm that German cars are well engineered with superior handling and performance, similar to the standard stereotype of German products. Japanese cars are reliable and fuel-efficient, the way most consumers see them. But there are also **country-of-origin biases** that have effects. As research has shown, there

G E T T I N G   T H E

Picture

This Bud Is Not for You, Anheuser

ITS MARKET SATURATED in the United States, St. Louis–based beer maker Anheuser-Busch, the world's largest brewer, is trying to market its leading Budweiser brand globally. But the rights to the Budweiser name in Europe belong to a much smaller beer maker, Budejovicky Budvar, the original Czech brewer of Budweiser. The Czech company has the leading market share at home and has a growing export business to other European countries as well.

Since beer marketing is very brand oriented, Anheuser-Busch has long made efforts to acquire the rights to the Budweiser name globally. After the fall of communism, when the Czechs started to privatize industry and sell off government-owned businesses, Anheuser-Busch tried to buy the local beer maker and the trademark.

But the Czech managers and workers did not want any part of a company that they suspected would pull the plug on their operation, siphon the profits, and try to take their beer off the market.

To soften up the Czechs, Anheuser-Busch opened up a $1 million cultural center in Ceske Budejovice, the town where the brewer is located, inaugurated baseball and basketball teams, opened a marble-floored café, and offered scholarships and English lessons. But to no avail. Listen to Frantisek Nedorost, a 52-year-old electrician: "I absolutely disagree with the Americans buying part of our company. I like Americans, their culture, their films. But I know American beer doesn't reach the quality of Czech beer. It's much poorer, much weaker."

Anheuser-Busch has just about given up hope of ever being able to sell its Budweiser in all of Europe, and instead uses only the shorter "Bud" in selected markets.

Sources: Perlez, 1995; Koenig, 1995.
http://www.anheuser-busch.com

---

is a tendency on the part of consumers to overstate positive and negative product attributes. Japanese cars may not be quite as fuel-efficient as people think, German cars not quite as outstanding technologically as many expect, and American cars not quite as bad as some would say.[26] Over time, as global competition intensifies and objectively the products become more comparable, many of these misperceptions are likely to be corrected. Still they may linger on for some time, rewarding or penalizing a country's companies accordingly.

There is also an *emotional* aspect of country-of-origin effects, when people feel pressured to buy (or not buy) products from a certain country. This can happen, for example, because of a media campaign ("Buy American") or because of social norms operating on the buyer. Research shows that in most countries, people like to buy products from their own country, everything else being equal.[27] The "everything else equal" condition is of course the key: Imported global products will in general offer something special, and as experience has shown, it is imprudent for the domestic company to rely on the emotional attachment of people to homegrown, but inferior, products.[28]

LOCAL PRODUCTS AND SERVICES

The success of global brands of products and services does not mean that locally adapted products or services have no opportunity.

As the experiences of many travelers attest, even in open markets many local products and services survive and prosper next to global brands. Restaurants serving local specialties thrive. In audio products, shoes, apparel, and other consumer goods, local products coexist with well-known world brands. In business-to-business markets local vendors do well with custom software and supplies. Local beers are successful throughout North America and Europe, even though in some cases their market is directly targeted by global competitors (see box, "This Bud Is Not for You, Anheuser").

The typical reason for the success of local products and services is the customization involved. In *industrial goods* markets, personal attention, fast delivery, and prompt after-sales service are all factors tending to favor local products. This advantage is diminished to the extent global manufacturers pay attention to the localization of their offerings. With the growing trend toward global integration and coordination in customer organizations, industrial marketing tends to follow suit and favor global uniformity. Selling to a globalized customer forces suppliers to globalize as well.

In *consumer goods*, the sameness of global products creates a potential for local products in special niche segments of the market. These niches comprise consumers who are looking for ethnic color, uniqueness, and local tradition. There are people who still like stick shifts, cigarettes without filters, and hair spray. Local products and services provide variety for consumers in special situations for which the global product is not suitable. Thus, while global brands may capture a large segment of the market, local variants can coexist underneath the global umbrella.

POSITIONING RESEARCH

Marketing research in global product positioning suffers less from the weaknesses of market segmentation studies abroad. Good primary data are expensive to collect, but the number of respondents for positioning purposes can be more limited. Getting individuals to reliably and validly rate competing products on various features is not so difficult, even though pretesting is necessary to make sure that the salient attributes and evoked stimuli include the relevant items.

That consumers from different countries have different perceptions of a given brand or product is hardly surprising, since this can be true also of the market at home. As mentioned above, a product's or brand's country of origin can bias perceptions.[29] Attributes defining the product may differ from those at home. The marketer needs to make sure that the offering is acceptable on aspects that might have been unimportant in the home market.

For many Western marketers, it will be tempting to rely on the image of the brand name as a major positioning tool. The local marketer should do a "reality check" of the company's perceptions against those of the local market. It is common to hear a newly arrived marketer proclaim that everybody knows and admires the company brands. Such "facts" need to be corroborated by research in the local market, among middlemen as well as among ultimate consumers. For example, while the Olivetti slimline design of word processors makes for an elegant and sophisticated continental image, American customers found it to be "fragile" and "effeminate."[30] Though Swedish products are considered functional and well made by big Swedes, they can seem stodgy and clumsy to other people.

Only research can uncover such potential positioning problems. Such research does not have to be very elaborate and expensive, but it should be an image survey done with the usual care. The respondents have to be representative, and the sponsor should not be identified.

EMBRYONIC MARKETS

As we have seen, the product positioning framework is useful for analyzing how global products and services are received by local customers. But product space maps used to disentangle the multiple effects of global brands assume that consumers have a well-articulated view of the marketplace for a given product or service. This assumption is likely to hold only in the *mature* stage of the product life cycle. As in the case of forecasting sales (Chapter 4), very new or "embryonic" markets require a different approach, one based on how new markets evolve as innovations are diffused.

The **diffusion process** that new innovations pass through underlies the early stages of the product life cycle. As Exhibit 11.10 shows, the life cycle in fact represents the cumulative distribution of a typically normal distribution of buyers. As the new product appears on the market, most potential buyers tend to be unsure about the exact benefits and the ability of the product to live up to its promises. Only a small minority, known as the "pioneers," are willing to accept the risk involved in trying the new product.

At this stage, which segment to target is not easy to decide. The Sony Walkman was initially targeted toward professionals commuting to work who would be free to listen to music while reading the morning newspaper. The name chosen with this in mind was not "Walkman" but "Soundabout." After lackluster initial sales in the target market, especially in the United States and Europe where the intended target found the product too flippant and youthful, the company shifted to younger people who had shown some interest in simply using the product while walking, running, skateboarding, or rollerblading. Hence "Walkman" and a sturdier design, even though initial market research had shown that the younger segment would not be interested in a "tape recorder that did not record."[31]

TARGETING STRATEGIES

To get a grasp on how segmentation and positioning fit into the development of global marketing strategy, it will be useful to examine the alternative targeting strategies that a globalizing firm can contemplate for a global product. The cross-classification in Exhibit 11.11 will help identify the various alternatives. The classification shows how segmentation and positioning analysis can be used to extend Keegan's formulation of global marketing strategy presented at the beginning of the chapter.

In the exhibit two alternative market segmentation cases (universal and unique) are crossed against two positioning appeals (uniform, adapted). A **universal** segment refers to one that is basically the same across countries: "teenagers," say, or "young

EXHIBIT 11.10 The Product Life Cycle (PLC) and the Diffusion Curve

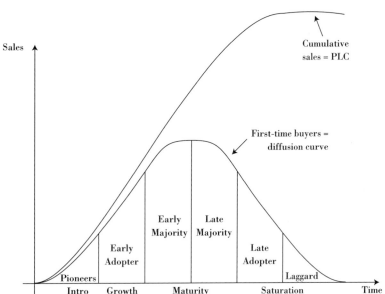

EXHIBIT 11.11 Segmentation and Positioning Examples for Global Products

Local Market Segment

		Universal	Unique
Positioning	**Uniform**	– Nike	– IKEA – Mobile phones
	Adapted	– Volvo – Pampers	– Levi's – Honda Prelude

professionals." A **unique** segment is one that differs across countries (for example, "college students" in country A and "families with children" in country B). For the product positioning dimension, **uniform** indicates a position that is the same across countries, while **adapted** indicates that the positioning theme differs across countries.

In the first cell, Nike's global brand appeals to young people and aspiring athletes, whether they play on the streets of Buenos Aires, Philadelphia, Seoul, or Helsinki. By contrast, in cell two the positioning is adapted. In the United States Volvo cars feature safety, while in Europe Volvo is positioned for sporty performance on less than perfect roads. Similarly, as we saw in Chapter 1, Pampers successful positioning message in Japan focused on happy babies rather than inconvenienced mothers.

In cell three, segments differ but the positioning appeal does not. Across the world IKEA offers the same furniture in self-assembled kits. But the target segment of young families with children is augmented in the United States with singles and homosexual couples. In the case of mobile phones, this "must-have" product for young professionals everywhere was in Scandinavia first used by delivery boys.

In cell 4 both segments and positioning are unique, with the product still standardized. Levi jeans are a status symbol in many countries, while the American home market takes a more prosaic view of the denims. The Honda Prelude, a small sport coupe for singles, became a woman's car in the North-American market, against the strategic intent.

These cases go to show that with proper segmentation and positioning it is possible to standardize products—and to some extent positioning—even though the segments targeted are not universal or even very similar in different countries.

SUMMARY

In today's global environment, careful segmentation of markets, at the macro as well as the micro level, becomes increasingly important. At the macro segmentation level the advantages of similarities between countries that cluster together need to be balanced against the possibility of diversification benefits and avoidance of

any domino effect should the economies of one country after the other topple.

At the microsegmentation level, where target segments within countries are identified, the increase in data availability is making it possible to use traditional marketing techniques to identify similar segments across countries. Because of differences in economic development, demographics, and culture, most companies still combine several criteria in forming the segments.

For positioning purposes it is common to look for—and target—universal segments that are similar across countries since those can be approached with relatively uniform marketing mixes. But the relationships are not that direct. As the chapter showed, even universally similar segments (such as teenagers) might need some adaptation of product or positioning. In other cases, globally coordinated strategies, standardized products, and even uniform strategies can be employed in cases where the segments are different. What matters is basically whether the product advantages—and how they are communicated—are appreciated by segment members. Fundamentally, Chapter 11 showed how the same product and the same message can have different meanings to different people.

The chapter also discussed the way an entering globally standardized product or service can affect the positioning of existing products or brands in a market. The advantages of brand name, quality/price ratio, and country of origin can sometimes outweigh the local brands' claim on their loyal customers.

The special case of embryonic markets where buyer preferences are yet to crystallize was also discussed. Here the marketer has much less use for the segmentation and positioning tools, since the market is still settling, and it becomes important for the marketer to decide whether first-mover advantages are sufficient to entice a risky entry.

The chapter ended with an extension of Keegan's original international strategy framework, focused on the case of a standardized product or service, the "bread and butter" of global marketing. The extension showed how different companies use different segmentation and positioning strategies when implementing global marketing.

KEY TERMS

adapted positioning   p. 360
attribute ratings   p. 351
cluster analysis   p. 343
country-of-origin biases   p. 356
diffusion process   p. 359
diversification   p. 347
dual adaptation   p. 339
embryonic markets   p. 338
evoked set   p. 351
focus strategy   p. 347
global communications   p. 340

macrosegmentation   p. 343
mispositioned   p. 355
opinion leaders   p. 359
preference   p. 351
product–communications
   extension   p. 339
product
   extension–communications
   adaptation   p. 339
product invention   p. 339

product
   localization–communications
   extension   p. 339
product space   p. 351
salient attributes   p. 351
segmentation criteria   p. 348
technology diffusion   p. 340
uniform positioning   p. 360
unique segment   p. 360
universal segment   p. 360

DISCUSSION QUESTIONS

1. Try to find a product or service for which the target segment can be the same all over the world. Try to find another one for which the target segments vary but where the product or service remains the same. What are the reasons for the difference? How would the difference affect the way the companies set up their Web sites?

2. When discussing product positioning, the chapter used the examples of the Japanese cars entering Western markets. Using this framework, how would you analyze the reception given to the Japanese luxury cars? What did change in people's perceptions, and what did not?

3. Use the Internet sites of a few companies to identify what their target segments seem to be. What positioning strategy do they seem to follow?

4. What country-of-origin *biases* do you think affect people's perceptions about these products: autos, rock music, classical music, hotels, shoes, and stereos. To what extent do you think the biases are justified by the facts? Are they changing over time?

5. The trade blocs represent "ready made" target segments. Discuss to what extent these blocs provide diversification benefits, and to what extent they do not.

NOTES

1. See Douglas and Craig, 1989.

2. This section draws on Keegan, 1969.

3. In Keegan's original formulation, the third strategy alternative involved product adaptation rather than product localization as used here. When "adaptation" refers to actual *use* of the product, as is the case here, the term "localization" is preferable. Adaptation can then be reserved for the case of adapting to different customer *preferences*, a more complex question. As we will see in Chapter 12, localized products can still be standardized.

4. See Levitt, 1983. A precursor to Levitt was an insightful article by Buzzell, 1968.

5. The discussions concerning Levitt's 1983 article followed this line of attack. For an alternative point of view, however, see Boddewyn et al., 1986.

6. These and similar changes are reported every day in television news programs and print media. A good data source for up-to-date market information on spending patterns is the *Global Scan* publication from Bates Worldwide, along with other sources listed in Chapter 4.

7. The Reatta case discussion is from Urban and Star, 1991, and the Mazda Miata information from a class project by H. Schumpert, Georgetown University, Spring 1992.

8. From Johansson and Roehl, 1994.

9. From a personal interview with Mr. H. Ahnefeld, corporate planning, Bosch A. G., Stuttgart, January 17, 1989.

10. This term was first proposed by Wind and Douglas, 1972.

11. A compact and accessible treatment of both factor and cluster analysis can be found in Churchill, 1994.

12. See Cavusgil, 1990.

13. See Helsen et al., 1993.

14. See Zandpour and Harich, 1996.

15. From Johansson, 1982.

16. See Ayal and Zif, 1979.

17. See Piercy, 1982, and also Lee, 1987.

18. From De Mooij, 1994.

19. See Mitchell, 1983, Chapter 10.

20. The standard terminology is used here, with "product" positioning also covering services. Ries and Trout, 1982, give the classic account of the psychology of positioning. A good treatment of the basics of positioning techniques can be found in Urban and Hauser, 1980. The Reatta case in Urban and Star, 1991, is an excellent example of the empirical application of positioning.

21. This illustration is adapted from Koten, 1984.

22. Adapted from Johansson and Thorelli, 1985.

23. In an interesting study of consumers in France, Korea, and Spain, Du Preez et al., 1994, showed how ideal points and attribute importance in automobiles differed between the countries. A standardized car model offering similar features in all three countries would have been mispositioned in at least two.

24. This is the problem of extrinsic versus intrinsic motivations, a topic researched in consumer behavior. See, for example, George J. Szybillo and Jack Jacoby, 1974.

25. Global brand names also give the manufacturers more clout in international channels, a topic we will return to in Chapter 14.

26. See Johansson and Thorelli, 1985.

27. The Papadopoulos and Heslop, 1993, volume offers several examples of this effect.

28. See Yavas et al., 1992, for a very interesting study of how powerful global brands can be when properly localized.

29. See Johansson and Nebenzahl, 1986.

30. See Dichter, 1964.

31. From Johansson and Nonaka, 1996.

32. The traditional meaning of opinion leadership is one where there is face-to-face contact. But today the concept is usually expanded to include the impact from celebrities and media figures. The virtual reality of television and the Internet has blurred the distinction between interpersonal and mass media.

SELECTED REFERENCES

Ayal, I.; and J. Zif. "Market Expansion Strategies in Multinational Marketing." *Journal of Marketing* 43 (Spring 1979), pp. 84–94.

Baden-Fuller, Charles W. F.; and John M. Stopford. "Globalization Frustrated: The Case of White Goods." *Strategic Management Journal* 12 (1991), pp. 493–507.

Boddewyn, Jean J.; Robin Soehl; and Jacques Picard. "Standardization in International Marketing: Is Ted Levitt in Fact Right?" *Business Horizons*, November–December 1986, pp. 69–75.

Buzzell, Robert D. "Can You Standardize Multinational Marketing?" *Harvard Business Review*, November–December 1968, pp. 102–13.

Carpano, Claudio; and James J. Chrisman. "Performance Implications of International Product Strategies and the Integration of Marketing Activities." *Journal of International Marketing* 3, no. 1 (1995), pp. 9–28.

Cavusgil, S. Tamer. "A Market-Oriented Clustering of Countries." In Hans B. Thorelli and S. Tamer Cavusgil, eds. *International Marketing Strategy*, 3d ed. New York: Pergamon, 1990.

Churchill, Gilbert A., Jr. *Marketing Research: Methodological Foundations*, 6th ed. Fort Worth, TX: Dryden, 1994.

De Mooij, Marieke. *Advertising Worldwide*, 2nd ed. Englewood Cliffs, NJ: Prentice-Hall, 1994, p. 167.

Dichter, Ernest. *Handbook of Consumer Motivations*. New York: McGraw-Hill, 1964.

Douglas, Susan P.; and C. Samuel Craig. "Evolution of Global Marketing Strategy: Scale, Scope and Synergy." *Columbia Journal of World Business*, Fall 1989, pp. 47–59.

Du Preez, Johann P.; Adamantios Diamantopoulos; and Bodo B. Schlegelmilch. "Product Standardization and Attribute Saliency: A Three-Country Empirical Comparison." *Journal of International Marketing* 2, no. 1 (1994), pp. 7–28.

Green, Paul E.; Arun Maheshwari; and Vithala Rao. "Dimensional Interpretation and Configuration Invariance in Multidimensional Scaling: An Empirical Study." *Multivariate Behavioral Research* 4 (April 1969), pp. 159–180.

Halliburton, Chris; and Ian Jones. "Global Individualism— Reconciling Global Marketing and Global Manufacturing." *Journal of International Marketing* 2, no. 4 (1994), pp. 79–88.

Hanni, David A.; John K. Ryans; and Ivan R. Vernon. "Coordinating International Advertising—The Goodyear Case

Revisited for Latin America." *Journal of International Marketing* 3, no. 2 (1995), pp. 83–98.

Helsen, Kristiaan; Kamel Jedidi; and Wayne de Sarbo. "A New Approach to Country Segmentation Utilizing Multinational Diffusion Patterns." Journal of Marketing 57, no. 4 (October 1993), pp. 60–71.

Johansson, J. K. "A Note on the Managerial Relevance of Interdependence." *Journal of International Business Studies,* Winter 1982, pp. 143–45.

———; and Izrael D. Nebenzahl. "Multinational Expansion: Effect on Brand Evaluations." *Journal of International Business Studies* 17, no. 3 (Fall 1986), pp. 101–26.

———; and Ikujiro Nonaka. *Relentless: The Japanese Way of Marketing.* New York: HarperBusiness, 1996.

———; and Hans B. Thorelli. "International Product Positioning." *Journal of International Business Studies* XVI, no. 3 (Fall 1985), pp. 57–76.

———; and Thomas W. Roehl. "How Companies Develop Assets and Capabilities: Japan as a Leading Market." In Allan Bird, ed. *The Future of Japan's Business.* Greenwich, CT: JAI Press, 1994.

Keegan, Warren J. "Multinational Product Planning: Strategic Alternatives." *Journal of Marketing,* January 1969, pp. 58–62.

Koenig, Robert L. "Bud War: 2 Budweisers Square Off in Czech Republic." *St. Louis Post Dispatch,* October 22, 1995, p. 1A.

Koten, John. "Car Makers Use 'Image' Map as Tool to Position Products." *The Wall Street Journal,* March 22, 1984, p. 31.

Lee, Chong Suk. *Export Market Expansion Strategies and Export Performance: A Study of High Technology Manufacturing Firms.* Doctoral dissertation, University of Washington, 1987.

Levitt, Ted. "The Globalization of Markets." *Harvard Business Review,* May–June 1983.

Lim Say Boon. "The Shave of Things to Come." *The Straits Times,* April 11, 1993, Sunday Review, p. 4.

Mitchell, Arnold. *The Nine American Lifestyles.* New York: Macmillan, 1983.

Nash, Nathaniel C. "Bunge & Born: More Mindful of Latin-America." *New York Times,* January 3, 1994, p. C5.

Papadopoulos, Nicolas; and Louise A. Heslop, eds. *Product-Country Images: Impact and Role in International Marketing.* New York: International Business Press, 1993.

Perlez, Jane. "This Bud's Not for You, Anheuser." *New York Times,* June 30, 1995, pp. D1, D4.

Piercy, Nigel. "Export Strategy: Concentration on Key Markets vs. Market Spreading." *Journal of International Marketing* 1, no. 1 (1982), pp. 56–67.

Quelch, John A.; and Edward J. Hoff. "Customizing Global Marketing." *Harvard Business Review,* May–June 1986, pp. 59–68.

Ries, Al; and Jack Trout. *Positioning: The Battle for Your Mind.* New York: Warner Books, 1982.

Robinson, Eugene. "In Argentina, Private Firm a Power Player; Bunge & Born, a Multinational Wields Clout in Nation's Economy." *The Washington Post,* December 6, 1989, p. G1.

Samiee, Saeed; and Kendall Roth. "The Influence of Global Marketing Standardization on Performance." *Journal of Marketing* 56, no. 2 (April 1992), pp. 1–17.

Sorenson, R. Z.; and U. E. Wiechmann. "How Multinationals View Marketing Standardization." In D. N. Dickson, ed. *Managing Effectively in the World Marketplace.* New York: Wiley, 1983, pp. 301–16.

Szybillo, George J.; and Jack Jacoby. "Intrinsic versus Extrinsic Cues as Determinants of Perceived Product Quality." *Journal of Applied Psychology,* February 1974, pp. 74–78.

Takeuchi, Hirotaka; and Michael E. Porter. "Three Roles of International Marketing in Global Strategy." In Michael E. Porter, ed. *Competition in Global Industries.* Cambridge, MA: Harvard Business School Press, 1986.

Uchitelle, Louis. "Gillette's World View: One Blade Fits All." *New York Times,* January 3, 1994, p. C3.

Urban, Glen L.; and John R. Hauser. *Design and Marketing of New Products.* Englewood Cliffs, NJ: Prentice-Hall, 1980.

———; and Steven H. Star. *Advanced Marketing Strategy.* Englewood Cliffs, NJ: Prentice-Hall, 1991.

Wind, Jerry; and Susan Douglas. "International Market Segmentation." *European Journal of Marketing* 6, no. 1 (1972).

Yavas, Ugur; Bronislaw J. Verhage; and Robert T. Green. "Global Consumer Segmentation versus Local Market Orientation: Empirical Findings." *Management International Review* 32, no. 3 (1992), pp. 265–72.

Zandpour, Fred; and Katrin R. Harich. "Think and Feel Country Clusters: A New Approach to International Advertising Standardization." *International Journal of Advertising* 15 (1996), pp. 325–44.

Global Products and Services

"Best in the world"

Your takeaways from this chapter:

1. There is a difference between *localization* of a product or service to fit local regulations and usage requirements and *adaptation*, which is a matter of fitting the product to buyer preferences. A *standardized* global product or service is not adapted to customer preferences but must still be localized.

2. Product and service standardization is never 100 percent, but management must select which features of the offering to keep uniform and which to adapt to local markets.

3. Global brands are often the most valuable assets of a global firm. The administration of these brands has become a top management concern.

4. Most firms have a portfolio of global and local brands, which need to be managed for synergy and potential building strategies for increased brand equity.

5. Globalizing a service means identifying very carefully what the core advantages of the service are and whether they can be reproduced faithfully in a foreign market.

ONE OF THE FIRST QUESTIONS arising in global product management is, "Can this product (or service) be standardized globally?" While a customized offering is closest to the marketing ideal, there are cost savings in large scale that make global standardization preferable. There are also demand spillover effects from a uniform approach—in brand name recognition, trade support, prestige, and word of mouth. This chapter discusses the management of globally standardized products and services, including the building of strong global brands.

Montblanc Bets on World-Class Reputation

When is a pen not a pen? When it is an "art form." This is how Switzerland's Compagnie Financière Richemont positions its Montblanc pens. The fancy writing instruments boast individually numbered gold nibs and are topped with a white mark representing a bird's-eye view of snow-capped Mont Blanc, a mountain in the Alps. A single fountain pen will set you back $235 to $13,500 (for one made of platinum).

Apparently, the pen's style and quality have succeeded in making it more than just a status symbol. The upscale readers of *Robb Report*, a monthly magazine that rates products associated with an affluent lifestyle, voted Montblanc the best writing instrument in the world.

For Richemont subsidiary Montblanc North America, this reputation presents an opportunity to extend the product line. The company recently announced plans to open stand-alone boutiques offering jewelry and leather accessories such as wallets, briefcases, organizers, and garment bags.

To support the brand extension, the company plans marketing communications reinforcing Montblanc's image of fine quality. This promotional effort includes magazine advertisements that link the Montblanc pen with the "art of writing." Newspaper ads announce the opening of the boutiques and the introduction of new products. Cultural events at the boutiques include displays of rare manuscripts, letters, and autographs. Together, such efforts are intended to convey, in the words of the ad agency's creative director, "an image that Montblanc isn't only a writing-instrument company but a European luxury brand. . . . We hope that the Montblanc brand will stand not just for a pen, but for a certain lifestyle."

Decisions about product design and image are also at the core of other marketers' efforts to expand international product lines. At Reebok International, Angel R. Martinez is leading an effort to rejuvenate the company's Rockport subsidiary, a maker of comfortable casual shoes. Martinez, formerly Reebok's vice president for global marketing, is betting that more exciting styles, coupled with advertising that conveys the shoes' high quality, will fuel a big upturn in sales and make Rockport a global brand. And at General Motors, management hopes that sharing design ideas across brands and national boundaries can help the company produce "world cars" from its Opel plant in Germany that will appeal to buyers on more than one continent. The stakes are high, but so are the expected rewards.

Sources: Glenn Collins, "Montblanc Expands on Gertrude Stein to Suggest That Sometimes a Pen Is More Than a Pen," *New York Times*, July 27, 1995, p. D9; Glenn Rifkin, "Does This Shoe Fit?" *New York Times*, October 14, 1995, pp. 33, 36; David Woodruff, "Can Opel Deliver the 'World Cars' GM Needs?" *Business Week*, December 4, 1995, pp. 52–53.
http://www.reebok.com
http://www.gm.com

INTRODUCTION

As we saw in Chapter 11, globalizing marketing involves global *coordination* of marketing activities. It means taking a *global strategy* perspective on the marketing operations in any one country. It involves a certain degree of marketing *standardization*, maintaining a degree of *uniformity* in product, advertising, distribution, and other marketing mix elements across country markets. In this chapter we will deal with the implications of globalized marketing for products and services.

First some definitions. Marketers generally make a distinction between "global" and "regional" products and brands. As we saw in Chapter 11, **global products** are usually standardized with some uniform features in all countries. In particular, brand names are often the same across countries. **Global brand** examples include Gillette razor blades, Colgate toothpaste, Sony television sets, and Benetton sweaters. By contrast, **regional** products and brands are unique to a particular trading region, such as Honda's "European" car model Concerto, P&G's Ariel and Vizir in Europe, the Mexican beer brewer Corona's "pan-American" market, and Korea's ginseng tea makers covering the Asian market. These regional products are latently global, as global expansion occurs and customers learn more about the products. Also, the marketing issues raised by regional products are similar in *kind* to those raised by global products, only the *degree* of complexity and the magnitude of the task are different. Where the regional market is large enough to offer the cost savings associated with standardization—reaching a "minimum efficient scale"—the marketing issue is to what extent the local markets can accept one standardized product. "Pan-European standardization" essentially poses the same problems as "global standardization."

This chapter first discusses the pros and cons of standardization and how managers balance the demand for local adaptation against the benefits of uniformity. The important distinction between localization and adaptation is clarified. Then the chapter discusses some pitfalls of companies that have practiced product standardization and describes what research on standardization versus adaptation involves. A section on global product lines leads into the important role that global brands play in products and services. The way companies build and manage a global brand is discussed in depth. A section on the very real threat of counterfeit products is followed by a discussion of services and the specific marketing problems encountered in globalizing services.

THE PROS AND CONS OF STANDARDIZATION

For most companies some product standardization is unavoidable. Cost savings from longer product series often outweigh the disadvantages of not being perfectly adapted to customers' precise requirements. At the same time, the customer satisfaction advantages of a high level of adaptation are well understood by most companies. Where the combined costs are at minimum (see Exhibit 12.1) is the optimal level of standardization. Finding this point in practice is often a delicate balancing act.

EXHIBIT 12.1 The Trade-Off between Standardization and Adaptation

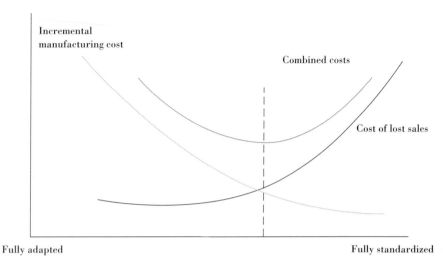

To evaluate the potential benefits of a standardized product or service strategy, it is useful to first summarize and review the advantages and drawbacks of standardized offerings. There are several pros and cons of standardization.[1]

The Advantages of Standardization

COST REDUCTION Cost reductions gained by **scale economies** constitute one major benefit from product standardization. Because of the longer production series there are considerable savings to be gained in manufacturing as well as purchasing. Product development costs can be spread over a larger number of units. Unnecessary duplication of effort, with minor variations in color or design of a product, can be avoided. Centralizing the purchase of media spots for advertising generates quantity rebates and other savings. When one global brand name is used in several countries, there are savings in media advertising and sales efforts. Furthermore, there are **scope economies** in marketing. The use of a globally standardized advertising campaign makes it possible to exploit good creative ideas to their fullest potential. Benetton's goodwill can be extended from apparel to sports gear. Advanced technology and new features can be used across a whole product line. New carbon material can be used for all tennis rackets, not just the upper end of the market.

IMPROVED QUALITY The standardized product or service is likely to offer improved quality in terms of functioning. Since additional resources can be focused on the product development effort and the design, the standardized product or service is likely to be more thoroughly tested. Investment in state-of-the-art production processes is justified. This leads to higher quality in terms of durability and reliability. The customized product may have more status and extra quality features—an expensive luxury car, for example, may have more expensive wood on the dashboard—but in terms of functionality, a standardized product is more likely to function well.

ENHANCED CUSTOMER PREFERENCE The firm can also enhance customer preferences by standardization. Positive experiences with a product in one country naturally encourage a consumer to buy the same brand elsewhere. One attractive feature of a camera can be that the same model is available in other countries, increasing the chance of getting service. Standardized advertising messages and slogans capitalize on spillover effects in marketing communications. Seeing attractive ads for the same camera at home and in a foreign country reinforces a customer's purchase decision. Canon, capitalizing on the recognition value of Andre Agassi, the tennis player, features him endorsing Canon cameras in airport advertisements around the world.

GLOBAL CUSTOMERS   There is also a special advantage to standardization because of global customers who demand uniform quality and services wherever they happen to be and buy. In consumer goods, global communications and the growth of international travel and tourism have helped spawn global markets for products as diverse as chocolate, watches, and apparel. In business-to-business markets, as firms grow more global and their purchasing function is centralized on a global basis, standardization of requirement specifications becomes necessary.

GLOBAL SEGMENTS   Finally, standardization has the advantage that it fits with the emergence of global customer segments. As we have seen, the customer segments in one market can often be similar to those in other markets. In technology-based product categories—computers, cameras, televisions—there are customer segments in various countries who all want similar products, and as these segments grow, the potential benefits of standardization grow as well.

The Drawbacks of Standardization

OFF-TARGET   One drawback of standardized products or services is that they are likely to miss the exact target in terms of customer preferences in any one country. Where needs and wants across countries are homogeneous, this is not a problem. The problem is obvious in markets where customers in different countries have widely different tastes or needs. Offering only jumbo-sized packages of bathroom tissue makes no sense where storage capacity in the homes is limited.

Standardization may mean that some segments of the market are not targeted correctly, and the resulting positioning of many global products may be in the larger core segments of the market (the typical American and Japanese case) or in specialty niches (the more common approach for Europeans). Thus, IBM, Microsoft, Xerox, Sony, Panasonic, and Toyota tend to offer standardized products for core market segments in many countries, while Mercedes, Armani, Chanel, and Leica offer standardized products to upscale segments everywhere.

LACK OF UNIQUENESS   There is also a drawback in the lack of uniqueness of standardized products. If customization or exclusivity is one of the overriding purchase considerations, a standardized offering is by definition in a weak position. As markets grow more affluent, uniqueness is likely to become increasingly salient. By contrast, in a period of recession, the luxury of being "special" might be forgone by the consumer.

VULNERABLE TO TRADE BARRIERS   In order to reap the benefits of standardization open trade regimes are necessary. The scale economies are difficult to realize unless production can take place in one or two countries, with plant capacity at least of the minimum efficient scale and with the standardized product exported globally. Where country markets are protected by trade barriers, local manufacturing may be necessary and the scale benefits from standardization can't be reaped. Then it may be better to target the local market specifically with an adapted product in order to avoid mispositioning.

STRONG LOCAL COMPETITORS   Standardization can also fail simply because local competitors are capable and manage to mount a strong defense. By offering customized products, and working closely with local channel members and offering special services, the local competitor can hold off an attack from a global company. If, in addition, the global company is not able to execute effectively at the local level, the global strategy is likely to fail.

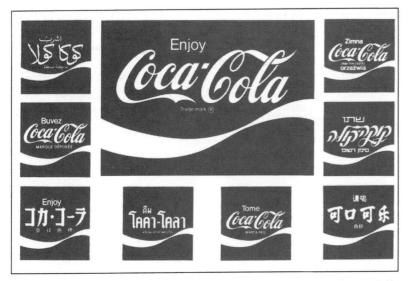

1. Arabic   5. Spanish
2. French   6. Chinese
3. Japanese   7. Hebrew
4. Thai   8. Polish

The Coca Cola name in eight different languages. A brand name takes on different meanings in different countries, a potential hazard. After research, the Chinese Mandarin translation became "kou-kee-koulee," suggesting "happiness in the mouth." Courtesy The Coca-Cola Company.

WHICH FEATURES TO STANDARDIZE?

In practice, 100 percent standardization is rare. Usually some features of a product need to be adapted.[2] For example, packaging needs to show information in the native language. Some global firms solve this problem by providing information in three or four languages on the same package. Most personal care products in Europe typically come in packages with up to four languages (English, French, German, and Spanish, for example), making it possible to produce longer series and gain scale economies.

Product Standardization

Standardization usually starts with a **core product** as the foundation. In automobiles this core is the "platform" chassis that forms the basic structure of the model. Then various features are added to the core product to complete the marketed product. These features may or may not be identical across countries. In the case of autos, for example, suspensions in Europe tend to be stiffer than in the United States, to accommodate the more aggressive European driving habits. In the case of soft drinks, the adaptations may involve the development of smaller package sizes for some markets or a slight change in sugar levels. For example, Coca-Cola lowers the sugar content and uses smaller packages in Asian markets.

Standardization can also involve a **modular design.** Here the various features are prepackaged as modules that can then be assembled in different combinations to target different markets. For example, most cameras are now assembled from a few modular components such as lenses, film winder, body casing, flash unit, telescope motor, and various electronic chips for focus, aperture, and the like. These modular components can be produced in long series and then assembled to build a line of models at different prices. The flexibility created has also meant that companies are able to offer slightly different models in different countries, not only to adapt to demand differences but also to discourage gray trade—all at no loss of standardization advantages.

Service Standardization

The standardization of services also starts with a certain "core" service. Most fast-food restaurants, following McDonald's, focus on the basic principles of friendliness ("smile"), cleanliness of the premises, and quick service. But given the cultural diversity in the world, the human element becomes an obstacle to **service standardization.** Thus, the consensus among many service marketers is that one can globally standardize the "**back room**" aspects of the service—quality control in fast-food restaurants, computerized bookings within a hotel chain, inventory control for retailers—but not necessarily the customer interactions, the "**front line**" meeting of consumers with the service providers.[3] The front-line personnel in even the most global service companies are usually natives, whose command of language and customs enables them to deliver the service appropriately.[4]

LOCALIZATION VERSUS ADAPTATION

Successful companies often find that even the most standardized product or service usually requires some local changes. Every country has a few regulations not found elsewhere. For example, a country may demand certain product information on a package not needed in other markets. A case in point is the U.S. warning on cigarette packages about the health hazard associated with smoking, not required in many Asian countries. Cars in Sweden need to drive with the parking lights on, and the lights are turned on automatically when the ignition key is turned. The United States is particularly confusing to foreign entrants since the individual states often feature separate requirements, such as the stricter pollution controls on cars registered in California compared with most other states.

Basic Requirements

But these differences do not mean "no standardization." Adhering to them involves **localization** more than true adaptation, an important difference in global marketing. *Localization refers to the changes required for a product or service to function in a new country.* For example, when a fax machine is fitted with a new type of telephone jack for a foreign country, it is "localized." *When products are adapted, changes are made to match customer tastes or preferences.* When the fax machine comes with a lighter handset for the Italian market, it is "adapted." Generally speaking, localization avoids having potential customers reject the product out of hand, while **adaptation** gives customers a positive reason for choosing it. Localization is a positive for all potential customers in the country, while adaptation aims to target some special segment or segments. Localization is necessary for consumers to even consider the product; adaptation tries to make them prefer it over other choices.[5]

In practice there is sometimes not a sharp and definite distinction between localization and adaptation as the Kentucky Fried Chicken experience in Japan shows (see box, "KFC Goes to Japan").

Nevertheless, the distinction is very useful in analyzing the pros and cons of standardization. *Even a "globally standardized" product needs to be localized.* It would basically offer an unchanged core design and simply be refitted to a country's requirements.[6]

Compatibility Requirements

Localization is in many ways equivalent to compatibility. It represents the adjustments in the product specifications necessary for it to function in the foreign environment. With TV broadcast systems differing between European countries and the United States, VCRs need to be adapted. The sleeves of Western clothing need to be shortened for the Japanese market. Shampoos for the softer northern European hair are chemically different from those for southern Europeans' thicker hair. Effective skin care products need to be biogenetically different depending on the food of a nation's people. And so on.

Multisystem Compatibility

In many products today, localization is accomplished by building in compatibility with multiple systems at the outset. Thus VCRs and TV sets are designed to operate in many system environments. Word processing software offers multiple formatting op-

KFC Goes to Japan

IN THE EARLY 1970s when Kentucky Fried Chicken entered Japan, it faced the task of creating a market for its version of fast food. The Japanese fast-food market consisted mainly of small noodle and sushi restaurants with lunch served at counters and with free home or office delivery (on moped or bicycle). The original recipe for KFC chicken was left unchanged (it is still the same worldwide, in the more than 9,500 KFC restaurants in the 20 plus countries KFC has entered since the 1970s). But developing a market for KFC in Japan involved some changes in side dishes to appeal to the Japanese palate,

such as lowering the sugar content of the coleslaw. KFC also added fish to the menu, redesigned the outlets, and stressed the American origin in the advertising. Appealing especially to children, a life-size plastic model of Colonel Sanders was placed outside the restaurants, creating an immediately recognizable mascot. In many respects—the logo, the visual layout, the buckets and bags, the appearance of the servers, the food, and the drinks—the stores remained true to the original concept.

Source: *http://www.kfc.com*

tions, making it possible to transfer files between programs. Hardware developers offer built-in adapters and transformers that help make fax machines portable worldwide.

Multisystem compatibility ensures that localization requirements are satisfied. Products designed for easier construction are usually modularized, making the manufacturing more of an assembly task than before. Thus, building a camera or a motorcycle becomes something resembling the kit assembly of a model airplane. It is easy, then, to separate out those components requiring localization and incorporate multiple options for those components alone. Laptop and notebook computers now come with adapters for various electric voltages. PCs offer expansion slots for floppy discs, sound cards, CD-ROM, and various other accessories, letting the buyer do the customization. IKEA, the furniture store chain, offers modular systems the customers can use to design different living environments in their homes. Multisystem compatibility makes it possible to generate the savings associated with long and standardized product series—even without the use of advanced robotics and flexible manufacturing systems.

PITFALLS OF GLOBAL STANDARDIZATION

Given the pros and cons of standardization, it is not surprising to find that companies do not always succeed with standardized product and service strategies. By systematically comparing the winners and losers, one researcher found that five factors explain why standardized products fail.[7]

1. Insufficient market research
2. Overstandardization
3. Poor follow-up
4. Narrow vision
5. Rigid implementation

Insufficient Market Research

Good marketing research helps a standardized product strategy in two ways: (1) by correctly identifying commonalities and (2) by winning support from the local organizations involved in the research. In contrast, insufficient research means not only that similarities among customers are assumed rather than proved but also that the local subsidiaries feel stepped on. For example, when Polaroid introduced its path breaking SX-70 camera in Europe, the company employed the same advertising strategy—including TV commercials and print ads—it had used in its triumphant launch in the United States. When the local Polaroid executives protested that TV testimonials from unknown people would not be very useful for consumer perceptions in Europe and asked for a chance to do more research on possible replacements, headquarters refused. The subsequent lack of awareness and acceptance of the camera in Europe did not come as a surprise to the disenchanted local managers.

Overstandardization

Even though many technologically intensive products lend themselves to functional standardization, the same is not necessarily true of their positioning. The Canon AE-1 camera, the first automatic single-lens reflex introduced in the mid-1970s, was first positioned as an expert's choice in all markets. After a less than successful entry, the company decided to gamble and reposition it as a fun camera in the United States, taking on the then prevailing 110 standard Kodak camera. TV commercials were used, the first time ever for a single-lens reflex camera, using as a spokesman tennis player John Newcombe. The success of the new strategy led the company to reposition the camera in other markets as well, creating a much larger market for single-lens reflex cameras worldwide.

Poor Follow-Up

Impressive kickoff meetings, splashy presentations to country managers, and the personal appearance of the CEO are important attention getters at the start of a global branding campaign. But these efforts need to be followed up diligently with communications, visits, and local effort if the campaign is to succeed. For example, after the German company Henkel to great fanfare launched a global campaign for its stick glue "Pritt" as an umbrella brand for related products, it failed to capitalize on the initial momentum. Instead of supplying extra resources and incentives to local units, the company left the implementation to be covered under the normal budget, forcing country managers to cut existing programs. Needless to say, as initial results proved weak, the resources were quickly reallocated to existing brands.[8]

Narrow Vision

There are two main approaches to organizing campaigns for standardized products. One is to direct the campaign from headquarters; the other, to designate a lead country, usually an important market for the product. Both approaches have their strengths, the main advantage of each being the clear focus of responsibility. However, the vision at the headquarters or in the lead country should not be narrow and inflexible. When Unilever introduced a new household cleaner Domestos, standardized for the pan-European market, the UK unit took on the lead role for global implementation. The problem was that the product was most successful in West Germany, where the local subsidiary had shifted the positioning from a "germ killer" to a "dirt remover." But this change in positioning was ignored by the UK unit, and its potential was lost, since other countries' organizations were not informed of it.

Rigid Implementation

When uniformity of marketing programs is dictated from headquarters, there needs to be some flexibility in implementation retained by local units. Not all local requests for deviations need to be accepted, but shrewd managerial judgment is required to decide how far to go. When the U.S. subsidiary of Lego reported that an American competitor, Tyco, offered toys in a plastic bucket that could be easily used for storage and requested to be allowed to replace the globally standardized paperboard cartons with similar buckets, the Danish headquarters refused. After a two-year slide in market share, the headquarters finally relented. The Lego toys are now sold in plastic buckets worldwide.

Generally speaking, empirical research tends to show equivocal results as to the benefit of standardization. One study found that when standardized strategies were properly matched against homogeneous markets, sales growth improved but return on investment (ROI) did not.[9] Another study reported similar results, with sales growth affected positively by standardization strategies but with return on assets worse.[10] This study also found that the attractiveness of product standardization declined when market growth was slow; customization seems more promising in mature markets. In general, standardization seems to be associated with increased sales, while the effect on the bottom line is less clear.

STANDARDIZATION RESEARCH

Standardization research in a local market usually involves usage analysis (to see what *localization* is necessary) and preference identification (to assess the profitability of *adaptation*).

Observation and Focus Groups

Product localization research requirements consist of finding out what factors affect the usability of a product. The size of parking spaces, the narrowness of streets, and the gasoline prices affect what size car is acceptable. Voltage levels, fire regulations, and circuit overloads affect what changes may be necessary in electrical products. Language, operating systems, and functions used affect what PC software applications may or may not be acceptable. When it comes to localization of a product (that is, removing obstacles to its convenient and proper local use), the research is not about user preferences but about usage constraints.

Observation is a particularly powerful method for uncovering localization requirements in an existing product. But it is important to recognize that the observer has to pay attention not only to unusual things, such as driving a car barefoot, but also to unremarkable manners, such as how much elbow room the driver uses. The hollowing out of doors in cars today came about not only because safety can still be ensured with stronger materials but because observation showed that with automatic transmissions, men drive with wide swings of the elbows.

In product adaptation research, the focus is on the adaptations that may give the product an advantage in the local customer's eyes. Such research is much more akin to product research at home. The techniques involve focus groups, concept testing with selected users, and test marketing.[11] These activities tend to be important in any developed market. One question often is, however, whether the uncovered preferences for an adapted product will be adhered to by headquarters.

When doing product research abroad, many companies find it useful to simply observe customers using the product. If the product is new on the market, recruited subjects can be given the chance to try it in their homes for a period of time and then report their experiences. This was done by Procter and Gamble when they introduced Pampers in European and Asian markets. It is done routinely by consumer goods companies going into emerging and developing markets, since it allows localization requirements to be uncovered. For example, when German electric irons were first introduced in Asia, their cords were too short. In Europe there are usually several electric outlets in the wall, while in Asia at that time electric outlets connected to the one bulb in the ceiling.

Traditional product research is based on the assumption that the individual consumer has well-developed preferences, that these can be identified and measured, and that then the design of a new product can target an unfulfilled need or provide a new benefit. When successfully accomplished, the results of the process can be impressive. But in many new markets the assumption of well-developed preferences is unfounded. In new markets preferences may be embryonic or nonexistent. In many foreign markets the solicitation of preferences is flawed, as was seen in Chapter 7. Competitive reaction or preemptive introductions may make the process too slow as well.[12]

Target Product Research

An alternative Japanese-style approach short-circuits the process and speeds it up. By analyzing the leading brands and their attributes, they are able to understand what appeals to their consumers. Targeting one of the brands, that brand's customers can be questioned directly for possible improvements. By reverse engineering the brand, and producing a new version incorporating the existing leader's strengths minus the weaknesses—a so-called me-too-plus product—the Japanese have been able to capture large market shares abroad. Examples include the Toyota Lexus, Camry, and Corona, the Canon Sureshot, and the VHS development by Matsushita.[13]

In developed countries with mature markets, the **target product research** approach has the drawback that a striking innovation which completely changes market preferences will be missed. Targeting some leading brand and offering minor improvements is generally not enough to establish a sustainable advantage. The leading brand is likely to respond, and a cycle of actions and reactions will push prices down. This is a typical result of a Japanese entry in many markets. For the local marketer, it is important to recognize that establishing customer loyalty is as important in the foreign market as at home. The aim should not be the quick kill but the sustained satisfaction of the customer.

Test Marketing

In emerging and developing local markets it is difficult to generate data prior to entry. There are quite formidable barriers to effective primary data collection, and secondary data are of uncertain consistency and may be lacking altogether. It is of course difficult to develop a marketing plan and proceed with a well-coordinated introduction in such markets. Accordingly, companies tend to approach these countries with care and use the initial entry points as **test markets** to learn more about the customers and competitors and to adapt the marketing program as sales results flow in.

The fact is that market response to new products is hard to predict anywhere.[14] Whether the markets are emerging, developing, or developed, the new local marketer faces uncertainties that are difficult to erase simply by doing more research. The customers can't give reliable and valid responses without direct experience with—or at least exposure to—the new product.

The test marketing of a new global product candidate is naturally different from the domestic case. Usually several different country markets are used, to ensure that potential problems are detected early. For example, in the case of Colgate's new Total toothpaste, a recent global introduction, six different markets were used: Australia, Colombia, Greece, New Zealand, the Philippines, and Portugal.[15] The positive results in all six markets indicated that the product's taste and unique positioning benefits—a long-lasting antibacterial formula that fought plaque, tartar, and cavities—could be the same throughout the world.

Emerging and developing markets are likely to exhibit the typical product life cycle characteristics of an introductory period followed by a growth period. In these cases, market research prior to test marketing is best focused on leading users and markets in other countries and on leading brands and products. As discussed in Chapter 4, leading markets may be used to develop a forecast by analogy, which then can help set expectations and targets for test marketing.

GLOBAL PRODUCT LINES

Product lines in even the most global company are rarely identical across countries. Procter and Gamble has not introduced its detergents Ariel and Vizir in the United States. Coca-Cola sells its Georgia ice coffee and Aquarius isotonic drink in Japan but not at home. Honda's Concerto automobile is sold in Europe but not in North America.

There are varied reasons why product lines differ. Many are simply historical accidents.

- *History.* The different local products were well established before standardization and coordination were feasible and the benefits recognized. Several of P&G's brands in soaps and detergents fall into this category.
- *M&A.* If the product lines are formed through mergers and acquisitions, complete integration is usually difficult. Although the company has tried to sell off unrelated businesses, after acquiring Findus, Nestlé found itself in the canning business in Europe.
- *Preferences.* Differences in market preferences provide the fundamental strategic rationale for these product line differences. Many American sport utility vehicles are too big and gas-guzzling for Europeans, who have to pay high prices for gasoline.
- *Capacity.* Global product lines need large production capacity, often through plant locations in several countries. A firm will take some time to develop that capacity, especially since forecasting demand is not without uncertainty. Because of strong demand in the North American target market, Toyota initially did not have enough capacity to sell its Lexus model in Japan.
- *Channels.* Differences in channel structure can make it difficult to support the same product lines. Coca-Cola's isotonic drink Aquarius is a "me too" version of a popular Japanese drink, Pocari sweat. By introducing Aquarius in addition to Georgia, the ice coffee, Coca-Cola made sure that its vending machines could be stocked with the variety demanded by the Japanese consumer.

As with all product line management, well-managed global lines also need to offer a certain rate of new product introductions. To be successful in globally competitive markets, a significant percentage of sales and profits should come from new products.

GLOBAL BRAND MANAGEMENT[16]

A company's principal brands are major assets, worth billions to their firms. In a 1995 study, the median value assigned by 153 senior managers to their principal brand was $5.3 billion.[17] Exhibit 12.2 shows the world's best-known brands as tabulated from one

EXHIBIT 12.2 The World's Best-Known Brands

1. Coca-Cola	3. Pepsi-Cola	6. Toyota	8. Disney
2. McDonald's	4. Sony	7. Nestlé	9. Honda
	5. Kodak		10. Ford

Source: Kashani, 1992.

EXHIBIT 12.3 The 10 Most Effective Global Brand Managers*

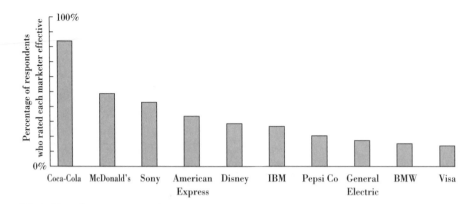

*Ranked by senior corporate executives.

Source: Elliott, 1995, with data from the *Brands at the Crossroads* study by Bozell Worldwide and Fortune Marketing, New York, 1993.

large-scale survey in the United States, Europe, and Japan.[18] Other surveys tally roughly the same set of brands, although the ranking varies by region. As can be seen, all of the brands belong to companies that market standardized products.[19]

The growing impact of global brands makes **global brand management** of crucial importance. In the 1995 study the senior managers ranked the 10 most effective global brand managers (see Exhibit 12.3). The results confirm Coca-Cola's preeminence as a global marketer. In fact, the most striking fact about Exhibit 12.3 is perhaps the sharp drop-off after the leader. Managing a global brand is not necessarily easy.

While brand managers in individual markets still manage the local execution of the marketing strategy, global brand management is necessarily a strategic function at headquarters.[20] In the senior management study mentioned, fully 91 percent of the 153 executives had a "definite plan or strategy" for enhancing their brand in the next two years. The basic thrust of these plans was similar across the companies. With quality and functional performance comparable across brands and therefore expected by the customers, differentiation would come from customer service and increased promotional support for the brand image.

Brand Equity

The monetary value of a brand constitutes its **brand equity,** the net revenues the brand can be expected to generate over time.

In brand equity measurement, the basic idea is the same as in the valuation of equity shares. Although the exact formulas differ between analysts (and details are held proprietary), the basic approach is similar. First, a brand's awareness, knowledge, and attractiveness levels are combined into a measure of brand *stature*. For example, Landor Associates, a branding research firm, uses survey respondents' "Knowledge" and "Esteem" scores combined as a measure of stature. This measure is then usually coupled with a measure of actual and potential market size and leverage. Landor uses "Differentiation" and "Relevance" combined to get the leverage or *vitality* of a brand. Brand equity rises with stature and vitality.[21]

The development of the formulas was spurred by the need to assess company value in acquisitions, mergers, and takeovers. Gradually, what has emerged is a sense that a strong brand might be the most valuable asset a firm has. For example, in the 1998 sale of Rolls Royce by Vickers of England to German Volkswagen, the name itself ("Rolls Royce") was sold separately to BMW, a transaction that led some observers to claim that Volkswagen got cheated.[22]

Brand equity assets are still off the corporate balance sheets in most countries, the United Kingdom being one significant exception. Nevertheless, the creation of brand equity measurement methods has had a profound effect on global marketers and how they manage their brand assets.

Global Brands

There are several advantages for companies using global brands. The three major factors are:

- Demand spillover
- Global customers
- Scale economies

Demand spillover is an important factor favoring the global brand. Sales in one country market generates demand in another country. Media coverage spills over into new country markets, and the brand name becomes well known and easily recognized. What people in one country buy is what other people want; they know about it through news reports, television coverage, and magazines. To capitalize on spillovers the brand name needs to be the same everywhere, so a global brand has a clear advantage over local brands.

A second way that benefits are gained is through *global customers*. In business-to-business markets, where the consumers might be large multinational firms, global customers are common. But this is also the case in consumer goods markets. As people travel internationally for business or pleasure, airport shops become important distribution outlets for product categories such as cosmetics, cameras, and fashion goods. These global customers are naturally more attracted to global brands that they can find in many places.

Scale economies constitute a third reason favoring a global brand. The standardization of logo, packaging, and production lowers manufacturing costs. As for promotional expenses, the cost for producing a global TV commercial can easily run into more than U.S. $1 million, much higher than a local campaign. Playtex "Traumbuegel" commercial ran a good U.S. $2.5 million. But when used as a prototype for campaigns all over the world, the production costs can be spread over a much larger volume, making global TV commercials very cost-effective. The same goes for the volume discounts in global media and global distribution.

However, the high brand awareness for a global product can have its drawbacks. Intel, the PC chip maker, used a "piggybacking" approach to promote its name by asking hardware manufacturers to indicate "Intel inside" on advertising materials. Consumer awareness, though, helped exacerbate the negative public relations damage when the company had problems with its Pentium chip. In addition, the "Intel inside" branding requirement on licensees has irked companies such as Compaq, which complain that their own brand name's uniqueness and brand equity are diminished by the Intel dominance.

Procter and Gamble has long avoided the use of company-identified brand names: There is no "P&G" detergent, for example, only several global or regional brands— Tide, Cheer, Vizir. This helps when difficulties occur, such as when its sanitary napkin brand Rely was found to induce toxic shock. On the other hand, the goodwill from linkage to a reputable company is lost. Although in American markets this factor can count for less because mergers and acquisitions blur the connection between ownership and market presence, in other countries the connection is more valuable.

The Brand Portfolio

At any point in time, especially among packaged goods companies with a history of growth through mergers and acquisitions, companies are likely to have a portfolio of a few global brands and several local brands. Exhibit 12.4 shows the **brand portfolio** of

EXHIBIT 12.4 Brands of Six Multinational Companies
in 67 Countries

Company	Total number of brands	Brands found in 50% or more countries (%)	Brands marketed in only one country (%)
Colgate	163	6 (4%)	59 (36%)
Kraft GF	238	6 (3%)	104 (44%)
Nestlé	560	19 (4%)	250 (45%)
P & G	217	18 (8%)	80 (37%)
Quaker	143	2 (1%)	55 (38%)
Unilever	471	17 (4%)	236 (50%)
Total	1,792		

Source: Betsy V. Boze and Charles R. Patton, "The Future of Consumer Branding as Seen from the Picture Today," *Journal of Consumer Marketing*, 12(4) (1995), p. 22.

six major multinational companies across 67 countries. The exhibit shows that less than 10 percent of the brands can be considered truly global.

The brands are typically managed in a hierarchical fashion. The **brand hierarchy** can take several forms. In one, the most important global brands are at the top, followed by regional and local brands. This is the typical branding scheme of companies such as Nestlé and Sara Lee. Alternatively, the top can be the corporate brand, possibly global, followed by sub-branded model names, also possibly worldwide, and specific model designations, possibly worldwide. This is the typical hierarchy of auto companies such as Honda and Mercedes. In the case of Sony, the hierarchy starts with the corporate name and cascades down through the various divisions (consumer electronics, entertainment, business markets . . .) to specific product lines and finally to models. The hierarchies mirror the levels in the organization where brand responsibility is lodged, top management focusing on the global brands, often the corporate brand.[23]

Brand awareness tends to follow a cycle similar to the product life cycle: After introduction and growth in awareness, saturation is reached as the penetration of a market rises to a certain level (although a *decline* stage is not necessarily part of the **brand cycle,** with many older brands doing well).[24] It is much harder to raise awareness levels from 80 to 85 percent of the market than from 35 to 40 percent. Because of this "ceiling" effect, raising brand equity in a given market tends to be difficult for established brands. Instead, it is usually more effective to extend the brand in two ways: new products and new markets.

Brand extensions into new product categories are a common but risky strategy that sometimes fails when the new product category is too different.[25] Coca-Cola's efforts in jeans and other apparel have not been very successful, and neither was Nike's excursion into brown leisure shoes. Expansion into new markets is often the simpler and safer alternative, especially when media spillovers have created a latent demand for the brand. Globalizing the brand by introducing the products in new markets overseas becomes the natural solution to growing brand equity.

Brand Globalization Potential

To evaluate the **globalization potential** of a local brand, it is useful to systematically go through a checklist of factors.[26] First are some questions about appropriateness or **brand fit**:

1. Does the brand name make sense outside of the source country? What does it mean? What associations are generated? Nokia from Finland, a leading company in

The Swiss Army brand name has been extended to a new product line of watches as well as other products. Originally made famous by its versatile and high quality pocketknives, the Swiss Army brand has extended into products where its country-of-origin cachet can be fully exploited. Courtesy Swiss Army Brands.

mobile phones, is not unaware of the fact that its name sounds vaguely Japanese: The Finnish and Japanese languages come from the same roots.

2. If the name suggests a country association, is the effect positive? Is the source country a leading market or a follower? The name of GM's German subsidiary ("Opel") may be preferable to "Chevrolet" with its American heritage.

3. Is the name available legally in many countries? Philips, the Dutch electronics giant, has been hampered continuously in the North American market because the Philips oil company was the first to register its brand name there.

If the answers to these questions are positive, the strong local brand is a good candidate for globalization. Next, its place in the brand portfolio needs to be considered.

4. Does the brand complement other global brands in the portfolio or compete directly against them? Because of resource demands and the threat of cannibalization, it is seldom justifiable to keep two directly competing global brand names, which is one reason why Sony decided to drop the Columbia record label after acquiring CBS's music business. On the other hand, Sony supports Aiwa—a subsidiary, which is a global brand with electronic goods at a lower price than the Sony parent—on the premise that cannibalization is minimal. And of course the brand may simply help extend the product line, as in the case of Campbell Soup's acquisition and globalization of Godiva, the Belgian chocolatier.

5. Should the growth be limited to the creation of a regional brand? Even if the brand portfolio has a direct global competitor, or if some local brands cannot be changed, the possibility of creating a regional brand should be considered. A regional brand can be a stiff competitor for the global brand in its region and will also help the company gain a larger and more defensible position in a region. For example, apart from its global "Kronenbourg" label, the Strasbourg-based beer maker also markets its "1866" label in southern Europe.

Implementation

Implementing the globalization strategy raises its own issues. A basic consideration is whether local brands elsewhere can and should be replaced:

1. Is the globalization product-based, involving product entry into new markets, or can the brand be globalized by simply changing other local brand names? If the product category is unique in the company, the global expansion involves mainly product introductions into other markets. If the corporation already has local brands in the product category, those might need to be changed to the globalizing name. In the drive to globalize the Nokia name, the Finnish company used its name for all the telecommunication products manufactured by its acquired foreign firms.

Product-based globalization of a brand engages all the global marketing skills of a business. Changing existing *local brands* requires far less resources but raises its own thorny problems:

2. Which local brands should be chosen for the changeover? Can the local managers be persuaded to drop one of their brands? The local brand to be changed has to offer a product line that matches the globalizing brand's product line. Furthermore, it should preferably not be a very strong brand locally so as not to lose loyal customers and discourage local managers. Electrolux, the appliance maker intent of globalizing its name, has met resistance in India where it owns Kelvinator, a locally strong brand. By contrast, Merrill Lynch has had little problems among either customers or employees in using its name in Japan after acquiring the local branch network of failed Yamaichi Securities.

Changeover Tactics

Once the target brands have been identified, standard **brand changeover** tactics can be employed.[27]

The *fade-in/fade-out* gradual option is the most common. The global brand is linked to the local brand for a time, after which the local brand is dropped. The time involved varies from months to a couple of years. Frequently purchased products require less time because the exposure penetrates faster. The approach usually involves a dual branding tactic:

- "Endorsement branding," with one brand introducing the new brand. Messages such as "From the makers of . . ." or "From the folks who brought you . . ." or simply "From . . ." or "By . . ." establish the connection and the legitimacy of the new brand. Mars, the American-based confectionery maker, used "Pedigree by Pal" to prepare the way for global Pedigree to replace local Pal dog food.

- "Double-branding," where both names are reproduced faithfully to their old logos and simply placed next to each other. This can be somewhat confusing but avoids losing loyal customers and channel members. Both the Whirlpool and Philips names appeared on appliances when Whirlpool took over Philips' white goods division, and after a transition period the Philips name was dropped. Black and Decker used the same approach to put its name on the acquired GE product line of appliances.

A less gradual approach, sometimes called *summary axing*, simply drops the local brand name and introduces the new brand. Although simpler to manage, this approach can create problems. In 1986 Mars pulled its Treets brand off the European market and introduced the product as M&Ms, using the same Treets slogan: "Melts in your mouth, not in your hand." Reaction among adult customers was negative, and sales and profits suffered. Learning the lesson, when Mars changed its local Raider brand to global Twix, the company used extensive *forewarning*, another approach to name changeover. TV commercials explained that "Now Raider becomes Twix, for it is Twix everywhere in the world."

COUNTERFEIT PRODUCTS

Counterfeits or knockoffs are fake products designed and branded so as to mislead the unwary customer into assuming that they are genuine.[28] Counterfeit products should be distinguished from "gray trade" or parallel trade. **Gray trade** is parallel distribution of genuine goods by intermediaries other than authorized channel members. Gray trade as related to exchange rates and pricing will be discussed in Chapter 13, "Global Pricing," and gray trade distribution will be discussed in Chapter 14, "Global Distribution."

Extent of Problem

Counterfeit products pose an ominous problem in the global marketplace. According to expert estimates, worldwide company losses due to counterfeit products are over $20 billion annually. The traditional cases of counterfeit products involve luxury goods with global brand names. Gucci wallets, Louis Vuitton bags, Cartier watches, and Porsche sunglasses are typical examples. But counterfeit products are no longer confined to designer jeans and watches. Items now routinely counterfeited include chemicals, computers, drugs, fertilizers, pesticides, medical devices, military hardware, and food—as well as parts for airplanes and automobiles.

Counterfeiters operate at all levels of the economy. As foreign direct investment transfers technology and manufacturing to new countries, these countries acquire the skills to turn out bogus goods. But not all counterfeits come from developing countries. For example, experts estimate that perhaps 20 percent of all fakes are made in the United States by producers who can't make a profit otherwise or who see the opportunity of a quick kill.

With today's advanced technology, pirating products is nowadays almost as easy as photocopying. The labels can be the trickiest part. These Korean counterfeits allow the buyer to choose which label to stitch onto the new sports shirt. Mark Richards/Contact Press Images, Inc.

Counterfeit Goes High-Tech

AS COMPUTERIZED CAD-CAM techniques become ever more sophisticated in design and manufacturing, the possibility of producing exact copies of apparel designs increases proportionately. This poses a headache for global brand names in particular, because of the price premium they fetch.

The counterfeit products from Hong Kong's and Taiwan's many small factories have long been a problem for global brands. But even in New York's Soho district, the heart of the city's large business in the fashion trade, high-tech machinery is used by some business operators to produce illegal copies of branded apparel. Given a specimen of a new Polo shirt, for example, the machinery has the capability to photographically analyze the material, the design, and the stitching, and then "reverse engineer" the

process to produce an almost exact copy, including the logo stitching of a polo player and the label inside the collar.

Only a specialist will be able to spot the copy's minor differences from the original. Buyers from the stores can't usually tell the difference, nor can a regular customer. Of course, since there is no discernible difference, the consumer might well be satisfied. For the owner of the brand name, however, the sale of the counterfeit items means a considerable loss of revenues, and the companies pay to have guards go through merchandise and interrogate store owners to find the illegal makers, prosecute them, and destroy fake merchandise.

Sources: *New York Times*, December 13, 1994; *Business Week*, December 16, 1985, pp. 48–53.

Some knockoffs can be almost as good as the original and hard to detect, especially since counterfeiters now know how to faithfully reproduce the identical labels (see box, "Counterfeit Goes High-Tech").

For the global marketer trying to build and sustain a global brand name's equity, such practices are naturally alarming. In Korea knockoffs of designer clothes are sold in some stores with various designer labels offered separately so that the customer can stitch the desired label on at home.

A particularly intriguing case is that of software piracy, the duplication and sale of software programs for personal computers. The practice of copying diskettes is widespread, and it is very difficult to enforce the copyright limitations indicated on the packages. One research study, however, found that the quicker diffusion of the software programs made possible through pirating can actually help penetration. In England, where six of every seven adopters of popular spreadsheet and word processing programs utilize pirated copies, the pirates were responsible for generating more than 80 percent of new software buyers.[29]

Actions against Counterfeits

What can the global marketer do? For some, the counterattack has been a two-pronged "search and destroy" mission. Firms make an effort to find the factories that turn out the counterfeits, and they track down the fakes in the stores. Private investigation outfits have emerged to offer their services to multinational companies.

To help identify fakes, some firms have resorted to various coding devices. Levi Strauss, the jeans maker, weaves into its fabric a microscopic fiber pattern visible only under a special light. To deter pirates, Microsoft launched a $1.09 million print media campaign in Hong Kong, claiming that Windows 95 is coded so that counterfeits can be tracked.

Many companies also appeal to their government for assistance, although the cases have to be well documented before most governments react. The recent agreement between the United States and China concerning piracy in the entertainment industry has received much publicity, although the ultimate success is uncertain (see box, "China's Video and Audio Pirates").

China's Video and Audio Pirates

IN THE SPRING OF 1995, the U.S. Trade Representative's Office scored a major diplomatic victory, convincing China's government to agree to strongly enforce a ban on copyright and trademark violations in that country. Chinese entrepreneurs had long copied popular videotapes and compact disks from the West for resale on the streets and in the small shops of Beijing and Shanghai. Other copies were trucked or shipped by boat into Hong Kong and other Southeast Asian cities. The American government had been pressured by the artists' organizations to help stop the practice, since it resulted in lost revenues and undermined the authorized distributors.

Although in principle this was a victory for the United States, many observers remain skeptical about the real effect of the agreement. For one thing, the amount of lost revenues is hardly great, given China's difficulty in paying hard currency. In addition, with regular prices many of the products would have a hard time making it against local competition: Mandarin and Cantonese artists are more popular than Western performers, and their CDs, many of them also pirated copies, cost a fraction of Western CDs at regular price. A third difficulty is the sheer number of small factories and outlets. New factories are easily established, and the manufacturers and the street salesmen are often entrepreneurial young people.

While Western companies concede that the effect is probably minimal, they consider the principle important for the development of a better business climate in China.

Sources: *New York Times*, February 27, 1995, pp. D1, D6, and May 17, 1995, pp. D1, D5; "Business Beams on IPR Breakthrough," *South China Morning Post*, March 17, 1995, p. 7.

GLOBAL SERVICES

Services marketing has received increasing attention lately as its importance in the developed economies has grown considerably. The share of GNP attributable to services has risen over the last few years, and in particular the employment share in the service sectors has increased a great deal in the advanced economies. The international trade and foreign direct investment in services have grown, as new communications technology makes global service delivery possible (see box, "Any Vacancy?").

The service industries include hotels and other lodging places; establishments providing personal, business, repair, and amusement services; health, legal, engineering, and other professional services; educational institutions; finance, insurance, and real estate; wholesale and retail trade; and general government, transportation, communication, and public utilities. Although some of these services are not very significant globally, only a few have no international involvement.

Our discussion will first center on the issues that make global services marketing different from physical goods marketing abroad. We will then consider how service quality is determined and how a service concept can be globalized. Finally we will focus on two illustrative examples: franchising and professional services. (It should be pointed out that this section does not deal with services associated with the sales and support of products. The after-sales service guaranteed with the sale of an automobile, for example, or the in-store explanations offered by a camera salesperson, both important activities for customer satisfaction, are not the focus of this section.)

A Marketing Equivalence

From a marketing viewpoint there are actually many similarities between physical goods and services. For example, one standard definition of a product is "a bundle of benefit-generating attributes." There is nothing inherently physical about this bundle. The same definition can be applied to an intangible service such as an insurance package. In fact, the similarities can be so strong that for some purposes there is no difference. In many ways the *product* is simply the packaging of a problem-solving *service*. For

Any Vacancy?

THE BUSINESS TRAVELER in Berlin going to Prague on the early morning train can reserve a hotel room there by simply calling the local Marriott phone number in Berlin. There might be no hotel with the Marriott marquee in Prague, but the American hotel chain has a number of affiliates in Eastern Europe. These independent hotels have allied with Marriott to attract customers from abroad. In turn, Marriott can provide foreign visitors with Marriott-warranted accommodations. In the future, when people from Eastern Europe want to travel in the United States, Marriott will be able to draw on the same network to attract them to U.S. Marriott hotels.

An important ingredient in this global expansion has been the creation of efficient telecommunications and computerized reservation lines. If the Berlin connection is attempted after-hours, reservations can still be made. In fact, many of Marriott's international reservation calls—from Eastern Europe, Japan, or Buenos Aires—are routed through its central reservation office in Salt Lake City, Utah, where telephone operators with different language capabilities serve the customers. The operators can check room availability through the computer and confirm the reservation. The local hotel staff receives confirmation via e-mail from Utah.

Sources: Bruce Wolff, vice president of distribution sales, Marriott Hotels.
http://www.marriott.com

example, a book replaces the telling of a story, a car offers transportation, a cash machine replaces a teller, and so on.

The similarities and differences that affect the marketing management of services can be identified clearly with reference to the traditional product discussion in standard marketing texts. Adapting the product discussion of these texts, we distinguish between the "core service," the "basic service package," and the "augmented service."[30] Exhibit 12.5 demonstrates the relationships between these three concepts.

The **core service** is what the buyer is "really" buying. For instance, the person getting a tune-up for her car is really buying trouble-free operation and transportation. The individual checking into the Hilton in Manila is really buying comfort and reliable service. The first job of the global services marketer is to make sure that these service benefits can be delivered in the foreign markets. While this task establishes a necessary condition for expansion, it is not sufficient by itself for success.

The **basic service package** refers to the specified services offered the customer, which include service features, the price, the packaging, and the guarantees offered. The basic service package of a bank involves the various "products" the bank offers and their features, including free checking, high-interest certificates of deposit, and so on. An airline provides a set of more or less tangible in-flight services (food, drink, duty-free sales, special baby care, movies). The second job of the global services marketer is to develop a service package that can be appropriately localized and replicated in the various markets around the world. Offering innovative and hard-to-duplicate service packages, such as the Club Med all-inclusive vacations in its own villages in different parts of the world, can help develop a loyal customer base and a sustained competitive advantage.

The **augmented service** is the totality of benefits that the individual receives or experiences when buying the product. These benefits revolve around the service delivery, the way the provider is dressed, the tone of voice and body language used, the confidence and credence imparted, and so on. These benefits also involve the brand image and status of the service provider, as well as the physical surroundings of the service. The third job of the global services marketer is to create a customer-oriented augmented service package.

Although they do play a role for physical products as well, these augmenting features can make a big difference in relatively standardized services. They can become

EXHIBIT 12.5 The Service "Product"

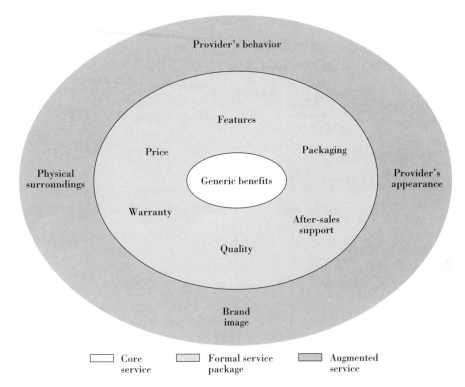

the FSAs (firm-specific advantages). For example, the hair stylist's appearance, the salon's furniture, the music played, and the other customers seen are all factors contributing to whether the hair styling itself will seem acceptable or not.[31] These augmenting benefits are often so inextricably linked to most services that without them the service can't be replicated properly elsewhere. Without such duplication, exporting to other countries is less likely to succeed. One key factor in global services marketing is not whether the core benefit is desired or whether the basic service package can be replicated but whether the total **service delivery system**—the linked activities, hardware and software, which make the service delivery work—can be successfully transplanted abroad. If not, quality and customer satisfaction are jeopardized.

Service Quality

The intangibility of services is typically assumed to make consumer evaluation of **service quality** more difficult than for tangible products.[32] This view is based on the natural hesitation of people to evaluate things they can't touch. The intangibility of services makes them much more *subjective*. Quality is a matter of how we feel and of our particular taste.

In global markets the difference between physical goods and services carries special relevance. What constitutes "high-quality service" can differ considerably between countries, while what constitutes a "high-quality good" often does not. The case of personal and cultural judgment about services comes into play.

In personal services, quality is determined partly by factors such as language spoken, tone and choice of words, body language (hand gestures, stance, distance), and ability of the provider to listen well, avoid confrontational arguments, and use other interpersonal communication skills. By comparing two culturally different places (say, New York City and Tokyo) great differences in approach—and "service"—can be easily seen. The direct, explicit, and "professional" approach of a New York department store clerk is far away from the Japanese clerk's kind and indirect demeanor. It is clear that one person raised in a particular service environment might be surprised by what passes for high-quality service in another.

Keeping the cultural factors well in mind and localizing where necessary, the global entrant can educate local customers about the potential quality of services in banking, restaurants, hospitals, hotels, and so on, revealing to the local consumers how culture and past experiences have limited their perspective unnecessarily. Just as past choices color what the customer has come to expect, new choices from global firms can open their eyes. New service opportunities can be created. And, as people say, once you have tasted luxury, it is no longer a luxury but a necessity.

SERVICE GLOBALIZATION POTENTIAL

The feasibility of globalizing a service business depends on some factors that are unique to services.

Life Cycle

As with a product cycle, development of a business service over time follows a cycle from birth through growth and maturity to decline. In the typical marketing illustration, the product life cycle follows an S-curve, with the growth period corresponding to where the "S" has its steepest ascent. This is when a new product is often introduced in foreign markets to capture first-mover advantages. However, for services, it is in the maturity stage that the potential for global expansion of the service concept is the highest.

In the early and growth stage of the cycle, the "production process" employed by the service company is often still under development. The concept is still being created. In maturity, the software and hardware ingredients in the service have been fully developed, and the standardization of key components and features takes place. It is this *standardization*—whether it be in advertising, medical care, fast-food restaurants, accounting, or hotels—that is the basis for global expansion of the service. FSAs in services are often in innovative standardization—from McDonald's strict procedures for cleanliness and friendliness, to Hilton Hotels' training of how to greet guests, to Boston Consulting Group's growth-share matrix.

Infrastructure

The global applicability of a service depends on whether the **infrastructure** through which the service is offered exists in foreign markets. In brokerage firms, for example, a very sophisticated service concept that works well under a certain type of regulatory and economic environment might lose all relevance when the financial regulations and/or the institutional members change character. The buying and selling of call and put options or other derivatives, for example, is not feasible where there is no futures market.

Localization

Another important inhibitor of services exporting is that many service systems exist as ingenious solutions to very special problems faced in the home country. The typical supermarket in the United States developed partly as a response to the growing availability of automobiles and parking lot space in many suburban areas of the nation. Similar idiosyncratic factors determine the specific shape of the service organizations found in many countries. This helps explain why Japanese service firms have been very slow in globalizing (see box, "Where Are the Japanese Services Industries?").

Where Are the Japanese Services Industries?

SINCE JAPANESE CORPORATIONS like Sony, Toyota, and Canon have been so successful in penetrating Western markets, one might have expected Japanese service firms to do equally well. After all, Japanese banks, brokerage houses, ad agencies, construction companies, hotel chains, and department stores are among the largest in the world in terms of assets and revenues. But so far there are only scattered signs of a "service invasion" abroad.

The basic problem limiting these companies' foreign expansion is the special conditions in their main domestic market. For example, the larger hotel chains are part of the keiretsu groupings, which virtually guarantees high occupancy rates. Established department stores are shielded from competition by laws limiting new stores' entry. Japanese banks can draw on a favorable savings rate, which has made abundant deposits available at low interest rates. Brokerage firms are protected by strict regulations preventing foreign competition. Ad agencies can control media in addition to producing advertising.

Yes, Japan has large service companies; and, yes, they have great service skills. But their ability to operate in a more open and free marketplace has simply not had a chance to develop. As Japan deregulates, this is likely to change—but only gradually, and with much pain for the established players.

Sources: Aaker, 1990; Johansson, 1990.
http://www.sony.com
http://www.toyota.com
http://www.canon.com
http://www.nikko.com
http://www.takashimaya.co.jp
http://www.mitsukoshi.co.jp
http://www.sumitomocorp.co.jp
http://www.nomura.com
http://www.dentsu.co.jp/DHP
http://www.youngandrubicam.com

What is needed for services export is (1) a reasonable similarity to the home country situation, (2) a distillation of exactly what the *key features of the service* concept are, and (3) the *localization of these* to another environment while still maintaining the FSAs of the firm.

Since the "production" of the service is typically inseparable from the distribution of the service, FDI (foreign direct investment) is usually needed to transfer the complete service delivery system. In particular, if the FSAs are lodged in augmented personal service, to globalize one needs to train the personnel delivering the service as well.

CLOSE-UP: TWO GLOBALIZED SERVICES

To show the variety in global services it is useful to examine two of them in more depth: global fast food for its amazing success and professional services for their unlikely globalization.

Fast-Food Franchising

The **franchising** of fast-food restaurants has witnessed an unprecedented growth in the last two decades. The brand names McDonald's, Kentucky Fried Chicken, Dunkin' Donuts, Wendy's, and others are well known the world over. How and why have these "exports" proved so viable?

The basic and necessary first step in franchising abroad is analogous to that of developing any geographically dispersed franchise organization. The core features of the service system and the firm's specific advantages have to be identified and then formulations developed that travel well. These features will form the basic building blocks for the system as exported. In the case of McDonald's it consists of not only the cooking method and serving procedure but also the training of the workers, their attire and attitude, and the management and bookkeeping system (see box, "The McDonald's Way").

The McDonald's Way

PERHAPS THE MOST SUCCESSFUL franchising system of all time is McDonald's, the home of the "Big Mac" hamburgers. Since the company has been very successful duplicating its early U.S. achievements elsewhere, its franchising system is of special interest for a global marketer.

Franchisees may invest as much as $600,000 (or the equivalent) in initial start-up costs for a franchise. McDonald's charges a 3.5 percent service fee and a rental charge of 8.5 percent of the franchisee's volume. The franchisees are also required to attend "Hamburger University" in a suburb of Chicago for three weeks to learn how to manage the business and how to train the staff. The franchisees must adhere to established McDonald's standards in quality of the ingredients and in preparing and selling the product.

With more than 11,000 outlets in 50 or so countries and more than $17.5 billion in annual sales, McDonald's sells more than double the hamburgers of its nearest rival, Burger King. Worldwide more than 19 million customers pass through the golden arches each day, and the company is rapidly expanding. In 1990, when McDonald's opened its first Moscow outlet, its 700-seat restaurant served 30,000 meals in one day.

It is hardly surprising that some non-Americans—as well as some Americans—consider McDonald's a threat to a country's traditions.

Sources: Barbara Marsh, "Franchise Realities: Sandwich-Shop Chain Surges, but to Run One Can Take Heroic Efforts," *The Wall Street Journal*, September 16, 1992, pp. A1, A5; Michael Specter, "Borscht and Blini to Go: From Russian Capitalists, an Answer to McDonald's," *New York Times*, August 9, 1995, pp. D1, D3.
http://www.mcdonalds.com
http://www.burgerking.com

Successful fast-food franchising firms provide a lot of preplanning tools to help the prospective local investor. These include analyses of key factors in choice of location (traffic patterns, competition and synergy from similar outlets, offices versus residential), checklists of positive and negative attraction factors in the market area (population mix, income levels, age and family size), and building advice (size, layout, construction materials).

Needless to say, these tools have to be localized to the conditions in the foreign markets. "Traffic pattern" in one country may refer to cars, in others to motorcycles, in still others to bicycles or pedestrians. "Population mix" is a nonfactor in homogeneous countries such as Norway but important and based on religion in countries such as Malaysia. "Building advice" in the desert sands of Kuwait is far different from that in North Dakota—not to speak of the building permits that of course differ across countries as well as between municipalities.

Professional Services

Despite local regulations that vary between countries, **professional services** have recently expanded in step with the expansion of global firms. A gradual move toward making regulations more homogeneous has also played a role. In the European Union, for example, certification of lawyers and doctors in one member country is recognized in other EU countries as well. As accounting standards converge, large Western firms, such as Arthur Andersen and Price & Waterhouse, are also going global. Their main customers are still multinationals from their own countries, but even this is changing. Large European firms such as Siemens and BMW retain American accountants, and Japanese firms such as Canon and Sony are now clients of the Tokyo offices of American accounting firms.

The global expansion of professional services has been facilitated by the increased sophistication in creating strategic alliances. Traditionally, professional services went global through the establishment of local branch offices administered by expatriates who would come and spend a few years as the country manager. The system worked but always made the branch office subservient to headquarters, not a useful arrangement to attract the best local professionals. Today, the firms often expand through the use of looser affiliations such as strategic alliances with local firms, allowing the local firm to keep much of its identity—and the fees. Even though sometimes this makes the service offered to global customers uneven in quality, the client is served in name by the same firm everywhere. The result is a lower-cost global reach for the main office and a motivated local force in the field.

SUMMARY

This chapter has discussed the emergence of standardized global products and services. It emphasized the distinction between localization to a country's infrastructure and adaptation to customer preferences. Localization is always necessary, but adaptation to customer preferences is more a matter of managerial judgment.

The chapter also discussed the management of the firm's brand portfolio, including the building and management of local and global brands. The global marketing successes almost always involve global branding, and the development of brand equity measures has helped to alert managers to the fact that strong local brands can often be leveraged in many overseas markets.

A global service is generally a more intricate and fragile export than a physical good. The difficulty for the marketer is re-creating the quality level of the existing service abroad. Issues that arise when going global involve defining what the service concept is "really about," how the same service delivery system can be reproduced abroad, whether the necessary localization to the new markets can be made without jeopardizing the firm-specific advantages, and how the necessary local personnel can be properly trained. Judging from the successes, many companies are up to the challenge.

KEY TERMS

adaptation   p. 370
augmented service   p. 384
"back room" service   p. 369
basic service package   p. 384
brand changeover   p. 380
brand cycle   p. 378
brand equity   p. 376
brand extensions   p. 378
brand fit   p. 378
brand hierarchy   p. 378
brand portfolio   p. 377
core product   p. 369

core service   p. 384
counterfeits or knockoffs
   p. 381
franchising   p. 387
"front line" service   p. 370
global brand   p. 366
global brand management
   p. 376
globalization potential   p. 378
global products   p. 366
gray trade   p. 381
infrastructure   p. 386

localization   p. 370
modular design   p. 369
professional services   p. 388
regional products   p. 366
scale economies   p. 367
scope economies   p. 367
service delivery system   p. 385
service quality   p. 385
service standardization   p. 369
target product research   p. 374
test markets   p. 374

DISCUSSION QUESTIONS

1.   What are the factors behind Disney's global success? What can other entertainment businesses learn from Disney about standardizing products and services?

2.   Analyze the reasons why some local products (such as local beers) might have an enhanced potential when standardized global brands enter the market. How does the Internet affect the competitiveness of the local producer? Is it a threat or an opportunity?

3.   In what ways are services different from products? How do these differences affect global expansion potential?

4.   Check out the Web sites of some service companies (for example hotels, brokerage firms, auto dealers), and analyze how they try to translate their offering to the new medium. Are services more or less adaptable to on-line shopping than products?

5.   Why is most personal service not easily globalized? Give some examples that show how a service has to be standardized before going global—and how standardized personal service is almost always *impersonal.*

NOTES

1. This section draws on Buzzell, 1968, and Yip, 1992.

2. Yavas et al., 1992, illustrate this point well with empirical data.

3. See, for example, Normann, 1984.

4. More on how to globalize services will be presented later in the chapter.

5. This difference is similar to the split between "practical" and "emotional" preferences cited by Du Preez et al., 1994. Practical preferences are desires associated with a country's infrastructure, climate, or physical environment (a desire for air-conditioning in a desert country, say). Emotional preferences involve more subjective taste, such as a preference for a certain color or designer name. Incorporating air-conditioning in an automobile is more of a localization strategy, while offering a pink Cabriolet version is more of an adaptive strategy to target some niche in the market.

6. In PC software, the word *localization* is commonly used, but the word *adaptation* is rare. Software is generally a globally standardized product. Adding umlauts and hyphens to word processing programs or changing from English to a native language in a spreadsheet are typical localization practices. Like changing the steering wheel of automobiles to the right side for countries where people drive on the left side of the road, such changes are not really a matter of preferences. There is always, of course, a "lunatic fringe" or "status at any price" part of every market who take pride in weird and dysfunctional features.

7. From Kashani, 1989.

8. From Robert J. Dolan, "Henkel Group: Umbrella Branding and Globalization Decisions," Harvard Business School, case no. 585-185, 1985.

9. See Carpano and Chrisman, 1995.

10. See Samiee and Roth, 1992.

11. See Thomas, 1993, Chapters 8 and 10.

12. See the Buick Reatta case in Urban and Star, 1991. Several months of sophisticated product positioning research was undone because the Mazda Miata, a small sports car, was introduced just before the launch of Reatta, a Buick sports car.

13. See Cooper, 1994, and Hanssens and Johansson, 1991.

14. See Thomas, 1993, Chapter 3.

15. See Kotabe and Helsen, 1998, p. 317.

16. Brand management has become a very "hot topic" in marketing in the 1990s. This section draws on several sources, including Aaker, 1996, Joachimsthaler, 1997, Kapferer, 1997, Keller, 1998, Macrae, 1996, and Schmitt and Simonson, 1997.

17. These and the subsequent figures are from the "Brands at the Crossroads" study by Bozell Worldwide and Fortune Marketing, as reported in Elliott, 1995.

18. From Kashani, 1992.

19. This does not mean that all standardized products are sold under global brand names. For example, the Unilever fabric softener called Snuggle in the United States uses the same logo and packaging in most countries, but its brand name is different everywhere (Yip, 1992, p. 98).

20. The value of global brands has not escaped potential global marketers. Although a 1989 study found that only about one-half of the top brands in the United States were used abroad (and some of them only in neighboring Canada), the strategic intent is for more global branding (Rosen et al., 1989, and Simmons, 1990).

21. Keller, 1998, pp. 162–3, discusses Landor's work in more detail.

22. See, for example, the business section of the *New York Times*, July 28, 1998.

23. The hierarchy has given rise to the notion of "brand architecture" to describe the task facing management; see, for example, Macrae, 1996, Chapter 11.

24. Kotler, 1997, p. 360, reports on Procter and Gamble's strong and long-lasting brands, including Tide, Ivory soap, and Crest toothpaste.

25. Keller, 1998, Chapter 12, discusses brand extension problems in detail.

26. From Kapferer, 1997, Chapter 12.

27. This section draws especially on Kapferer, 1997, Chapter 10.

28. These definitions and much of this section draw on "The Counterfeit Trade," 1985.

29. See Givon et al., 1995.

30. In Kotler's version, the product definition now takes five levels: core benefits, generic product, expected product, augmented product, and potential product (Kotler, 1997, p. 431). For global services, the more standard three-level split is sufficient.

31. See, for example, Bitner, 1992.

32. See, for example, Zeithaml, 1981.

SELECTED REFERENCES

Aaker, David A. "How Will the Japanese Compete in Retail Services?" *California Management Review* 33 (1990), pp. 54–67.

———. *Building Strong Brands*. New York: Free Press, 1996.

———; and Alexander L. Biel, eds. *Brand Equity & Advertising*. Hillsdale, NJ: Lawrence Erlbaum Associates, 1993.

Albrecht, Karl. *The Only Thing That Matters*. New York: Harper Business, 1992.

Andrews, Edmund L. "A.T.&T. Reaches Out (and Grabs Everyone)." *New York Times*, August 8, 1993, sec. 3, pp. 1, 6.

Bitner, Mary-Jo. "Servicescapes: The Impact of Physical Surroundings on Customers and Employees." *Journal of Marketing*, April 1992, pp. 57–71.

Bobinski, Christopher. "Polish License for Deutsche Bank." *Financial Times*, July 4, 1995, p. 24.

Boddewyn, J. J.; Robin Soehl; and Jacques Picard. "Standardization in International Marketing: Is Ted Levitt in Fact Right?" *Business Horizons*, November–December 1986, pp. 69–75.

Buzzell, Robert D. "Can You Standardize Multinational Marketing?" *Harvard Business Review*, November–December 1968, pp. 102–13.

Carlzon, Jan. *Moments of Truth*. Cambridge, MA: Ballinger, 1987.

Carpano, Claudio; and James J. Chrisman. "Performance Implications of International Product Strategies and the Integration of Marketing Activities. *Journal of International Marketing* 3, no. 1 (1995), pp. 9–28.

Cooper, Robin. *Cost Management in a Confrontation Strategy: Lessons from Japan.* Cambridge, MA: Harvard Business School Press, 1994.

Czepiel, J. A. "Managing Customer Satisfaction in Consumer Service." Marketing Science Institute, working paper, September 1980, pp. 80–109.

Du Preez, Johann P.; Adamantios Diamantopoulos; and Bodo B. Schlegelmilch. "Product Standardization and Attribute Saliency: A Three-Country Empirical Comparison." *Journal of International Marketing* 2, no. 1 (1994), pp. 7–28.

Elliott, Stuart. "Advertising." *New York Times,* June 21, 1995, p. D9.

Feder, Barnaby J. "The Unorthodox Behemoth of Law Firms." *New York Times,* March 14, 1993, sec. 3, pp. 1, 6.

Givon, Moshe; Vijay Mahajan; and Eitan Muller. "Software Piracy: Estimation of Lost Sales and the Impact on Software Diffusion." *Journal of Marketing* 59, no. 1 (January 1995), pp. 29–37.

Hanssens, D. M.; and J. K. Johansson. "Rivalry as Synergy? The Japanese Automobile Companies' Export Expansion." *Journal of International Business Studies* 22, no. 3 (1991), pp. 503–26.

Joachimsthaler, Erich A. "Managing Brands in the Global Village." Presentation at Georgetown University, November 7, 1997.

Johansson, Johny K. "Japanese Service Industries and Their Overseas Potential." *The Service Industries Journal* 10, no. 1 (January 1990), pp. 85–109.

Kapferer, Jean-Noel. *Strategic Brand Management.* 2nd ed. London: Kogan-Page, 1997.

Kashani, Kamran. "Beware the Pitfalls of Global Marketing." *Harvard Business Review,* September–October 1989.

———. *Managing Global Marketing.* Boston: PWS-Kent, 1992.

Keller, Kevin Lane. *Strategic Brand Management.* Upper Saddle River, NJ: Prentice-Hall, 1998.

Kotabe, Masaaki; and Kristian Helsen. *Global Marketing Management.* New York: Wiley, 1998.

Kotler, Philip. *Marketing Management.* 9th ed. Englewood Cliffs, NJ: Prentice-Hall, 1997.

LaBarre, Polly. "Quality's Silent Partner." *Industry Week* 243, no. 8 (April 18, 1994), pp. 47–48.

Lovelock, C. H. *Services Marketing.* Englewood Cliffs, NJ: Prentice-Hall, 1984.

Macrae, Chris. *The Brand Chartering Handbook.* Harlow, England: Addison-Wesley, 1996.

Normann, R. *Service Management.* New York: Wiley, 1984.

Normann, R.; and Rafael Ramirez. "From Value Chain to Value Constellation." *Harvard Business Review,* July–August 1993, pp. 65–77.

Rosen, Barry Nathan; Jean J. Boddewyn; and Ernst A. Louis. "US Brands Abroad: An Empirical Study of Global Branding." *International Marketing Review* 6, no. 1 (1989), pp. 7–19.

Samiee, Saeed; and Kendall Roth. "The Influence of Global Marketing Standardization on Performance." *Journal of Marketing* 56, no. 2 (April 1992), pp. 1–17.

Schmitt, Bernd; and Alex Simonson. *Marketing Aesthetics: The Strategic Management of Brands, Identity, and Image.* New York: Free Press, 1997.

Shelp, R. K. *Beyond Industrialization: Ascendancy of the Global Service Economy.* New York: Praeger, 1981.

Simmons, Tim. "A Global Brand of Dialog." *Supermarket News* 40, no. 28 (July 9, 1990), p. 2.

Sorenson, R. Z.; and U. E. Wiechmann. "How Multinationals View Marketing Standardization." In D. N. Dickson, ed. *Managing Effectively in the World Marketplace.* New York: Wiley, 1983, pp. 301–16.

Tanaka, Hiroshi. "Branding in Japan." In Aaker and Biel, 1993, pp. 51–66.

"The Counterfeit Trade." *Business Week,* December 16, 1985, pp. 48–53.

Thomas, Robert J. *New Product Development.* New York: Wiley, 1993.

Urban, Glen L.; and Steven H. Star. *Advanced Marketing Strategy.* Englewood Cliffs, NJ: Prentice-Hall, 1991.

Yavas, Ugur; Bronislaw J. Verhage; and Robert T. Green. "Global Consumer Segmentation versus Local Market Orientation: Empirical Findings." *Management International Review* 32, no. 3 (1992), pp. 265–72.

Yip, George. *Total Global Strategy.* Englewood Cliffs, NJ: Prentice-Hall, 1992.

Zeithaml, Valarie A. "How Consumer Evaluation Processes Differ between Goods and Services." In James H. Donnelly and William R. George, eds. *Marketing of Services.* Chicago, IL: American Marketing Association, 1981.

Thirteen

Global Pricing

"There are limits"

Your takeaways from this chapter:

1. Although centrally coordinated prices interfere with the local subsidiary's ability to target its market, it is necessary and possible to coordinate pricing at least by regions or trading areas.

2. To discourage gray trade, which attempts to take advantage of currency exchange shifts and local price differentials, companies try to keep prices in different countries within a narrow band or "corridor."

3. Transfer prices between a global company's plants in different countries can seldom be arbitrarily used to shift profits but should be used to motivate subsidiaries and measure performance, while remaining supportable to local tax authorities.

4. Countertrade, including barter, is a frequent pricing option in countries with a lack of hard currency, especially when global financial turmoil puts domestic currencies under pressure.

5. In the end, global pricing still has to pay attention to basic issues such as competition, price-quality relationships, and stage of the product life cycle.

PRICING GLOBALLY is much trickier than pricing in the home market. In the domestic market, deciding on price levels, promotional rebates to middlemen, and consumer deals requires careful analysis; but once the decisions are made, the implementation is straightforward. The opposite generally holds true for markets abroad. The level of price is often a minor headache compared with the problems of currency fluctuations and devaluations, price escalation through tariffs, difficult-to-assess credit risks, f.o.b. versus c.i.f. quotations, dumping charges, transfer prices, and price controls—all common issues in global pricing. In global marketing the actual height of the product price is sometimes less important than currencies quoted, methods of payment, and credit extended.

Global Forces Create Pricing Challenges for Mercedes-Benz

For customers of Mercedes-Benz, "Made in Germany" has long signaled high quality. Lately, though, it also signals a drag on profits.

One reason has to do with exchange rates, the relative value of nations' currencies. In the mid-1990s, the value of the German mark rose, meaning more and more dollars were needed to exchange for a given number of marks. For Mercedes, higher and higher dollar prices were needed to profitably sell a car valued at a certain price in marks. Or, if the price is fixed in dollars, the money Mercedes earns is worth less when converted to marks. The company therefore had to choose between continually raising prices or earning lower and lower profits.

The strong mark also makes German employees relatively expensive; Mercedes pays them in high-value marks, rather than in a weaker currency. However, this is only one of several factors contributing to high costs for Mercedes. Like other German automakers, its factories are less efficient than Japanese or American plants. Until recently, German producers were able to tout their superior engineering instead of keeping up with productivity improvements their foreign competitors were adopting to lower costs and reduce defects.

These environmental pressures have forced Mercedes to take a harder look at how to earn a profit without raising prices. The exchange rates have hurt sales somewhat, but Mercedes can minimize the damage by holding prices steady. To profit with this policy, Mercedes must cut its costs.

The company is therefore establishing production facilities outside Germany; almost all the new cars it is developing will be made in foreign plants. It is also making product-related decisions such as simplifying designs so that they involve fewer variations among cars. The merger with Chrysler has also allowed the company to extend both its product line and its U.S. market penetration.

The performance of Mercedes over the long haul depends less on exchange rates and more on how well the company can rebuild its own competitive advantages through innovation and product development, and the successful integration of the Chrysler culture with the Daimler-Benz ethos. Recent market share figures show it bouncing back very well.

Sources: Nathaniel C. Nash, "Loss by Daimler Shows Danger of Strong Mark," *New York Times*, July 29, 1995, pp. D1, D7; "Daimler-Benz Posts $1.06 Billion Loss," *New York Times*, September 12, 1995, p. D4; Nathaniel C. Nash, "Luxuries They Can't Afford," *New York Times*, September 13, 1995, pp. D1, D22; David Greising, "Weak Dollar, Strong Profits," *Business Week*, July 11, 1994, p. 39; Robert Hanley, "Car Buyers Play a Game of Beating the Tariff," *New York Times*, May 18, 1995, pp. D1, D5.

http://www.mercedes.com

INTRODUCTION

In theory, any student of microeconomics is well equipped to handle pricing problems. Given fixed and stable demand and cost curves, the derivation of optimal price allows the simultaneous identification of optimal quantity to produce. This is a wonderful situation, since other company functions become ancillary and the "firm's problem" is solved.

The "next generation" texts in applied areas such as marketing then go on to demonstrate that the basic price theory learned in normative economics is not very practical. Demand and cost curves are not easily estimated, they are not stable over time, the competitors influence the demand function unpredictably, the firm produces for more than one market, and prices and output can't be set simultaneously because of organizational constraints. Even though the economists are patching up some of these holes, their theories (if not their terminology) have been largely abandoned by pragmatic price makers in the firm's marketing function. Instead, new procedures much closer to heuristic "rules of thumb" have been devised for the job.

These practical heuristics are also prominent in global pricing. Here the conditions that limit the value of microeconomics are further magnified when new limitations stemming from cross-border transactions are encountered. As a result, the pragmatic guidelines for price setting that have been developed over the years for the home markets need to be revised and augmented. New approaches have evolved—and keep evolving—under pressure from legal and governmental forces in the various countries in addition to the traditional market forces. These approaches represent truly eclectic combinations of practical experience and more or less theoretical suggestions.

It is perhaps fair to say that it is in pricing that the existing know-how from domestic marketing is least valuable for global operations. Market segmentation and product positioning principles can be extended abroad. Advertising and sales campaigns can be standardized for foreign markets. But the practical and institutional know-how required for global pricing decisions is of a wholly different order of magnitude.

INSTITUTIONAL LIMITS

Many of the problems in global pricing concern host country institutional limitations (legal and financial) that constrain strategy.

It is useful to distinguish at the outset between pricing considerations facing the company as an exporter and the pricing problems specific to global coordination and integration. As we saw in Chapter 5, "Export Expansion," among the export pricing concerns are the currency exchange risk exposure and the credit risks, which can combine to make customer-oriented easy credit terms in local currencies financially irresponsible. Problems also arise relating to such matters as how to quote prices (f.o.b. versus c.i.f.) and whether all of the price escalation due to the tariff (and nontariff) barriers should be passed on to the customer, lowering competitiveness. As for positioning strategy, high prices and an "import" status image necessitate niche targeting but also slow down market growth and leave windows of opportunity for the competition.

On the other hand, choosing a low *penetration price*, the firm runs a risk of being accused of *dumping*, that is, selling its products below cost.

For the global company, there are additional problems of constraints on pricing strategy. The first strategic task is that of deciding in which *currency* to price and what hedging tactics to employ. Next is the task of determining *transfer prices*—the prices charged country subsidiaries for products, components, and supplies—that are fair in terms of performance evaluation between country units and still optimal from the overall network perspective, including a desirable profit repatriation pattern. But foreign tax authorities have grown increasingly impatient with pricing schemes that rob a country of "fair" tax returns and, consequently, subject transfer prices to great scrutiny. Then there is the problem (really a "headache") of coordinating pricing across countries, to satisfy multinational customers, without imposing a straitjacket on local subsidiaries and illegally fixing prices for independent distributors.

These and related issues will be discussed in detail in this chapter. As always, it is in the end the "final" price of the product as viewed by the buyer that matters, regardless of what ingredients have come together to make it up. Differences in trade barriers make some prices escalate abnormally, and a great competitor in some markets might simply be priced out of other markets. Foreign cars have long been more or less shut out of the Italian market by virtue of high tariffs and quotas to protect Fiat, Alfa Romeo, and the other domestic producers, a situation that is gradually changing as the European Union integration proceeds. Also complicating matters is that the stage of the product life cycle (PLC) will differ between countries for the same product. Furthermore, inflation and the selective price regulations imposed by governments will vary.

The chapter will also discuss countertrade and what to do about being paid in goods instead of hard currency. "Systems selling" and the questions that arise when pricing a complete system of hardware and software will also be covered. In global markets there are many "turnkey projects," which pose their own peculiar kind of marketing problems. For instance, one typical headache for management is whether the components should be priced separately or whether one system price should be quoted.

The chapter will start with the basics of pricing, then move to the financial issues of *currency exchange* and *hedging*, very salient problems in the turmoil at the end of the 1990s. The chapter will then turn to *transfer pricing*, *countertrade*, and *systems pricing*. The roles of the *price-quality* relationship and the product life cycle in positioning strategy are discussed next. This is followed by an assessment of the feasibility of a global or regional *price coordination* with particular emphasis on firms' "gray trade" experiences in the integrated European market.[1] The last section of the chapter deals with the relative merits of *polycentric*, *geocentric*, and *ethnocentric* pricing strategies in the global firm.

PRICING BASICS

The basic principles of global pricing derive from the traditional pricing approaches in home markets. These revolve around production costs, competitive factors, and demand considerations.

The Role of Costs

The standard pricing procedure for exporting consists of a **cost-plus** formula. The firm arrives at export prices by adding up the various costs involved in producing and shipping the product (cost-based pricing) and then adding a markup ("plus") to this figure to achieve a reasonable rate of return. The cost components include manufacturing costs, administrative costs, allocated R&D expenditures, selling costs, and the transport charges, customs duties, and requisite fees to various facilitating agencies (see Chapter 5).

There is a long-standing argument about whether full costs should be used or whether only direct costs should burden the product or, the ideal case from a theoretical viewpoint, whether the firm should simply attempt to estimate marginal costs and then use those. In practice most firms seem to use all or a combination of these and other related methods. The emphasis varies with the company strategy and the market situation. For an existing product entering a new market, direct costs tend to be a natural choice, since overheads are already covered at home and investments have been recouped. If the product is new but relates directly to the firm-specific advantages (FSAs) of the company, marginal costs will be more important and the potential of grooming a "star" dominates the strategy. In the decentralized company where profit center accountability is featured, the tendency is to let the individual product carry itself and to load it down with its full share of overhead and contribution requirements.

The sole reliance on a cost-based pricing system is acceptable only in rare circumstances. It is frequently resorted to in the firm starting its exporting, since the know-how and the financial resources are not yet sufficient for market-oriented pricing. In most cases, however, it becomes absolutely necessary that competition and demand be factored into the decision process.

Experience Curve Pricing

The use of a cost-based price has become more common after the discovery of the "experience curve" effect. The **experience curve** shows how unit costs go down as successively more units of a product are produced. Through the "learning by doing" that comes from experience, the company's employees develop skills and capabilities that translate into lower costs.[2] Thus, a firm entering new foreign markets will gain in capabilities and scope economies from accumulated production and market experience.

Under this scenario, the entry into a new local market might well be accompanied by a lower price than that maintained in other markets, even at home. With the new market providing a chance for increased output and thus lower unit costs, the anticipated gains might be passed along to the customers in the form of low introductory prices ("penetration" prices in the early stage of the PLC). Whether the introductory price will be raised later or not depends directly on the correctness of the anticipated cost declines. If experience effects are smaller than anticipated, costs might certainly rise later; but a very low "cutthroat" entry price might stay down for a long time (because of competition) and still generate positive profits because of the experience curve decline.

Experience curve pricing has been adopted primarily by companies entering an existing market in the maturity stage. Many Japanese firms operate with this strategy, since it allows them to maintain a penetration price level in foreign markets.[3]

Competition

The competitive analysis might be as simple as finding out what global and domestic competitors in the particular country market charge for their products. These prices tend to set the "reservation" prices in the local market, that is, those limits beyond which the firm's product will not be considered and people will avoid buying. The analysis can go further and attempt to isolate the differential advantages that the firm's product might have over these existing offerings, so-called perceived value pricing.[4] One way to do this, developed by DuPont, the U.S.-based manufacturer of artificial fibers and related products, consists of dividing price into a "commodity" part and a "premium price differential" part. The commodity portion of price relates to underlying demand factors, while the premium differential focuses specifically on the competitive factors.

The **premium price differential** refers to the degree to which the firm might be granted a higher price by the market because of the particular strengths of its product.

To find this out, the company needs to do market research in the local market, identify how important various product attributes are to customers, and assess how competition is perceived on the salient attributes. A company such as Caterpillar uses this approach to price its products in relation to those of Komatsu, its large Japanese competitor.[5] Although in domestic markets such research is typically done via comprehensive and in-depth marketing research, in foreign markets softer data from existing customers, distributors, and country experts can usually offer a preliminary guide.

Demand

Naturally, demand also needs to be considered when setting prices; and most firms do, however implicitly, pay attention to what the various local markets "will bear."

The **price elasticities** associated with the demand curve in economic theory identify how many customers are willing to buy how much of the product at various price levels. This curve yields the "commodity" price in the DuPont approach, reflecting the underlying willingness to buy and ability to pay among the potential customers across the market. In many cases, the assessment of this "generic" demand can be done using statistical analysis; in other cases, especially when the product is new on the market, the analysis has to be judgmental (see Chapter 4 for some of these techniques).

The more seasoned manager will tend to base prices on an analysis of the costs involved and adjust the emerging prices in view of competitive and demand conditions in the market country. This naturally leads to an approach in which prices are set on the basis of costs plus a variable markup. Where demand is strong and the competitive differential large, the markup can be higher. In countries where the premium price differential is weaker because of strong competition, and especially where demand is relatively soft, the markup will come down correspondingly. This type of variable markup is common among companies with global strategies since it lends itself well to global coordination.

FINANCIAL ISSUES

Exchange Rates

Fluctuating exchange rates will routinely create problems with revenues and prices in a foreign market and can powerfully affect the performance of local subsidiaries. A particularly potent threat is the chance of a government **devaluation,** as happened in Mexico (see box, "Mexico's Peso Problems").

In less severe cases, **exchange rate fluctuations** do not always affect prices in the manner postulated by economic theory. A rising currency does not necessarily mean higher prices, weakened competitiveness, and less exports. A simple example helps illustrate what might happen.

Take the case of trade between Germany and Japan. If the German mark or the euro depreciates against the yen, theory says that German automobiles will be cheaper in Japan, while Japanese automobiles will be more expensive in Germany. Because of existing inventories and lags between ordering and delivery times, the effect may not be immediate, but gradually the trade balance will shift. German automobiles will sell better in Japan, while Japan's market shares in Germany will diminish. The extent of the shift depends on the price elasticities in the two countries for the automobiles traded and thus on available substitutes from domestic producers and other foreign producers.

From a managerial perspective, this scenario depends on prices being set by the headquarters in the home country currency—and staying unchanged. In other words, German exporters are assumed to quote prices to their Japanese importers in terms of the same D-mark (Deutsche mark) or euro price as before the currency depreciation. Similarly, the Japanese are assumed to stay with the same yen prices for their German subsidiaries as before. Neither case is necessarily realistic for the company with global operations.

G E T T I N G   T H E   *Picture*

Mexico's Peso Problems

THE DEVALUATION of the Mexican peso in January 1995 was a prime example of how difficult pricing in foreign markets can be in an era of exchange rate volatility.

During the early years of the 1990s, Mexico was a fast-growing market and very attractive for foreign products. The economy was spurred by the creation of NAFTA, the North American Free Trade Agreement, which ensured free access for Mexican goods in Canada and the United States. With the peso pegged to the U.S. dollar, the purchasing power of the Mexicans increased apace with growth, and imports grew rapidly.

However, as the dollar rose the peso grew increasingly overvalued, the Mexican exports became high-priced and uncompetitive, and foreign investment slowed down. As the import surplus grew, the country's foreign exchange reserves were depleted, forcing a devaluation only days after a new government was installed. By mid-1995, the peso had lost in the neighborhood of 30 percent of its original value.

For the foreign marketer in Mexico, revenues were the same in pesos, but back home at headquarters, they often did not cover production costs. As pending orders from Mexican sales subsidiaries were filled at foreign prices, they became too expensive for the Mexican consumers to buy with their devalued pesos, and the multinationals faced the question of whether to support the Mexican market positions by introducing lower prices. Most opted to maintain prices, forcing the Mexican consumers to forgo imports. Firms with local manufacturing or assembly fared better, since their costs came down, which helped make exports from Mexico competitive again.

Sources: Lustig, 1995; Thurston, 1995; and various newspaper reports.
http://www.porsche.com
http://www.vw.com

First, the Japanese may decide that the German market is too important for them, and therefore they keep their D-mark and euro prices in Germany unchanged in an attempt to maintain market share. This strategy was common for the Japanese after the Plaza Accord in 1985 led to a yen appreciation of nearly 40 percent. Since the revenues from the automobiles sold in Germany will be lower than before, profits for the Japanese will tend to fall even as volume sales stay steady.

Second, the shrinking profitability will induce the Japanese to shift supply routes. Instead of shipping to Germany from Japan, which is now a more expensive producer, the Japanese companies will look for supplies from their manufacturing subsidiaries in a third country whose currency has moved with the German mark and euro. This is one reason why many Japanese companies have started to supply Europe from their North American–based subsidiaries.

Third, when the shift in the exchange rate is judged to be more or less permanent, management will explore the option of investing in production in Germany (or in another euro country). Although currency rate fluctuations are notoriously difficult to forecast and thus rarely "permanent," the relatively small appreciation of the Japanese yen of about 10 percent at the beginning of the 1990s had this effect, since it coincided with long-term structural changes in the Japanese economy.

As for German companies faced with a depreciating D-mark and euro they become more price-competitive in Japan and their exports are stimulated, much in the way economic theory suggests. Their incentive to invest abroad is reduced, and no trade-substituting foreign direct investment (FDI) is likely to occur. Nevertheless, to the extent that the German automobiles rely on components produced abroad, perhaps in their own foreign subsidiaries, the cost of such components may rise. The tendency will be for such components to be replaced by German domestic supplies where feasible, and German value added will be increased.

Russians in line to withdraw cash before the ruble drops lower. The Russian ruble was devalued by 34% in August that year. While hedging can protect a company's bottom line, dramatic shifts in the exchange rate play havoc with a company's global price coordination. Wide World Photo.

Thus, a depreciating currency often leads to an increased ability to lower prices abroad and increased competitiveness for the exporter. By contrast, an appreciating currency does not necessarily lead to higher prices and lower competitiveness, since the company can often shift supply routes and invest in overseas manufacturing.

This asymmetrical pattern is even more pronounced for the company that has a global network of manufacturing locations and a presence in many markets. Not only can alternative supplier locations help limit the damage from currency fluctuations, but a presence in multiple markets makes it possible to shift emphasis from one country market to another. As their competitiveness in German markets decreases, Japanese companies can simply allow their shares to go down and instead focus on other markets where the currency rate against the yen is more favorable. This was happening in the late 1990s as the strong U.S. dollar made American markets more attractive and the then weaker D-mark and euro made Germany a less attractive market.[6]

In the big picture, the effect of exchange rate fluctuations on the market prices of the products sold is limited not only by what managers can do but also by what they can't do. Prices can't be changed overnight, even if exchange rates do. Purchasing contracts for industrial products may be negotiated months in advance and remain in force for a prespecified period. Suppliers of high-quality components are sometimes asked to work closely with the company's designers and engineers and can't be easily dismissed. There are considerable start-up costs in organizing and managing a distribution channel in a foreign country, and a shift in exchange rates will often be viewed as a "windfall" profit or loss to the channel members without any adjustment in prices and costs quoted. To avoid the risk of wide fluctuations in short-term profits, the global company will often turn to hedging.

Hedging

Hedging involves the purchase of insurance against losses because of currency fluctuations. Such insurance usually takes the form of buying or selling "forward contracts" or engaging in "currency swaps" with the help of financial intermediaries (banks and brokerage houses).

A **forward contract** refers to the sale or purchase of a specified amount of a foreign currency at a fixed exchange rate for delivery or settlement on an agreed date in the future or, under an options contract, between agreed upon dates in the future. A **swap** may be defined as the exchange of one currency for another for a fixed period of time. At the expiration of the swap each party returns the currency initially received. While the forward contract represents a simple insurance policy against downside risk—the firm buys today so as not to lose by deteriorating exchange rates—the cost of the contract reduces the gain from a favorable change in rates.

Various combinations of these contracts are possible, and hedging has become a major financial activity of the international division in many MNCs. From a marketing viewpoint, the most desirable arrangement would be for the seller to assume responsibility for currency fluctuations and quote prices in the local currency. This is not done very often by Western companies, however. Their prices, especially in commodities and industrial markets, tend to be quoted in the "hard" currencies, in particular the U.S. dollar. A company such as Boeing, for example, quotes prices in U.S. dollars only and lets its customers worry about the exchange rate fluctuations and the conversion from the local currency.

Government Intervention

Different countries exhibit different rates of inflation, some like Israel and Argentina in the past showing hyperinflationary patterns. The currencies of such countries will continuously be losing their value against stronger currencies, while their governments will intervene in the workings of the financial system in order to bring some stability to prices. The standard solution is selective **price controls.** For the global marketer, price controls mean that prices can't be changed as frequently as might be desirable—in particular, inflationary erosion of revenues can't so easily be avoided.

Under price controls, increases in prices usually need to be officially sanctioned. To obtain such sanction it is typically required that price increases be directly related to costs. Accordingly, companies with exemplary accounting records tend to have a much better chance of getting their requests for increases in price sanctioned. But where inflation is very rapid, it is unlikely that cost increases alone are sufficient to justify price increases. In such a case, the company has to resort to the kind of currency management discussed above, getting involved in forward contracts and swap deals. Needless to say, such matters are best handled by financial, not marketing, officers of the firm.

There are other types of government intervention that affect pricing. Chief among these are the antitrust laws, in particular as they relate to price fixing and discrimination. Not much can be said here about these matters; the interested reader is referred to any international law book. The firm's legal counsel is the person most likely to be involved in these matters. In terms of price fixing it is important to point out that in certain countries price cartels are not forbidden per se as they are in the United States (there are several instances of cartels in Japan, for example). Under the current trend toward open markets and free international trade, however, cartels will be increasingly under attack. The 1994 flat glass agreement, in which American trade negotiators managed to break open a Japanese cartel to allow foreign firms to bid on new construction, is an example of how protective barriers gradually fall.

In terms of **price discrimination,** there are very few laws of the American Robinson-Patman type that prohibit discrimination unless justified by cost savings. However, many laws do question discounts not tied to specific functions performed: The issue of bribery surfaces easily. The firm needs to get some legal advice on what is acceptable and what is not in the particular country. In Japan, for example, it is customary to give large functional rebates to the many middlemen handling the product in that country's complex network of distribution.[7] It is usually necessary to offer such rebates for any newcomer who wants to enter the market.

TRANSFER PRICING

With a considerable amount of some countries' trade accounted for by shipments between headquarters and subsidiaries, the question of what the value of these shipments is and what the prices mean naturally arises. This is the problem of "transfer" prices.

Definition

The basic reason for **transfer pricing** is simple: There has to be a price paid for the products shipped between units of the same organization when the shipment crosses national borders so that the correct duties and related fees can be paid. However, since the transfer prices directly affect the amount of purchases in the cost accounting of a foreign subsidiary, they have a direct influence on the subsidiary's financial performance. Because of this they have also become a mechanism for the multinational company to shift profits from one country to another. If the headquarters of a company sets a high price on the shipment to a subsidiary in an African country, say, this subsidiary will have trouble showing a profit; and if the (quite arbitrary) price is set low, the subsidiary will be very profitable.

The use of transfer prices for the purpose of profit repatriation has come under the close scrutiny of many governments whose tax revenues have diminished because of it (see box, "How to Transfer Income?").

Reputedly, the use of transfer prices for tax-shifting purposes is not as widespread as it once was because the governments have now caught on to past abuses. Transfer prices have taken on an additional role as control mechanisms, however.

The Hertz company's uniform pricing approach appeals to global business customers who travel to many countries and want to simplify control over expenses. The prices in local currency will, of course, vary according to exchange rates, and local customers in countries with weak currencies against the dollar will find Hertz relatively expensive.
Courtesy The Hertz Corporation.

How to Transfer Income? Carefully

BECAUSE OF THE TAX and dumping implications of transfer prices and governments' insistence on transparent accounting rules, public accounting firms have developed strict guidelines for the transfer pricing process in large multinationals. The following 10 steps are typical of the recommended process:

1. Before the beginning of the annual business cycle, meet with outside advisers and agree on a game plan.
2. Compare third party (arm's-length) transactions with "related party" transactions. Adjust prices.
3. Prepare a financial model to test the method agreed on.
4. Make sure senior management understands the transfer pricing audit process, issues, and exposure.
5. Prepare internal documentation.
6. Prepare external documentation.
7. Spot-check the process within the company.
8. Simulate a transfer pricing audit by outside advisers.
9. Evaluate year-end or cycle-end tax position against goals.
10. Prepare tax returns.

Sources: Davis, 1994; Weekly, 1992.

Arm's-Length Price

From a theoretical point of view, the transfer prices set should reflect the prices the subsidiary might encounter in the open market—so-called **arm's-length prices.**[8] In this way the costs of the goods to the subsidiary will give the right "signals" to the buyer about how much to buy, and the consequent operating criteria (such as return on investment and profits) will be valid indicators of the subsidiary's performance. In the practical world there are times when such market prices are difficult to identify, usually because there are no substitutes in the open market. The practice also goes against the use of transfer pricing to shift profits from one country to another.

Judging from their public statements, many global American companies have given up trying to repatriate profits in this fashion and do indeed attempt to set market-related transfer prices. Several companies have even taken the logical step of introducing an option for the subsidiary to buy on the open market, should price and quality there be more favorable. Many of Ford Motor Company's subsidiaries around the world now have this option: To exercise it requires, however, a quite rigorous demonstration that the quality of components and parts is up to par.

Shifting Resources

There are other factors influencing the level of transfer prices, most related to the flow of funds between headquarters and the subsidiaries. Where the country suffers from rapid inflation, there is usually an attempt to keep the operating funds at a minimum. The shipments of intermediate goods going to the subsidiary in the country will be charged at a higher rate than otherwise, for example. This was the effect of the problems firms faced in Brazil in the 1980s and again at the end of the 1990s. If a country suffers from currency shortages (rationing of dollars, for example), this approach will not work since the payments are not convertible. Options then include currency swaps, forward contracts, countertrade, and so on. In the end, the global firm will attempt to reduce its dependence on the country, possibly pulling out its investments. This was why the Mexican devaluation in early 1995 was so threatening to Mexico and other countries in Latin America, and why the threat of Brazil's real being devalued at the end of 1998 was making foreign investors wary.

Transfer prices can also be used to support a subsidiary's competitive position in a local market. Where the market position is strategically important for the global position of the MNC, headquarters might well transfer more funds to the subsidiary by simply charging low prices for some key product components or parts. The approach is equivalent to government subsidies, but in this case it is carried out within a corporation. An example is the entry of many Japanese companies into the U.S. market. In the initial stages at least, the American offices are usually staffed by people paid directly from Japan without any attempt to make the subsidiary a profit center.

COUNTERTRADE

Countertrade is the term for transactions in which all or part of the payment is made in kind rather than cash. The practice has been known as *barter trade* throughout recorded history, but in the last few years new and ingenious wrinkles on the practice have emerged. The primary moving force has been the shortage of hard currencies available to developing countries, in particular those lacking a strong export sector to generate foreign earnings. In addition, the failure of the globally integrated financial markets to support the stability of domestic currencies has made countertrade again appear as a viable alternative payment.

It is useful to distinguish between five kinds of countertrade: barter, compensation deals, counterpurchase, product buy-back, and offset.

Barter is the oldest form of countertrade. It is the direct exchange of goods between two trading partners. A famous barter trade was the huge deal between Occidental Petroleum of the United States and the Soviet government back in the 1970s to exchange superphosphoric acid (from Occidental) for urea and potash (from the Soviet Union), an agreement valued at about $20 billion. No money changed hands and no third party was involved—a classic Armand Hammer transaction.

For barter to make economic sense, the seller must be able to dispose of the goods received in payment. In the case of Occidental this was no problem since the company could use the urea and potash in its own manufacturing plants. To assist companies that engage in barter trading and cannot count on such arrangements, several barter houses have been established primarily in Europe, where many of the exchanges are negotiated.

Compensation deals involve payment both in goods and in cash. In one case GM sold locomotives to former Yugoslavia for $12 million and was paid in cash plus Yugoslavian machine tools valued at approximately $4 million. The introduction of the cash portion is to make the deal more attractive to the seller, and most companies faced with the possibility of a countertrade agreement will in fact insist that at least some portion of the bill be settled in cash. As in the case of barter, the goods portion of the payment has to be sold in a third market, and the additional transaction costs should logically be added to the original amount invoiced.

Counterpurchases represent the most typical version of the countertrade. Here two contracts are usually negotiated: one to sell the product (the initial agreement) at an agreed upon cash price, and a second to buy goods from the purchaser at an amount equal to the bill in the initial agreement. This type of contract simply represents one way for the buyer to reuse valuable foreign currency and force exports and is usually introduced relatively late in the exchange negotiations. In practice the seller gets its money and then has a limited period of time (usually 6 to 12 months) before its purchases from the country must be completed. In some of these cases the second contract is sold (at a steep discount) to a third party (a barter house, for example), but this is not always easy. For a classic example, McDonnell Douglas, the American aircraft manufacturer now merged with Boeing, once had to buy and then resell ham from China in order to sell a few of its aircraft there.

Product buy-backs come in two types. Under one type of product buy-back agreement the seller accepts a certain amount of the output as full or partial payment for the goods sold. Alternatively, the seller can agree to buy back some of the output at a later date. Levi Strauss is accepting Hungarian-made jeans (bearing its brand name) in partial payment for setting up a jeans factory outside Budapest. Another Western company has established a tractor plant in Poland and agreed to buy back a certain number of Polish-built tractors as part of the deal.

In **offset** deals, the seller contracts to invest in local production or procurement to partially offset the sale price. In aircraft, for example, it is not uncommon for a national airline buying airplanes to demand that the manufacturer procure certain components, parts, or supplies in the buyer's country, or invest in some assembly operation there. This helps justify the purchase price paid to the manufacturer from cash-strapped nations.[9]

Business Evaluation

There are many multinational corporations and exporters that have found themselves in a situation where a countertrade represents the only feasible alternative for the buyer. In general, settlement in cash is preferable to the seller. Where there is no competition, the seller can insist on a cash settlement. But companies such as Coca-Cola and Ford have been forced to accept the "realities" of the international marketplace and will do countertrading if necessary. GM has even gone so far as to create its own in-house barter subsidiary, General Motors Trading Company. For Japanese companies, the close ties with the large trading houses have proved to be of vital importance for countertrade, giving the Japanese an edge in the marketplace.

Similarly, European companies rely on barter houses to provide the necessary expertise and contacts to sell the goods received. In the global marketplace of the 1990s, with the huge China market opening up and the former Soviet republics suffering because of slow economic progress and currency problems, the acceptance of countertrade proposals might be necessary in order to be able to compete at all.

A countertrade option means not only that the value of the offered goods must be assessed but also that the extra costs associated with the negotiations and future sale must be considered. It is usual, therefore, for the agreed upon price to rise considerably higher than the cash price. But for the buyer the gains are important; and in many situations the value to the buyer of the seller's products is much higher than the sacrifice in terms of domestic products, so the higher "price" is only a nominal figure.

For the seller evaluating a countertrade proposal, the following points are important to consider:

1. Is this the only way the order can be secured?
2. Can the received goods be sold?
3. How can we maximize the cash portion?
4. Does the invoiced price incorporate extra transaction costs?
5. Are there any import barriers to the received goods (so that we will have trouble disposing of the goods at home, say)?
6. Could there be currency exchange problems if we try to repatriate the earnings from sales in a third country?

If these issues receive a positive evaluation, countertrade might be a useful alternative. When the opposite happens, the firm might be better off curbing its appetite for foreign sales.

SYSTEM PRICING

One pricing issue of frequent relevance in global markets is the question of systems pricing. **Systems selling** or **turnkey sales** refers to the notion that in many instances the firm not only is selling some particular physical product or offering a single service but also is providing the buyer with a complete "package." Examples include the turnkey plants being built by firms from developed countries in many less developed countries (LDCs), for instance, the paper and pulp mill built in Japan and floated to the Manaus free trade zone on the Amazon river in Brazil.[10] Fiat's auto plant in Russia is another example. Many computerized office systems are sold as complete turnkey operations because of compatibility requirements. The German computer firm Nixdorf, now part of Siemens, has long specialized in complete information systems for banks in Europe. The driving force in these sales is not the hardware itself but the added value produced by wedding hardware and software into a functioning and complete system. The question is how such a system should be priced.

Exhibit 13.1 demonstrates how one firm has gone about analyzing this pricing problem.[11] The company deals with a varied set of customers in Southeast Asia in the telecommunications industry. The specific hardware sold is a mobile telephone, but the final sales to many customers also involve switching networks, computerized accounting and billing facilities, the construction of physical facilities, and the training of supervisors. The firm does not manufacture the switches or the telephones but serves basically as the prime contractor for the turnkey system, carries out the initial feasibility studies, develops the administrative software, and selects the hardware components and the construction subcontractor for the physical facilities. Its know-how and FSA lie in the experience accumulated in running these types of systems in the United States.

EXHIBIT 13.1 Pricing a Turnkey Package

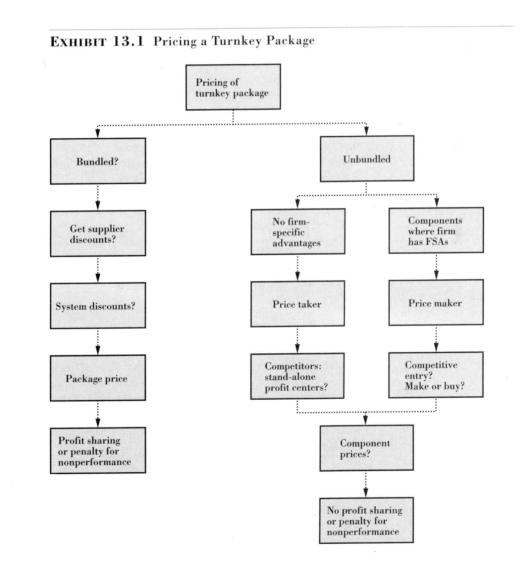

As Exhibit 13.1 demonstrates, an initial decision is made between offering an un-bundled system and a complete turnkey operation. The unbundling option is less preferable from the seller's point of view and is resorted to only when the customer insists it has certain skills that can be used for parts of the project. The seller attempts to direct the participation of the buyer into areas where the seller has no firm-specific advantages (FSAs), partly in order to protect against dissipation and also because alternative suppliers are available. This is done by pricing such components high, while areas where the firm's proprietary know-how and FSAs are lodged are priced more aggressively so as to discourage customers from going to outside firms or doing the work themselves. Thus, system design, an area in which the firm claims a great deal of expertise, tends to be sold aggressively, while the telephone hardware is less of a concern and accordingly priced higher.

In the preferred case the customer does not attempt to unbundle but allows the firm to become the supplier for the complete turnkey operation. In such a case the firm will identify the overall price by adding software and design charges as markups on hardware components. In addition, the seller will negotiate for possible supplier hardware discounts, using its previous connections with suppliers to obtain special rebates if possible. Where desirable, these discounts can then be passed on to the customer. The ability to obtain these special discounts is one argument used to convince the customer not to unbundle the package.

When the complete system is handled, the firm is in a position to guarantee its performance—a guarantee customarily not offered when unbundling has taken place (to accept responsibility the firm needs to be in complete control of the project). In its home market the firm has been willing to accept business risk on some projects, receiving full payment only after successful installation and marketing of the mobile telephone system. Such an exposure has not been deemed acceptable in foreign markets.

PRICE AND POSITIONING

Before deciding on the final price, some basics of pricing and positioning need to be kept in mind. In the final analysis, price is important because it represents the sacrifice for the potential customer contemplating a purchase. As such, price is no different whether we think of a consumer in Tanzania, in Thailand, or in Turkey. Most of the pricing discussions in traditional marketing texts are relevant at this stage. A few issues, however, do not translate so directly from the domestic to the foreign and global markets and need to be considered carefully when going abroad. They include the question of price-quality relationships in positioning of the product and the role of the product life cycle with its skimming versus penetration price.

Price-Quality Relationships

In many countries where the positioning objective of a product is for a high-quality niche in the market, it goes without saying that price has to be relatively high. What is assumed, often correctly, is that customers will attribute high quality to a product with high price. It would generally cost more to produce a high-quality product, and thus its price will be higher. Research has shown that this **price-quality relationship** varies in strength by products, standardized products being less affected. Also, a strong brand name or a strongly positive country-of-origin image can nullify the negative quality effect from a low price.[12]

The price-quality relationship is also weakened in markets protected by trade barriers. In such markets imported products will usually show an artificially high price (the price escalation phenomenon), and thus a high price signals an imported product, not only or even necessarily a high-quality product. In many cases such imports will be of higher quality (if they were not, why would they be imported?), so the high price is in a sense justified. In other cases, however, the escalated prices are simply too high to render a product competitive, and the imports will make no inroads against established domestic brands. An example is the situation in the Japanese market where high non-tariff barriers have made many markets "dualistic," with a domestic and an import segment.[13] The majority of the market falls to the domestic producers, between whom competition is intense, while the imports garner a small fringe segment of the market, whose primary buying appeal is "status." A typical case is cameras, where a Swiss Leica is priced at approximately 2.5 times the price of Nikon, a high-priced Japanese rival; or autos, where a BMW is priced at double its American price. Perhaps not surprisingly, for both companies Japan is their most profitable market.[14]

In this type of distorted marketplace, the assumption that high prices necessarily imply higher functional quality no longer holds, and the consumers will by and large learn this fact. Status is what matters. A high-priced Western luxury car, such as a Cadillac, has only recently been built with right-hand drive, for example, to accommodate the Japanese market. In Japan, the customers can usually buy more functional quality products at relatively low prices, by staying with domestic offerings.

The PLC Impact

It is generally agreed that in the introductory stage of the product life cycle (PLC) customers are relatively insensitive to price levels. The innovators and pioneers who venture to try the new product are not very much concerned with price but act out of a desire to experience new things. Thus, the firm entering a market in the early growth stage could possibly maintain a relatively high **skimming price,** charging what the market will bear.

This logic becomes much less clear in global markets. Even though a given local market might be new so that the product is in the introductory stage technically speaking, it might already have reached the maturity stage in other local markets and certainly in leading markets. If so, the existing producers in those countries will be potential entrants in the new market and thus serve to put a limit on prices. Furthermore, a "demonstration" effect serves to speed up the introductory phase of many products: Potential customers are prepared for the eventual arrival of the new product by exposure via television and related global media.

Consequently, the best entry pricing strategy in many markets will be a relatively low-priced **penetration** approach. This is also the one followed in recent years by most companies, including those as diverse as Microsoft with its office products, Compaq in PC hardware, Mercedes' new model autos, Olympus cameras, and Xerox copiers. The competitive rivalry is potentially intense, the buyers in the global village already know much about the product, and the producers use the experience curve argument to justify very low prices based on marginal costs. If the competitors consider the new entry to be in the potential "star" category, they will price aggressively for global strategic reasons.[15] All in all, the role of a skimming strategy in the introductory stage in the PLC is severely limited, although in the mature stage of the cycle a well-protected position can possibly still be used to generate cash in the short term.

PRICING RESEARCH

Pricing research asks two different kinds of management questions. One question refers to the *elasticity of demand* to price changes, a fine-tuning of what prices to charge. At home, these kinds of studies may involve in-store experiments or the analysis of historical time series data of prices and sales volume. The in-store data gathering often involves some kind of temporary promotional offering, to identify the extent to which deal-prone customers will react.

These studies are usually difficult to carry out in new local markets. Historical sales data are not available, and access to stores and promotional tracking are often limited. The new entrant may have to check competitive prices to identify realistic levels and then attempt the fine-tuning only after some data, perhaps from a test market, are in hand. Of course, in the case of a well-established multinational in a developed and mature market, the pricing research can easily be carried out in the more advanced typical way.

The second function of pricing research is to identify a *price level* congruent with the intended product position. This is usually a more important aspect of pricing research for the foreign local marketer. It involves less formal methods than price sensitivity studies. In the typical market the research involves finding out about competition's price points and the proper alignment of the firm's own prices given the competitive strengths and weaknesses of its brand. Advanced methods such as trade-off and conjoint analysis can be useful for these purposes, since the basic task of comparing products and brands is real enough for customers to give reliable and valid answers.[16]

In emerging and developing markets where competition has been hampered by trade barriers, pricing has to take into account the effect of price on image. Generally, these markets will be more receptive to a higher price because the quality of their past products was low. This is seen today in Eastern Europe, where Western entrants tend to be the high-priced alternatives. But it is important for the firm to monitor competitive quality improvements and customer reactions to these, since an unwarranted price premium is a recipe for failure. Consumers' confidence in their own product evaluations, regardless of brand image, will generally increase as markets mature, and prices might have to be adjusted downward from a high initial base. Even though Unilever introduced its superior Timotei shampoo at a premium price in Eastern Europe, it had to revise prices downward within six months as local competitors came back with improved products.[17]

Another kind of pricing research involves monitoring **"parallel" imports**, unauthorized middlemen importing the identical products and brands from countries whose prices are lower because of exchange rates. These imports are also called **"gray trade."** Regardless of the company's price policy, fluctuations in exchange rates tend to produce temporary misalignment in prices between countries. Entrepreneurial spirits in a country can exploit such arbitrage opportunities by purchasing the product abroad, shipping it to the market, and selling it at a discount. For example, it is estimated that as many as 20 percent of the Mercedes-Benz cars sold in Japan in 1992 were parallel imports from Europe and the United States.[18] Since these entrepreneurs are usually protected under antimonopoly laws, the firms can do little directly to stop them. Instead, they tend to monitor the levels, do research on customer sensitivity to the price differentials, and, as necessary, adjust their prices downward. The firms also attempt to block the parallel imports by more or less subtle tricks such as refusing to honor warranties, delaying repair work, and so on.[19]

GLOBAL COORDINATION

When a company manufactures in several nations and sells its products in many countries, the same product might appear on the market in different countries at widely different prices.

For many products there is a need to develop a formula for coordinating prices and avoiding confusion among customers and opportunities for gray trade. A global customer does not usually like to pay different prices for the same product in different parts of the world. If the customer finds it does, it might simply concentrate purchases where the price is lowest, ship to subsidiaries elsewhere, and cut costs. Or the customer might opt to put pressure on the manufacturer. For example, a leading manufacturer of consumer products distributed through large local and pan-European retailers had its biggest retail customer request that all products be supplied at the lowest European price. The company had to comply, but the 20 percent price decline across Europe resulted in a profit disaster.[20]

A coordinated pricing policy is obviously desirable but not so easily implemented. Generally, one can identify a polycentric, a geocentric, and an ethnocentric approach. But first companies have to decide what to do about gray trade.

Usually, the problem relates to exchange rate fluctuations. A good example is the pricing of a McDonald's hamburger. Although the company attempts to position the products as affordable and targets broad-based segments in most local markets, the resulting prices vary a great deal, as Exhibit 13.2 shows. The 1993 Big Mac prices ranged from $1.03 in China to $3.69 in Switzerland, and even between two relatively comparable countries such as Singapore and Korea the range is from $1.90 to $2.84.

EXHIBIT 13.2 The Hamburger Standard

	Big Mac prices				
	Prices in local currency*	Prices in dollars	Actual exchange rate 13/4/93	Implied purchasing power parity of the dollar	Local currency under (−)/ over (+)[†] valuation[‡], %
United States§	$2.28	$2.28	—	—	—
Argentina	Peso3.60	3.60	1.00	1.58	+58
Australia	A$2.45	1.76	1.39	1.07	−23
Belgium	BFr109	3.36	32.45	47.81	+47
Brazil	Cr77,000	2.80	27,521	33,772	+23
Britain	£1.79	2.79	1.56 ‖	1.27 ‖	+23
Canada	C$2.76	2.19	1.26	1.21	−4
China	Yuan8.50	1.50	5.68	3.73	−34
Denmark	DKr25.75	4.25	6.06	11.29	+86
France	FFr18.50	3.46	5.34	8.11	+52
Germany	DM4.60	2.91	1.58	2.02	+28
Holland	F15.45	3.07	1.77	2.39	+35
Hong Kong	HK$9.00	1.16	7.73	3.95	−49
Hungary	Forint157	1.78	88.18	68.86	−22
Ireland	I£1.48	2.29	1.54 ‖	1.54 ‖	0
Italy	Lire4,500	2.95	1,523	1,974	+30
Japan	Y391	3.45	113	171	+51
Malaysia	Ringgit3.35	1.30	2.58	1.47	−43
Mexico	Peso7.09	2.29	3.10	3.11	0
Russia	Rouble780	1.14	686#	342	−50
S. Korea	Won2,300	2.89	796	1,009	+27
Spain	Ptas325	2.85	114	143	+25
Sweden	SKr25.50	3.43	7.43	11.18	+50
Switzerland	SwFr5.70	3.94	1.45	2.50	+72
Thailand	Baht48	1.91	25.16	21.05	−16

*Prices may vary locally.
†Purchasing-power parity: local price divided by price in United States.
‡Against dollar.
§Average of New York, Chicago, San Francisco, and Atlanta.
‖Dollars per pound.
Market rate.

Source: *The Economist*, April 17, 1993, p. 79, with data from McDonald's. © 1993 The Economist Newspaper Group, Inc. Reprinted with permission. Further reproduction prohibited.

G E T T I N G   T H E

Checking Gray Trade the Hard Way

Picture

IN 1994 SOME CAR MODELS cost 30 to 40 percent less in Italy than in Germany because of the recent devaluation of the lira. The flood of reimports prompted one German automaker to drastic action. To control reimports from Italy, where prices were much lower than at home in Germany, the company bought back a number of reimported cars from the gray traders and offered them as a "special series model" to authorized German dealers at gray import prices. Next, headquarters limited the number of cars to the Italian dealers, who were no longer able to supply both local customers and gray trade demand. With a limited supply the prices in Italy moved up, and with the exception of a few gray reimports by private owners, the so-called pipeline control worked out well.

Pricing Actions against Gray Trade

The problem of gray trade is particularly acute in trade areas where barriers have recently been dismantled and exchange rates fluctuate, the EU being one example. According to one report, for identical consumer products, prices typically deviate 30 to 150 percent, creating big **arbitrage** opportunities and **"consumer tourism,"** with people traveling to another country for the purpose of shopping.[21] By the mid-1990s, if you lived in France but bought your car elsewhere in Europe, you could have saved 24.3 percent on a Citroen, 18.2 percent on a Peugeot, or 33 percent on a Volkswagen Jetta (see box, "Checking Gray Trade the Hard Way").

Against this background it is not surprising if the drive toward a common European currency (the "euro") was sustained despite many countries' misgivings. But the euro is not without its own problems (see box "The Euro: An Opportunity Creates Problems").

As will be seen in Chapter 14, "Global Distribution," controlling gray trade involves more than trying to set prices that eliminate price differentials between countries, an impossible task in a world of floating exchange rates. Nevertheless, some pricing actions can be taken to help reduce the gray trade problem.

Four approaches to coordinating prices under the threat of gray trade can be identified.[22] They are not mutually exclusive, since a company can pursue them in combination:

ECONOMIC CONTROLS   The company can influence price setting in local markets by changing the prices at which the product is shipped to importers or by outright rationing of the product as in the German auto case (described in the box, "Checking Gray Trade the Hard Way"). This usually is most feasible in the case of transfer prices to wholly owned subsidiaries.

CENTRALIZATION   The company can attempt to set limits for local prices. These usually involve so-called **price corridors,** a range between maximum and minimum prices within which all local prices in a trading area must fall. The corridor should consider market data for the individual countries, price elasticities in the countries, currency exchange rates, costs in countries and arbitrage costs between them, plus data on competition and distribution.[23] The United Distilleries example shows how the process can be implemented (see box, "Portfolio Pricing of Spirits").

GETTING THE *Picture*

The Euro: An Opportunity Creates Problems

THE INTRODUCTION of the euro on January 1, 1999, has meant that many firms have to start quoting euro prices on their products. (Although the bills and coins won't be in circulation until the year 2002, credit cards can be used to buy at euro prices.) While this change has eliminated the problem of floating exchange rates within Europe, it has created its own hazards.

First, firms are now forced to do integrated pan-European pricing, avoiding excessive price differentials (since the prices in different countries can now be directly compared). Because costs of transportation and distribution still vary for different parts of Europe, one single European price cannot be justified for most products. Instead, the companies are opting for an acceptable range of maximum and minimum prices.

Second, while Euro-brands have become commonplace, the same brand in all countries makes price comparisons easier. So, to limit the arbitrage opportunities, some manufacturers are reconsidering their brand policies and contemplate introducing different brands in different countries—for the identical product. If the brands are different (even if the products *are* identical), consumers will hesitate before buying a foreign brand.

A third complication is that in some regions of Europe where incomes are lower (Spain, Portugal), a low price is necessary for affordability. But such low prices cannot be maintained when the euro makes prices directly comparable, and there is no currency exchange rate to adjust for the difference. Accordingly, prices must be raised, possibly out of reach of local customers. The end result may be that some products will be withdrawn from the poorer markets.

Other changes are minor but create additional work. New price points cannot be routinely computed but need to be adjusted so that consumers' habitual cutoffs are maintained. For example, if a price changes from DM 4.99 to some new level of euro 2.48 (the initial exchange rate was at about 1 euro for 2 Deutsche marks), the psychological rounding effect is lost. Should the new level be set at euro 2.39 or 2.49—or even 2.99? The introduction of the euro creates a lot of work for marketers, and it is small wonder if many see it as one big headache.

Source: Bacher et al., 1997. Adapted with permission from "The Concept of Euro Pricing: Theoretical Approach and Practice Implications," by Matthias Bacher, Heger, and Richard Kohler, CEMS BUSINESS REVIEW, Volume 2, No. 4 (1998), pp. 237–362. © 1998 by Kluver Academic Publishers.

FORMALIZATION Headquarters can standardize the *process* of planning and implementing pricing decisions in order to direct the pricing at the local level.

INFORMAL COORDINATION The company can institute various informal coordination mechanisms, including explicit articulation of corporate values and culture, human resource exchanges, and frequent visits to share experiences in other markets.

The choice between these approaches is affected by many factors, but two have been identified as particularly important: level of marketing standardization and strength of local resources. The diagram in Exhibit 13.3 helps identify how these factors affect choice of method.[24]

Several different situations can be assessed from the exhibit:

1. When marketing standardization is high, target segments and the elements of the marketing mix are known well enough for headquarters to help set local prices.
2. If local resources are on a high level, *economic controls* tend to be preferable, since raising and lowering transfer prices or rationing will send clear signals to local representatives without imposing final prices.
3. But if local resources are weak, *centralization* of the pricing decisions may be necessary, creating limits beyond which prices may not deviate.
4. In the low standardization case, when marketing is multidomestic in orientation with locally adapted mix elements, headquarters' role will be less directive.

G E T T I N G   T H E   *Picture*

Portfolio Pricing of Spirits

IN THE EARLY 1990S, UNITED DIS-
TILLERS of Britain, one of the most profitable spirits companies in the world, reanalyzed its pricing policies in order to optimize global performance.

A careful analysis of the demand structure of several local markets showed that:

1. The *specific price elasticities* of brands were much different from the generic price elasticities of a market as a whole. *Brand loyal* customers followed a brand as its price went up, even if as a whole consumers were sensitive to the price level in the product category.

2. There were *price ranges* within which each brand could move without much effect on sales (price elasticity was low), but with wider swings price elasticity could suddenly jump, as the brand moved into another set of competitive brands.

3. Sales of one brand *without a loyal following* could be affected greatly by shifts of prices of competing brands with higher awareness.

United Distillers first developed subsets ("portfolios") of brands whose cross-elasticities were high and which therefore justified coordination on a global scale. Then managers for the various brands agreed on price ranges or corridors that maximized the portfolio's overall sales and profit performance rather than the performance of the individual brands.

Sources: Sims, Phillips, and Richards, 1992; Simon, 1995.
http://www.diageo.com/operatingcomps/UDV.htm

EXHIBIT 13.3 Coordinated Pricing Strategies

Level of Marketing Standardization

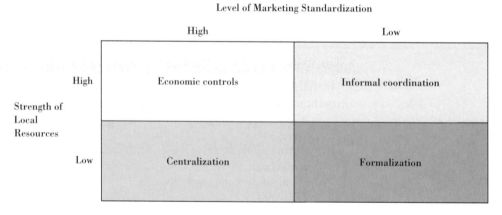

	High	Low
High	Economic controls	Informal coordination
Low	Centralization	Formalization

Strength of Local Resources

Local managers are likely to be better informed about local conditions than headquarters.

5. When local representatives are less resourceful, *formalization* of procedures can be helpful in ensuring that the appropriate factors are taken into account when local prices are set.

6. With strong local resources, *informal coordination* is likely to be preferred, preserving local autonomy—but still using a stick if the carrot is not enough (see box, "Informal Coordination").

Informal Coordination:
Using the Carrot and the Stick

ONE COMPANY in high-tech medical equipment was faced with a sticky problem. In some countries, doctors needed extensive service support to operate the equipment, while in other countries hospitals had more trained staff. The transfer prices to these latter countries were set higher since sales costs for the subsidiaries were lower. But hospital purchasing managers in these countries were able to lower procurement costs by ordering equipment directly from subsidiaries in countries with lower transfer costs.

To solve the problem, headquarters first organized discussion groups with subsidiary managers to find an acceptable solution. After several meetings, the following strategy was adopted. First, the three most important markets were defined as lead countries. The main pricing authority was given to the local managers in the lead countries, who were to set prices so that gray trade would not be lucrative. Second, the country managers were trained and rotated between countries to better understand local competition and profit responsibility. Third, the reward system was changed by basing part of the local manager's annual bonuses on the success of the whole group. Managers who were uncooperative and hindered progress were laid off.

After one year, the problems were solved. Prices were coordinated, and profitability increased by more than 10 percent.

Source: Assmus and Wiese, 1995.

GLOBAL PRICING POLICIES

Apart from the global coordination of prices on specific products and services, firms usually adopt one of three alternative pricing policies that cuts across all their product lines. These pricing policies can be classified as polycentric, geocentric, and ethnocentric.

Polycentric Pricing

Polycentric organizations are those firms that leave a wide margin of discretion to local management. In these firms, prices are set at their appropriate levels in each local market separately, without constraints from headquarters. Naturally, prices might vary considerably between countries in **polycentric pricing.** On the other hand, there is the undeniable advantage of really being able to adjust prices to the particular conditions facing the product in any one country.

Geocentric Pricing

The most common **geocentric pricing** scheme revolves around the use of a global or regional standard plus a markup that is variable across countries. The comparison price is derived for the home country or some other lead country for the world or a regional trading bloc. This base price is computed from a cost-plus formula. The markup is then adjusted for the particular situation the product faces in each country. When demand is strong and competition is weak (a "cash cow" situation), the added-on markup will be high; if competition is strong, the markup will come down. A Swedish pharmaceutical company with a successful ulcer drug uses this approach in its European markets.[25] The coordination is not easy, because the company has to take into account not only competition and demand but also regulatory factors and reimbursement formulas that differ between countries. Of course, the possibility of gray trade across country borders also needs to be taken into account, especially after the European Union

(EU) integration. The overall consistency across EU countries is ensured by periodically reviewing the prices at headquarters and comparing them to the base price.

The biggest headache in geocentric pricing is the question of **product line pricing.** The markup deemed reasonable for one product in the line might not be very appropriate for another item in the line with a different competitive situation. Consequently, the assigned markup will differ across products in a local market. The strategy followed by United Distillers is instructive (see box, "Portfolio Pricing of Spirits," in this chapter).

Philip Morris, the American tobacco company, tried for years to maintain a premium price image for its world-leading Marlboro brand. Because of widely varying tariffs and pricing regulations—and tobacco tax differences—the actual prices on Marlboro varied considerably across countries, but the premium image was consistent across the Philip Morris product line. This policy was finally abandoned in 1993, when competitive pressure and increased taxes in some states in the United States forced the company to discount Marlboro.[26] The premium positioning is still attempted in foreign markets, but the global coordination of prices is no longer in effect.

Product line pricing is very much influenced by varying competitive conditions. When IBM competes with Digital Equipment Corporation (DEC) in some particular country, only minicomputers might be involved. Accordingly, IBM could lower its prices on these units alone in the countries in question. The problem is that in terms of the overall product line, lower prices for the large-scale units will make its smaller-scale units seem overpriced. Furthermore, if the unit prices are lowered in some countries but not in others (where DEC does not have a sales office, for example), some large MNC might easily concentrate its computer purchases in the lowest-price country and do its own distribution to different countries—parallel trade again. The solution adopted by IBM is to avoid changing prices but rather increase the marketing (including service) support in the countries under competitive attack.

In contrast to IBM, Hewlett-Packard, another computer maker, has shifted from a "standard plus markup" approach to a more global system (see box, "Hewlett-Packard's New Global Pricing System").

Ethnocentric Pricing

In **ethnocentric** pricing the same price is charged to all customers regardless of nationality. It provides a standard worldwide price, usually derived on the basis of a full-cost formula to ensure that general overhead, selling expenses, and R&D expenditures will be covered. This type of pricing approach is most useful when the company is producing a relatively standardized product with uniform usage patterns across many countries.

This is the typical pricing scheme for large-ticket items in industrial goods. Examples include aircraft and mainframe computers. IBM maintains this type of pricing policy, partly for the reasons stated above. Boeing, the aircraft company, is pricing its commercial aircraft in this fashion, only making adjustments because of special customization requirements and quantity discounts—as well as Airbus competition.[27] Ethnocentric pricing is also a natural pricing procedure when the company is small and the international sales are few and far between. This is the kind of pricing scheme most acceptable to global customers since homogeneity of prices worldwide makes planning easier and concentrated purchases from central headquarters possible.

Managerial Trade-Offs

The ethnocentric approach to pricing in global companies has the great advantage of simplicity and allows headquarters to coordinate prices at the subsidiaries. But its drawbacks, primarily in terms of nonadaptation to the individual local markets, usually make it not useful to the multinational facing multidomestic markets and different competitive situations in each country. The polycentric approach is the one favored by most local managers of subsidiaries since it increases their control and allows complete attention to

Hewlett-Packard's New Global Pricing System

I N 1992, faced with a globalizing marketplace, Hewlett-Packard, the computer maker based in Cupertino, California, realized that its international pricing system no longer worked. H-P's old system relied on two parts. The first was a *base* price, quoted in U.S. dollars and derived on the basis of production costs at home and estimated price elasticities in the U.S. market. On top of the base price each country's sales organization would charge an "uplift," taking into account price escalation due to transportation, tariffs, and their own sales costs. There was little attempt to analyze the differences in demand between countries and across the various products (minis, PCs, notebooks, printers, and so on).

In changing the global pricing system, the first move was to make each product division into a business unit respon-

sible for pricing and profits worldwide. The base price was changed to reflect transfer costs to the various countries, and the local subsidiaries set final prices on the basis of their own sales costs, demand conditions, and competitive situations. But headquarters has final say in pricing, over possible protests by locals, in order to be able to optimize worldwide performance. Held responsible for worldwide performance, business unit managers at headquarters are expected to set transfer prices and sales incentives to local managers so as to maximize overall profits.

Sources: "The Price Is Right at Hewlett-Packard," *Financial Executive* 10, no. 1 (January–February 1994), pp. 22–25; Gates, 1995.
http://www.hp.com/

competing in the local market. Nevertheless, the lack of control and coordination from headquarters makes the polycentric strategy suboptimal in the global context, missing out on potential synergies and advantageous trade-offs. It also leaves the company open to the arbitrage possibilities of gray trade, with entrepreneurial middlemen buying up products in a low-price country, transporting the shipment back to a high-price country, and undercutting regular resellers at a profit. Many different product categories such as cameras, watches, jeans, and compact disks suffer from parallel imports. Even though these middlemen in a sense help markets become more efficient and equalize prices, they create a headache for multinationals trying to manage their regular distribution channels and motivate authorized resellers to support and service their products.

Geocentric pricing, especially as regionalized by trading blocs, emerges as a well-balanced compromise between global coordination and local adaptation. The variable markup, or the use of price corridors, allows the subsidiaries to adapt to the specific conditions within their particular local markets, including the threat of parallel imports from a neighboring country. The markup adopted for a particular product and country can be based on both the demand conditions in the country and the role the subsidiary is supposed to play in the MNC's overall global strategy. In this way it allows synergies to emerge and a global perspective is naturally adopted by both headquarters management and managers at local subsidiaries.

SUMMARY

This chapter has dealt with the many complex pricing issues facing the global marketer, showing how institutional limitations constrain purely strategic considerations in global pricing. Building on the discussion in Chapter 5 on export expansion, this chapter placed the global pricing question in the context of pricing in economic theory and in marketing theory and practice, and then focused on issues and problems related to transfer prices and the global coordination of prices.

Many factors combine to determine what the actual price of a product will be when it finally appears on the market abroad. This final price might be quite different from the intended positioning: In global marketing it is not always easy to control what the final price will be because of regulatory limitations, exchange rate fluctuations, the number of independent middlemen and facilitating agents, and the need to motivate managers in local subsidiaries. Transfer prices to local subsidiaries have various functions over and above that of stimulating local sales, in particular a role in performance evaluations of the subsidiaries. Another complicating factor is the need to evaluate countertrade options and, in business-to-business settings especially, the possibility of bundling software and hardware together in larger systems.

As one ingredient of the product positioning mix, global pricing still has to take into account how customers in different countries evaluate high and low prices, as well as the stage of the PLC in the particular market. At the same time, the pressure from multinational customers to be quoted the same price anywhere in the world, along with the specter of gray trade, means that global coordination of prices is a necessary task of the global marketer. The chapter discussed the pricing aspect of the gray trade problem with special reference to the EU market, along with various schemes that companies use to counter gray trade. In the last section of the chapter we described the relative merits of polycentric, geocentric, and ethnocentric pricing strategies in the global firm.

KEY TERMS

arbitrage p. 410
arm's-length prices p. 402
barter p. 403
compensation deals p. 403
"consumer tourism" p. 410
cost-plus pricing p. 395
counterpurchases p. 403
countertrade p. 403
devaluation p. 397
ethnocentric pricing p. 414
exchange rate fluctuations
     p. 397

experience curve pricing
     p. 396
forward contract p. 400
geocentric pricing p. 413
"gray trade" p. 408
hedging p. 400
offset p. 404
"parallel" imports p. 408
penetration price p. 407
polycentric pricing p. 413
premium price differential
     p. 396

price controls p. 400
price corridor p. 410
price discrimination p. 400
price elasticities p. 397
price–quality relationship
     p. 406
product buy-backs p. 403
product line pricing p. 414
skimming price p. 407
swap p. 400
systems selling p. 404
transfer pricing p. 401
turnkey sales p. 404

DISCUSSION QUESTIONS

1. With the coming of the global marketplace on the Internet, will all prices be the same all over the globe? Why or why not? What are the ways in which the prices in local markets can still be different?

2. Why are so many foreign-made products cheaper in the United States, while very few American-made products are cheaper abroad? How will global electronic commerce change this?

3. As a marketing manager for a non-European business, what obstacles would you face in attempting to coordinate prices between European countries? Why would you attempt it?

4. From a marketing viewpoint, what are the advantages and disadvantages of allowing local units to set their own prices?

5. What are the problems in implementing a coordinated pricing system to control gray trade?

NOTES

1. The logistics aspects of the gray trade problem will be covered in Chapter 14, "Global Distribution."

2. See Abell and Hammond, 1979, Chapter 3.

3. Because the experience effect can't be documented in advance, companies that price on the basis of anticipated costs can be convicted of dumping based on historical costs.

4. See Anderson et al., 1993.

5. See Kotler, 1997, pp. 505–6.

6. See Johansson, 1989, for a discussion of the Japanese reluctance to raise prices after the yen appreciated in the late 1980s. The trade conflict between the United States and Japan in mid-1995 concerning luxury cars again illustrated that exchange rate shifts alone will not necessarily change prices; see Pollack, 1995, and Tagliabue, 1995.

7. This practice lies behind the charges from foreign entrants that Japan's market is closed, as in, for example, the ongoing battle between Kodak and Fuji. See "Fuji Denies," 1995.

8. This discussion of transfer prices draws on the excellent treatment by Rutenberg, 1982, Chapter 5.

9. These are only highlights of the countertrade options. The book by Alexandrides and Bowers, 1987, can be suggested for further reading.

10. Because of the difficulty of transportation into an area such as Manaus and the standardized manufacturing processes involved,

most of the plants built for this booming free trade zone are basically turnkey operations. See Brooke, 1995.

11. Adapted from Mattsson, 1975.

12. See Chao, 1993.

13. See Johansson and Erickson, 1986.

14. See Terry, 1994.

15. The pressure of aggressive competitive pricing at entry is perhaps most commonly observed in new electronics products. See, for example, "The Fight for Digital TV's Future," *New York Times*, January 22, 1995, section 3, pp. 1, 6; and "Digital Innovator Pays a Price for Being First," *New York Times*, February 1, 1995, p. D4.

16. See Urban and Hauser, 1980.

17. From "A New Brand of Warfare," *Business Central Europe*, April 1994.

18. Personal interview in Tokyo with Hans Olov Olsson on July 12, 1994. Mr. Olsson was then president of Volvo Japan.

19. The parallel trade into Japan tends to increase dramatically as the yen rises in value, but rigid distribution channels attempt to maintain domestic profits.

20. From Simon, 1995.

21. The figures for the European Union come from Simon, 1995.

22. The following discussion draws on the excellent study by Assmus and Wiese, 1995.

23. See Simon, 1995.

24. Adapted from Assmus and Wiese, 1995.

25. See "Pharma Swede: Gastirup," case no. 14, in Kashani, 1992.

26. The move to discount Marlboro was seen gloomily as the "end of the brand names" in the advertising world. More recently, however, brand names, including Marlboro, have staged a comeback; see Elliott, 1994.

27. See "Boeing Launches Stealth Attack on Airbus," *Business Week*, January 18, 1993, p. 32.

SELECTED REFERENCES

Abell, D. F.; and J. S. Hammond. *Strategic Market Planning.* Englewood Cliffs, NJ: Prentice-Hall, 1979.

Alexandrides, C. G.; and B. L. Bowers. *Countertrade: Practices, Strategies, and Tactics.* New York: Wiley, 1987.

Anderson, James C.; Dipak C. Jain; and Pradeep K. Chintagunta. "Customer Value Assessment in Business Markets: A State-of-Practice Study." *Journal of Business-to-Business Marketing* 1, no. 1 (1993), pp. 3–29.

Assmus, Gert; and Carsten Wiese. "How to Address the Gray Market Threat Using Price Coordination." *Sloan Management Review* 36, no. 3 (1995), pp. 31–42.

Bacher, Matthias Richard; Thomas Heger; and Richard Köhler. "Euro Pricing by Consumer Goods Manufacturers." Institut für Markt- und Distributionsforschung, Universität zu Köln, 1997.

Brooke, James. "Brazil Looks North from Trade Zone in Amazon." *New York Times*, August 9, 1995, p. D3.

Chao, Paul. "Partitioning Country of Origin Effects: Consumer Evaluations of a Hybrid Product." *Journal of International Business Studies* 24, no. 2 (Second Quarter 1993), pp. 291–306.

Davis, H. Thomas, Jr. "Transfer Prices in the Real World—10 Steps Companies Should Take Before It Is Too Late." *The CPA Journal* 64, no. 10 (October 1994), pp. 82–83.

Elliott, Stuart. "From the Optimists' Ball, a Consensus That Happy Days Are Indeed Ahead." *New York Times*, December 6, 1994, p. D22.

"Fuji Denies Kodak's Contention of Unfair Trade." *New York Times*, August 1, 1995, p. D2.

Gates, Stephen. "The Changing Global Role of the Marketing Function: A Research Report." The Conference Board, report no. 1105-95-RR, 1995.

Hofmeister, Sallie. "Used American Jeans Power a Thriving Industry Abroad." *New York Times*. August 22, 1994, p. A1.

Iritani, Evelyn. "For Japanese, Hawaii's Hottest Spot May Be a Discount Mall." *Los Angeles Times*, September 25, 1995, p. D1.

Johansson, Johny K. "Stronger Yen and the United States—Japan Trade Balance: Marketing Policies of the Japanese Firms in the United States Market." In Tamir Agmon and Christine R. Hekman, eds. *Trade Policy and Corporate Business Decisions.* New York: Oxford University Press, 1989.

———; and Gary Erickson. "Price-Quality Relationships and Trade Barriers." *International Marketing Review* 3, no. 2 (Summer 1986).

Kashani, Kamran. *Managing Global Marketing.* Boston: PWS-Kent, 1992.

Kotler, P. *Marketing Management.* 9th ed. Upper Saddle River, NJ: Prentice-Hall, 1997.

Lustig, Nora. "The Outbreak of Pesophobia." *Brookings Review* 13, no. 2 (Spring 1995), p. 46.

Mattsson, L. G. *Systemforsaljning.* Stockholm: Marknadstekniskt Centrum, April 1975.

Pollack, Andrew. "U.S. and Japan Again Pull Back from the Brink." *New York Times*, June 22, 1995, pp. 31, 34.

Royal, Weld; and Allison Lucas. "Global Pricing and Other Hazards." *Sales & Marketing Management* 147, no. 8 (August 1995), pp. 80–83.

Rutenberg, D. P. *Multinational Management.* Boston: Little, Brown, 1982.

Shulman, J. S. "Transfer Pricing in the Multinational Firm." Reading no. 40 in Thorelli and Becker, *International Marketing Strategy*, pp. 316–324.

Simon, Hermann. "Pricing Problems in a Global Setting." *Marketing News*, October 9, 1995, p. 4.

Sims, Clive; Adam Phillips; and Trevor Richards. "Developing a Global Pricing Strategy." *Marketing & Research Today* 20, no. 1 (March 1992), pp. 3–14.

Tagliabue, John. "For Japan Auto Makers, It's Tougher in Europe." *New York Times*, June 28, 1995, p. D4.

Terry, Edith. "Japan: Where the Prices Are Insane!" *Fortune*, October 31, 1994, p. 21.

Thurston, Charles W. "Surprise! It's Devaluation Time Again." *Global Finance* 9, no. 2 (February 1995), pp. 48–50.

Urban, Glen L.; and John R. Hauser. *Design and Marketing of New Products.* Englewood Cliffs, NJ: Prentice-Hall, 1980.

Weekly, James K. "Pricing in Foreign Markets: Pitfalls and Opportunities." *Industrial Marketing Management* 21 (1992), pp. 173–179.

Fourteen

Global Distribution

"Here, there, and everywhere"

Your takeaways from this chapter:

1. Global logistics and transportation are important determinants of financial performance, and their efficiency has been improving dramatically.

2. Parallel distribution and gray trade create control problems for the global firm and resellers, but they are not always negatives.

3. The wholesale and retail structure of a local market reflects the country's culture and economic progress and the way business is done in that country, but new channel modes may be successful if timing and conditions are right.

4. Channel management is very much a matter of local execution, and therefore local subsidiary managers need to play important roles in implementing any global distribution strategy.

5. The creation of globally coordinated channels has to start with a clear understanding of how the firm-specific advantages (the FSAs) depend on distribution channel design.

THE GLOBAL MARKETER faces a complex problem in designing globally coordinated channels through which to market the product. The distributors and agents used for initial entry may not be suitable any longer when global expansion proceeds further, and new channels may have to be found. Which alternative intermediaries are available and what functions they perform vary across different local markets. The channel strategies successful at home might not be effective abroad—and might not even be feasible. The global logistics of transporting products between various countries increase in speed and flexibility but also become more difficult to manage, with diverted gray trade creating problems for manufacturers as well as local distributors. The global marketer attempting to create synergies and cost savings by rationalizing global distribution faces a formidable task.

Retail Chains Seek to Clothe the World

For marketers who want to serve consumers around the world, channels are often already in place. Retailers, like producers, have been going global as never before.

In the case of The Gap, successful global retailing involves offering American fashion not only in clothing but also in store design. The chain has determined that the way products are presented to customers is even more important in Europe than in the United States, and Gap stores apply that knowledge. In London, The Gap's interiors are white with light wood floors and chrome fixtures. This striking design, which is not typical of British retailers, has generated attention—and sales.

Woolworth credits responsiveness to global changes for much of its recent growth. To serve its international customers, Woolworth identifies product categories that will be profitable and then sets up stores targeting those categories. A Woolworth format popular in many countries is Foot Locker and Lady Foot Locker, specialty stores offering athletic footwear and clothing.

Stocking U.S. brands can give these stores an edge. Explains Frederick E. Henning, Woolworth's president and chief operating officer, "Consumers worldwide recognize and want American labels like Nike." The demand, Henning says, is fueled by the popularity of American movies and television. Woolworth therefore designs stores that reflect the images promoted by these media.

In contrast, Wal-Mart's global expansion has capitalized on the chain's exceptional management of logistics and distribution. The discounter is the first retailer in the United States to have its own foreign trade zone. Located in Buckeye, Arizona, where Wal-Mart has a massive distribution center, the zone allows the company to receive imports without paying duties until the products are shipped to stores, to avoid paying duties on exports and on any imports it rejects, and to pay lower duties on products assembled from imported components. Wal-Mart requested government approval of the free trade zone not only as a way to save half a million dollars a year but also to fulfill what it called its "ultimate goal of truly global distribution and sales."

Of course, U.S. retailers are not the only ones with global ambitions. Thailand's two largest stores merged as a way to strengthen their ability to compete in China and other Asian countries. By joining forces, the two companies (Central Department Store and Robinson Department Store) became Southeast Asia's largest retailer chain. Management completed the merger to help the stores fend off increasingly heated competition, and although suffering, they are holding their own in the Asian downturn at the end of the 1990s.

In distribution, bigger definitely seems to be better.

Sources: Jai Ok Kim, Mary Barry, and Carol Warfield, "Gaining Ground in a Globalized Market: U.S. Clothing Industry," *Bobbin*, *Bobbin* Blenheim Media Corp., May 1994, p. 60; Arthur Markowitz, "Wal-Mart Zones In on Foreign Trade," *Discount Store News*, April 19, 1993, p. 1; Ron Corben, "Thailand Megamerger Is Expected to Shake Up Retail Trade in Asia," *Journal of Commerce*, May 22, 1995, p. 5A.
http://www.gap.com
http://www.venatorgroup.com
http://www.nike.com
http://www.wal-mart.com/

INTRODUCTION

In Chapter 5, "Export Expansion," the importance of finding good distributors for an exported product was emphasized. The capability of the distributor chosen is critical for two reasons. One, the distributor is the gateway to the new country market, the "face" of the exporter's firm and the avenue through which the marketing effort is channeled. Two, because of contractual obligations it is often difficult to change distributors later when a global strategy favors an alternative.

In this chapter the issue of global distribution will be faced by the marketer who wants to impose some coordination on local distribution channels. The chapter shows how the attempt might involve reconfiguring channels by introducing new alternatives or by establishing parallel channels. Multiple distribution channels are often a fact of life anyway for the global marketer because of the growth of gray trade. As for the distribution of products between countries, technological development and competition have made independent global logistics companies crucial players in the firm's global strategy.

The chapter starts with a discussion of *channels in different countries* and the possibility of rationalizing local distribution. It also covers *globalization of retailing*. Then we shift our attention to *global logistics* and recent advances in global transportation. We then turn to the issue of gray trade and the threats and opportunities from multiple channels in *parallel distribution*. The chapter finishes with a discussion of the potential for coordinated *global channels*.

RATIONALIZING LOCAL CHANNELS

Channel networks once designed do not stay the same forever. It is in the very nature of the open market system that competitive and countervailing forces assert themselves and force change. The global marketer will want to try to rationalize distribution by introducing some uniformity across countries.

Changing Distributors

The distribution channel configuration created for entry into a foreign market is rarely optimal once the product is established on the market. In some cases the success of the distributor in selling the product contains the seeds of his or her undoing. Then the exporter may move aggressively to usurp some of the power of the distributor and grab some of the profits. But the traditional reason for termination of a distributor is the sense on the part of the exporting firm that the distributor is not doing a good enough

G E T T I N G   T H E
....

Picture

Nike's "Do It Yourself" Switch

N I K E, the Oregon-based athletic shoe maker, first entered foreign markets in the late 1970s using independent distributors. But as the company grew successful at home, it began putting pressure on overseas distributors to invest more in the sales of its brand. Whereas Nike spent about 8 to 9 percent of sales on advertising, overseas distributors were reluctant to spend more than 4 percent.

Starting with Europe in the early 1980s, Nike began to establish overseas sales subsidiaries and take control of its overseas distribution. It now controls all of its distribution in Europe and has marketing subsidiaries in Australia, New Zealand, Hong Kong, Malaysia, and other Asian countries. In some markets the subsidiaries were created from acquired distributors, while in other cases they were new units.

To maintain high-quality service and support for the trade, in the various country markets, Nike feels it is necessary to bring the subsidiary managers to headquarters for briefings and product training four times a year. Taking control also means taking charge.

Sources: *Business Asia*, July 27, 1992, p. 263; M. S. Salter and M. J. Roberts, "Nike: International Context," Harvard Business School, case no. 9-385-328.
http://www.nike.com

job in the market.[1] Nike's experience is a case in point (see box, "Nike's 'Do It Yourself' Switch").

As in the Nike case, typically the channel changes initiated by the manufacturer involve the termination of independent distributors' or authorized dealers' contracts and creating a wholly owned sales subsidiary. But termination often involves conflict.[2] As we saw in Chapter 5, it is useful to formulate the distribution contracts in such a fashion that conflicts are resolved in an orderly manner. And we saw in Chapter 6 how some joint venture distribution agreements even go so far as to include "divorce clauses" specifying how the dissolution of the "marriage" should take place if necessary.

When conflicts do arise, some painful and scarring experiences often result. One reason is the different view that people from different countries have of proper conflict resolution methods. In the United States, legal proceedings are resorted to rather quickly. By contrast, in many foreign countries such proceedings are invoked only as a last resort. Whereas certain cultures view the business relationship between manufacturer and middleman in terms of antagonism that readily engenders conflict, others view it in terms of cooperation and are willing to forgo immediate individual gratification for the benefit of a harmonious relationship in the longer run. When these two viewpoints clash, as they often do in global channel agreements, the whole channel design is in jeopardy.

Dual Distribution

The channel changes that occur do not necessarily involve termination of contracts. In some cases multiple channels emerge or are created.[3] For example, Lucky Goldstar's entry from Korea into the U.S. television market was made via original equipment manufacturing (OEM) agreements with retailers such as Sears; later a **dual distribution** system was initiated with sales under its own brand name, Goldstar. Often the manufacturer tries to differentiate the offerings in different channels. Italian apparel maker Giorgio Armani has set up a number of stores in the West under a separate name, AX Exchange, carrying more casual clothes and lower-priced items than the regular Armani's at his own specialty shops and department stores.

Changing to direct sales might solve the overseas distribution problem for the industrial goods multinational. The global marketer of consumer goods, however, also has to deal with the wholesalers and retailers that provide the link to the ultimate consumer.

EXHIBIT 14.1 Size and Number of Wholesalers in Selected Countries

	Number of enterprises (thousands)	Persons employed (thousands)	Turnover (billions ECU)
Belgium	48.0	201.8	85.0
Denmark	35.8	166.2	60.0
Greece	28.0	115.4	—
France	132.4	1,049.0	312.0
Ireland	3.5	40.4	12.0
Italy	192.6	1,084.0	—
Luxembourg	1.9	10.8	5.0
Netherlands	71.9	360.0	135.0
Portugal	31.3	200.0	—
United Kingdom	142.7	921.0	310.0
United States	469.5	4,578.0	1,260.0
Japan	436.4	4,332.0	2,651.0

Source: *Retailing in the European Single Market, 1993.* These figures are adapted from Table EUR1a: "Importance of Commerce in the EC—Absolute Values (1987–91)."

WHOLESALING

Wholesalers sell to retailers or industrial users. Their main functions involve making contact, negotiating, buying, selling, and warehousing; but they might also be involved in shipping, financing, and packaging as well as other middleman functions. Wholesaling is a major component of a country's infrastructure, and its structure reveals important clues as to the country's stage of development. The data presented in Exhibit 14.1 demonstrate how the number and size of wholesalers vary in different countries.

Perhaps the most striking fact in Exhibit 14.1 is the large number of people employed in wholesaling in Japan. While most European countries are on par, relative to the population, and the United States has relatively few establishments, each of larger scale, the Japanese have many units and a large number of people in wholesaling. The notoriously complex Japanese distribution system involves at least three levels of wholesalers.[4] This system is gradually being streamlined under pressure from direct imports and new technology, and the savings can be considerable even for a relatively mundane product such as Italian spaghetti, as Exhibit 14.2 shows. Initiatives for direct imports (buying directly from overseas suppliers, bypassing the established importer) come not only from foreign entrants into the Japanese markets but also from individual Japanese entrepreneurs as well as established channel members who recognize and capitalize on the new trends.

Vertical Integration

POWER AND COMPETITION The size distribution of wholesalers in many countries seems to approximate the well-known "80–20" rule: 80 percent of the transactions are handled by 20 percent of the firms. In Malaysia, for example, fewer than a dozen European merchant houses handle over half the import trade, while hundreds of small local trading companies handle the remaining volume. The giant Israeli wholesaler Hamashbir Hamerkazi handles all kinds of products and has full or partial ownership of 12 major industrial firms, representing approximately one-fifth of all Israeli wholesaling trade.[5]

The financial power of large wholesalers coupled with a good infrastructure and lack of government regulation has meant that in some countries they operate on a nationwide basis; Japan, Israel, and Australia are only a few examples among many. In other countries, however, the preponderance of small wholesalers means that in order

EXHIBIT 14.2 Japanese Import Distribution Alternatives—
Distribution Route of Italian Spaghetti

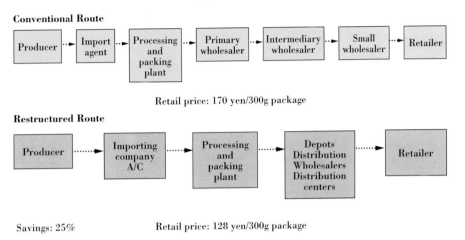

Conventional Route

Producer → Import agent → Processing and packing plant → Primary wholesaler → Intermediary wholesaler → Small wholesaler → Retailer

Retail price: 170 yen/300g package

Restructured Route

Producer → Importing company A/C → Processing and packing plant → Depots Distribution Wholesalers Distribution centers → Retailer

Savings: 25%   Retail price: 128 yen/300g package

Source: Reprinted with permission from *Unlocking Japan's Markets*, by Michael Czinkota and Jon Woronoff, p. 104.

to cover the whole country, more than one wholesaler is used: The smaller ones cover at most a regional portion of countries such as Italy, Turkey, and Egypt.

The U.S. trend toward **vertical integration** in channels—with large food wholesalers such as SuperValu and Associated Grocers controlling the production and distribution of farm produce, for example—has now spread to other countries. There are cases in which wholesalers have organized retail chains (in Britain for soft goods, for example) and also cases in which wholesalers have integrated backward into manufacturing (as in Japan for certain food products).[6] This integration sometimes makes it difficult for an importer to gain access to a wholesaler. In India, the large wholesalers in several markets are entrenched "monopsonists," monopolistic buyers. If you don't deal through them, you don't deal.

EFFICIENCY   The trend toward integration is based on the technological developments that have made large-scale economies and technical coordination feasible. It is an example of technological diffusion across the globe. The emergence of freezing equipment, automatic (and computerized) materials handling, models of optimal inventory control and large-quantity reordering, and reliable and fast communications (telecommunications and transportation) has made the growth of the large individual wholesaler possible and economically desirable. As the infrastructure in various countries has improved with economic development, the introduction of these technical innovations has become feasible. As entrepreneurial wholesalers adopt the new technology, they leave others behind; and if the wholesalers don't do it, there are always eager retailers and manufacturers who are keeping a watchful eye on possible cost savings or improved service in the middleman levels. In many countries the wholesalers have, in fact, been too slow to innovate and have been pushed aside by aggressive retailers integrating backward and manufacturers eager to simplify their distribution channels.[7] The functions carried out by the wholesalers still remain necessary for the movement of the product from producer to consumer: It is just that wholesalers are not always the most efficient at it, especially with the new direct importers providing stiff competition.

Types of Wholesalers

In most developed countries it is customary to identify a wide variety of wholesalers, and one can usually count on finding some wholesaler that will fill the bill when it comes to distributing the product. But this variety reflects more the aggressive nature of the entrepreneurial instinct and the particular nature of the market system in each of the countries rather than a homogeneous trend toward which all economies move. In general, the so-called **full-service wholesalers** can usually be counted on in most countries. But because of their size and tie-ins with existing brands and chains, they might not be willing, or the best ones, to distribute the firm's product. The full-service concept should be carefully assessed for each country entered. *Full-service* might mean "take title" (and thus ownership) to American sellers, but it might not prohibit a Middle Eastern wholesaler from returning a product that does not sell well in expectation of a full refund. Full service might not include service backup in European countries, but in India retailers expect to be able to hand over defective products to the wholesaler rather than the manufacturer.

Even practices in developed countries can vary considerably; see Exhibit 14.3. As can be seen, in a country such as Japan it is common that unsold goods can be returned to the manufacturer. This is in stark contrast to the practice in Western countries. While European countries offer some open and fixed rebates on purchases, and the United States allows functional discounts, Japan has a much more complex system of rebates, some of which are not open but only extended to favored customers. Suggested retail prices do not exist in principle in Europe (although price competition is usually less intense than in the United States), are allowed in the United States, and are

EXHIBIT 14.3 International Comparison of Wholesale Trade Practices

Practice	Japan	United States	Britain	France	Germany
Returned goods	• Returning unsold goods is common	• Doesn't exist except for imperfect or damaged goods	• Doesn't exist except for imperfect or damaged goods	• Doesn't exist except for imperfect or damaged goods	• Doesn't exist except for imperfect or damaged goods
Rebate system	• Various and complicated structure (volume, fixed date, evaluation, promotion) • Long term in pay unit (yearly, half-year, etc) • Rebates are not necessarily open	• No rebates but discounts and allowances exist • Open rule • Pay unit depends	• Quantitative and date fixed rebates exist • Open rule • Pay unit depends	• Quantitative and date fixed rebates exist • Open rule • Pay unit depends	• Quantitative and date fixed rebates exist • Open rule • Pay unit depends
Quotations	• Manufacturer's suggested retail prices exist • Written materials and certain drugs and cosmetics are allowed to maintain resale prices	• Manufacturer's suggested retail prices exist	• Doesn't exist in principle • Books and drugs are allowed to maintain resale prices	• Doesn't exist in principle • Books and certain cosmetics, ski equipment, and some consumer electronics are allowed to maintain resale prices	• Doesn't exist in principle • Books, newspapers, and magazines are allowed to maintain resale prices
Forward integration	• Exists (consumer electronics, auto, cosmetics)	• Uncommon	• Exists (auto)	• Exists (auto)	• Exists (auto)
Others	• Loaned sales staff • Frequent and small-amount delivery • Perpetuates business relation • Unclear contracts	• Uncommon	• Uncommon	• Uncommon	• Uncommon

Source: Distribution Economics Institute, *Survey on International Comparison on the Distribution Industry*, May 1990.

not only common in Japan but quite vigorously enforced by some manufacturers (although the practice of cutting off supplies to uncooperative retailers has been successfully challenged in court). Manufacturers in Japan have also engaged in forward integration to a greater extent than elsewhere and tend to offer more sales support to the distribution channel members. Needless to say, complete standardization of channel design across these countries by a global marketer is not feasible without creating a new channel.

Between-country differences are perhaps even more common for the various limited-line wholesalers that specialize in one or two of the wholesaling functions. For example, a very unique institution in the U. S. economy is the rack jobber, the wholesaler that delivers the product to the retailer's shelf directly. Many supermarkets overseas do not have this system, and the chain drugstores (another semi-unique U.S. invention) where products such as compact disks and women's hosiery might be sold through displays rented to, and stocked by, the rack jobber are not yet common in many other countries. The reason a product such as L'eggs pantyhose has been accepted only slowly in overseas markets is not resistance to the product among buyers. A greater obstacle has been that the innovation (the firm-specific advantage) lies in the convenient packaging and the "front door" delivery system via rack jobbers through which the product is distributed.[8] Without the same channel linkage operating well in other countries, market penetration is difficult.

RETAILING

Retailers are those middlemen who sell directly to the ultimate consumer. They fulfill similar functions as other middlemen, including ordering, creating assortments, presenting the merchandise, storing and packaging, and perhaps also shipping and financing. The variety in retailing across countries is, if anything, greater than in wholesaling. In some countries such as Italy and Algiers, retailing is composed largely of small specialty houses carrying a narrow line of products. By contrast, in the northern European countries there are many stores with a broad assortment of products. The large Japanese chain of department stores, Mitsukoshi, maintains retail outlets around most major capitals in the world and attracts an average of 100,000 customers per day. The bazaars of the Middle East, on the other hand, contain as many shops as customers on some days.[9]

Exhibit 14.4 presents a statistical picture of the number of retail outlets in a selected number of countries. The United States has an unusually large number of people employed in retailing (relative to the population), with each store quite large (the United Kingdom is the closest country in this regard). Most European countries have fewer people in retailing relative to the population and have smaller stores. Japan is quite similar to the British pattern, with more stores than the United States but relatively few persons employed in each store.

Retailing and Lifestyles

Because retailers cater to the individual consumer, it is hardly surprising that there are so many of them and such wide differences between countries. The retailing structure has to adapt to the varying living conditions (the lifestyles) of individual households. Shopping represents both a tiresome job and a leisure activity for individuals everywhere and is both a reflection of and a formative influence on the lifestyle of the people in a country. Where living standards differ between countries, one would therefore expect retailing structures to differ; and where lifestyles are similar, these similarities will be reflected in more homogeneity in the respective retailing structures. Retail stores are, in a sense, the most obvious indication of a country's economic achievement and thus are a most informative indicator of the lifestyles of a country's citizens.[10]

Over time, economic progress is likely to lead to a convergence of the retail structures, as the large chains globalize their operations (see below). In the meanwhile, however, the global marketer has to face the differences and learn to work through them.

EXHIBIT 14.4 Size and Number of Retail Outlets in Selected Countries

	Number of enterprises (thousands)	Persons employed (thousands)	Turnover (billions ECU)
Belgium	127.8	274.7	35.0
Demark	48.1	199.7	24.0
Greece	175.0	338.2	20.0
France	461.8	2,090.0	260.0
Ireland	29.3	131.4	11.0
Italy	929.7	2,401.0	230.0
Luxembourg	3.5	18.1	3.0
Netherlands	95.0	637.5	45.0
Portugal	173.3	366.3	20.0
United Kingdom	348.2	3,030.0	280.0
United States	1,503.6	19,085.0	1,350.0
Japan	1,619.8	6,851.0	682.0

Source: *Retailing in the European Single Market, 1993.* These figures are adapted from Table EUR1a: "Importance of Commerce in the EC—Absolute Values (1987–91)."

For example, the standardized Gillette blades sold through drugstores in the United States are sold in tobacco shops in Italy, department stores in Germany, on the street in Moscow, at movie counters in Thailand, and from traveling vans in India.

Creating New Channels

But retailing is dynamic. As economic growth takes place and global trade expands, new alternatives emerge. Even the least developed countries experience dramatic changes in distribution channels as innovations such as self-service, discounting, vending machines, mail-order houses, and fast-food outlets are diffused globally.[11] Today, convenience stores such as 7-Eleven and its emulators, fast-food restaurants such as McDonald's and its similar offshoots, discount stores such as Tower Records and Virgin stores, and catalog merchandisers such as L. L. Bean and Eddie Bauer can be found in a number of countries around the globe.

Global Retailing[12]

Retailing is, in fact, being globalized at a fast rate. In addition to increasing affluence in global markets, helping to spark this trend is the logistical and operational know-how of leading retailers around the world. As was mentioned in the section on wholesaling, throughout the 1980s the rapid deployment of **point-of-purchase information technology**—including bar coding, scanner data, and inventory controls—shifted the power in the channel toward large retailers. Leading stores—such as Wal-Mart and Kmart in the United States, Marks & Spencer in Britain, Carrefour in France, Delhaize in Belgium, and Daiei and Ito-Yokado, owner of 7-Eleven, in Japan—integrated upstream, established their own sourcing abroad, introduced point-of-purchase (p-o-p) technology, and created data banks on product and brand turnover that gave them power over both wholesalers and manufacturers. The sheer volume of product channeled through these large store chains, coupled with immediate access to sales data, gave the retailers a strong hand in negotiating for functional discounts and preferential services. Global expansion has become the large retailer's avenue to growth in the 1990s.

In the mid-1990s Yaohan, the now bankrupt Japanese retailer built the largest shopping center in Asia, the 21-story Nextage Shanghai Tower, just east of Shanghai's harbor. Opened in December 1995, the shopping center covered more than 1 million

A 7-Eleven outlet in Denmark decorated for the Christmas season. Even as the convenience store chain introduces new forms of retailing into traditional markets, its exterior design, display windows and entrance attempt to meld into the existing surroundings, facilitating local customer acceptance. Courtesy of The Southland Corporation.

square feet under one roof. Yaohan's main owner and chairman, Kazuo Wada, in fact believed so strongly in Asia and the Chinese market that he moved his company's headquarters from Tokyo to Hong Kong as other businesspeople were moving out in anticipation of the 1997 communist takeover. He was the first foreign retailer to receive a license in China, and before the Asian crisis hit, Yaohan planned to open more than 1,000 stores in China, in addition to expanding in the United States and into Europe.

Perhaps the largest retail group in Southeast Asia is Dutch-owned Makro, a wholesale club operator specializing in warehouse stores. Its sales in the region topped $2 billion in 1994, and the chain has revenues of more than $10 billion worldwide. Other Europeans are also active globally. Carrefour, the French hypermarket chain, is a leading retailer in Brazil and Argentina. Marks & Spencer, the English chain that sells affordable quality clothing under its own brand names at good prices, had six stores in Hong Kong that (before the Asian crisis) were even more profitable than the high 12 to 13 percent profit on sales the chain racks up in Britain. Before the crisis at the end of the 1990s, the trend involved retailers not only in the "triad" countries but in other countries as well, such as Thailand.[13]

Of course, global expansion is not always successful. France's Carrefour has introduced the hypermarket concept to the East Coast of the United States with little success so far. Japan's Takashimaya department store has established a branch on Fifth Avenue in New York City but has still to turn a profit. Its compatriot Isetan developed an even less successful collaboration (joint venture, dissolved in 1997) with Barney's of New York for men's and women's upscale apparel and brought a Barney's store to Tokyo. Belgium's Delhaize, a successful top-of-the-line supermarket at home, has had trouble in the United States, where its Food Lion's supermarkets have tried against odds to penetrate the market in the South. Marks & Spencer, which seemed a sure bet in Canada, encountered a lot of difficulties and has pulled out. Timing is important— and so is focusing on what you do best (see box, "Benetton's Turnaround").

Even though the emergence of **global retailers** would seem to offer the global marketer a chance for central coordination of worldwide channel activities, it is important to remember that these retailers tend to become powerful "channel captains." It is more than likely that the manufacturers (and wholesalers) will have to adapt to their needs; They want to be treated as customers. Selling through them will involve "relationship marketing"—offering special services, discounts, emergency supplies as necessary, and so on. To tilt the balance to a more even playing field, the manufacturer with a strong global brand has an advantage: The giant retailers need them as much as they need the retailers.[14]

G E T T I N G   T H E

Picture

Benetton's Turnaround

IN THE EARLY 1980s, Benetton, the Italian apparel maker that had been very successful in Europe, was poised to enter the U.S. market. The company quickly expanded using its tried-and-true formula of franchising individual owners, providing them with supplies from Benetton's own factories in Europe. But the distance between Europe and the United States created delays in shipments, and even with the company's rapid market feedback system it proved difficult to replicate the European success. Benetton franchised too many dealers too fast (and too close to each other), information about the fast-selling (and slow-selling) items was not always timely or accurate enough from the novice franchises, and shipments were slow in coming.

Regrouping, Benetton reengineered the whole business system. Focusing on apparel design, its original strength,

the company exited manufacturing and shifted to contract manufacturing with centralized warehousing in Italy. It stopped franchising dealers and instead became a wholesaler to independently owned stores around the world. It operates one huge distribution center in Castrette, Italy, from which its robots can supply the latest fashions to 120 countries within 12 days—very fast for the apparel industry. Benetton is no longer in retailing but in "apparel service," as the company brochure has it. And its controversial advertisements seem to put its name in the headlines even more often than before.

Sources: Rapoport, 1995; "Benetton (A)," Harvard Business School, case no. 9-685-014, 1984.
http://www.benetton.com

DISTRIBUTION RESEARCH

When arriving in the local market, the marketing manager will naturally need to visit stores and dealers—**hands-on research**—to learn firsthand what the current state of the market is. Inspecting store shelves, observing customers in the stores, talking to dealers and to customers will be natural ways of conducting informal market research.

What products are on the shelves will give the marketer a quick feel for the competitive situation. It is easy to learn which are the leading brands and what the retail prices are. Middlemen can help explain the standard margins in the trade and what functions are performed by the various players. Coupled with sales data for competing brands and products, such information is a natural beginning to understanding the distribution system. Chapter 5 discussed the research activities which are necessary before electing or changing distributors in a foreign market.

The hands-on activities employed by the Japanese have been described by Johansson and Nonaka (see box, "The Japanese 'Hands-On' Approach").

GLOBAL LOGISTICS

Global logistics can be defined as the transportation and storage activities necessary to transfer the physical product from manufacturing plants and warehouses in different countries to the various local market countries. Global logistics is a subset of global distribution, which also involves the management of the channels within a country. It is a useful distinction for the global marketer, since the management of channels within a country requires a lot of interactions with local subsidiaries, distributors, and agents. By contrast, the distribution between countries is usually a matter for headquarters and the trading partners alone.

Supply chain management, that is, coordinating and rationalizing the global logistics function of the firm involved in many markets is not a simple task. The company might have located manufacturing facilities in various countries, each specializing in only part of the complete product line, so that a particular local market needs to be supplied from a number of countries. The Nissan trucks sold in France might come

G E T T I N G T H E ....

Picture

The Japanese "Hands-On" Approach

WHEN AMERICAN SALES of Minolta cameras overtook Canon in the early 1970s, Canon sent a three-man team to the United States. Their job was to suggest an alternative distribution strategy. The original American distributor had been less than interested in pushing Canons in new camera stores and had been content with a few accounts where its own business in film cameras was strong. In contrast, Minolta's aggressive entry through discount store chains had been very successful. The three-man team trekked across the United States, visiting camera stores, talking to distributors, and posing as customers in many places.

After two months, the new strategy crystallized. Detecting a strong ethnic prejudice on the part of the dis-

tributor against the new camera dealers, mainly European Jews, and little or no support in established specialty stores, Canon created a wholly owned subsidiary to import and distribute their cameras. Hiring and training a sales and service force of Americans, the company mounted a counterattack through the specialty camera shops. Crisscrossing the country to offer the dealers incentives and gathering customer information, Canon was back on top in sales with a premium product in less than one year.

Sources: Johansson and Nonaka, 1986.
http://www.canon.com
http://www.minolta.com

from the company's United States plant in Tennessee, the Micras from its Sunderland plant in England, while the Maximas are imported from Japan by its European subsidiary located in Amsterdam. Furthermore, Nissan's engine plant in the U.K. might be supplying engines to its American and Spanish plants. From a marketing perspective this might seem quite irrelevant, but it means that parts for after-sales service and repairs have to be ordered from factories in several different countries. Global logistics in the heavily globalized automobile industry might be particularly complicated, but similar problems afflict most companies that attempt to implement a global strategy.

Competition and Technology

Considering the difficulties involved, many firms are reluctant to try to reengineer their global logistics. A decentralized solution, building on whatever localized solutions have gradually emerged during the global expansion, seems preferable, especially since the local managers know their customer requirements better anyway. But this goes counter to two external forces pushing the company: competition and technology.

As we have seen throughout this book, global competition requires more efficient operations, greater flexibility, and quicker response time. Global transportation is an area where considerable savings are often possible. Consolidating shipments, eliminating duplication in cross-border procedures, including shipping documents and customs declarations, and investing in specialized equipment at transfer points are only a few of the areas in which reengineering can help. Furthermore, inventory management can often be improved through rationalized global logistics, creating savings through just-in-time practices and adding customer value by reducing delivery times.

Also, because of new technology—global communication possibilities and computerized operations, in particular—more efficient logistics operations have become possible. Benetton, the Italian apparel company, has long been known for its fast market response. A competitor such as Levi's is now using point-of-sale terminals in some European locations, linked directly to regional headquarters in Brussels. Transactions and sales of its apparel can be traced quickly, and new and revised orders transmitted to factories as demand fluctuates and according to workloads. Order lead time is lowered, faster response is made possible, and inventories are reduced.[15]

The technology has spawned a number of new global distribution options available for the global marketer. Freight forwarders, ship lines, air express outfits, and airlines now offer more reliable and faster services than before and also offer services not available before, such as tracking of shipments and overnight delivery.

Air Express

Technical innovations in computerized inventory systems and numerically controlled machines for goods handling, including robotics, coupled with the speed and reliability of the jet aircraft, made possible the growth of air express systems exemplified by American-based Federal Express (now simply FedEx), DHL, UPS, and Airborne. Typically, the logistics involve shipment systems offering local pickups, the transportation of packages in the evening to a single transshipment point, sorting according to addresses during the night, and then shipping out to their destination by the early morning for local delivery.

These new **air express** freight services are growing rapidly. With the increased penetration of modern telecommunications and fax machines in developing and newly emerging markets, these shipping services have been very active in foreign markets. Overnight delivery is usually not available, since there is a need for a transshipment point in the country of destination. Typically, one or two more days are needed. For example, Atlanta to Frankfurt requires two days, while Detroit to Hiroshima takes three days. As technology is applied further, these limits are likely to change (see box, "UPS on the Next Flight Out").

Today, shipping computer software, cameras, many consumer electronic products, and even apparel overseas often starts with a call to the local express mail office for a pickup. Instead of taking one to two weeks or much more in the case of ocean shipping, the merchandise can arrive in a couple of days. The goods are cleared through customs faster by using the express carrier's dedicated access ports at the point of transshipment, usually away from crowded entry ports for general merchandise. The computerized system makes it possible to track the packages, monitor the progress, and resolve obstacles or trouble.[16]

Ocean Carriers

The development of fast and efficient air transportation has opened up new international distribution channels, in particular for items high in value per unit weight. For shipments of bulky and low-value-per-unit products—such as automobiles, produce, dry goods, beer, and soft drinks—ocean-going vessels are still the most economical carrier alternative overseas. A few of these products—autos, oil, grain—are transported in specially designed ships owned by the producers, but the shipping is done largely by independent ship lines through containers, ship-to-truck, or rail. But even here global requirements have made for changes.

Because of the savings involved in sharing resources and the advantage in providing integrated one-stop services to the shipper, there have been a number of **global carrier alliances** in the shipping industry. American President Lines (APL), Orient Overseas Container Line from Hong Kong, and Mitsui O.S.K. Lines from Japan have joined in a global alliance consortium. APL and Matson Navigation Co., another American ship line, share vessels in a U.S.—Hawaii—Asia service since 1996. In another alliance, Sea-Land Service in Seattle and Maersk Line of Denmark have started a world partnership.[17]

The advantages of these alliances are similar to those in the airline industry. Sharing routes, vessels, and port facilities, better utilization of fixed assets is made possible, cargo destinations are expanded, and economies in documentation and customs clearing can be realized. The larger scale makes investment in specialized assets economically justified, reducing transfer costs further and offering lower prices to users.[18] These specialized assets—involving large-capacity lifting cranes, up-to-date storage

---

G E T T I N G   T H E

Picture

UPS on the Next Flight Out

T O G A I N a (possibly short-lived) competitive edge on its international rivals, UPS (United Parcel Service, an American express delivery carrier based in Atlanta) has started a round-the-clock, next-flight-out service from the United States to Europe, Asia-Pacific, and Latin America.

UPS's new service is intended as another weapon in the fierce international express war being waged between UPS, Federal Express, DHL Worldwide Express, and TNT Express Worldwide. As business finds new markets abroad, these companies are indicating a need to add the rush premium service they're now offering domestically.

While convenient, the new service is not cheap. It will cost $365 for the first 10 pounds according to a company spokesman. Most companies attempt to avoid such ship-

ments in order to keep costs down, and the market may be small. But there is a strategic angle to it. As one industry analyst says, "You don't want to be in a position of a shipper telling you, 'Here, this is my most critical package,' and you having to tell them, 'Well, I don't do that. Call someone else.' "

Moral: Global competition requires speed and flexibility.

Sources: Johnson, 1995b; "DHL Worldwide Express," Harvard Business School, case no. 9-593-011.
http://www.ups.com/
http://www.fedex.com
http://www.dhl.com
http://www.tnt.com/

---

facilities, and ever larger and faster ships—put pressure on competitors and ports as well. While competitors respond with alliances of their own, the future of ports is thought to depend on the building of **megaports,** which can accommodate huge ships, speed up container loading and unloading, and reduce the "dwell time" while the unloaded containers wait on the dock for further transportation via truck or rail.[19]

Overland Transportation

The increasing volume of international trade has put the system under pressure not only in ports but also inland. There is of course a direct link. For example, containers with tobacco products from Richmond, Virginia, are unloaded in Bremerhaven, put on trucks, and speeded overland to Poland on the German Autobahn—creating traffic problems, safety hazards, and long lines at the border. With so many new products entering the Eastern European markets, the traffic problems are getting worse, and German authorities are contemplating placing a steep toll on trucks.[20]

One North American solution to this problem has been the **roll-on-roll-off (RORO)** system, in which a loaded container is simply rolled onto a railcar and shipped by rail for part of the way, avoiding congested freeways. Even quicker is the new RoadRailer system, in which a rail wheel carriage can be attached to the bottom of the trailer carrying the container on the road. Then the container can go directly on the rail and be hooked up to a train without the need for a railcar.

These North American solutions have not yet been introduced in many places elsewhere, mainly because of the costs involved in transferring from the existing systems. In Europe, the typical overland transportation involves trucking, and the changeover to rail requires a special truck/rail terminal with a capability of lifting the container off the trailer and then placing it on a railcar. The special equipment required and the time lost in the transfer mean that European roads are likely to be clogged by trucks for some time to come.[21]

Warehousing

The competitive need on the part of global companies to be "close to the customer" and provide fast and efficient service has placed increased demand not only on transportation but also on **warehousing** and **inventory management.** While increased

A distribution center in Germany for Mattel, the American toy maker. The computerized center located in the middle of the continent makes it possible to efficiently consolidate routes and deliver orders throughout Europe. All photos used with permission of Mattel, Inc.

speed on the part of independent carriers has made it possible to fill orders faster and cut response time for parts requests, increased competition has escalated customers' demands for service. SKF, the Swedish roller-bearing company, has centralized its European distribution system, reducing its distribution points in Europe from 24 to 5 and creating a new **distribution center** in Belgium, thereby cutting costs, increasing speed, and improving service.[22]

Thus, locating several warehouses close to customers is not necessary any longer for the customer-oriented firm. And if the company does not want to invest in its own distribution center, some of the middlemen in global logistics provide inventory services. For example, Federal Express, DHL, and also smaller outfits offer warehouse space for rent at their transshipment points.[23] Companies rent the space to store products in high demand. A company such as Eddie Bauer can stock some of the more popular catalog items in Memphis at the FedEx central location and ship directly from there, lowering the shipment time significantly.

Such options are useful for the company attempting to cut down the time required to respond to customer requests. In addition, companies attempt to speed up the manufacturing-to-market process further, not only by reengineering inventory management but by streamlining their own handling of shipments to multiple markets. The Kodak approach is instructive (see box, "Kodak's Own Air Freight Hub").

It is not surprising that senior managers from major manufacturing companies now consider logistics one of the key areas for company profitability.[24] The cost savings and the value added made possible by rationalized global logistics can be considerable.

PARALLEL DISTRIBUTION

Developments in logistics coupled with floating exchange rates and widely different prices in different countries have led to the emergence of gray trade through **parallel distribution** channels.

Gray Trade[25]

As opposed to the trade in counterfeit products discussed in Chapter 12, **gray trade** is parallel distribution of *genuine* goods by intermediaries other than authorized channel members. Gray marketers are typically brokers who buy goods overseas either from the manufacturer or from authorized dealers at relatively low prices and import them into a country where prevailing prices are higher. The gray marketers sell the merchandise at discounted prices in direct competition with authorized local distributors, often advertising the lower prices openly in print media and direct mail. The practice

GETTING THE *Picture*

Kodak's Own Air Freight Hub

Eastman Kodak, the world's largest maker of photography products, has formed its own air freight hub at home in Rochester, New York. To minimize product handling and shipping errors, Kodak, which ships its products worldwide, is consolidating all outbound air freight at an on-site gateway in Rochester.

After consolidation, the shipments are loaded on trucks at Rochester bound for different airports, and all customs documentation and shipping paperwork are completed at Rochester. Flight approval is obtained electronically before the shipment arrives at the airport.

In the past Kodak's air shipments were cobbled together at New York's John F. Kennedy International Airport. But this proved unwieldy because shipments were repeatedly handled, sometimes came up short, or airlines rejected certain Kodak products—such as certain processing chemicals—as unsafe. In addition, some shipments were being pilfered on the way to or at the airport.

Sources: Johnson, 1995a; *Washington Post*, June 26, 1995, p. A12.
http://www.kodak.com
http://www.fujifilm.co.jp

is not illegal per se except under certain circumstances, but the activities tend to disturb existing trading relationships and are usually fought by manufacturers as well as authorized distributors.

As we saw in Chapter 13, gray trade tends to serve as an arbitrage mechanism, equalizing prices between markets in different countries. Three main factors motivate entrepreneurs to engage in gray trade:

1. *Wide price discrepancies.* There are substantial price differences between national markets, for example, because of currency fluctuations (see Chapter 13).

2. *Limited availability.* There is limited availability of certain models or versions in one market. Demand outstrips supply and is likely to push local prices even higher relative to other markets. Certain Mercedes-Benz and Porsche models are unavailable in the United States, for example, as were originally some Lexus models in Japan, which stimulated gray trade. Localization requirements, such as local certification of emissions controls on cars, have a dampening effect, but with sufficient margins gray traders will invest in conversion equipment (although sometimes the buyer gets stuck with the job).

3. *Inexpensive logistics.* Transportation and importation can be accomplished with relative ease. The increased availability of global modes of transportation and the added services offered by carriers and freight forwarders have meant that the logistics problems are usually few. Gray traders can use the independent middlemen as well as any manufacturer.

Exhibit 14.5 shows some of the ways in which gray traders infiltrate the global distribution of Japanese watches. The Japanese companies export watches to the importer, often a sales subsidiary, in the various countries. From there the watches are shipped to the distributors and on to retailers. These are the authorized channels where the company offers merchandising support and sales training and in turn demands service support.

As can be seen in the exhibit, the gray trade arises from several sources. Some of the distributors in price-competitive markets, such as Hong Kong, will divert part of their shipment to more lucrative markets. They may sell directly to unauthorized (or even authorized) European or American distributors or retailers, getting higher prices that more than offset any transportation charges. Alternatively, Japanese distributors and retailers backed by a strong yen can go abroad to get watches from overseas distributors or retailers for sale at home. And for new models in great demand, a Hong

EXHIBIT 14.5 Seiko's Authorized and Unauthorized Channels of Distribution

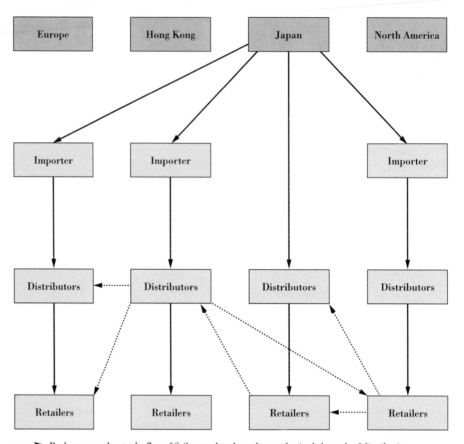

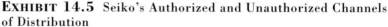

--------▶ Broken arrow denote the flow of Seiko watches through unauthorized channels of distribution.

———————▶ Solid arrows denote the flow of Seiko watches through authorized channels of distribution.

Source: Jack Kaikati, "Parallel Importation: A Growing Conflict in International Channels of Distribution." Symposium on Export-Import Interrelationships, Georgetown University, November 14–15, 1985.

Kong distributor may send people to Tokyo to buy at retail, sometimes in duty-free shops, and bring back watches that fetch premium prices.

The company's control over distribution is lost when gray trade proliferates. Sales statistics for individual country markets are misleading or meaningless. The Japanese watch, camera, and electronics makers try to do something about it. Apart from monitoring their independent importers and authorized distributors more closely, they also change model names, mix features differently, and generally make the styles for different regions (Europe, North America, Asia) slightly different. Such a solution represents "cosmetic" localization, since it does not involve adaptation to consumer preferences or needs.

Gray trade is extensive for global brands in certain product categories. Although exact figures are hard to come by, since identification of gray goods is uncertain and the volume varies annually by exchange rate changes, the following are some estimates from U.S. industry sources:[26]

10 percent of IBM PC sales.

20 percent of Sharp electronics.

22 percent of Mercedes cars.

Total volume has been estimated at $10 billion. In cameras, a notorious gray trade product category since value per unit is high and brands are well recognized, the aver-

Do Gray Goods Get Serviced?

JAPAN'S NOTORIOUSLY TIGHT distribution system has been jolted throughout the 1990s by the appearance of gray goods in several product categories. Taking advantage of a strong yen, which has cheapened imports, the reduction in tariff rates, and the reluctance of existing distributors to pass savings on to consumers, Japanese entrepreneurs have set up purchasing offices overseas and established direct import channels that sell products at savings as high as 50 percent.

One example is Steinway grand pianos directly imported from New York and Hamburg. The ensuing surge in sales of Steinways has created problems for Steinway's sole authorized distributor in Japan. Rather than reducing prices to compete with the direct imports, the distributor has opted for a more subtle strategy.

The gray pianos, easily identified because of their serial numbers, are the last to be serviced. Generally, a grand piano requires comparatively little service except for tuning. But there are some localization matters to take care of. The high humidity of Japan's summers requires expensive reconditioning of grands prepared for European or American conditions. In severe cases the entire soundboard, the key to the grand's sound, may have to be refinished. Also, tuning the pianos during the initial one to two break-in years requires specialists trained by Steinway, and they are now suddenly in "short supply."

Disgruntled Steinway owners in Japan have taken the distributor to court. But since service is not denied, only delayed, the legal outcome is uncertain. Japan's "impenetrable" distribution system may yet win another one.

Sources: *New York Times*, June 23, 1995, p. D1; Assmus and Wiese, 1995.
http://www.steinwaymusical.com

---

age manufacturer might have recently lost sales of about \$7.4 million annually. The volume is increasing as the opening of the communist blocs has further stimulated gray trade (as well as piracy). However, firms are reluctant to discuss gray trade since the legal recourse is uncertain, and the fear is that as the general public learns more, the practice may become more widespread.

Effects of Gray Trade

The damage from gray imports falls into four categories. Gray trade threatens to:

Erode brand equity.

Strain relationships with authorized channel members.

Lead to legal liabilities.

Complicate global marketing strategies.

The eroding of brand equity can happen if the gray goods do not perform to the level expected. For example, products with date marks, such as film and batteries, may be resold in gray markets with dates changed or obliterated, and the unwary buyer will find photos ruined and batteries dead. The strain with channel members arises from the fact that they will face intrabrand competition, the identical brand sold at lower prices elsewhere, and they will be asked to do service and repairs for gray imports. They may not have a legal basis for refusal and will have to be inventive (see box, "Do Gray Goods Get Serviced?").

The legal liabilities problem usually involves warranties that can't be honored and performance criteria that can't be fulfilled. These problems are especially acute for pharmaceutical products because of the potential injuries involved. Taking medication that has expired or whose dosages are meant for adults can severely harm children.

Gray trade affects global marketing management in a number of ways. Forecasted sales in a market may not be realized when there is a sudden influx of gray goods. Rollout campaign plans for new product introductions might have to be

GETTING THE Picture

The Silver Lining on Gray Trade

TWO ACADEMICIANS, Anne Coughlan at Northwestern University in the United States and David Soberman at INSEAD in France, set out to analyze the effects of gray trade on company and authorized resellers' sales and profits. The researchers were able to show that gray trade can actually be of benefit not only to the consumer but also to the firms.

Coughlan and Soberman demonstrated that under two conditions gray trade may in fact yield more profits to the manufacturer and the retailers. The conditions relate to consumers' price sensitivity.

Condition 1. There should be a *price-insensitive* market segment. In this segment price is no object, but service and other things matter.

Condition 2. The price-*in*sensitive segment should be large. "Large" here means relative to the price-sensitive segment. In other words, the people who buy on price represent a minor share of the total market.

The professors argue that the low price of the parallel imports will help attract the price-sensitive segment into the market. The authorized resellers can focus on the price-insensitive customers, providing value-adding items such as extra service, delivery, and special options.

One caution from the professors to the authorized resellers: Don't let the extra service eat up all the profits.

Sources: *Harvard Business Review*, September–October 1998, pp. 22–23.
http://www.nwu.edu
http://www.insead.fr

---

changed if gray traders introduce the product prematurely, as happens frequently in film videos and popular music. And as was seen in Chapter 13, "Global Pricing," while gray trade means that the need for uniform pricing across countries grows, exchange rates need to be monitored and fluctuations may force a realignment. But not all effects might be negative. It is also possible to gain some advantages because gray trade tends to enlarge the market for a product through lower prices (see box, "The Silver Lining . . .").

Channel Actions against Gray Trade

What can global marketers do in the distribution channels about gray trade? There are a number of actions available to help reduce the volume of gray trade and limit the damage done.

SUPPLY INTERFERENCE   Most companies engage in some interchange and relationship building with their distributors in various countries, asking them to help stop gray trade at the source by screening orders carefully and being careful how they dispose of surplus inventory. Lotus, the American software maker, in an effort to stop dealers from ordering large quantities of its popular 1-2-3 program at volume discounts and then selling the excess to gray traders, has announced its determination to terminate any distributor that supplies the product to unauthorized dealers. These practices have to be done with care, since putting pressure on suppliers can easily turn into an illegal restriction of trade.

DEALER INTERFERENCE   A more drastic measure is to search for gray imports at the gray traders' outlets in the importing country and then ask the dealers—or help them—get rid of their inventory. Companies sometimes attempt to simply destroy gray merchandise in the stores. This kind of "search and destroy" action requires a substantiated legal justification, such as an illegal change in the valid dates or improper packaging, and is more common for counterfeit goods (see Chapter 12).

DEMAND INTERFERENCE Some firms use advertising and other promotional means to educate potential customers about the drawbacks of gray goods and the limitations on warranties, returns, and service. Companies such as Rolex, Seiko, Mercedes, Microsoft, and IBM have engaged in these practices. There are two problems. One is the legal problem of threatening to limit service to products sold through authorized dealers only, not an acceptable practice in most countries. Second, firms are reluctant to call attention to the gray trade phenomenon and create hesitation on the part of potential buyers of the brand.

STRATEGIC ATTACK A more constructive solution is to go on the attack and create stronger reasons for customers to patronize authorized dealers. As we saw in Chapter 13, this might involve aggressive price cutting, but other measures should be considered as well. Supporting authorized dealers in offering innovative credit plans, improved service, and other customer-oriented initiatives is a possible tactic. Caterpillar, the heavy machinery company, helped authorized dealers develop customized warranties the individual buyer could tailor to his or her own special needs.

Manufacturers also support their dealers by regionalizing their offerings, differentiating model features and numbers between trade areas to make it possible to spot gray imports and restrict servicing liability. Most Japanese camera makers use different model numbers and introduce slight differences in features between their Asian, North American, and European markets. By stressing features and model numbers in the advertising, their global advertising copy can remain uniform with the same brand name (Minolta, Canon, Nikon) while at the same time alerting buyers when a gray import does not correspond to an "authentic" model.

Multiple Distribution Channels

Given the increased speed and service in global logistics, the breakdown of single-channel distribution regimes, and the prevalence of gray trade, it is not surprising to find that multiple distribution channels are now common. The initiators are sometimes middlemen who decide that attack is the best defense. While authorized intermediaries appeal to the manufacturer to help block parallel importing, they also attempt to bypass some middlemen on their own. Local distributors, wholesalers, or retailers can now order directly from overseas distributors, bypassing one or more of the levels in the local link between the manufacturer and the ultimate consumer. In fact, these options are available not only to middlemen but often to ultimate consumers as well. There is an increase in **direct buying,** with consumers in different countries ordering directly from overseas stores and catalog houses, which ship the products through independent carriers.[27]

This means that there are many ways for a buyer to purchase a particular product or brand. For example, a Madrid father of two, busy filming his small children playing, could have bought his Sony videocam in any one of the following outlets:

A Madrid specialty store (expensive but secure).

A Madrid discount house (cheaper but outside of town).

In Portugal across the border, duty-free and no sales tax.

In Frankfurt, at the airport, duty-free and with all-Europe service.

In Barcelona from a street vendor who smuggled it off the Hong Kong ship in the port (cheap but risky—could be a knockoff).

G E T T I N G   T H E

Picture

Duty-Free Shopping in Manila

IN THE EARLY 1990s Philippine authorities changed the standard duty-free shopping regulations, which make duty-free alcohol, tobacco, and perfume available only to departing airline passengers. Recognizing that a large portion of the more than 4 million Filipinos working overseas returned home on vacations and holidays with food and household appliances for relatives, the government decided to get some of that business for itself. Now, at the airport in Manila, *incoming* passengers can spend up to $1,000 ($2,000 for returning Filipinos) at the duty-free stores and bring the goods duty-free into the country.

Most travelers would have trouble recognizing the duty-free scene that has grown up around the Manila airport. Much of the merchandise would never fit into an aircraft cabin's overhead storage bins: motorcycles, big-screen TV sets, brass beds, freezers, washing ma-

chines, air conditioners, even farm equipment. The grocery section includes large packages of Kellogg's Rice Krispies, Kool-Aid, Cheez-Whiz, Budweiser beer, and other mainstream American brands.

While it makes a lot of consumers happy, the new system has infuriated Philippine manufacturers and retailers who are crying unfair competition.

"We're getting battered by duty-free," says Roberto S. Claudio, vice president of the Philippine Retailers Association. "It makes a mockery of retailing."

Whether viewed as a boon for consumers or a bust for local retailers, duty-free sales are soaring. Duty-free has passed the Shoe Mart chain as the Philippines' number one retailer.

Sources: Lambert, 1995; Foster, 1995.
http://www.dutyfree.com

By fax order from 47th Street Photo in New York (cheap and no fake—and freight at $45 might be acceptable for a $700 videocamera).

And, no longer in a distant future, the Madrid father's videocamera might in fact have been bought on Internet.

Some of these alternative channels, which may seem minor and of limited potential in the large picture, can become important under special circumstances. An example is **duty-free shopping** as done in the Philippines (see box, "Duty-Free Shopping in Manila").

Although some manufacturers do try to control their channels completely with a strong in-store sales effort—Swatch and Rolex are two that do—for many manufacturers the job is too big, and they concentrate on trying to keep the abuses and damages at acceptable levels. By managing global logistics they try to steer these forces—via slight model changes, pricing and advertising support, and interpersonal appeals—in a direction that minimizes interchannel conflict and enables synergy to develop between the parallel channels through which the product moves.

GLOBAL CHANNEL DESIGN

Despite the idiosyncrasies of each individual country's channel structure, it can still be possible to identify what middlemen should be used in a country to ensure that the strategic objectives of the marketing mix—the target segmentation and the desired product positioning—are reached. To do this requires an analysis of what the important functions in the channel network are (identification of what the key success factors are as they relate to channel choice) and then ensuring that the chosen intermediaries in each country measure up on those criteria. The Swatch watch strategy demonstrates how the same intermediaries might not be used everywhere (see box, "Swatch's Globally Limited Distribution Strategy").

G E T T I N G   T H E   *Picture*

Swatch's Globally Limited Distribution Strategy

S W A T C H, the Swiss watch company whose fashionable but well-functioning watches appeal to a mainly young mindset across national boundaries, practices what it calls "global but limited distribution." The company's national sales organization works closely with local distributors and dealers to control distribution, build and sustain the brand image, and avoid retailer discounting.

In Europe, Swatch watches are sold by the few existing up-market department stores, but mainly through traditional jewelers and some specialized sports, gift, and fashion boutiques, mail-order houses, and duty-free shops. In the United States, Swatches are sold mainly through "shops in shops" at up-market department stores, some specialized watch retailers, sports shops, and boutiques.

Discounting by distributors is not allowed, and the trade is warned repeatedly about counterfeits. In-store merchandising is considered fundamental to the strategy, and retailers are assisted with sales promotions that include color-coordinated display racks, in-store videos, upbeat music tapes, and ample supply of product brochures.

Sources: Christian Pinson, "Swatch," INSEAD-Cedep case no. 589-005-IN, 1987; Susan W. Nye and Barbara Priovolos, "The Swatch Project," Imede, 1985.
http://www.swatch.com

The FSAs Revisited

To identify the channel requirements, the natural first step is to decide whether any of the firm-specific advantages are uniquely lodged in the distribution channels to be used. In the case of fast-food franchising, the answer is clearly yes: Without control over the outlets afforded by the franchising contracts, there would be little point in expanding globally. The product sold is a homogeneous (and therefore reliable) meal located at a convenient place. A less obvious example would be automobile sales. Without a strong dealer network providing after-sales service, some auto manufacturers find it difficult to export. Part of the problem that British cars like MG, Triumph, and Rover faced in the United States was the weak service network available. Companies recognizing that such drawbacks will make sales difficult and might give the product a bad reputation sometimes refuse delivery into the countries where no service network exists. Toyota avoided Algiers as a market for its trucks until a sufficiently strong service network was built (in the meantime the Mitsubishi trading company sold its trucks in the country in a kind of gray import market).

Key success factors and FSAs may vary across countries. For example, many of the convenience products in Western markets (packaged foods, cigarettes, soft drinks, and so on) require intensive distribution coverage, precisely because customers want them to be conveniently available. One might infer, therefore, that the absence of such intensive convenience channels in some countries would lower the sales of these products there. But as has been mentioned, what constitutes a convenience good in one country might be a shopping good (or even a specialty good) somewhere else. Consequently, there might really be people who would be willing to "walk a mile" just to buy a Camel cigarette.

Availability of Channels

Once the critical features of the channel network have been identified, the question is whether the country market analyzed possesses channels that will provide the necessary service. Are there financially strong franchisees available, if they are needed? Can dealers provide after-sales service? Are there boutiques where designer apparel is sold to an upscale market niche? Are there middlemen that can store frozen juice in sufficient quantities?

Where the answer is no, the firm needs to consider whether such outlets can be created, that is, whether the firm might invest in a dedicated network in order to supply the market. This is usually a big investment question, and as we have seen, there is no certainty of success. When the market is sufficiently large, as the U.S. market almost always is, it might pay for the company to develop its own distribution network, as Honda has done for its motorcycles. But where the market is smaller and the gains consequently less, the investment might not be worth the risks involved.

Channel Tie-Up

Where channel members are available to provide the functions necessary, they still might be unwilling to sign on with the new product unless special trade allowances bigger than those offered by the competition are made. There are reasons for making sure at this stage that the best units available are tied into, and it is customary for new entrants to pay a premium to established dealers to get them to accept the new product. One reason for the resistance on the part of auto dealers in the United States to small cars was the lower margins offered on them. Cognizant of this fact, the Japanese small car makers entered with higher dealer margins than customary for that size of auto. The thrust behind signing up good distributors and dealers is not only that sales will be high but that they are the ones most likely to sustain the FSAs identified as necessary for the competitive success of the company.

Coordination and Control

With a good distribution network established, coordination and control from a centralized headquarters location might now be feasible. The task is large even in small firms, making sure that shipments arrive on time, that the distributors are notified, that a standardized advertising campaign to middlemen across a number of countries is on schedule, that the sales reports for the last quarter have all been received, that the required reporting format is followed so that comparisons between budgeted and actual sales can be made, and so on. It is quite clear that before the advent of global telecommunications and LAN computer networks the control and coordination of distribution across different countries was a very difficult task.

SUMMARY

In this chapter various aspects of a global distribution strategy have been discussed: first some of the differences in wholesaling and retailing in various countries, the feasibility of rationalization and creation of new channels, and the emergence of global retailing; then the independent organizations that facilitate global logistics between countries, emphasizing how competition and technology have pressured them to increase speed, reliability, and service; next problems with parallel distribution, especially gray trade, showing how multiple channels into a country have become a fact of life; and finally issues of coordinated global channel strategies.

In the end, the degree to which channel policy in different countries should be made consistent through a global strategy hinges on the degree to which FSAs are explicitly lodged in distribution channels and the degree to which the channel members' activities can be coordinated and controlled. If channels are very important because of FSAs, the company has to evaluate the alternatives very carefully and decide whether the available channels provide sufficient support. If they do not, the firm might have to establish its own distribution network, or else forgo entry. The channel strategy is only part of the overall business strategy of the global firm, and where the costs of control and coordination are too high, the global approach might have to yield to a polycentric approach in which the company takes a different angle on distribution in each local market.

KEY TERMS

air express   p. 430
direct buying   p. 437
distribution center   p. 432
dual distribution   p. 421
duty-free shopping   p. 437
full-service wholesalers   p. 424
global carrier alliances   p. 430
global retailers   p. 427

gray trade   p. 432
hands-on research   p. 428
inventory management   p. 431
megaports   p. 431
parallel distribution   p. 432
point-of-purchase information
   technology   p. 426

rock-on-roll-off (RORO)
   p. 431
supply chain management
   p. 428
vertical integration   p. 423
warehousing   p. 431

DISCUSSION QUESTIONS

1. Compare and contrast the food retailing system in two countries you are familiar with. Why have the differences occurred? Is a convergence under way?

2. Why is coordination of global logistics so complex? What technological innovations have made coordination easier?

3. Discuss how the phenomenon of gray trade affects the ability of the global marketer to control distribution. How can the difficulties be overcome? How will the emergence of the Internet spawn more gray trade, or will it?

4. Use the Web sites of FedEx, DHL, and UPS to analyze how the service is marketed. What are the competitive advantages of each? How do the firms attempt to keep air freight distribution from becoming a commodity?

5. Using library and Internet resources, investigate one of the successful cases of an introduction of a new approach to channels in foreign countries (Avon, 7-Eleven, Toys R Us, or L. L. Bean, for example). What customer factors were important determinants of the success? What did competition do? What are some lessons for other companies?

NOTES

1. See Rosson, 1987.

2. Rosson, 1987, demonstrates some of the conflicts that can arise between manufacturers and independent distributors and how they lead to termination of contracts.

3. As the empirical study by Bello et al., 1991, demonstrates, where the multiple channels are not in direct competition, independent distributors can still provide strong benefits to the manufacturers in terms of market knowledge and specialized services.

4. This does not mean, however, that the Japanese system necessarily exhibits low productivity. Although this is a common assumption, and is the case for most productivity measures, it can be argued that because of high value added relative to low wage rates, Japan's complex and multilayered distribution system is not particularly inefficient by international standards; see Maruyama, 1993.

5. Although this consolidation has perhaps gone furthest in the United States, even Japan with its notorious large numbers and levels of wholesalers is moving toward larger units; see Czinkota and Kotabe, 1993.

6. See Munns, 1994.

7. Typical examples include, from the retailing end, Kmart and Sears in the United States, Virgin stores in Britain, and the FNAC chain in France. Manufacturers moving forward include Compaq and Dell in personal computers, both selling their products mainly through telemarketing; Benetton with its franchised stores; and many luxury goods makers such as Cartier, Louis Vuitton, and Dunhill with their boutiques (see also the global retailing section below).

8. See "L'eggs Products, Inc," Harvard Business School, case no. 9-575-090, 1979.

9. Alexander, 1990, discusses the variety among national retailers in more detail.

10. A good example of the kind of difficulty created in retailing by different consumer in-store behavior and different expectations about store service is the early resistance to computer stores in Europe, overcome only gradually. See "What's Holding Back Computer Chains," 1984.

11. For a striking example, see "Dell," 1992.

12. This section draws on the excellent survey by Rapoport, 1995.

13. See Corben, 1995.

14. This power advantage has become one reason why manufacturers aim to develop more global brands; see, for example, Simmons, 1990.

15. See "How Levi's Works," 1993.

16. The emphasis on speed has made even small savings important. For example, in mid-1995 Federal Express induced the U.S. Trade Representative to pressure Japanese authorities for landing rights at Kobe's New International Airport even though other Japanese airports were available and landing in Japan was no longer a necessity on Far Eastern routes from FedEx's hub in Memphis. Rather, Federal Express, which got access, plans to use Kobe from its new hub in Subic Bay in the Philippines. See Pollack, 1995.

17. See Tirschwell, 1995.

18. Price competition among ocean carriers is guided by "conferences," loose agreements between industry participants, sometimes aided by governments, which attempt to regulate competition. These conferences have at times lost power as individual carrier lines refused to go along, but deregulation is not

as far-reaching as in the airline industry, and there are still successful attempts to control prices. See, for example, Fabey, 1995.

19. These megaports may have to be built away from existing port sites because of a lack of land area, and they may also be built by the global alliance partners rather than the port authorities since the latter are limited in their actions by local governments. See DiBenedetto, 1995.

20. See Koenig, 1995. As was discussed in Chapter 10, when P&G found its truck shipments delayed at the border, the company helped invest in improved port facilities in St. Petersburg and shipped products to Russia from Germany by boat across the Baltic.

21. Change is possibly under way, however. As of 1995, the RoadRailer system is being tested in Bayern in the south of Germany, with the first train going from Munich across the Alps

through the Brenner Pass with BMW cars destined for Milano and Verona in Italy, a trip of eight hours (see Barnard, 1995a).

22. See "SKF," 1993.

23. The smaller companies can be competitive by focusing on certain key routes and terminals and offering specialized services, a niche strategy; see Barnard, 1995b.

24. From a study reported in *The Journal of Commerce;* see Johnson, 1995c.

25. This section draws on Cavusgil and Sikora, 1988.

26. Figures from ibid.

27. Direct marketing will be discussed in more detail in Chapter 16, "Global Promotion, Direct Marketing, and Personal Selling."

SELECTED REFERENCES

Alexander, Nicholas. "Retailers and International Markets." *International Marketing Review* 7, no. 4 (1990), pp. 75–85.

Assmus, Gert; and Carsten Wiese. "How to Address the Gray Market Threat Using Price Coordination." *Sloan Management Review* 36, no. 3 (1995), pp. 31–42.

Barnard, Bruce. "RoadRailer Trailer to Make European Intermodal Debut." *Journal of Commerce,* May 18, 1995a, pp. 1A, 2A.

———. "Jan Jansen Leading Ogden's 'Ground Troops' into Europe." *Journal of Commerce,* June 19, 1995, p. 14A.

Bello, Daniel C.; David J. Urban; and Bronislaw J. Verhage. "Evaluating Export Middlemen in Alternative Channel Structures." *International Marketing Review* 8, no. 5 (1991), pp. 49–64.

Cavusgil, S. Tamer; and Ed Sikora. "How Multinational Can Counter Gray Market Imports." *Columbia Journal of World Business,* Winter 1988, pp. 75–85.

Corben, Ron. "Thailand Megamerger Is Expected to Shake Up Retail Trade in Asia." *Journal of Commerce,* May 22, 1995, p. 5A.

Czinkota, Michael R.; and Masaaki Kotabe. *The Japanese Distribution System.* Chicago: Probus, 1993.

"Dell: Mail Order Was Supposed to Fail." *Business Week,* January 20, 1992, p. 89.

DiBenedetto, William. "Giant Ship Terminals Are Coming; The Question Is: Who'll Build Them?" *Journal of Commerce,* June 21, 1995, pp. 1A, 2A.

Fabey, Michael. "TACA Finds Cargo Surge Making Up for Rollback." *Journal of Commerce,* June 19, 1995, pp. 1A, 8A.

Foster, Peter. "The Capital of Duty-Free." *The Times,* September 28, 1995, Features, p. 1.

"How Levi's Works with Retailers." *Business Europe,* July 19, 1993.

Johansson, Johny K.; and Ikujiro Nonaka. "Marketing Research: The Japanese Way." *Harvard Business Review,* March–April 1986.

Johnson, Gregory S. "Eastman Kodak Forms Own Air Freight Hub." *Journal of Commerce,* May 17, 1995a, pp. 1A, 7A.

———. "UPS Leaps Ahead with Next-Flight-Out International Service." *Journal of Commerce,* May 25, 1995b, p. 3A.

———. "Survey: Companies Consider Logistics a Key to Profits." *Journal of Commerce,* May 31, 1995c, p. 2B.

Kale, Sudhir H.; and Roger P. McIntyre. "Distribution Channel Relationships in Diverse Cultures." *International Marketing Review* 8 (1991), pp. 31–45.

Kim, Jai Ok; Mary Barry; and Carol Warfield. "Gaining Ground in a Globalized Market: U.S. Clothing Industry." *Bobbin* 35, no. 9 (1994), p. 60.

Koenig, Robert. "Tenfold Increase in Truck Traffic Fuels German Plans for Toll Hike." *Journal of Commerce,* June 7, 1995, p. 1A.

Lambert, Bruce. "In Philippines, Duty-Free with a Difference (or Two)," *New York Times,* June 24, 1995, p. 34.

Lyons, N. *The Sony Vision.* New York: Crown, 1976.

Markowitz, Arthur. "Wal-Mart Zones In on Foreign Trade." *Discount Store News* 32, no. 8 (April 19, 1993), p. 1.

Maruyama, Masayoshi. "The Structure and Performance of the Japanese Distribution System." In Czinkota and Kotabe, *The Japanese Distribution System,* pp. 23–42.

Morita, Akio. *Made in Japan.* New York: NAL Penguin, 1986.

Munns, Peter J. S. *Marketing and Distribution in Japan Today.* Master's thesis, Graduate School of Management, International University of Japan, 1994.

Pollack, Andrew. "U.S. and Japan Again Pull Back from the Brink." *New York Times,* June 22, 1995, pp. 31, 34.

Rapoport, Carla; with Justin Martin. "Retailers Go Global." *Fortune,* February 20, 1995, pp. 102–8.

Rosson, Philip. "The Overseas Distributor Method." In P. Rosson, and S. Reid, eds. *Market Entry and Expansion Mode.* New York: Praeger, 1987.

"SKF to Centralize Distribution." *Business Europe,* April 12, 1993, p. 7.

Simmons, Tim. "A Global Brand of Dialog; Food Products Manufacturers Moving to Market Products Globally." *Supermarket News* 40, no. 28 (July 9, 1990), p. 2.

Tirschwell, Peter M. "APL Seeks Shift to Terminal Adjacent to Partners." *Journal of Commerce,* June 23, 1995, p. 1A.

"What's Holding Back Computer Chains in Europe?" *Business Week,* November 12, 1984, p. 120.

Global Advertising

"One voice, many languages"

Your takeaways from this chapter:

1. As the affluence of countries grows, new products and services appear, and customers need more information. Advertising becomes more important, and advertising expenditures as a percent of the GDP increase.

2. As markets integrate, global communications expand, and customers become more similar, pan-regional advertising campaigns will become increasingly cost-efficient and more effective than multidomestic advertising.

3. Rather than trying for complete uniformity, global advertising tends to follow a pattern standardization approach with unified slogan, visualization, and image but with local execution in terms of language, spokespersons, and copy. This helps to avoid the pitfalls of standardized and translated messages.

4. The global advertising agency is often at an advantage over local rivals when global or regional advertising is contemplated. But independent local advertising agencies have combined with others to form multinational networks and can sometimes offer stronger local talent.

5. The development of a global campaign takes time, effort, and planning. The process should involve headquarters and ad agency managers but also local representatives whose knowledge will help formulate the global communication strategy.

GLOBAL PROMOTION involves a variety of activities, ranging from in-store point-of-purchase displays and Sunday newspaper coupons to satellite TV advertising and sponsorship of symphony orchestras, athletic events such as the Olympics, soccer's World Cup, and major tennis tournaments.

All of these various tools need to be integrated and project a consistent message and image for maximum effectiveness. This is a stiff challenge for global marketers since the tools are not equally effective everywhere and some are not even available in certain country markets.

The most visible promotional activity is perhaps *global advertising*, the topic of this chapter. *Global sales promotion*, *public relations*, and *publicity* have also become powerful promotional tools because of developments in global communications and the opening up of new markets. Then there is participation in *international trade fairs*, *direct marketing*, and *personal selling*, the last typically much more localized but still important. These other promotional tools will be discussed in Chapter 16. Promotion on the Internet will be covered in a separate section in Chapter 18.

This chapter will start by discussing the extent of advertising and media spending that exists in various countries and will then focus on global advertising issues. It will discuss the pros and cons of global versus multidomestic advertising, what is involved in doing global advertising, the role of the advertising agency, and the problems of global advertising management. The chapter concludes with an illustration of how one company has gone about developing a pan-regional advertising campaign.

Provocative Ads Give Benetton Global Impact

"Do you play safe?" asks an advertisement for Benetton Sportsystem, picturing Ektelon eyeguards on one page and a condom on the other. A different ad juxtaposes an Asolo climbing boot with a picture of Jesus' crucifixion ("Do you play alone?"), while another combines Kastle skis with photos of German and American Olympic athletes giving Nazi and black power salutes in 1936 and 1968 ("Do you play race?").

These ads are undeniably provocative; many people find them offensive. They build on Benetton's experience that controversial images give the retailer worldwide recognition despite modest advertising budgets. These benefits convinced Benetton to stick with the provocative ad campaigns for the company's clothing stores as well as its sporting goods.

The earlier Benetton campaigns were classic examples of global marketing. They paired multicultural groups of models with the logo "United Colors of Benetton," promoting global harmony as much as Benetton's clothing. Because of the ads' ethnic diversity and freedom from words, they worked around the world, and Benetton gained a reputation for caring about high-minded values like global unity.

Extending the focus on values, Benetton's ads became more hard-edged. One showed a man dying of AIDS, another a priest and nun kissing. Some consumers bristled, and many critics doubted the messages could stimulate sales. In the United States, where sales slipped, Benetton began using more conventional advertising to ensure that consumers know what its stores offer. A television ad describes a minidress as "your best dress . . . the one you sometimes think you love more than your boyfriend." Provocative as that message is, it's a lot more like other fashion ads than the earlier Benetton billboards.

2 Short
1 Short
Normal
1 Long
2 Long

Even as Benetton diversifies its advertising, debate continues over whether global ads can succeed. To promote the Flore line of fragrances, New York agency Ally & Gargano and Spanish agency FMRG collaborated on a global campaign with the theme "A World Within." The ads use soft-focus photos of a woman—images the agencies believe universally convey intimacy. Eastman Kodak, too, uses global advertising, although it allows local ad agencies to adapt campaigns to local needs. In contrast, Colgate-Palmolive Company shifted from a global strategy to advertising tailored to each country for some of its brands. Kellogg Company also targets its advertising—a logical step in its Latin American markets, where eating breakfast cereal (or breakfast, for that matter) is not part of the culture.

Either way, marketers need advertising agencies with international expertise. The ideal agency? One that knows whether to use a single global message or target messages geographically. That kind of knowledge is literally worth its weight in gold.

Sources: Stuart Elliott, "Benetton's Unrepentant Adman Vows to Keep Pushing the Envelope," *New York Times*, July 21, 1995, p. D4; Marshall Blonsky and Contardo Calligaris, "At Benetton, a Retreat from Revolution," *Washington Post*, April 30, 1995, pp. H1, H7; Stuart Elliott, "Creative Agencies That Feel at Home in the Global Village Are Writing Their Own Tickets," *New York Times*, September 30, 1994, p. D17; Laurie Freeman, "Colgate Axes Global Ads; Thinks Local," *Advertising Age*, November 26, 1990, pp. 1, 59.
http://www.benetton.com/
http://www.ektelon.com/
http://www.asolo.com/
http://www.kodak.com
http://www.colgate.com
http://www.kelloggs.com/

THE GLOBAL ADVERTISING JOB

The global advertiser faces a complex task. The communication has to be appropriate for each local market, while at the same time there is a need to coordinate campaigns and control expenditures across the globe. Because of the varying media availability in different countries and differing effectiveness of global media, the feasible channels for advertising will differ. Furthermore, the variations across country markets in customer behavior make for variable receptivity to advertising and message construction. But customizing the advertising to each individual country leads to increased costs and unwieldy control procedures. This chapter deals with these managerial issues in-depth and attempts to show how the optimal balance between the two extremes of ethnocentrically global and polycentrically multidomestic advertising can be achieved.

Global advertising can be defined as advertising more or less uniform across many countries, often, but not necessarily, in media vehicles with global reach. In many cases complete uniformity is unobtainable because of linguistic and regulatory differences between nations or differences in media availability, but as with products, **localized advertising** can still be basically global. In contrast, **multidomestic advertising** is international advertising deliberately adapted to particular markets and audiences in message and/or creative execution.[1]

There are several traditional problems facing the decision maker in global advertising. One is how to allocate a given *advertising budget* among several market countries. Another is the *message* to use in these various markets. A third is what *media* to select.

But even before tackling these management decisions, the advertiser needs to define the *objectives* the advertising in the different countries. And before doing that it is imperative that the decision maker identify what can conceivably be expected from the global advertising effort. Thus, the logical starting point in global advertising management is the assessment of the *role of advertising* in the country markets and the availability of alternative advertising media.

THE INTERNATIONAL WORLD OF ADVERTISING

Advertising Volume

Judging from most published figures, there is a role for advertising to play in all economies, socialist as well as capitalist. At the same time, there is little doubt that the role of advertising in the United States is considerably greater than in many other places. The advertising-to-GDP percentages in Exhibit 15.1 illustrate this.

- Advertising intensity varies a great deal between countries. Advertising is simply not a very common form of communication in some countries and may not be an effective promotional tool there.

- Generally the higher the GDP, the more is spent on advertising in percentage terms. The more developed the country, the more money is allocated to advertising. The association, however, is not necessarily uniform across the globe. Brazil, for example, shows a higher figure than most European countries, possibly reflecting its large geographical spread.

- Religion matters. Muslim countries such as Indonesia tend to show low figures for religious reasons. Since advertising attempts to stimulate desire for products, it runs counter to Muslim religious convictions.

- Advertising is an unusually important medium in the United States, partly a result of the cultural diversity that makes social norms and interpersonal communication (word of mouth) relatively less reliable. This has now been recognized by many foreign companies, which find that they have to spend much more on advertising in the United States than elsewhere. To illustrate, for German BASF and Siemens, both makers of industrial products, corporate advertising in the United States far outstrips that done by the two companies elsewhere.[2]

EXHIBIT 15.1 Advertising Intensity in Selected Nations, 1993

Country	Advertising as percent of gross domestic product
North America	
Canada	1.17%
United States	2.49
Latin America	
Argentina	1.08
Mexico	0.16
Asia	
India	0.28
Indonesia	0.39
Japan	0.82
Malaysia	0.85
South Korea	1.21
Australia	1.20
Europe	
Belgium	0.54
France	0.65
Germany	0.82 (1990)
Italy	0.57
Sweden	0.63
United Kingdom	1.35

Sources: Calculated from *International Marketing Data and Statistics 1996* and *European Marketing Data and Statistics*, Euromonitor Plc. 1996.

The global advertising manager also needs to remember that different cultures and target segments have different receptivity to advertising. This affects the desirability of having a job in advertising as well. In parts of Asia and the Middle East, advertising agencies have difficulty hiring the best people.[3] But things are changing over time; free market advertising crowds out traditional norms and inefficient ways of communicating. Even Italians are taking to voice mail. But differences persist.

The point is one can't assume that global market receptivity to advertising is already the same everywhere, because it isn't. Global advertising allocated equally across countries will lead to misallocated resources. Allocating so that the last dollar spent yields equal returns everywhere, a good rule of thumb, means that there will be widely different levels of coverage across markets, with countries like Korea and the U.K. getting more than their GDP share, and Italy and India less (using the figures in Exhibit 15.1). At the same time, the global marketer has to judge whether historical data for a country such as India are a good guide for the future; there might be a good opportunity for an expanded advertising effort there.

Media Spending

It is useful to sketch out what media are important in different countries. In Exhibit 15.2 expenditures in five basic media types (TV, print, radio, cinema, and outdoor/transit) are shown for selected countries. Some differences stand out:

- *Outdoor* advertising is much more important in Japan and South Korea than in the West, probably a reflection of the fact that such media can reach the large number of people in the big cities.

- Special media such as *cinema* can be of great value in some countries such as Argentina and India (not shown on the exhibit), where films are popular pastimes and advertisers have access to theaters.

- *Print* media in France, Germany, and Sweden are strong, probably attributable to a high literacy rate and relatively limited commercial broadcasting.

- The Europeans avoid the use of *radio* for advertising. This is perhaps primarily a reflection of lack of opportunity. Many of the European radio stations are still government-controlled near monopolies with no commercial base.

- *Television* advertising is strong in the United States, Asia, and South America. An unusually large share of Japanese advertising expenditures are for TV ads, reflecting the complete penetration of that medium in Japanese homes. The Latin American figures reflect a general tendency among Spanish-speaking countries to rely heavily on audiovisual rather than printed communication.

EXHIBIT 15.2 Media Usage in Various Countries*

Nation	TV	Print	Radio	Cinema	Transit
Argentina	148	155	43	16	47
Brazil	126	77	10	—	4
France	2,712	4,717	611	57	1,108
Germany	2,826	13,423	641	157	550
Japan	13,434	12,900	1,913	—	5,231
South Korea	1,083	1,755	188	—	708
Spain	2,386	4,569	873	62	384
Sweden	143	1,560	—	13	82
United Kingdom	4,621	9,071	287	84	530
United States	45,410	67,536	14,022	—	1,672

*In U.S. dollars.

Sources: *International Marketing Data and Statistics 1995* and *European Marketing Data and Statistics 1995*, Euromonitor Plc, 1995.

Global Media

The figures in Exhibit 15.2 do not show the degree of global advertising spending nor do they depict the emergence of truly global media. Global media are emerging:

- In *television*, for example, Cable News Network (CNN) reaches into many of the globe's remote corners. The British Skychannel can be seen in most of the EU countries.

- In *magazines* such as U.S.-based *Time*, *Newsweek*, *Cosmopolitan*, and *Playboy*, overseas editions in the English language have editorial content adapted to the local country. For major markets they also have more completely localized editions and offer, for example, Japanese-language editions.

- In *newspapers*, *The Financial Times* and *The Wall Street Journal* have global reach; *The Wall Street Journal* has an Asian and a European edition.

- The arrival of the *Internet* and the *World Wide Web* heralds further developments in global media. Publishing houses and broadcast networks are teaming up with on-line services to create a global multimedia environment. Electronic commerce will be dealt with in Chapter 18.

By and large, however, global advertising does not depend on the emergence of global media. Even the most global advertising campaigns have to be scheduled in local media vehicles with the help of media planners in the local ad agencies. A global 30-second television commercial for British Airways, which may run unchanged in a dozen or so countries (with some voice-over translation), still needs to be scheduled in the local media in these countries. Although cross-country media ownership is growing (Rupert Murdoch, the Australian media mogul, owns a number of newspapers, magazines, and television stations in various countries, but intended takeovers are often thwarted by government regulations that limit foreign media ownership), at the present advertising space in foreign media is still largely bought and paid for locally.

Strategic Implications

The global statistics are indicators of important differences between country markets. They have some important strategic implications:

1. Advertising expenditures create barriers to entry into an industry. A new firm bent on entering a market usually needs to match the advertising expenditures of existing firms in order to enter successfully. A global firm with established presence can use high advertising spending to "raise the ante" and make competitive entry difficult.

2. There are some countries where a scarcity of available media has made advertising a competitive weapon of limited usefulness. Since advertising represents mass communication and thus requires mass media, successful advertising campaigns are very dependent on a well-developed and functioning infrastructure.

3. The communication objectives realistically achieved through various media differ among countries. The so-called **hierarchy of effects**—which traces the effects of advertising through brand awareness to knowledge, attitude, liking, trial, and adoption (see Exhibit 15.3)—can be used to illustrate this fact as the following examples show:

TELEVISION Whereas television is a true mass medium in the United States and Western Europe and thus a reasonable avenue for creating *awareness* for a new product, in many other markets (including some European countries with limited time availability) it provides a status association for the brand and is thus better as an *attitude change* agent.

EXHIBIT 15.3 The Hierarchy of Effects

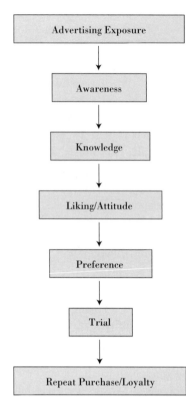

RADIO   Similarly, radio is a true mass medium in many countries and thus useful for awareness campaigns, but it is very focused on specific segments (such as teenagers) in the United States and aimed at the direct action or *trial stage* rather than more general objectives.

NEWSPAPERS   Newspapers are the only available medium in some countries and will thus have to fulfill their standard role (in Western markets) of a direct action influence as well as establishing more general *knowledge* and *liking* of the brand.

OUTDOOR   Where literacy levels are low (such as in Bangladesh), broadcast and outdoor advertising plus relatively odd media such as cinema advertising will outweigh print media in importance regardless of objectives of the campaign.

WHAT DOES GLOBAL ADVERTISING INVOLVE?

It is helpful to distinguish between four components of global advertising:

1. *Strategy.* Global advertising often involves products and services that are positioned similarly across markets, that is, those whose advertised benefits can be the same. As we saw in Chapter 11, it is not necessary that market segments or usage conditions be identical, but the product's appeal should be the same. The positive spillover won't happen unless certain elements of the product are standardized. Brand name should be identical or recognizably similar.

2. *Organization.* Global advertising is typically directed from headquarters with the help of advertising agencies with a global network. The need for central control of the global advertising campaigns has been one of the driving forces behind

Collezionali tutti e 5.

Collect all five.

Il nuovo iMac. Ora in 5 colori. Think different.

Think different.

Italian and English language ads for Apple, the maker of the new iMac personal computer. The advertisements are virtually identical, with only translation needed to communicate the same message across different regions. Courtesy Apple Computer, Inc.

the ad agencies' expansion abroad, and this in turn has stimulated agencies to promote the use of more global advertising (more on this below).

3. *Media.* Global advertising draws on media with global reach such as satellite TV and international editions of magazines and newspapers to create spillovers in two ways: (*a*) crossing borders to reach customers in different countries and (*b*) following traveling customers around the globe.

4. *Message and creative.* The copy and visualization go to the heart of the global campaigns. Global advertising is basically uniform in copy and visualization across markets. Three levels of gradually decreasing uniformity can be distinguished: identical ads, prototype advertising, and pattern standardization.

Identical Ads

The ads can be **identical,** usually with localization only in terms of language voice-over changes and simple copy translations. Pan-European advertising featuring Exxon gasoline's tiger in the tank and Marlboro cigarettes' cowboy is an example. In some cases the identical ads or commercials can be used without any translation at all. Levi's, the jeans manufacturer, uses cartoons with rock music and unintelligible, vaguely Esperanto-sounding vocals in one commercial where the Levi's-wearing hero rescues a beautiful woman from a burning building, an easily comprehended message. In other cases the commercials simply carry subtitles. IBM shows Italian-speaking nuns discussing the pros and cons of Internet surfing with subtitles translating the conversation: global ad, with a local touch.

Prototype Advertising

Then there are **global prototypes** in which the voice-over and the visual may be changed to avoid language and cultural problems; the ad may also be re-shot with local spokespeople but using the same visualization. Drakkar Noir, a man's fragrance, in an Arab print ad shows a woman's hand caressing a man's hand holding the product; in the United States the same hand grasps the man's wrist. Colgate-Palmolive and Coca-Cola often use prototypes of actual commercial and advertisement samples that demonstrate what headquarters wants in the ads with specific written guidelines for acceptable deviations from the prototypes in terms of story and message (usually limited flexibility) and creative aspects (layout, color, symbols—usually more flexibility), with suggestions for appropriate media.

Pattern Standardization

A similar but less structured global approach involves **pattern standardization,** in which the *positioning theme* is unified and some alternative creative concepts supporting the positioning are spelled out but the actual execution of the ads differs between markets. This has become perhaps the most common approach, since it allows creative flexibility at the local level. In particular, it allows the local execution to reflect differences in the use of copy versus visuals. The European ads for Xerox, the copier maker, often carry more copy than their corresponding ads in the United States, for example. To ensure the desired degree of uniformity, companies might send along photos showing the manner in which the product line should be illustrated. Electrolux, the European white goods manufacturer, sends CD-ROMs to its various subsidiaries from which the product displays can be downloaded and printed by each subsidiary's local agency.

Globalization Examples

There are many examples of successful campaigns based on global advertising. For many of its cola brands, Coca-Cola develops prototypes of advertising messages and layouts in the United States and ships them to its representatives abroad. The local offices are allowed to make changes so as to accommodate language differences and possible differences in regulations, but they are generally expected to follow the main script for the campaign. The result is a congruent presentation of the product throughout the world in a manner that is judged to yield the best payoffs. The synergy is naturally high, and unless the slogans are totally inappropriate for the target market, the possible loss due to lack of local adaptation is more than counterbalanced by the instant recognition of the brand name and the slogans (sometimes in English, even in non–English language countries). Added to that are the savings from the use of similar materials across the globe and the scale returns to globalization. It is easy to see that globalization might well pay off.

Other companies (and products) that are practitioners of global standardization of advertising are the Revlon company (cosmetics), Philip Morris (tobacco) with its Marlboro brand, the Ralph Lauren Polo and Chaps brands (men's clothing and accessories), Kodak film products, most high-fashion companies such as Yves Saint-Laurent and Dior, and home electronics companies such as Sony. There are others from which one might expect globalized campaigns but which do not use them. The Canon AE-1, a "world camera," employs different campaign material in Japan, Europe, and the United States, as do the Japanese automobile companies. The European car manufacturers develop special campaigns for their North American markets even though many of the selling propositions remain the same.

Investigating a cross section of 30 print campaigns and 16 television campaigns from ad agencies in the United States, Germany, and Japan, one researcher found that standardization is more common for advertisements transferred between Western markets than for messages transferred between Western and Eastern markets.[4] Interestingly, the product type played a much smaller role than the market distance. Message standardization was much more common for television commercials than for print ads, regardless of country, probably because of the relatively higher cost of producing TV commercials.

Naturally, global advertising is not always the correct strategy. By far the most advertising spending in the world is for ads adapted to the local marketplace. In a recent study of 38 European and U.S. multinationals, it was found that only three practice complete standardization of advertising.[5] Another three reject any attempts at standardization. The majority of the companies practice some degree of standardization, from "standardizing strategy but not execution" (23.5 percent) to "limited standardization" (31.5 percent) to "standardize in most cases" (29.5 percent). The most common approach was that of "pattern standardization," employing a unified positioning theme but allowing local variation.

PROS AND CONS OF GLOBAL ADVERTISING

There are several reasons why global advertising might be beneficial—and why it might not be. The most immediate benefit usually centers around the cost advantages of unified campaigns.

Cost Advantages

From a cost viewpoint a globally uniform campaign is usually advantageous.[6] The creative ideas once developed can be used globally; the illustrations and messages can be developed once and for all or employed with only minor modifications. Media availability forces some changes, since a broadcast approach might not be directly translatable into print, but generally costs can be held down below those generated by original work for the local market.

Globalized campaigns can also be the basis for savings in media buying. Several media provide global services, especially print, through their international editions. Because media ownership is becoming multinational (so that newspaper owners in one country control newspapers in others—for example, Murdoch's string of newspapers in Australia, the United Kingdom, and the United States), there are sources of scale returns available to a globalized campaign not easily tapped by local buyers.

Global Markets

In general, global advertising will be most useful when the market itself is global. Air travel is a case in point. International airlines offer a typically standardized "product"— or service—and compete for passengers in a global marketplace. The various international airlines attempt to differentiate themselves by superior preflight, in-flight, and postflight service. Global advertising has become an important competitive weapon and a prime source of differentiation. British Airways' famous "Manhattan landing" TV commercial from 1982 has become a landmark in global strategy.

Desperate to make inroads in a competitive market, airlines have pushed the limits of what can be accomplished within a relatively small range of possibilities. Singapore Airlines offers unparalleled in-flight service based on an extensive customer satisfaction program and uses global ads in business magazines to emphasize the attractiveness of its stewardesses. The drive to be noticed and stand out was taken to new heights by South African Airways as it tried to break into the European and American markets (see box, "The Airline That Cares").

G E T T I N G   T H E
Picture

The Airline That Cares

AFTER SOUTH AFRICA rejected apartheid and Nelson Mandela became its president, the country started a drive to convince companies that had left to return and to attract tourists and new business. One side benefit was increased air travel between South Africa and the advanced economies. South African Airways wanted to be the airline of choice and needed to establish a much better known image in an industry where anonymity is associated with lack of safety.

A global advertising campaign seemed the best vehicle to create awareness and a caring image for the airline. To carry the message, a TV commercial was created that drew on a 1982 event on a South Africa Airways 747 en route from Johannesburg to London. A passenger, assisted by flight attendants, gave birth to a healthy baby boy. The spot, produced by Sonnenberg Murphy Leo Burnett, the South African affiliate of the Leo Burnett Company of Chicago, shows a woman, seven months' pregnant, going into labor as her husband watches nervously. After a successful delivery, and as the aircraft continues aloft, the pilot says: "Ladies and gentlemen, this is your captain. We'd like to welcome a new passenger on board."

The commercial was broadcast in the major European and American markets and received considerable atten-

tion. The spot's drastic departure from the standard "feel good" airline advertising and its graphic coverage of the birth led to highly negative reviews among creative agency directors, who felt it had gone beyond the bounds of good taste. In *Adweek*, one critic stated: "I don't see flight assistant–assisted birth as an appropriate selling tool, unless you are trying to promote Lamaze Airlines," referring to the well-known birthing technique.

Consumers in various countries were divided, but not along country lines. For every consumer who praised it as heartwarmingly on target, there was another who damned it as tasteless and irrelevant. But in all countries, the awareness goal was reached and surpassed. The negative press coverage in fact helped, so that even though the image conveyed was not entirely positive among all target consumers, on balance the follow-up research showed consistently high ratings for being noted and liked. And traffic on the routes between the points where the commercial has aired has never been higher.

Sources: Elliott, 1995a; Wentz, 1994.
http://www.saa.co.za/
http://www.leoburnett.com/
http://www.adweek.com/

Global Products

It might be assumed that global products need global advertising. This is often true. The campaigns for Swatch watches, Club Med, Benetton, and Reebok are very similar across continents. But there is often a need to do some local adaptation of global campaigns. For example, a global product and brand such as Levi's jeans targets specific segments with different appeals in each local market, since the positioning of the product and brand varies as the target markets differ (see box, "The Localization of Levi's").

Sometimes a brand's global campaign has misfired and the company has retreated to a more multidomestic adaptation. Parker Pen, a globally recognized American brand name, shifted to global advertising in the mid-1980s only to return to multidomestic advertising (and renewed success) after sales slumped badly. The cause of failure was the lack of cooperation on the part of the company's country subsidiaries, whose previously successful campaigns were discontinued.[7]

In summary, global advertising is most powerful under the following conditions:

The *image* communicated can be identical across countries.

The *symbols* used carry the same meaning across countries.

The product *features* desired are the same.

The *usage* conditions are similar across markets.

If all of these conditions hold, as they do in the case of the airlines, global advertising is a natural. When one or more are not fulfilled—as in the case of Levi's—even standardized products may need adapted multidomestic advertising. If the conditions

G E T T I N G   T H E

Picture

The Localization of Levi's

LEVI'S JEANS are among the most global of products and brands. But most of Levi's advertising is local, even though recently some of the best local ideas have been used in other parts of the world.

In North America Levi's are part of a particularly active outdoor lifestyle and advertised as such, showing healthy, slightly square individuals pursuing their version of the American dream in a variety of outdoor settings. By contrast, in Japan Levi's are fashionable and emphasize this by using James Dean as a symbol. Levi's in Japan are for the young and restless "shinjinrui," the new generation of men and women. In turn, Levi's advertising in Britain stresses (as so common in British ads) the humorous and cheeky aspects of the product, with a male in his underwear washing his Levi's in a laundromat, Levi's in Britain are targeted toward young college students and their ilk having fun. Same product, different images.

Lately, however, Levi's has attempted to create more global consistency. For example, its British ad agency,

Bartle Bogle Hegarty of London, developed a very successful animated campaign that Levi's has used without adaptation in Asia, Latin America, and the United States. The animated spot features a character called Nick Clayman who rescues a woman from a burning building by taking off his Levi's 501 jeans and using the strong, durable jeans to parachute through an adjacent building's window to a bathroom where the two bump into an elderly man sitting on the toilet. Set to music with a strong, persistent beat, and only vaguely intelligible Caribbean-style vocals, the arresting spot clearly communicates the benefits of Levi's while also sustaining its rebel and fun image.

Sources: David B. Montgomery, "Levi Strauss Japan K. K.," Stanford Business School case, 1994; Clio International Awards, 1992: TV Commercials from Japan and Britain; Belch and Belch, 1998, p. 635.
http://www.levi.com

are not right, global advertising will fail, which helps explain why there is still so much controversy about global versus multidomestic advertising.[8]

THE GLOBAL ADVERTISER'S DECISIONS

To describe what is involved in global advertising decision making, a useful start is with the basic mass communication process as it has to be adapted for the international context. This will help explain why the advertiser has to rely to a large extent on local people (agency people and local representatives of the firm) when doing global ads. Advertising, being so close to the cultural traditions of a country, was long one of the more decentralized decisions in the multinational company. Headquarters would perhaps be setting the budget, but the basic positioning strategy would be determined by the local subsidiary and approved by headquarters. When it came to execution, including message creation and especially media selection, the advertising agency and its local branch were the prime movers.

The global advertiser, aiming to gain some benefits from a unified approach, has to take charge of this process more effectively. Positioning strategy has to be unified across countries and the unique selling propositions of the brand made clear—and the same—everywhere. That is the strategy part. As for execution, the global advertising manager needs to work closely with local personnel in the subsidiaries and in the agency network to get consensus on a message that transcends borders, reflects the brand accurately, and has punch everywhere. As for media, although the agency still must be the main actor, the global advertiser will want to make sure that cost factors such as media discounts are properly taken into account. While doing all this, the global advertiser also needs to keep an open eye and open mind to suggestions from the local people, to quickly diffuse information through the various local affiliates, and to be flexible enough to change when new information and market research suggest so. A challenging task!

The International Mass Communication Process

Communicating well through mass media is hard enough when populations speak the same language and come from the same culture. When such homogeneity is missing, everything becomes even more complicated. The global advertiser starts with the same basic communications model and then adapts it by introducing cultural context and language differences (see Exhibit 15.4, which uses the common sender–encoding–channel–decoding–receiver paradigm, but also shows what the specific tasks are at different stages). The *encoding* involves the formulation of translated messages that properly reflect the underlying positioning themes selected by the advertiser. Needless to say, there are problems putting into exact words what the communication is trying to achieve, especially since themes for foreign markets can need a subtly different slant. Then there are language problems. For example, an English word such as *assertive* has no counterpart in many foreign languages, which also means that the sentiment is hard for people in those cultures to recognize and feel. By contrast, the many-hued variations in the meanings of the multipurpose English word *love* need to be precisely translated into languages in which *love* has a certain and unmistakable connotation and various synonyms and alternatives can be found as needed. It's crucial to be clear not only about what the advertising is supposed to convey but about whether this has been adequately translated into another cultural and linguistic context.

The *decoding* on the part of the receiver is similarly complicated by differences in context. While the encoding translation may be correct and apt, the receiver's situation may be very different from what has been envisioned by the sender. For example, television messages are usually intended to be one-on-one with the viewer, but in societies where television watching is more of a social activity as in many emerging markets, intimate-sounding messages about feelings tend to be less effective and in danger of being interpreted with snide remarks when the audience is a group. Even if the language is correct and the message is perfectly understood at one level, hidden or double meanings may surface. Having a good-looking blonde female show her perfect smile and white teeth in a magazine ad for a man's cologne might not increase the attractiveness of the product for males in certain cultures. While pink for a baby boy's shirt might not seem wrong to many Asians, increased exposure to Western cultures has made them more sensitive. Some of these problems can be caught by diligent pretesting of ads, but it is difficult to predict audience reactions when cultural distractions from a message are not well understood.

Exhibit 15.4 A Model of the International Mass Communication Process

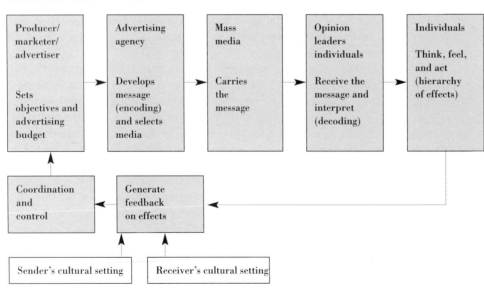

The decoding is likely to involve word of mouth from *opinion leaders* and to follow the so-called *two-step-flow of communication.*[9] This means that the message is first decoded (the first step) by individuals with special interest or expertise whose opinions are valued by other members of the same social groups. These peers evaluate and then pass on (the second step) their version of the message to followers in the groups, creating positive or negative *word-of-mouth* information. The advertiser needs to find out who the opinion leaders are, at what level they should be spoken to in the message, and what selling propositions they would judge important. This requires clear understanding of the cultural context. Even though the majority of ultimate buyers in a country may be without particular product expertise, their opinion leaders are likely to be very knowledgeable. Marketing PCs to upper-level European households, for example, might be very much a matter of creating image and status, but the advertising needs to provide information useful to the opinion leaders of the target segments.

Given these complications, it is not surprising that complete standardization of message and visualization is usually unrealistic. Some adaptation is often necessary, and pattern standardization allowing local variation has become the norm.

In the end, these communications problems mean that the quality of the local talent in the ad agency is very important. The agency's local branches and the firm's local representatives have to be depended on to bridge the gap between different cultural contexts.

Strategic Objectives

Most managers approach global advertising with the intention of using the global reach of media and the similarity of message to enhance the awareness and unique positioning of the brand or product. The boost to the **brand image** and global brand equity is usually the most immediate benefit. When the target market involves global consumers, the ability to reach these customers in many places on the globe helps sustain a positive image of the brand. The traveler who recognizes a brand advertised in a foreign resort location may pay more attention to it there than at home. Global advertising helps create goodwill.

But the effect of global advertising can also be more direct and come closer to **buyer action.** Global customers, such as businesses with a multinational spread, will usually be able to act on buying intentions even when away from the purchasing center. The manager visiting a plant in Malaysia can still place purchase orders through the head office in Honolulu, New York, or London. Global communications—telephone, fax—makes this possible and even likely, considering the global manager's typical traveling schedule. In fact, the effect of advertising might be enhanced when the manager encounters it overseas, simply because of the pleasant surprise of recognition. For global customers, global advertising can be a trigger to action, not just goodwill.

What about consumers exposed in their home country? Does global advertising make any difference? Does locally adapted advertising get closer to the buying stage, while global advertising is good for image only? Again, the answer is perhaps surprising. Yes, local advertising in newspapers and on local broadcast stations can run a tag line with local outlets' phone numbers and addresses, which is harder and more expensive to do—although it can be done—with globally directed advertising. Also, where technical information on attributes needs to be passed along, the copy may have to be redone in the local language; changing voice-overs may not be sufficient. The visual memory, seeing the words, will enhance the consumer's aural memory from the voice-overs. But global ads are often superior in execution. Since more money and creative resources can be spent on them, global ads can support more special effects. In addition, they tend to use only the best creative ideas. In all likelihood, the consumer exposed to a global ad will see something more impressive than in a local effort (see box, "Global Ads Taking Flight").

More recent than the "Manhattan Landing" commercial, the Coca-Cola commercial with a huge number of young people on a hilltop in Italy and the similar British Airways commercial with thousands of extras creating a mosaic flag pattern somewhere

G E T T I N G   T H E
···
Picture

Global Ads Taking Flight

O N E   O F   T H E   F I R S T   examples of global advertising, the "Manhattan Landing" TV commercial by Saatchi & Saatchi for British Airways, has achieved legendary status in the ad world. The commercial, developed in 1982, was inspired by the success of the Steven Spielberg film *Close Encounters of the Third Kind*. The long 90-second commercial showed Manhattan, with its well-known skyscraper skyline, landing slowly in an English village, lights blinding astonished onlookers, engines decelerating, and no voice-over during the first 40 seconds. As the island spaceship descends, the announcer intones, "Every year, we fly more people across the Atlantic than the entire population of Manhattan."

Although British Airways attempted to induce all its country managers to run the commercial, not all cooperated. In India, there were questions about the relevance of Manhattan to Indian customers. Japan rejected the com-

mercial as inappropriate because the challenge for advertising was first to make Britain attractive as a destination, then turn to British Airways as the best choice. In South Africa, 90 seconds were not available for commercial time.

In the end, the commercial was launched in 20 countries. The results showed positive improvement in most local markets. In the United States, especially, awareness of the company rose significantly and unaided recall of the advertising was high. Most important for the advertising industry, the campaign showed that the extra money spent on superior execution of global TV commercials could produce strong effects in local markets even without adaptation.

Sources: Quelch, 1984; Stuart Elliott, "British Air Joins a Flight to New Saatchi," *New York Times*, May 3, 1995, pp. D1, D9.
http://www.saatchi-saatchi.com
http://www.british-airways.com

in India are ads people talk about and are not easily forgotten.[10] Global advertising carries more emotional impact.

Furthermore, as we saw in Chapter 14, people in many parts of the world are starting to buy more items over the phone or from catalogs, using credit cards and avoiding stores. This means the advantage of localized advertising will diminish. Chinese customers in Hong Kong call—or fax—L. L. Bean in the state of Maine to place orders for outdoor boots using their Visa cards. They learn about L. L. Bean (and Eddie Bauer and REI) from travel in the United States, from Hong Kong media reports, and from advertising in international editions of English-language magazines. Global sources of information are available everywhere, in airplanes, dentists' offices, stores, and homes.

Budgeting for Global Advertising

In *domestic* markets, a common method for advertising budgets is **percentage-of-sales,** setting a certain percentage of last year's sales as next year's budget. The figure arrived at can be adjusted by considering a changing competitive situation, increasing growth objectives, or a squeeze on company profits; but percentage-of-sales has the advantage of establishing a stable and predictable expenditure level tied to revenues. The percentage chosen can be calibrated against the industry average ratio of advertising-to-sales, making for easy comparisons with competitors.

Although percentage-of-sales is popular among firms from most countries, it is not a very useful method for setting *global* advertising budgets. Even if total worldwide revenues can be used as a base, it is not clear what the appropriate percentage would be. Which country's industry average should be used as a starting point, for example? Different countries show widely different levels of advertising-to-sales ratios for the same industry, depending on media availability, competitive situation, and so on. Since the percentage-of-sales approach sets advertising on the basis of past sales, it is of little use

An ad for mbcTV, a television station targeting the Arab world. With the emergence of satellite broadcasting, TV channels can now reach across regions to capture culturally homogeneous segments, offering advertisers extraordinary reach and coverage. Courtesy The Advertising Practice.

The Arab world is watching, tell them something!

MBC is not just famous for news and sport, its variety shows with live music, celebrity appearances and exciting competitions have become compulsive viewing for millions throughout the Arab speaking world.

It's coverage like this, that makes

MBC the most popular Satellite TV network in the Middle East today and that's confirmed by PARC research.

So, if you're planning a cost effective advertising and sponsorship campaign, phone for details today and let MBC put your brands in the picture!

mbCTV puts your brands in the picture

For advertising information please contact:
Marketing Dept., MBC, 80 Silverthorne Road, London SW8 3XA. U.K. Phone: (0171) 501 1214 Fax: (0171) 501 1602 or

when a shift from multidomestic to global advertising is contemplated. **Competitive parity** approaches, where advertising budgets are set on the basis of what competitors spend, are also of less relevance in global advertising. The main difficulty is to identify the appropriate parity to actual and potential competitors from different countries, many of which have very different FSAs and market presence. Competitive parity is most appropriate when the major global competitors are from the same countries, as with Coca-Cola and Pepsi-Cola, or with Sony, Matsushita, Sharp, and other Japanese players in consumer electronics.

Budgeting for global advertising typically involves some version of the so-called **objective-task** method favored domestically by more sophisticated marketers. In this method the objectives of the advertising are first made explicit and quantified, after which the requisite media spending to reach the required exposure levels is specified. Although precise calibration of spending is difficult because of the uncertainty in gauging worldwide audiences of media vehicles, the basic logic is sound. After the initial specification of the job to be done by advertising (target percentages for awareness, for example, or certain reach and frequency figures), the creative solutions and the media schedules likely to attain the levels desired are developed.

This is work requiring the expertise of an ad agency with a global network. The budgeting done for global advertising involves an unusually large amount of agency input, since assessing the feasibility and cost of global campaigns requires input from the local branches in the agencies' global network. Partly for this reason, the drive toward global advertising is often spearheaded by an agency with global reach.[11]

THE GLOBAL ADVERTISING AGENCY

As mentioned earlier, the drive toward global advertising has to a large extent been spearheaded by **global advertising agencies** that have developed worldwide networks of subsidiaries or affiliates.

Agency Globalization

Most large agencies in the United States and Europe today have more or less global reach (by contrast, the Japanese agencies, including large Dentsu, are very minor players outside of Asia), but the ability to execute a global campaign can vary because of uneven local capability. A more established and tightly knit network of branches and joint ventures around the globe has paid off very well for large integrated agencies in

EXHIBIT 15.5 Coca-Cola's Agency Network

A growing cast

Since 1991, the Coca-Cola Company has changed its relationships with Madison Avenue. Instead of using a handful of advertising agencies to create campaigns for its brands, the company has hired almost a score, including Creative Artists Agency, the powerful Beverly Hills, California, talent agency.

Following a "think global, act local" strategy, Coca-Cola shifted several assignments from McCann-Erickson, its main worldwide agency for 30 years, and instead relied on local talent to create exciting and trendy advertising under the overall tagline of "Always Coca-Cola." With the arrival in 1993 of Sergio Zyman as chief marketing officer, the Coca-Cola agency roster grew even larger. Freely reshuffling the agency roster throughout the 1990s, Zyman kept the pressure on creative talent. The advertising successes have included Classic Coke from Edge Creative, Creative Artists Agency's new name, in Los Angeles, and Diet Coke from Fallon McElligott of Minneapolis and Lintas Paris. Both brands are global leaders in their categories, Diet Coke marketed in many countries as Coca Cola Light.

Before 1991 . . .

Principal assignment(s)	Agency
Diet Coke/Coca-Cola Light	Lintas Worldwide
Sprite, Mello Yello, Fresca,	Lowe & Partners
Minute Maid, Hi-C	
Coca-Cola Classic/Coca-Cola,	McCann-Erickson Worldwide
Fanta, Cherry Coke, Mr. Pibb	

Since 1991 . . .

Principal assignment(s)	Agency
Aquarius	Casadevall Pedreño & PRG
Fruitopia	Chiat/Day (New York)
Cherry Coke	Chiat/Day (Venice, Calif.)
Coca-Cola Classic/Coca-Cola	Creative Artists Agency
Fanta, Latin America	D'Arcy Masius Benton & Bowles/Americas (Mexico)
Fanta, Asia-Pacific, and local service	D'Arcy Masius Benton & Bowles (Hong Kong)
Coca-Cola Classic/Coca-Cola, campaigns promoting contoured bottles	Fallon McElligott
Coca-Cola Light	Lintas Paris, Fallon McElligott
Fanta, Europe	Lowe Howard-Spink
Diet Coke, Sprite, Fresca, Minute Maid, Hi-C	Lowe & Partners/SMS
Fresca (sugared)	Lowe/SMS de Mexico
Mello Yello, Mr. Pibb	The Martin Agency
Georgia Coffee	McCann-Erickson (Japan)
Powerade	McCann-Erickson (Seattle)
Five Alive	McKinney & Silver
Caffeine-Free Diet Coke/Caffeine-Free Coca-Cola Light	Publicis Conseil (Paris)
OK Soda	Wieden & Kennedy

Sources: Benezra and Parpis, 1998; Gramig, 1998; Wells, 1998.

Benezra, Karen and Eleftheria Parpis. "Chasing Coca-Cola. As he exits, how does Zyman's performance rate?" *Brandweek*, March 30, 1998, pp. 1, 5–6.

Gramig, Mickey. "Coca-Cola to release new ads, but retain multiagency approach." *The Atlanta Journal and Constitution*, May 14, 1998, p. 5F.

Wells, Melanie. "Coke Classic ads have life." *USA Today*, October 19, 1998, p. 8B.

the new global environment. This meant that a firm such as McCann-Erickson, the largest global player before the mergers, gained business in the early 1990s from independent local agencies in Europe and Asia. In 1994, IBM centralized all its advertising to the global network of Ogilvy & Mather Worldwide, one of the large New York–based agencies.[12] However, as always, some buck the trend (see Exhibit 15.5, "Coca-Cola's Agency Network").

As ad agencies expanded their global reach, many advertisers started to centralize their advertising spending and appointed a single firm as the global agency. This meant that many smaller agencies lost accounts as large firms consolidated their ad spending. As a result, smaller agencies merged and became part of larger global networks. Even large agencies were gobbled up—the WPP Group, in 1992 the world's largest, consisted of J. Walter Thompson and Ogilvy & Mather in the United States; Brouillard Communications in France; as well as Scali, McCabe, Sloves; Fallon McElligot; and the Martin agency—all from Britain. Among the 16 largest global agencies now are Cordiant and the WPP Group PLC in Britain; Publicis and BDDP Group in Paris; Dentsu and Hakuhodo in Tokyo; and Interpublic Group and Omnicom (now owner of Chiat-Day) in New York (see Exhibit 15.6).

With the members of the groups being large agencies in their own right and often with a proud history, most mergers have retained the independence of the individual units as far as possible. This strategy has been all the more important as many mergers placed accounts from competitors under the same roof. But it also means that the combined units, although large and well represented in many countries, tend to have some difficulty in making the parts work together. The Saatchi & Saatchi breakup is an example (see box, "Saatchi & Saatchi's Global Management Problems").

The Agency's Job

The global advertiser will generally develop the message and media schedule working intimately with an advertising agency that has local representation in the various markets. The creative development and the production of a prototype ad or standardized commercial are usually centralized at an agency with headquarters in the company's home country and branch offices in the relevant market countries.

The large multinational with entries in many country markets will generally find it advantageous from a control and coordination perspective to rely on a worldwide agency. Unilever, the large packaged goods company headquartered in London, employed J. Walter Thompson, now part of the WPP Group, to handle most of its

EXHIBIT 15.6 The World's 16 Largest Global Agencies, 1997 (in millions of $)

Rank 1997	Ad organization	Headquarters	Worldwide gross income 1997	Worldwide gross income 1996	% change
1	Omnicom Group	New York	$4,154.3	$3,750.8	10.8
2	WPP Group	London	3,646.6	3,430.2	6.3
3	Interpublic Group of Cos.	New York	3,384.5	3,037.1	11.4
4	Dentsu	Tokyo	1,987.8	1,929.9	3.0
5	Young & Rubicam	New York	1,497.9	1,356.4	10.4
6	True North Communications	Chicago	1,211.5	996.7	21.6
7	Grey Advertising	New York	1,143.0	1,027.7	11.2
8	Havas Advertising	Paris	1,033.1	974.3	6.0
9	Leo Burnett Co.	Chicago	878.0	866.3	1.4
10	Hakuhodo	Tokyo	848.0	897.7	-5.5
11	MacManus Group	New York	842.6	756.2	11.4
12	Saatchi & Saatchi	London	657.0	616.9	6.5
13	Publicis Communication	Paris	625.0	672.4	-7.1
14	Cordiant Communications Group	London	596.7	577.0	3.4
15	Carlson Marketing Group	Minneapolis	285.2	255.8	11.5
16	TMP Worldwide	New York	274.1	222.5	23.2

G E T T I N G   T H E

Picture

Saatchi & Saatchi's
Global Management Problems

IN EARLY 1995 Saatchi & Saatchi, part of Cordiant and then one of the world's largest advertising agencies and the one that spearheaded the drive toward global advertising, was in trouble. Three years of recessionary economies around the world had led to lowered billings. The expansion of the agency business into marketing consulting had to be cut short. The acquisitions of several large agencies, including Compton's and Ted Bates, had placed a heavy debt burden on the London-based home office. And the bondholders and stockholders of the publicly listed company included professional money managers of pension funds who demanded high returns on their portfolios. In a coup engineered by American shareholders, Maurice Saatchi, an advertising wizard who had founded the agency in 1970 together with his brother Charles, was ousted as chairman. Global advertising campaigns, the force behind the creation of powerful global brands, are difficult to implement without the help of agencies like Saatchi with global reach. But these wide-reaching organizations that try to combine creative talent and business skills are difficult to manage. As analysts tried to diagnose Saatchi & Saatchi's problems, one thing stood out: A large company might need strong financial managers, but could it allow enough freedom for the creative people and still be a successful ad agency?

Sources: *Washington Post*, January 4, 1995; *New York Times*, January 12, 1995.
http://www.saatchi-saatchi.com

products and markets. Volkswagen was so impressed by Doyle Dane and Bernbach, an American agency, in its handling of Volkswagen's U.S. account that it gave the agency responsibility for its other country markets, including the home market in Germany.

It is also common for companies to allot their advertising money to agencies in the local market when conditions in a country are particularly difficult or unique. Thus, Japanese multinational companies rely on the giant Dentsu or Hakuhodo agencies of Tokyo to handle many of their markets in Asia, but not the American market. Most of the personnel in a particular branch office (even a wholly owned subsidiary) of a multinational agency will be natives of the branch country. Even so, the avoidance of the home country agency by the Japanese is simply a step to ensure that the campaign will have no ethnocentric overtones. At the same time, the tendency for the U.S. multinationals is to prefer dealing with American agencies abroad. This practice might be questioned, since in the annual Clio awards given by an international jury to well-crafted and imaginative advertising, American ads tend to fare less well. But then, American-based advertising agencies rely largely on local talent in their offices abroad.

Research shows that the extent to which local branches focus on global advertising is relatively limited. In a survey of 347 foreign branches of U.S. agencies it was found that about two-thirds (232) had at some time participated in multicountry advertising initiated by the home office.[13] Of these multicountry campaigns, most were regional in scope, followed by major-markets-only campaigns, with less than 10 percent truly global (see Exhibit 15.7). According to the researchers, the emphasis on **pan-regional** campaigns (evidenced by the figures in Exhibit 15.7) is mainly due to the emergence of regional groupings and trading blocs.

Local agencies are often preferable (and sometimes the only ones willing to accept the assignment) when the account is small. The reason is that global agencies, owing to their sheer size, tend to neglect smaller accounts. Even though payment agreements differing from the standard commission fee of 15 percent can be negotiated, the multinational agencies still tend to concentrate on the more important large accounts. This drawback for small local campaigns can be eliminated with the help of globalized cam-

EXHIBIT 15.7 Scope of Advertising Agencies' Participation in Multicountry Campaigns

Market scope	Number of agencies	Percent of total
Agencies doing one type of multicountry campaign		
Global	15	6.5%
Major	35	15.1
Regional	103	44.4
	153	66.0
Agencies executing more than one type of multicountry campaign		
Global-major	5	2.2%
Global-regional	16	6.9
Major-regional	29	12.5
Global-major-regional	29	12.5
	79	34.1
Total	**232**	**100.0%**

Source: Adapted from Hill and Shao, 1994, p. 39.

paigns directed from headquarters and managed through the local branch office of a multinational agency. Even though a particular country shows a small account size, the globally pooled advertising budget can be substantial.

One particular headache of agency–advertiser relations is the across-country variability in financial arrangements and payments. Advertisers in some countries insist on paying for the agency services with the product advertised or some other type of "countertrade." The agency then has to arrange the media payments. It is not surprising that some of the highly leveraged global agencies exhibit rather low levels of profitability, creating pressure from irate bondholders and shareholders, as the Saatchi & Saatchi experience demonstrates.

Message Creation

For good reasons, message creation and language translation are the aspects most consistently and thoroughly discussed in the literature on global advertising. Even experienced ad people commit mistakes with ease. And once committed, the faux pas are painfully obvious. The examples are legion (see box, "Translated Messages Have Their Pitfalls").

But there are also examples of successful advertising messages used in many different countries with only a modicum of modification. A classic example is Exxon's "Put a tiger in your tank." Unilever's Lux soap was long advertised around the world as "the soap used by 9 stars out of 10"; "Coke is refreshing" in many countries of the world; Sony positions itself as "the innovator" in most country markets; and Marlboro is from the same "cowboy country" whether you are in Asia, Europe, or Latin America.

Message translation is complicated because of the cultural diversity among the various countries of the world. Language difference is only the most obvious manifestation of this diversity. Other factors, more subtle and therefore treacherous, include the use of idiomatic expressions to signify other matters than the ones literally expressed. An example is the slogan "Avoid embarrassment—use Quink" for an ink product, which translated into Spanish became "Avoid pregnancy—use Quink." Cultural symbolism makes darkened teeth very attractive among some Asian people, creates difficulties in employing an animal as a trademark across cultures (even the tiger had to be given up by Exxon in some countries such as India), and forces close scrutiny of numbers and colors (4 is the number of death in Japan, so is 3 in the Philippines, 13 is not acceptable in the United States and Western Europe, black *and* white are funerary

G E T T I N G   T H E   *Picture*

Translated Messages Have Their Pitfalls

SMALL NUANCES in words sometimes matter a lot. An American manufacturer in the auto industry advertised its batteries as "highly rated." In Venezuela the translation made it "highly overrated." A shirt manufacturer advertising in Mexico also had trouble with the Spanish language. Instead of declaring, "When I used this shirt I felt good," the character in the advertisement asserted. "Until I used this shirt I felt good."

Sexual connotations under the surface of day-to-day language create pitfalls. Chrysler tried to use its American slogan "Dart Is Power" in Latin American markets only to find that the message implied that drivers of the car lacked sexual vigor. An airline advertising its "rendezvous lounges" on its flights did not realize that to many Europeans a rendezvous carries the distinct connotation of meeting a lover for an illicit affair. Otis Elevators promoted parts of its line in Russia as "completion equipment," which in Russian became "tools for orgasms."

Brand names are well known stumbling blocks. Chevrolet's Nova car meant "won't go" in Spanish markets. In Mexico "Fresca" is slang for "lesbian." "Pinto," the Ford car, had to be renamed "Corcel" in Brazil after it was discovered that pinto was slang for the male appendage. The Japanese, on the other hand, have maintained several of their domestic names (in order to keep the Japanese connection) even though experts warned them that names such as "Facom" and "Datsun" ("That soon?") elicit snide remarks among English speakers. Such examples demonstrate why it is desirable to employ local agencies rather than rely on a home country agency that works at a distance from the market.

Sources: Ricks, 1993, and personal interviews.
http://www.chryslercars.com
http://www.otis.com/
http://www.chevrolet.com/
http://www.ford.com

American tobacco companies have aggressive marketing campaigns in most developing countries. Many challenge the ethics of this practice. Munshi Ahmed.

colors in Asia, white is happiness in Europe, red is a masculine color in Italy and feminine in northern Europe, and so on).[14]

Media Selection

If message creation needs the collaboration of the agency and the advertiser (to ensure a unified positioning theme), **media selection** is one area where the agency and its local representative rules. The reason is primarily expertise. Local knowledge of the availability of media alternatives is absolutely necessary so that the optimal media, given the constraints, are chosen. It might be possible to direct an advertising campaign from overseas insofar as budgeting, message creation, and general direction go, but the media choices must be negotiated and made locally.

Varying media usage across regions was shown in Exhibit 15.2. As noted earlier, rates of media usage are determined by a number of factors—such as availability of commercial TV and radio, level of economic development, literacy rates, religion, and so forth—and reflect directly, of course, the actual media selection decisions made by the advertisers and agencies for the country in question.

What type of media to select hinges (within the availability constraints) very much on the objectives and target segment(s) of the campaign.

For *awareness*, television serves well in many countries where it is generally available. In markets with lower rates of TV penetration, radio can often be used to supplement television advertising. Television in most cases has the advantage of a high-attention value, especially in countries where it is relatively rare.

Effective communication of *knowledge* about a product usually requires the use of words, whether spoken or written. If illiteracy is a problem, knowledge will have to be transmitted through the spoken word and radio would be a logical candidate. Where literacy is high but the number of appropriate magazines low, newspapers might have to serve. In most Western nations the best medium for knowledge creation is the magazine, where specific selling points about the product can be well communicated. It is no coincidence, as noted earlier, that it is in these same countries that "rational," multiattributed product evaluations seem to be most applicable.

For *attitude* change and *image* building, newspapers and radio advertising are generally inferior to television and magazines. Cinema and outdoor advertising are important in certain countries. In Argentina, cinema is an important medium precisely because of the affective spillover from the movie's context and, of course, because of the captive audience (Argentines unlike Americans don't seem to mind). In most countries television is the most important medium for emotional communication, since it combines visual and verbal stimuli.

To affect *behavior* directly, the media chosen have to be timely; that is, they have to reach the audience near the time of purchase. Newspapers fulfill this function well in most cultures. Magazines (and TV) tend to be less useful here, unless the product can be sold through the special direct marketing channels opened up in some countries. An example of the latter is the United States, where credit cards are used to pay by telephone for goods advertised on TV.

Once the media types have been decided upon, the particular vehicles to be used within each type are usually selected on the basis of some efficiency criterion, such as "cost per thousand" (CPM). The use of an efficiency criterion requires information about how much advertising in a vehicle costs and how many people (in the target market) will be reached. Here a major problem is encountered in many markets. The available audience measurements are either incomplete (lacking audience demographics, for example) or unreliable or even nonexistent. Even in developed countries it is sometimes hard to find accurate figures properly validated by independent agencies. As a result, it is often very difficult to be precise about the computation of an index such as the CPM. Again, local people with in-depth knowledge of the various media vehicles should be consulted before choices are made.

On the cost side, the rate schedules for advertising may provide great discounts for large quantity and special rebates, often to domestic agencies over foreign agencies. Again the local connection becomes important in negotiations about proper pricing and payment procedures.

CLOSE-UP: GOODYEAR IN LATIN AMERICA

The way in which the headquarters managers, the local subsidiaries, and the ad agency work together to generate a global advertising campaign can be illustrated through Goodyear's development of a pan-regional campaign for Latin America.

Goodyear, the large American tire company headquartered in Akron, Ohio, has long taken a standardized approach to its advertising. Under the assumption that customer needs and wants in tires are largely dependent on basic factors such as climate and road conditions, the company has centrally coordinated its international advertising since the early 1970s. Goodyear's present regional approach has evolved into a prototype standardization program that involves the local subsidiaries in decision making more than previously. Its Latin American market advertising gains global scale advantages while remaining responsive to local conditions.[15]

Planning for a unified regional advertising strategy that properly involves local subsidiaries needs to start early. For Goodyear, prompted by a reorganization in 1992, the process began about 12 months before the new campaign rolled out. The planning process involved six stages (see Exhibit 15.8).

1. Preliminary Orientation (September)

The beginning stage was an educational one, allowing both headquarters and local subsidiary staff to understand each other's perspectives. Headquarters informed the subsidiaries of the benefits expected from a pan-regional approach, and the subsidiaries were asked to provide information about their current and planned communication strategies. To emphasize the pan-regional benefits, the regional director of Latin American sales and marketing described the cost reductions from lower trade barriers for advertising materials and the advantage of having available a bank of high-quality standardized commercials. Each national sales director was asked to provide answers to several strategic business questions, including brand image perceptions in their respective markets.

2. Regional Meeting to Define Communications Strategy (October)

An informal two-day working conference was organized in Miami where the communications strategy could be developed. From headquarters came the regional vice president for Latin America, the director of sales and marketing communications, and the manager of marketing research. From the subsidiaries came the sales director and the advertising manager for each country. Also participating were regional account execu-

---

EXHIBIT 15.8 Goodyear's Latin American Campaign
Development Stages

1. Preliminary orientation, September 1992
Subsidiary strategic information input on business and communications strategy on country-by-country basis. Home office review.

2. Regional communications strategy definition meeting, October 1992
Outputs: Regional positioning objective, communication objectives, and creative assignment for advertising agency.

3. Advertising creative review meeting, November 12, 1992
Outputs: Six creative concepts (storyboards). Research questions regarding real consumer concerns to guide research.

4. Qualitative research stage, November–December 1992
Consistent research results across five countries on purchase intentions and consumer perceptions of safety.

5. Research review meeting, January 15, 1993
Sharply defined "consumer proposition" identified and agreed upon with new creative assignment for agency.

6. Final creative review meeting, March 12, 1993
Campaign adoption.

Source: David A. Hanni, John K. Ryans, Jr., and Ivan R. Vernon (1995), "Executive Insights: Coordinating International Advertising—The Goodyear Case Revisited for Latin America," *Journal of International Marketing*, Vol. 3, No. 2, p. 88. Reprinted by permission of Michigan State University Press.

G E T T I N G   T H E   *Picture*

"Smile and Say 'Tires' "

G O O D Y E A R has identified four different ways to say "tires" in Latin America, and a fifth way to say it in Puerto Rico. In some of these countries one of the expressions occurs less frequently, while in other countries expressions other than the main one either will not be understood or may convey an entirely different meaning. It's important to pick the right word for each local market.

Spanish word for tires	Countries using each word
Cauchos	Venezuela
Cubiertas	Argentina
Gomas	Puerto Rico
Llantas	Mexico, Peru, Guatemala, Colombia, and elsewhere in Central America
Neumaticos	Chile

Source: David A. Hanni, John K. Ryans, Jr., and Ivan R. Vernon (1995), "Executive Insights: Coordinating International Advertising—The Goodyear Case Revisited for Latin America," *Journal of International Marketing*, Vol. 3, No. 2, p. 96. Reprinted by permission of Michigan State University Press.

tives and creative directors from Leo Burnett Worldwide, the recently appointed global ad agency based in Chicago with offices in Latin America.

The purpose was to develop an "umbrella" campaign theme that would fit all countries but with subsidiary autonomy to prepare retail, promotional, and product advertising to meet local requirements. The umbrella theme would make sure that local creative concepts reinforced common positioning and would make possible centralized (and thus cost-effective) production of a pan-regional pool of television commercials and print advertisements.

Everyone involved at the October meeting was requested to look at tire advertising afresh, disregarding previous regional campaigns to the extent possible. The various participants were happy to discover that no one country's problems were in fact unique, a common base soon emerged, and participants were able to agree on a unified positioning strategy to build brand equity throughout the region. At the same time, needs for local adaptation were uncovered. For example, even though Spanish is a common language among all the countries except Brazil, national differences in word choice and pronunciations made localized voice-over necessary (see box, "Smile and Say 'Tires' ").

Using local talent would enable the country units to employ spokespeople with regional appeal. On the basis of the subsidiaries' input, a pattern standardization solution of the regional advertising campaign seemed logical.

Involving the ad agency at this early stage facilitated development of the creative brief for the pan-regional ads. To follow up on the development of creative alternatives, a task force was organized, consisting of advertising managers and sales directors from each country, the regional sales and communications directors from headquarters, and agency people (including creative teams from five countries).

3. Advertising Creative Meeting (November)

The task force met to consider six alternative concept or storyboards developed by the creative teams. Each of the five creative teams explained and defended its particular concept or storyboard, and lengthy discussions ensued. The outcome was a decision to collect more data on the concepts from customers in the respective countries. Specifically, more marketing research was judged necessary to identify the extent to which the campaigns were targeted correctly at real consumer concerns.

4. Qualitative Research Stage (November–December)

The research on the proposed concept storyboards focused on two main issues. One was customers' degree of concern about safety and security of the tires. The second issue involved consumer reactions to four different creative themes:

a. Authority based on an emotional appeal.
b. Leadership positioning.
c. Technology transfer.
d. Advanced technology with rational appeal.

Using focus groups in five countries (Brazil, Chile, Colombia, Mexico, and Venezuela) to test the alternatives, the company found that the results were consistent throughout the region, with safety and security a strong theme everywhere, and with support for an emotional authority-based approach. It was also found that the typical "We are not the same" local sentiments were overstated: The respondents in each country rated their roads "the worst in Latin America."

5. Research Review Meeting (January)

The task force met to consider the research results. The aim was to reach a consensus on one unique selling proposition, a convincing argument why consumers should change their beliefs about tires and choose Goodyear. This theme would be the recurring motto serving to unify the various local executions.

The outcome of the meeting was a succinctly worded "consumer proposition," a theme that was assigned to the ad agency for the development of a full pan-regional campaign. In a subsequent meeting, the task force reviewed the creative proposals from the agency and its local creative teams, and further directions for the work were issued.

6. Final Creative Review (March)

At this final decision-making meeting of the task force, each team's concept was presented without indicating the team identity or the country in which the campaign originated. A regionwide creative team presented all the proposals, with the supporting material reflecting an entire campaign from print to outdoor media. This was done to avoid the "not invented here" syndrome and reduce the inclination to defend one's own particular proposal at all cost.

The process worked smoothly, as one of the campaigns was judged clearly superior in capturing the positional theme and creative concept. This campaign was adopted, and the agency and its local offices were instructed to proceed with full-fledged development of the campaign material and local executions. The production of the commercials, advertisements, and other support material took place through the summer months, and media buys were completed by the start of the campaign at the end of August.

Lessons

There are several points to emphasize about this illustration of a recent approach to pattern standardization in pan-regional advertising.

First, by focusing on regions it may be possible to reap the scale benefits and cost efficiencies of global advertising without sacrificing too much on the side of local adaptation. The recent emergence of new trading blocs suggests that this perspective can be generally useful.

Second, the early involvement of country subsidiaries and agency professionals not only facilitates later acceptance of unified themes but helps broaden the sources of powerful campaign concepts. This is especially useful since in most cases the local subsidiaries can be expected to have greater market knowledge than headquarters.

Third, and very important, the process by which pattern standardization is arrived at needs to allow open and free exchange. In the Goodyear case, it is striking how local differences seemed to be based on misperceptions that vanished once participants interacted without pressure to defend the home turf. By the same token, headquarters can't assume to know more about the markets involved than its local units but should focus on explaining carefully why standardization might be beneficial. The way the local operation fits into the whole needs to be clarified, and headquarters should not expect local units to sacrifice for the common good without a compelling rationale. Then headquarters should be flexible when the local units suggest alternative options.

Fourth, even when the company has operated for years in a market, research is still necessary, especially when conditions are changing. Yesterday's solutions were perhaps good for yesterday's problems, but new times need new information and new solutions. A planning process that is systematic, thorough, and flexible—such as the one implemented by Goodyear—is far more likely to generate successful advertising campaigns than one based on a static and unchanging perception of the environment.

SUMMARY

Despite the pitfalls of standardized and translated messages, global ads have become an important alternative to adapted multidomestic advertising. The technological advances in global communications, the growth of global media, and the strength of global advertising agencies have combined to make global advertising possible. And the positive spillovers from unified messages and the increasing homogeneity of many markets have made global advertising desirable.

As the affluence of countries grows, new products and services appear and customers need more information. Advertising becomes more important, and advertising expenditures as a percentage of the GDP increase. For the global marketer, faced with increasing spending needs in all markets, a coordinated effort with synchronized campaigns, pattern standardization, and unified image across trade regions is usually more effective and cost-efficient than multidomestic campaigns. We took note of the advantages, problems, and pitfalls of global advertising and discussed how the advertiser and ad agency can jointly develop a regional or global campaign, using as illustration a case study of one company Goodyear.

KEY TERMS

brand image, p. 457
buyer action, p. 457
competitive parity, p. 459
global advertising, p. 446
global advertising agencies, p. 460

global prototypes, p. 452
hierarchy of effects, p. 449
identical ads, p. 457
localized advertising, p. 446
media selection, p. 464
message translation, p. 463

multidomestic advertising, p. 446
objective task, p. 459
pan-regional advertising, p. 462
pattern standardization, p. 452
percentage-of-sales, p. 458

DISCUSSION QUESTIONS

1. Using library sources and the Internet, find three examples of global advertising. What characteristics make these campaigns global?

2. Using the same sources, can you find examples of global advertising for which the markets are not global but "multidomestic"?

3. Discuss what an advertiser may do to avoid conflicts with country managers when a global advertising campaign is contemplated.

4. How can an advertiser use the company Web site to create global advertising? How can the message be localized?

5. Rather than enforcing complete uniformity, global advertising tends to follow a "pattern standardization approach." What does this mean? How does this help avoid the pitfalls of standardized and translated messages?

NOTES

1. These definitions are necessarily crude. Some "global" advertising, such as the pan-European ads done by Pioneer car audio products, is perhaps better seen as "regional." Even the most multidomestic advertising, such as that done for Budweiser beer in many countries, retains a certain similarity across markets, with the featured packaging and brand name remaining constant. As in the case of product standardization, global advertising is a matter of degree.

2. From Greyser, 1992.

3. See DeMooij and Keegan, 1991.

4. See Mueller, 1991.

5. From Harris, 1994.

6. Although not always as advantageous as one would initially assume. In one case an American company wanted to use the same TV commercials abroad as the ones used at home, without any dubbing or change of language. But the actors employed for the U.S. commercials demanded so high a compensation for the world rights that reshooting the commercial with local talent became the cheaper option.

7. From Lippman, 1988.

8. See, for example, the contrasts between Banerjee, 1994, and Elliott, 1995c.

9. The two-step-flow communication model, first developed in sociology, is usually attributed to Austrian sociologist Paul Lazarsfeld and his colleagues at Columbia University in the 1940s; see Kotler, 1994, p. 610.

10. These were TV commercials aired during 1994–95.

11. See, for example, the role of Saatchi & Saatchi in the British Airways' decision to use global advertising.

12. See Johnson, 1994.

13. From Hill and Shao, 1994.

14. Many of these culturally based idiosyncrasies are documented by Ricks, 1993.

15. The following account draws on the excellent article by Hanni et al., 1995.

SELECTED REFERENCES

"Advertisers Seek Global Messages." *New York Times*, November 18, 1991.

Banerjee, Ashish. "Global Campaigns Don't Work: Multinationals Do." *Advertising Age* 65, no. 17 (April 18, 1994), p. 23.

Belch, George E.; and Michael A. Belch. *Advertising and Promotion*, 4th ed. Boston, MA: Irwin/McGraw-Hill, 1998.

DeMooij, M. K.; and Warren Keegan. *Advertising Worldwide*. London: Prentice-Hall International, 1991.

Elliott, Stuart. "What's in a Name? Perhaps Billions." *New York Times*, August 12, 1992, p. D6.

—. "South African Air Gets Results from a Much-Debated Commercial." *New York Times*, January 11, 1995a, p. D9.

—. "At Coke, a Shift to Many Voices." *New York Times*, January 20, 1995b, pp. D1, D6.

—. "Creative Agencies That Feel at Home in the Global Village Are Writing Their Own Tickets." *New York Times*, September 30, 1995c, p. D10.

"Firms Opt for Pan-Regional Marketing Strategies in EC." *Business International*, October 29, 1990.

Freeman, Laurie. "Colgate Axes Global Ads; Thinks Local." *Advertising Age*, November 26, 1990, sec. 1, pp. 1, 59.

Greyser, Stephen A. *Siemens: Corporate Advertising*. Harvard Business School, case 593–022, 1992.

—. and W. S. Schille. *British Airways: The World's Biggest Offer;* Harvard Business School, case 592–051, 1993.

Hanni, David A.; John K. Ryans; and Ivan R. Vernon. "Coordinating International Advertising—The Goodyear Case Revisited for Latin America." *Journal of International Marketing* 3, no. 2 (1995), pp. 83–98.

Harris, Greg. "International Advertising Standardization: What Do the Multinationals Actually Standardize?" *Journal of International Marketing* 2, no. 4 (1994), pp. 13–30.

Hill, John S.; and Alan T. Shao. "Agency Participants in Multicountry Advertising: A Preliminary Examination of Affiliate Characteristics and Environments." *Journal of International Marketing* 2, no. 2 (1994), pp. 29–48.

Johnson, Bradley. "Tumult Ahead for IBM, Ogilvy." *Advertising Age* 65, no. 23 (May 30, 1994), pp. 36–37.

Kotler, Philip. *Marketing Management*, 9th ed. Upper Saddle River, NJ: Prentice-Hall, 1997.

Lippman, Joanne. "Marketers Turn Sour on Global Sales Pitch Harvard Guru Makes." *The Wall Street Journal*, May 12, 1988, p. 1.

Mårtensson, Rita. *Innovations in Retailing*. Lund, Sweden: Liber, 1983.

Mueller, Barbara. "Multinational Advertising: Factors Influencing the Standardised versus Specialised Approach." *International Marketing Review* 8, no. 1 (1991), pp. 7–18.

Quelch, John. *British Airways*. Harvard Business School, case 585–014, 1984.

Ricks, D. A. *Blunders in International Business*, Cambridge, MA: Blackwell, 1993.

Solomon, Michael R. *Consumer Behavior*. 2d ed. Needham Heights, MA: Allyn & Bacon, 1992.

Sorenson, R. Z.; and U. E. Wiechmann. "How Multinationals View Marketing Standardization." In D. N. Dickson, ed., *Managing Effectively in the World Marketplace*. New York: Wiley, 1983, pp. 301–16.

Wentz, Laurel. "Global Village." *Advertising Age*, November 21, 1994, p. I3.

"World's Top 50 Advertising Organizations." *Advertising Age*, April 15, 1992, pp. 5–10.

Global Promotion, Direct Marketing, and Personal Selling

"In your face"

Your takeaways from this chapter:

1. In addition to media advertising there are now a number of alternative promotional tools for creating global presence and visibility. But global marketing communications need to be integrated so a unified image and message is communicated.

2. The global promoter should be aware that local regulations can kill the implementation in any one country. Use local representatives to find out exactly what the limits are.

3. With advances in the Internet, telecommunications, and express mail—as well as the development of address lists and the availability of credit cards—direct mail is transformed from a simple promotional tool to a low-risk direct marketing option, a new mode of entering a market, and a new way for small business to promote and sell its products abroad.

4. Personal selling may be the last frontier of globalization, with local people necessary for customer contact. With the globalization of industries and markets, local salespeople will also be part of the front-line service providers for global customers.

5. As promotional activities increase in the newly opened markets, local "How to do business" customs can be expected to converge, as cultural bonds and personal likes and dislikes are no longer a sufficient basis for a buyer–seller relationship.

THE MAIN COMPONENTS of the promotional mix besides advertising are sales promotion, public relations, and publicity, as well as personal selling. This chapter will cover these plus some special international promotions, including international trade fairs and the use of direct marketing in a global setting. Internet advertising is treated separately in Chapter 18.

Because of widely different local trade regulations and the obstacles of local customs and culture, at first sight many of these promotional activities don't seem good candidates for globalization. Global coordination of promotion is complicated by the fact that implementation and execution are in the hands of local employees. Local salespeople are necessary for running promotional schemes such as in-store displays, free samples, and contests. But globalized promotional activities have become very important in global marketing. The main reasons involve the globalization of markets, the growth of global media reach, and the resulting emergence of megastars and megabrands. Globally recognized endorsers and brand names are opening doors for global promotions.

The Windows 95 Launch: Promotion as a Global Event

When you introduce a product that retailers forecast will boost overall sales by 20 percent, expect store owners to make a fuss over it. When you spend $200 million on promotion, expect the media to make a fuss, too. That's just what happened in 1995 when Microsoft Corporation launched its Windows 95 operating system.

What the *New York Times* called "the splashiest, most frenzied, most expensive introduction of a computer product in the industry's history" started in New Zealand. Microsoft had announced it would release Windows 95 on August 24, and it kept that promise to the minute. Windows 95 went on sale at midnight in the first English-speaking country to greet the new day. As midnight arrived in one time zone after another, stores joined the hoopla with late-night hours, balloons, and special sales.

In the United States, CompUSA kept stores open past midnight for the first time in its history. The stores offered free pizza and discounts on American Airlines tickets. Computer City Supercenter ran late-night specials on Windows-related merchandise, such as discounts on a Microsoft mouse from 11 p.m. till midnight.

Microsoft didn't rely on its retailers to generate all the excitement. In New York, the company arranged for the Empire State Building to be lit with spotlights in colors from the Windows logo. In Toronto, the landmark CN Tower bore a Windows 95 banner. And in a move that dismayed some, Microsoft underwrote the cost of distributing the *Times of London*. A box at the top of the first page read, "Windows 95 Launch—Today The Times Is Free Courtesy of Microsoft." At the bottom of the first page was this ad: "Windows 95. So Good Even The Times Is Complimentary." The paper also carried an editorial supplement sponsored by Microsoft.

Meanwhile, in the Redmond, Washington, home of Microsoft, Bill Gates was throwing a party. Jay Leno hosted the introductory ceremonies, the product's theme song ("Start Me Up" by the Rolling Stones) was played, and commemorative T-shirts sold briskly. Those who didn't get an invitation could attend electronically. Microsoft made the party's sights and sounds available over the Internet (thereby promoting the product's easy-to-use Internet connection, known as the

Microsoft Network). Forty-five Microsoft employees wielded digital cameras, sound digitizers, and other electronic equipment to record the festivities for anyone able to navigate the World Wide Web. And though the real-world party was a day long, the on-line version lasted over two weeks.

Perhaps the clearest indicator of Microsoft's promotional success was that other companies bought advertising on the infomercial introducing Windows 95. Who would run ads on an ad? Coca-Cola Company, Compaq Computer Corporation, CompUSA, and Eastman Kodak Company. Explained a Coca-Cola spokesperson, "The whole launch is a happening . . . a place we ought to be." Perhaps mindful of the monopoly accusations against the company, Microsoft's launch of Windows 98 was a decidedly less glitzy event.

Sources: Carey Goldberg, "Midnight Sales Frenzy Ushers in Windows 95," *New York Times*, August 24, 1995, pp. A1, D6; Richard W. Stevenson, "Software Makes Strange Bedfellows in Britain as Microsoft and Murdoch Team to Push Windows 95," *New York Times*, August 24, 1995, p. D6; Peter H. Lewis, "Microsoft Has Windows 95 Party; the Internet Shows Up," *New York Times*, August 25, 1995, p. D4; Stuart Elliott, "So Much Stock, but So Little Liquidity," *New York Times*, August 25, 1995, p. D4; Amy Cortese, "The Software Resolution," *Business Week*, December 4, 1995, pp. 78–90. *http://www.microsoft.com*

INTRODUCTION

While global advertising has been around for a few years, other global promotions have only recently come into their own. Although businesses have long sponsored sports and arts events—including World Cup soccer, tennis tournaments, auto racing, and painting exhibitions—companies have recently taken to creating events and news with the promotions being the main purpose. Disney's gala film openings or video releases, Swatch's parties when launching new lines, Benetton's ultrahip advertisements, and Microsoft's launch of Windows 95 are global events created for the purpose of maximum visibility for products. In the beginning they may have reflected the 1980s unabashed hedonism, but their continuation into the 1990s suggests that they reflect a structural change in the way promotions will be done in the future. With the emergence of the Internet as a genuine global and accessible communications medium, one can only assume that these promotional stunts will increase in frequency over the next few years.

But global promotions also involve more mundane and traditional tools, such as point-of-purchase merchandising, public relations, and personal selling. There is also the new development of global direct marketing, emerging from the old direct mail campaigns, and, of course, the "tried and true" international trade fairs where prospective buyers and sellers get together to check out new products and establish ties. It is the purpose of this chapter to discuss these various promotional tools and give the global marketer a sense of where they can be most useful.

The chapter will start by discussing global *sales promotion*, covering in-store promotions, events and sponsorship, and cross-marketing. Then the discussion will shift to *publicity*, recently emerging strongly in global marketing communications, and global *public relations*. The role of international *trade fairs* will be dealt with briefly before discussing *direct marketing*, a tool enabling even the smallest firm to go global. The last part of the chapter will focus on *personal selling* and the problems and opportunities in a global sales effort. Since its emergence is so recent, the Internet and its promise will be dealt with in Chapter 18, "The Future of Global Marketing."

GLOBAL SALES PROMOTION

Sales promotion involves a variety of activities, ranging from point-of-purchase displays and trade promotions to Sunday newspaper coupons and the sponsorship of symphony orchestras and athletic events such as the Olympics, soccer's World Cup, and major tennis tournaments.

In-Store and Trade Promotions

In-store or point-of-purchase (p-o-p) **promotions** refer to promotional activities inside the store; trade promotions are targeted at channel intermediaries ("the trade"). Both are important in the U.S. market and are becoming more important in many other markets as well.

Typically, in-store sales promotion is a much more localized activity than advertising, which uses global media such as cable television and international magazines. Sales promotion needs to be localized because its use is often more rigidly regulated than advertising. Cents-off coupons, free samples, and two-for-one offers can be prohibited in some countries where regulation is aimed at ensuring orderly markets and steady margins for local retailers. Premiums, gifts, and competitions are sometimes allowed but with major restrictions. As Exhibit 16.1 shows, outright prohibition is unusual, but most countries impose limits on what can be done. These restrictions vary

EXHIBIT 16.1 Regulations Regarding Premiums, Gifts, and Competitions in Selected Countries

Country	No restrictions or Category	Authorized with major minor ones	General ban with important restrictions	Almost total exceptions	prohibition
Australia	Premiums	X			
	Gifts	X			
	Competitions		X		
Austria	Premiums				X
	Gifts		X		
	Competitions		X		
Canada	Premiums	X			
	Gifts	X			
	Competitions		X		
Denmark	Premiums			X	
	Gifts		X		
	Competitions			X	
France	Premiums	X			
	Gifts	X			
	Competitions	X			
Germany	Premiums				X
	Gifts		X		
	Competitions		X		
Hong Kong	Premiums	X			
	Gifts	X			
	Competitions	X			
Japan	Premiums		X		
	Gifts		X		
	Competitions		X		
Korea	Premiums		X		
	Gifts		X		
	Competitions		X		
United Kingdom	Premiums	X			
	Gifts	X			
	Competitions		X		
United States	Premiums	X			
	Gifts	X			
	Competitions	X			
Venezuela	Premiums		X		
	Gifts		X		
	Competitions		X		

Source: Jean J. Boddewyn, *Premiums, Gifts, and Competitions*, New York: (International Advertising Association, 1988). © 1988 International Advertising Association.

between countries. In France, for example, a gift can't be worth more than 4 percent of the retail value of the product. In Germany, requiring proof of purchase for participation in a competition is illegal.[1]

Apart from constraining regulations in many countries, several other factors influence the effectiveness of in-store promotions:

COOPERATION FROM THE TRADE   In-store promotions to the consumer need to be supported by trade promotions, that is, promotions to channel intermediaries. The aim of in-store promotion is to "move product," and retailers and upstream wholesalers need to be induced to cooperate and increase the product flow. This is usually done through trade discounts, cooperative advertising, and sales support. If the trade is not compensated, middlemen may not cooperate. For example, A. C. Nielsen tried to introduce cents-off coupons in Chile, but the nation's supermarket union opposed the project and asked its members not to accept them.

ATTITUDES TOWARD COUPONS   The retailers need to handle promotions such as coupons professionally and not embarrass the consumers, often difficult in countries with a history of producers dominating the customers.

LIMITED CAPABILITY   Since distribution infrastructure is often different between countries, some promotions may simply not be feasible. Procter and Gamble tried to introduce its Cheer detergent in Japan using the type of trade promotion employed in the United States, including coupons, cents off, and trade discounts. The stores in Japan, however, were too small to handle the necessary volume and quickly ran out of stock. Consumers were disappointed, retailers were frustrated, and the introductory campaign was a failure.

PRESOLD CUSTOMERS   In-store promotions work best when the consumer expects to make choices in the store. In some cases the choice is already made before entering the store: Preselling a product through advertising or newspaper coupons, for example, often means that no in-store choice is necessary. Brand loyalty has the same effect. But when channels are dominated by manufacturers (as used to be the case in Japan), stores may feature only one brand and the store choice dictates which brand will be bought.

Trade promotions have their own problems. When General Electric broke into the air-conditioning market in Japan, the company offered overseas trips to outstanding dealers and a free color TV set to purchasers of high-end models. The successful campaign drew complaints from the trade association, and new rules to limit promotions were approved by the Japanese Fair Trade Commission. A limit was set on the size of the premium that could be offered, and no overseas trips were allowed as dealer incentives for any home appliances.[2]

Calculating the cost of a promotion relative to its revenue-raising potential is not always easy. It involves not only the actual cost of the promotional material and the accompanying marketing communications as well as a forecast of anticipated sales but also an estimate of the amount of sales that would have been made without the promotion. Simple mistakes can ruin the projections. One British firm created a very successful promotion by offering free airline tickets to buyers of its home appliances. However, the firm neglected to eliminate some longer routes from the offer and found that most customers opted for an expensive trip from London to New York. Once the losses started to mount, the promotion had to be broken off, leading to legal entanglement and the promotional manager losing his job.

Sponsorships

With the advent of global media the possibilities for global **sponsorships** are opening up. Sponsoring a World Cup match by plastering the brand name on the bleachers and

The French national soccer team celebrating after an early round World Cup victory. The 1998 event was notable for its increased size (32 teams) and first-time winner (host France). The cumulative television viewership of the four-week event was estimated at close to 50 billion. With relative newcomers (and large markets) Japan and the United States both qualifying, companies sponsoring the event got a lot of valuable exposure. Allsport.

piggybacking on the television broadcasts has helped companies such as Hitachi, Kodak, Siemens, and Volvo establish a strong identity in the global marketplace.[3] More direct spending involves sponsoring tennis tournaments (Volvo, Virginia Slims), Formula One race cars (Coca-Cola, Marlboro), single-man treks to the South Pole (Nordic track), and athletic team wear (Nike, Reebok). The Olympic sponsorship, which reached new heights in Los Angeles in 1984, has spilled over into promotional sponsorship of Russian hockey players (Visa) and Italian basketball teams (Sony). It is somewhat unsettling to see newspaper pictures of Juergen Koehler, the all-German national player from Koeln AS, and find Toshiba, the name of the Japanese electronics company, on his jersey. Global promotion knows no boundaries.

The global reach of sporting events, which has created possibilities for products to become associated with globally recognized sports figures, has made the sports figures rich in addition to famous. Michael Jordan, the basketball player, receives more money from his endorsements than from his playing. Andre Agassi, the tennis player, is an effective spokesperson for Reebok sports gear and Canon cameras and has also put his name on a line of products. These, however, need to be marketed well and can't stretch too far: Tennis star Bjorn Borg's adventure in personal hygiene products and leisure wear was not successful, for example.

The use of well-known personalities has its downside. The Pepsi-Cola company used Michael Jackson as a global spokesman until his legal troubles started. Luciano Pavarotti was used by the American Express card until his fee became too high. O. J. Simpson, Magic Johnson, and Bo Jackson are three athletes whose subsequent problems limited their usefulness, to the despair of sponsors like Hertz and Nike.

The 1995 track and field world championships in Gothenburg, Sweden, represented another step in the increasing promotional role of athletic events. For a period of two weeks the Swedish organizers created a number of exhibition booths, restaurants, and well-equipped business offices in a city block across the street from the main entrance to the stadium. For a fee, businesses could rent a space and invite existing customers, potential prospects, or employees for business entertainment as well as serious negotiations, interspersed with attendance at the events and meals in the restaurants. The available spaces were quickly snapped up, mostly by European firms. The Mercedes-Benz company entertained a number of its salespeople and their spouses during a two-day visit.[4]

Cross-Marketing

As markets have globalized and regulations have been harmonized, promotion has become a very active area of competition. The varied promotional tactics in the globally successful American entertainment industry are illustrative. The **cross-marketing** of related products from successful events and stars represents one of many tactics. There is a big global business in selling products associated with Elvis Presley, James Dean, various successful films (*Beauty and the Beast, Forrest Gump*), and TV shows ("Star Trek," "Sesame Street"). It is possible to buy T-shirts, lunch boxes, pencils, hats, bags, puzzles, music tapes, and a CD-ROM game featuring Disney's film *The Lion King*.[5] The leveraging of a strong brand name by product-line extension has been done for a long time by luxury brands such as Dunhill, Gucci, and Burberry. Other brands are getting into the act, combining global advertising to sustain the brand name with product-line extensions that make it economically feasible to open separate boutiques.

The practice of using popular success for promotion has spilled over into media advertising and has been adopted by non-U.S. companies. Honda, the Japanese auto firm, introduced its new minivan Odyssey using characters based on the work of Keith Haring, the New York artist—and sold more units than forecast despite a premium price.[6] Japan Air Lines, a most staid organization, has painted two of its 747s used on the Hawaii route in bright and irregular patches of color. The sky is the limit—if regulation opens up.

PUBLICITY

Publicity, the publishing of news about the company and its products, is an increasingly important part of global companies' promotion function.

"Good News . . ."

Publicity is more credible than paid advertising, and since a global expansion effort is inherently more newsworthy than expansion at home, global companies often get featured in news media. The press coverage can even be orchestrated by the firm as we saw in the opening vignette about Windows 95. Many of the products and services involved represent high technology, of importance for security reasons or for national competitiveness, which also enhances potential reader interest. And managing publicity—including coordination with the public relations function—is important when foreign direct investments or trade barriers become news, as they often do.

Publicity has the obvious advantage that there is no need to pay for air time or press coverage. But it is not always without cost. Publicity requires some management and can be labor-intensive. Media contacts need to be created, nurtured, and maintained. Press coverage of the opening of a plant or warehouse in a new market involves travel, food, and sometimes lodging for journalists. The preparation of **press releases,** copy written for immediate news publication, requires skill, especially when the information is about a technical breakthrough. Making top managers available for personal interviews takes their time and diverts their attention. Still, the payoff in goodwill and free advertising can be considerable and the investment well worth it (see box, "Total Communication Inc.").

" . . . and Bad News"

Even "negative" publicity can have its rewards since it serves to keep the brand name in the public eye. Benetton, the Italian apparel maker, is one example. Through its famous (or infamous depending on one's views) realistic TV commercials and large full-page magazine ads of a man dying from AIDS, a priest kissing a nun, an automobile ablaze after a car bomb, and a boatload of refugees without copy but with the brand logo displayed after the commercial or below the picture, Benetton has garnered plenty

GETTING THE *Picture*

Total Communication Inc.

IN THE WORLD of high technology, global publicity counts as a major promotional medium. The introduction of the Macintosh personal computer was accompanied by a "full-court" media blitz with Apple press conferences, customer contests, educational "giveaways," appearances of software producers (Microsoft, Lotus) giving assurances of program designs, and of course personal interviews with *Time*'s "Man of the Year," Steve Jobs, Apple's chairman. The international press duly reported on the American developments, in fact preparing an entry mat for Apple into many European and Asian countries.

High-tech companies often create news as a matter of course in their daily business, and the press is a ready channel to tell the world about it. The release of a new product occasions a press conference, where pictures, models, technical summaries, and prototypes are available for publicity purposes. The hoopla and excitement are orchestrated to create an event and atmosphere worthy of Hollywood—and of news coverage. Charismatic business leaders are company assets, and the worldwide media help give well-recognized public persona a global impact.

Consulting firms help companies manage this important function. The large PR firms, such as Hill & Knowl-ton in the United States, have global reach, following their customers around the world. Smaller companies that specialize in certain countries and industries offer unique services.

San Francisco–based Autodesk, which sells LAN software for networked PCs, uses smaller publicity consultants extensively in its global markets in addition to the large global media relations firms. By releasing newsworthy items about its products, the company aims to create curiosity among potential customers. Using local consultants, the company is able to draw on people with intimate ties to local journalists who can adapt the global press releases to the needs of the local media. Through frequent travels and personal appearances at conferences and industry seminars, the president of Autodesk makes herself available for local interviews.

Sources: Smith, 1994; *New York Times*, June 14, 1994; Jan Segerfeldt, personal communication.
http://www.apple.com/
http://www.microsoft.com
http://www.lotus.com/
http://www.hillandknowlton.com/
http://www.autodesk.com/

of publicity, mainly negative. The ads seem to be in bad taste, and Benetton has been accused of exploiting human suffering to sell its products. In Germany, irate store owners refused to stock Benetton products unless the advertisements were withdrawn, claiming that the ads kept customers away. But the company argues that it is doing a positive thing, and to help prove it, it has opened a new store in war-torn Sarajevo.[7]

Events

Companies also help arrange **events** at which their brands can be promoted through unpaid-for publicity. An extreme example of creating an "event" associated with a brand was the launch of Microsoft's Windows 95 computer operating system as described at the beginning of this chapter. Similar strategies, although perhaps less extravagant, are used by other companies. The Swiss watchmaker Swatch relies extensively on sponsorship of special events. The company has a policy of spending a major share of its promotional budget on special events promotion. Exhibit 16.2 shows the range of the typical events sponsored by the company. As can be seen, some events, such as the large Swatch on a Frankfurt building, are simply "happenings" created to draw attention to Swatch and generate free publicity for the brand. The company organizes "launch parties" in various countries, such as the one in Barcelona in November 1985, when a new collection of Swatches is introduced. The company has positioned its watches as fashion products, and its product policy is to keep the Swatch designs fresh by introducing new styles twice a year, in the spring and in the fall.[8]

Exhibit 16.2 Major Special Events Organized or Sponsored by Swatch

Date	Country	Event
March 1984	Germany	13-ton giant Swatch on Commerzbank building, Frankfurt
April 1984	France	"Urban Sax" saxophonist group at the "Eldorado" theater in Paris to celebrate launch, first *Swatch* Magazine
August 1984	USA	Ivan Lendl U.S. Tennis Open
September 1984	USA	World Breakdancing Championship: "The Roxy" New York
September 1984	France	First street art painting show with the French artists "Les Fréres Ripoulin," "Espace Cardin" theater, Paris
November 1984	USA	The Fat Boys music sponsorship, "Private Eyes," New York, to introduce "Granita di Frutta" to the trade
Oct 84–Jan 85	USA	New York City Fresh Festival: breakdancing, rapping, graffiti artists
January 1985	USA	World Freestyle Invitational/Celebrity Classic, Breckenridge, Colorado
March 1985	France	IRCAM "copy art" show, Paris; limited education (119) Kiki Picasso design watches; second *Swatch* Magazine
Spring 1985	USA	Hi-fly freestyle windsurfing team sponsorship
May 1985	England	Second street art painting show, Covent Garden, London, with "Les Fréres Ripoulin" and English street artists
June 1985	Switzerland	Art fair in Basel; third street art painting show with 50 European artists
Summer 1985	Sweden	Oestersjö Rallyt (Segel-Rallye)
September 1985	France	Cinema festival, Pompidou Center, Paris with Kurosawa's film, *Ran*; Mini City Magazine
September 1985	France	"Le Défilé": Jean-Paul Gaultier & Régine Chopinot fashion/dance show, "Pavillon Baltard," Paris
September 1985	England	Andrew Logan's Alternative Miss World, London
October 1985	Belgium	"Mode et Anti-Mode" fashion show, Brussels
Fall 1985	USA	Thompson Twins concert tour sponsorship
November 1985	Spain	Swatch launch party, the "Cirque," Barcelona

Source: Pinson and Kimball, 1987. Copyright © 1987 INSEAD-CEDEP, Fontainebleau, France. Reproduced with the permission of INSEAD-CEDEP.

Product Placement

The last few years have seen an increase in the use of **product placement** for promotional purposes. Product placement refers to the use of branded products in films and television. For example, in the movie *ET: The Extraterrestrial*, an alien creature was seen eating "Reese's Pieces" a peanut-flavored candy; Sales of the product subsequently increased by 70 percent. Sales of Ray-ban Wayfarer sunglasses tripled after Tom Cruise wore them in the movie *Risky Business*.[9] The very successful introduction of BMW's new roadster, the Z3, was credited partly to its use by James Bond in the *GoldenEye* movie.

Product placement involves contracting with producers about using the branded product as a natural prop in the film or TV program. In many cases the product is offered free, and no guarantees about its use are made by the producers. Partly because of this, the impact can be negative as well as positive. A Mercedes car used as a prop in one film was set on fire, not a particularly successful product placement.

The use of product placement has been stimulated largely by the global success of American entertainment vehicles, ensuring wide exposure across the world. Nike, the athletic shoe maker has managed to place its swoosh logo on many true and "wannabe" athletes around the world, resulting in a lot of almost free publicity. But again the results can veer out of control, and have, especially as the financial crises have raised anti-American sentiments in various countries. When a 1997 demonstrator in Mexico City burned the American flag, the photograph transmitted over the news wires showed him in a Nike cap. The stone-throwing Korean rebel in a 1998 wire photo similarly sported the Nike swoosh in big print on his bloodied T-shirt. And when the 39 members of the Heaven's Gate religious cult in southern California committed joint suicide in March 1997, they were equipped with new Nike shoes "for the life beyond." This is more like product *mis*placement—and Nike sales have predictably dipped, as we saw in the opening vignette to Chapter 2.

GLOBAL PUBLIC RELATIONS

Similar to publicity, **global public relations** is a form of indirect promotion of products and services that focuses on creating goodwill toward the corporation as a whole. The corporate communications staff at headquarters and its counterpart in the various host countries serve as promoters of the corporation to various stakeholders interested in the company's foreign expansion. These stakeholders can include a wide variety of groups:

Stockholders

Employees

Customers

Distributors

Suppliers

Financial community

Media

Activist groups

General public

Government

These groups can lay some legitimate claim on a company to conduct itself ethically and to operate with a certain level of transparency in accordance with the free market system. However, because of the many countries in which a global company is likely to do business, ethical standards and customary business secrecy can vary considerably. This easily creates conflicts between host country stakeholders' claims and headquarters' policy guidelines. One job of the public relations staff is to make sure that such potential conflicts do not erupt and, when they do, to carry out "damage control."

Conflicts typically arise when a firm enters a new country by acquiring a local company or by investing in manufacturing. When American companies such as Ford, GM, IBM, Xerox, Honeywell, and General Electric became big investors in Europe in the 1950s and 60s, Europeans became alarmed by the "American challenge."[10] As Japanese companies like Nissan (trucks), Mitsubishi (real estate), Matsushita (electronics), and Honda (automobiles) established presence in the United States by large investments, many Americans voiced misgivings.[11] Even though the economic justifications of these and other FDI entries are usually sound, and the host countries also benefit, the companies' PR departments have to work hard to establish the "good local citizen" image among stakeholders such as the general public. This involves compiling statistics about the number of natives employed, the local content of the products, and the tax contribution made to the local municipality—and publicizing this information.

From the global marketing perspective, the critical issue is whether alarm or misgivings about corporate strategy spill over into a negative brand evaluation and lower sales. According to company research, the negative evaluation against Japanese investments in the United States did lead to some temporary loss of American market share for Honda in the early 1990s.

Effective **damage control,** actions taken to limit the spillover into a negative public opinion, requires both public relations and timing. When a Volvo TV commercial in the United States was found deceptive because the car used in a demonstration of

Nestlé and Babies: Who Was Right?

THE LARGE SWISS MULTINATIONAL Nestlé is a major global company in the food industry. Its Nestlé instant tea, Nescafe coffee, Libby's juices, and Carnation milk products are household names all over the world.

The company got its baptism in global PR by fire in the latter half of the 1970s. Having developed a superior infant formula that could effectively supplant a breastfeeding mother, the company saw great potential among malnourished Third World children. Distributing the formula through clinics and wet-nurses, the company was able to tap into the market effectively. There was only one problem. Some mothers, partly to offset the relatively high cost of the formula, took to diluting it with water. As a consequence, many babies on formula did not get the requisite nourishment, and in a few cases, the water used for the dilution was infected and there were some deaths.

Through various sources, activist groups in Europe and North America soon learned about the situation. As initial appeals to the company in Vevy, Switzerland, were rebuffed, the groups started a massive international campaign against Nestlé and its products.

Through press conferences and media releases as well as in direct meetings with activist leaders, Nestlé argued that withdrawing a beneficial product would do more harm than good. The company undertook scientific research projects designed to establish the superiority of the product against weak mothers' milk and projected the expected death rates should the product be withdrawn.

In the end, the activists were fought off and the company prevailed, succeeding in maintaining its product in the Third World markets and reducing the damage to its brands. But the process, which extended for several years, was a lesson for the company and should be a lesson for other global firms as well. Ethical conduct and corporate standing that might seem spotless and self-evident at home need to be explained, justified, and defended actively in other places. And in all cases, flexibility and respect for local norms are a must.

Sources: Shirk, 1991; C. B. Malone and N. Harrison, "Nestlé Alimentana S.A.—Infant Formula," Harvard Business School, case no. 9-580-118.
http://www.nestle.com

Volvo's body integrity was reinforced, the company first publicly admitted the mistake, retracted the advertising, and then moved to dismiss the advertising agency.[12] The German automaker Audi, by contrast, stood firm in defending its Audi 4000 model design against repeated accusations of malfunctioning. Several accidents had happened because drivers mistakenly (as the courts found) stepped on the gas pedal instead of the brakes. The Audi engineers won their court case, but consumer PR damage was not contained, and Audi market share slipped badly.

A recent example of how a company can mishandle public relations was the problem Intel had with its Pentium chip at the end of 1994. At first belittling the importance of the flaw, which led to miscalculated long divisions, the company rallied after a week and offered apologies to the public, explanations to media, and free replacements to users.[13] This quick about-face in a relatively straightforward case can be contrasted with the much more complicated PR problem of Nestlé's infant formula in the Third World (see box, "Nestlé and Babies").

INTERNATIONAL TRADE FAIRS

As we saw in Chapter 5, participation in **international trade fairs** is a way of identifying potential distributors in a new local market. But the 1,500 or so international trade fairs that take place in over 70 countries each year also serve other purposes. Whether at the traditional Fotokina photo show in Cologne, Germany; or the famous Hannover fair, also in Germany, "largest in the world" with its 5,000 or so major exhibitors; or the annual New England Auto Show in Boston; or the Comdex computer fair in Las Vegas; or any of the other large events, the fairs' attraction is the chance to introduce a company's latest products and models, to discover industry trends, and to spot new competitive developments. This holds true whether the fair is open to the general public, quite common in the United States, or attendance is limited to industry members, the more common European approach.

For the global marketer, fairs are an excellent promotional avenue. Participation enhances and sustains visibility and local presence. The Comdex computer fair, for example, is the major avenue through which new hardware and software companies get known and where established players such as Microsoft, Novell, and Lotus show their new products. The prestige of Comdex has grown to the point where 90 percent of the exhibition space is rented one year in advance, and the event returns a sizable profit to the organizers. In 1995, the fair was sold to a Japanese investor, Masayoshi Son, for $800 million. Mr. Son plans to expand the fair by holding Comdex shows in Asia and Europe in addition to the traditional Las Vegas location.[14]

DIRECT MARKETING

Direct marketing refers to sales from the producer directly to the ultimate consumer, bypassing the channel middlemen. More formally, direct marketing is an interactive system that uses one or more advertising media to generate a measurable response (usually an order) from a customer. Direct marketing is not so much a promotional tool as a new distribution channel, but it grew out of direct mail, which is a traditional advertising medium. The traditional direct mail promotions of various products often offered "direct response" options, including requests for more information, redeemable cents-off coupons, and participation in contests and lottery drawings. It was only a small step to a completed sale, and especially since credit cards became common, direct mail has become an important sales and promotion channel.

The standard direct marketing medium is **mail order,** with catalogs and sales offers sent directly to individual households, which then order via mail. The names and addresses are drawn from various lists—in the beginning often from subscription lists of newspapers and magazines but today more often from commercial data banks that can screen for key words and develop lists of qualified prospects. In recent years **telemarketing,** selling via the telephone, has grown fast in the United States, and so has **direct response television** (DRTV), where TV commercials will list telephone numbers to let viewers call for purchases. With the growing presence of the World Wide Web, direct marketing has become a very important channel.

Direct marketing is growing rapidly because it is fast, safe, convenient, low-cost—and eliminates the job of going to the store. Express mail delivery means that most goods can arrive within one or two days. Return privileges are generous. Payment can be made by simply giving a credit card number. The liability for improper use of a card number is limited. Toll-free 800 numbers make it possible to use the telephone free of charge.

Can direct marketing be globalized? The answer, despite the need for fast delivery and efficient communications, is an emphatic "Yes, absolutely!" First of all, the postal systems of many countries, despite otherwise weak infrastructures, seem to function quite well. Second, countries' telephone systems are growing increasingly reliable and have in many cases penetrated into remote rural areas. This has not escaped the attention of international long-distance carriers. AT&T International Service 800 S.A. now offers toll-free dialing to more than 50 countries on five continents. Third, as we saw in Chapter 12, credit cards have gone global, and people pay by American Express, MasterCard, or Visa all over the world. Finally, as we saw in Chapter 14, the express carriers have globalized their operations and now reach most places on the globe.

Because of advances in communications technology, the number of conversations handled by the transatlantic cable between Europe and North America has increased from 138 per hour in 1966 to over 100 million per hour in 1994. The volume will have tripled by the year 2000.[15] The increase in coverage of global communications has

Picture

In Global Direct Marketing, Small Is Beautiful

TO GET A GRIP on how global direct marketing works, have a look at Acton Ltd. for an object lesson. A typical company in global direct marketing, Acton is a small (48 employees) direct marketer in the publishing and financial services industries. The firm is located in Lincoln, Nebraska, in the heart of Buffalo Bill and Wild Bill Hickok country.

Acton's direct marketing operation started by marketing U.S. client banks' checking accounts and related services across the country and gradually developed or acquired address lists of prospects and leads at home and overseas. One of the lists it has exclusive rights to includes 14 million households in Japan, developed from client contacts over a few years. The address files are digitalized and can be transferred back and forth on the Internet. For any particular direct marketing campaign, the company will work with a local agent who is part of Acton's emerging global network.

About 70 percent of the company's clients are large banks on the East and West Coasts of the United States that are primarily interested in expanding their credit card customer bases overseas. Says Cheri Pettet, vice president of international sales: "Our marketing programs for credit cards . . . work so well we can almost guarantee the client will gain customers."

Sources: Kelly, 1994; Egol, 1994a.
http://www.acton.com/

meant not only that customers almost everywhere can be reached but that the marketer can be located in any small place on the map, not needing a major metropolitan location for its headquarters or a large staff (see box, "In Global Direct Marketing, Small Is Beautiful").

Regional Developments

Direct marketing opportunities in mail order have been boosted by the recent privatization of many postal services around the world. Direct mail is one of their top cash-generating "products." In Germany, for example, newly privatized Die Deutsche Post A. G., or "Bundespost," is moving quickly to become a major international player, with the rich U.S. market as a key target. The new executive team at the top of Bundespost—mostly from private business—has charged a wholly owned subsidiary with the task of easing entry into the German market for prospective U.S. companies.[16] The subsidiary updates address lists, develops new lists working with Bertelsmann (the world's largest media company), and sells computer software to help with presorting mail and bulk-mail preparations. The Bundespost offers a 25 percent discount on bulk mailing, provided the presorting corresponds to official regulations. The postal subsidiary even offers assistance with shipments to 14 other European countries. A shipment to France, for example, can be sent via air to Frankfurt and loaded there—without time-consuming inspection—onto a truck for Strasbourg on the French border, where it is inserted into the French mail stream. Packages can reach Paris or Marseilles within a day or two, depending on the shipper's choice, one day being more expensive.

Latin America is another area where the direct marketing possibilities are opening up as a result of improved infrastructure.[17] The telecommunications system in Chile is said to be world-class. The Brazilian postal service is, perhaps surprisingly, famous for its service and efficiency. Cable TV has excellent penetration in Argentina with more than 50 channels available to most subscribers. Data banks with address lists are being developed at a rapid pace, often with technology transferred from U.S. database companies in alliances with local software firms.

Japan with its high per capita income, well-developed post and telecommunications, and complex distribution system has become a natural target for direct marketers. Foreign catalog sales are booming. The U.S. Department of Commerce has

G E T T I N G   T H E   *Picture*

Asia: Direct Marketing Requires Smarts

MANY COUNTRIES in the then booming Asian economy offered good potential for direct marketers in the mid-1990s, even though China was—and remains—"problematic." But to get the most out of the effort, the marketer had to be (and still has to be) smart, according to James Thornton, managing director of Mailing Lists Asia. He recommends a two-step entry strategy, first testing multinational lists that include several countries to find out which markets are responsive to your offers. Only after that determination has been made does he recommend step two, which involves going after a specific local market. For example, he suggests skipping Hong Kong,

Singapore, and Malaysia if the offer involves merchandise rather than publications. In Singapore and Hong Kong, especially, financial offers and self-improvement books and courses seem to work well, while catalogs with merchandise will usually fail. By contrast, consumers and businesspeople in Indonesia and Thailand seem to be responsive to all products regardless of type or country of origin. And as a bonus for global direct marketers, many people in the region are English-speaking or at least readers of English.

Sources: Egol, 1994b; "Thais and Indonesians," 1995.

even organized a unit that offers lists of catalogs to Japanese consumers in three locations: Tokyo, Osaka, and Sapporo. Consumers can browse through the list and then pay about $5 for any one catalog they are interested in. Catalog houses pay the Commerce Department $600 to participate in the program. Japanese language information about ordering, payment, and return policies is available. Credit card orders can be faxed to the companies the same day they are filled out by Japanese customers, and they usually receive their packages within a few days, depending on the delivery option chosen.

About 200 American companies participate in this program, ranging from jewelry to candy to sporting goods catalog houses. For many of them, this is a first-time entry into the Japanese market, and many plan to invest more, perhaps in a Japanese-language catalog, if sales take off.[18]

Japan is not the only Asian country with promise. Even though China so far seems to offer less opportunity because of a lack of infrastructure and few customer lists, other countries show potential (see box, "Asia").

Global Strategy

Although direct marketing is relatively new, early experiences suggest that there are basically three alternative ways of implementing a global strategy.[19]

- *"Do it yourself."* The most obvious method is the company developing the market and the necessary contacts on its own. This involves time, travel, and expense. At some point when volume justifies it, it also involves developing a relationship with a local company to handle "fulfillment," that is, dealing with customs as necessary, some delivery, lost goods, and other incidental services. This is a labor-intensive and costly method for a small company, with a typical overseas business trip lasting two to three weeks and costing easily $5,000.

- *Marketing intermediary.* A second way to go is to turn the product over to a direct marketing company specializing in international marketing and to let it act as a general contractor (akin to an export management company). The intermediary will be responsible for establishing infrastructure and setting up local representatives to handle inventory as needed, order taking, and fulfillment. These intermediaries often work through a global network of local entrepreneurs. Going this route, the company will need to establish a consistent global pricing structure, to prohibit reexporting, yet offer the intermediary sufficient margin to realize a profit.

- *Strategic alliance.* A third option is to develop a strategic alliance with a direct marketing company in the local market. Such a company will have better knowledge of the local market and may be able to help with neighboring country markets. It will also have the required infrastructure capabilities in place.

To date, the second option seems to be the one chosen most often by smaller companies. It enables the direct marketer to get into foreign markets quickly and without major expense. It is the natural alternative when the company is starting out and learning how global direct marketing works. Established catalog houses, such as L. L. Bean and Eddie Bauer, seem to prefer the first option since it offers more control over the local marketing effort. Technology-based companies also seem to favor this option. Sun Microsystems (office computer systems) has created its own direct marketing division in Europe, Sun Express, which currently mails 60,000 quarterly catalogs in three languages along with direct mail, places direct response ad space and fax ads, and participates in local trade shows. Telephone response filters directly to the Netherlands, but callers dial a local number. Orders are fulfilled from the United States usually within three days.[20]

The three options are likely to vary in attractiveness across local markets, and most companies find it useful to examine all three alternatives for any one market. In Europe, a relatively difficult direct marketing region because of fragmentation of languages and cultures, alliances tend to be common. One American publisher tackled the U.K. market by partnering with Direct Marketing Services, a British firm, which adapted the American promotional material and address list characteristics to those in Britain with good success.

Direct marketing is emerging as a new global option for many companies. It is an option capitalizing directly on the technological advances in global communications and transportation during the last two decades, opening up global opportunities for even the smallest companies.

PROMOTIONAL RESEARCH

The role of advertising in the acceptance of a product or brand and the effectiveness of various sales promotion techniques are important factors to ascertain in local markets. Neither is easy without primary research, but a crude measure may be gotten by examining the advertising-to-sales ratios of major competitors and the level of in-store promotional activity. Reliable media data are often difficult to get, and the spending levels can't be easily assessed with certainty, but rough guesstimates of the magnitudes can usually be derived from middlemen and trade experts. It is important to develop a sense of the amount of spending needed to break into the market successfully so that the appropriate funds can be requested from headquarters.

Since market communications play an important role in any local marketing effort, the manager needs to thoroughly investigate the options available. Even in emerging and developing markets, TV and magazine advertising can be very influential in shaping customer evaluations. Research on copy and visuals is crucial in making sure to avoid the many pitfalls associated with foreign languages and cultures and especially translations from home country materials.

Major faux pas can usually be avoided by having local staff in the subsidiary and in the local agency review any proposed communication, but more careful testing of campaigns is always warranted. Focus groups with potential customers, pretesting of alternative storyboards, and follow-up with recall scores and attitude surveys are all useful tools regardless of the level of market development. Remember that people in poor countries are also looking for emotional satisfaction, and image-related factors such as choice of spokesperson and background music can have a powerful differential impact that needs to be tested.

GLOBAL PERSONAL SELLING

As we saw in Chapter 3, culture affects the "people skills" of the global marketer. Because of the importance of personal factors in selling, it is not surprising to find that good **salesmanship** varies across countries. Personal selling is usually the least global of all the marketing activities. As Percy Barnevik of ABB puts it: "When you are selling in Germany, your salesmen have to be German."[21]

Managing a Sales Force

When the company is simply an exporter using independent distributors, management of the **sales force** is not an issue. However, when more control over local marketing is desired, the local company agent needs to work with the distributor's salespeople, help train them, and offer incentives to push the company's products. When the company takes over distribution in the country, it will usually end up establishing its own sales force.

Establishing the company's own sales force in a foreign country requires faith in the market and considerable resources. But some companies, especially those for which the selling function is a key success factor, have decided to take the plunge and have done it successfully. As we've mentioned, firms such as Avon and Mary Kay (cosmetics), Amway (miscellaneous products), and Electrolux (vacuum cleaners) have managed to create viable direct sales forces in various countries by following the selling practices back home. This has typically meant that the sales force has been started from scratch, with the company hiring people whom it can train from the beginning.

In the more general case, where personal selling is used primarily to sell to middlemen and large customers, the practice is often to hire some of the people who used to work for the distributor in order to avoid high start-up costs as well as interruptions in service. When Microsoft decided to open its own sales subsidiary in Japan, the people who previously had worked at ASCII, its distributor, were given the chance to interview for positions in the new outfit. Since switching jobs in Japan is a sensitive matter, following Japanese tradition, these interviews were kept secret so as not to jeopardize the person's status in his or her current position.

The major question facing the manager trying to coordinate the global sales effort is the transferability of the selling strategies and techniques used in the home market. Interviews with multinational managers and reviews of published literature have shown that there are basically four factors that affect transferability:[22]

1. *Geographic and physical dimensions.* The geographical spread of a country, its climate and terrain, as well as roadways and transportation conditions are obvious factors in determining the size of the territories that can be economically covered by one salesperson and the expense of individual calls. In cases such as rural India, for example, a single salesperson will rarely be able to cover more than a village area. Advanced techniques for optimizing territorial limits need considerable adaptation to provide guidance in such countries.

2. *Degree of market development.* In countries where customers are sophisticated and demanding, with high potential, in-depth training and specialization of the sales force are both necessary and possible. By contrast, where the life cycle is at an early stage, customers are less knowledgeable and require more information and education. Products tend to be less advanced, and the salesperson has to be more broadly trained and sell a wider product line. In the EDP industry, for example, Burroughs compresses its sales territories in smaller markets and each salesperson carries a broader line and assumes servicing tasks in addition to sales tasks.

3. *Differing regulatory environments.* In some countries where fringe benefits—such as medical coverage, severance pay, and pension funding—may be high, the cost for a salesperson will escalate. Since such benefits are usually accompanied by a high tax rate

Much of a salesperson's activities fall under the rubric of 'relationship marketing.' Here Nestlé salespeople from the Thailand subsidiary explain new products and help check the stocking levels for retailers in Bangkok. Peter Charlesworth/SABA.

on individuals, offering high commission rates to a salesperson may be ineffective in comparison with special gifts, a free car, or housing, all of which offer opportunities for tax avoidance.

4. *Differing human relations.* In many societies the job of a salesperson is looked down on as relatively unworthy. Hierarchical cultures such as Hindu India, Muslim Iran, and the Shinto culture in Japan tend historically to be aristocratic, favoring military castes, the priesthood, and feudal landowners over businesspeople or "merchants." Even in more democratic societies there may be some remnant of this pattern, and there is often a subtle ranking that puts a salesperson below engineers and the professions. The effect is to make it difficult to attract the best people to a sales job, and for those who accept the challenge it is often difficult to remove a certain aura of defensiveness in them that can mar the sales presentation. Commissions, contests, and bonuses are less effective since they make obvious the extrinsic monetary motivation behind salespeople's behavior. Research shows, for example, that in Thailand straight salary is considered more "respectable" than commission-based remuneration.[23]

These fundamental factors affect sales force recruiting, hiring, training, compensation schemes, and territorial allocation. The global marketer also needs to understand more specifically what can be realistically expected from the salespeople in different countries. What constitutes good salesmanship?

Personal Salesmanship

Salesmanship is the art of making a sale to another person. There are a few key personal characteristics of good salesmanship. One is enthusiasm, another self-confidence, still another appearance. These and other related factors all refer to the **salesman as a person.**[24]

There is no doubt that appearance is a very important factor in international business dealings, perhaps more so than domestically. Since the business relationship crosses cultures, to use a person's appearance as a clue to his or her personality is much more common globally than at home where it is easier to "look through" the surface appearance. But the important features of a person's appearance are not the same everywhere: Even those features that are relevant are often given a different interpretation. Asian nationals tend to be much less preoccupied with "good looks" and more concerned about appropriate clothing for the occasion than Westerners, whose individualism is usually given much more play. Whereas wide, large shoes with thick soles (the much maligned "wingtips") might be viewed by Americans as conservatively masculine, the no less tall or large people of northern Europe regard such shoes as clumsy and in bad taste. There are naturally a great many such small differences of style (which might make a large difference to the business relationship), and the astute salesperson will learn in-depth about the host country's particular customs.

As for enthusiasm and self-confidence, these factors are always important abroad but tend to go over best in "hard sell" situations of the kind typically encountered in New York, Bombay, or Tel Aviv. To the extent that enthusiasm reflects an interest in showing one's company and product in a positive light, it is certainly an asset in most countries. But excited delivery, loud voice, and fast talking do not sit well in many cultures. The energy of enthusiasm needs to be carefully tempered in many cases so that it is not released at inopportune moments.

The same is valid for self-confidence, that great asset of Western individualists. In cultures where group decisions are the norm, the role of self-confidence is appropriately reduced. A knowledgeable individual possessing confidence can make his voice heard, but self-confidence is no necessary requirement for an influential presentation: The product and the company are what the individual has to sell, and the "self" should not get in the way.

Especially in high context cultures, there are other characteristics of the salesperson as an individual—quite distinct from the role as a spokesperson for the product and the firm—that are important in overseas markets. In many cultures the objectives of the business transaction go beyond the immediate business proposition. In such cultures, the relationship is so important that the "personal worth" of the salesperson becomes a much bigger issue than it is customarily in the American tradition.

This important point seems paradoxical at first. The salesperson and his or her self-confidence are unimportant since the individual only represents a company, but personality and "worth" are important at the same time. This needs to be explained.

Representing the Country

In American salesmanship books one is usually told that "the salesperson is the company." This means that the customer is presumably identifying the company with the individual—and that the two are indistinguishable. It is the latter part of the presumption that falters in many foreign markets. Yes, the person traveling abroad is, in a sense, the company. But to the customer in foreign markets he or she is so much more. Precisely because this salesperson is from another country, the individual implicitly becomes associated with many of the ideas, facts, stories, and images that the customer has of that country. To see why this is so—for Americans too—visualize a German salesman visiting a prospect in New York City as a representative of a company like Siemens, the electronics giant. Yes, he is at the moment the company to the American customer. But the latter sees in him much more: "How is the German mark?" "What will happen in the next election?" "I spent last June in Berlin visiting some of the places I saw in the War." Naturally the conversation turns to Germany. The salesman is not just representing Siemens, but to some extent all of Germany, in fact, possibly all of Europe. In this nonbusiness conversation the two persons end up showing much more of themselves as human beings than the standard "good salesmanship" text would suggest.

Imagine the conversation when the same American prospect receives a salesperson from an American competitor, say General Electric in Bridgeport, Connecticut. There may be less reason now to spend much time on incidental, nonbusiness matters, since they both possess approximately the same access to information about social, cultural, and political events and don't want to waste time.

The standard approach to preparing for a sales call by focusing on (1) the product, (2) the customer's needs, and (3) the competition should be augmented abroad by a wider definition of the "customer's needs." The "good salesperson" will have to become a "good individual" in a general sense. At the minimum, one needs to study up on those aspects of one's own country that might be of personal interest to the customer. More broadly, the person sent abroad should get in touch with some genuine interest in nonbusiness matters he or she has that could be of interest to the customer. In many countries such "human worth" needs to be established first before more serious, focused business discussions can take place.[25]

Once these discussions start, the salesperson then can calmly play down individual worth, repressing the self, as it were, in favor of presenting his or her company and product in the best light. The salesperson functions as the conduit through which the company wants to attract the new customer. As a conduit, the salesperson's only role is to transmit the necessary information and present the product as well as possible. He needs to leverage the company and the product, not sell himself! The biggest mistake for the individually oriented salesperson from the United States in some of these markets is to let enthusiasm and self-confidence place ego in the way of the company and the product.

The Western type of salesmanship, enthusiastic and confident individuals asserting themselves as the "face" of their companies, is successful in Western cultures, in particular the United States. The opposite type of salesperson—a simple conduit when it comes to business, an interesting human being outside of business—is more successful in Eastern cultures, in which individualism is subdued and the ultimate objectives of the business transaction are more than just economic.

The Presentation

The presentation made during a sales visit in domestic markets is typically viewed as consisting of five distinct stages:

> *Stage 1—Attention.* Get the customer to listen to you.
> *Stage 2—Interest.* Get the customer interested in what you have to say.
> *Stage 3—Desire.* Get the customer to desire what you are selling.
> *Stage 4—Conviction.* Get the buyer convinced that the offer is a good deal.
> *Stage 5—Action.* Get the customer's signature on the contract.

In global marketing these stages are in a superficial sense still valid, but their relative importance and the way an individual salesperson goes about moving the customer through them deviate considerably from the home market.

First of all, the attention and interest stages are often less critical when making sales calls abroad. The obvious investment in time and travel plus the "exotic" flavor of the visitor naturally arouses the curiosity of the prospect. The exception to this rule is the salesperson representing a country not too well known for the particular product sold, such as a Brazilian visitor to France selling loudspeakers, a new export product from Brazil. In general, however, the first two stages are easier to surmount in global markets.

By contrast, the next three stages are for the same reasons less easily traversed in global transactions. The distances involved, geographically and psychologically, and the consequent difficulties in establishing reliable supply and payment systems, not to mention future service support, all combine into obstacles for a successful agreement. These global factors create an environment in which the traditional salesmanship virtues of "preparedness," "handling objections," and "closing tactics" take on new and deeper meanings.

Be Prepared!

There is no shortcut to effective sales presentations abroad, and the most fundamental building block in this process is preparation. The visitor must be knowledgeable with respect to her or his product and the competition, as well as the customer's situation and needs, but must also be able to handle questions concerning tariff and nontariff barriers and other trade complications affecting shipments. In many cases the requirements for an effective sales call are such that a single individual simply can't be expected to handle all the questions alone. Teams of visitors are therefore dispatched (at consequently higher expense), or a representative of the consulate in the country may be asked to join. The important fact here is usually not that specific information can be instantaneously accessed and questions answered right away but that the salesperson demonstrates that he or she has paid close attention to the customer's specific situation and the special requirements for doing business in the country. Such a demonstration, again, comes down to not only specific knowledge about the "strictly business" aspects of the transactions but also the "nonbusiness" aspects of the relationship. Learning about Subhas Chandra Bose ("Netaji") and his role in Bengal during the first half of this century is "good for business" in India in the broadest sense. For the visitor it generates an understanding of the complex social and political forces at work in the country that in turn leads to a deeper appreciation of similar anticolonial movements and postcolonial societies elsewhere. It tends to make the individual a more compassionate and less prejudiced human being, and that is always useful.

Handling Objections

Handling objections is a difficult task in any sales presentation, and it is more so in global settings where communications are more easily garbled. In fact, there is perhaps no other area of the sales presentation in which the cultural differences are more pronounced. The best procedures for handling objections vary considerably from country to country.

Generally speaking, some pointers can be suggested. It is important that the objections not be escalated into an argument. Even in very contentious societies—as in Israel, for example—it is better to allow for the fact that most objections do have merit. Rather than attempting outright refutation and persuasion based on facts and figures, it is more effective to suggest the direction in which the answer lies and lead the customer toward it rather than pushing.

The best way to handle objections is to avoid having them raised in the first place. Whether this can be done hinges very much on the amount of "ego" that the salesperson presents. The self-confident salesperson so highly praised in American textbooks is told to "keep standing so that the prospect can be dominated," or at least be equal to the customer: "I know you are busy. I am busy myself."[26] It goes without saying that such tactics might be inappropriate in countries where the "customer is the king" and where the use of confrontation and intimidation is highly counterproductive. Even though in many such countries the presentation will meet no overt objections, it is likely to fail miserably. In such cases the unfortunate salesperson is often back in the hotel room before long wondering, "What hit me?"

Closing Tactics

The **closing tactics** also vary considerably between countries. Most infuriating for foreigners, it is not always easy to discern when exactly the "decision to buy" is made or when a felicitous moment for closing is at hand. There are times when the senior manager on the customer's side leaves a meeting without any particular agreement with the salesperson, who is expected to continue the presentation without his presence. Some quietly whispered words in the native tongue not understood by the salesperson can easily be misinterpreted as a polite way of saying "no" when in fact they mean "yes." A direct question from the salesperson to gauge interest and reaction of the customer may be given an evasive answer, again yielding mixed and exasperating signals.

When closing is seemingly within reach, some person with intimate knowledge of the country's customs should be present to assist the salesperson. It is in these later stages that the particular cultural norms have been set down most precisely. Generally, cultural norms can be suspended more easily in matters of low importance. Since the signing of the contract is the most serious action to be taken during the whole of the negotiations, most customers (and salespeople) tend to lean on standard, formal procedures when committing themselves and their company. The presence of a knowledgeable person (often with legal expertise) to assist in the final stages therefore becomes very important.

But this same person might be useful throughout in indicating to the salesperson what is going on among the customer's people by listening in on their discussions and also interpreting what their nonspeaking, their silences, mean. Silence has a particularly strong effect in international presentations as a closing technique. Sometimes the "final offer" is modified when the customer remains intimidatingly silent, although the offer would have been quite acceptable. This is common in Japan when American salespeople get impatient and give unnecessary concessions, but it occurs often enough in Europe and even in the United States. A salesman for industrial products related how he had closed a sale to the U.S. manufacturing operation of a European ski producer: "I had made all my points, laid out the whole situation, answered the questions. I saw he was thinking, thinking hard, so I shut up and just sat there. Seconds stretched into minutes. I sensed that the first man to speak would lose, so I let it ride. We sat there for perhaps 15 minutes, not saying a thing. Suddenly he said, 'Let's do it,' and I had a sale."

Global personal selling has to be localized and adapted; but with sensitivity, persistence, preparation, and a good product, most cultural obstacles can be overcome.

INTEGRATED MARKETING COMMUNICATIONS

Any one customer, whether global or local, receives information about a brand from a number of sources. It is naturally important that the message coming through be consistent. The promotional tools discussed in this chapter need to be integrated with each other and also with the media advertising covered in Chapter 15. This is the task of **integrated marketing communications,** or IMC for short.

The IMC concept stresses the need to combine the various communication disciplines—for example, media advertising, direct marketing, sales promotion, Internet advertising, and public relations—to ensure clarity, consistency, and maximum communications impact. It argues for a broad perspective that takes into account all sources of brand or company contacts that a customer has with a product or service. Instead of seeing media advertising or in-store promotion as the major promotional vehicle, with other communication tools ancillary, IMC says that all tools need to be managed jointly to achieve maximum impact.[27]

The IMC concept is difficult to implement globally since it enlarges the number of communication functions that need to be coordinated. It also runs up against the problem that, as we have seen in this chapter, different rules and regulations govern the use of promotional tools in different countries. Nevertheless, the IMC concept is valuable globally since it forces the company to define the brand identities and communication platforms more clearly. It may not be possible to use the same promotional tools in different countries, but the message put across can be uniform and consistent.

In fact, IMC forces advertising and promotional specialists to "think outside the box," that is, to take a broader view of their communication means and goals. This can be particularly useful when entering new markets where communication media are different. Intel, the chip maker from Silicon Valley, placed television and billboard ads throughout China to establish brand awareness for its microprocessors. The company also distributed nearly 1 million bike reflectors—which glow in the dark with the words "Intel Inside Pentium Processor"—in China's biggest cities. Taiwan-based Yonex Corporation pays $2 million annually to be the exclusive equipment sponsor for Indonesia's powerful national badminton team. Nike sponsors four teams in China's new professional soccer league, including one owned by the People's Liberation Army.

Citibank captured 40 percent of Thailand's credit card market relying on a sales force of 600 part-timers who are paid a fee for each applicant approved.[28]

The same realization that there are usually several means of reaching a given objective pervades the global marketing function at Levi Strauss, the jeans maker. Robert Holloway, the new vice president, is moving the company toward a "think globally, act locally" approach with campaigns that carry a unified message but with looks that mirror their individual markets. He says global marketing brings very powerful benefits to the brand and is also important to the bottom line, since global images can be more cost-efficient than local ones. Using the same campaign in multiple markets saves production costs of $100,000 to $1 million for a 30-second commercial. But local managers are allowed to select their own ad agencies with no pressure from headquarters. "How can I possibly know all the local markets?" Holloway says.

As part of its IMC strategy, Levi Strauss is also examining its worldwide media mix, 75 percent of which goes to television. It plans on spending fewer TV ad dollars in mature markets (where TV is losing share) and allocating more in emerging markets (where TV is more efficient). In mature markets the stress is shifting to newer media, in particular the Internet. Levi's Web sites feature brand history, fashion tips, games, and youth trends. The American-style, pioneer brand identity of Levi's fits well with the new media, and plans are to expand the Web spending as the Internet reach increases.[29]

SUMMARY

Although much of the execution of promotional strategies needs to be localized because of varying regulations in different countries, the growth of global communications, global media, and global events in sports and other areas has made global promotion feasible. Sponsorship and creation of global events, participation in international trade fairs, and a global public relations perspective, including global publicity, are promotional tools for the company's global marketing effort. The increasing feasibility of direct marketing helps even smaller companies capitalize on global opportunities.

As for the promotional regulations that often force localization, the growth of integrated trading blocs is gradually forcing harmonization of regulations. Challenges from global companies to arcane legislation designed to protect local businesses have been successful.

The trend has been toward increasing importance of global recognition and reputation, as evidenced by the growth of global brand names. The various promotional tools discussed in this chapter play an important role in developing and sustaining the equity in such global brand names. This is accomplished by globally integrated marketing communications, with all promotions based on a unified brand identity and global copy platforms, but with room for local implementation taking into account differing promotion regulations and availability of promotional tools.

Many people around the world do not like the way promotional hoopla seems to have become more important than what is promoted—the game or the product itself. However, with open global markets, democracy, and capitalism, promotion is unavoidably part of the game.

KEY TERMS

closing tactics   p. 491
cross-marketing   p. 478
damage control   p. 481
direct marketing   p. 483
direct response television
    (DRTV)   p. 483
events   p. 479
global public relations   p. 481

handling objections   p. 491
in-store promotion   p. 475
integrated marketing
    communications   p. 492
international trade fairs   p. 482
mail order   p. 483
press releases   p. 478
product placement   p. 480

publicity   p. 478
sales force   p. 487
salesman as a person   p. 493
salesmanship   p. 487
sponsorship   p. 476
telemarketing   p. 483
trade promotions   p. 476

DISCUSSION QUESTIONS

1. What is it that makes a created media event such as a Disney opening a powerful promotional tool? Trace the effect of such an event on the individual consumer decision process discussed in Chapter 7, "Local Buyer Behavior" (for example, identify to what extent the effect is cognitive, affective, and socially normative). What does this tell you about when such events should (or should not) be attempted by the global marketer?

2. Analyze how some companies' Web sites serve as both a source of information and a point-of-purchase promotional site. What do the companies do in order to create an interactive, highly involved encounter? How do they try to induce "action"?

3. As we saw in the opening vignette to Chapter 2, Nike's high visibility and publicity have had some negative effects. Use the Internet and other media sources to find out what they are. What can Nike do to counter the product "misplacement" effects?

4. What are the forces that have led to the success of direct marketing? What are the threats against its continued success? What has helped the globalization of direct marketing? Do you see any obstacles now or in the future?

5. Drawing on the cultural discussion in Chapter 3 and your own cultural background, compare the salesmanship skills needed to sell an automobile in Germany, in the United States, and in Japan (or some other countries of your own choice). What skills would be most advantageous? Which ones could land you in trouble?

NOTES

1. See Boddewyn, 1988.
2. From Terpstra and Sarathy, 1994, p. 508.
3. Such "serendipitous" advertising, broadcasting of brand names through TV coverage of the events, is coming under scrutiny, at least in the United States. The rental rates for stadium advertising space have risen to reflect the TV coverage, at the same time that broadcasters are starting to complain about the "free ride" they are giving to nonpaying advertisers. But although cigarette advertising such as Marlboro's has been curtailed (see McKinley, Jr., 1995), it will probably be some time before Monica Seles' Yonex stickers disappear from view.
4. From the *Washington Post*, August 12, 1995, E1, 2.
5. See, for example, the Gump mania discussed in Farhi, 1995.
6. See Bennet, 1995.
7. See Levin, 1994, and Case 4.3.
8. The Swatch material is drawn from two case studies, Pinson and Kimball, 1987, and Jeannet et al., 1985.
9. See Belch and Belch, 1998, p. 431.
10. Jean-Jacques Servan-Schreiber's *The American Challenge* became a great bestseller in the late 1960s.
11. Many of the negative attitudes have been documented and shown to be based on a one-sided view of Japanese management as all-powerful; see Sullivan, 1992.
12. See Stephen A. Greyser and N. Langford, "Volvo and the Monster Mash," Harvard Business School, case no. 9-593-024.

13. See Markoff, 1994.
14. From Pollock, 1995a and 1995b.
15. See Parke, 1994.
16. See Weyr, 1995.
17. See McNutt, 1995.
18. See Boyd, 1995.
19. This section draws on Sacks, 1995.
20. See Egol, 1994a.
21. From an interview in *Harvard Business Review* (Taylor, 1992).
22. This section draws on Hill et al., 1991.
23. See Still, 1981.
24. Much of the noninternational material in this section comes from Buskirk and Buskirk, 1992, a leading text on salesmanship.
25. Hall, 1960, has an extended example of a telecommunications deal in a Latin American country that is fun reading as well as instructive.
26. From Buskirk and Buskirk, 1992, pp. 266 and 331.
27. As defined by the American Association of Advertising Agencies; see Belch and Belch, 1998, pp. 9–10.
28. These examples come from Warner and Hsu, 1996, and "Sticky Wickets . . . ," 1995.
29. The Levi Strauss example is from Fannin, 1996, and Belch and Belch, 1998, p. 635.

SELECTED REFERENCES

Belch, George E.; and Michael A. Belch. *Advertising and Promotion*, 4th ed. Boston, MA: Irwin/McGraw-Hill, 1998.

Bennet, James. "An Auto Maker Uses a Cult Artist's Colorful Images to Make Its Minivans Stand Out from the Pack." *New York Times*, January 19, 1995, p. D23.

Boddewyn, Jean J. *Premiums, Gifts, and Competitions.* New York: International Advertising Association, 1988.

Boyd, Terry. "Sweet Surrender? Candy Company Hopes Federal Program Will Help It 'Invade' Japan." *Business First—Louisville* 12, no. 1 (August 7, 1995), sec. 1, p. 14.

Buskirk, R. H.; and B. Buskirk. *Selling: Principles & Practice.* 13th ed. New York: McGraw-Hill, 1992.

Egol, Len. "Europe: Uncommon Market." *Direct* 6, no. 10 (October 1994a), p. 83.

————. "Is China Ready for U.S. Mail, U.S. Direct Marketers?" *Direct* 6, no. 12 (December 1994b), p. 55.

Fannin, Rebecca A. "Levi's Global Guru Shakes Up Culture." *Advertising Age International*, November 1996, pp 120, 123.

Farhi, Paul. "Selling Is as Selling Does." *Washington Post*, April 30, 1995, pp. H1, H6.

Goldberg, Carey. "Midnight Sales Frenzy Ushers in Windows 95." *New York Times*, August 24, 1995, pp. A1, D6.

Hall, Edward T. "The Silent Language in Overseas Business." *Harvard Business Review*, May–June 1960, pp. 87–96.

Hill, John S.; Richard R. Still; and Unal O. Boya. "Managing the Multinational Sales Force." *International Marketing Review* 8, no. 1 (1991), pp. 19–31.

Jeannet, Jean-Pierre; Susan W. Nye; and Barbara Priovolos. "The Swatch Project." Imede, 1985.

Kelly, Gene. "Direct Marketing Going Overseas." *Lincoln Evening Journal*, June 1, 1994, business sec.

Levin, Gary. "Benetton Ad Lays Bare the Bloody Toll of War." *Advertising Age*, February 21, 1994, p. 38.

Markoff, John. "In About-Face, Intel Will Swap Its Flawed Chips." *New York Times*, December 21, 1994, pp. A1, D6.

Mårtenson, Rita. *Innovations in Retailing*. Lund, Sweden: Liber, 1983.

McKinley, James C., Jr. "The Garden Agrees to Curb Cigarette Ads." *New York Times*, April 5, 1995, p. C2.

McNutt, Bill III. "DM in South America Can Be as Easy as ABC." *DM News*, November 13, 1995, Supplement, "Global Views," p. 22.

Parke, Jo Anne. "The Case for Going Global: Globalization in Direct Marketing." *Target Marketing* 17, no. 11 (November 1994), p. 8.

Pinson, Christian; and Helen Chase Kimball. "Swatch." INSEAD-CEDEP, 1987, case no. 589–005–IN.

Pollock, Andrew. "Computer Exhibition Purchased." *New York Times*, February 14, 1995a, pp. D1, D8.

————. "A Japanese Gambler Hits the Jackpot with Softbank." *New York Times*, February 19, 1995b, sec. F, p. 10.

Sacks, Douglas. "Entering the Asian Living Room: Direct Response Television." *Target Marketing* 18, no. 2 (1995), p. 12.

Segal, David. "With Windows 95's Debut, Microsoft Scales Heights of Hype." *Washington Post*, August 24, 1995, p. A14.

Servan-Schreiber, Jean-Jacques. *The American Challenge*. New York: Atheneum, 1968.

Shirk, Martha. "Simple Formula No Answer for Hungry Children." *St. Louis Post-Dispatch*, September 23, 1991, p. 18.

Smith, Dawn. "Putting Soul into the Machine." *Marketing Computers* 14, no. 7 (July 1994), p. 38.

"Sticky Wickets, but What a Future." *Business Week*, August 7, 1995, pp. 72–73.

Still, Richard R. "Cross-Cultural Aspects of Sales Force Management." *Journal of Personal Selling and Sales Force Management* 1, no. 2 (1981), pp. 6–9.

Sullivan, Jeremiah J. *Invasion of the Salarymen*. Westport, CT: Praeger, 1992.

Taylor, William. "The Logic of Global Business: An Interview with ABB's Percy Barnevik." In Christopher A. Bartlett and Sumantra Ghoshal, *Transnational Management*, Homewood, IL: Irwin, 1992, pp. 892–908.

Terpstra, Vern; and Ravi Sarathy. *International Marketing*. 6th ed. Fort Worth, TX: Dryden, 1994.

"Thais and Indonesians Are Good Direct Mail Targets." *Market Asia Pacific*, February 1, 1995.

Warner, Fara; and Karen Hsu. "Intel Gets a Free Ride in China by Sticking Its Name on Bicycles." *Wall Street Journal*, August 7, 1996, p. B5.

Weyr, Thomas. "Germany Flexes Postal Muscle, Expects to Become a Major Player." *DM News*, June 19, 1995, Supplement, "Dateline Europe," p. 7.

Organizing for Global Marketing

"Making it all work"

Your takeaways from this chapter:

1. The global network of the multinational firm is a marketing asset that can be leveraged with a global strategy, but only if the appropriate organizational linkages to the local market are created.

2. The most important aspect of any organizational solution is to make sure that local motivation is not diminished, negatively affecting the implementation of a global strategy. Because of this, local managers need to be consulted early in the strategy formulation process.

3. The local managers not only have better knowledge of the local market but can assume a more global view given the chance. In the "transnational" company, local subsidiaries become centers of excellence, with global responsibilities for a particular product line—local globalization.

4. The coordination mechanisms that companies institute range from creating a common global culture, sharing information, and establishing personal relations to the creation of new organizational units such as global account managers and global teams.

5. The organizational structure and the systems need to be designed to serve one common purpose: to bring the global company closer to the local customer—global localization.

TO IMPLEMENT A GLOBAL marketing strategy, the organization's structure—the solid and dotted lines connecting management positions, departmental staff, divisional units, and subsidiaries on the organizational chart—often needs to be changed. The typical multinational organization with an international division and semi-independent country subsidiaries can work well in the multidomestic case when coordination across local markets is of less importance. As markets globalize, the central coordination requirements grow stronger, and country subsidiaries' autonomy must be reined in. In matrixed organizations, where coordination across product divisions and countries is explicit, global marketing can be implemented more easily. However, since a global marketing strategy tends to focus on the "market served" and limit the role of local adaptation, in global companies the product dimension of a matrix tends to dominate the country dimension. It is the global counterpart of "product management." Needless to say, this creates conflicts at the local country level, and firms have to find a way to tilt the balance, for example, by placing strong managers at regional centers.

This chapter deals with the organizational aspects of global marketing. It explains how to structure centralized coordination and integration and how to manage the potential conflicts at the local level. As in all organizations, the *organizational structure*, the *management systems* installed, and the *people* in the organization are the critical ingredients in the successful implementation of global marketing strategies.

ABB Structures Its Way to Success

For almost a century, Swedish Asea was an international leader in the heavy electrical equipment industry. But despite rapid growth, its future was cloudy. Asea had a score of competitors in the European electrical industry, half of them losing money—a sign of substantial overcapacity. Percy Barnevik, then Asea's managing director, thwarted decline by pioneering a dramatic restructuring.

The transformation began when Asea merged with Switzerland's Brown Boveri, forming a giant international provider of electrical systems and equipment. The new company, ABB Asea Brown Boveri, acquired or took minority positions in 60 companies, primarily in Europe and the Americas. As ABB grew, it structured itself to simultaneously capitalize on each subsidiary's unique strengths and unite the work of its 240,000 employees.

ABB is what Barnevik and his successor Goran Lindahl call "multidomestic." Each of its operations maintains deep roots in its home country, yet ABB has managers who specialize in setting global objectives to which the various groups must contribute. Its local plants have global mandates, and the organization shares knowledge and other resources across national boundaries.

Consider the business of transportation, in which ABB is the market leader, selling locomotives, subway cars, trolleys, signaling systems, and more. To serve this market, ABB draws on technology expertise from its international network of labs and facilities. Because it has several specialized facilities among which to allocate production orders, ABB can capitalize on economies of scale and compete by offering exceptional value. Because its operations are in a variety of countries, ABB also offers in-depth knowledge of its markets—for instance, the Swiss concern for the environment, or the effects of a region's temperature changes on its locomotives.

Tying the enterprise together at the top are a few ABB executives in Zurich with a global outlook. For these positions, the company develops and selects people with patience and open-mindedness. To ensure that everyone has equal access to information, they are expected to communicate in English, ABB's official language.

The need for radical change is hardly unique to ABB. Rapid globalization eliminates companies that settle for business as usual; somewhere in the world a competitor will find a way to deliver better value. At AlliedSignal, change has involved reorganizing the company around the core processes that deliver value to customers rather than around functions like marketing or engineering. Illinois-based Thermos has moved away from a functional structure to product development by cross-functional teams that take their cues directly from customers. General Electric, too, uses teams, plus a flatter structure, strategic alliances, and closer links to suppliers, all to break down the boundaries that stifle innovation. Ironically, change is the only certainty in global business. So flexibility is crucial to survive as well as thrive.

Sources: William Taylor, "The Logic of Global Business: An Interview with ABB's Percy Barnevik," *Harvard Business Review*, March–April 1991, pp. 90–101; Stratford Sherman, "Are You as Good as the Best in the World?" *Fortune*, December 13, 1993, pp. 95–96; Brian Dumaine, "Payoff from the New Management," *Fortune*, December 13, 1993, pp. 103–104; Noel M. Tichy, "Revolutionize Your Company," *Fortune*, December 13, 1993, pp. 114–15.
http://www.abb.com
http://www.alliedsignal.com
http://www.ge.com

INTRODUCTION

The *formulation* of a global marketing strategy for a product line is primarily an intellectual challenge for managers. The *implementation* of the strategy, by contrast, involves much more interpersonal discussion and persuasion. The global marketing manager needs to become an internal salesperson and champion. And the global organization needs to be structured carefully to be able to respond to the challenge. The local units have to be motivated to *execute* the global strategy effectively.

The focus of this chapter is the organizational problems of global marketing. We start by establishing the *context* in which the organizational decisions are made, then spell out the *job* that needs to be done, along with the tools that exist to do it. We discuss some common organizational *structures* found in multinational firms and look at the global *network* as a firm-specific advantage. A section on *globalizing management* leads into a discussion of management *systems* and the role of *people and culture* in global marketing management. We deal with the special case of organizing to serve *global customers*, and finally, we present techniques for *resolving conflicts* between headquarters and local units.

The Context

To see why implementing global marketing is generally difficult, it is important to first understand the managerial context. The typical situation is one where:

1. The company is already present in many markets.
2. The company is successful in at least some of the major markets (global marketing is usually *not* a crisis solution).
3. There is a history of quite successful operations with local autonomy.
4. The country managers have experience and status at home and in the organization. For administrative and control reasons the subsidiaries may be run by expatriates, but the local marketing effort is run by a local marketing manager (and/or by the country manager, when a native).
5. The *legitimacy* of the global marketing "imperative" is not all that obvious in the organization—unless successful competitors have forced the issue.
6. The global advantage derives from (*a*) cost savings, (*b*) demand spillover effects, and (*c*) serving global customers. Only in the last category will the benefits be unequivocal.

7. One obvious effect of a global strategy will be less autonomy for the local subsidiary.

8. The initiative for the global strategy comes from the top.

Given this context, it is not surprising if local country managers have to be dragged into globalization against their will.

The Task

There are essentially three main organizational requirements when a global marketing strategy is implemented. The organization needs to provide:

1. *Communication.* An effective *multiple-way communication system* needs to be set up to carry directives from the center to the local markets and to feed back information to headquarters and other subsidiaries.

2. *Motivation.* The local country managers need to be given *incentives* to implement the global strategy even though it often involves a reduction in local autonomy and resources.

3. *Flexibility.* The organization structure and/or systems need to be *flexible* so that changing conditions and new developments can be responded to and capitalized on as they arise.

The typical organization has several *organizational* tools to accomplish these tasks:

*   *Creating new organizational units.* The most common new units are perhaps *global teams*, drawing members from headquarters and country subsidiaries, with the team leader from a major lead country.

*   *Creating new positions* (or reformulating existing position descriptions) that emphasize global responsibilities. A typical example is the creation of a *global marketing director.*

*   *Changing the reporting lines.* The organization can change the existing *structure*, that is, the formal lines of reporting and authority. This is in some ways the most clear-cut change toward centralization and the most far-reaching and dramatic change in the local organization. For example, one company wanting to create a pan-European marketing strategy directed its local marketing managers to report to European headquarters instead of the country managers, who saw themselves as losers.

*   *Creating new systems.* The organization can create *new systems* and procedures within the given structure. Generally, this means that local managers retain formal authority and reporting lines but are forced to work harder and/or differently. For example, among globalizing firms it is very common to initiate periodic global meetings among country managers to explain and reinforce the global strategy.

*   *People adapting.* The organization can rely on *people* to change their behavior and accommodate the changes. In one technology-intensive firm, the global "change agent" was the marketing manager at headquarters who spent most of his time on the road explaining the global strategy and sharing information from other subsidiaries.

ORGANIZATIONAL STRUCTURE

There is no single best way to organize for global marketing. There is simply too much variety in product lines, customers, and country environments. Even companies with similar product lines and global reach will organize differently. The diversity and flexibility of people and existing systems differ between firms, and the global organization

EXHIBIT 17.1 The Export Department Structure

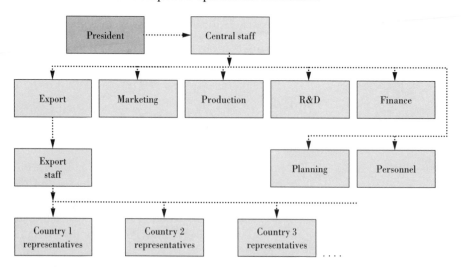

is a product of the historical evolution of the company. Naturally, it is easier to implement global marketing when people and systems in the company have previous experience with marketing in foreign countries.

The key issue for **organizational design** tends to be how to strike an appropriate balance between headquarters' need for central coordination and the local subsidiary's motivation for implementing the global strategy.

The firm can organize its international coverage in different ways. Most have gone through a sequence of these stages as they change their structure to expand overseas.

- *Export department.* The creation of an **export department structure** is usually the first step in the functional organization toward entry into foreign markets. Export departments are typically cost centers without independent authority in product and marketing mix decisions. The typical export department structure is given in Exhibit 17.1.

- *International division.* As the export revenue share increases (a common threshold value is around 10 percent of total revenues) and there are several countries in the strategic portfolio, the firm changes to a full-fledged **international division structure,** where the general manager has profit-and-loss responsibilities. The international division is often a **strategic business unit** (SBU), an operating unit functioning basically as a freestanding business. It competes with the domestic units for resource allocations, buying services from the central headquarters' staff and demanding a say on product design, product positioning, and other decisions affecting its effectiveness abroad. Exhibit 17.2 shows the typical structure with an international division.

- *Geographical/regional structure.* As overseas sales expand and the management of the countries takes more time and resources, the firm usually subdivides the international division into country groups or trade regions. Typical areas are Western Europe, Latin America, Africa and the Middle East, East Asia and the Pacific, and Eastern Europe and Russia. The international division is still usually intact, and a new organizational level is introduced to coordinate within the newly established regions. This **regional organization** is common among Japanese companies, whose home market is large and structured separately. When the home market is minor compared with the overseas sales, as in many European companies, the home market is simply subordinated in the area and there is no domestic division as such. A regional structure is shown in Exhibit 17.3.

EXHIBIT 17.2 The International Division Structure

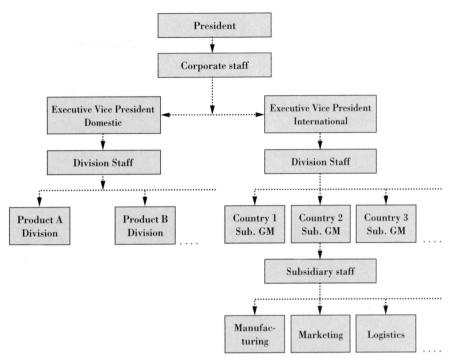

Note: Sub.GM = subsidiary general manager.

EXHIBIT 17.3 The Regional Structure

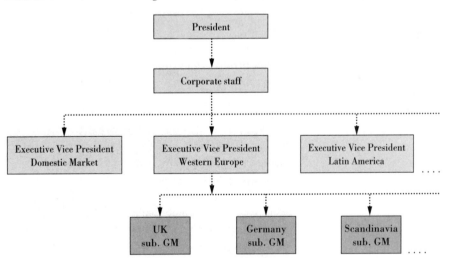

Note: Sub.GM = subsidiary general manager.

- *Global product divisions.* The attempt to develop a truly global strategy for a firm's product line tends to force a rejection of the international-versus-domestic split. The solution is often a **global product division,** where regional and local managers' authority is subordinated to that of the global division chief, who approves and directs. Although the structure has a strong logic behind it and the implementation of global marketing is facilitated, this structure demands a lot from the division manager.[1] The reason is simple. The division manager's staff is often too far away from the local market to have a very secure understanding of

EXHIBIT 17.4 The Global Product Structure

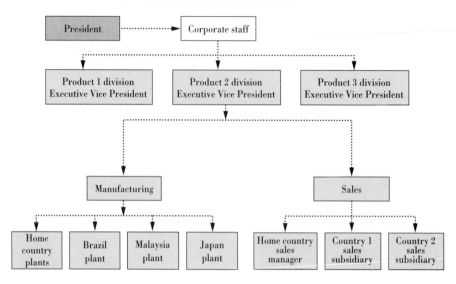

the local issues and differences. Furthermore, the need for speed and responsiveness to local competitive moves and customer requests makes central direction of operations difficult. One common solution has been for the division chief to set only broad policy goals and formulate the global strategy and then allow the local managers a great deal of autonomy in implementing the strategies. Even though global uniformity might be less than otherwise, the positive effect on the motivation of the local country managers often makes up for it. The global product structure is displayed in Exhibit 17.4.

• *Matrix organizations.* Matrix structures are those in which both country and product receive equal emphasis. Marketing of one product in a given country has to report to both the global product manager, who oversees all the countries for that product, and the country manager, who is responsible for all the products in the country. The local marketer has to respond to two bosses, an undesirable feature but often workable if the people are experienced and the management systems are handled flexibly. This is the essence of coordination and integration, and the **matrix organization,** whether formally established or not, is a natural structure for the global marketer. The global matrix structure at Honda Motor Company is shown in Exhibit 17.5.

• *Transnational organizations.* As globalization requirements increase in reach and scope, global strategies involve not only manufacturing and marketing but also R&D, design, and engineering. This has led especially technology-intensive companies to develop organizational structures in which different parts of the firm's value chain are located in different parts of the world. These are called **transnational organizations** to emphasize their cross-country network character.[2]

For example, companies such as Ericsson from Sweden in telecommunications can place its R&D for certain products in one country, manufacturing of the product somewhere else, and then do global sales and marketing from a third location. Other firms have gone even further, splitting up country subsidiaries into specialized units. Honeywell, the U.S.-based multinational in electronic measurement, has distributed its functions for design, engineering, sales, and marketing throughout Europe, allowing each country subsidiary to specialize. The reorganization of former full-fledged country subsidiaries into "special resource centers" is not particularly easy on the people displaced

EXHIBIT 17.5 The Global Matrix Structure: Honda's Global Organization

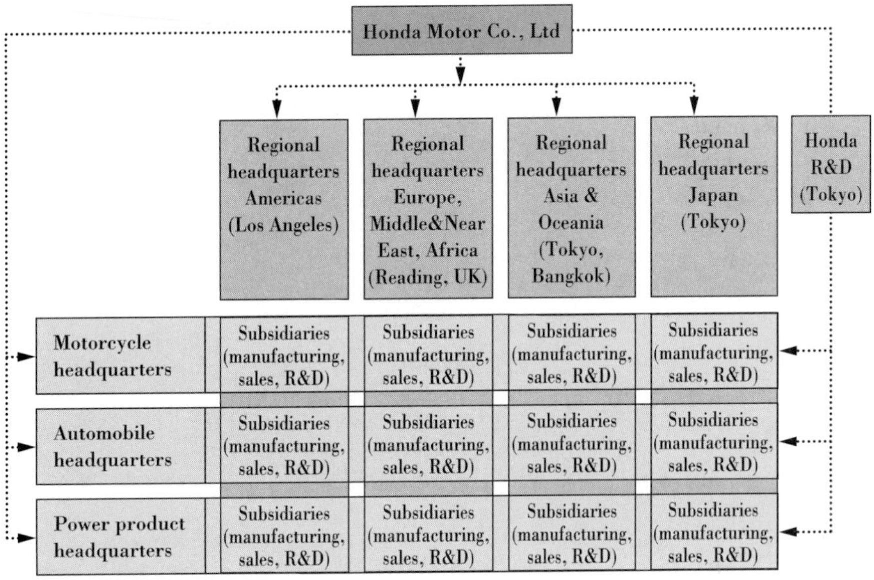

Source: Osamu Iida, executive vice president, Honda North America.

because their specialty is now in a new country location. Nevertheless, given some flexibility in the implementation of the new structure, many firms have succeeded in developing global networks with the country units drawing on the particular strengths of the local economy. How the transnational structure involves all units of the global network is shown in Exhibit 17.6.

- *Horizontal networks.* The natural result of the recent emergence of transnational expertise, effective global communications, and the drive toward "lean" organizations, **horizontal networks** have become the new "ideal" type of organizational structure. In these networks, the traditional hierarchical arrangement—with a decision maker at the top of the international division or global product division, directives flowing out to the various country subsidiaries, and performance results fed back up—has been replaced by a much less pyramidal structure. In horizontal networks, not only do local managers implement global strategies but the local subsidiaries are also involved in the formulation of the strategy, often in fact initiating the global approach. In the horizontal network structure local and central managers are virtually indistinguishable, as flows are generally horizontal from the periphery into the home country center and directly between country subsidiaries. In practice, the picture is not quite so simple, of course (see box, "The Pan-European Effect").

Although very few corporations have yet attained the perfect equality implied between all parts of the network, the structure itself is enabling the emergence of such horizontal or "democratic" relationships. In actual organizational life, even if the *structural* reporting lines are horizontal and management *systems* encourage free participation, *people* do not always respond to the implied equality. Leadership and charisma still matter. An organization has a tradition and a culture, which enable certain behaviors and discourage others. It is not surprising to find the horizontal organization working in new start-up companies, such as in computers and software, but not very far advanced even in such high-tech industries as telecommunications, where old and established companies still dominate.

EXHIBIT 17.6 Integrated Network: The Transnational Structure

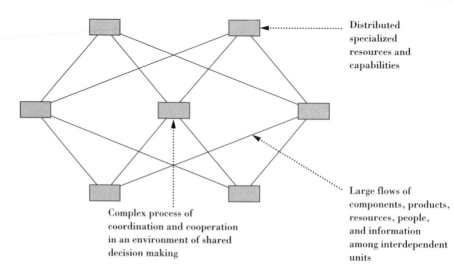

Distributed
specialized
resources and
capabilities

Complex process of
coordination and cooperation
in an environment of shared
decision making

Large flows of
components, products,
resources, people,
and information
among interdependent
units

Source: Reprinted by permission of Harvard Business School Press. From *Managing Across Borders: The Transnational Solution* by Christopher A. Bartlett and Sumatra Ghoshal. Boston, MA, p. 89. Copyright 1989 by the President and Fellows of Harvard College, all rights reserved.

THE GLOBAL NETWORK AS AN ASSET

Many companies think of their global network of country subsidiaries as an "invisible resource" or "hidden asset." The network is one of their FSAs. After the years it has taken to develop presence in the many separate country markets, the companies start contemplating how to further leverage the investment. This is a natural development for entrepreneurial managers. For example, as we saw in Chapter 15, advertising agencies that develop global reach to follow their clients abroad start attracting new business because of their network. Procter and Gamble used its global network to be the first to introduce condensed detergents in major countries, beating the innovator, Japan's Kao, to the market.

The strategic view of the **global network as an asset,** as an FSA, is doubly useful since it tends to make local units more important, helping to counter the problem when country managers feel their local authority is being compromised by a shift to global strategy. Treating the network itself as an asset means that the global strategy becomes more of a "win-win" proposition for both headquarters and subsidiaries.

Painful History

To understand how companies may leverage network resources, we can learn from the past history of multinational expansion. It teaches some painful lessons.

The increased need for an integrated global strategy has come about partly because of the successful attacks on world markets by newly emerging multinationals, especially the Japanese. A key ingredient in their success has been their lack of existing foreign subsidiaries, allowing their global expansion to take place through well-coordinated exporting from Japan and other home countries. As Western companies have tried to emulate the Japanese successes, their efforts at globalized strategies have been hampered rather than helped by their traditionally independent country subsidiaries. The European multinationals, in particular, had long allowed local subsidiaries to run their own operations, a historical accident partly due to Europeans' bent for respecting different local customs.

G E T T I N G   T H E

Picture

The Pan-European Effect

THE EFFECT of global marketing on organization structure is well illustrated by the attempts of companies to capitalize on the European integration.

Many companies have developed pan-European structures and processes. Lever Europe, the regional headquarters of Unilever in Europe, added a general manager for strategic development to whom Europewide product group managers report. The strategic European group complements the existing geographic structure with country managers responsible for operating profits. The company is developing Euro-brands for which Europewide product managers have responsibility to develop marketing strategy, package design, and advertising. The Europewide product managers have their own budgets, operate as cost centers, and have to "sell" the country managers on the introduction of the Euro-brands through the existing channels in each country. Additional reporting lines represent a simple coordinating device.

Dell Computer is asking its product marketing managers in the various European countries to report to the pan-European head office in addition to the country managers. Going halfway is sometimes not enough. 3M, the

Minnesota-based maker of videodisks and tapes and related products, tried to develop Euro-products by creating small European product teams that had to draw on functional expertise in local units. This structure became too weak, and the company shifted to full-fledged Europewide business units.

When a company dominates its markets and products are standardized, centralized direction is facilitated. Gillette's international headquarters in the United States is responsible for all marketing in Europe, including product positioning, advertising, and public relations. The head man at Gillette spent a long time with the firm in Germany, so the European market conditions are not unknown at headquarters. Gillette's effort in Japan, which is managed with much more local autonomy, is unfortunately less successful, Schick being the market leader there.

Sources: Gates, 1995; Uchitelle, 1994.
http://www.unilever.com
http://www.dell.com
http://www.gillette.com

American companies have traditionally operated with stronger central authority than the Europeans, which means that many American brand names are well recognized globally while European brand names differ between countries. But even American companies have had trouble coordinating global marketing, involving as it does more limited independence for local subsidiaries. As late as the early 1990s, Western companies still lagged behind Japanese firms in their level of global marketing integration.[3] Subsidiary managers balk and refuse to cooperate, citing differences in customer preferences and the lowered motivation among local personnel as impenetrable barriers to coordination with headquarters. Norelco, the American subsidiary of Dutch Philips, is still largely run as an independent company; the head of Ford's operation in Germany resigned; and even Procter and Gamble's decade-long struggle for pan-European product teams has encountered some fierce resistance.

The Win-Win View

Perhaps not surprisingly given this history, the win-win solution to the problems involved in implementing a global strategy against local resistance has come primarily from companies and researchers in Europe. Scandinavian academicians in particular have been active in promoting what has become known as "the network theory" of global enterprise.[4]

The central tenet of the **network theory** is that the linkages between actors in the global network—not only between headquarters and subsidiaries but also between company and suppliers, marketers and channel members, and company and loyal customers—constitute the true source of competitive advantage for the firm. Rather than thinking of the firm as "we" and the other actors as "they," the approach

G E T T I N G   T H E

Picture

Researching the Power of Networks

SINCE THE NETWORK APPROACH places the key competitive advantages in the linkages between players rather than in individual companies, it is natural to replace the topic of organizational behavior with that of network behavior, an approach suggested primarily by Swedish researchers. Network researchers study how networks are created, grow, and change over time. For example, researchers have dealt with how companies get new trade contacts (often quite haphazardly, as through random encounters while traveling), how often and for what purposes face-to-face meetings are necessary (common when a subsidiary adopts an innovation), and how "sleeping" relationships can be activated by new opportunities (such as when the Berlin Wall's dismantling allowed Swedish companies to reactivate past contacts in Eastern Europe).

In the same stream of research, there is relatively little discussion of leadership. The reason is that traditional leadership is typically a top-down activity with followers being motivated by leaders. The network view is much more egalitarian and fits nicely into the newer organizational frameworks of empowerment and decentralized authority. The businesses that have shown themselves particularly adept at global networking involve high-technology products or services with skills distributed throughout the network, and many of them can be quite small. Size is no object in networks—quite the contrary. The so-called virtual corporation is one extreme form of the network approach with company employees attached to the center by virtue of only a computerized communications link. It remains to be seen whether such communication links can be strong enough to completely replace face-to-face encounters. But the fact remains that the computer-linked global network competitor is here to stay.

Sources: Forsgren and Johanson, 1992; Hakansson, 1989; Hertz and Mattsson, 1998.

is inclusive. The best way to gain advantages is for the network to be strong, not only the individual participants. "What is good for them is good for us."

In this view, *competition occurs mainly between networks of businesses.* Analyzing Japanese competitors, for example, the network approach suggests that Nissan and Toyota compete not only directly but also through their related keiretsu (or network) suppliers. This view is shared among many businesspeople inside and outside Japan. Another factor of importance in the network view is the enlarged role of a country subsidiary in communicating and supporting other subsidiaries—and not only reporting to headquarters. The role of headquarters, in the network view, becomes one of sharing knowledge, disseminating innovations, and facilitating communication among network members rather than giving orders and directing from the center (see box, "Researching the Power of Networks").

From a global marketing viewpoint, the most striking benefit derived from the network approach is the fresh recognition of *what* the firm's resources and FSAs are and *where* new ideas and innovation might emerge. Remember, knowledge assets are a critical resource in competitive markets. The existence of the network opens up new possibilities, rather than constraining solutions. The so-called core competencies of the corporation involve not simply what the company can do but what the network can do. The network can do more things than the individual company; and, conversely, an absence of a global network reduces management strategy options.

The ideas for expansion and growth can come from anywhere in a network, which is why communication is so important? Sharing information, news, and knowledge via the firm's e-mail system—and even via the public Internet—managers inside the network learn about the capabilities of other members; new visions open up, and imaginative innovations emerge. It is small wonder that most multinational companies today spend huge amounts to create internal communication links through so-called **intranets,** protected communication systems that help tie together a global firm's network.

As global competition heats up and companies are faced with "hypercompetition" (see Chapter 2), the global network is a key source of competitive advantage and new possibilities.[5] Rather than viewing the network members as out-of-date and obstacles to progress, their local know-how and motivation need to be allowed to impact the member companies and the network as a whole. This takes much less "leadership" from the center but requires facilitation and sharing of knowledge. The marketing manager whose organization operates with a "network as an asset" not only uses the most up-to-date telecommunications and videoconferencing equipment but also spends considerable time on the road, cajoling and persuading and sharing. Global integration is not a matter of centralized command over an army of exporters, as in the Japanese system, but rather a matter of inspiring individual network members to share in the win-win philosophy.

GLOBALIZING MANAGEMENT[6]

Because of the large home market, many American companies come to global marketing with an international division structure separating domestic and overseas markets. This structure tends to prohibit global integration of marketing effort, since the home country occupies a special position. For integrated marketing, the home country needs to be viewed as part of the global market. To accomplish this, companies are shifting to global marketing directors.

Global Marketing Directors

In companies organized along the lines of global product divisions or separate business units, the **global marketing director** naturally becomes the head of marketing for both the home country and overseas. In Chapter 16, for example, we met Levi Strauss' global marketing director, Robert Holloway. Each product division will then have a global marketing manager reporting to the director. Even without a global product structure, global marketing directors may be appointed to operate in a matrix fashion across a geographic structure. In either case, the global marketing director is generally given the following responsibilities:

- *Strategy.* Strategic planning, budgeting, and implementation with functions and regions.
- *Systems.* Design, creation, and maintenance of global marketing systems.
- *Coordination.* Coordination of all functions affecting business and major product lines.
- *Performance evaluation.* Participation in performance evaluation of functional and regional managers.
- *Profitability.* Profit accountability for individual lines of business and major product lines.

These are major tasks and may demand that national marketing managers in the main markets report directly to the global marketing director. New product specifications, positioning, advertising, and distribution choices may become centralized decisions, while lower-level execution questions such as local sales and logistics remain a national responsibility. All major accounts are handled centrally.

Even without such a dramatic change in the reporting lines of the organization, global marketing directors can still exert considerable influence as staff members by sheer force of personality and access to information. They can bring vast experience to bear on a particular situation. For example, one manager exerted strong influence over the country managers simply by explaining why their advertising ideas had failed in other countries and by sharing where they had succeeded. Arguments about the particular tastes of a local market and the need for special advertising often dissolve when the success of a campaign in a neighboring country is demonstrated.

A transnational product development team in 3M's European Business Center for medical products in Brussels. From left: Valori Seltz, a U.S. citizen; Philippe Husson, French; Kurt Wiethoff, German; Inge Thulin, Swedish; and Stig Eriksson, Finnish.
© Steve Niedorf photography.

Global Teams

One of the commonest organizational changes for global marketing is to create **global teams.** The responsibilities can vary from specific programs or activities, such as the advertising campaign for a new product, to more wide-ranging responsibilities, including the whole marketing mix. The European integration has spawned many examples of global teams. For example, a French manufacturer of security devices uses a team of country managers, with the different countries playing the lead role for different products. While this approach is time-consuming, the company has found that the reliance on line managers makes it easier for various countries to accept input from other countries.

Similarly responding to the European integration, Minnesota-based multinational 3M initially used "European Management Action Teams," one for each of its 50 product lines. Each team had eight to fourteen members representing several functions and different countries, and each was chaired by a Brussels-based product manager. As the integration proceeded and customers demanded more extensive pan-European sales and services, the teams eventually were succeeded by "European Business Centers" (EBCs). A 3M EBC has responsibility and accountability for managing a business throughout Europe, from planning and manufacturing to selling and delivering the product to the customer. One such business center is the "Consumer and Office Markets EBC." The center's six product lines (home care, consumer stationery, do-it-yourself/paint and drywall products, commercial care, visual systems, and commercial office supply) are managed by separate European Business Units (EBUs) with pan-European responsibility. These six product lines are coordinated in each of 3M's eight European regions, with a local organization that mirrors that of the pan-European structure. For example, the German consumer and office markets EBC manager coordinates sales and marketing for six EBUs in that region.[7]

MANAGEMENT SYSTEMS

Companies can also implement global marketing within their existing organizational structure by instituting new **management systems** as integrating mechanisms. Global budgeting, global performance reviews, and global accounting are some of the general systems that create a basis for globalized strategies. Companies can also achieve greater global emphasis with integration mechanisms such as meetings and informal networks, committees and task forces, and coordinating staff groups and information sharing on a global basis. The advent of electronic communication media such as videoconferencing and electronic mail has also helped develop a global culture in companies.

The choice of integration mechanism depends on the intensity of the global marketing activity.

Informal Coordination

Information sharing about similar experiences in different markets is a first step in achieving integrated strategies. Most companies today are involved in these types of informal exchanges, and they are one reason why the global marketer has to travel so often and so far. Experiences are rarely the stuff of formal reporting, and it usually takes some time spent in mutual discussion before the relevance of a particular experience is recognized.

This type of informal management interaction is difficult to systematize. It is akin to MBWA (management by walking around) on a global scale. The outsider has to come to the country subsidiary as a consultant and friend rather than as a boss on an inspection tour. Such informal cooperation can't be achieved through telecommunications or through written memos. In one study of managers in Swedish multinational firms traveling to subsidiaries abroad, it was found that as many as 44 percent of the managers traveled without specific problem or action objectives, but in order to "cultivate the network."[8]

Coordinating Committees

A number of companies attempt to achieve more effective implementation systems by creating joint committees of regional or country managers that meet on a regular basis. These high-level meetings serve to reinforce ties at the top levels, creating umbrellas for operational coordination and integration between units. Many large multinationals have used such committees for a long time. IBM, GE, and ITT are some of the well-known examples of this; but so are Philips, Siemens, and Volvo in Europe, and well as Sony, Honda, and Matsushita of Japan. Swapping new-product information and competitive data, sharing market research, selecting which brands to promote as regional or global, setting international standards for sales performance, and synchronizing product launches—it is from these joint committees that more permanent organizational fixtures such as Euro-brand groups or global advertising units develop.

In many cases the higher-level committee efforts are followed up by regular meetings between functional managers or task forces with professionals at various levels. Temporary personnel transfers are also used, although not so commonly. In one study of 35 European multinationals, only 5 sent their head office marketing managers for a stint in a foreign subsidiary, and only 9 transferred their local marketing managers to the head office.

Coordinating Staff

As the so-called global imperative (or, for some companies, the "limited global imperative" discussed in Chapter 11) is endorsed at top management levels, its implementation usually leads to temporary arrangements of meetings between the various country subsidiary managers. The coordination will initially consist of simple consultation, exchange of information, and informal cooperation, but soon the need for a more systematic approach will be clear.

The emergence of permanent coordinating mechanisms from initial temporary management processes is typical of the incremental character of much of the global integration efforts in companies. For example, product design may require a unified task force of designers and engineers from various countries, drawn together in some central location. In automobiles, many companies from various countries have a design office in southern California, where many of the new design ideas originate. Similarly, they have engineering offices in Germany, where technology is strong.

The need for global marketing thus often leads to the creation of a new staff group with global integration responsibilities but without line authority. The group may facilitate shared new-product development in lead countries, an approach now common in companies such as Procter and Gamble, Nissan, and Nestlé. The group may also facilitate the wedding of global brands to the existing lineup of brands in local campaigns, such as adding Euro-Vizir to P&G's detergents in Britain. The staff may also help develop a more coordinated campaign across the globe, such as when the Sony Walkman was rechristened replacing the "Soundabout" name already launched in Europe. The global staff group can be responsible for organizing the many global meetings that oil the mechanism of the global management effort. There is a need for travel arrangements, hotel accommodations, alignment of schedules, and simple caretaking that can tax the energies of many organizations. The visits from headquarters are expensive distractions unless real business can be transacted—with global marketing and business decisions made at the meetings.[9]

PEOPLE AND ORGANIZATIONAL CULTURE

In the end, the implementation of global marketing stands or falls with the capability of the people involved. Because of the complexity of the task and the inherent conflict with local management, **people skills** matter a lot.

If the organizational *structure* is the body and the chassis that hold the car together and the management *systems* are the engine and the gearbox, *people* provide the necessary lubrication that makes the pistons pump and the car run smoothly. And "people" means everybody in the organization, from top management down.

Local Acceptance

Global marketing strategies almost always require a leap of faith on the part of local managers, because local conditions are almost always different from other places.[10] A skilled manager must persuade the local managers and motivate them to work for the success of the global strategy. Simply forcing the strategy on the local office leads to surreptitious efforts to undermine the global brand, as Henkel found with its Pritt product line (as we saw in Chapter 12). While paying lip service to the global branding concept, the local subsidiary manager went about supporting the existing brands in direct competition with the new global brand.

Research on the acceptance of global strategies demonstrates the importance of allowing country managers to participate in the global strategy formulation process. The acceptability of a global directive from headquarters is directly related to the perceived fairness of the process.[11] Where local managers have been involved in formulating global marketing strategies, they have been much more likely to accept and to implement them. Regardless of the management incentives and penalties adopted to promote local implementation, the major factor in acceptance was what managers call "due process." If a global strategy did not have sufficient local input, managers felt ignored—and acted accordingly. The "people" factor is important.

Another factor is the level of agreement with the "global imperative" at the local level. In many globalized firms, the local managers are well aware of their dependency on the global network of the organization and are quite willing and able to assume a

G E T T I N G   T H E

P&G's Vizir Experience

Picture

THE 1983 SUCCESSFUL LAUNCH of Vizir, Procter and Gamble's liquid detergent, in Germany, Holland, and France was spearheaded by a novel organizational innovation, a Euro-team. In order to develop and test the new product, the company had appointed one manager from Germany as the head of a Europewide team of experts and managers. With Germany the largest market in Europe and since the new product development had originated there, Germany became a natural lead country in the product development effort.

Even though the product launch was a success, there were some setbacks in the organization of the team. The local country managers were reluctant to participate, since the periodic meetings were time-consuming. As a result, the team members were not always given adequate support in their home countries, participation in the Euro-team changed frequently, and attendance at meetings fluctuated. The solution was to distribute Euro-team responsibilities among the various countries to motivate their participation and to make local managers more sensitive to the difficulties involved in the integrated effort.

Procter and Gamble is pursuing the global team further, and the company is instilling a global perspective in all product managers by regular meetings to share ideas of potential value elsewhere. For example, the product modifications to the Pampers diapers originating in Japan have been introduced globally. The new condensed detergents, also from Japan, have been quickly expanded elsewhere. The global perspective has been further strengthened by the appointment of a CEO with extensive experience abroad.

Sources: Bartlett, 1983; Bartlett and Ghoshal, 1989, pp. 93–94; Yoshino, 1990.
http://www.pg.com/

global perspective.[12] Giving more global responsibility to local managers, however, requires some organizational changes. The headquarters role is not so much that of pushing a global strategy as facilitating interaction between various local managers who will be directly dependent on each other. The Euro-brand managers at Procter and Gamble provide one example of this process (see box, "P&G's Vizir Experience").

People skills and country cultures do not always work in predictable ways. As BBD&O, the advertising agency, expanded its Brussels office in anticipation of the European Union, the intent was to draw in talent from several continental countries. Instead, the agency found that British and American employees were much more effective, partly because of the language facility but also because the continental Europeans tended to remain close to their home culture. Southern Europeans, in particular, with their high context cultures, tend to be less flexible when asked to jettison preconceived and culture-bound ideas.[13] The French and Italians' attention to dress, for example, tended to blur their appreciation of easygoing, casual spokespersons.

The people factor directly affects the execution of global advertising strategies. Telling the local marketing manager to work with the branch office of a global agency rather than with a longtime friend in a local agency is not a pleasant job. If handled badly, the local manager will leave the company, as happened when Pioneer, the consumer electronics company, centralized its European marketing in Antwerp with advertising given to BBD&O's expanded Brussels office.

Many of these personnel losses are motivated by personal as well as professional reasons. Ford Werke AG in Cologne lost its top marketing manager in Germany when it instituted pan-European product development strategies and pulled in design responsibilities from Germany and gave them to the European headquarters in Dagenham, England, even though a promotion to England was offered. The head of market research at Brown Boveri, the Swiss electrical machinery manufacturer, left when Swedish Asea took over to create ABB, not wanting to work for a company dominated by Swedes.

Corporate Culture

The fact is that since global strategies often involve centralization, they are also prone to make a company's culture ethnocentric. While the old-style multinationals—companies like Philips of Holland, Nestlé of Switzerland, Beiersdorf (Nivea) of Germany, and Singer (sewing machines) of the United States—offered products that many consumers around the world vaguely thought were local brands, the new global emphasis has placed nationality in the forefront. The global marketer who carries the orders from the home office needs a lot of interpersonal skill to get the necessary cooperation. While 20 years ago the local manager for an American multinational in Germany had credibility as a local figure, today the position is undermined by the home office's insistence on direct control. It is hardly surprising when the experienced local managers quit as global strategies get implemented.

Many coordination and integration activities involve communication. Firms use people and **organizational culture** to enhance communication in different ways, such as to:

- *Build a strong corporate culture internationally.* IKEA, the furniture retailer, does this by fostering its Swedish values of egalitarianism, frugality, hard work, and simplicity among its employees worldwide (and IKEA has had more problems doing this in the United States than in Western Europe and Canada).
- *Build a common technical or professional culture.* Elf-Aquitaine, the French oil company, sets high standards for professionalism and technical knowledge to create group affiliation.
- *Build strong financial and planning systems.* Emerson Electric promotes careful planning, financial reporting, and cost reduction as company values.

The key notion is that managers in different countries should be induced to communicate and interact more in line with company values than to rely on their different national cultures. Honda's way is a good example (see box, "Honda's Global Management by Culture").

The Expatriate Manager

The discussion so far has treated the local manager as a native of the country. This is the usual case if the manager in question has the marketing responsibility. But for control and communication purposes, many country subsidiaries are run by **expatriates** from the home country, typically executives who have been sent to the foreign subsidiary after several years with the firm at home. What is their role in the implementation of the global strategy and the local marketing effort?

Apart from being the headquarters' "envoy," the expatriate country managers in a global company have three typical marketing *leadership* roles to fill.[14]

Role 1. Customer representative. The expatriate manager must serve as a high-level contact with existing customers, prospects, and suppliers *in the local market.* The local marketing effort can then be carried out by locals, who can follow up at operating levels on contacts provided by the expatriate. This part of the job relates directly to the "relationship marketing" function so prominent in today's customer-oriented firm.

Role 2. Local champion. The expatriate manager must be a champion for the local office at *headquarters.* Local requests such as product modifications, advertising approvals, and additional resources need to be explained and justified back home by the manager.

Role 3. Network coordinator. The expatriate manager must provide *linkages* with the firm's other offices in the *worldwide network* of the firm. Coordinating product launches in different countries, production scheduling, and exchange of market information are examples of the kinds of issues that require close communication links between the various country managers.

Honda's Global Management by Culture

HONDA IS A COMPANY with a strong global vision. The impetus derives partly from its founder, Soichiro Honda, who was blocked out of the Japanese home market by powerful and well-established competitors. This pushed the company overseas, and the United States became its primary market. Recognizing its dependence on foreign countries, the company has attempted to create a corporate culture of "three world headquarters": Japan, the United States, and Europe.

The company attempts to be an "insider" in all three areas by assembling cars in several different locations (Swinton, United Kingdom, and Marysville, Ohio, are the major sites) and hiring local workers as well as local managers. There is little or no "selling" of the global strategy

necessary because the company avoids being "Japanese." Products are standardized but often designed outside of Japan; some are developed for specific non-Japanese markets (such as the Concerto for Europe), and cars built abroad are exported back to Japan (such as the Accord from Ohio). The company also takes workers and supervisors (the "associates," as the company calls its employees) from its plants abroad for stints in factories in Japan—and sends many Japanese workers and managers abroad.

Sources: Sakiya, 1987; Pearson and Ehrlich, 1989.
http://www.honda.com

The last two tasks are critical when implementing global marketing strategy. While the local representative task is often similar to the task of marketers anywhere, it is the linkage with headquarters and other country offices that provides the added sources of advantage for the global marketer. The strength of these linkages depends on the expatriate as much as on the native people.

When strategies are globalized, the expatriate manager is often put in a delicate position, since the strategy often reduces the autonomy of the local subsidiary. Being the connecting link with headquarters, it is natural that the expatriate must be the one to explain and implement the strategy locally. This usually involves limiting the local marketing manager's authority and may force a change of ad agency, new directions in sales efforts, and termination of distribution contracts. Since in many cases certain parts of the business are consolidated and placed with other country units or at headquarters, the strategy may involve layoffs and voluntary retirements. Often these measures are a threat to an expatriate's authority in the firm and to the existing network of contacts outside. In one fairly typical case in which the expatriate manager was asked to fire 20 percent of the local work force, the manager decided to quit since his standing in the local business community, as well as in the firm, was jeopardized.

When strategies are globalized, expatriate managers may need (or want) to be replaced, rotated to another country, or promoted. It is often more difficult to transfer the native marketing manager or the country manager if a native. In these cases, the companies have options available, discussed below, which can help avoid the low morale that globalization often incurs.

GLOBAL CUSTOMERS

As we have seen repeatedly throughout Part Four, a very clear-cut rationale for the introduction of a globalized marketing strategy is the emergence of global customers. It is easiest to recognize the advantages of a coordinated offering to multinational buyers that can choose in what country to make their purchases. A consistent image; well-recognized brand; assurance of parts, supplies, and service; and coordinated pricing—all are obvious benefits to a company selling to global customers. With the emergence of global purchasing on the part of individual customers as well, the benefits of coordination are increased further. When an individual buyer of a personal computer in Toronto, say, can choose between the local stores, buying through a direct import house, shopping at home via catalog from New York, or a duty-free purchase at Tokyo's Akihabara district or Frankfurt's airport, the need for the computer company to coordinate product specifications, pricing, warranties, and parts distribution is quite clear.

Global Account Management

In practice, however, the coordination is not that easy. The typical solution for the multinational buyer is for companies to organize **global account managers** or account groups whose sole responsibility is to serve that customer globally. The account managers serve primarily a coordinative function, usually without direct line responsibility over functions. Their tasks involve the coordination of orders from the customer's various locations, the negotiations for uniform prices, the coordination of communications from various sources inside the firm (R&D, manufacturing, parts) to the various customer locations, and, above all, the provision of consistent after-sales service and follow-up from the seller in all countries. The account managers are the global counterparts to the account groups serving similar functions with domestic customers, such as P&G's large account group (over 60 people strong) focused on Wal-Mart.

Global customers naturally force a coordinated marketing approach, with the marketer's local subsidiaries asked to execute similar strategies as elsewhere. These coordinated strategies involve **relationship marketing,** with the account managers and their groups providing special services. Instead of treating the customer as one among many, relationship marketing increases customer satisfaction by treating the customer as a special client.

This means that extra services can be offered on demand and that the SOPs (standard operating procedures) may be altered for this customer. Banks change opening hours for their corporate customers, packaged good manufacturers help manage inventories for their top wholesalers, and auto companies offer vacation trips for their largest dealers. For some large and favored customers, the global account manager at the head office is the guy they can squeeze to get the lowest global price.[15]

Needless to say, some of these "relationship marketing" tools can be demoralizing for the local subsidiaries, as the buyer actively tries to play headquarters against local sellers. To carry these activities out on a global scale is a challenge, requiring a lot of information sharing and coordination across the seller's subsidiaries. The global account manager needs to have people skills in dealing not only with the customer but also with the managers in the local subsidiaries (see box, "H-P's Global Account Management").

Coordination of marketing activities for smaller customers and individual buyers who purchase globally is usually more narrowly focused on avoiding the pricing arbitrage possibilities we discussed in Chapter 13. As for distribution control, rather than relying on innovations in organizational structure, firms tend to attempt coordination via more ad hoc measures and specific interventions in the channels as discussed in Chapter 14. Global account clients can be selected on the basis of several criteria. They are often industry leaders, in terms of both technology and sales. This creates a competitive advantage where it counts and spreads the awareness of the program throughout the industry. The global accounts should have active operations in several countries, including manufacturing and design. This is the source of the advantage of cross-country coordination. There should be an expressed desire for worldwide procurement, price, service, and support agreements. The global buyer, in effect, needs to be organized for centralized buying.

Retail Trade Groups

Retailers who are resellers of the manufacturer's product lines are a special type of global customer. They are also becoming globalized.[16]

In most developed countries, the leading five or six retailing chains control well over 50 percent of the total food and drink volume. They are also expanding abroad.

G E T T I N G   T H E

Picture

H-P's Global Account Management

IN 1991 HEWLETT-PACKARD launched a global account management program to meet six customers' need for more standardization and support on a global basis. The global account manager (GAM) reports to the field sales manager and the subsidiary manager in the country of the client's home office and works to achieve coordination and to satisfy the performance goals of the account.

Since the GAM often takes over the country manager's best and most profitable client, conflicts arise. After a couple of years, H-P decided to offer the country managers an option to have their performance tied partly to the success of the GAM account. In addition, the directive from the center is strongly worded to the country manager: Cooperate or else.

The GAM contact point at the H-P head office is a headquarters account manager (HAM) who works jointly with the GAM on technical, pricing, and strategy issues. They also support business development efforts and share best practices from throughout the H-P organization with the country subsidiaries and with the global clients.

The program has grown from 6 to 26 global accounts in three years. Its success is measured in terms of increased orders and satisfaction among the global clients. Internally, the program's success is attributed to top management support, the dual reporting system from the GAM to the field operations and the country manager, and the selling of the system inside as a competitive advantage.

Sources: Gates, 1995; Royal and Lucas, 1995 (See also Case 4.5) *http://www.hp.com*

Tengelman, the German retailer, owns A&P in the United States; French Carrefour is a leading retailer in Spain and Brazil; and American Safeway is a leading supermarket in Britain. The heavy investments in computer equipment needed for scanners to streamline inventory control and stock the shelves have required these retailers to hire highly qualified staff people who do not hesitate to make strong demands for service from suppliers. For example, the Wal-Mart success in the United States is partly the result of its managers' insistence that manufacturers supply just-in-time inventory. The success of high-quality private labels and store brands is helping fuel the retail chain's expansion. In some European countries store brands account for more than 30 percent of the total market.

In response, consumer goods manufacturers are creating a special form of **retail trade marketing groups.** These groups attempt to meet the powerful retailers' need for customized product design, advertising, direct marketing, and sales promotions. Trade marketing groups learn which of their company's services and products are most needed by a customer, spot opportunities, and detect problems. Members of these groups include personnel from sales, service, manufacturing, logistics, management information systems, and other business activities. Nestlé's cooperation with French retailer Casino and the 7-Eleven experience in Japan illustrate these points (see box, "Manufacturers Pay Attention to Retailers").

CONFLICT RESOLUTION

Coordinating the marketing function on a global basis usually means consolidation of local staff, reduced budgets at subsidiaries, and less local autonomy. This naturally threatens to demoralize country managers, who typically lose control first over manufacturing and then gradually over strategic marketing decisions. What remains are usually tactical decisions about sales, promotions, and local advertising.

The local units are crucial for effective execution of global programs. This is where the middlemen are contacted, advertising media are bought, customers are encountered, and sales are made. Even in the case of global customers, whose negotiations may be with a headquarters global account group, the deliveries of the goods or

G E T T I N G   T H E   *Picture*

Manufacturers Pay Attention to Retailers

A CONSUMER GOODS company such as Nestlé has unique contributions to bring to its partnerships with retailers. Its leading global brands offer strong appeal. The products offer high quality at competitive prices. The company's market research provides detailed knowledge of consumer habits and requirements, and R&D generates a stream of improvements and new products.

When Nestlé encountered some conflict about shipments and service with Casino, a large French retailer, the company decided to leverage these resources by establishing a retail trade group focused on Casino. The trade group initiated a series of cooperative meetings to develop joint marketing, logistics, and sales efforts. For example, the partners agreed to test a joint breakfast promotion, with 10 Nestlé brands matched against 10 store brands to help determine which products sell well. The companies will jointly analyze bar code information and scanner data to create a database of how to build customer loyalty for brands and stores while reducing costs. Casino will get help to find out which products need to be stocked more (and which less), while Nestlé will get help to reduce supply channel delays (in France goods-to-market time for breakfast cereals is 11 weeks compared with 3 weeks in the United States).

A similar type of alignment that helps manufacturers offer low prices without jeopardizing their clout in regular channels is represented by the various tie-ins arranged by 7-Eleven in Japan. Companies such as Philip Morris, Hershey, and Häagen-Dazs will make specially designed products available for sale in 7-Eleven stores only. For example, under one arrangement, the Kraft division of Philip Morris will sell smaller-sized cheesecakes through the convenience store chain. Although reflective of the power of 7-Eleven in Japan, the alliances are also illustrative of how Western manufacturers seem more able to cope with the new distribution outlets in Japan than their domestic counterparts.

Sources: Gates, 1995; Johansson and Hirano, 1995; Simmons, 1990.

---

services are usually local. To counter the threat of lowered morale and to resolve actual or potential conflicts, companies have introduced some or all of the following **conflict resolution** practices:

1. *Let country managers retain local brands and marketing budgets.* In many companies country managers maintain a local product and brand portfolio. While they may have little control over global or regional brands, they have full responsibility for the marketing programs of their local brands. They control promotional budget allocations between the brands and the amount allocated to specific tactics such as sales contests and in-store couponing. Also, they have a role to play in global brands. Even though the ad agency choice may be made higher up, they can choose the agency for sales promotions and for direct marketing efforts.

2. *Solicit country managers' input for new-product development.* Country managers, especially in leading markets, are well positioned to develop and test new products. Especially where new products are market rather than technology driven, the local managers' inputs become crucial. Companies in which the local product manager reports to the country manager rather than to a global product manager tend to have a higher success rate for new products.[17]

Bausch & Lomb, the optics and glass maker, improved its new-product development success by switching from a global to a regional substructure. Each region has its own product development team, and each local manager participates in the regional level's decisions about priorities for new-product development. New product ideas from local markets are encouraged, and after the idea is presented and evaluated at the regional level, it passes to a global product coordinating committee for worldwide sharing.

3. *Give country managers lead roles in global teams.* To create mutual dependence and improve implementation, it is important that over time different country managers

take responsibility for a global brand or at least one component of the global marketing. As in the Vizir case, the country managers are often at the receiving end of the stick, so to speak, when they have to persuade other country managers to participate in a global program, and this helps make them sympathetic in turn to the requests of other global team leaders. It is important that the country managers assume responsibilities in the global teams, so that the local subsidiary's role is endorsed by the boss. Lower-level managers, such as the local product manager and advertising manager, will then have the requisite support and legitimacy to implement the local part of the global campaigns.

4. *Provide international transfers for country managers.* A clear perspective on foreign local markets helps when making global marketing decisions. Consequently, global marketing groups at the head office would benefit from foreign national marketing team members. Unfortunately, frequent international transfers of marketing managers are still rare. There is even less exchange between subsidiaries in different countries. In a recent study, only 4 of 35 companies reported any regular transfers of marketing people between country subsidiaries.[18]

Foreign marketing managers are caught in a double bind.[19] A lack of experience at corporate headquarters limits the foreign managers from reaching the upper echelons where their different perspective could be very valuable. However, since most global companies do not offer the marketing managers the opportunity to work at the home office, there is no way to accumulate the required corporate experience.

If neither marketing nor country managers rotate, their experiences remain parochial. This can be a disadvantage since the implementation of global strategies requires local sacrifices for the benefit of the entire company. Creating alternative career opportunities for country managers outside their home market can broaden their perspectives and lessen conflict with global or regional managers.

5. *Involve the country managers in the formulation of the global marketing strategy.* In the end, the best medicine against local subversion of global marketing is to co-opt the country managers by inviting them to help design the global marketing strategy. The impetus for a globalized strategy is almost always from the top, since headquarters marketers are the ones who most easily notice the potential savings and gains. But once the start has been made, country managers from, at the least, the leading countries and the markets most directly affected should be directly involved in the strategy formulation. The implementation success of global strategies tends to be directly proportional to the level of local involvement in strategy formulation.[20]

There are, of course, obvious problems associated with having managers from several countries involved in the strategy formulation:

- Local managers propose strategies without a full understanding of the global situation.
- Country managers feel forced to put their local interests first.
- Communication between managers of different nationalities is not always easy.

These obstacles have made many companies reluctant to involve too many country managers in their global strategy development. Instead of relying on foreign managers, many companies rely on home office nationals with experience abroad. This is the common style in Japanese corporations, with the global strategies developed in Japan and disseminated to local subsidiaries. The local perspectives are mainly represented through Japanese managers with experience in the various countries, a solution made possible because Japanese multinationals consistently try to develop top career paths that include rotations to overseas sites. Unfortunately, the local perspectives brought to the home office for the formulation of the global strategies are sometimes quite biased and unreliable, especially when based on only one or two individual experiences.

Japanese companies are doing well in the Americas where most of the Japanese corporations can draw on a number of senior internal advisers with direct country experience for the strategy formulations. By contrast, in the European market most Japanese companies are dependent on a few individuals with direct experience in any one country. But the language and cultural barriers—and the Japanese consensus-style decision making—make such relative outsiders' advice difficult to assimilate. Not surprisingly, the Japanese are baffled by the fragmented European markets, and the EU integration has been warmly welcomed by them.

The **ethnocentricity** of the Japanese corporations is paralleled in some global European companies: Mercedes and Siemens have strong German identities, Philips is Dutch at the core, and Ikea is Swedish, while Marks & Spencer is English, and Benetton is Italian. This situation arises from the desire not only to avoid conflict in strategy formulation but also to draw strength from the cultural heritage of the country.

American companies sometimes, though not always, show less ethnocentricity in the handling of their country managers. This is commonly attributed to the openness and multiculturalism of the American society. Regardless, a lack of ethnocentricity becomes desirable and beneficial because the American multinationals do have such a large share of their resources located overseas. As data show, both in absolute value and in terms of proportions, the American global companies have more assets abroad than any other country. About one-fifth of the output of American firms is produced offshore, and about a quarter of all U.S. imports and exports represent intrafirm transfers. There is an accompanying cadre of foreign nationals in management positions in the local subsidiaries, providing a rich source of local market information and know-how. Some observers argue that future American competitive strength will come increasingly from the judicious use of these national managers inside the global organization, and that the absence of promising global careers in European and Japanese companies will make it impossible for them to attract the best local managerial talent.[21]

Involving the country managers in the formulation of global marketing strategies not only is good for the quality of the strategy designed and the collaboration that makes local implementation easier but also makes the country manager's job more interesting, attracting the best local talents.

SUMMARY

The inherent conflict between local country managers and the top-down imposition of global marketing needs to be recognized and handled very candidly throughout the organization. The limits of the resources allocated to the local marketing budgets need to be justified to the local managers, and appropriate compensating measures in terms of new global team responsibilities should be considered. In addition it is important that local managers be consulted early in the global strategy formulation process to get their input and stimulate acceptance of the globalization as well as to encourage cooperation with the local implementation of the strategy. Not many companies can go as far as GE and ABB, whose strong and single-minded CEOs virtually force local

implementation of the global strategy, but any globalizing effort involves a certain overcoming of local resistance.

Of the various organization structures that the large multinational firm can operate with, a split between a domestic and an international division is consistently a negative factor in implementing globalized marketing. Having global product divisions without a division between the domestic and the foreign markets is more conducive to a global strategy, but there is almost always a need to consider a strengthening of the foreign market perspective. This has led many globalizing companies into a matrix structure with a geographic dimension cutting across the product divisions, which has meant that local country managers are charged with coordination of the firm's involvement in the country while global product managers are responsible for the global marketing program for each particular product line.

While a firm may globalize marketing strategy, marketing tactics usually need to be adapted to local conditions. Thus, the implementation of a global strategy involves a considerable amount of local activity, and it is important that the local subsidiary manager is motivated to support the global brand. This is often accomplished by the creation of global teams focusing on specific brands, on specific tactical measures, or even special global campaigns. These teams can take the temporary form of task forces rather than becoming permanent fixtures in the organizational structure. However, over time the success of such teams has tended to make them the prime vehicle for global marketing implementation, and compa-

nies have come to institutionalize them. The added advantage is that serving on a global team is a good way for a country manager to become familiar with corporate headquarters and other country managers, creating a basis for future promotions up the corporate ladder.

The role of people and organizational culture in the implementation of global marketing is also crucial. Regardless of how globalized the organizational structure and the management systems are, there is always need for people skills to lubricate the relationships and make the organization function. Global communications require the telephone, faxes, and perhaps multimedia, but in the end the global marketer needs to travel and meet with people face to face. This also has the advantage that the marketer can stay closer to the customer, a particularly important factor when organizing for global consumers.

KEY TERMS

conflict resolution p. 516
ethnocentricity p. 518
expatriates p. 512
export department structure p. 500
global account managers p. 514
global marketing director p. 507
global network as an asset p. 504

global product divisions p. 501
global teams p. 508
horizontal networks p. 503
international division structure p. 500
intranets p. 506
management systems p. 508
matrix organization p. 502
network theory p. 505
organizational culture p. 512

organizational design p. 500
people skills p. 510
regional organization p. 500
relationship marketing p. 514
retail trade marketing groups p. 515
strategic business unit p. 500
transnational organization p. 502

DISCUSSION QUESTIONS

1. Discuss how a global team would work to create the kind of pricing "corridor" to control gray trade mentioned in Chapter 13. How would it work with the local subsidiaries to create and implement the kind of global advertising campaign created by Goodyear in Chapter 15?

2. "Global managers are made, not born. This is not a natural process. We are herd animals. We like people who are like us. But there are many things you can do. Obviously, you rotate people around the world. There is no substitute for line experience in three or four countries to create a global perspective. You also encourage people to work in mixed-nationality teams. You *force* them to create personal alliances across borders. This is why we put so much emphasis on teams." So says Percy Barnevik, CEO of Asea Brown Boveri (ABB), the large Swedish-Swiss multinational in electrical machinery.[22] Discuss what is gained by such

rotation and forced personal alliances. Are there any risks involved? What alternatives to the team concept are there?

3. Discuss how a multinational can use its Web site home page to share information with its employees around the world. Will the emergence of electronic communication links make it more or less difficult to implement a global strategy?

4. Why are people skills so important in the implementation of global marketing? Will the emergence of electronic communications over the various networks (Internet, intranets) make people skills more or less important than before?

5. What are the pros and cons for a native country manager to drop a strong local brand in favor of a global brand. How would you go about presenting the need for the global brand to your local staff?

NOTES

1. The burdensome tasks are well documented by Davidson and Haspeslagh, 1982.

2. This is the terminology proposed by Bartlett and Ghoshal, 1989.

3. There is some evidence that the Japanese managers' people skills and company commitment help motivate subsidiaries to adopt a global strategy; see Yip and Johansson, 1993.

4. See Forsgren and Johanson, 1992.

5. The "hypercompetition" concept was first advanced by D'Aveni, 1994.

6. Much of this and the following section draw on Gates' excellent review (Gates, 1995).

7. These examples are taken from the review by Gates, 1995, and from 3M corporate publications.

8. From Axelsson et al., 1992.

9. Huddleston, 1990, shows vividly why visits from headquarters can be a real distraction for local management.

10. It is useful to remember that a uniform global strategy more or less explicitly assumes that headquarters has better information than locals. In specific instances, such as the degree of price sensitivity on the part of local customers, the notion that headquarters "knows better" than the locals is debatable; see Assmus and Wiese, 1995.

11. The importance of local "ownership" of the strategy formulation process for fairness evaluations was empirically demonstrated by Kim and Mauborgne, 1993.

12. See Hanni et al., 1995.

13. The example of Goodyear's development process of pan-regional advertising in Latin America discussed in Chapter 15 shows how a global mindset can be instilled—and how local knowledge can be integrated into the strategy formulation—by repeated interactions between local subsidiary managers and headquarters personnel (Hanni et al., 1995).

14. Thanks to Norio Nishi of Canada's Commonwealth Bank in Tokyo for suggesting the three roles.

15. See Royal and Lucas, 1995, for a rather cynical view of global account management.

16. This section relies heavily on Gates' up-to-date research on current practices among multinationals. See Gates, 1995.

17. This was one of the empirical findings of Theuerkauf et al., 1993.

18. This surprising finding is reported by Gates, 1995. Despite the many reasons why experiences in different countries are good for management development, especially in marketing, relatively few companies seem to be able to create effective programs to induce people to take a stint abroad.

19. This dilemma is well illustrated in the *Business International* 1990 report.

20. From Kim and Mauborgne's 1993 findings.

21. This point is forcefully made by Ferdows, 1993.

22. See Taylor, 1992.

SELECTED REFERENCES

Assmus, Gert; and Carsten Wiese. "How to Address the Gray Market Threat Using Price Coordination." *Sloan Management Review* 36, no. 3 (1995), pp. 31–42.

Axelsson, Bjorn; Jan Johanson; and Johan Sundberg. "Managing by International Traveling." Chapter 7 in Forsgren and Johanson, 1992.

Bartlett, Christopher. "Procter & Gamble Europe: Vizir Launch." Harvard Business School, case 384–139, 1983.

———; and Sumantra Ghoshal. *Managing across Borders: The Transnational Solution.* Boston: Harvard Business School Press, 1989.

Business International. "Marketing Strategies for Global Growth and Competitiveness." October 1990.

D'Aveni, Richard. *Hypercompetition.* New York: Free Press, 1994.

Davidson, William H.; and Philippe Haspeslagh. "Shaping a Global Product Organization." *Harvard Business Review,* July–August 1982, pp. 125–32.

Ferdows, Kasra. "Leveraging America's Foreign Production Assets." Working paper, Georgetown University, School of Business Administration, OPMT-1977-01-293, 1993.

Forsgren, Mats; and Jan Johanson, eds. *Managing Networks in International Business.* Philadelphia: Gordon and Breach, 1992.

Gates, Stephen. "The Changing Global Role of the Marketing Function: A Research Report." *The Conference Board,* report no. 1105-95-RR, 1995.

Hakansson, Hakan. *Corporate Technological Behavior: Cooperation and Networks.* London: Routledge, 1989.

Halliburton, Chris; and Reinhard Huenerberg. "Pan-European Marketing—Myth or Reality?" *Journal of International Marketing* 1, no. 3 (1993), pp. 77–92.

———; and Ian Jones. "Global Individualism—Reconciling Global Marketing and Global Manufacturing." *Journal of International Marketing* 2, no. 4 (1994), pp. 79–88.

Hanni, David A.; John K. Ryans; and Ivan R. Vernon. "Coordinating International Advertising—The Goodyear Case Revisited for Latin America." *Journal of International Marketing* 3, no. 2 (1995), pp. 83–98.

Hertz, Susanne; and Lars-Gunnar Mattsson. *Mindre foretag blir internationella: Marknadsforing i natverk* (Smaller Firms Go International: Marketing in a Network). Lund, Sweden: Liber Ekonomi, 1998. (In Swedish).

Huddleston, Jackson N., Jr. *Gaijin Kaisha: Running a Foreign Business in Japan.* Tokyo: Charles E. Tuttle, 1990.

Johansson, Johny K.; and Masaaki Hirano. "Japanese Marketing in the Post-Bubble Era." *International Executive,* Vol. 38(1), Jan-Feb. 1996, pp. 33–51.

Kim, W. Chan; and Renee A. Mauborgne. "Making Global Strategies Work." *Sloan Management Review,* Spring 1993, pp. 11–27.

Mazur, Laura; and Judie Lannon. "Crossborder Marketing: Lessons from 25 European Success Stories." *Economist Intelligence Unit,* February 1994.

Pearson, A. E.; and S. P. Ehrlich. "Honda Motor Co. and Honda of America (A)." Harvard Business School, case no. 9-390-111, 1989.

Royal, Weld; and Allison Lucas. "Global Pricing and Other Hazards." *Sales & Marketing Management* 147, no. 8 (August 1995), pp. 80–83.

Sakiya, Tetsuo. *Honda Motor: The Men, the Management, and the Machines.* Tokyo: Kodansha, 1987.

Simmons, Tim. "A Global Brand of Dialog." *Supermarket News* 40, no. 28 (July 9, 1990), p. 2.

Taylor, William. "The Logic of Global Business: An Interview with ABB's Percy Barnevik." Reprinted in Christopher A. Bartlett, and Sumantra Ghoshal. *Transnational Management.* Homewood, IL: Irwin, 1992, pp. 892–908.

Theuerkauf, Ingo; David Ernst; and A. Mahini. "Think Local, Organize . . ." *McKinsey Quarterly*, no. 1 (1993), pp. 107–114.

Uchitelle, Louis. "Gillette's World View: One Blade Fits All." *New York Times*, January 3, 1994, p. C3.

Yip, George; and Johny K. Johansson. "Global Market Strategies of U.S. and Japanese Business." Working paper, Marketing Science Institute, Cambridge, MA, 1993, pp. 93–102.

Yoshino, Michael. *Procter & Gamble Japan (A)(B)(C).* Harvard Business School, case nos. 9-391-003, 004, 005, 1990.

The Future of Global Marketing

"Point and click"

Your takeaways from this chapter:

1. The Internet has emerged as a strong force in marketing, and its global reach supports global expansion of many businesses, large and small. Its main drawback is the lack of technological infrastructure and Internet access in many countries.

2. Electronic commerce is growing rapidly, especially in services. Marketers are starting to view on-line users as a special target segment in different countries.

3. The main threat against *global* marketing is a possible rise of protectionism associated with the current global financial crisis, and its potential for generating political and military conflict.

4. The threat against *local* marketing, especially in emerging markets, is the naturally unequal distribution of benefits from open markets and free trade among the average citizens. The frustrations can lead to a backlash against free market practices, and thus further restraints.

5. In most markets of the future, strong global marketing needs to be localized, and strong local marketing needs to be globalized. This is the task of global localization and local globalization, respectively.

GLOBAL MARKETING is in many ways still only at the beginning. Global brands have been around for a long time, and globally standardized products are certainly not new. But what has emerged in the last decade is a much more emphatic stress on the centralization and coordination of marketing strategies and tactics around the world to take advantage of scale savings and demand spillovers. Will this development continue and intensify, or are there threats against global marketing that will limit its progress? And how can the firm achieve "global localization," the popular expression reflecting the need to be global and local at the same time?

In the early 1990s, for most companies the answers to these questions were obvious. The global imperative meant that marketing in the future has to be global to succeed.

Marketers had to adopt a global perspective or else be left behind. Companies from Microsoft in PC software to Ford in automobiles, Unilever in toiletries, Beck's in beer, Marriott in hotels, Armstrong in wall paneling, Bridgestone in water tanks and tires, and innumerable others all shared this perspective.

In the late 1990s, by contrast, the global financial crisis has severely tested the faith of many believers. Although most companies still maintain a global posture, as we have seen, some are adopting a more cautious and "limited global" attitude.

This chapter will critically examine the global imperative and how the financial crisis coupled with developments in information technology and the Internet may affect global marketing in the future. As the reader will find out, despite threats against the global economic system and problems in local marketing, the future of global management is still bright.

Building Brands on the Internet: Not Yet?

By 1998, most major multinationals had created their own home page on the World Wide Web, ranging from simple greetings and company logos to virtual storefronts and full-fledged interactive shopping possibilities. In addition, the companies had created banner ads and linkages from various popular sites to attract browsers and surfers to their home pages. But few companies seemed to know what the economic value of these ads or the home pages might be. In the words of the typical marketing manager, it was simply a case of "everybody has to be on the Web."

What's the value of a presence on the Internet? In August 1998, in an effort to find out how best to use the Web, Procter and Gamble assembled a group of 400 top executives from Internet and consumer marketing companies, including America Online and Coca-Cola, at a "summit" conference in Cincinnati. Spurred by the increased penetration of Internet access into households, was it possible, P&G asked, to use the Web for sales, for promotions, and as a new advertising medium? Could the Internet replace television commercials, in-store promotions, and even the stores themselves?

By the year 2000, the number of households with Internet access in the United States alone is forecasted to be about 40 million. Add the number of individuals with Internet access at their workplace, and add also the numbers from other countries around the world, and P&G's query becomes understandable. If the numbers so far are any guide, many of these Internet customers will use the Web to find out more about the products they consider purchasing. In 1996,

85 percent of Internet users in the United States said they intended to surf the Web the next time they bought an automobile. Denis Beausejour, P&G's vice president for advertising, suspected that if it was possible to advertise and sell cars, airplane tickets, and books on-line, could detergent, soap, and toothpaste, P&G's staples, be far behind?

Most of the companies at the meeting had spent only a very small share of their promotional budget on the Internet. Procter and Gamble's own 1997 spending was $2.1 million, out of an advertising budget of $1.7 billion, or much less than 1 percent. Even a car company such as Ford spent only about 0.5 percent of its total 1997 ad budget on the Internet.

As it turned out, most of the participants agreed that until the technology is further advanced, it will be difficult to develop the kind of brand building capability that traditional media have. The typical banner ads flashing on top or on the side of the screen are simply not emotionally involving. For example, John Sculley described the brand building strategy used when he was the CEO at Pepsi-Cola in the 1980s: "When we created the Pepsi Generation, we needed to make Pepsi a drink that says something about the people who drank it. The Web is not ready for that emotion yet." The consensus at the meeting was that the Web ads will be good for specific product information (including prices) and as reminders of brands and events, but not as a primary medium for creating brand image and identity.

So far, apparently, the Web as a promotional medium supports and reinforces the images already created through other media. A good case in point is the multimedia campaign developed in 1995 for the launch of the BMW Roadster, the Z3. The sporty mid-priced car ($28,000 list price) was targeted to the young and restless, including those in their middle age who wanted to recapture some of their (lost) youth. Using a product placement strategy, BMW launched it with great media fanfare as the James Bond car in the film *GoldenEye*, starring Pierce Brosnan. Free loaners were offered to TV personalities (Jay Leno) and radio DJs. It was featured as a pricey gift in the Christmas catalog of Neiman-Marcus, an upscale department store (generating 5,000 orders!). On its Web page, BMW displayed Pierce Brosnan, the catalog insertion, and reports on Leno's and others' reactions to the car.

According to research, the brands that are already well known tend to attract the largest number of Web site visits. Advertising on the Internet is likely to grow—but not, apparently, at the expense of other media that have proven capability to build brands.

Sources: Saul Hansell, "Selling Soap without the Soap Operas," *New York Times*, August 24, 1998, pp. D1, 7; "1998 On-Line Advertising Report," Jupiter Communications; Susan Fournier and Robert J. Dolan. "Launching the BMW Z3 Roadster," Harvard Business School, case no. N9-597-002.
http://www.pg.com
http://www.aol.com
http://www.coca-cola.com
http://www.cokecce.com
http://www.ford.com
http://www.pepsiworld.com
http://www.bmw.com
http://www.neimanmarcus.com/

INTRODUCTION

In the 1997 edition of this text, the final chapter warned of growing protectionist sentiment in various countries and also extolled the virtues and promise of the Internet marketplace. In this second edition, three years later, these two themes need to be emphasized even more.

The protectionist forces have been kindled further by the global financial crisis that started in Thailand in 1997. As the crisis spread like wildfire first across Asia and then into Russia and Brazil, it threatened to eclipse other economies as well. The result has been devastating for countries and their people at the end of the 1990s.

Item. The Asian currency collapse has forced companies into bankruptcy, stoppage of foreign payments, unemployment, and loss of incomes and savings.

Industrial and consumer goods markets have virtually disappeared in Asia as individual households and consumers regroup. Riots and ethnic strife accompany individual frustrations in Indonesia, Korea, and elsewhere.

Item. Russia is embroiled in economic and political chaos as oil revenues dip, government tax collection falters, and foreign investors pull out.

Item. Brazil is temporarily shifting to a barter economy as foreign investment exits, putting a squeeze on the real currency and forcing companies and consumers to reduce spending.

The result. Global companies that throughout this book have been held up as carriers of the global marketing torch are suffering. From Coca-Cola and Citibank to ABB, Sony, and Siemens, firms reported lower revenues and profits in 1998. The companies are still firmly wedded to the global concept—but, as we have seen earlier in this book, they have become more cautious and some are weighing carefully the advantages of a more limited global involvement.

Contrast this with the continued "Up, up and away!" spirit of the Internet and electronic commerce. Even though some of the Internet-related businesses have yet to make a solid profit, the values of their outstanding shares, measuring the expected value of their future business revenues, have grown far beyond the more traditional businesses.

Item. Amazon.com, the on-line book seller that, despite huge revenue growth, has yet to show any profits (inventory costs are still high and prices are set lower than retail outlets to make up for transportation charges and delivery time), had a market value in December 1998 well above the combined value of the top book-selling retail rivals, Barnes & Noble and Borders.

Item. Charles Schwab Corporation, the leading on-line discount stockbroker based in San Francisco, has a market value higher than Merrill Lynch & Company, even though the latter showed 1997 revenues of $17.1 billion, more than seven times those of Schwab.

Item. Microsoft, the leading software company whose Windows provides the basic operating system for most desktops and whose Explorer program for Internet browsing has edged out Netscape in the race for market share, is making record profits and shows continued high share prices despite pending monopoly charges in U.S. courts.

The result. Any business enterprise involving the Internet seems promising enough to attract venture capital funding and entrepreneurial workers. And since the Internet is inherently global, providing a boundary-less marketplace, electronic commerce on the Internet is growing by leaps and bounds.

Ironically, these dual developments move in opposite directions: one threatening global marketing, the other offering new opportunities. If one would dare make any predictions in this context, it would be that both trends are extreme. The bad state of the global economic system at the end of 1998 is likely to shift into calmer and warmer waters by the beginning of the next century (Asian stock markets showed hopeful signs of recovery in early 1999, for example), while the expansive dreams attached to some Internet entrepreneurial efforts will turn out to be a bit too rosy as reality sets in.

In what follows, the chapter will first discuss some of the potential protectionist dangers resulting from the global financial crisis. It will also touch on the ethics of free markets and how local reception for a global marketer in some countries may be more negative than expected. The chapter will also briefly discuss how the advances in global communications and information technology help companies integrate their far-flung operations and the implementation of global strategies through intranets. Then the chapter will shift to Internet and electronic commerce, discussing the global implications of the rapid increase in on-line marketing. The chapter concludes with a discussion of global localization, the role of strategy execution, and how companies manage to be global and local simultaneously.

POLITICS AND GLOBAL MARKETING

Protectionism

There should be little doubt on the part of a marketer about the threat to the global trade regime from **protectionist forces,** wherever and whenever they arise. Tariff barriers and quotas keep more efficient *exporters* away from domestic competitors in home markets. There are various ways of getting over the hurdles, but they invariably lead to higher costs. Investing in *overseas manufacturing* may not be economically justified unless protective barriers force the issue. *Licensing* and *strategic alliances* transfer technologies but carry risks that need to be compensated. Demands for government equity shares in *joint ventures* jeopardize entry and complicate management of the local operation.

From a marketing perspective, these issues take on a different color. As we saw in Chapter 6, in principle it is possible to do global marketing under any mode of entry. Whether exporting (Mazda), licensing (McDonald's), joint venturing (Xerox), or running wholly owned subsidiaries (IBM), a company can globalize its marketing. The problem is that the company's products and services may not be competitive in the protected markets because of the price escalation caused by entry barriers. As we have seen, global marketing almost always involves a certain amount of uniformity across countries. Trade barriers distort the markets and the positions of the products, making uniform marketing difficult if not impossible. In protected markets, imported low-end products automatically become positioned as high-priced luxuries (Chrysler cars in Japan, Budweiser beer in Asia, Levi's jeans in Europe, to name a few).

With protected markets, most local marketing is necessarily unique to the country environment. It is designed to deal with the markets' distorted price structures, and it attempts to nullify domestic producers' artificial advantages. It is hardly a coincidence that in the many protected markets after World War II, marketing became a matter of adaptation to local customs. In protected markets, imposing global uniformity will be suicidal. Open and free markets are a precondition for global marketing.

The current political difficulties in Russia, Asia (including China), Brazil, and elsewhere—which stem from disappointment with free markets, a nationalistic impulse, and a desire to return to a nostalgic past—are threats to global marketing because they encourage protectionism. At the same time, the liberation of South Africa, the free market conversion of India, the strengthening of democracy in Latin America, and the thrust toward free markets in former communist countries are all positive signs. On balance, the picture still looks positive, with the World Trade Organization, the new GATT, poised to rebuff any threats. The high cost of protectionism has been recognized all over the world.[1] Nonfree markets are a luxury.

Free Trade Areas

The regional free trade areas (EU, NAFTA, APEC, etc.) have made "regional" a midway stop between "country" and "global." In principle, dividing the globe into several trade regions is inefficient when compared with pure free trade among all nations. In practice, however, regional trade areas justify globalization strategies, offering sufficient *size* for scale returns in manufacturing and marketing, and sufficient market *similarity* for standardization of products and services and uniformity of the communications mix.

Whether or not regional integration becomes a stepping stone toward further integration remains to be seen. The experience in Europe is positive in this regard. As the EU integration gained momentum, several EFTA countries (members of the European Free Trade Area) initiated negotiations toward EU membership. By the beginning of 1999 the European Union had 15 members: Austria, Belgium, Finland, France, Germany, Ireland, Italy, Luxembourg, the Netherlands, Portugal, Spain, England, Denmark, Sweden, and Greece—all but the last four members of the new euro currency regime. Countries are apparently not willing to let existing membership loyalties stop them when a better deal is available. From this perspective, one would expect free trade areas to gradually expand to include new members and in the process become more global. The negotiations about NAFTA's inclusion of Chile and other South American countries are typical examples. Free trade areas are a step toward global free trade, not an effort to place barriers between regional members and nonmember countries.

THE DARK SIDE OF MARKETING

With the failure of the planned economies around the world, marketing is rapidly becoming a household word in the remotest parts of the globe. In advanced countries it is spreading from the field of private business into hospitals, symphony orchestras, and even government agencies. Marketing is riding high in countries where it is traditionally viewed with aversion. But some people still focus on what they see as the dark side of marketing.

The Legitimacy of Free Markets

Marketing requires free markets, and free markets are proving to be a big headache for many of the emerging nations. **Free markets** require supplies of products, information about demand, a currency of exchange—and, basic but easy to forget, a legal framework for the transfer of private ownership from seller to buyer. Emerging countries have a short supply of these ingredients because of the planned economy in the past. This means the countries have trouble creating working marketplaces, where exchanges can be transacted. This holds for stock exchanges as well as for retail stores and business-to-business markets. An example of how the marketplace can be distorted by these factors is McDonald's approach in Moscow (see box, "McDonald's Two Faces").

Needless to say, these problems of free markets create frustrations and anger among many people who happen not to be among the lucky ones. In Russia, crime has become a major problem for Western businesses. Shipments to stores regularly get hijacked, store owners have to pay bribery "fees" to distributors to get access to merchandise, and there is a black market for most Western goods. Not surprisingly, various Mafia-style organizations have sprung up, making life and commerce very difficult.[2] The solution clearly lies in economic progress with shared benefits, but that promise is as yet largely unfulfilled. To engage in heavy marketing activities under such conditions is not only bad business but bad politics. The result is likely to be more regulation, less free enterprise, and a return to the past.

The Ethics of Marketing

In some countries, there is in fact a question about the extent to which the whole **ethics of marketing** thinking and practice is acceptable. In many newly opened markets, customers are not used to the ways of Western marketing, and many can be expected to voice opposition to the unabashed trumpeting of a firm's product. It is not just the hard-hitting advertisements that may cause problems; people may find the notions that

G E T T I N G   T H E   *Picture*

McDonald's Two Faces

IN ITS MOSCOW fast-food outlets opened in the early 1990s, McDonald's initially introduced a system of two separate entrance doors, one for customers with hard currency, and one for customers with rubles only. The customers with hard currency got preferential treatment and were given quicker service and more waiters. Many locals were not served when there were hard currency customers still in line.

As long as the Russians saw only foreigners in the hard currency line, things went relatively smoothly. This was, after all, the ways thing used to be. But as some of the Russians with luck and hard work managed to get access to hard currency and appeared in the "foreign" line, the mood changed. The frustrations and envy on the part of the local currency line began to take their toll, and the out-

lets started to encounter some violent reactions. Words were exchanged, and fights between the people in the two lines became a common occurrence.

McDonald's outlets were forced to introduce security guards to keep order. For a few years, as economic growth was strong, the ruble stabilized; Russian fast-food competition appeared, and the altercations between the two lines temporarily evaporated. But in 1998, as the Russian foreign exchange crisis erupted, the happy days were over. Fighting about standing in line had become a nonissue: Few Russians could afford McDonald's hamburgers any longer.

Sources: Saito, 1991; Specter, 1995, LaFraniere, 1998.
http://www.mcdonalds.com

"anything can be bought," "everything has a price," and "at some price the market will clear" abhorrent. Certain promotional activities are likely to become regulated as the free-for-all euphoria in the new countries recedes. It will be important for marketers to correctly gauge the mood of the populace and to not engage in practices that will stir up negative sentiments. Ethical marketing constraints are likely to be enforced much more in some of these countries than in the United States.

The playbook for the company's strategies might well be taken from the responses to the various problems encountered in the consumer movement in the United States. When Lotus Corporation proposed a database development drawing on individual credit records and social security numbers, the ensuing uproar from privacy advocates forced the company to abandon the plan.[3] The calls for boycotts of brands because of offensive advertising (for example, the Joe Camel cartoon character to sell cigarettes, discontinued after 1998, and the Powermaster malt liquor with extra strong alcohol content aiming for the black minority), the loss of consumer goodwill on the part of Intel because of the Pentium chip problem, and the imposition of fines for misleading advertising by Volvo (where a truck was dropped on a reinforced Volvo to demonstrate its safety) are only a few examples.

A complicating factor for management is that Internet companies will find it increasingly difficult to contain negative publicity. For example, at the end of the 1990s both Nike and Disney were targeted by Internet boycotters arguing that the brands and the corporations were indecent and immoral, Nike for using forced labor in Asia and Disney for allowing homosexual celebrations in its theme parks and extending family benefits to gay couples. These kinds of grass-roots drives have been greatly facilitated by the Internet's ability to quickly spread information globally.

But these issues will seem tame when compared with the more basic problems in emerging markets. The marketer in China is likely to find it difficult to protect a successful brand from imitators, while at the same time people will challenge the foreign influence of a global brand. When Levi's jeans first attempted to uphold the control of its branded jeans against knockoffs in China, the government questioned the idea that a brand name could be copyrighted and then challenged Levi's to leave the country.[4] Similar anticapitalist sentiments are likely to surface elsewhere, as ethical marketing

The Strategic Value of Information Networks

HARDWARE COMPUTER MAKERS such as Compaq and PC software companies like Novell have the same marketing target: the connected corporation, a networked organization with operations distributed globally. To win the coming battle against software competitors, Novell is turning to marketing and global branding.

Denver-based Novell Inc. is the company behind Netware, the leading PC network operating system.

In order to create better recognition and a stronger global presence, in early 1995 Novell hired a new senior vice president for corporate marketing with global responsibilities. Christine G. Hughes came from the Xerox Corporation where she was head of integrated marketing. She understands the role for corporate marketing worldwide: "If you look not just at the industry but at where societies and businesses are going, the ability to get information and to really digest it and make it applicable to what you are doing is the most overriding theme we have had in the computer industry in many years. . . . We have to be higher up in the buyer's organization and address the chief information officers and the chief executive officers."

Sources: Fisher, 1995; La Polla, 1995.
http://www.compaq.com/
http://www.novell.com
http://www.microsoft.com
http://www.xerox.com

questions are raised. Global marketers in emerging markets ignore ethical concerns at their peril.

IT AND STRATEGY IMPLEMENTATION

Before dealing with the impact of the Internet on global markets and marketing, it is useful to discuss briefly the impact of **information technology (IT)** on the multinational firm. The main point to emphasize is that the explosive growth of IT has facilitated company implementation of global strategies tremendously. In fact, it is hard to imagine that global marketing would have gotten very far without global telecommunications, satellite TVs, and the ubiquitous fax machines.

Today, as we saw in Chapter 17, the various locations of a multinational's operations are likely to be connected through an internal **network** of mainframe computers, transmission cables, and desktops. An **intranet** is like a smaller (and password protected!) version of the global Internet, but typically also ties in with the Internet.

With these electronic networks or the cost of communicating with any overseas location has been cut dramatically, often little more than a local phone call. The communications can be real-time, like a telephone call conversation via a keyboard, or sent as electronic mail (e-mail), with the message delivered within seconds to the receiver's computer. The feasibility of sending directives, making inquiries, coordinating shipments, and requesting information—all standard administrative actions in a company implementing a global marketing push—has become much greater. On the other hand, as always with new innovations, established firms tend to be slower on the uptake than new and more agile competitors. For example, a UK study shows that new exporters are more likely to adopt the Web as a marketing tool than established exporters.[5]

Furthermore, not only are global marketing strategies easier to execute through these new implementation tools, but they are more effective as the organization linked electronically necessarily ends up with a common language of communication, usually English. The first task for some country managers today is often to learn how to create access to the network and how to express themselves in written English.

Internet Basics I

THE FIRST BASIC COMPONENTS of the Internet are the **servers,** the large mainframe computers that provide the memory space and processing capability to house the home page visuals, text, data, and interactivity that allow us (the users) to access Internet sites, send e-mail, and chat. These computers can be located anywhere in the world: in foreign countries, in small towns, in the desert. They are similar to broadcasting towers in that space on them is simply leased to companies and individuals who need to establish an Internet site.

The second Internet component is the digital **fiberoptic cable** that links different servers—and also links to us, the users. This is where the old telephone companies come into the picture. They already have access to home and office telephones from electronic switchboards: Now they also lay cables that link to the server computers. This is

why we users need **modems**—to call up the servers. The newer the cables, the faster the connections, and the faster the Internet responds (although with a lot of requests on a site, you may get a busy signal).

The third component of the system is the **desktop computer,** typically a PC or Macintosh. It is needed so that we users can "talk" to the servers, and express ourselves in language they understand. When we "point and click" on an icon on our screen, we are, in a way, using sign language. Our own desktop translates the simple action into a request the mainframe computer can decipher and respond to.

Source: For more information on Internet topology, check out *http://navigators.com/internet_architecture.html* to find a very good description of the Internet.

Information technology has also meant global business for computer and software companies. The new communication hardware and software created by high-technology firms need marketing to succeed. Marketing forces the software sellers to explain to business customers and individuals exactly what benefits will come from the new technology. And as the new products broaden the market base by entering foreign markets, marketing must be globalized (see box, "The Strategic Value of Information Networks").

High-technology communication products and the marketing efforts in their behalf tend to follow the Vernon international product cycle (discussed in Chapter 2) that characterized the initial American overseas entries. The inventing company from any country marches abroad, markets its new product in many countries, and over time globalizes its marketing.

Since the network architecture of an intranet is similar to that of the Internet (only smaller in scale), and since the Internet's World Wide Web serves as the "marketplace" in electronic commerce, it is useful to know a little about how the mechanics (actually the electronics) of the Internet functions (see box, "Internet Basics I").

ELECTRONIC COMMERCE

The Internet has created a new marketplace on the World Wide Web. This development is still in its early stage but has recently been growing at a rapid rate. It is likely to grow immensely in importance for global marketing in the future. This section will provide an overview of the main developments of relevance to global marketing and assess the promise for the future. The best place to start is perhaps with some definitions of the new concepts and the new terminology that Web-based marketing has brought along.

Some Definitions

The **Internet marketplace** started as companies and individuals realized the commercial potential of the vast Internet network. Initially, companies began offering general product information and placing want ads for systems analysts and the like.

Each and every day, thousands of businesses build their sites on the Internet and wonder: When does the excitement begin? Where are the new customers, the improved relationships, the lower overhead? Surprise, surprise. You can't expect it to happen automatically.

It takes a solution. The good news is, a call to IBM can help put things in motion. **IBM Internet solutions** provide a unique combination of technology, professional services and know-how that's enabling a world of e-business opportunities, changing the way business is done. Here are a few customers already reporting results:

Japan Airlines: uses Internet reservations to boost ticket revenue by $4 million.

NHL: online store attracts more than a million hits per month.

Arena di Verona: online ticketing expands opera house audience.

Supervox: French wholesaler finds an $8 million opportunity in previously untapped market.

Find out how **the Internet can transform your business.** Just drop by www.ibm.com/internetsolutions or give us a call at 1 800 IBM-7080, ext. NC01, for our free brochure on commerce solutions.

"the "yippeee... we're on the Internet! now what?" solution

IBM.
Solutions for a small planet™

An IBM ad targeting firms that have just established their Websites. The Internet has already become the information super-highway it was predicted to be, and actual business transactions are growing exponentially. The next step is to understand how a company can make the most out of its 'must-have' homepage presence on the net. Courtesy IBM.

Gradually, as the technology developed and **hits** (the number of requests for a site) started to get recorded, companies moved into customer and market research. As the **cookie** technology emerged (a *cookie* is a memory device that can track a user's activity on a Web site and customize the information provided), the research moved into questionnaire surveys and focus groups via interactive **chat boxes,** text-only boxes that allow typed exchanges between several people at various remote locations. As the accessibility and versatility of the medium has grown, its capabilities as a true global market are becoming realized. It is now an arena for complete electronic commerce.

Electronic commerce refers to buying and selling goods and services on-line, usually on the Internet. It is sometimes also called **on-line marketing.** Electronic commerce shows phenomenal growth particularly in services, those "goods" that can be broken down into chips and bits and "shipped" electronically to the destination. It is also big in business-to-business marketing, where the one-to-one linkages between buyer and seller tend to be stronger and long established.[6] But electronic commerce has become an increasing force in "real products" for consumers as well, including books, cameras, computer software, and even automobiles.

Actually, electronic commerce defined broadly includes more than just buying and selling on the Internet. It can also refer to simple informational or service exchanges, such as those between a government agency and its constituents, teacher-student relationships, and fund-raising. As in marketing generally, electronic commerce refers to the "exchange" between a provider and a customer, this time using electronic communications.

Success Examples

To grasp what the opportunities in electronic commerce are, a few examples of the successes are helpful:[7]

- Dell's on-line customers buy $6 million worth of products each day, customized to their own specifications. These products provide a 30 percent higher profit margin than those bought by its traditional customers.

- Targeting a new on-line market segment, *The Wall Street Journal* has grown its customer base and also retained 85 percent of these new subscribers to its on-line edition.

- American Airlines sends a weekly e-mailing of last-minute discounted ticket offers, specials for the upcoming weekend. The company reaches 1.7 million prospects who subscribe to the listing. American spends virtually no promotional money.

- California-based Wells Fargo has halved its cost per transaction, enjoys higher average balances per customer, and has reduced customer defections by 50 percent for on-line customers.

- Cisco Systems, the maker of the "routers" that help guide user commands and site requests through the electronic network, has saved over $550 million annually in customer service for the last three years and now does 62 percent of its $5 billion annual business over the Internet.

- National Semiconductor, a leading chip maker, provides targeted current information to one-third of its potential global market by offering technological news on its Web site. Over 500,000 design engineers visit its site every month.

Fast Market Growth

Although exact figures for the total transaction volume are not available yet, all indications are that the World Wide Web marketplace has grown by leaps and bounds. The amount of *business-to-business* electronic commerce is allegedly vast but difficult to estimate because sales data tend to be proprietary. The amount of *consumer* electronic commerce so far is assumed to be much smaller. According to Forrester Research, a market research firm in Cambridge, Massachusetts, the 1998 on-line retail market sales were about $4.8 billion, a fairly respectable amount. The firm's forecast for the year 2001 is for total retail sales of more than $17 billion, for an annual growth rate of about 50 percent.

The Forrester firm expects 86 percent of the consumer sales growth to come in just five categories, all of them already established on the Internet: computers, software, entertainment, books, and travel.[8] And by far the largest share will be within North America. Although promising, the global growth for on-line retailing is apparently still in its infancy (see box, "The Internet Global Promise").

Marketing Strengths and Weaknesses

When properly implemented, there are several **marketing strengths** to electronic commerce. For example, on-line marketing:

- Makes it easy and convenient for the customer to do business with you.
- Creates a natural one-to-one relationship between buyer and seller, with customization of products and services.
- Fosters customer loyalty and increases customer retention rates.
- Helps the company focus on providing customer value.

GETTING THE *Picture*

The Internet Global Promise

ALTHOUGH *GLOBAL* ELECTRONIC COMMERCE is still in its infancy, its rapid rise in advanced economies gives some hints of what is to come. Not surprisingly, perhaps, most transactions so far have involved *services* rather than products. While products need to be shipped to the buyer's location, services can often be transmitted electronically to any destination. Some promising high-potential examples include:

Airline tickets. Buy on-line and pick up at the airport ticket counter.

Tourist packages. Compare prices and features, then order for express delivery of tickets to the home.

Banking services. Transfer money, check credit card balances, pay bills.

Brokerage services. Buy and sell shares.

Rental cars. Reserve a car at the airport upon arrival.

Hotel reservations. Get lodgings anywhere in the world.

Because of the need for shipment, global on-line *product* purchases involve the usual logistics costs—from warehousing and transportation to customs clearing and home delivery (see Chapter 14). Still, a few examples show tantalizing promise:

Personal computers. Dell's customized direct sales have been very successful.

Books. Amazon.com is perhaps *the* best example of on-line product marketing.

Computer software. A natural!

Cameras. Catalog sales of cameras were a forerunner of on-line selling.

Leisure apparel. L. L. Bean, Lands' End, and Eddie Bauer are well established through catalogs and are now on-line as well.

Sports equipment. Another natural, although the category faces obstacles in the form of stiff tariff barriers and exclusive distributorships in many countries.

Compact discs. The global Internet music business is fighting against old and well-established local price cartels in many countries. It is also threatening the music industry itself through new technology that allows digital downloading of CDs from the Web.

Sources: Hansell, 1994; Markoff, 1994; Siwolop, 1998.
http://www.dell.com
http://www.amazon.com
http://www.llbean.com
http://www.landsend.com
http://www.eddiebauer.com

- Lowers costs for buyers and sellers in the whole process from prepurchase stage to postpurchase stage.
- Facilitates price comparisons. In fact, proponents of electronic marketing argue that the Internet will make for more efficient markets. Probably so: Preliminary research findings suggest that price competition is heating up for goods on the Web.

At the same time, electronic commerce has some **marketing weaknesses:**

- It can only reach a certain segment of the total market, those with desktops and Internet access. Globally, this is still a severe limitation.
- It cannot (yet) provide the full tactile experience with the product or the personal interaction in service. This limitation is not a drawback for many of the services already successful on the Internet, such as banking and airline travel.
- For effective implementation, electronic commerce needs good electronic communication links. Faulty technology will ruin customer relationships.
- Many customers are put off by computers and technology. The degree of aversion varies across cultures, but the on-line customers will constitute a minority-only in many markets for years to come.
- The perceived risks involved can be great. Who can buy a car simply on the basis of a picture on the Web? (Some apparently can, though even the typical Internet car shopper will visit a dealer before committing to a purchase.)

G E T T I N G   T H E   *Picture*

Global Expansion with Borders

THE BORDERS GROUP, the second largest American bookstore chain after Barnes & Noble, is the first to expand outside the United States. The company, based in Ann Arbor, Michigan, has established a superstore on busy Oxford Street in London and has opened a total of five stores in Britain, Australia, and Singapore during 1997–98. It has plans to open another 10 stores abroad before the year 2000. But it has stayed away from the Internet.

While its main rivals Barnes & Noble and German Bertelsmann are trying to compete head on with Amazon.com in the on-line bookselling market, Borders has opted for a more traditional expansion. While its competitors have been preoccupied with the new business model presented by the Internet challenge, which so far has not been very lucrative for any of the participants, Borders has simply stayed with what it does best: creating large and comfortable store interiors with a huge selection of books and magazines where customers can browse, lounge in huge armchairs, and order house-blend coffee or chilled chardonnay and relive the nostalgia of those darkly lit cafés where the literary elite of past decades did their talking, reading, and sometimes even writing (but, this being the 1990s, "No Smoking" please).

With their store sales booming, the lack of Internet exploration by Borders has not cost the company any lack of revenues. But the stock market sees danger ahead, apparently expecting the Internet market to be a dominant book channel in the future. Accordingly, despite its success, Borders' share prices are down, while those of Barnes & Noble, Bertelsmann, and Amazon.com are up. In fact, even though the European countries have been relatively slow in ramping up their electronic commerce—stymied by traditional prohibitions against discounting and high costs of communication tie-ups—1998 was a year when on-line commerce took hold in Europe. For example, Amazon.com's new UK and German sites established in the fall of 1998 proved immediate successes.

Which strategy is right remains to be seen. Only the future will tell whether traditional retail stores can coexist with electronic commerce.

Sources: Carvajal, 1999; Kahn, 1998; Strassel, 1998.
http://www.borders.com/
http://www.barnesandnoble.com
http://www.bertelsmann.de
http://www.amazon.com
http://www.waterstones.com/
http://www.emigroup.com

- The credit card problem is still with us. Without credit cards, electronic commerce would be unthinkable. Many purchases now on the Internet are as routine as paying with the card in a shop or in a restaurant. Also, the card-issuing banks by and large extend the standard limits and exposure rules to their global customers. Still, many individuals balk at putting their card numbers into cyberspace. The security procedures put in place by different companies seem to be working, although some level of credit card fraud will presumably always be with us.

Given these weaknesses, it is not surprising that so far at least most companies are using the Internet mainly for marketing research and relationship building rather than for outright sales. Marketing research using questionnaires and randomly intercepted Web-site visitors has in fact become very common. Such studies are also facilitated by the "cookie" technology which allows a company to customize responses and interactive messages to each visitor separately. The potential for deception and misuse of the information has induced ESOMAR, the European association of market researchers, to issue a code of ethics for Web-site research. The code stresses in particular the need to inform the visitor that he or she is being monitored, and to offer an option of rejecting the cookie attached to their screen name.

The uncertainties surrounding electronic commerce have prompted at least one bookseller to avoid the Internet when going abroad (see box, "Global Expansion with Borders").

G E T T I N G   T H E
Picture

Internet Basics II

IN "ANCIENT" TIMES, before the Internet, what you could accomplish with your desktop depended simply on how much memory and processing capacity it had.

With the Internet network of computers this has changed dramatically. This is where the **World Wide Web** comes in. Web technology helped connect the network efficiently. The data and information that could be acquired through the Internet were now more accessible. Companies worldwide quickly established Web sites to make themselves known to the world. Universities and public agencies opened Web sites to provide information.

But navigating between the different Web sites— "surfin' the Web"—was initially not easy. This is where Netscape came in. Netscape provided the first easy-to-understand **browser**, the translating "interface" between your desktop and the Web. It offers clear options to users and helps the Web respond to the users' choices. Many of these options have been developed by independent companies, including **search engines** such as Yahoo and Infoseek, which help us look for information about things.

Where do **on-line service providers** such as America Online (AOL) fit in? Basically they allow you—typically for a flat monthly fee—to have your own office on the network. You get an identity, an e-mail address, and the ability to interact with friends and colleagues using chat boxes. The service also provides easy access to the Internet and offers news alerts, film reviews, and shopping tips. This is a service with global potential, especially since local dial-ups allow you to chat with a friend on another continent for a local telephone fee.

Sources: Angell, 1995; Allen et al., 1998.
http://www.netscape.com
http://www.yahoo.com
http://www.infoseek.com
http://www.aol.com

Promotion

The first step for a company to get into electronic commerce is to create a **storefront,** usually the Web **home page.** The home page is the first screen image that pops up when a user accesses a particular company site. It typically shows the company name, logo, and representative product line. On the home page the user can then usually point and click to get further information about company products, to request information to be mailed, to fill out a research questionnaire, or sometimes to play a game. Some car companies (Honda, BMW, Volkswagen) allow the users to design their own version of a car. The new VW Beetle was in fact designed using suggestions from a large number of on-line "wannabe" car designers—and presumably potential buyers.

Specialized software developers design the home page for companies and also maintain and update the site for a fee. The home page is physically located on the server computer and is also registered with the appropriate browsers and search engines, creating a recognized **Web site** (see box, "Internet Basics II").

Once the store is "open for business," advertising will be necessary to let potential users know about it and request it. This is usually done by adding the **URL (Universal Resource Locator)** address to all of the company communications (the Web sites given for most of the companies mentioned in this book). This address can also be added to traditional media advertisements and placed on product packages. In addition, however, to reach the on-line target segment, it is useful to advertise on-line.

The ads on-line are those (to some people, annoying) boxes with various offers and company products that seem to appear every time you get on the Internet or access a company's home page. There are several types of ads, but they all have one simple purpose: to get your attention and entice you to access the company's storefront (see box, "Web Advertisements").

Web Advertisements

Picture

WEB ADS are those boxed "inserts" on the screen that pop up as you arrive on the Internet or at a Web site. They are **interactive** in the sense that you can point to them with the mouse and click to get more information about the product or service advertised. You are typically whisked electronically to the company home page.

- There are several kinds of Web ads:

- **Banner ads.** These are the most common and simplest types of ads. The largest appear as elongated boxes on the top or the bottom of the screen, covering about two-thirds of the screen width—hence the name. They actually come in various sizes (measured in pixels) with the smaller ones placed at the sides as square boxes or "buttons."

- **Interstitial ads.** These are the ads that flash on the screen during the time your request is being handled. Loading a site can take several seconds, and these ads fill up the void. Again, clicking on it will shift your request to the advertised site.

- **Pop-up ads.** These are the ads that appear once a site has been loaded but before you get access. They usually contain messages from the site company but are increasingly sold to independent entrepreneurs who want to take advantage of a popular site. Amazon.com appears in many pop-up ads.

- **Transactional ads.** These ads let you order or request something without leaving the Web page you are on. They are getting increasingly popular as advertisers realize that users typically want to stay on the site requested but still explore the advertised offer.

- **Rich media ads.** "Rich media" are any Web ads that move, talk, beep, or flash. As communication lines improve and desktop computers get more powerful, transmission times shorten and become less of an issue with users. This opens the door for these kinds of ads that require more processing capability—and provide the first glimpse of what filmed commercials on the Web would be like.

Source: *http://www.amazon.com*

Companies pay to get their ads on popular sites and especially on the **portals,** those sites that lead into the search machines. The theory is that even if the user has a definite intention to search only for something very specific on the Internet—such as an address of a hotel in Madrid—seeing a pop-up ad for a special discount on a video camera can generate a visit to the camera retail site. For many users, being on the Internet is like "going where the tide takes you," which is why it's called "surfin' the Web."

Not much is known yet about how effective these various Internet ads are. Research is under way, but in the meantime companies are struggling with assessing whether Web ads can really replace traditional advertising. So far the answer seems to be negative, as we saw in the opening vignette. The typical measure used is the number of "hits" or visits a site receives, but this can be misleading since the time spent may be very brief (and sites get requested by mistake). But the hit numbers can be staggering. In one case, Honda Accord reported that as a result of an interstitial ad running for 2.5 weeks, the Accord Web site received 193,500 visitors, of which over 24,500 signed up for future updates.

At the present, Web ads are seen as basically supportive of other advertising and simply good at providing a road map to a company home page for a "store visit." Users apparently respond mostly to brand names they are already familiar with.[9]

Threats and Opportunities

In an ideal world, the network created by the Internet nodes and links provides an efficient marketplace through which global exchanges could be transacted efficiently. The build-up of the system is uneven, however. While servers can be made available, the leases can be expensive. Fiberoptic cable links might not exist, and old cables often cannot carry the required signals or, at best, are very slow. Furthermore, the penetration of desktop computers is uneven around the globe. With the financial crises around the world at the end of the 1990s, the improvement of these components has slowed or stopped altogether in many places. In principle, the Internet is global—but not all global members are players yet.

One interesting aspect of the potential for electronic commerce on the Internet is that some products can be "digitalized" and sent via electronic mail, bypassing traditional trade barriers that focus on the physical product shipped. Nicholas Negroponte's book *Being Digital* lucidly explains this process.[10] Good candidates for digitalizing information include newsprint, financial transactions, legal documents, and technical blueprints—all of which are already crossing national borders electronically. More promising (or threatening, depending on one's viewpoint) is the digital transmission of complete books, compact discs, videotapes, and computer software.[11] The digital technology is one reason why piracy of certain products is so common, as the copies can be as good as the originals.

Further into the future, one can visualize the elimination of "exports" and "imports" of manufactured goods such as computer hardware components, including semiconductors, as market-based local plants are guided by remote control. According to Negroponte, that future will come sooner than we think, and companies are now pushing the frontier. For example, the design of some automobile models is already done by global teams working on the same "blueprint" through terminals located in different countries. The same is happening (or is likely to happen) with apparel design, advertising campaigns, and financial services.

Marketing on the Internet is necessarily a global effort. As communication links with all countries, offices, and homes around the world get access to the **information superhighway,** anyone anywhere can log on a computer and "go shopping" in any "country." It is still amazing to imagine consumer in Japan ordering a briefcase online from Lands' End in Wisconsin or a Finnish customer buying a video camcorder from Hong Kong. Of course, the availability of terminals and required investments in infrastructure—such as fiberoptic cable—will limit access for many countries and individuals. As important, trade and tariff barriers will still make some transactions prohibitively expensive.[12] The point here, however, is that a global marketing strategy will prove very beneficial for the company, since it can get a lot of demand spillover effects on the "information superhighway."

GLOBAL LOCALIZATION AND LOCAL GLOBALIZATION

The need for companies to have "local presence" even when they are global reflects the fact that most, if not all, markets today are still local. We do our shopping in our hometown or in some airport in a given location, and the company needs to be "there."

In this final section, the question of how to be global and local at the same time will be addressed. **Global localization** refers to the notion that a global marketer needs to be close to the customers locally to be able to compete effectively with local firms. Because of the centralization of many decisions, the firm with a global marketing strategy is in danger of losing touch with the consumer and needs to find ways to avoid this. A key role is played by the execution phase of the strategy.

The Importance of Execution

It is important to recognize that many failures in global marketing are failures of *execution*. Global strategies are not "right" per se. As Swatch, Ikea, Benetton, Honda, and countless other success stories show, decisions are "made right" by luck, persistence, and constant improvement. The foreign entry process might seem scientific and well structured in retrospect, and local marketing analysis is similar to sound analysis elsewhere; however, in the end, failure and success are often determined less by strategy formulation than by implementation—and, in global strategy especially, execution.

Execution means having the nerve and talent (the hidden and not so hidden assets) to do the things the strategy as formulated and implemented intends (remember that implementation has to do with how to do it, while execution is the doing of it). Some examples stand out. The slow and tortured beginning of GM's Japan-inspired Saturn project—now a success—was not the result of bad strategy or weak implementation. It just asked American management and workers to do things that they had not yet mastered. When IBM ventured into the PC market, its initial execution was not flawed (although it took a special task force project organization separate from the company to do it), but the logical (and strategically sound) follow-up was not executed properly because the company was not experienced in consumer marketing. The many Japanese companies that have successfully entered Western markets have been very careful to tailor their strategies to their execution skills, not the other way around. Their so-called incremental entry strategies are examples of scaled-down aspiration levels and longer-term visions while markets are learned and execution skills are developed.

If the company can't execute, even a good strategy will fail. It also works in reverse. Good execution of bad strategy really demonstrates the flaws of the strategy.[13] The Mitsubishi automobile entry into the United States via Chrysler's dealerships was bad strategy, as has been the strategy of Korean firms to do OEM manufacturing for Sears, GE, and others, and Ricoh's decision to enter OEM with Savin copiers in the United States. The problem is that the effective execution of these strategies has put the companies in a bind. When Chrysler bought Lamborghini, it was bad strategy. Luckily, the deal was not executed properly, and Chrysler got out without major damage. It remains to be seen how the $36 billion acquisition of Chrysler by Mercedes in 1998 will play out.

Localized Global Marketing

Execution is what makes or breaks effective localization. Strategies and systems may be multidomestic or global: In the actual marketplace, what matters is execution.

Companies from Sony to ABB to Microsoft strive hard to become good local citizens wherever they design, manufacture, or market their products. In marketing, this means, as we have seen, that products are localized even if standardized. It means that distribution places the products where consumers can get them easily, even if this is done by Federal Express from a faraway warehouse. It means that pricing is competitive and payment conditions fair, even though the prices are synchronized across the globe and credit checks are done electronically overseas. It means that media advertising speaks in terms that appeal to the target segments, even though the message might be uniform throughout the hemisphere.

The challenge in *global localization* is to make sure that global marketing restraints do not become a disadvantage in the local marketplace. Even though certain options are forced out—no more locally produced slogans, no further modification to the product—standardized features originating from other countries prove more effective also in the local market. To accomplish this is a tall order, but proper execution helps make it come true. And since local country managers will be responsible for the execution of the strategy, their motivation is all-important.

Sony, as one example, attempts to ensure local presence in several ways.[14] Its German subsidiary outside Cologne is a case in point. The German manager of the subsidiary came up the ranks through marketing. The subsidiary is given considerable say in product development through, among other things, travel to Japan, visits from Japan, and frequent videoconferences. Product design has partly shifted to Europe, with special European features, styles, and colors added. The advertising draws heavily on Sony's global brand name, using pan-European images, which in contrast to Sony's lighter Japanese advertising emphasize innovative product features and styling with darker colors suggesting quality. As in other countries, the global slogan "It's a Sony" appears everywhere, in commercials, advertisements, and even as a sticker on many of the products.

Using free publicity about its innovations (Walkman, compact disks, camcorders, videodisks) and creating an aura of higher-end status by consistently pricing slightly above competitors (Matsushita's Panasonic, Toshiba, Hitachi, Philips, and others), Sony is positioning its products in Germany and across the globe as a premium brand. In surveys, its brand name is consistently one of the best known in the world, and for many people it is not a Japanese brand. The company does not deny its Japanese roots, but does not play on them either. Sony is a global brand that is local everywhere.

Globalized Local Marketing

ABB (Asea Brown Boveri), the Zurich-based merger of a Swedish and a Swiss company in the electrical and electric machinery business introduced in the opening vignette of Chapter 17, faces an altogether different set of markets.[15] Its customers range from national governments for its hydroelectric power plants, to local governments for its levitating trains, to large multinationals for its robotics, to local repair shops for its electric draining pumps. Although its size makes the ABB name well known among many of these customers, its global marketing strategy is more limited in scope than Sony's. Strong local presence is absolutely necessary to secure many of the governmental contracts, and in most of the markets, delivery times, service, and repairs need to be quick, with distribution pipelines for components and spare parts well developed.

The solution at ABB has been to place the plants in various countries around the world on a stand-alone profit basis. Each of its 35 plants in Germany is organized as an independent subsidiary with a general manager responsible for profitability. The local marketing is done through the sales force, and market communications, product customization, and pricing are basically each manager's responsibility.

Where does global marketing come in? In two ways. First, the subsidiaries can draw on the ABB distribution networks and sales contacts in other countries, getting access to markets they could not get to before. Second, through global rationalization of production, the subsidiaries have become more specialized, making a globally standardized product for which they have special plant-specific or country-specific advantages (for example, Strombergs, one subsidiary in Finland, focuses entirely on one important product group, electric drives, for which it is the center of excellence in ABB). That product is then marketed throughout the world using the existing ABB network. This is **local globalization.**

ABB's extreme localization is backed up, in effect, by a global organization. If Sony has localized its global marketing, ABB has globalized its local marketing.

The Global Markets' Case

In the Sony and ABB cases the localization depends directly on executing the strategies at the local level. The name of the game is having good local people, good local systems, and good local marketing, classic cases of competing in mature markets.

Microsoft, the PC software producer, is in a different strategic situation.[16] Its global potential depends very much on its dominance in the world's leading market, the United States. Its ventures abroad involve diffusion of new technology into new and growing markets, a classic example of the international product cycle. The software market is also a good example of a fundamentally **global market,** even if local differences in standards sometimes complicate the development of uniform products.

The global marketing effort aims at leveraging first-mover advantages and brand reputation overseas.

In these cases the local presence is not so much a matter of skillful execution. Strategic choice in terms of entry mode becomes more critical, especially since it often involves finding independent licensees or joint venture partners that can provide the management know-how and market knowledge lacking at the head office. Microsoft's initial 1983 entry into Japan took the form of a joint venture with ASCII, a small independent software company in Tokyo. Created after a chance meeting on an airplane between Bill Gates of Microsoft and Mr. Nishi, ASCII's founder, the joint venture allowed Microsoft to enter Japan with its Multiplan spreadsheet program before Lotus 1-2-3, making Multiplan the market leader.

As these markets evolve and customers become more demanding, however, effective local presence takes on a more important role. What worked as an initial setup may no longer be sufficient. The relationship gets strained as local customer preferences for product modifications and new features are passed on to the home office. The selected partner may or may not be able or willing to provide them. Local capability must be increased.

In the Microsoft case, the strain occurred after ASCII demanded that its big customer NEC of Japan be offered special customization of some Microsoft software. Microsoft's home office refused to allow such a close tie to one customer. The company broke off its relationship with ASCII and started a wholly owned subsidiary in Tokyo in 1987. A wholly owned subsidiary for Europe was also established in London. These two subsidiaries form the centers for the local marketing efforts in Asia and Europe, respectively. A major task of the subsidiaries is also to aggressively pursue copyright infringements, software products being easily copied and distributed.

Microsoft's marketing effort involves standardized products localized by translations done at the company headquarters in Redmond, Washington. Very little adaptation is done locally: The products are basically exported as finished goods from the United States, although display boxes and retail packaging are done locally. Customer information, advertising, in-store displays, and flyers are localized. But there is little input from the local offices to Redmond in terms of product modification, design, or new-product ideas. The American market being the leading market, Microsoft's global marketing consists of making its brand names well known through its new-product announcements as well as the publicity value of its chairman and then introducing the new products abroad as soon as possible. In a global market, being the leader in the largest market simplifies the global marketing strategy.

SUMMARY

It is difficult not to be "guardedly optimistic" about the future of global marketing. The basic philosophy of free markets has proved stronger than the planned economy alternatives. Active marketing efforts to capitalize on the new opportunities by bringing products and services to all corners of the globe, although questioned in some places, are still basically encouraged locally. The bumps in the road relate to the possibility of continued financial turmoil and slow economic progress in emerging and new growth nations, a consequent negative political fallout from frustration with free markets and a nostalgia for the past. On the upside, the rise of the Internet and electronic commerce, global mass communications, and innovative product and process technology all combine to make the "megatrends" very favorable.

It seems likely that the drive toward global strategies in marketing will require stronger local presence in the future. No firm can avoid the need to be locally strong. As the information superhighway evolves, it will create a truly global market alternative for some exchanges. In the foreseeable future, however, local conditions will always require localization, if not adaptation, to the customer's situation. Even global marketers have to be close to the customer.

KEY TERMS

banner ads   p. 536
browser   p. 535
chat boxes   p. 531
cookies   p. 531
desktop computer   p. 530
electronic commerce   p. 531
ethics of marketing   p. 527
fiberoptic cable   p. 530
free markets   p. 527
global localization   p. 537
global markets   p. 539
hits   p. 531
home page   p. 535
information superhighway
   p. 537

information technology (IT)
   p. 529
interactive   p. 536
internet marketplace   p. 530
interstitial ads   p. 536
intranet   p. 529
local globalization   p. 539
marketing strengths of
   electronic commerce   p. 532
marketing weaknesses of
   electronic commerce   p. 533
modem   p. 530
network   p. 529
on-line marketing   p. 531

on-line service providers
   p. 535
pop-up ads   p. 536
portals   p. 536
protectionist forces   p. 526
rich media ads   p. 536
search engines   p. 535
server computer   p. 530
storefront   p. 535
transactional ads   p. 536
URL (Universal Resource
   Locator)   p. 541
Web site   p. 535
World Wide Web   p. 535

DISCUSSION QUESTIONS

1. Check out the advertising done on the Internet for the Web site of a company of your choice. What different types of advertising can you find? What seems to be the main purpose of the ads? How effective do you think the ads are? Can you suggest any improvements?

2. Access the World Wide Web and track down some companies' "storefronts." How difficult/easy is it to get to the store? What do they offer—information, games, survey questionnaires, products, services? How big a market do you think they potentially reach? Map out some of the various possibilities for further marketing by the company on the Internet.

3. From the Internet, marketing journals, and newspapers (*Advertising Age*, *The Wall Street Journal*) find examples of consumer backlash against marketing practices in some emerging or new growth market(s). Assess

whether these are isolated incidents or represent a trend.

4. In the local consumer market for a product such as beer, imported and local brands (including microbreweries) often compete. Discuss how their marketing strategies differ in terms of segmentation (by usage situation, demographics, and the like) and in terms of positioning (high end, core, and so on). Can you find examples of successful global localization? A not so successful example?

5. From current newspaper reports, assess how likely it is that trade barriers around the various trade regions (EU, NAFTA, ASEAN) will be raised or lowered. What do you think the impact will be on global marketing practices?

NOTES

1. In the mid-1990s, several of these threats came from the bilateral disputes between the United States and Japan, spawned by a new "get tough" attitude on the part of the Americans. In the end, free trade sentiment seemed to reign. See, for example, Nash, 1995.

2. See, for example, Shapiro, 1994.

3. See Culnan, 1994.

4. This is only one of the problem areas; see Sanger, 1995b.

5. See Bennett, 1997. Every day newspapers are rife with stories about new technological developments, and for established businesses the problem is often to evaluate what the gains are over existing procedures. New firms have less to lose. See, for example, Lewis, 1995a. A good guide to the way communication capabilities influence company organization is "The Virtual Corporation," 1993.

6. For one-to-one Web marketing, see Allen et al., 1998, and also Peppers and Rogers, 1993. The article by Quelch and Klein, 1996, demonstrates the cost-efficient use of the Internet and intranets for customer service and supplier contacts.

7. These examples are taken from Seybold (with Marshak), 1998, pp. 5–6.

8. Data as reported in Siwolop, 1998.

9. Evidence from the auto industry provided by Honda. According to syndicated sources, there seems to be a strong correlation between market share and number of hits.

10. See Negroponte, 1995, especially Chapter 1 and the Epilogue.

11. As one example of how the Internet can bypass official barriers, a book written by the personal physician to the late French President François Mitterand, but banned by a French judge because of privacy violations, can be downloaded from the Internet.

12. There is also a question whether customers want to buy this way. If history is any guide, however, once there are real advantages to the consumer—whether in the form of convenience, cost, or

availability of products—early misgivings are likely to evaporate; see Rushbrook, 1995.

13.   The notion that good execution uncovers strategic flaws is similar to Bonoma's notion that good implementation of a bad strategy unmasks flaws in the strategy; see Bonoma, 1985.

14.   The Sony discussion draws on "Sony Corp.: Globalization," 1990, and also on personal interviews in Cologne and Tokyo.

15.   The ABB discussion draws on Taylor, 1992.

16.   The Microsoft discussion draws on Lewis, 1995b, and "Microsoft Corp.," 1987.

SELECTED REFERENCES

Allen, Cliff; Deborah Kania; and Beth Yaeckel. *Internet World: Guide to One-to-One Web Marketing.* New York: Wiley, 1998.

Angell, David; and Brent Heslop. *The Internet Business Companion.* Reading, MA: Addison-Wesley, 1995.

Bennett, Roger. "Export Marketing and the Internet." *International Marketing Review* 14, no. 5 (1997), pp. 324–44.

Bonoma, Thomas V. *The Marketing Edge: Making Strategies Work.* New York: Free Press, 1985.

Carvajal, Doreen. "2 Peoples Separated by Ocean, Not by Borders." *New York Times*, January 1, 1999, pp. C1, C3.

Culnan, Mary. "Privacy Guidelines for the 'New' Direct Marketer." *Privacy and American Business* 1, no. 4 (1994), p. 5.

Fisher, Lawrence M. "A Unifying Force at Novell." *New York Times*, February 5, 1995, p. F9.

Hansell, Saul. "Banks Go Interactive to Beat the Rush of Services." *New York Times*, October 19, 1994, pp. D1, D4.

Kahn, Joseph. "Schwab, for Now, Bests Merrill on Strength of On-Line Trading." *New York Times*, December 29, 1998, pp. C1, C5.

Komenar, Margo. *Electronic Marketing.* New York: Wiley, 1997.

LaFraniere, Sharon, " 'Every Day We Are Angry': Russian City Discovers the High Price of Free Market." *Washington Post*, September 13, 1998, pp. A1, A40.

La Polla, Stephanie. "Compaq Turns Eye on the Enterprise." *PC Week*, October 30, 1995, p. 49.

Lewis, Peter H. "Paperless Cash to Be Tested for Internet Use." *New York Times*, October 19, 1994, p. D4.

———. "Prodigy Is Leading Its Peers onto the World Wide Web." *New York Times*, January 18, 1995a, pp. D1, D7.

———. "Microsoft Has Windows 95 Party; the Internet Shows Up." *New York Times*, August 25, 1995b, p. D4.

Markoff, John. "A Credit Card for On-Line Sprees." *New York Times*, October 15, 1994, p. 39.

"Microsoft Corp.: The Introduction of Microsoft Works." Harvard Business School, case no. 9-588-028, 1987.

Nash, Nathaniel C. "The Lonely Americans Isolated in a Trade War." *New York Times*, May 26, 1995, p. D2.

Negroponte, Nicholas. *Being Digital.* New York: Alfred A. Knopf, 1995.

Peppers, Don; and Martha Rogers. *The One-to-One Future: Building Relationships One Customer at a Time.* New York: Currency Doubleday, 1993.

Perlez, Jane. "Fast and Slow Lanes on the Capitalist Road." *New York Times*, October 7, 1994, pp. A1, A12.

Peterson, Robert A., ed. *Electronic Marketing and the Consumer.* Beverly Hills, CA: Sage, 1997.

Quelch, John A.; and Lisa R. Klein. "The Internet and International Marketing." *Sloan Management Review*, Spring 1996, pp. 60–74.

Rushbrook, Lewis. "Buying in the Cybermarket." *Marketing*, March 2, 1995, pp. 20–21.

Saito, Akiko. *My Husband Is My Rival.* Tokyo: Yuhisha, 1991.

Sanger, David E. "Trade Fight Aside, U.S. to Sell China More Wheat." *New York Times*, February 8, 1995a, pp. D1, D18.

———. "This Is a Trade War! Get Your Popgun!" *New York Times*, February 12, 1995b, sec. 4, pp. 1, 5.

Seybold, Patricia B.; with Ronni T. Marshak. *Customers.com: How to Create a Profitable Business Strategy for the Internet and Beyond.* New York: Times Business, 1998.

Shapiro, Margaret. "New Russia: A Country on the Take." *Washington Post*, November 13, 1994, pp. A1, A36–37.

Siwolop, Sana. "Books Did It for Amazon, but What's Next?" *New York Times*, August 23, 1998.

"Sony Corp.: Globalization." Harvard Business School, case no. 9-391-071, 1990.

Specter, Michael. "Borscht and Blini to Go: From Russian Capitalists, an Answer to McDonald's." *New York Times*, August 9, 1995, pp. D1, D3.

Stevenson, Richard W. "Foreign Investors in Russia Brush Risks Aside." *New York Times*, October 11, 1994, pp. A1, D6.

Strassel, Kimberley A. "E-Commerce Finally Blooms as Europe Takes to the Net." *Wall Street Journal*, Interactive edition, December 7, 1998.

Taylor, William. "The Logic of Global Business: An Interview with ABB's Percy Barnevik." In Christopher A. Bartlett and Sumantra Ghoshal. *Transnational Management* (Homewood, IL: Irwin, 1992), pp. 892–908.

"The Virtual Corporation." *Business Week*, February 8, 1993, pp. 98–102.

Cases

Four

Case 4.1

P&G's Pert Plus: A Pan-European Product?[1]

Procter & Gamble (P&G), the U.S. manufacturer of consumer packaged goods, is considering the introduction of a new haircare technology (BC-18) into the European market. The technology combines a shampoo and a conditioner in one product with the same effect as a shampoo and conditioner used separately. The product was launched in the U.S. haircare market in 1986 as Pert Plus and its success provided the impetus to consider a "roll-out" launch in Europe.

COMPANY BACKGROUND

Procter & Gamble was founded in the U.S. in 1837. Today it is the world's biggest manufacturer of packaged consumer goods and a global leader in health and beauty care products, detergents, diapers, and food. P&G products include Pampers, Ariel, Mr. Proper, Camay, and others. More than one-third of P&G's total profit is generated by its international operations, which are the fastest growing part of its total business. To strengthen its health and beauty care division, P&G in 1985 bought the Richardson-Vicks Company (with

brands like Vidal Sassoon and Pantene) and in 1987 bought the German Blendax Group (dental-care products). These acquisitions resulted in a leading position in health and beauty care products in Europe.

Over its more than 150-year history, P&G has accumulated a broad base of industry experience and business knowledge. A great deal of it has been formalized and institutionalized as management principles and policies. One of the most basic principles is that P&G's products should provide "superior total value" and should meet "basic consumer needs." This has resulted in a strong commitment to research to create products that are demonstrably better than others. In contrast to the conventional product life cycle mentality, P&G believes that through continual product development, brands can remain healthy and profitable in the long term.

Perhaps the most widely known of P&G's organizational characteristics is its legendary brand management system. The brand management team, usually a group of three or four people, assumes general responsibility for its brand. They plan, develop, and direct their brand in its market. The group develops business objectives, strategies, and marketing plans. It selects advertising copy and media, develops sales promotion activities, manages package design and product improvement projects, and initiates cost savings. To carry out their responsibilities, members of the brand management team draw on the resources available to them. These include the other disciplines within and outside the organization (e.g., manufacturing, product development, market research, sales, advertising agencies).

[1]Source: This case was written by Dr. Wolfgang Breuer and Professor Dr. Richard Köhler, University of Cologne (Germany). It was devised together with the German P&G office. It is based on real facts but the figures have been partly changed for teaching purposes. A more detailed version of the case was published by Sage Publications, Ltd., London, in the volume Marketing in Europe: Case Studies, ed. Jordi Montaña, 1994. Reprinted with permission.

Summing up, it may be said that they know more about their product than anyone else, and they feel a real sense of ownership as they strive to develop business opportunities in their local market.

But in the early 1980s it became more and more obvious that greater coordination was needed between local markets in Europe. Increasingly, competitors had been able to imitate P&G's innovative products and marketing strategies, and had preempted them in national markets where the local subsidiary was constrained by budget or organizational limitations. Therefore, closer coordination was important, particularly for new brands, to ensure they reached the marketplace first. Marketing strategies had to be thought through from a European perspective. This meant also the possibility of simultaneous or closely sequenced European product introductions. Furthermore, the European approach, through maximizing efficiency across countries, pooling know-how, and manufacturing with better economies of scale, could give a big advantage over the competition.

As a main forum for achieving this goal the Eurobrand team meetings were introduced chaired by the brand management of the so called "lead country." This European perspective did not necessarily mean Europe-wide standardization. Market conditions still vary widely within Europe. P&G's concept is that of "Euro-balancing," meaning as much standardization as possible, as little localization as necessary. A P&G senior manager comments: "It is occasionally better to allow some complexity to get a better overall result."

PERT PLUS

The most important P&G shampoo brands were losing U.S. market share in the years up to 1986. Therefore, it was decided to introduce a new technology, called BC-18, in the U.S. market at the beginning of 1986 by replacing the brand Pert with Pert Plus.

The long-term marketing goal of Pert Plus was to take over the leading value position in the U.S. shampoo market, with a market share of at least 10 percent by the end of the fiscal year 1989/90. For the first year the specific target was a market share value of 5 percent.

In order to achieve this, Pert Plus was positioned as the shampoo that offered attractive hair in a convenient way. This was backed up by the unique Pert Plus formula, which combined a mild shampoo with a fully effective conditioner in one wash.

The target group was to be all people. The source of business would also come from the group of people who had not used Pert or a conditioner before. Pert Plus was introduced with a price of U.S. $3.20 (for the 15 oz. size).[2] Pert Plus was an instant success, doubling Pert's market share in one year, and growing steadily after that.

MARKET DEVELOPMENT AND COMPETITIVE ENVIRONMENT

In Europe a steady growth of the shampoo market and the conditioner market could be seen. There was evidence of increased hair-washing. However, the conditioner market was still, compared with the U.S.A., relatively undeveloped. The share of shampoo users who also used conditioner was still below the 44 percent which had been reached in the United States. This was particularly true for Southern European countries. Therefore, the initial focus was on West Germany, Great Britain, France, Scandinavia, and Benelux. An underdeveloped conditioner market was, however, also evident in France (in terms of sales volume only 10 percent of shampoo consumption). Among the European countries considered, Great Britain, with 42 percent, showed the strongest user share (see Exhibit 1).

With respect to the number of suppliers and brands, the European market was even more crowded than the U.S. market, undoubtedly a function of the different nationalities. The most important competitors for P&G were Unilever, Colgate, and L'Oréal. Some brands could be found in all countries, others only in their domestic markets (see Exhibit 2).

The gap between the top and bottom price classes was even bigger than in the U.S. market. Between brands there were price differences of over five times for the same quantity, which meant that the value-based market share of a shampoo brand was very important (see Exhibit 3).

In order to carry through the brand message, media support would be a key driving force (see Exhibit 4).

---

[2]US $ = 2.17 DM; 15 oz. (ounces) = 425 ml.

EXHIBIT 1 Market Sizes, Shampoo/Conditioner, Europe, 1988

	West Germany	Great Britain	France	Scandinavia	Benelux
Shampoos					
Value (TDM)	650,000	485,000	700,000	250,000	200,000
Volume (MSU)	20,000	18,000	20,000	7,000	7,500
Use per head	325	325	350	300	300
(SU/1,000 of population)					
Conditioners					
Value (TDM)	230,000	250,000	100,000	85,000	60,000
Volume (MSU)	4,500	7,500	2,000	1,700	1,500
Use per head (SU/1,000 of population)	70	140	35	70	70

1 MUS 5 1,000 SU (statistical units).
1 SU 5 2.5 litres.
TDM 5 Thousand German marks.

EXHIBIT 2 Percentage of Market Shares, Shampoo, Key Brands, Europe 1988

	West Germany		Great Britain		France		Scandinavia		Benelux	
	Volume	Value	Volume	Value	Volume	Value	Volume	Value	Volume	Value
P&G brands										
Vidal Sassoon	0.5	1.3	1.1	3.6	N/A		1.0	2.4	N/A	
Pantene	N/A		N/A		1.0	2.1	N/A		N/A	
Petrole Hahn	N/A		N/A		3.0	2.1	N/A		0.6	
Shamtu	11.0	6.3	N/A		N/A		N/A		N/A	
Head & Shoulders	1.1	1.7	6.5	12.0	1.1	1.6	1.0	1.4	2.9	5.4
Competitor brands										
Timotei (Unilever)	5.0	5.7	8.5	11.8	4.9	5.2	7.5	7.8	3.8	5.3
Nivea (Beiersdorf)	9.0	9.2	N/A		N/A		2.5	2.3	4.4	5.5
Schauma (Schwarzkopf)	21.0	10.0	N/A		N/A		N/A		7.0	4.1
Palmolive (Colgate)		N/A	4.6	2.7	12.3	5.4	7.0	3.0	18.2	10.6
Elsève/El' Vital (L'Oréal)	3.3	4.6	N/A		4.5	5.8	6.5	8.2	5.0	8.4

N/A 5 product not on offer in this country.

EXHIBIT 3 Sizes and Shelf Prices, Shampoo, Europe 1988 (in German marks)

	West Germany	Great Britain	France	Scandinavia	Benelux
P&G brands					
Vidal Sassoon	6.99	6.99	N/A	6.99	N/A
(200 ml)					
Pantene	N/A	N/A	4.99	N/A	N/A
(200 ml)					
Petrole Hahn	N/A	N/A	2.99	N/A	2.99
(300 ml)					
Shamtu	2.99	N/A	N/A	N/A	N/A
(400 ml)					
Head & Shoulders	5.99	5.99	5.99	5.99	5.99
(300 ml)					
Competitor brands					
Timotei (Unilever)	2.99	2.99	2.99	2.99	2.99
(200 ml)					
Nivea (Beiersdorf)	3.99	N/A	N/A	3.99	3.99
(300 ml)					
Schauma (Schwarzkopf)	2.49	N/A	N/A	N/A	2.49
(400 ml)					
Palmolive (Colgate)	N/A	2.49	2.49	2.49	2.49
(400 ml)					
Elsève/El' Vital (L'Oréal)	4.49	N/A	4.49	4.49	4.49
(250 ml)					

N/A = product not on offer in this country.

To simplfy matters, the retail prices have been rounded off to a European average. However, price relations within a country have been retained.

EXHIBIT 4 Media Spending, Shampoo, Europe 1988 (in thousands of German marks)

	West Germany	Great Britain	France	Scandinavia	Benelux
AP&G brands					
Vidal Sassoon	1,000	3,000	N/A	1,000	N/A
Pantene	N/A	N/A	0	N/A	N/A
Petrole Hahn	N/A	N/A	3,000	N/A	0
Shamtu	4,000	N/A	N/A	N/A	N/A
Head & Shoulders	3,000	3,000	2,000	800	2,800
Competitor brands					
Timotei (Unilever)	6,500	6,500	3,000	3,000	1,500
Nivea (Beiersdorf)	8,000	N/A	N/A	2,000	1,000
Schauma (Schwarzkopf)	10,500	N/A	N/A	N/A	N/A
Palmolive (Colgate)	N/A	4,000	4,000	1,000	1,000
Elsève/El' Vital (L'Oréal)	5,000	N/A	7,000	2,000	2,000
TOTAL	80,000	80,000	60,000	60,000	50,000

N/A = product not on offer in this country.

EXHIBIT 5 Consumer Test, Europe

Positioning statement	Price/Pack size
Vidal Sassoon Wash & Go—for great-looking hair in a convenient way	4.99 DM/200 ml
Shamtu 2 in 1—shampoo and conditioner in one—silkiness and bounce in one step	4.99 DM/200 ml
Shamtu 2 in 1—shampoo and conditioner in one—silkiness and bounce in one step	4.99 DM/250 ml
Pantene—shampoo with built-in vitamin conditioner—the perfect hair care in one step	4.99 DM/200 ml
Pantene—shampoo with built-in vitamin conditioner—the perfect hair care in one step	5.99 DM/200 ml
Pert Plus Wash & Go—for great-looking hair in a convenient way	4.99 DM/200 ml

THE GO DECISION

In 1988, Procter & Gamble decided to introduce BC-18 into the European market. The opportunity for easy, time-saving, and convenient everyday use of the product was a strong competitive advantage and essential when considering positioning. There was also no doubt about placing the new product in the premium-priced segment. As with Pert Plus, a premium price was necessary to be consistent with the high-quality product concept. The main question was still, however, under what brand name to introduce the product in the individual European markets. There was also the question of whether a 200 ml bottle, used in the United States, would be accepted by the European consumer and the question of price sensitivity at premium pricing.

CONSUMER RESEARCH

It was decided, therefore, to undertake some consumer research. Obviously, it was impossible to test all possi-

ble product concepts with respect to brand names, positioning alternatives, pack sizes, pack designs, and price alternatives, for all European countries. So, in a prescreening phase, the possible brand alternatives were reduced to four. In any case, there was to be a brand which, already present in the United States and several European markets, had so far shown a certain European potential (Vidal Sassoon). The U.S. brand Pert Plus, unknown in the European market, was also to be tested. The two other alternatives were national brands firmly established in their domestic markets (Pantene and Shamtu). Price and packaging alternatives were tested on only two brands: one brand from the lower-price segment and another brand that had a high-quality product concept (i.e., product concepts where possible price sensitivity would be easily detected). An abridged version of the positioning statements can be found in Exhibit 5. The consumer tests were carried out in the relevant European countries (for average results, see Exhibit 6; there were no significant differences between countries).

EXHIBIT 6 Consumer Test, Europe, Results (*percent*)

Product concepts	Vidal Sassoon Wash & Go 4.99DM/ 200ml	Shamtu 2 in 1 "silkiness and bounce" 4.99DM/ 200ml	Shamtu 2 in 1 "silkiness and bounce" 4.99DM/ 250ml	Pantene "perfect care" 4.99DM/ 200ml	Pantene "perfect care" 5.99DM/ 250ml	Pert Plus Wash & Go 4.99DM/ 200ml
"Would definitely buy"	29%	20%	27%	28%	17%	28%
"Is very new"	41	40	41	39	40	40
"Is very convincing and relevant"	70	73	72	73	72	70

EXHIBIT 7 Overview, Economics/Profits, Europe, 1988

		W. Germany VS 200 ml	W. Germany Shamtu 400 ml	Great Britain VS 200 ml	France Pantene 200 ml	Scandinavia VS 200 ml	Benelux H&S 300 ml
Volume	MSU	100	2,000	300	200	100	400
Shelf price	DM/pack	6.99	2.99	6.99	4.99	6.99	5.99
Manufacturer's list price	DM/pack	4.50	2.40	4.50	3.20	4.50	4.80
Manufacturer's list price	DM/SU	56.25	15.00	56.25	40.00	56.25	40.00
Discount	DM/SU	5.60	1.50	5.60	4.00	5.60	4.00
Manufacturer's net price	DM/SU	50.65	13.50	50.65	36.00	50.65	36.00
Production costs (incl. transport)	DM/SU	30.00	8.00	28.00	22.00	30.00	18.00
Overheads (sales, R&D, etc.)	DM/SU	5.60	1.50	5.60	5.00	5.60	4.00
Advertising costs for trade	DM/SU	2.80	0.75	2.80	2.00	2.80	2.00
Budget for advertising and sales promotion	DM/SU	20.00	2.50	14.00	6.00	14.00	10.00
Profit	DM/SU	−7.75	0.75	0.25	1.00	−1.75	2.00

VS = Vidal Sassoon

H&S = Head & Shoulders

DM = German marks

MSU = 1,000 SU

SU = statistical unit

ECONOMICS

The basis for cost planning for the BC-18 introduction in individual European countries was the cost structure of the existing P&G shampoo brands. This also gave an idea of the profitability of the brands tested in the consumer test, which might be one of the deciding factors in the choice of an introductory brand name for BC-18 (see Exhibit 7).

The costs of producing the new product, including average transport costs, were relatively easy to estimate, since the decision had been made to locate production for the whole European market in England. However, it had still not been decided whether to use the available 200 ml bottle or a 250 ml bottle still in development. Two figures were therefore used in the plans: production costs would be roughly 22 DM/SU;[3] for the small bottle and 20 DM/SU for the larger bottle. These figures presumed a work capacity of 50 percent, and it was assumed that working at higher capacity would not generate lower costs because of the special production technology. To determine total costs it was necessary to consider also advertising and sales support budgets, which depended on the individual countries and their chosen introduction program (see Exhibit 8).

[3]2DM = German mark; 1 SU (statistical unit) = 2.5 litres; 1,000 SU = 1 MSU.

EXHIBIT 8 Media and Promotion Costs

	W. Germany	Great Britain	France	Scandinavia[2]	Benelux
Media (TDM per month)[1]					
TV normal advertising month	600	600	600	—	200
strong advertising month	800	800	800	—	250
Radio normal advertising month	400	400	400	—	130
strong advertising month	500	500	500	—	160
Print normal 3-month campaign	3,000	3,000	3,000	1,000	1,000
strong 3-month campaign	5,000	5,000	5,000	1,600	1,600
Sample distribution (DM per piece)					
Sample costs	0.40				
Distribution costs					
Door-to-door	0.10	(same as for West Germany)			
Hypermarkets	0.20				
Via other products	0.15				
Additional promotions (TDM)					
Hypermarket—display activities	500	600	500	200	200
Consumer competition	100	100	100	50	50
Wheel of Fortune competition	300	300	300	100	100
Additional Costs (TDM)					
Production TV	400	400	400	—	400
radio	30	30	30	—	30
print	50	50	50	50	50
Listing funds	1,000	1,000	1,000	400	300
Material for sales representatives	50	50	50	400	300
Number of households (millions)	26	22	21	20	20

[1]*Strong advertising month means that the frequency (number of spots) is about one-third higher than in a normal advertising month.*
[2]*TV and radio advertising not possible for legal reasons.*

DM = German marks.

TDM = 1,000 German marks.

DECISION CONSTRAINTS

The first restrictions arose in the available production capacity. For the first year a capacity of 2,000 MSU was available. This could have been increased to 4,000 MSU in the second year and to 8,000 in the third year. Nevertheless, in case of difficulties, with six months notice it would have been possible to get an extra 500 MSU capacity, but with 2 DM/SU higher production costs.

Lead times for alternative pack sizes and designs were also a restriction. The development of a new 200 ml bottle would take a lead time of 12 months. Although development of a new bottle containing 250 ml was underway, it would still take six months before it could be used. By contrast, using the existing U.S. bottle for Pert Plus would not require any lead time.

DISCUSSION QUESTIONS

1. How attractive is the European market for Pert Plus in terms of demand potential?

2. How competitive is the European market? What competitive advantages does Pert Plus have? Disadvantages? Any country-of-origin effect?

3. Which countries are the leading markets in Europe? What are the advantages or disadvantages of entering a leading market first?

4. What does the marketing research tell about the price and positioning decision for Europe?

5. What are the possible alternative brand name strategies? Should the BC-18 technology be introduced with a pan-European name, or with local brand names, or even with a mixture of both approaches? Should a new brand be created, or should an existing brand be relaunched in a new formulation?

Case 4.2

Texas Instruments Global Pricing in the Semiconductor Industry

Mr. John Szczsponik, Director of North American Distribution for Texas Instruments' Semiconductor Group, placed the phone back on its cradle after a long and grueling conversation with his key contact at Arrow, the largest distributor of Texas Instruments' semiconductors. With a market-leading 21.5% share of total U.S. electronic component distributor sales in 1994, Arrow was the most powerful distribution channel through which Texas Instruments' important semiconductor products flowed. It was also one of only two major American distributors active in the global distribution market.

Arrow's expanding international activities had made it increasingly interested in negotiating with its vendors a common global price for the semiconductors it sold around the world. In the past, semiconductors had been bought and sold at different price levels in different countries to reflect the various cost structures of the countries in which they were produced. Semiconductors made in European countries, for example, were usually more expensive than those made in Asia or North America, simply because it cost manufacturers more to operate in Europe than in the other two regions. Despite these differences, large distributors and some original equipment manufacturers were becoming insistent on buying their semiconductors at one worldwide price, and were pressuring vendors to negotiate global pricing

terms. Szczsponik's telephone conversation with Arrow had been the third in the past month in which the distributor had pushed for price concessions based on international semiconductor rates:

> Yesterday they discovered that we're offering a lower price for a chip we make and sell in Singapore than for the same chip we manufacture here in Dallas for the North American market. They want us to give them the Singapore price on our American chips, even though they know our manufacturing costs are higher here than in the Far East. We can't give them that price without losing money!

In anticipation of increased pressure from Arrow and other large distributors, Szczsponik had organized a meeting with Mr. Kevin McGarity, Senior Vice President in the Semiconductor Group and Manager of Worldwide Marketing, to begin developing a cohesive pricing strategy. They were both to meet with Arrow executives in four days, on February 4, 1995, to discuss the establishment of common global pricing for the distributor.

Szczsponik knew that he needed to answer some basic questions before meeting with Arrow:

> Global pricing might make Arrow's job of planning and budgeting a lot easier, but our different cost structures in each region make it difficult for us to offer one price worldwide. How do we tell Arrow, our largest distributor, that we aren't prepared to negotiate global pricing? Alternatively, how can we reorganize ourselves to make global pricing a realistic option? And what implications will a global pricing strategy have in relationship to other international customers?

With only two hours to go before his meeting with McGarity, Szczsponik wondered how they could respond to Arrow's request.

EXHIBIT 1 Top Ten Semiconductor Manufacturers

1980		1985		1990		1992	
Company	**Sales $**	**Company**	**Sales $**	**Company**	**Sales $**	**Company**	**Sales $**
1. Texas		NEC	1,800	NEC	4,700	Intel	5,091
Instruments	1,453	Motorola	1,667	Toshiba	4,150	NEC	4,700
2. Motorola	1,130	Texas		Motorola	3,433	Toshiba	4,550
3. Philips	845	Instruments	1,661	Hitachi	3,400	Motorola	4,475
4. NEC	800	Hitachi	1,560	Intel	3,171	Hitachi	3,600
5. National	745	National	1,435	Texas		Texas	
6. Intel	630	Toshiba	1,400	Instruments	2,518	Instruments	3,150
7. Hitachi	620	Philips	1,080	Fujitsu	2,300	Fujitsu	2,250
8. Fairchild	570	Intel	1,020	Mitsubishi	1,920	Mitsubishi	2,200
9. Toshiba	533	Fujitsu	800	Philips	1,883	Philips	2,041
10. Siemens	525	Advanced		National	1,730	Matsushita	1,900
		Micro Devices	795				

Source: Analysts' reports.

THE SEMICONDUCTOR INDUSTRY

Semiconductors were silicon chips which transmitted heat, light, and electrical charges and performed critical functions in virtually all electronic devices. They were a core technology in industrial robots, computers, office equipment, consumer electronics, the aerospace industry, telecommunications, the military, and the automobile industry. About 80% of semiconductors consisted of integrated circuits made from monocrystalline silicon imprinted with complex electronic components and their interconnections. The remainder of semiconductors were simpler discrete components that performed single functions.

The pervasiveness of semiconductors in electronics resulted in rapidly growing sales and intense competition in the semiconductor industry. Market share in the industry had been fiercely contested since the early 1980s, when the once-dominant U.S. semiconductor industry lost its leadership position to Japanese manufacturers. There followed a series of trade battles in which American manufacturers charged their Japanese competitors with dumping and accused foreign markets of excessive protectionism. By 1994, after investing heavily in the semiconductor industry and embarking on programs to increase manufacturing efficiency and decrease production costs, American companies once again captured a dominant share of the market (refer to Exhibit 1 for the top ten semiconductor manufacturers).

In 1994, total shipments of semiconductors reached $99.9 billion, with market share divided among North America (33%), Japan (30%), Europe (18%), and Asia/Pacific (18%). The industry was expected to reach sales of $130 billion in 1995, and $200 billion by the year 2000. To capture growing demand in the industry, many semiconductor manufacturers were investing heavily in increased manufacturing capacity, although most industry analysts expected expanding capacity to reach rather than surpass demand. Combined with record low inventories in the industry and reduced cycle times and lead times, a balancing of supply and demand was causing semiconductor prices to be uncharacteristically stable. The last three quarters of 1994 had brought fewer fluctuations and less volatility in the prices of semiconductors (refer to Exhibit 2 for a history of semiconductor price stability) despite their history of dramatic price variations.

Regardless of price stability, most semiconductor manufacturers were looking for competitive advantage in further cost reduction programs, in developing closer relationships with their customers, and in creating differentiated semiconductors which could be sold at a premium price. Integrated circuits were readily available from suppliers worldwide and were treated as commodity products by most buyers. Any steps manufacturers could take to reduce their production costs, build stronger relationships with customers, or create unique products could protect them from the price wars usually associated with commodity merchandise.

EXHIBIT 2 History of Semiconductor Stability

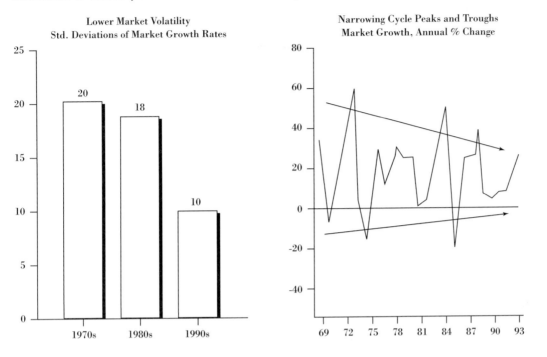

TEXAS INSTRUMENTS INCORPORATED

Established in 1951 as an electronics company serving the American defense industry, by 1995 Texas Instruments was a leading manufacturer of semiconductors, defense electronics, software, personal productivity products and materials, and controls. Its 1994 sales of $10.3 billion, a 21% increase from the previous year, was split among components ($6.8 billion), defense electronics ($1.7 billion), digital products ($1.66 billion), and metallurgical materials ($177 million). 1994's profits of over $1 billion came almost entirely from its components business. Components made a profit of $1.1 billion, while defense electronics made $172 million (refer to Exhibit 3 for income statements).

1994's performance was record-breaking for Texas Instruments. It marked the first time the company exceeded sales of $10 billion and over $1 billion in profit, and followed a history of volatile financial results. Although Texas Instruments was often considered the pioneer of the American electronics industry—it was one of the first companies to manufacture transistors and developed the first semiconductor Integrated circuit in 1958—it struggled to maintain its position in the electronics industry through the intense competition of the 1980s. After receiving market attention with its de-

velopment of such innovative consumer products as the pocket calculator and the electronic wrist watch, Texas Instruments lost its business in both markets to cheap Asian imports. Meanwhile, it struggled to keep up with orders for its mainstay business in semiconductors through the 1970s, only to see demand for its pioneer semiconductors shrink during the recession of the early 1980s. Faced with heavy losses in many of its core areas, Texas Instruments reorganized its businesses to foster innovation and embarked on a program of cost-cutting. By 1985, the company had refocused its efforts on its strengths in semiconductors, relinquishing market dominance in favor of greater margins. While the company continued to grow its technological leadership, it also sought to build stronger relationships with its customers.

By 1995, Texas Instruments had developed a strong position in the electronics industry, despite its reputation as a technological leader rather than a skilled marketer of its products. The company continued to remain powerful in the semiconductor industry, in part because it was the only American company that continued to manufacture dynamic random access memory chips in the face of fierce Japanese competition in the 1980s. The company had manufacturing sites spread

EXHIBIT 3 Income Statements

	Texas Instruments Key Financial Numbers				
	1994	1993	1992	1991	1990
Sales ($ millions)	10,200	8,523	7,049	6,628	6,395
Operating margin (%)	17.5	16.8	9.1	5.0	0.7
Net Profit ($ millions)	715	459	254	169	0.7
Working Capital ($ millions)	1,800	1,313	961	813	826
Long-Term Debt ($ millions)	800	694	909	896	715
Net Worth ($ millions)	2,975	2,315	1,947	1,955	2,358

throughout North America, Asia, and Europe, and was pursuing its strategy of increasing manufacturing capacity and developing manufacturing excellence.

The Semiconductor Group

In 1958, Texas Instruments engineer Jack Kilby developed the first integrated circuit, a pivotal innovation in the electronics industry. Made of a single semiconductor material, the integrated circuit eliminated the need to solder circuit components together. Without wiring and soldering, components could be miniaturized and crowded together on a single chip. Only a few years after Kilby's invention, electronics manufacturers were demanding these integrated circuits, or chips, in smaller sizes and a lower costs, a move that led to unprecedented innovation in the electronics industry. Soon chips became a commodity, and chip manufacturers relied on high-volume, low-cost production of reliable chips for success. Only a few manufacturers had strong positions in the production of differentiated semiconductors.

Forty years after its discovery, Texas Instruments still remained dependent on its semiconductors sales, which fell primarily in integrated circuits. The Semiconductor Group, a part of the Components Division, had total sales of $2 billion in 1994, the third consecutive year in which Texas Instruments' semiconductor revenues grew faster than the industry. The company's return to financial success in the early 1990s was based on its strong performance in semiconductor sales and profits, both of which were at record levels in 1994. Management in the company expected semiconductor sales to continue to grow strongly and was planning heavy capital expenditures on new or expanded plants in the United States, Malaysia, and Italy to increase the company's capacity.

The Semiconductor Group divided its business into two segments: standard products and differenti-

ated products. Standard semiconductors, which accounted for 90% of the Group's sales, included products which could be substituted by competitors. Standard semiconductors performed in the market much like other products for which substitutes were readily available. Texas Instruments, like its competitors, competed for market share in these commodity products based primarily on the price it offered to original equipment manufacturers and distributors. The remaining 10% of the company's semiconductor business came from differentiated products, of which Texas Instruments was the sole supplier. Because substitutes for these products were not available in the marketplace, differentiated products commanded higher margins than their standard counterparts and were receiving greater strategic emphasis on the part of Group management. While the company continued to hold a strong position in standard semiconductors, it was searching for a strategy that would allow it to achieve a higher return on development and manufacturing investments. Managers at Texas Instruments believed that higher returns were possible only by developing more successful differentiated semiconductors.

ELECTRONICS DISTRIBUTION MARKET

Texas Instruments sold its semiconductors through two channels: directly to original equipment manufacturers and through a network of electronics distributors. Szczsponik estimated that 70% of the Group's U.S. customers dealt directly with Texas Instruments. The remainder bought their semiconductors through one or more of the seven major semiconductor distributors that served the North American market (refer to Exhibit 4 for information on the top electronics distributors). Whether an original equipment manufacturer dealt directly with Texas Instruments or bought from a distributor de-

EXHIBIT 4 Top Electronics Distributors

Company		1994	1993	1992	1991	1990
Arrow Electronics	Sales ($ billions)	3.973	2.536	1.622	1.044	971
	Share (%)	21.5	17.4	14.8	11.0	10.2
Avnet	Sales ($ billions)	3.350	2.537	1.690	1.400	1.429
	Share (%)	18.1	17.4	15.4	14.8	15.0
Marshall Industries	Sales ($ billions)	.899	.747	.605	.563	.582
	Share (%)	4.8	5.1	5.5	6.0	6.1
Wyle Laboratories	Sales ($ billions)	.773	.606	.447	.360	.359
	Share (%)	4.2	4.2	4.1	3.8	3.8
Pioneer Standard	Sales ($ billions)	.747	.540	.405	.360	.343
	Share (%)	4.0	3.7	3.7	3.8	3.6
Anthem	Sales ($ billions)	.507	.663	.538	.420	.408
	Share (%)	2.7	4.6	4.9	4.4	4.3
Bell Industries	Sales ($ billions)	.395	.308	.282	.257	.239
	Share (%)	2.1	2.1	2.6	2.7	2.5

Source: Lehman Brothers, "Electronic Distribution Market," December 22, 1994.

pended on the manufacturer's size. The largest original equipment manufacturers were able to negotiate better prices from semiconductor manufacturers than were the distributors and therefore bought directly from the manufacturers. Because mid-sized and small original equipment manufacturers were fragmented, and thus more difficult to serve, these customers were served more efficiently through the distribution channel. Szczsponik explained:

> *The semiconductor market can be divided into three tiers. Fifty percent of our sales in semiconductors go to the top tier of perhaps 100 large electronics manufacturers who deal with us directly. The next 46 percent of sales come from 1,400 medium-sized companies at the next level, half of whom deal directly with us and half of whom buy through distributors. The remaining 4% of sales are to 150,000 smaller companies at the bottom tier in the market, who deal only through distributors. Distributors have a clearly defined role in servicing mid-sized and small buyers.*

Distributors were considered to be clearinghouses for the semiconductor industry. Each distributor dealt with products from all the major semiconductor manufacturers. For example, Arrow Electronics sold semiconductors manufactured by Motorola and Intel as well as those made by Texas Instruments. The distributors specialized in handling logistics, material flows, sales and servicing for electronics manufacturers who were either too small to negotiate directly with the major semiconductor manufacturers or lacked sufficient expertise in logistics management. In addition, the distributors sometimes knitted packages of different products together for the smaller original electronics manufacturers as an added service. Some also performed varying scales of assembly operation.

The electronics distribution network had originally consisted of a large group of smaller companies. By 1995, however, industry consolidation had left almost 40% of the distribution market in the hands of its two largest competitors, Arrow Electronics and Avnet. The seven largest distributors captured 58% of sales in the market (refer to Exhibit 5 for the sales and market shares of the top distributors). This trend toward consolidation had had a major impact on the nature of the relationships among semiconductor manufacturers and the distributors through which they sold their products. According to Szczsponik:

> *Fifteen years ago, 30 distributors were active in the industry and it was clear that the semiconductor manufacturers controlled the distribution network. With the consolidation of the distribution network into only 7 or 8 powerful players, however, power is shifting. It's hard to say if we are more important to them or they are more important to us.*

Price Negotiations and Global Pricing Issues

Since the vast majority of semiconductors were considered commodity products, the buying decisions of distributors were based almost entirely on price. Distributors forecast the demand for the various semiconductor products they carried and negotiated with vendors for their prices. Since semiconductor prices were notoriously volatile, the price levels negotiated

EXHIBIT 5   Total Sales and Market Share of Top Distributors

		1994	1993	1992	1991	1990
Industry Total	Sales ($ billions)	16.22	12.95	10.18	9.06	9.17
Top 25	Sales ($ billions)	13.41	10.69	8.11	7.10	7.20
	Share (%)	82.7	82.5	79.7	78.4	78.5
Top 7	Sales ($ billions)	10.75	8.42	6.36	5.05	5.00
	Share (%)	58.0	57.9	57.9	53.5	52.5
Top 2	Sales ($ billions)	7.32	5.07	3.31	2.44	2.40
	Share (%)	39.6	34.8	30.2	25.8	25.2

Source: Lehman Brothers, "Electronic Distribution Market," December 22, 1994.

between manufacturers and distributors played a vital role in the distributors' profitability. The Semiconductor Group at Texas Instruments combined the practices of forward pricing and continuous price negotiations to set prices with its distributors.

FORWARD PRICING   The cost of semiconductor manufacturing followed a generally predictable learning curve. When a manufacturer first began producing a new type of chip, it could expect only a small percentage of the chips it produced to function properly. As the manufacturer increased the volume of its production, it both decreased the costs of production and increased the percentage of functioning chips it could produce. This percentage, termed "yield" in the industry, and the standard learning curve of semiconductor manufacturing together had a large impact on the prices semiconductor manufacturers set for their products (refer to Exhibit 6 for the price curve of semiconductor products). This yield was important to TI; a 7% increase in overall yield was equivalent to the production of an entire Water Fab plant, an investment of $500 million.

According to Jim Huffhines, Manager of DSP Business Development in the Semiconductor Group, managers could predict with considerable accuracy the production cost decreases and yield improvements they would experience as their production volumes increased:

We know the manufacturing costs for any given volume of production. We also know that these costs will decrease a certain percentage and our yields will increase a certain percentage each year. These predictions are the basis of the forward prices we set with both original equipment manufacturers and distributors.

CONTINUOUS PRICE ADJUSTMENTS   Production costs and yield rates were not the only contributing factors to price levels for standard semiconductors:

market supply and demand also played a powerful role in establishing prices. As a result of volatile prices caused by shifts in supply and demand, distributors often held inventories of semiconductors that did not accurately reflect current market rates. To protect distributors from price fluctuations, most semiconductor manufacturers offered to reimburse distributors for their overvalued inventories. Szczsponik explained:

Semiconductor prices have fallen by 15% over the past 9 months. If Arrow bought semiconductors from me for $1.00, nine months ago, they are worth only 85¢ now. Arrow is carrying a 15% "phantom" inventory. If Arrow sells those semiconductors now, we give it price protection by agreeing to reimburse it the 15¢ it has lost per semiconductor over the past three quarters.

At the same time, distributors had at their disposal sophisticated systems for monitoring semiconductor prices from each of the major manufacturers, and were constantly in search of price adjustments from vendors when placing their orders. Szczsponik continued:

Distributors have access to the prices of products from all the semiconductor manufacturers at any given time, and some anywhere in the world. The largest distributors have a staff of 20 to 30 people shopping around continuously for the best prices available for different types of semiconductors; add to this group a staff of accountants managing the price adjustment transactions. For example, they may call us to say that Motorola has quoted them a certain price for a semiconductor, and ask us if we can beat their price. In total, we get close to 150,000 of these calls requesting adjustments from distributors a year, and do over 10% of our sales through price adjustments. I have 10 people on my staff who negotiate price adjustments for distributors: 5 answer their calls, and 5 work with our product managers to make pricing decisions. These decisions are critical: if we make a mistake in our pricing, we lose market share in a day that can take us 3 months to recapture. At the same time, through our negotiations with distributors, we capture masses of data regarding the pricing levels of our competitors

EXHIBIT 6 Forward Pricing Curve

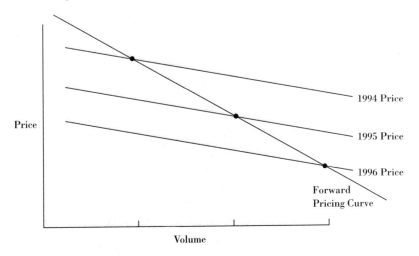

Forward Pricing Curve

Price

Volume

1994 Price

1995 Price

1996 Price

Forward
Pricing Curve

and the market performance of our different products. These data are critical to our ability to set prices.

As the distribution network consolidated into a small number of powerful companies, Szczsponik had begun to notice that his price negotiations were increasingly focused not only on beating the competition in North America, but on beating prices available around the world, including those of TI in other regions. With distributors becoming more active in the global market, they were more often exposed to semiconductor price levels from Europe and Asia. Industry analysts expected North American distributors to become more active in global markets as they pursued aggressive expansion campaigns in Europe and Asia. Although Texas Instruments' current contracts with its distributors prevented them from selling semiconductors outside of the region in which they were purchased, distributors were becoming insistent on access to freer global supplies and markets. While the concept may have appeared reasonable to the distributors, it was somewhat more complicated for Texas Instruments. Kevin McGarity elaborated:

> *Because business is different everywhere in the world, our international distribution channels have evolved independently. They aren't subjected to the same costs, and don't operate under the same methods and calculation models. In the United States, for example, we offer a 30-day payment schedule for our customers. If they don't pay us within 30 days, we cut off their supply, no matter who they are. Italy operates under a 60-day schedule. Europeans include freight in their prices; we don't in North America. Finally, the cost of producing semiconductors varies by country. Europe tends to*

be more expensive than North America or Asia, simply because their infrastructure is more costly. So when one of our large distributors phones with the Singapore price for semiconductors manufactured in Düsseldorf, he is crossing boundaries that may be invisible to him but are very real to us.

Preparing for the Meeting with Arrow

With sales of almost $4 billion in 1994, Arrow Electronics was the largest semiconductor distributor in North America, of which TI products accounted for approximately 14%. Its aggressive growth had taken the company into global markets and had given it increased exposure to fluctuating price and exchange levels in different international markets. Seeking to minimize its costs, Arrow had begun to pressure semiconductor manufacturers to set standard global prices for each of their products. Motorola, one of Texas Instruments' largest competitors in the semiconductor industry, was rumored to be preparing for global pricing. Management at Texas Instruments, however, was unsure of the wisdom of moving toward global pricing. According to Szczsponik, the pros and cons to global pricing seem unevenly balanced:

> *The large distributors want global pricing to reduce their costs and simplify their planning. But does it make sense for us? Right now our organization's calculation systems and costs in each country are too different for us to offer standard global prices. There are other things to consider as well. If we set global prices, we will no longer continue our price adjustment negotiations with the distributors. This may save us the cost of staffing our negotiations team, but it also takes away from us a powerful tool for gathering information on*

our customers' prices and our product performance. As soon as we stop negotiating price adjustments, we lose our visibility in the market.

To prepare for his decision with McGarity and the forthcoming meeting with Arrow Electronics, Szczsponik knew TI had to make some fundamental decisions regarding global pricing. Who held the power in the relationships Texas Instruments had with its distributors? What was the source of the negotiating strength each party would bring to the meeting? Finally, what position should the Semiconductor Group take with its distributors regarding global pricing? And what organizational implications would such a decision imply?

DISCUSSION QUESTIONS

1. What are the reasons the semi-conductor market is global? Why is it so difficult to create an FSA or CSA? Are there any differential advantages?

2. What drives the need for global pricing? Any options apart from global pricing?

3. Who has most power in the value chain from manufacturers through distributors to customers?

4. How would you try to manage the global pricing process—by formalization of the pricing process, economic controls, centralization or informal persuasion? Any other options?

Case 4.3

United Colors of Benetton

It was October 1995. Luciano Benetton, chairman of Benetton Group S.p.A, prepared to address yet another audience of business leaders. This tall, smiling yet reserved man with very blue eyes and longish hair was the guest speaker at a dinner held by the Italian Chamber of Commerce for France in Paris. Over the past 40 years, Benetton had become famous for its technological advances and novel approach to retailing. By 1995, it had become one of the world's best-known brands, with 8000 shops world-wide, and a successful winning Formula One racing team (key financial data can be found in Exhibit 1). For most people, however, Benetton was synonymous with its communication strategy—one of the world's most visible and controversial, almost always provoking reactions of outrage or praise and, quite often, both.

Rather than advertising its products, Benetton used its communications budget to provoke debate on broad social issues such as racism, AIDS, war and poverty. A number of observers had criticised its 'use of social problems to sell knitwear'. Luciano knew that he would have to explain one more time why he spent Benetton's L115 billion[1] communication budget on 'penetrating the barriers of apathy', and that, inevitably, some of his audience would remain unconvinced.

THE BENETTON GROUP

Benetton Group S.p.A. was the world's biggest consumer of wool and Europe's largest clothing concern, with 1994 sales or L2,788 billion and net income of L210 billion. Its largest markets were Italy (34% of sales), Germany (12%), Japan (11%) and France (9%). 64 million items were sold world-wide in 1994, up 12.7% on 1993. Outside the EU, the increase was 36%. Aided by several devaluations of the lira, Benetton had cut prices by up to 40 percent over the previous two years.[1]

This is an abbreviated version of a case developed by Christian Pinson, Professor, and Vikas Tibrewala, Associate Professor at INSEAD, with the assistance of Francesca Gee. It is intended to be used as a basis for class discussion rather than to illustrate either effective or ineffective handling of an administrative situation.

[1]On 16 October 1995, US$ 1 = L1602.10

EXHIBIT 1 Benetton Group SpA: Financial Highlights 1986–1995 (millions of lire[1])

	Italy	Other Europe	The Americas	Other Countries	Consolidated
1986 Revenues	388,872	470,530	173,322	19,558	1,089,983
Operating profits	99,680	86,160	16,180	4,030	206,050
Net Income					113,029
Share price/MIB[2]					15,900/104.8
1987 Revenues	437,101	609,973	222,780	12,050	1,261,077
Operating profits	108,426	117,071	8,928	(2,526)	249,839
Net Income					130,291
Share price/MIB					10,460/99.6
1988 Revenues	641,633	702,462	236,372	35,266	1,475,282
Operating profits	111,937	115,196	16,134	(2,361)	239,673
Net Income					130,171
Share price/MIB					10,560/80.3
1989 Revenues	665,530	672,635	222,874	96,460	1,657,519
Operating profits	120,986	99,462	(637)	5,560	225,307
Net Income					115,412
Share price/MIB					8,720/99.3
1990 Revenues	749,930	819,825	220,463	268,830	2,059,048
Operating profits	147,477	142,820	(8,265)	9,952	266,180
Net Income					133,271
Share price/MIB					8,580/100.0

	Italy	Other Europe	The Americas	Other Countries	Consolidated
1991 Revenues	790,339	933,751	215,409	364,265	2,303,764
Operating profits	150,374	151,368	(12,255)	35,123	311,757
Net Income					164,783
Share price/MIB					10,320/84.7
1992 Revenues	862,495	987,603	237,798	424,745	2,512,641
Operating profits	170,770	172,533	(12,029)	43,106	356,639
Net Income					184,709
Share price/MIB					13,870/70.5
1993 Revenues	850,609	1,062,823	270,021	568,005	2,751,458
Operating profits	165,003	204,150	(22,418)	74,490	407,926
Net Income					208,038
Share price/MIB					26,730/83.5
1994 Revenues[3]	882,744	1,019,478	227,302	658,148	2,787,672
Operating Profits	151,153	175,040	(19,138)	93,841	388,740
Net Income					210,200
Share price/MIB					12,038/104.1

Note: Results for 1995: revenues of L 2,940 billion with net income of L 220 billion.
Share price on 31.12.95: 18,890 lire

[1] Exchange rate Lire/US$: 1986 = 1358; 1987 = 1169; 1988 = 1306; 1989 = 1271; 1990 = 1130; 1991 = 1151; 1992 = 1471; 1993 = 1704; 1994 = 1626

[2] MIB = MIB Index, calculated by the Milan Stock Exchange and based on the average of all stocks traded on that exchange, 1990 = 100.

[3] On 1 February 1994, Benetton had a capital issue of 10 million shares at L 26,500/share.

In 1995 Benetton had three main brands:

- United Colors of Benetton (clothing for men and women) which also included Blue Family (with an emphasis on denim) and Benetton Undercolors (underwear and beachwear): 60.8% of sales

- 012 United Colors of Benetton (clothing for children under 12) including Zerotondo (clothing and accessories for babies): 18.5% of sales

- Sisley (higher-fashion clothing): 11.8% of sales

Over two-thirds of their clothing was for women, who represented 80% of Benetton's shoppers. Fabrizio Servente, head of product development, commented:

> *'The "objective" target for the adult Benetton stores is the 18–24 year old, but of course there is no age ceiling. Our product takes into account quality and price. It's clean, international, with a lot of attention to design. It can be worn just as easily by Princess Diana and by her maid, or her maid's daughter . . . The way young people dress is becoming more and more "uniform", but there are differences from one region to another. Benetton must still be Italian in Italy, Brazilian in Brazil, Indian in India.'*

THE BENETTON SYSTEM

Benetton operated through a complex system of over 500 sub-contractors and several joint ventures specialising in design, cutting, assembling, ironing or packaging, plus thousands of independent retail outlets. Benetton's success was largely attributed to this ability to combine fashion with industry.

Benetton's unique distribution philosophy was an important reason for its success. 'We didn't want to become directly involved in the selling side,' Luciano Benetton said, 'so in the beginning it was friends with financial resources who moved into this part of the business'. By 1995, from over 8,000 retail outlets Benetton owned and operated fewer than 50 'flagship stores' in cities such as Milan, New York, Paris and Düsseldorf. The rest were owned by independent retailers who typically ran five or six outlets.

The company dealt with these retailers through a network of 83 agents, controlled by seven area managers reporting to Benetton's commercial director. The agents, who were independent entrepreneurs, had exclusive rights over a territory; they selected store owners, and received a 4% commission on orders placed with them. They supervised operations in their territory, kept an eye on the market and offered guid-

ance to store owners on product selection, merchandising and the location of new stores, making sure that Benetton's policies were respected. Another important responsibility of the agents was to find new retailers who 'fit' the Benetton culture. They were themselves encouraged to re-invest their earnings in new stores of their own.

BENETTON'S COMMUNICATION

Benetton's early advertisements were rather conventional, focusing on the product and stressing the quality of wool.

The logo, a stylised knot of yarn and the word 'Benetton', were later united within a green rectangle with rounded corners. During the 1970s, the company reduced its advertising consistent with its decision to adopt a low profile in Italy. The first US advertising campaigns, handled by a small agency (Kathy Travis) stressed the European origins and international success of Benetton. 'Last year we made 8,041,753 sweaters . . . sold through 1573 Benetton stores internationally.' These campaigns contributed less to Benetton's breakthrough in the US than the runaway success among students of a simple model (the rugby polo) and the awakening of Americans to fashion 'Made in Italy.'[2]

In 1982 Luciano Benetton met Oliviero Toscani, a well-known fashion and advertising photographer who lived in Tuscany and had studios in Paris and New York. His clients included, among others, Jesus Jeans, Valentino, Esprit, Club Med and Bata. Toscani convinced Luciano that Benetton ought to promote itself as a lifestyle, not a clothing business. At Toscani's suggestion, Benetton retained Eldorado, a small Paris agency with which Toscani had often worked as a photographer.

ALL THE COLOURS IN THE WORLD

The first campaigns were conventional in style ing social status and conformism, and feat of young people wearing Benetton cl departure came in 1984 with a n Colours in the World'. This of teenagers from diffe

[2]Benetton's sales have al
For example, in 1994, the c.
of the winter sales in France.

groups dressed in colourful knitwear. The print and billboard campaign was distributed by J. Walter Thompson (JWT) in 14 countries.

The campaign was greeted with enthusiasm and Benetton received hundreds of letters of praise. But it prompted shocked reactions in South Africa, where the ads were carried only by magazines catering to the black community. A few letters, from England and the US reflected hysterical racism. 'Shame on you!' wrote one correspondent from Manchester in the north of England, 'You have mixed races that God wants to keep apart!'

UNITED COLORS OF BENETTON

In 1985, a UNESCO official visited the studio where Toscani was photographing a multi-racial group of children and exclaimed: 'This is fantastic, it's the United Colors here!' This became the new slogan: 'United Colors of Benetton'. The posters reconciled instantly recognisable 'enemies': a German and an Israeli, a Greek and a Turk, and an Argentinean and a Briton. Another poster showed two small black children bearing the US and Soviet flags.

The multi-racial message was made clearer still with the theme chosen for the 1986 and 1987 campaigns: 'the globe'. One ad showed a white adolescent dressed as an Hassidic Jew holding a moneybox full of dollar bills, next to a black teenager dressed as an American Indian. 'In the eyes of Eldorado's directors, all of them Jewish, the picture was humorous enough to make it clear that we were taking aim at the stereotype [of the money-grabbing Jew],' wrote Luciano Benetton.[3] Benetton was flooded with protests, mostly from France and Italy. In New York, Jewish groups threatened to boycott Benetton shops. Benetton replaced the ad with a picture of a Palestinian and a Jew, which was also criticised.

Luciano commented:

'I was a bit discouraged, but I had learned a fundamental lesson. We had chosen to promote an image that touched very deep feelings, identities for which millions of people had fought and died. We had reached the limits and felt the responsibilities of commercial art. Everybody was now watching us, and even a small dose of ingenuity could hurt us and irritate others. I promised myself I would control our image even more rigorously.'[4]

[3]Luciano Benetton and Andrea Lee, *Io e i miei fratelli*, Sperling e Kupfer Editori, 1990 (translated by the authors).

[4]*Io e i miei Fratelli*

The 1987 autumn/winter campaign, 'United Fashions of Benetton', showed models wearing Benetton clothes with accessories that evoked the great names in fashion. 'United Superstars of Benetton' was the slogan for the 1988 campaign, featuring pairs dressed up as Joan of Arc and Marilyn Monroe, Leonardo da Vinci and Julius Caesar, or Adam and Eve—two-long haired teenagers dressed in denim.

A MESSAGE OF RACIAL EQUALITY

1989 marked a turning point in Benetton's communication activities. The company terminated its relationship with Eldorado.[5] 'From the beginning, Luciano Benetton wanted image to be an in-house product, so that it would reflect the company's soul,' Toscani explained later. United Colors Communication would soon handle all aspects of Benetton's communication including production and media buying. The entire process was managed by less than ten people; Toscani's visuals would be discussed by the advertising team, then shown to Luciano for final approval. This allowed Benetton to produce advertisements which cost about one-third of those of its competitors.[6] Benetton did not usually advertise on television because of the high costs but used print and outdoor media extensively. It limited itself to two series of campaigns (Spring and Fall). Each campaign would typically last a couple of weeks, and consist of a small number of visuals shown in an increasing number of countries. By 1995, Benetton spent about 4% of turnover on communication, which included campaigns for United Colors of Benetton and Sisley, sports sponsorship, a quarterly magazine, *Colors*[7] and funding for its communications school, *Fabrica*.

This shift to in-house communications was accompanied by a radical change in approach. The 1989 ads no loner showed the product, didn't use a slogan and replaced the knot logo with a small green rectangle that was to become the company's trademark. Hard-hitting images began to deliver an unambiguously political message championing racial equality. One ad showing a black woman nursing a white baby generated controversy in South Africa and in the US,

[5]Two years later, Benetton fired JWT and set up United Colors Communication as a full-service agency.

[6]*Financial World*, 17 September 1991, p. 41

[7]In 1993, spending amounted to 5.7% to finance the TV launch of Tribù, a line of scents and cosmetics. The complete Benetton fragrance business was restructured in 1995.

where it was seen as a throwback to the era of slavery. Benetton withdrew the ad in the US, explaining that 'the campaign is intended to promote equality, not friction'.

This became Benetton's most praised visual ever, winning awards in five European countries. Another ad, showing a black man and a white man handcuffed together, offended British blacks, who thought it showed a white policeman arresting a black. London Transport refused to show the poster in its network.

The 1990 campaign continued the theme, with softer images: the hand of a black child resting in a white man's hand; a white wolf and a black lamb; a small black child asleep amid white stuffed bears; the hand of a white relay runner passing a baton to a black team-mate.

Benetton's attempt to show two babies on their potties on a 770 square meter billboard opposite Milan's cathedral was banned by the city authorities and the Roman Catholic cardinal. That year, Benetton won its first advertising award in the USA.

SOCIAL ISSUES

By 1991 Benetton's campaigns, which now tackled issues beyond racism, were reaching audiences in more than 100 countries. A picture showing a military cemetery, released at the start of the Gulf war, was turned down by all but one newspaper, *Il Sole 24 Ore* in Italy.

An ad displaying brightly coloured condoms ('a call for social responsibility in the face of overpopulation and sexually transmitted disease') was intended to 'demystify condoms by displaying them in a playful and colourful way, like fashion items.'

Simultaneously, condoms were distributed in Benetton's shops world-wide. Benetton also distributed HIV guides in the shanty towns of Rio 'because it was importance that even people who could never buy a Benetton sweater should get the basic communication.'

Other ads included a white boy kissing a black girls, a group of Pinocchio puppets in different hues of wood, and a multi-ethnic trio of children playfully sticking out their tongues.

While this last ad won awards in Britain and Germany, it was withdrawn from display in Arabic countries, where it was considered offensive.

Later that year, Toscani chose to focus on: 'love, the underlying reason for al life'. The campaign featured, among others, a priest and a nun kissing; and Giusy, a screaming new-born baby with her umbilical cord still attached.

Courtesy Benetton Group, S.p.A. Reprinted with permission.

In the US, the Anti-Defamation League condemned the priest-and-nun ad for 'trivialising, mocking, profaning and offending religious values', and several magazines rejected it.

In France, the Bureau de Vérification de la Publicité (BVP), a self-regulating advertising body, recommended the removal of the priest-and-nun ad in the name of 'decency and self-discipline', whilst in England, it won the Eurobest Award. Others were also positive: Sister Barbara Becker Schroeder from Alzey, Germany, wrote to Benetton: 'I feel the photo expresses great tenderness, security and peace . . . I would be grateful if you would let me have one or more posters, preferably in different sizes.'[8] In November 1991, Benetton won a court case initiated by AGRIF (L'Alliance générale contre le racisme et pour le respect de la famille française) where it was accepted that the nun and priest poster was not racist or anti-Christian.

In Britain, Benetton ignored a warning issued by the Advertising Standards Authority (ASA) concerning the Guisy ad and within days, the authority received some 800 complaints. The offending posters were withdrawn—and replaced with an ad showing an angelic blond-haired child next to a black child whose hair was styled to evoke horns, which the ASA also criticised.

In the USA, Giusy elicited some negative reactions but was accepted by *Parenting*, *Self* and *Vogue*. It was rejected by *Child*, *Cosmopolitan*, and *Elle*. The posters were not displayed in Milan where the city of-

[8]This is one of 100 letters (positive and negative) published at Benetton's initiative in P. Landi and L. Pollini, eds. *Cosa C'entra L'Aids Con i Maglioni?*, A. Mondadori Editore, 1993.

Courtesy Benetton Group, S.p.A. Reprinted with permission.

ficials complained of 'the excessive impact and vulgarity of the subject.' The local High Court ruled that 'the picture offended public order and general morality.' Giusy was also banned in France, Germany and Ireland, where the advertising space was donated to the Association for the Fight Against Cancer. These reactions surprised Benetton, as well as a number of others:

> 'We should ask ourselves the question of why such a natural, vital and basic image as that of a baby being born, offends the public. Every day we are confronted with pictures of death, often meaningless, and we put up with them in silence, or very nearly. Yet we are afraid to see an image of life.' (L'Unita, 10/9/91)

> 'Why must beer be drunk topless on the deck of a sailing boat and the smiling, happy mum always be half-naked as she swaddles the baby in a nappy like a scented pastry? Isn't all this rather ridiculous?' (Il Giornale Nuovo, 26/10/91)

According to Benetton, 'Once the period of rejection was over, the picture began to be understood and appreciated.' Giusy won an award from the Société Générale d'Affichage in Switzerland and Bologna's General Clinic asked for a copy to decorate its labour room.

THE 'REALITY' CAMPAIGNS

In 1992, Benetton broke new ground with two series of news photographs on issues such as AIDS, immigration, terrorism, violence, and political refugees. The use of real-life pictures showing, for example, a bombed car, Albanian refugees, a Mafia-style killing and a soldier holding a human bone provoked controversy around the world, despite Benetton's repeated claim that it was trying to prompt debate of serious social issues.

This claim was supported by Patrick Robert, a photographer with the Sygma agency, some of whose pictures had been used in the campaigns: '. . . the absence of an explanatory caption on my photographs [soldier with human bone, truck bulging with refugees] does not bother me . . . for me the objective of the campaign is reached . . . to draw the public's attention to these victims.'[9]

A picture showing David Kirby,[10] an AIDS patient, surrounded by his family on his deathbed, stirred particularly strong emotions.

In Britain, the ASA described the ad as 'obscene' and 'a despicable exploitation of a tragic situation' and asked magazines to reject it. Benetton donated the use of 500 paid UK poster sites to the charity *Trading*. Maggie Alderson, the editor of the UK edition of *Elle*, which ran a statement on two blank pages instead of the ad, commented:

> 'It is an incredibly moving image in the right context, but to use it as an advertisement for a fashion store selling jumpers is incredibly insulting. They have stepped out of the bounds of what is acceptable and what makes this so sickening is that they have touched up the photograph to make it look biblical because the AIDS victim resembles Jesus Christ.' (The Guardian, 24/1/92).

In France, the BVP took an unprecedented step: without even waiting for the ad to be printed, it threatened to exclude any publication that dared carry it. Only one publication ignored the ban: *Max*, a magazine for young people. Its editor, Nicolas Finet, commented, 'Our readers, those between 15 and 30 years old, are directly affected by this topic. This campaign is one way of approaching the AIDS problem whilst avoiding the socio-medical aspect. Our readers' letters have shown that we were not wrong' (quoted in the French advertising weekly *Stratégies*, 18/2/92). In Switzerland, *Schweizer Illustrierte* decided to accept the ad saying that it did not hurt mass sensitivity but 'wounded only one thing: the rules of the games according to which the message must be dull, stale even.'

Many organisations and advocacy groups for homosexuals charged Benetton with callous exploitation, saying it offered no information about prevention. However, some AIDS activists felt it gave the issue a higher public profile, an opinion which others shared:

[9]In *Benetton par Toscani*, Musée d' Art Conetmporain, Lausanne, 1995.

[10]The photographer Therese Frare won the World Photo Award for this picture

'For the large majority of the population which thinks that AIDS is not their business, Benetton's ads will be a slap in their face . . . and I am sure it will be more effective than every campaign to date by any public or private body.' (L'Unita, 25/1/92).

'The company estimates that between 500 million and one billion people have seen the AIDS image, far more than ever saw it when it came out in Life. A public that is reading fewer newspapers and believing fewer broadcasts might begin to swallow tiny doses of information between the ads for liqueur and lingerie.' (Vicky Goldbert in The New York Times, 3/5/92).

'The picture . . . has done more to soften people's heart on the AIDS issue than any other I have ever seen. You can't look at that picture and hate a person with AIDS . . . As far as the comment that it was "touched up to look like Jesus Christ" . . . I know that at Pater Noster [hospital], several times, with several patients through the years, nurses have made the same comment, "he looks like Jesus" ' (Barb Cordle, David Kirby's nurse in Interview, 4/92).

The Economist (1/2/92) felt that the ads targeted the young and,

'what better means to appeal to them than by offending their elders . . . expect no repentance, or tamer ads, from Benetton unless its sales start to drop.'

Asked about the campaign's impact on sales, Peter Fressola, Director of Communications, Benetton Services New York, emphasised that individual ads were not geared to boost sales and that Benetton was aware that

'people are not going to look at an image of a burning car, and then make a best-seller out of our fuschia sweater.' (The Wall Street Journal, 28/5/92).

Reacting to the charges of exploitation, Benetton argued that the David Kirby visual increased awareness of the need for collective and personal solidarity with AIDS patients, created a media tribune for HIV organisations and others involved in the issue, and encouraged a debate on how best to communicate on AIDS.[11] They also stressed that David's family was in favor of the photo being used. In support of the ad, the Kirby family went on the record:

'It is what he would have wanted . . . We don't feel used. Rather it is we who are using Benetton. David is speaking louder now that he is dead than when he was alive.' (Il Mattino, 22/3/92).

The second 1992 campaign once more used hard-hitting news pictures: an oil-covered bird from the Gulf; an albino Zulu woman ostracised by other Zulus; a grime-smeared Salvadoran child carrying a white doll; pigs in a trash heap in Peru; children building a brick wall; KGB agents arresting a suspect; an empty electric chair in a US jail.

The *Financial Times* commented:

'Like its previous campaign, Benetton has again focused on the downbeat and the unhappy, this time selecting a set of apparent outcasts to sell its colourful jumpers.' (17/9/92)

THE CLOTHING REDISTRIBUTION PROJECT

The spring 1993 campaign showed Luciano Benetton, newly elected to the Italian Senate and named as Italy's leading entrepreneur, stark naked, modestly screened by a caption reading 'I want my clothes back.' A second ad followed: 'Empty your closets.'

People were invited to donate clothes of any brand at Benetton stores. The campaign, which ran in about 1000 magazines and 150 dailies, was widely welcomed: 'It is a clear break from Benetton's self-serious attitude of the past. It also marks the first time the company has engaged in direct action to support a cause.' (The Wall Street Journal, 27/1/93).[12]

Some 460 tons of clothes were collected in 83 countries and re-distributed world-wide with the help of charities such as Caritas, the International Red Cross and the Red Crescent.

THE VENICE TRIPTYCH

In June 1993, Toscani exhibited a 400 square meter triptych at the Venice Biennial art show. A specially restored chapel housed the work, which showed 56 close-up photos of male and female genitals—blacks and whites, adults and children. Benetton added its logo and published the picture as an ad in *Libération*.

That day the newspaper sold an extra 40,000 copies. The BVP threatened to sue. Two days later, French men's underwear-maker Eminence published a

---

[11] Around this time, Benetton started advertising in gay magazines, which were generally ignored by major corporations.

[12] Pascal Sommariba, Benetton's International Advertising Director, countered charges of a lack of charitable giving, saying: 'If a company makes 10% profits and takes 20% of it for charity, this is 2% of its turnover. If you take just 1/3rd of a communication budget of, say 5% of turnover, you are already there and it does not look like a charitable company, it is fairer.'

double page in *Libération* showing as many (male) crotches with the same layout and the slogan: 'We like dressing them.'

THE HIV-POSITIVE CAMPAIGN

A near-unanimous outcry greeted the Fall 1993 campaign, which consisted of three stark photographs showing an arm, buttock and crotch, each branded with the words 'HIV Positive'.

Benetton explained that the pictures referred to the three main avenues for infection, as well as to the ostracism of AIDS victims. In Singapore, Danny Chow (President, ASA) dismissed the ads as 'easily another ploy to get free publicity' (*Straits Times*, 27/9/93). The Italian advertising watchdog, the Giuri della Pubblicità, condemned the campaign for 'not respecting the dignity of human beings.'

The AIDS association LILA (*Lega Italiana per la Lotta control l'AIDS*) didn't approve of it but took a pragmatic approach and decided to use it in its fight against AIDS. In the USA, reactions were mostly negative. David Eng (Gay Men's Health Crisis, New York) felt that 'the ad can fuel hatred and disempowerment . . . people can get the message that this [i.e. branding] is what we should be doing to people who are HIV positive.' (*The New York Times*, 19/9/93). The *National Review* refused the ad without seeing it. The British ACET (AIDS Care Education and Training) demanded the ad's withdrawal.

The *Association Française de la Lutte contre le Sida* (AFLS), a French government-sponsored AIDS group, sued Benetton, for 'hijacking a humanitarian cause for commercial ends.' Four HIV sufferers joined in the lawsuit, with charges of 'humiliation' and 'debasement'. According to their lawyers, the brandings were an implicit call to discriminate against patients, and evoked the Nazi death camps.[13] A representative of AIDES, another French association, felt the ad could be misinterpreted: 'It is clearly stated that sodomy or intravenous drug abuse are the [major] causes of AIDS. . . . Such short cuts are misleading and stupid.' (*CB News*, 20/9/93).

The brother of one sufferer bought a full page ad in *Libération*, and published a picture of his brother's emaciated face with the caption: 'During the agony,

---

[13]On 1 February 1995, a Paris court ruled against Benetton and awarded damages of about US$32,000. On 6 July 1995, a German court ruled that these pictures offended the dignity of HIV-infected people.

the selling continues. For the attention of Luciano Benetton, from Olivier Besnard-Rousseau, AIDS sufferer, terminal phase.' There were increasingly strident calls to boycott the firm, including one from a former cabinet minister. Arcat Sida, a French AIDS support group headed by Pierre Bergé, CEO of Yves Saint Laurent, sponsored a poster showing a condom stuffed with bank notes next to a 'United Boycott' logo in Benetton's signature typeface and green colour. Stores were vandalised and sprayed with graffiti leading some store owners to complain that 'Mr Benetton listens to nobody.' (*Le Nouvel Observateur*, 20/12/93).

Luciano Benetton was himself surprised and hurt by the violence of these reactions. In the Group's defence, its long-standing commitment to the fight against AIDS and the extent of its actions were cited. On December 1, 1993 (World AIDS Day), Benetton in cooperation with the association Actup had a 22 metre pink condom placed over the obelisk in the Place de la Concorde in Paris. In early 1994 Luciano received an award given by the President of South Korea in recognition of the consciousness-raising role played by the company.

THE KNOWN SOLDIER

In February 1994, a Benetton ad showing bloodied battle fatigues appeared on billboards and in newspapers across 110 countries.

The clothes had belonged to a Croatian soldier killed in Bosnia, as a caption in Serbo-Croat indicated:

> '*I, Gojko Gagro, father of the deceased Marinko Gagro, born in 1963 in the province of Citluk, would like that my son's name and all that remains of him be used in the name of peace against war.*'

The advertisement was greeted by an immediate uproar. While it became an instant success in Sarajevo, where the *Oslobodenje* newspaper printed it, leading dailies such as the *Los Angeles Times*, *Le Monde*, and the *Frankfurter Allgemeine Zeitung* refused to carry it, and the Vatican denounced Benetton for 'image terrorism.' Reactions among the combatants and people in the war zones depended on whether Gagro was seen as a victim or an aggressor and whose cause the ad was perceived as helping. Indignation reached a climax in France, where the minister for human rights and humanitarian action urged consumers to stop buying Benetton clothes and to 'rip them off the backs of those who wear them.' Once again, several Benetton stores were vandalised, causing a growing sense of unease among some retailers.

The French advertising weekly *Stratégies* announced it would not write about Benetton's advertising as long as it remained in the same vein: 'Besides the disgust it causes, this [latest] ad raises the issue of the responsibility of advertisers. Can one do anything, use anything, to attract attention?' (25/2/94). Marina Galanti, Benetton's spokeswoman reacted to the outcry: '. . . If we were trying to sell T-shirts, there probably would not be a worse way of doing it. We are not that naïve. It's meant to question the notion of institutionalised violence and the role of advertising.' (*The Guardian*, 16/2/94). The autumn 1994 worldwide campaign featured in print media and billboards showed a mosaic of 1000 faces arranged to softly highlight the word AIDS at its centre. This campaign attracted little attention.

THE ALIENATION CAMPAIGN

The spring 1995 campaign featured two visuals based on the theme of 'alienation'. One showed lines of barbed wire, coming from a variety of troubled countries such as Bosnia, Lebanon and Israel as well as from private gardens.

The other showed a jungle of TV antennae symbolising the 'invisible barriers erected by the overcrowding of video images, which not only affect interpersonal relationships, but also people's perception of reality.' Billed as 'an invitation to an open discussion on real and virtual prisons, on the mental and televisual dictatorships which restrict freedom', the campaign did not elicit strong reactions. Benetton denied that the ads reflected a softer, toned-down communications strategy.

Around the same time, Benetton's US retailers launched a campaign developed by Chiat/Day of New York, designed to appeal to more conservative audiences. The new US campaign focused on clothing and included TV spots as well as eight-page magazine inserts. Luciano explained that this initiative was not an alternative to their international campaign, but an additional support to its US store owners.

THE GERMAN LAWSUITS

The furore over the recent Benetton campaigns reached a peak in Germany. Here 12 retailers being sued by Benetton for non-payment[14] defended their case by accusing Benetton of provoking adverse reaction in consumers through their ads, with a consequent drop in sales. Benetton stated that '. . . total sales in Germany have remained stable in 1994 . . . 1992 was a record year . . . 8 million items were sold in 1993 and 1994 versus 4 million in 1985.' While the group of retailers claimed that the number of Benetton stores had dropped form 650 to 500, with 100 more dropouts expected, Benetton maintained that it had 613 stores in Germany in 1994 as opposed to 650 in 1993. Marina Galanti explained that, 'What we are talking about is a lawyer's trick to use a *cause célèbre* as a peg on which to hang every kind of grievance . . . these store owners may not like the ads, but the Frankfurt Museum of Modern Art has them on permanent exhibition.' (*The Independent*, 6/2/95).

Threats of legal action in France and other European countries had also been made. A body called The Benetton Retailers Interest Group had been formed to co-ordinate the various actions against Benetton. However, other retailers formed the 'Pro-Benetton' group in Germany to 'fight the discredit done to Benetton by the disgruntled retailers.'

In October 1995 Luciano indicated that all twelve cases had been won by Benetton and that 'the affair was now over.'[15] Financial analysts were generally optimistic about Benetton's prospects as they felt the markets had already discounted any possible negative impact due to the controversies. Salomon Brothers issued a 'Buy' recommendation on Benetton stock on 17 October 1995.

The visibility and uniqueness of Benetton's communications had prompted a number of advertising agencies and publishing and market research companies to conduct independent studies of their effectiveness, very often without Benetton's knowledge. These studies evaluated specific Benetton campaigns (Exhibit 2) together with the image of Benetton and other leading brands across a variety of countries (Exhibit 3).

[14]Ulfert Engels, the lawyer co-ordinating the 12 cases said: '. . . Our tactic was to get Benetton to sue, otherwise we would have had to fight in an Italian court and we prefer to fight in Germany.' *Marketing Week*, 3/2/95

[15]'Germany: Benetton ends dispute with retailers'. *Handelsblat*, 12 October 1995

EXHIBIT 2 Ipsos Tests of Benetton Campaigns in France (billboards, Paris and suburbs), 1985–1993

	Recognition[2]	Attribution[3]	Confusion[4]	Liked	Disliked
Overall sample (N=300)	57	29	3	73	23
18–34 year olds (N=150)	63	36	3	73	21

Date of Campaign: 1-20/3/85
Date of Test: 20/9/85
Cost[1]: 2,000,000 FF and 4,000,000 FF ($223,000 and $446,000)

[1]Estimated cost of the campaign in French Francs (US$). This refers only to billboards and does not include print.
[2]Respondents were shown a folder containing several ads with the brand name blocked out. As they leafed through, they were asked which ads they remembered seeing. The recognition score is the % of respondents remembering having seen (at least one of) the ads listed.
[3]For each ad recognised, respondents were asked whether they remembered the name of the brand blocked out.
[4]Percentage of respondents who incorrectly identified the brand.

N= 301	Recognition	Attribution	Confusion	Liked	Disliked	Indifferent
Overall sample	75	64	2	79	20	1
Gender						
Men	75	60	3	77	23	1
Women	75	68	1	81	17	2
Age group						
18–24	81	77	1	83	16	1
25–34	81	76	1	83	15	3
35–55	69	53	3	75	25	—
Income group						
Higher	83	72	3	81	18	1
Medium	72	60	2	77	22	1
Lower	65	58	2	77	20	3
Ipsos standards[5]	43	18	—	60	35	5

Date of Campaign: 1989
Date of Test: 28/9 to 3/10/89
Cost: 2,396,000 FF ($375,543)

[5]Average score of all other billboard campaigns tested by Ipsos within the same industry and with similar budgets.

N= 302	Recognition	Attribution	Confusion	Liked	Disliked	Indifferent
Overall sample	79	72	1	32	66	2
Gender						
Men	76	67	1	34	64	2
Women	83	77	—	30	69	1
Age group						
18–24	84	75	1	34	64	2
25–34	80	77	1	38	62	—
35–55	79	67	1	26	70	3
Income group						
Higher	80	71	—	44	56	1
Medium	82	78	1	23	75	3
Lower	75	63	2	27	71	2
Ipsos standards	43	18	—	59	35	6

Date of Campaign: 2/9 to 11/9/91
Date of Test: 19/9/91
Cost: 2,440,000 FF ($432,463)

EXHIBIT 2 (*cont'd*) Ipsos Tests of Benetton Campaigns in France (billboards, Paris and suburbs), 1985–1993

N= 193	Recognition	Attribution	Confusion	Liked	Disliked	Indifferent
Overall sample	64	59	1	59	38	3
Gender						
Men	67	60	1	60	38	2
Women	60	58	–	58	39	3
Age group						
18–24	65	63	–	65	29	6
25–34	67	65	–	60	36	4
35–55	60	53	1	58	41	1
Income group						
Higher	67	63	1	56	43	1
Medium	60	53	–	66	30	4
Lower	66	62	–	48	48	3
Ipsos standards	43	18	–	59	35	6

Date of Campaign: 2/9 to 11/9/91 and 14/10 to 21/10/91
Date of Test: 24/10/91
Cost: 2,440,000 FF ($432,463) and 1,097,000 FF ($194,431)

N= 301	Recognition	Attribution	Confusion	Liked	Disliked	Indifferent
Overall sample	81	77	2	23	70	7
Gender						
Men	78	72	3	22	70	8
Women	85	81	1	24	70	6
Age group						
18–24	86	84	–	21	69	10
25–34	82	79	1	22	71	7
35–55	81	75	3	24	68	7
Income group						
Higher	86	85	1	20	75	6
Medium	82	75	4	25	68	7
Lower	69	60	–	28	62	10
Ipsos standards	44	21	–	61	31	8

Date of Campaign: 14/9 to 21/9/93
Date of Test: 23/9/93
Cost: 2,200,000 FF ($338,473)

Source: Ipsos Publicité, Paris, France.

DISCUSSION QUESTIONS

1. What are the explanations for the global success of Benetton?

2. What is the marketing logic behind the "United Colors of Benetton" campaign? Do the Toscani photographs "add value" to the Benetton brand name or dilute it?

3. Why do some people (including Benetton's own distributors) react so negatively to some of the advertising? Judging from the research, some of the ads score high on "Liking" while others are clearly "Disliked." What is it in the ads which makes for this?

4. To what extent is the communicated message universal? To the extent the message is universal, one would expect a uniform global ad campaign to be successful. Would this be the case here? Why/Why not?

5. Discuss the ethical aspects of using human suffering in ads. Does your answer influence how likely you would be to buy a Benetton product? Why/Why not?

EXHIBIT 3 Overall Awareness and Use of Some Clothing Brands in 21 Countries, 1994 (*A Young & Rubicam Brand Asset*™ *Valuator Study*)

	Benetton		Chanel		Dior		Esprit		Gap		Armani		Lacoste		YSL	
	Aware[1]	Use[2]	Aware	Use	Aware	Use	Aware	Use	Aware	Use	Aware	Use	Aware	Use	Aware	Use
Australia	59	2/81	93	4/84	94	11/73	87	7/63	12	1/93	43	2/95	74	4/65	82	16/76
Brazil	54	3/81	51	1/93	42	4/86	30	0/98	9	0/98	20	1/97	29	6/85	34	5/88
Canada	61	2/78	97	11/69	89	2/89	83	22/58	57	5/79	60	2/92	41	2/78	84	15/64
Czech Rep	69	1/77	92	3/38	91	6/36	32	1/45	23	1/70	22	0/47	51	1/57	37	2/44
France	91	8/53	98	16/64	98	14/65	21	1/96	25	2/91	37	3/91	97	24/30	99	19/58
Germany	71	8/51	80	5/66	83	3/70	68	8/54	19	1/79	44	4/72	66	4/54	63	2/71
Hungary	73	3/87	78	7/87	75	7/87	31	2/95	13	1/95	35	2/93	60	4/67	45	4/91
Italy	94	21/35	85	15/67	83	13/68	25	1/97	16	1/96	93	25/49	86	19/37	73	14/70
Japan	75	3/64	98	21/63	93	27/50	47	3/93	28	1/90	75	6/85	88	6/36	93	29/49
Mexico	66	8/74	90	13/63	79	17/59	73	5/86	22	4/86	33	7/82	60	7/57	47	14/69
Netherlands	74	1/53	93	10/70	86	5/73	66	3/41	11	0/10	36	3/31	78	2/54	78	6/64
P.R. China	19	2/95	15	1/97	23	1/98	6	0/99	12	0/99	7	0/100	9	0/99	13	1/98
Poland	40	0/81	69	2/50	58	4/52	13	0/59	9	0/76	31	2/57	27	1/70	32	2/55
Russia	17	0/99	53	4/91	67	4/91	5	1/99	11	1/98	22	1/98	22	0/93	12	1/98
S. Africa	25	3/88	29	3/91	49	13/72	56	3/89	25	1/89	12	1/97	29	2/86	22	5/88
Spain	73	9/48	85	6/69	86	7/65	28	1/79	12	2/77	55	5/72	87	18/36	59	7/66
Sweden	74	0/62	93	1/65	92	1/61	54	1/74	14	1/91	58	1/74	89	18/42	83	2/63
Switzerland	89	11/50	91	14/56	93	14/63	69	11/55	19	2/92	65	12/68	89	10/50	87	14/61
Thailand	55	3/18	51	3/25	64	5/37	14	1/6	37	2/12	23	0/12	49	6/20	39	2/17
UK	88	2/65	96	7/78	94	7/77	35	1/93	27	1/87	70	5/85	55	2/78	87	8/77
US	53	1/30	90	11/51	86	15/51	76	16/58	77	12/24	61	5/51	51	2/23	70	12/51

The data base consists of a survey of 30,000 consumers in 21 countries across 6,000 global and local brands and 120 product categories

[1] Awareness: respondents were asked to rate on a 7-point scale (1 = never heard of, 7 = extremely familiar) their "overall awareness of the brand as well as their understanding of what kind of product or service the brand represents". The figures correspond to the % of respondents answering 2 or above.

[2] First figure: % of respondents indicating that they "use or buy regularly/often"; 2nd figure: % of respondents indicating that they have "never used or bought".

Source: A Young & Rubicam Europe, Brand Asset™ Valuator Study, 1994.

567

Case 4.4

Cathay Pacific Airways and the China Syndrome

In the early 1990s Asia Pacific was the fastest growing region in the world of the airline industry. Cathay Pacific Airways (Cathay) in Hong Kong was strategically located at the "heart of Asia," and was repeatedly ranked as one of the most profitable airlines in the world. However, the competitive environment in which Cathay operated was challenging. The company was facing the issue of whether to become a truly global carrier, or whether to stay regional by concentrating on the China market and anticipate developments after the 1997 Chinese takeover of Hong Kong.

COMPANY BACKGROUND

Cathay Pacific Airways was founded in 1946 by an American and an Australian who used a DC-3 to offer passenger and cargo services to southeast Asian countries. In 1948, the company was incorporated, and Butterfield and Swire, later the Swire Group, became the largest shareholder. In 1959, Cathay acquired Hong Kong Airways and became Hong Kong's true "flagship" carrier.

The Swire Group, one of the two largest British conglomerates in Hong Kong, exercised its control over Cathay through the provision of management support services. Cathay was first listed on the Hong Kong exchange in May 1986. Swire Pacific continued as a holding company, although its shareholding declined from 70% to 54.25%. The Hong Kong and Shanghai Banking Corporation (HSBC) reduced its stake to 23.25%.

Source: This case was prepared by Eddie Yu and Anthony Ko, associate professors, Department of Business & Management, City University of Hong Kong, as a basis for class discussion. It is not intended to illustrate either correct or incorrect handling of administrative problems. The authors gratefully acknowledge case materials provided by Angela Wong and other students in their strategic management class. Copyright 1996 by Eddie Yu and Anthony Ko, City University of Hong Kong, Kowloon Tong, Hong Kong. Case taken from the 1994/95 Annual Report of the Director of Civil Aviation.

Cathay continued to expand rapidly and profitably in the second half of the 1980s. The number of aircraft grew from 21 in 1986 to 41 in 1990, destinations from 36 to 38, revenue passengers carried from 4.2 million to 7.7 million, and consolidated net profit from US$158 million to 384 million. Exhibit 1 shows selected financial results for the 1981–1995 period.

Apart from benefitting from the emergence of Hong Kong's Kai Tak Airport as an international hub, Cathay's success was also attributed to its good marketing and operating efforts. Cathay won *Air Transport World* magazine's "Airline of the Year Award" in 1987. It maintained an outstanding reputation for in-flight service. Its marketing programs were designed to secure a major share of the normal full-fare market sector.

By the mid-1990s, Cathay served 46 destinations in 27 countries and territories. The breakdown by destinations of passengers served at Kai Tak from April 1994 to March 1995 is given in Exhibit 2.

THE ASIAN MARKET

In the past two decades, the Asia Pacific region has undergone significant economic, social, and political changes conducive to the business development of the civil aviation industry.

During this period the region managed to have a relatively stable political climate, which in turn encouraged both local and foreign investments. As a result, the Asia Pacific region was ranked the highest GDP growth region in the world in the period 1970 to 1991, with a compound growth rate of 7.1% against the world average of 3.2%. The region is forecasted to outstrip other regions again in the period 1991 to 2000 at 6.1%, against the world average of 3.4%. Thus, with the region's population representing approximately 55% of the world total, the need for business and leisure travel by air is rapidly increasing.

EXHIBIT 1 Financial and Operating Statistics of Cathay Pacific Airways

Year ending 31/12		1981	1982	1983	1984	1985	1986	1987	1988	1989	1990	1991	1992	1993	1994	1995
Group turnover																
Passenger	US$M		568.8	581.7	683.9	740.7	859.5	1145.7	1509.9	1769.6	2010.3	2095.9	2332.0	2341.4	2564.8	2835.6
Excess baggage	US$M		10.0	9.9	11.1	11.5	13.8	18.3	17.4	19.1	21.2	22.1	30.0	26.9	26.7	25.2
Cargo	US$M		126.3	146.7	167.8	169.4	229.8	273.4	335.9	350.1	402.2	443.7	483.0	524.2	699.4	836.7
Mail	US$M		6.7	7.9	8.6	9.9	13.5	17.3	19.6	21.5	25.5	28.7	30.4	28.7	27.3	29.3
Traffic turnover	US$M		711.8	746.3	871.5	931.7	1116.6	1454.7	1882.8	2160.4	2459.2	2590.4	2875.3	2921.1	3318.2	3726.8
Other turnover	US$M		23.4	26.0	31.3	34.1	44.3	46.8	51.4	54.7	85.1	103.6	135.4	182.3	203.4	210.3
Total turnover	US$M		735.2	772.3	902.8	965.9	1161.0	1501.5	1934.2	2215.1	2544.4	2694.0	3010.7	3103.4	3521.6	3937.2
Consolidated net profit	US$M	23.2	44.8	82.9	112.4	99.8	158.1	271.4	361.8	425.8	384.5	379.6	388.6	296.4	309.0	385.0
Dividends	HK$M	10.2	24.7	42.7	196.8	49.9	67.9	102.8	132.1	154.2	154.4	154.8	155.4	155.5	155.7	177.8
Fixed assets																
Other long-term assets & investments	US$M						96.0	95.8	100.1	87.7	151.9	140.9	188.3	204.0	245.1	269.2
Current & other assets less current liabilities	US$M						272.3	377.0	347.4	325.3	583.6	755.0	1192.7	1216.1	1085.0	1057.8
Deferred taxation	US$M						−71.8	−62.6	−73.4	−84.5	−103.6	−45.7	−124.3	−252.2	−389.0	−511.2
Deferred exchange differences & other items	US$M						364.7	665.4	544.3	359.2	367.4	308.1	193.3	222.7	293.0	126.8
	US$M						1409.7	2000.1	2057.3	2143.2	2809.0	3360.3	4098.3	4316.8	4395.8	4760.1
Shareholders' funds	US$M						243.2	547.1	776.2	1048.2	1257.2	1483.1	1720.7	1862.7	1999.7	2206.1
Long-term financing	US$M						1166.5	1453.1	1281.1	1095.0	1551.8	1877.2	2377.6	2454.1	2396.1	2554.0
	US$M						1409.7	2000.1	2057.3	2143.2	2809.0	3360.3	4098.3	4316.8	4395.8	4760.1

EXHIBIT 2 Number of Passengers In and Out of Kai Tak Airport, April 1994 to March 1995 (in 000s)

Markets	Arrivals	Departures
Amsterdam	22.5	28.7
Auckland	40.2	42.4
Bangkok	362	362.3
Kaohsiung (Taiwan)	243.0	236.0
Kuala Lumpur	95.4	87.4
London-Heathrow	160.8	147.8
Los Angeles	113.1	120.0
Manila	335.1	342.2
Melbourne	60.6	63.8
Osaka-Itami	72.4	71.9
Osaka-Kansai	96.9	97.5
Paris-De Gaulle	93.3	90.6
Penang	31.4	34.3
Rome	42.3	44.3
Seoul	178.3	173.8
Singapore	207.8	191.1
Sydney	99.5	94.9
Tokyo-Narita	288.7	274.3
Toronto	34.7	40.4
Vancouver	119.6	130.4
Total (others included)	4,477.6	4,476.2

Source: 1994/95 Annual Report of the Director of Civil Aviation.

Other factors have contributed to the substantial growth of airline business in the region. It has vast areas of ocean so that air transport provides a natural means of both commerce and social interaction. As Asia is distant from a number of its major international trading partners, air transport is an obvious choice for businessmen. Asia is also the fastest growing international tourist destination.

Not surprisingly, the region also has the world's highest growth rate in international scheduled passengers' kilometers (9% annually for the next five to ten years), greater than Europe and North America (at 5.6% and 4.0% respectively). The most profitable airlines in the world can also be found in Asia, including Singapore Airlines and Cathay.

REGULATORY ENTRY BARRIERS

Unlike the United States, liberalization of the airline industry in the region is proceeding very slowly. Access to the Asia Pacific market is closely regulated by governments, and the majority of airlines are state-owned.

Similar to practices in other regions, the rights to fly into and between Asian countries are regulated by bilateral agreements that are a requirement of the Chicago Convention. At the international level, the airline operators are also required to comply with the International Civil Aviation Organization's standards and recommended practices, and at the national level, they are required to comply with the Civil Aviation Acts, Civil Aviation Regulations, and other airport and airline operators' requirements.

Air services agreements are regarded as trade agreements, as they are carefully negotiated between governments, each of which seeks to secure the best possible deal for its designated national airline(s).

Asia Pacific carriers are characterized by their strong national connection, and to some extent their image mirrors national characteristics, such as Singapore Airlines, Korean, Japan Airlines, and Qantas (Australia). They have been able to cope with strong growth, and several are considered dynamic competitors by other airlines in other regions of the world.

Since 1987, there have been some moves towards privatization. Recently, Philippines Airlines was privatized, Thai Air is currently undergoing privatization, and the Government in India also recently announced the privatization plan for Air India.

One feature that reflects developments elsewhere is the move towards deregulation in domestic airline operations. A number of countries in the region are now allowing new carriers to start up to fill market niches and compete with existing flag carriers. Newly emerging carriers, such as Asiana of Korea, EVA of Taiwan, Ansett of Australia, and Japan Air Services, have increasingly exerted competitive pressure to both their countries' flag carriers and other regional airlines.

In addition to the 1997 takeover of Hong Kong by China, the early 1990s presented Cathay with some new challenges.

PROFITABILITY SQUEEZE

After a good run in the last years of the 1980s, Cathay started encountering some problems in 1990. A slowdown of the world economy, costs rising due to inflation in Hong Kong, uncertainties caused by the Gulf War, and worldwide excess of capacity led to decline and stagnation of Cathay's profit during the period from 1991 to 1995. The consolidated net profit declined 10% from the peak achieved in 1989. The 1993 profit dropped 23.8% from that of 1992. Cathay was also hit by an industrial action by flight attendants in January 1993, which was estimated to have cost the company around US$31 million.

STRONG ROUTE COMPETITION

Cathay also faced increased competition. The market shares for the various destinations are shown in Exhibit 3. As can be seen, the company's strongest competitors on its main routes were some of the major global airlines:

Australian route

Qantas, the Australian national airline was the dominant competitor. Qantas had global ambitions and had established alliances with Swissair and other airlines.

China route

Air China, the Chinese national airline, was the main carrier for customers into China. However, from Hong Kong, the largest market share was held by Dragonair (which is partly owned by Cathay), with China having a controlling interest. In 1990, Cathay had transferred its Shanghai and Beijing routes to Dragonair, de facto withdrawing from the Chinese market. It was not clear, however, what the opportunities would be after the Chinese takeover of Hong Kong on July 1, 1997.

Japan route

An important link in Cathay's global network, the Japan route was dominated by Japan Airlines (JAL). JAL's strongest features were its in-flight service and the preferential treatment it received at Narita and Osaka international airports.

London route

This route was another historically important link for Cathay, as its importance was not declining despite the end of British rule, since it linked Hong Kong to Europe. British Airways was the leader on this route, and British-based Virgin Atlantic Airways was a new challenger. British Airways had a strong global network, with high customer recognition, but still lacked a strong ally in East Asia. Virgin Atlantic competed mainly on price, but also provided special services, such as door-to-door transportation and in-flight events.

Singapore route

Although a relatively short distance route, Singapore was an increasingly important link as Asian economies continued to flourish. The main competitor was Singapore Airlines, who had dominant share and preferred landing rights. Singapore had long been viewed as a top service provider, and served as a benchmark when Cathay expanded its own customer satisfaction effort.

United States route

This was a weak link for Cathay's global plans, but was an important route in any global network. This route featured strong competition from national airlines in Asia (including Thai Airlines and Korean Air) and

EXHIBIT 3 Inbound (to HK) Market Share Distribution by Place of Origination

	1985	1986	1987	1988
Inbound market share (worldwide) %				
Cathay Pacific Airways	28.7	29.9	30.9	31.5
China Airlines	8.3	8.4	9.2	11.9
Japan Airlines	10.8	10.6	11.6	11.6
Thai International	7.5	7.5	7.2	6.5
Singapore Airlines	7.3	6.7	6.2	4.9
United Airlines	5.6	5.1	5.2	4.2
HK Dragon Airlines	—	—	—	—
China Southern Airlines	—	—	—	—
British Airways	—	—	—	—
Qantas Airways	—	—	—	—
Combined PRC airlines/CAAC (2)	6.2	6.2	6.1	7.4
Inbound market share (S. E. Asia) %				
Cathay Pacific Airways	25.7	24.8	26.8	29.0
Thai International	10.4	9.8	11.1	9.9
Singapore Airlines	13.0	13.7	13.4	12.3
Philippine Airlines	8.3	9.3	10.2	10.5
China Airlines	11.9	12.3	12.0	11.1
Dragonair	—	—	0.3	0.4
Combined PRC airlines/CAAC	5.7	6.2	6.2	6.4
Inbound market share (USA) %				
Cathay Pacific Airways	16.2	18.4	20.2	21.0
United Airlines	18.5	19.2	17.3	17.9
Northwest Orient Airlines	10.7	11.3	11.4	10.5
China Airlines	7.3	6.7	7.6	6.8
Singapore Airlines	11.4	9.6	10.5	9.1
Dragonair	—	—	0.3	1.1
Combined PRC airlines/CAAC	9.7	9.9	9.4	11.0
Inbound market share (Canada) %				
Cathay Pacific Airways	35.9	39.3	44.1	44.1
Canadian Airlines Int'l	9.9	13.6	12.1	15.1
United Airlines	3.2	3.9	3.9	4.2
Dragonair	—	—	0.3	1.0
Combined PRC airlines/CAAC	6.5	6.3	5.0	7.0
Inbound market share (United Kingdom) %				
Cathay Pacific Airways	38.0	36.4	40.9	41.8
British Airways	20.7	22.9	16.4	16.8
Virgin Atlantic	—	—	—	—
Emirates Airlines	—	—	—	—
Thai International	3.7	4.1	4.8	4.4
Qantas Airways	2.6	4.0	4.4	5.8
Dragonair	—	—	0.2	0.5
Combined PRC airlines/CAAC (2)	5.6	5.0	4.8	4.5
Inbound market share (Australia) %				
Cathay Pacific Airways	47.6	48.3	48.9	49.2
Qantas	16.1	23.3	22.5	22.8
Dragonair	—	—	0.2	0.3
Combined PRC airlines/CAAC	3.4	3.1	3.4	3.4
Inbound market share (Taiwan) %				
Cathay Pacific Airways	—	—	26.3	28.4
China Airlines	—	—	42.2	43.1
Thai International	—	—	12.6	6.7
Dragonair	—	—	0.1	0.9
Combined PRC airlines/CAAC	—	—	1.5	11.6
Inbound market share (Japan) %				
Cathay Pacific Airways	33.7	36.8	33.9	33.7
Japan Airlines	42.1	41.3	40.0	42.0
All Nippon Airways	3.0	1.4	2.8	4.7
Dragonair	—	—	0.7	1.8
Combined PRC airlines/CAAC	5.0	5.2	4.7	4.2

1989	1990	1991	1992	1993	1994	1995
33.5	33.7	33.4	34.1	32.7	34.0	35.1
11.5	11.7	10.9	11.1	11.6	9.8	9.4
11.3	11.1	11.5	9.5	8.4	8.6	9.3
6.6	5.6	5.5	6.0	5.7	5.9	5.8
4.6	4.4	4.5	4.3	4.3	3.9	4.0
—	—	4.4	3.8	3.8	3.6	3.9
1.5	2.0	2.3	2.5	2.7	3.6	3.8
—	—	2.2	2.4	2.5	2.2	2.1
—	—	2.1	2.4	—	2.0	1.9
—	—	1.9	2.3	3.0	2.7	2.3
5.7	7.6	—	—	—	5.3	4.7
31.3	32.2	27.1	29.2	29.9	29.2	30.9
11.3	10.5	12.3	11.7	10.3	12.0	11.7
10.4	10.8	10.7	10.9	11.1	10.2	11.1
11.9	8.7	8.1	8.8	8.8	7.9	9.8
9.5	11.3	9.9	8.5	8.0	5.6	5.2
0.5	1.0	1.2	1.6	2.2	2.9	2.8
3.4	5.1	5.0	4.6	5.5	4.8	3.7
22.4	20.7	21.5	24.2	24.2	23.0	24.0
17.9	21.0	21.7	20.2	19.1	19.4	21.4
12.1	10.9	8.8	7.6	5.1	5.2	5.5
6.6	7.2	6.5	6.9	7.7	7.3	6.6
10.6	10.1	7.7	7.0	6.3	6.2	6.2
1.3	2.4	3.6	4.3	4.7	5.4	5.6
6.8	8.9	7.0	7.2	8.5	7.1	6.6
45.6	41.8	39.6	42.1	42.0	42.2	41.7
16.6	14.2	18.5	19.8	18.5	15.6	15.7
3.3	9.1	6.7	4.9	5.4	5.8	6.5
1.1	1.7	3.3	2.9	4.4	4.6	5.3
4.2	6.4	5.1	4.9	5.1	4.9	4.5
43.3	45.6	45.8	41.8	36.9	36.5	35.7
25.2	25.0	23.1	21.0	17.9	15.8	15.9
—	—	—	—	—	3.6	8.6
—	—	0.5	2.5	3.3	2.8	3.2
5.0	4.4	4.6	4.2	4.3	3.5	3.0
6.2	4.9	4.3	7.9	13.6	9.4	8.8
0.9	1.5	2.6	2.7	2.9	3.7	4.5
2.8	3.3	2.8	3.4	3.7	3.4	2.9
52.6	56.0	53.4	50.6	46.3	43.5	45.1
21.1	20.1	23.3	27.1	30.0	28.8	25.3
0.6	1.0	2.0	2.0	2.5	4.1	4.1
2.7	3.0	2.5	2.8	3.7	2.9	3.0
31.1	28.9	33.1	37.7	36.1	42.2	42.4
40.0	41.0	38.4	36.5	39.3	36.0	37.4
5.6	3.6	4.3	5.5	5.3	5.3	5.2
2.7	3.1	3.0	2.4	2.3	2.1	1.6
11.8	17.3	10.7	10.5	10.0	7.1	6.4
34.2	35.8	34.6	35.5	33.2	33.6	35.8
41.9	39.5	40.8	39.5	36.5	36.4	35.4
6.0	5.8	5.1	5.1	7.0	6.7	6.9
1.7	1.8	1.7	1.8	2.1	4.3	5.2
2.8	2.9	2.5	2.9	3.5	3.5	2.9

Source: Annual Reports by the Director of Civil Aviation, Hong Kong Government.

from American airlines, including Delta, Northwest, and, in particular, United Airlines. United's strong domestic presence in the United States, coupled with a strong network across the Pacific (a PanAm heritage), made the company a dominant competitor.

Among the rapidly growing destinations, Japan and China were the most important ones. To be successful, an Asia Pacific air carrier would have to obtain access to the two economic powerhouses of the region, Japan and China. The right to fly from Japan to other Asian nations would thus be an important asset. In addition, the opening of the new Kansai International Airport on Osaka Bay would offer more growth opportunities for domestic and international carriers.

GROWTH STRATEGY

Despite its profit problems, Cathay focused on growth during the first half of the 1990s. The fleet was increased from 41 aircraft in 1990 to 57 in 1995, destinations from 38 to 44, and revenue passengers carried from 7.7 million to 10.4 million. It entered into a joint venture to provide ground handling services at Kansai Airport in Osaka, Japan, in 1990, and acquired 10% of Taikoo (Xiamen) Aircraft Engineering Co. Ltd. to enter the aircraft maintenance services in Xiamen, China. In 1994, it consolidated its position in the cargo business by acquiring 75% of Air Hong Kong, a cargo airline owned by a locally listed company.

The company also started an ambitious fleet renewal and expansion program. Nine Lockheed L1011 passenger aircraft were replaced by newer and more efficient Airbus models in 1995. Between 1996 and 1999, 22 Airbus A340/330s and Boeing 777s were scheduled to be delivered. Besides making capital investment, Cathay has made other efforts to make management more efficient and to reduce operating costs.

INCREASED DIFFERENTIATION

To support its growth strategy, Cathay campaigned vigorously under a "Heart of Asia" slogan, emphasizing its central position in the Asian market. The aim was to increase the differentiation from other global airlines and also to change its British-related image to that of a Asian carrier. The campaign involved TV spots and newspaper ads, press briefings, and executive interviews to broadcast the new message. The airline further differentiated itself by changing in-flight service to include menus with more Asian foods, Chinese-language films, and redesigned seats for the typical Asian body proportions.

To improve customer satisfaction, market research was used to pinpoint areas of concern. As a result, some changes were made, including new counters at Kai Tak Airport to handle customer complaints "on the spot," providing personal TVs in first class, establishment of a frequent flyer program, and club premises at airports. Decision-making power was pushed towards the front-line employees, empowering them to make quick decisions about customer problems. The resulting customer satisfaction level, measured as the percent of passengers rating themselves satisfied or better with their Cathay flight experience, reached as high as 94%, comparable to the best in the industry.

As Cathay faced the question of whether it should become a truly global airline or stay regional and await the developments after the 1997 China takeover of Hong Kong, a number of issues caused concern.

ALLIANCE ISSUES

"Mega carrier" was a trendy strategic concept in the international airline industry. To develop an effective market network, international airlines were eager to exchange maintenance services, share ticketing and operations systems, and group together to negotiate better deals from aircraft manufacturers and other suppliers. In early 1992, British Air and KLM Royal Dutch Airlines and Northwest of the United States entered into a strategic alliance. Singapore Airline swapped stakes with U.S.-based Delta Airlines, Swissair had allied with Qantas Airways of Australia, and Japan Airlines allied with Hawaiian Airlines. However, Cathay did not have any alliance arrangement with other international airlines. Should it pursue one?

MARKETING ISSUES

It was difficult to differentiate Cathay from the rest of the Asian airlines. "The Heart of Asia" slogan had been stressed consistently in the past two years. How strong was this in changing the corporate identity from a colonial British image to a modern Chinese one?

How should the cabin crew work force, who came from over eleven nations and cultures, be trained to appreciate and pursue a quality service goal?

How could the company better link up with the various intermediaries, including travel agents, in selling the passenger and cargo space?

AIRPORT ISSUES

The existing Hong Kong International Airport Kai Tak was saturated and limited the business growth opportunity of Cathay. Cathay represented around 25% of inbound and outbound flights, and this would not be improved until 1998, when construction of the new airport Chek Lap Kok on Lantau island would be completed. What, if anything, should be done in the meantime?

As Kai Tak was located in an urban area, the flight hours were restricted, and only certain low noise aircraft were allowed to fly over the residential areas during early morning and late evening. How could Cathay increase its flights?

TECHNOLOGICAL ISSUES

The airline industry was increasingly being driven by technology. Computer reservations systems (CRS) and management information services (MIS) were becoming indispensable competitive tools for the airlines. CRS allowed users, including the airlines, travel agents, and other intermediates, to process bookings for seats on flights anywhere in the network. Travel agents and other sales intermediaries would give preference to airlines who provided efficient CRS access. CRS also enhanced the marketing capability of an airline. When linked to MIS it could also offer a range of product and performance enhancements. Cathay needed to upgrade its system, but MIS and CRS required millions of dollars to develop and maintain the hardware and software systems as well as train the users. Assuming the financing was available, how big would the customer advantage be?

THE CHINESE TAKEOVER

On July 1, 1997, the British Government had to relinquish sovereignty over Hong Kong to the Chinese government. The Joint Declaration and the Basic Law of the Hong Kong Special Administrative Region (SAR) provided for Hong Kong to maintain a high degree of autonomy in aviation matters and "for the maintenance of the status of Hong Kong as a center for international regional aviation." Still, great uncertainties remained.

CATHAY'S NIGHTMARE

Putting the best face on a difficult situation, Cathay announced in its 1995 annual report that "We look forward to operating in the new Hong Kong aviation environment and playing our full part as a member of the Chinese aviation community." But inside the organization managers and employees were still wondering about what might happen and what the company should do.

With the British Government's protection vanishing, Cathay's status after 1997 was uncertain to say the least. In the past decade, China, by direct and indirect moves, had sought to have direct influence on the strategic industries in Hong Kong. These industries included banking, airlines, telecommunications, container terminals, and shipping. In banking, The Bank of China had successfully secured the chairmanship of the Hong Kong Banking Association. The position had been previously monopolized by the two British banks—Hong Kong and Shanghai Banking Corporation and Standard Chartered Bank—since its inauguration. China International Trust & Investment Corporation Hong Kong (Holdings) Limited (CITIC HK), in which China had controlling ownership interests, became a big player in Hong Kong financial markets.

Through CITIC HK and other red chip companies ("red chip companies" was the popular terminology for companies with strong ties to China, if not entirely China funded), the Beijing government was stepping up the holdings in other strategic industries. As all operators of these strategic businesses also had substantial investments in China, the share acquisition processes had been smooth and friendly for most of the cases. But such deals were not necessarily made on a purely commercial basis.

With the Chinese takeover, Chinese airline operators were likely to move into Hong Kong to compete head-on with Cathay. The state-owned airlines could be expected to have certain privileges hampering fair competition. For example, the China National Aviation Corporation (CNAC), the commercial arm of the regulatory Civil Aviation Administration of China, was widely regarded as the most likely candidate to replace Cathay as the territory's flagship carrier after the transfer of sovereignty. CNAC already owned 51% of start-up carrier Air Macao, the flag carrier of Macao, Hong Kong's neighboring Portuguese colony until 1999. Maintaining a good relationship with the key officials in China and related state enterprises was clearly of strategic importance for the future. Cathay's parent company, the Swire Group, had in the past decade has actively developed an amiable relationship with China. The relationship had grown out of their joint venture, the Dragonair airline.

DRAGONAIR

Hong Kong Dragon Airlines (Dragonair) was founded in 1986 by Hong Kong Macao International Investment Ltd., a company controlled by K. P. Chao and his family, who owned a major textile business. Chao was joined by the prominent Sir Y. K. Pao and other investors in November. However, after Dragonair's initially disappointing performance, the Pao family withdrew from Dragonair in 1989 and sold the shares back to the Chao family.

Realizing the need to get closer to industry insiders and to get better access to the Chinese market, Chao decided to invite the Swire Group and CITIC HK to become partners. In January 1990, Cathay Pacific and Swire Pacific acquired 30% and 5% of Dragonair's issued capital. The cost to Cathay was approximately US$38 million. The Chao family retained 22% of the shares, while CITIC HK with its ties to China became the largest shareholder with 38% (increased to 46% in 1992).

Dragonair's move to invite powerful partners from China was not a novel strategy. Swire Pacific had actually employed the same strategy in February 1987 when CITIC HK acquired a 12.5% stake in Cathay Pacific and thus became Cathay's second largest shareholder. This was the beginning of the close relationship between Swire and Chinese officials.

Cathay also entered into a management service agreement to manage Dragonair. As part of this move, some personnel, including a senior executive, were transferred to Dragonair. Cathay also transferred its China routes, consisting of Shanghai and Beijing services, to Dragonair starting on April 1, 1990.

THE CHINA MARKET

For China, since its inauguration of the Open Door policy in 1979, the rapid growth of economic activities in some 30 cities led to a great demand for air travel. The outbound travel potential of 1.25 billion people,

EXHIBIT 4 Weekly Schedule of Flights for Hong Kong to China

Route	PRC Airlines	Dragonair
Beijing	28 flights	14 flights
Shanghai	28 flights	16 flights
Xiamen	14 flights	9 flights

and the several hundred thousands of foreign businessmen going in and out of China each year, presented a great attraction to all regional and international airlines. And as China was speeding up the quest for readmission to the World Trade Organization, China offered the largest potential for airline business development in the next decade.

The Beijing government still controlled key operational areas, such as fares, routes, and aircraft acquisitions of all airlines. However, since the early 1990s, the Civil Aviation Administration of China (CAAC) had gradually decentralized the civil aviation rights to newly established regional airlines in order to meet the increased demand for air travel. In addition to Air China, the flagship carrier, new airlines included China Eastern (Shanghai based), China Southern (in Guangzhou), and China Northwest (based in Xian).

Because of the booming Chinese market, the first half of the 1990s was great for Dragonair—in contrast to Cathay and the global airline industry. By 1992, Dragonair was serving 13 cities in China and 4 cities in North and South Asia. It established itself as the preferred carrier for passengers traveling to and from China. With expanding services and high load factors, Dragonair reported record profits in 1993. By 1994, it was providing services to 14 cities in China and 8 cities elsewhere in Asia by a fleet of nine aircraft.

By the mid-1990s, the weekly schedule of flights between Hong Kong and three main Chinese cities showed the relative strength of Dragonair against all the PRC airlines combined (see Exhibit 4).

TROUBLED SKIES

Past history and CNAC's aggressive posture suggested the possibility of international expansion by a new Chinese flagship carrier based in Hong Kong. As the chairman of the Cathay repeatedly emphasized to the press, Cathay would not be afraid of fair competition, as it had already competed successfully with over 61 airlines, many world class. Cathay was simply afraid that the new entrant would have distinct privileges in competing with Cathay, especially since CNAC was also China's regulator of the airline industry. If such worries were realized, no matter how good Cathay's strategic planning, it would have major difficulties in coping with the powerful political forces.

In March 1995, CNAC announced that it had been applying for licenses to operate airline services, initially flying between China and Hong Kong, and Hong Kong and Taiwan (a very profitable route for Cathay) with a new airline company. Sensing that its worst nightmare was coming true, Cathay protested, claiming a conflict of interest in having a regulator run its own airline in Hong Kong. The Chinese rule-maker could easily create obstacles by favoring CNAC and penalizing Cathay, or stripping it of its primary landing slots at the new Hong Kong airport. Unfortunately, Cathay could not rely on Chris Patten, the last British Governor of the colony, to negotiate these issues with China. In addition to his "lame duck" status, the relationship between the Governor and the Beijing government was frayed, due to some last-minute democratic reforms introduced by Patten.

In July 1995, Cathay, in its role as the flagship carrier of Hong Kong, announced that it had reached a preliminary deal with the Taipei Airlines Association to license a second carrier in both Taiwan and Hong Kong. The additional carriers were expected to be Dragonair and Taiwan's EVA Airways. The Chinese were not happy. The general manager of the CNAC, Wang Guixiang, stated that Cathay was not authorized to negotiate the deal, and that the Basic Law had been violated.

In September 1995, CITIC HK sold their holdings of Cathay shares. In mid-March 1996, CNAC was rumored to have off-loaded its 5% stake in Cathay. The market considered these activities as a vote of lack of confidence in the future of Cathay, anticipating that its flagship carrier status would soon be replaced by a powerful China airlines company.

On April 3, 1996, one of the most influential financial newspapers in Hong Kong reported that the Swire Group planned to sell its stake in Cathay. The report claimed that the Swire family had approached five potential buyers, among them United Airlines, Northwest, and Lufthansa. Although the report was categorically denied by the Swire Group's Hong Kong chairman (and chairman of Cathay), Peter Sutch, the rumor persisted.

DISCUSSION QUESTIONS

1. Considering "the global option," in which regions should Cathay look for alliance partners, if any? What does Cathay have to offer a potential partner?

2. How does the positioning theme "Heart of Asia" fit in with Cathay's global aspirations? Is the image a plus or minus for going global?

3. What are the advantages and disadvantages of staying regional? How can marketing help leverage the advantages?

4. How attractive is the China market? How should Cathay deal with the China market—by trying to enter and developing it further, or by focusing on the global market?

5. If the decision is to penetrate the China market, how should Cathay go about it—develop its interest in Dragonair further, or attempt some alliances, for example with Chinese airlines? Any other alternatives?

6. Will Cathay survive? What protection from a direct takeover by CNAC can Cathay count on? To what extent does its firm-specific advantages (including marketing skills) protect it? How?

Case 4.5[1]

Hewlett-Packard's Global Account Management

*I*n a November 1989 interview, John Young, president and chief executive officer, Hewlett-Packard, summarized the situation in the computer and electronics industry that was the mainstay of this $11.9 billion multinational corporation:

"Customers no longer want a box, they want solutions."

In Young's view, the industry was moving from an era in which the product defined the solution, to one in which the customer defined the solution. A pure technological focus was no longer appropriate as customers were demanding more standardization and support. In addition, industry growth was slowing in the United States, which represented just less than half of the global market for computers and electronics. Challenges were particularly evident in H-P's largest division, the computer systems organization (CSO).

One CSO executive, Greg Mihran, manager, industry marketing, and a fourteen-year H-P veteran, summarized H-P's position as follows:

"H-P has a long history of success with a product-oriented, country-based sales and support organization. While considerable progress had been made during the past two years toward an account focus, ongoing efforts to adjust the balance between account and geographic strategies continued. It seemed evident, however, that the right answer was somewhere in between these two extremes. Both strategies must coexist to ensure success and respond to the complex mix of country and global account priorities."

COMPANY BACKGROUND

H-P, incorporated in 1947 as successor to a partnership formed in 1939, designed, manufactured, and serviced electronic products and systems for measurements and computation. The company was committed to a set of core values: leadership in technology, quality and customer service, financial stability, and uncompromising integrity in all business dealings. H-P sold nearly all of its products to businesses, research institutes, and educational and healthcare institutions and was one of the United States's largest exporters. H-P's basic business purpose was to provide the capabilities and support needed to help customers worldwide improve their personal and business effectiveness. In 1990, the company employed over 92,000 people and operated product divisions in 53 cities and 19 countries with over 600 sales and support offices in 110 countries and generated revenues of $13.2 billion. In 1990, net revenue grew by 11 percent following a 21 percent increase in 1989. In 1990, H-P experienced a slower net revenue growth in most of its product areas and declines in operating profit and net earnings when compared to amounts reported in 1989. H-P maintained manufacturing plants, research and development facilities, warehouses, and administrative offices in the United States, Canada, West Germany, France, Spain, Italy, Switzerland, The Netherlands, Australia, Singapore, China, Japan, Hong Kong, Malaysia, Mexico, and Brazil. H-P had a strong market presence in Europe with net revenue for European operations equal to approximately five billion dollars. H-P's market participation was weaker in Latin America but strong in Asia. The geographic distribution of H-P's orders was as follows: 46 percent—United States, 35 percent—Europe, and 19 percent—Asia Pacific (includes Latin America).

INDUSTRY TRENDS

In 1990 the computer industry was moving away from a geographic focus to more of a customer focus with an emphasis on global strategy. As customers demanded

---

[1]Source: This case was developed by George S. Yip and Tammy L. Madsen, Anderson Graduate School of Management, University of California at Los Angeles (UCLA). Copyright George S. Yip.

more standardization, hardware producers were being driven into complex and occasionally secret alliances. For example, AT&T, creator and owner of the Unix operating system, teamed up with Sun Microsystems to promote its standard. On the other side of the fence, IBM, Digital Equipment, and a few others were trying to promote another version of Unix, possibly the one used by Steve Jobs, Apple Computer founder, in his new workstation. These two groups then began to discuss working together on a common version of the operating system.

In addition, customers also wanted to work with vendors that provided consistent service and support across geographic regions and industries. Multinational customers demanded that vendors be strategic partners who could demonstrate an understanding of specific international needs and deploy solutions to these needs on a global basis. H-P executives increasingly saw the need for "one platform common across vendors and across many industries." While competitors appeared to be interested in taking a more global approach to the business, one of H-P's senior executives indicated that "the industry looked at 'global' as a buzzword." Many at H-P saw the need to integrate the current geographic approach with a global strategy.

Alternative sales channels such as dealers, two-tier suppliers, systems integrators, or resellers had become prevalent throughout the industry. Thus, companies in the industry needed to identify strategies to maximize these alternative channels and the opportunities presented by them. In H-P's case, the organization needed to couple industry/customer focus with an all-channel strategy as well as develop ways to measure and develop alternative channels.

ACCOUNT MANAGEMENT PROGRAM

In 1990, H-P's account and sales management program was product focused, organized on geographic lines, and supported approximately one thousand accounts worldwide. Under this structure, sales responsibility did not extend beyond geographic boundaries and according to one executive, the amount of business tended to shift up and down from year to year.

The organization structure consisted of four levels. First, there were field operations managers for each of the three worldwide sectors: Europe, Asia Pacific, and the Americas. Second, each sector was divided by countries and/or regions, and managers were identified for each country or region. The number of country/region managers was a function of country

size and business. For example, the United States was divided into four regions: the West, South, Midwest, and East. Each country or region manager reported to the field operations manager.

Third, the regions or countries, depending on size, were further divided into areas. Area sales managers reported to the country or region managers. Fourth, district sales and account managers reported to the area sales managers. Just as area sales manager responsibility did not extend beyond the area geographic lines, district manager responsibility did not extend beyond district lines. District managers were designated as the major account managers for the largest accounts in their districts but were also responsible for the entire geographic area. In addition, there were approximately eight sales representatives per district manager. Distinct geographic boundaries existed within this framework such that sales activity did not cross boundaries. Minimal interaction occurred between regions and districts and there were no mechanisms in the system to encourage interaction across areas, districts, or regions.

In addition to the field operations sales and account structure, headquarters account managers were located at corporate headquarters. Headquarters account managers reported to the product divisions while the rest of the sales staff reported to the geographic operations. Account managers utilized these contacts to gather information and determine if H-P had sufficient resources to support their customers. One of the executives interviewed indicated that since the headquarters account managers reported directly to the different product divisions they did not always act in the interests of the district or region managers. As a result, many of the geographic account managers were not sure if they could trust or would benefit from the use of a headquarters account manager.

PERFORMANCE MEASURES

Under the geographic structure, performance measures were based on product quotas. Managers focused on meeting product line targets within their designated region, area, or district. For many years H-P had set sales quotas and tracked performance by product lines solely within geographies. This was an important metric to quantify product performance but lacked clear differentiation of account quotas and expenses. Expenses and account quotas were reported and managed together within all other product quotas and costs in each country and region. As a result, within the product focus structure, it was difficult to differentiate individual account performance at any level and there was a lack of a complete measure of global account performance. In 1990, when H-P began to shift more to a customer focus, one senior executive indicated that it was very difficult to get the sales team to shift to an account focus while they still were required to satisfy product line targets.

The organization structure and the performance measures did not facilitate the development of new accounts outside regional boundaries. Area and district managers had no incentive to provide information to other district or area sales managers regarding new account development, as their primary focus was meeting product quotas in their own designated region or district. In many ways, different regions, areas, and districts competed with each other. Ken Fairbanks, district sales manager, indicated that if managers wanted to help develop business for a customer in another region, the manager was forced to use a "tin cup approach." For example, if an account manager for the Northwest region of the United States needed to coordinate activities for his customer in another region in the United States, he or she had to provide an incentive to the account manager in the other region if they wanted any assistance. Mr. Fairbanks indicated that he had to approach managers in other regions with a "tin cup" or "beg" for support. Managers often spent considerable amounts of time trying to convince managers in other regions of the benefits that would result from their support. Managers in different regions had no incentive to coordinate activities of major customers across regions because their performance was measured only on product quotas for their region and was not differentiated for particular major accounts. Under this system new account development was lacking and product sales fluctuated from year to year.

GLOBAL ACCOUNT MANAGEMENT

In January 1991, Franz Nawratil, vice president and manager, worldwide marketing and sales, computer systems organization (CSO), Hewlett-Packard, received approval to implement a pilot program based on a proposal for global account management. At this time, Mr. Nawratil asked Alan Nonnenberg, director of sales, Asia-Pacific, to help head the pilot program and appointed Greg Mihran as the new director of sales, global account management, CSO.

The program proposal envisioned a critical role for the global account manager (GAM). Accordingly, the pilot program focused on providing the GAM with the authority, power, and tools to manage the global account. GAMs were responsible for defining the global account sales and support needs and budget, developing an account plan, and identifying the goals and objectives for the account and the strategies and resources necessary to achieve those goals and objectives.

THE PILOT PROGRAM

The first step of the pilot program involved selection of the global accounts based on various criteria. Good executive relation ships between the customer and H-P were required to exist and H-P had to hold a strong defensible position in the account. The global customer needed to be interested in developing a global account program and to also be demanding more global consistency and support than were other customers. From a financial perspective, global accounts were required to have greater than $10 million in current annual sales and support. The first six major global accounts identified were four American companies—AT&T, Ford, General Motors, and General Electric; one Canadian company—Northern Telecom; and one European company—Unilever. Within five of the six accounts, 5–10 percent of each customer's total spending on information technology was allocated to H-P. In the sixth account, H-P was heavily installed with 70 percent of that customer's business.

The dual structure defined in the proposal empowered the GAM to manage his or her sales team to meet the global needs of the customer. The GAM jointly reported to the country manager of the customer's HQ country and to the field operations manager, but was empowered to make decisions independent of geography. In addition, the GAMs were evaluated on worldwide performance of a single account while a country manager was evaluated on sales performance in a single geography.

To facilitate visibility of the program, a quarterly report, the Global Account Profile, documented by the headquarters account managers (HAMs), summarized the status of the global accounts. This report diffused information about the global accounts throughout the entire organization and worked as an internal awareness document. The Global Accounts Profile was not a problem-solving tool but informed executives of the opportunities and strategic issues related to each global account. It provided the GAMs with a vehicle to communicate the status of the account to the rest of the organization. In addition, GAMs held quarterly meetings to bring district sales managers together to share best practices.

THE HAM PROGRAM

The headquarters account management (HAM) program was redefined during the first year of the pilot program and provided a point of contact at H-P headquarters for the customer. The HAMs represented the global account at headquarters, assumed global responsibility and ownership, and were the link between account assigned executives and the global account. In this role, HAMs were seen as an investment by the global sales team to maximize success of the account. HAMs were selected during the development of the pilot program and two were identified by the end of fiscal 1991. Mr. Mihran, Mr. Nawratil, and Mr. Nonnenberg all agreed that sales and field experience was a requirement for all HAMs.

The HAMs worked closely with the GAMs to address technical, pricing, and strategy issues and basically to do whatever was necessary to support the customer. While the HAMs' role was to provide a point of contact at headquarters, they also traveled to customer locations about 30–50 percent of the time depending on the account. Mr. Mihran indicated that initially they did not realize how important it was to keep the HAMs together. But he soon found that locating the HAMs at H-P's headquarters facilitated the sharing of knowledge as well as the development of an important network of resources across industries.

While representing the GAM at H-P headquarters, HAMs also supported business development opportunities presented by the global account and shared H-P best practices with the global account. One headquarters account manager, Teresa Clock, emphasized that the program provided business development opportunities that otherwise might have been missed. For example, Ms. Clock developed an alliance with a third party in Singapore to support the global account with Shell. This would not have been possible without the global account program structure because the country managers previously had no incentive to extend sales operations outside their region. Another HAM, Ann Johnson, on the Northern Telecom account, believed that a main benefit of the program was the sharing of best practices with the customer. In this case, Northern Telecom's operations were organized similarly to

H-P's, and the sharing of best practices provided value-added support to the global account.

INTERNAL ACCEPTANCE OF HAMS

HAMs as well as the entire sales staff for each global account were funded by the global account. During the pilot program, not all accounts funded HAMs and several GAMs were skeptical of the value added by the HAMs' role. Initially many GAMs hesitated to invest in a HAM because of negative experiences with headquarters account managers and sales personnel prior to the GAM program. Within the previous account management organization, headquarters account managers had reported directly to individual product divisions and did not always represent the best interests of the major accounts they supported. As the global account program evolved, most GAMs came to see the value added by the HAMs' role in the new structure, and began utilizing HAMs where funding allowed. HAMs' value-added activities included the development of new business opportunities, sharing of best practices, account visibility at headquarters, and being the eyes and ears of the GAM. Some customers began to recognize the value of having a presence at H-P headquarters.

Other product divisions within H-P also questioned the HAMs' role. Many product division managers initially saw the HAMs as just another layer of management to deal with. Even after the pilot program, many product marketing managers were still not thinking along global lines. But most changed their view once the organization began to better understand the GAM program and the HAMs' role, and product marketing managers began to change their internal approach, emphasizing a more global strategy.

In fiscal 1992, 50 percent of the global accounts funded half a HAM, 20 percent funded a full HAM, and 30 percent did not use a HAM. In contrast, by fiscal 1993, 57 percent of GAMs funded half a HAM while 31 percent funded a full HAM.

COUNTRY REACTIONS TO THE GAMS

Within the first year, many managers at H-P saw the program as a fad and this presented a large challenge to the GAM team. But by 1993, approximately 80 percent of the people who viewed the program as a fad or did not believe in it were no longer in their positions with H-P. Upper management did not tolerate anyone who did not support the program. Further, individuals in key country management positions that were seen as obstacles to the success of the program were encouraged to pursue other opportunities. H-P did not expect automatic buy-in from everyone, and gave senior management two or three opportunities to buy into the program.

During the first two years of the program, the difference in performance measurements often created conflict between GAMs and country managers. Country managers continued to focus on their geographic regions and felt threatened by the GAMs. Field operations managers often had to step in to resolve conflicts or assist in negotiations between the GAMs and country managers. Many executives considered this as one of the problems with the performance measurement system. As a result, the global account performance measurements were revised in fiscal 1993. The new system linked the country managers' evaluation to the worldwide performance of global accounts headquartered in his or her country in addition to the geographic region. This change reduced conflicts and provided country managers with an incentive to coordinate and collaborate with the GAMs.

Beyond the performance measurement system, country managers felt threatened by the GAM program as a whole. Outside the United States, the country managers controlled all accounts within their geographic region. With the initiation of the pilot program, some of the country managers' largest and most profitable accounts were now under the control of a global account manager. While GAMs dually reported to country managers, the GAM was empowered to manage the global account to satisfy the account goals. In addition, because the program received a large amount of top-down support and visibility, GAMs were seen as having an advantage over the country managers. Country managers felt their territory was being encroached upon and this adversely impacted coordination between country managers and GAMs. Country managers that did not buy into the GAM program were given several opportunities to accept the program and work with the GAMs. If managers did not eventually buy into the program they were encouraged to pursue opportunities elsewhere in the organization or outside H-P.

Overall, H-P's senior management felt the program was successful, although during the first two years of the pilot program a few global accounts changed. In one case, the customer had funded the account, then pulled the funding out, and the global account manager was no longer needed. In other cases, the global account manager was not the right person for the job. For example, an area sales manager was successful at managing several accounts in one geography but was not effective at managing one account across multiple geographies.

The GAM program had a high profile at H-P and as the program evolved and diffused to more accounts, its success became highly visible. While Mr. Nawratil's proposal was designed to use the current sales force, he did not intend to create an elite group or autonomous division, but this occurred to some extent. During 1992 and in early 1993, the success of the program was heavily promoted and in mid-1993, Mr. Mihran was requested to "tone down" the promotion to avoid conflicts within H-P. As the program received more visibility there was a concern that the success of the program might create tension between the CSO and other product divisions.

CUSTOMER REACTION

The initial response from customers was positive. Some customers identified the Global Account Program as a strong differentiator between H-P and its main competitors, IBM, Sun, and Digital. Ms. Clock, headquarters account manager, commented that the global account program positioned H-P as more than just a first-tier or second-tier supplier: "The customers feel value in the linkage with product groups and headquarters executives."

The HAM for Northern Telecom, Ms. Johnson, believed that her customer encouraged the global account concept and wondered why it had taken so long for H-P to develop the program. Ms. Johnson indicated that the program made a significant impact by breaking down barriers between regions and field operations. She emphasized that the strength of the program stemmed from the program promotion and visibility to other levels at H-P, and stated that Mr. Mihran had played a critical role in championing the program with executives. Ms. Johnson commented that this type of headquarters presence was an essential feature of the program.

Overall, H-P believed the program was extremely effective. The pilot program began with 6 accounts, evolved to 20 accounts in fiscal 1992, and 26 accounts in fiscal 1993. Mr. Mihran believed that customers were extremely happy with the program. H-P saw the program as a competitive differentiator and this was reinforced by the company's inclusion in Fortune's 1993 ranking of America's most admired corporations. In the category of computers and office equipment, H-P was identified as the organization with the best managers: "Apple is judged more innovative, IBM a better corporate citizen, but H-P's managers are tops."[2]

[2]*Fortune*, February 8, 1993.

DISCUSSION QUESTIONS

1. What obstacles to global synergy do you see in the current sales organization?
2. How does the GAM program solve some of the global synergy problems of H-P?
3. What is the role of the HAMs?
4. How would you attempt to make the GAM program acceptable to the current sales managers?
5. Would you say that the program was a success? Any negatives?

AUTHOR INDEX

COMPANY INDEX

$\mathscr{S}$UBJECT INDEX

A
....

Absolute advantage, 34, 35
Access barriers, 129, 131–132.
    See also Relationship
    marketing
Account management, 514,
    579–580
Acquisitions, of manufacturing
    subsidiary, 163–164
Adaptation. *See also*
    Nonadaptation; Product
    policies
    of automobiles, 162, 281
    cultural, 62
    dual, 339
    versus localization, 370
    research process, 373–375
Adapted positioning, 355, 362n
Address lists, 484–485, 486
Advantages. *See also* Country-
    specific advantages; Firm-
    specific advantages
    comparative and absolute,
    34, 35
    of domestic competitors, 30
    of electronic commerce,
    532–533
    locational, 37–38
    marketing skill, 40–42
    sourcing, 15
Advertising. *See also* Global
    advertising
    in Asia, 273, 274 (*see also*
    China; India; Japan)
    in Australia and New
    Zealand, 246
    basic decisions, 446
    budgeting, 458
    controversial, 559–564
    corporate, 302, 447
    credibility, 290
    cultural differences, 448,
    456–457, 463–464
    in emerging markets, 283

Advertising (*cont.*)
    global, 46 (*see also* Global
    advertising)
    in Latin America, 264–265
    local versus global agencies,
    462–463
    in magazines, 449, 562n
    in mature markets, 229
    multidomestic, 446
    in the Netherlands, 230
    in newly democratized
    countries, 290
    in North America,
    250–251
    outdoor, 283, 448, 450
    pan-European, 238
    and standardization,
    367–368
    volume per nation,
    447–448
    on World Wide Web, 449,
    535–536
AF (ASEA Regional Forum),
    269
Affluence, 10, 73, 101
Africa, 258, 280, 282. *See also*
    South Africa
AFTA (ASEAN Free Trade
    Area), 270, 275
After-sales support
    country differences, 17
    in emerging markets, 49,
    281, 288
    and foreign entry, 144
    as globalization issue, 439
    on gray trade products, 435
Agents. *See also* Distributors;
    Middlemen
    appointment checklist, 145
    legal, 144
    for marketing, 168, 170
Agreements, 62, 142. *See also*
    Contracts
AIDS, in advertising campaign,
    561–562, 563
Air freight services, 430
Aircraft, 404, 414

Airlines
    Cathay Pacific example,
    568–577
    distribution alliances, 160
    and electronic commerce,
    532, 533
    and global advertising,
    453–454
Analogy method, 115–116
ANCOM (Andean Common
    Market), 261
Antitrust laws, 400, 408
APEC (Asia-Pacific Economic
    Cooperation), 269, 275,
    526
Appliances
    standardization, 341, 342
    Whirlpool experiences,
    85–91, 88, 337–338
Arbitrage, 410
Argentina, 264, 265–266, 448
Arm's-length price, 402
ASEAN (Association of South
    East Asian Nations), 257,
    269, 275
Asia. *See also specific countries*
    advertising, 448
    and brand names, 61
    Cathay Pacific Airways case,
    568–577
    clothing market, 271–272
    country differences, 268
    culture, 270–271, 271–272,
    273
    direct marketing, 485
    distribution, 273
    economic crisis, 8, 524–526
    as leading market, 272
    local marketing, 268–275
    major country markets,
    273–275
    market segmentation,
    270–271
    pan-regional marketing, 275
    pricing, 272–273
    product adaptations,
    271–272